I0083748

# INHABITANTS

*of*

# NEW YORK
## 1774 - 1776

*Thomas B. Wilson*

**CLEARFIELD**

Copyright © 1993
Thomas B. Wilson
All Rights Reserved

Published by Genealogical Publishing Co., Inc.
Baltimore, Maryland
1993

Library of Congress Catalogue Card Number 93-79752


Reprinted for Clearfield Company by
Genealogical Publishing Company
Baltimore, Maryland
2011

ISBN 978-0-8063-1396-2

*Made in the United States of America*

# INTRODUCTION

In the course of doing research on the American Revolution many years ago, several lists of names were encountered which would be of value to historians and genealogists if they were readily available. There are several lists in Peter Force's *American Archives*, a series of nine massive volumes published between 1837 and 1853. The names on these lists were not indexed. Many other lists are included in the *Calendar of Historical Manuscripts Relating to the War of the Revolution* published by the New York Secretary of State (Albany, 1868). This publication contains the invaluable census of Suffolk County taken in 1776.

While the above sources contain lists relating to New York City, they were particularly valuable for Queens and Suffolk Counties. The balance was redressed, however, by two important lists relating to New York published in other sources. A petition signed by nearly 3,000 "of the principal male inhabitants of New York" in 1774 was published as an appendix to the *Manual of the Common Council of New York, 1850*. Nearly a thousand inhabitants of New York signed an address to Admiral and General Howe which was published in *New York City During the American Revolution* (Mercantile Library Association of New York City, 1861). Additional lists relating to New York were found in other sources which are listed in the references on the following pages.

All of the above publications are well over a hundred years old, but the lists of names contained in them are little known to genealogists. In the case of Peter Force's *American Archives* even if the volumes are available in a library, it takes many research hours to discover what is in them and to locate names of interest. To make all these names available to researchers was the inspiration for this compilation.

The lists used are of widely varying length, ranging from a few names to several hundred while, as indicated above, one contains nearly 1,000 names and another, spectacularly, nearly 3,000 names. The total is over 13,000 names.

As most of the documents which form the basis for this work were previously published, albeit decades ago, and many of them are quite lengthy, it was decided not to reprint the text of each of them. Every effort was made, however, to indicate fully and accurately in the references the nature of each record cited. Needless to say, perhaps, this statement refers only to the body of the document and not to the list of names.

In the following pages the columns list respectively: name; county (New York, Queens or Suffolk); town or address when known; and a code indicating the source of the information. The code begins with a year (1774, 1775 or 1776). Thus one can tell at a glance the county and year involved for each name on this list.

The codes always relate to the county named. The reference 75-E for Queens, for example, is entirely different than the reference 75-E for a resident of Suffolk County. The references are listed by county on pages v - xx.

Numbers in square brackets following a name indicate the number of persons with the same name who appear on a particular list.

Thomas B. Wilson
Lambertville, N.J.

# REFERENCES

The codes for the references begin with a year (1774, 1775 or 1776) which always relates to the county. The reference 75-E for a resident of Queens, for example, is entirely different than the reference 75-E for a resident of Suffolk. The codes are listed below by county.

## CITY AND COUNTY OF NEW YORK
### 1774

74-A    "Names of the Principal Male Inhabitants of New York, Anno 1774" published as an appendix to the *Manual of the Common Council of New York, 1850*, pp. 427-442. In response to an act of the Legislature directing that all buildings to be erected in the City of New York should be of stone or brick, covered with slate or tiles, a petition signed by nearly 3,000 persons (2977 by actual count) was presented to the governor on 2d May 1774 praying for a suspension of the act. The prayer of the petition was not granted. The citizens later paid dearly for their opposition to the act as a fire broke out in 1776 which destroyed 500 buildings including Trinity Church.

74-B    Insolvent Debtors Confined in the Gaol of New York City in September 1774. A list of names published in Rivington's *New York Gazetteer*, 22 Sept 1774 and extracted in Kenneth Scott's *Rivington's New York Newspaper, Excerpts from a Loyalist Press 1773-1783*. (New York Historical Society, *Collections*, v.84, 1973).

74-R  *New York City Court Records, 1760-1797; Genealogical Data from the Court of Quarter Sessions*, by Kenneth Scott. (National Genealogical Society, Special Publication no. 52, 1983). The contents of the book for the year 1774 were treated here as if it were a list a names. The officers of the court and all the jurors are also included in the list. As the book is well indexed, data relevant to a person named here will be easily found. Names from this same source were also extracted for 1775 and 1776, referenced, below, as 75-R and 76-R.

74-T  *Rivington's New York Newspaper, Excerpts from a Loyalist Press 1773-1783*, by Kenneth Scott. (New York Historical Society, *Collections*, v.84, 1973). The data relating to all persons who are named in these extracts as being residents of New York (city or county) were treated here as a list of names. Occupations and addresses were included when possible. As the book is well indexed, data relevant to a person named in this list will be be easily found. Names from this same source were also extracted for 1775, referenced, below, as 75-T. (This newspaper was not published in 1776, although it was re-established in 1777). Scott did not extract all ads inserted by business and trades men, but these omissions have been added here under a separate reference designation: 74-T2 (below). See also 75-F, a list of names which Scott referred to but did not include in his book.

74-T2 *New York Gazetteer*, the newspaper edited and published by James Rivington. Many business advertisements were not extracted by Scott in his book named above, but they are included here with occupation and address when possible. These names are referenced as 74-T2 followed by the date of issue of the newspaper in which the name first appears. Two lists were omitted by Scott which have a bearing on the political history of the revolutionary era. In the issue of 24 November 1774 a list of the sixty members of the Committee for New York was published, and in the issue of 4 May 1775 the names of the members of the new Committee, which had been increased to 100, were published. While many of the names are well known to students of history, others are obscure, and, considering that New York was occupied by the British from 1776 to 1783, membership on one or the other of these committees may represent the only patriot service known for some of the members. For other members, such as Nicholas Hoffman and Anthony Van Dam, it is surprising to find that they had any patriot service at all as later in the war they were tories. This newspaper has been microfilmed and is available in many libraries or through interlibrary loan.

74-V *Genealogical Data from Colonial New York Newspapers*, by Kenneth Scott. (Baltimore, Genealogical Publishing Co., 1982). The names extracted for this list were taken from the section of Scott's book dealing with the *New York Gazette; and the Weekly Mercury*. The treatment here is the same as that for Rivington's newspaper (see 74-T, above). Many news items were published in both newspapers. Names duplicated in the *Gazette* are not included here unless there is differing detail. As Scott's book is well indexed, data relevant to a person who is named here will be easily found. Names were also extracted for 1775 and 1776, referenced, below, as 75-V and 76-V. No attempt was made to compare Scott's extracts with the original newspaper.

## CITY AND COUNTY OF NEW YORK
### 1775

75-A "Return of Officers Elected in the City of New York, 29 August 1775." (New York Secretary of State. *Calendar of Historical Manuscripts Relating to the War of the Revolution*, Albany, 1868, v.1, p.129). Names 24 each of captains, 1st lieutenants, 2d lieutenants and ensigns.

75-B "Petition of New York Officers, 21 September 1775." (New York Secretary of State. *Calendar of Historical Manuscripts Relating to the War of the Revolution*, Albany, 1868, v.1, pp. 152-153). A petition to the New York Committee of Safety signed by 63 officers (rank not stated) who, being convinced that "the safety of a nation may be preserved by every citizen being a soldier," request that the several companies in the city and county of New York may meet more frequently than previously mandated.

75-C Petition of James Arden and others, tradesmen and labourers of the City of New York, to the Provincial Congress. (New York Secretary of State. *Calendar of Historical Manuscripts Relating to the War of the Revolution*, Albany, 1868, v.1, p.157). The document, not dated but probably drawn up in the autumn of 1775, states that the petitioners are willing to engage in the service of their country, but being in want of the necessaries of life because of the exigencies of the time, they pray for speedy relief.

75-D1 New York City Militia, 25 April 1775. Names 405 inhabitants of the City and County of New York who acknowledged having received a musket and accoutrements from the Corporation of the said City and who promised to return the same on demand. (New York Historical Society. *Collections* for the year 1915, v.2, pp.498-505). This record is one of a trio of complementary documents (see 75-D2 and 75-D3, below).

75-D2 "A List of Five Hundred Inhabitants of New York City in

1775 with their Occupations and Addresses" by Dorothy C. Barck. (New York Historical Society *Quarterly Bulletin*, v.23 [1939], pp. 23-31, 60-62, 109-110, 138-142). This is a list of 498 militiamen who in July and August 1775 returned the muskets which had been given to them in April 1775 (see 75-D1, above). The discrepancy in the number of men named in each of the records may be accounted for in part by the fact that the Provincial Congress did not have the names of all those who received arms from the corporation of New York but took stern measures to ensure that they were returned, not the least of which was to declare as an enemy to his country anyone who did not do so.

75-D3 "A List of the Guard for April 28, 1775." The guard in this case is very broad in meaning as it includes guards posted at many different stations throughout the City and also includes reliefs who came on duty at various times of day and night. This record is part of the same document listed above as 75-D1 and was published in the same source, pp.504-513. Those names which were also on the preceding two lists are not repeated here unless there was a variation in the name, or a rank was stated (as those lists did not indicate rank).

75-E Captains of the City of New York, appointed by the Provincial Congress, engaged in recruiting, 6 July 1775. (Peter Force's *American Archives*, Series IV, v.2, p. 1592). The captains were assigned locations for recruiting, in each case at an inn or tavern. Thus any name appearing with this reference (75-E for New York) who is not listed with a rank, that is to say, captain, may be considered as having been an innholder.

75-F Business and trades men willing to accept Connecticut bills of credit, 10 July 1775. This list of 147 names was published in James Rivington's *New York Gazetteer*, 21 July 1775. (This list was mentioned, but not published, in Kenneth Scott's *Rivington's New York Newspaper*.)

75-R *New York City Court Records, 1760-1797; Genealogical Data from the Court of Quarter Sessions*, by Kenneth Scott. (The same reference as 74-R).

75-T *Rivington's New York Newspaper, Excerpts from a Loyalist Press 1773-1783*, by Kenneth Scott. (The same reference as 74-T).

75-T2 *New York Gazetteer*, the newspaper published by James

Rivington. (The same reference as 74-T2).

75-V *Genealogical Data from Colonial New York Newspapers*, by Kenneth Scott. (The same reference as 74-V).

# CITY AND COUNTY OF NEW YORK
# 1776

76-A   Address to Admiral and General Howe, 16 October 1776. (*New York City During the American Revolution*, Mercantile Library Association of New York City, 1861, pp. 117-137). A memorial to Admiral Lord Richard Howe and General Sir William Howe signed by 948 inhabitants of the City and County of New York expressing loyalty to King George the Third and praying that they, the Howe's, would restore this city and county to His Majesty's protection and peace.

76-B   "Prisoners in the Upper Barrack Guard, New York, 13 January 1776." (New York Secretary of State. *Calendar of Historical Manuscripts Relating to the War of the Revolution*, Albany, 1868, v.1, p. 212). These prisoners for the most part appear to have been former militia men.

76-C   "Vote of Col. Lasher's Battalion to go into the Continental Service, 29 January 1776." (New York Secretary of State. *Calendar of Historical Manuscripts Relating to the War of the Revolution*, Albany, 1868, v.1, pp. 223-224). Names several officers of the battalion as well as some non-commissioned officers and privates.

76-D   "Petition of Col. Lasher's Regiment" to the Provincial Congress of New York, 30 January 1776. (New York Secretary of State. *Calendar of Historical Manuscripts Relating to the War of the Revolution*, Albany, 1868, v.1, pp. 225-226). A memorial from the non-commissioned officers (none of whom are identified by rank) of the first battalion of Minute Men of the City of New York stating that they have equipped themselves at their own expense and have served without pay. Now that the battalion has been established on a new footing and they are to receive pay, they are are willing to continue in the service on condition that they are reimbursed for their previous expenses.

76-E "Petition of Sundry Soldiers" to the Provincial Congress of New York, 15 February 1776. (New York Secretary of State. *Calendar of Historical Manuscripts Relating to the War of the Revolution*, Albany, 1868, v. 1, p. 240). A petition from soldiers who had served in the Northern Campaign praying for a redress of grievances in that their captain deducted from their wages a sum for their clothing which they conceived to have been a bounty and in addition stopped their wages on 27 January when they were in Albany rather than on the date that they returned to New York.

76-F "Disaffected Persons in New York City, 10 March 1776." (New York Secretary of State. *Calendar of Historical Manuscripts Relating to the War of the Revolution*, Albany, 1868, v. 1, pp. 259-261). A list of loyalists who had been disarmed, with descriptions of the arms and accoutrements which had been taken from them.

76-G "Officers and Privates of Different Beats in New York at work 17 March 1776." (New York Secretary of State. *Calendar of Historical Manuscripts Relating to the War of the Revolution*, Albany, 1868, v.1, p. 267). The list also names twelve blacks at work with the militia and indicates by whose authority (presumably their master's) that this was permitted.

76-H "Persons that have Paid Duty of the Excise for 1776" a list drawn up 22 April 1776. (New York Secretary of State. *Calendar of Historical Manuscripts Relating to the War of Revolution*, Albany, 1868, v.1, p. 287). It isn't made clear whether those named on the list were tavernkeepers or retailers, that is to say, storekeepers. There are 78 names on the list of whom 12 were women. Some names are also entered on the following list, 76-I.

76-I "List of Liquor Sellers in New York City." (New York Secretary of State. *Calendar of Historical Manuscripts Relating to the War of the Revolution*, Albany, 1868, v.1, pp. 287-292). This list is not dated, but apparently it was drawn up at approximately the same time as the preceding list, 76-H. There are 268 names on the list of whom 41 are women.

76-J The Poor of the Parish of New York Who Came to Bedford on 28th August 1776. (Peter Force. *American Archives*, Series V, v.2, p. 1272). The document is a letter from the Bedford Committee, 28

October 1776, to the New York Convention stating the charges which have arisen for the care of the poor since they arrived in Bedford and asking for instructions for their care in the future.

76-K Soldiers' wives, whose husbands are absent in the Continental Service in the Northern Department, who received their husbands' pay in New York, March 8th, 1776. (Berthold Fernow, ed. *Documents Relating to the Colonial History of the State of New York*, v.15, Albany, 1887, p. 82). A list of 23 names.

76-L Firemen of the City of New York under the Command of Jacobus Stoutenburgh, Engineer. June 1776. (New York Secretary of State. *Calendar of Historical Manuscripts Relating to the War of the Revolution*, Albany, 1868, v.1, pp. 315-316). This list was also published in Peter Force's *American Archives*, Series IV, v.6, p.1408, as an appendix to the Minutes of the Provincial Congress of New York for 15 June 1776. From this source it is clear that these men were formed as a separate company of militia for the preservation of the City in case of invasion. The list has 106 names.

76-M Prisoners Confined in the City Hall, July 1st 1776, Suspected to be Enemies to American Liberties. This list was sent to General Washington along with two memorials dated 9 July 1776, and it is now preserved in the George Washington Papers, Series IV (microfilm reel 36). It lists fifteen men suspected to be loyalists as well as four men described as money makers, that is, persons who charged more for goods than was permitted.

76-N The Memorial of sundry Inhabitants of New York, and other friends to the peace and safety of the United States of America, to His Excellency George Washington, 9 July 1776, stating that they have been vigilant in finding out the enemies to the American States and praying that all such persons may be removed to some distant parts of the country. There are two copies of the memorial, each signed by different persons. They are preserved in the George Washington Papers, Series IV (microfilm reel 36). Peter Force published the two as a single document in his *American Archives*, Series V, v.1, p.335. However, the originals were used for entering the names into this book.

76-P The Poor Who Came out of the City of New York, August 1776. (*New York in the Revolution as Colony and State, Supplement*, ed. by Frederic G. Mather. Albany, 1901. pp. 118-125). In anticipation of the arrival of British forces, people began leaving New York City in such numbers that the Provincial Congress took measures to create an orderly exodus and to provide for the maintenance of the poor. It is clear, however, that not all the persons named on the list were poor as one man, for example, went out with his family and three loads of goods. Others, apparently, were the wives and children of soldiers. The list is divided into sections naming those who removed to Dutchess, Ulster and Westchester Counties, followed by a much longer list in which the place of destination is not stated. There is some duplication of names in the various sections perhaps indicating persons who went first to one county and then removed to another. There are 542 names on the list including the duplicate entries.

76-R *New York City Court Records, 1760-1797; Genealogical data from the Court of Quarter Sessions*, by Kenneth Scott (the same reference as 74-R).

76-S Officers appointed for the Militia of the City of New York, 8 January 1776. A list of 19 names which appeared in the minutes of the New York City Committee, published in Peter Force's *American Archives*, Series IV, v.4, p. 690).

76-V *Genealogical Data from Colonial New York Newspapers*, by Kenneth Scott (the same reference as 74-V).

76-Y Officers of the Regiment and Independent Companies of New York Militia. A list of loyalist officers commissioned 23 October and 15 November 1776. (*New York Genealogical and Biographical Record*, v.2, pp. 156-157 with corrections on p. 208).

# QUEENS COUNTY
## 1775

75-A Poll List of those in favor of, or opposed to, sending deputies to the Provincial Congress, 7 November 1775. (New York Secretary of State. *Calendar of Historical Manuscripts Relating to the War of the Revolution*, Albany, 1868, v.1, pp. 181-186. Also published in Peter Force. *American Archives*, Series IV, v.3, pp. 1389-1392). This lengthy list clearly defines those who were in favor of the revolutionary movement and those who were opposed to it. Those who were in favor of sending deputiies are marked as "associator" in the list in this book. All others named with this code (75-A), were opposed to sending deputies. The latter were by far in the majority. A copy of this poll list was sent to the Provincial Congress. See 75-I, below.

75-B  Inhabitants of Newtown, Queens County, who signed a remonstrance disapproving of the Continental Congress, 19 January 1775. (*Rivington's New York Newspaper, Excerpts from a Loyalist Press 1773-1783*, by Kenneth Scott. New York Historical Society, *Collections*, v.84, 1973, p. 99).

75-C  The Jamaica Declaration of Loyalty to King George III, 27 January 1775. (Peter Force. *American Archives*, Series IV, v.1, p. 1191. The names of the signers were also published in *Rivington's New York Newspaper*, cited above, pp. 102-103). The signers, by far the majority of the inhabitants of Jamaica, denounced a self-styled "committee" of that township and stated that they did not acknowledge any other representatives but the General Assembly of the Province.

75-D  Vote of the Town of Jamaica on the expediency of choosing a deputy. Presented to the Provincial Congress 21 April 1775. (Peter Force. *American Archives*, Series IV, v.2, pp. 838-839). Of the inhabitants, 94 voted under the heading "No Committee - No Deputy", that is, against having a town committee and against sending a representative to the Provincial Congress, whereas 85 voted for sending a deputy. In the list in this book all those named with the code 75-D who voted to send a deputy are marked "associator". All others with that code were opposed.

75-D1  Deputies chosen to represent Queens County in the Provincial Congress, 22 May 1775. (Peter Force. *American Archives*, Series IV, v.2, p. 838).

75-E  Minutemen of Jamaica, 1775. (New York Secretary of State. *Calendar of Historical Manuscripts Relating to the War of the Revolution*, Albany, 1868, v.1, pp. 186-187). The document only bears the date 1775, but it appears that it may have been drawn up in November of that year.

75-F  Freeholders of Oyster Bay who voted to send Zebulon

Williams as a delegate to the Provincial Congress, 12 April 1775. (New York Secretary of State. *Calendar of Historical Manuscripts Relating to New York in the Revolutionary War*, Albany, 1868, v.1, pp. 39-40). A list of 42 names. A preamble to the document states that the majority of the inhabitants of Oyster Bay did not choose to send a delegate, but they, the signers, were determined to keep in unity with the Provincial Congress and the United Colonies.

75-G   Freeholders of Newtown who voted to send Col. Jacob Blackwell as a delegate to the Provincial Congress, 20 April 1775. (New York Secretary of State. *Calendar of Historical Manuscripts Relating to the War of the Revolution*, Albany, 1868, v.1, p.40). A list of 100 names.

75-H   Disaffected Persons in Queens County, 12 December 1775. (New York Secretary of State. *Calendar of Historical Manuscripts Relating to the War of the Revolution*, Albany, 1868, v.1, p.202). The Provincial Congress, having received undoubted information that a number of disaffected persons in Queens County were supplied with arms and ammunition from on board the *Asia*, ship of war, and were arraying themselves in a military manner to oppose the measures taken by the United Colonies, thereupon ordered that the principal men among them (the men named on this list) attend the Provincial Congress on 19th December to answer the premises.

75-I   Delinquents in Queens County, 21 December 1775. (Peter Force. *American Archives*, Series IV, v.4, pp. 372-375). This list, drawn up by the Provincial Congress, is a clerical rearrangement of the Poll List of 7 November 1775 (item 75-A, above). Theoretically the names should be the same on the two lists, but some names do appear on the later one which are not on the first, while in other cases distinct variations in the names occur. Only those names which are in either of these categories have been incorporated into this book. (See also 76-B, below).

75-T   *Rivington's New York Newspaper, Excerpts from a Loyalist Press 1773-1783*, by Kenneth Scott. (New York Historical Society, *Collections*, v.84, 1973). Names relating to Queens County for the year 1775 were excerpted. The newspaper was not published in 1776. For a fuller description, see 74-T under the City and County of New York.

# QUEENS COUNTY
## 1776

76-A Associators of Queens County, 1776. (New York Secretary of State. *Calendar of Historical Manuscripts Relating to the War of the Revolution*, Albany, 1868, v.1, p. 209). The document only bears the date 1776, but it may have been drawn up in January of that year. The signers pledged to defend with arms the measures of the United Colonies. It was signed by only 17 men, however.

76-B Declaration of Sundry Inhabitants of Queens County, 19 January 1776. (New York Secretary of State. *Calendar of Historical Manuscripts Relating to the War of the Revolution*, Albany, 1868, v.1, pp. 215-218). The signers of this declaration were disaffected persons who had been disarmed by a regiment of soldiers from New Jersey under the command of Col. Nathaniel Heard. They declared (undoubtedly under duress) that they would obey all orders and instructions enjoined by the Provincial and Continental Congresses, and that they would not aid or assist in any way the army of the King. (See also the next document, 76-B2, below). In determining those who were opposed to the revolutionary measures, Col. Heard used, among other records, the Poll List of 7 November 1775, item 75-A, above.

76-B2 Oath Subscribed to by Sundry Inhabitants of Queens County, 19 January 1776. (Papers of the Continental Congress, item 67. Microfilm reel 81). Signed by disaffected persons who declared that the arms delivered up to Col. Heard were all the arms in their possession and that none had been concealed. In a note to the document it is stated that all those who signed the preceding document (76-B) also signed this one. That may be true, but there are upwards of forty names which either are not on the first list or else are variants of names which are. Only those names which are in either of these categories have been incorporated into this book.

76-C Return of the Jamaica Company of Militia, 22 March 1776. (New York Secretary of State. *Calendar of Historical Manuscripts Relating to the War of the Revolution*, Albany, 1868, v.1, pp. 271-272).

76-D    Petition of Inhabitants of Hempstead to the Provincial Congress 1776. (New York Secretary of State. *Calendar of Historical Manuscripts Relating to the War of the Revolution*, Albany, 1868, v.1, pp. 460-461). While the petition is not dated, it undoubtedly was drawn up in late August or in September 1776. The prayer of the petition was for relief from a regulation made by the Provincial Congress 24 August 1776 for the removal of all cattle and sheep from the township so that they would not fall into the hands of the British army.

76-E Petition and Representation of Queens County to Admiral Lord Richard Howe and General Sir William Howe, 21 October 1776. (Peter Force. *American Archives*, Series IV, v.2, pp. 1159-1163). A document signed by 1281 persons declaring that they bear allegiance to his Majesty George the Third and praying that the Howes would declare the County at peace with his Majesty thereby enabling the inhabitants to receive the benefits from that protection.

76-V  *Genealogical Data from Colonial New York Newspapers*, by Kenneth Scott. (Baltimore, Genealogical Publishing Co., 1982). Only a few names relating to Queens County appeared in this source. For fuller bibliographical detail, see the reference 74-V under the City and County of New York on page vi.

## SUFFOLK COUNTY
## 1775

All lists for Suffolk County in 1775, with one exception, item 75-H1, were published in New York Secretary of State. *Calendar of Historical Manuscripts Relating to the War of the Revolution*. (Albany, 1868), volume 1. Thus in the references below, the page numbers refer to this volume. (These lists were also published in Peter Force's *American Archives*, Series IV, v.3, pp. 610-618. A word of caution is necessary. Two lists were published in this same volume by Force which are headed Suffolk County, one being a long list beginning on p. 607, the other a short list on p. 615. A check of the names on these lists indicates that despite the headings they are not of Suffolk County.)

75-B1  Brookhaven, 16 May 1775. Men of the 4th Company of Militia of who voted to send a representative to the Provincial Congress, followed by a list of eleven men who refused to sign the association. The latter are indicated as non-signer, or n.s. (pp. 46-47)

75-B2  Brookhaven, 17 May 1775. Men of the 2nd Company of Militia who voted to send a representative to the Provincial Convention. (p. 45)

75-B3  Brookhaven, 17 May 1775. Men of the 3rd Company of Militia who voted to send a representative to the Provincial Convention. (pp. 45-46)

75-B4  Brookhaven, 19 May 1775. Men of the 1st Company of Militia who voted to send a representative to the Provincial Convention. (p. 44)

75-B5  Brookhaven, 23 May 1775. Men of the Middle Island Company of Militia who refused to vote to send a representative to the Provincial Convention. (p. 47). They were described as being neutral.

75-B6  Brookhaven, May 1775. The names of those who signed the association. (p. 57)

75-B7  Brookhaven, 8 June 1775. Men within the bounds of the 4th Company of Militia who signed the association. Those who refused to sign are marked non-signer, or n.s. (pp. 47-49)

75-B8  Brookhaven, 8 June 1775. Men of Brookhaven who signed the association. (p. 53)

75-B9  Brookhaven, *June and July*, 1775. Men of the 2nd Company of Militia who signed the association. Those who refused to sign are marked as non-signer, or n.s. (p. 47)

75-B10  Suffolk County, *June, July and August*, 1775. A list of those who signed the association. (pp. 63-64). This list is clearly headed Brookhaven, Suffolk County, but it appears that persons from other towns, particularly Southold, are named on it. Perhaps, despite the heading, it was intended as a general list for Suffolk County and not just for Brookhaven.

75-B11  Brookhaven, 3 August 1775. Men within the limits of the 1st Company of Militia who did not sign the association. (pp. 44-45)

75-B12  Brookhaven, 3 August 1775. Men within the limits of the

3rd Company of Militia who refused to sign the asssociation. (p. 46)

75-E Easthampton, 5 May 1775. A list of those who had signed the association. It was noted that every male within the town capable of bearing arms did sign. (pp. 55-56)

75-H Huntington, 8 May 1775. A list of those who had signed the association. Those who refused to sign are marked non-signer, or n.s. (pp. 50-53). See the note regarding Huntington under Islip, item 75-I, below.

75-H1 *Huntington Town Records*, by Charles R. Street. Records for 1775 are in v.2 (1888) and v.3 (1889). These records are treated here as if they were a list of names, but as the volumes are well indexed there should be no difficulty in locating data relating to a specific name. (A note to genealogists: the use of the word "records" in the title of this book does not refer to vital records).

75-I Islip, 13 May 1775. A list of those who had signed the association. Those who refused to sign are marked non-signer, or n.s. It also contains the names of Quakers of whom it was remarked that not one had signed the association. (pp. 54-55). It was noted on the list that some of the inhabitants of Islip signed the association at Huntington and Smithtown. The lists for those towns, however, do not specifically identify any signers as being of Islip. Perhaps these men signed the general list for Suffolk County, item 75-R, below, which does not indicate place of residence.

75-K Shelter Island, *May*, 1775. A list of those who had signed the association. (p. 62)

75-L Smithtown, *May*, 1775. A list of those who had signed the association. Those who refused to sign were described as recusants. The list also names the members of the Smithtown Committee who are noted here as Committee. (pp. 53-54). See the note regarding Smithtown under Islip, item 75-I, above.

75-M Southampton, 19 July 1775 and 1st August 1775. A list of those who had signed the association. (p. 59). It was noted that all males 16 years of age and upwards signed the association with only two exceptions.

75-N Southold, *May and June*, 1775. A list of those who had signed the association. Those who refused to sign are marked as being a non-signer, or n.s. (pp. 61-62)

75-R  Suffolk County, *May, 1775*. A list of inhabitants of Suffolk County, not identifed by town, who had signed the association. (pp. 49-50, 58-61)

# SUFFOLK COUNTY
# 1776

The only source used for Suffolk County in 1776, with the exception of Huntington, is the *Census of Suffolk County, New York, 1776*. This census was included in *Calendar of Historical Manuscripts Relating to the War of the Revolution*, published by the New York Secretary of State (Albany, 1868) v.1, pp. 378-417. It was published as a monograph by Hunterdon House (Lambertville, NJ) in 1984.

The census names the head of a household and gives a statistical abstract of the other members by age groups. For most households these age groups were indicated by five columns, or set of figures. Those households which included blacks required seven columns to distinguish the various members. These figures are:

- males above 50 years of age
- males above 16 years of age
- males under 16 years of age
- females above 16 years of age
- females under 16 years of age
- negroes, male and female, above 16 years of age
- negroes, male and female, under 16 years of age

## *Huntington*

The Town of Huntington was not included in the above census record. Whether the record for that town is missing or the census was never taken is unknown. To help make up in part for this absence, the following is offered.

76-H1 *Huntington Town Records*, by Charles R. Street. (Published jointly by the Towns of Huntington and Babylon in 3 vols., 1887-1889). Records for 1776 were published in volume 3. For additional detail, see the reference 75-H1 for Suffolk County.

76-H2 "Return of the Company of Capt. John Wickes, Huntington, for serving in Col. Josiah Smith's Regiment from July 29 to Aug. 31, 1776." Published in the above source (76-H1), p. 11. This list provides patriot military service for all who are named.

76-H3 "A List of Capt. Platt's Company under Command of Col. Josiah Smith." Published in the above source (76-H1), p. 12. This list, of course, also provides patriot military service for all who are named.

# A GUIDE TO THE DATA

The columns in the following pages list respectively: name; county (New York, Queens or Suffolk); town or address when known; and a code indicating the source of the information. The code begins with a year (1774, 1775 or 1776). Thus one can tell at a glance the county and the year involved for each person on this list.

The codes always relate to the county named. The reference 75-E for Queens, for example, is entirely different than the reference 75-E for a resident of Suffolk County. The references are listed by county on pages v - xx.

Numbers in square brackets following a name indicate the number of persons with the same name who appear on a particular list.

| | | | |
|---|---|---|---|
| , Cato [Mr. Fine] | N | New York | 76-G |
| ——, Ceasar [Mr. Laight] | N | New York | 76-G |
| ——, Cubitt [C$^n$ Lighburn] | N | New York | 76-G |
| ——, Elizabeth, widow | S | Southold | 76:0.0.0.3.0 |
| ——, Jo [Mr. Drake] | N | New York | 76-G |
| ——, Jo [Mr. Walton] | N | New York | 76-G |
| ——, Johan | N | New York | 74-A |
| ——, John [Mr. Lamb] | N | New York | 76-G |
| ——, Lodwick | N | New York | 76-A |
| ——, London, negro | N | to Dutchess Co. | 76-P |
| ——, Pero alias Shadreck | N | New York | 74-R free negro |
| ——, Peter [Benj Moore] | N | New York | 76-G |
| ——, Peter [C$^n$ Lighburn] | N | New York | 76-G |
| ——, Phyllis, a wench | N | to Dutchess Co. | 76-P |
| ——, Pierot, mulatto | N | Haerlaem | 74-T |
| ——, Pomp [Mr. Lott] | N | New York | 76-G |
| ——, Sam [Benj. Moore] | N | New York | 76-G |
| ——, Simms [C$^n$ Lighburn] | N | New York | 76-G |
| ——, Tom [Fred$^k$ Bassett] | N | New York | 76-G drummer |
| Aaron, Haob | N | New York | 76-A |
| Abbet, James | S | Huntington | 75-H non-signer |
| Abbet, James | S | Huntington | 76-H3 |
| Abbet, John | S | Huntington | 75-H |
| Abbet, Joseph | S | Huntington | 75-H |
| Abbet, Timothy | S | Huntington | 75-H |
| Abbett, Stephen | S | Huntington | 75-H |
| Abeel, Garret | N | New York | 74-A, 75-F |
| Abeel, Garret, Capt. | N | New York | 75-A |
| Abeel, Garret, juror | N | New York | 75-R, 76-R |
| Abeel, James | N | New York | 74-A, 76-N |
| Abeel, James, merchant | N | Maiden Lane | 75-D2 |
| Abeel, John | N | New York | 76-A, 76-N |
| Abeel, John, juror | N | New York | 74-R, 75-R |
| Abel, James, juror | N | New York | 74-R |
| Abell, William | N | New York | 74-A |
| Able, Jane | N | New York | 75-R |
| Able, Jane | N | removed upstate | 76-P |
| Abrahams, Daniel | Q | ........ | 76-B |
| Abrahams, Jacob | N | New York | 74-T |
| Abrams, Charles | Q | ........ | 75-A |

| | | | |
|---|---|---|---|
| Abrams, Daniel | Q | ........ | 75-A, 76-B2 |
| Abrams, Henry [2] | Q | ........ | [on] 75-A |
| Abrams, James | Q | ........ | 75-A |
| Abrams, John | Q | ........ | 75-A |
| Abrams, Jonas | Q | ........ | 75-I |
| Abrams, Joseph | Q | ........ | 75-A |
| Abrams, Samuel | Q | ........ | 75-A, 76-E |
| Abrams, William | Q | ........ | 75-A |
| Abramse, Abm. J. | N | New York | 76-A |
| Abramse, Anthony | N | New York | 74-A |
| Abramse, Anthony and Jac. | N | New York | 75-F |
| Abramse, Jacob | N | New York | 74-A |
| Acker, Philip | N | George Street | 76-H, 76-I |
| Acker, Sarah | S | Brookhaven | 76:0.0.1.2.1 |
| Acker, Sybert | N | New York | 76-N |
| Ackerly, Anthony, constable | N | New York | 74-R to 76-R |
| Ackerly, Benjamin | Q | ........ | 75-A associator |
| Ackerly, Benjamin | Q | ........ | 76-E |
| Ackerly, Joseph | Q | ........ | 76-E |
| Ackerman, David | N | New York | 74-A |
| Ackerman, Nicklass | N | New York | 74-A |
| Ackert, Philip | N | New York | 76-A |
| Ackles, Elisabeth | N | removed upstate | 76-P |
| Ackley, Anthony | N | New York | 74-A |
| Ackley, Jeremiah | N | New York | 76-A |
| Ackley, John | N | New York | 74-A, 76-A |
| Ackley, Stephen | S | Brookhaven | 76:0.1.1.1.2 |
| Ackron, Mary | N | removed upstate | 76-P |
| Acle, Martin | N | New York | 76-I |
| Acley, Philop | S | Brookhaven | 76:1.1.0.2.0.1.2 |
| Acley, Robard | S | Brookhaven | 76:0.2.2.1.5 |
| Adams, Abraham | N | New York | 76-A |
| Adams, Amos | S | Brookhaven | 75-B6 |
| Adams, Amos | S | Brookhaven | 76:0.1.3.1.2 |
| Adams, John | N | New York | 74-R |
| Adams, John, carpenter | N | James Street | 75-D2 |
| Adams, John, executed | N | New York | 74-T, 74-V |
| Adams, Jonas, taylor | N | Beekman Slip | 75-D1, D2 |
| Adams, William | N | New York | 76-N |
| Adams, William, Sergt. | N | Fly Market | 75-D1, D2 |

| | | | |
|---|---|---|---|
| Adams, Wm | S | Shelter Island | 75-K |
| Addoms, John | N | New York | 74-A |
| Adolphus, Isaac | N | New York | 74-T |
| Adolphus, Philip | N | New York | 74-T |
| Adriance, Elbert | Q | ........ | 75-A, 76-B |
| Adriance, Jacob | Q | ........ | 75-A, 76-B |
| Adrianse, Elbert | Q | ........ | 76-E |
| Aersson, Aaron | N | New York | 74-A, 75-D3 |
| Agar, Edward | N | New York | 76-A |
| Agar, Edward, 2d Lieut. | N | New York | 76-Y |
| Ahers, Chapman, smelter | N | New York | 74-T |
| Ahner, John | N | New York | 74-A |
| Aillin, Wm | N | New York | 74-A |
| Aim, George, taylor | N | Fair Street | 75-D1, D2 |
| Aim, Martin | N | New York | 74-A |
| Aimes, Ernest | N | New York | 76-A |
| Airs, Elisabeth | N | (d. at Bedford) | 76-J |
| Airy, Cornelius | N | New York | 74-R |
| Aitkin, Charles Esq. | N | Haerlaem | 74-T |
| Akemsen, Jeronimus | N | New York | 76-A |
| Akerly, Arthur | S | Brookhaven | 75-B10 |
| Akerly, Elijah | S | Brookhaven | 75-B10 |
| Akerly, Elijah | S | Brookhaven | 75-B11 n.s. |
| Akerly, John | S | Brookhaven | 75-B10 |
| Akerly, John | S | Brookhaven | 75-B11 n.s. |
| Akerly, Nathanael | S | Brookhaven | 75-B10 |
| Akerly, Nathaniel & his son | S | Brookhaven | 76:1.1.2.2.0 |
| Akerly, Philip | S | Brookhaven | 75-B10 |
| Akerly, Robart | S | Brookhaven | 75-B10 |
| Akerly, Robert | S | Brookhaven | 75-B11 n.s. |
| Akerly, Stephan | S | Brookhaven | 75-B10 |
| Akerly, Stephen | S | Brookhaven | 75-B11 n.s. |
| Akerly; see also Ackley; Acley | | | |
| Alban, John | S | Brookhaven | 76:1.1.2.4.3 |
| Albertson, Albert | Q | ........ | 76-E |
| Albertson, Albert | Q | Oyster Bay | 75-F |
| Albertson, Charity, widow | S | Southampton | 76:0.1.1.4.1 |
| Albertson, Daniel | Q | ........ | 75-A |
| Albertson, Daniel | Q | ........ | 76-B, 76-E |
| Albertson, Daniel | S | ........ | 75-R |

| | | | |
|---|---|---|---|
| Albertson, Daniel | S | Southampton | 76:0.1.2.1.2 |
| Albertson, Derick | Q | ........ | 76-E |
| Albertson, Derrick | Q | ........ | 76-E |
| Albrson, John | S | Southampton | 76:1.2.1.4.0 |
| Alburtus, Peter | Q | ........ | 76-E |
| Aldredge, Gershom | S | Southold | 75-N |
| Aldrich, Garshum | S | Brookhaven | 75-B10 |
| Aldrich, Jacob | S | Brookhaven | 75-B10 |
| Aldrich, Stephen | S | Brookhaven | 75-B10 |
| Aldridge, Daniel | S | Southold | 75-N |
| Aldridge, Enos | S | Southold | 75-N |
| Aldritch, Daniel | S | Southold | 76:0.3.2.2.0 |
| Aldritch, Gershom | S | Southold | 76:0.1.2.1.2 |
| Aldritch, Jacob | S | Southold | 76:1.2.1.3.0 |
| Aldritch, Stephen | S | Southold | 76:0.2.3.1.2 |
| Alexander, Robert | N | Hunter's Quay | 75-T |
| Allaby, William | S | Huntington | 75-H non-signer |
| Allan, William | N | New York | 74-A |
| Allbeen, John | S | Brookhaven | 75-B1, 75-B7 |
| Allen, Abraham | Q | ........ | 76-E |
| Allen, Andrew | Q | ........ | 75-A, 75-I |
| Allen, Andrew | Q | ........ | 76-A, 76-B |
| Allen, Andrew | Q | ........ | 76-E |
| Allen, Baruch/Brauch | Q | ........ | 75-A, 75-I |
| Allen, Baruch/Brauch | Q | ........ | 76-B, 76-E |
| Allen, Benjamin | S | ........ | 75-R |
| Allen, Benjamin | S | Southampton | 76:1.0.0.1.0 |
| Allen, Daniel | Q | ........ | 75-A, 75-I |
| Allen, Daniel | Q | ........ | 76-B, 76-E |
| Allen, Darius | Q | ........ | 76-B, 76-E |
| Allen, David | Q | ........ | 76-E |
| Allen, Elias | Q | Oyster Bay | 75-A, 75-I |
| Allen, Henry | Q | ........ | 76-E |
| Allen, Henry Sr. | Q | ........ | 76-E |
| Allen, Jacamiah | N | New York | 75-B; 75-R juror |
| Allen, John | Q | ........ | 75-A, 75-I |
| Allen, John | Q | ........ | 76-B |
| Allen, John [2] | Q | ........ | [on] 76-E |
| Allen, Letty | N | New York | 76-K |
| Allen, Nathaniel | S | Huntington | 76-H2 |

| | | | |
|---|---|---|---|
| Allen, Philip [2] | Q | ........ | [on] 76-E |
| Allen, Richard, Sergt. | N | New York | 75-D3 |
| Allen, Robert | Q | ........ | 75-A, 75-I |
| Allen, Robert | Q | ........ | 76-B, 76-E |
| Allen, Samuel | Q | ........ | 76-E |
| Allen, Stephen | N | New York | 76-A |
| Allen, Thomas | N | New York | 76-A |
| Allener, Appolone, Mrs. | N | rem to Ulster Co. | 76-P |
| Allener, Prudence | N | rem to Ulster Co. | 76-P |
| Allesby, Arthur | S | Brookhaven | 75-B11 n.s. |
| Allgelt, Jacobus | N | New York | 74-A |
| Alliben, John | S | Brookhaven | 75-B6 |
| Allicocke, Joseph | N | New York | 74-A |
| Allicoke, Joseph | N | New York | 74-T2, 6/22 |
| Alliner, James | N | New York | 75-D2 |
| Alling, Pruden, blacksmith | N | Broad Street | 75-D1, D2 |
| Allison, Edward | Q | ........ | 76-E |
| Allison, Robert | N | New York | 74-A, 76-A |
| Ally, Henry | S | Huntington | 75-H non-signer |
| Alner, Apolonia | N | to Dutchess Co. | 76-P |
| Alner, James | N | New York | 75-B |
| Alner, James, Capt. | N | New York | 76-C |
| Alner, Jas., Sergt. | N | New York | 75-D3 |
| Alner, John | N | New York | 74-T2, 12/22 |
| Alner, John | N | New York | 76-M |
| Alner, Mary | N | to Dutchess Co. | 76-P |
| Alsop, John | N | New York | 74-T2, 11/24 |
| Alsop, Richard | Q | ........ | 76-E |
| Alsop, Richard, J.P. | Q | Newtown | 75-B |
| Alsop, Thomas | Q | ........ | 76-E |
| Alstine, Harmanus | N | New York | 74-A |
| Alstyne, Jeronemus | N | New York | 74-A |
| Alstyne, Jeronemus | N | New York | 76-A, 76-L |
| Alstyne, John | N | New York | 76-A |
| Alstyne, _____ widow | N | Maiden Lane | 75-T2, 7/27 |
| Amar, James | N | New York | 76-A |
| Amar, John | N | New York | 76-F |
| Ambeman, Dirck | S | Huntington | 75-H |
| Amberman, Derrick | Q | ........ | 76-E |
| Amberman, Isaac | Q | Jamaica | 75-A, 75-D |

| | | | |
|---|---|---|---|
| Amberman, Isaac | Q | Jamaica | 75-I |
| Amberman, Isaac | Q | Jamaica | 76-B, 76-E |
| Amberman, Isaac Jr. | Q | ........ | 76-B, 76-E |
| Amberman, Isaac Sr. | Q | ........ | 75-A |
| Amberman, John | Q | ........ | 75-I |
| Amberman, John | Q | ........ | 76-B |
| Amberman, John [2] | Q | ........ | [on] 75-A |
| Amberman, John [2] | Q | Jamaica | [on] 75-C |
| Amberman, John [3] | Q | ........ | [on] 76-E |
| Amberman, Nicholas | Q | ........ | 76-B, 76-E |
| Amberman, Powell/Powall | Q | Jamaica | 75-A, 75-C |
| Amberman, Powell/Powall | Q | Jamaica | 75-D, 75-I, 76-E |
| Amberson, Simon, shoemkr | N | New York | 75-D2 runaway |
| Amerman, Albert | N | New York | 74-A |
| Amerman, Cornelius | Q | Jamaica | 75-E |
| Amerman, Derick | Q | Jamaica | 75-E |
| Amerman, John | N | New York | 76-A |
| Amerman, Paul | Q | ........ | 76-B |
| Amia, Mary | N | to Westchester Co | 76-P |
| Amiel, John Jr. | N | New York | 74-A |
| Amiel, John Jr., storekeeper | N | Smith Street | 74-T2, 1/27 |
| Amon, Harry, shoemaker | N | Golden Hill | 75-D2 |
| Amory, John | N | New York | 74-A, 76-A |
| Amory, John, whipmaker | N | New York | 75-T2, 9/21 |
| Amos, Daniel | N | New York | 76-A |
| Andarese, Nich⁴ Jr. | N | New York | 74-A |
| Anderiese, John | N | New York | 76-A |
| Anderrese, Stephen | N | New York | 76-A |
| Anderson, Abᵐ | N | New York | 75-D2 |
| Anderson, Abraham | N | New York | 74-A |
| Anderson, Alex, Corp'l | N | New York | 75-D3 |
| Anderson, Alex'r | N | New York | 74-A, 76-D |
| Anderson, Alex'r, cordw'r | N | Fresh Street | 75-D2 |
| Anderson, Alexander | N | New York | 76-V |
| Anderson, Alexander, joiner | N | Maiden Lane | 75-D2 |
| Anderson, Andrew, servant | N | New York | 75-T runaway |
| Anderson, Ann, Mrs. | N | to Dutchess Co. | 76-P |
| Anderson, Anne, Mrs. | N | rem to Ulster Co. | 76-P |
| Anderson, Elbert | N | New York | 74-A |
| Anderson, Elias | N | New York | 74-A, 74-T |

| | | | |
|---|---|---|---|
| Anderson, Elias, wheelwrt | N | New York | 75-D1, D2 |
| Anderson, Elisabeth | N | rem. to Bedford | 76-J |
| Anderson, Elizabeth | N | New York | 76-H, 76-R |
| Anderson, Elizabeth | N | to Westchester Co | 76-P |
| Anderson, Elizabeth | N | to Dutchess Co. | 76-P |
| Anderson, George | N | New York | 74-A |
| Anderson, John | N | New York | 74-A, 76-N |
| Anderson, John | N | to Dutchess Co. | 76-P |
| Anderson, John, printer | N | Beekman's Slip | 74-T2, 5/26 |
| Anderson, Mary | N | removed upstate | 76-P |
| Anderson, Peter, joiner | N | William Street | 75-D1, D2 |
| Anderson, Peter Jr. | N | New York | 74-A |
| Anderson, Peter [3] | N | New York | [on] 74-A |
| Andres, Jacob | S | Brookhaven | 75-B6 |
| Andres, Jacob | S | Brookhaven | 76:0.1.3.1.1 |
| Andrews, Jeremiah, jeweller | N | Hanover Square | 74-T2, 9/15 |
| Andrews, Robt. | N | New York | 74-A |
| Anne, Mary | N | to Westchester Co | 76-P |
| Annely, Richard, gunsmith | N | Dock Street | 75-D1, D2 |
| Anno, Marcia | N | to Dutchess Co. | 76-P |
| Anno, Mary | N | to Westchester Co | 76-P |
| Anter, Samuel | N | removed upstate | 76-P |
| Anthony, Jno. | N | in The Swamp | 75-D2 |
| Anthony, John | N | New York | 74-R juror |
| Anthony, John | N | New York | 74-T2, 11/24 |
| Anthony, John | N | New York | 75-B, 76-N |
| Anthony, John, Supt. | N | New York | 75-D3 |
| Anthony, John, tanner | N | William Street | 75-D1, D2 |
| Anthony, ---- Lieu* | N | New York | 76-C |
| Anthony, Nicholas Jr., juror | N | New York | 74-R, 75-R |
| Anthony, Nich* N. | N | New York | 74-A |
| Anthony, Nich* N., Capt. | N | New York | 75-A |
| Anthony, Theophilus | N | New York | 74-A |
| Anthony, Theophilus | N | New York | 74-T2, 11/24 |
| Anthony, Theophilus | N | New York | 76-R juror |
| Antill, John | N | New York | 76-A |
| Antill, Lewis | N | New York | 76-A |
| Apple, Anthony | N | New York | 74-A |
| Apple, Anthony, baker | N | Prince Street | 75-D1, D2 |
| Applebey, Thomas | Q | ........ | 76-E |

| | | | |
|---|---|---|---|
| Applegate, John | N | Coenties Market | 75-T2, 4/6 |
| Applegate, John | N | New York | 74-A |
| Applegate, Zebulon, shoemr | N | William Street | 75-D1, D2 |
| Apthorpe, Chaˢ Wᵈ | N | New York | 76-A |
| Archer, James | N | New York | 75-R |
| Archer, John | N | New York | 74-A, 76-A |
| Arcularius, Philip | N | New York | 76-A |
| Arden/Arding, Charles, Dr. | Q | Jamaica | 75-A, 75-C |
| Arden/Arding, Charles, Dr. | Q | Jamaica | 75-D, 75-H |
| Arden/Arding, Charles, Dr. | Q | Jamaica | 75-I, 76-E |
| Arden, Francis | N | New York | 76-A |
| Arden, Francis, butcher | N | Georges Street | 75-D1, D2 |
| Arden, Francis [2] | N | New York | [on] 74-A |
| Arden, Jacob | N | New York | 74-A, 75-D1 |
| Arden, James | N | New York | 74-A, 75-C |
| Arden, John | N | New York | 74-A |
| Arden, Thomas | N | New York | 74-A, 74-T |
| Arden, Thomas and James | N | New York | 75-F |
| Arden, Thomas Jr. | N | New York | 74-A |
| Arding, John, Lieut. | N | New York | 75-A |
| Arelf, Peter | N | New York | 74-A |
| Areson, Anne | N | Pecks slip | 76-I |
| Areson, James | Q | ........ | 76-E |
| Areson, Samuel | N | New York | 74-A |
| Arisson, Benjamin | Q | ........ | 76-E |
| Arisson, William | Q | ........ | 76-E |
| Armbruster, John | N | New York | 74-A |
| Armitage, James | N | New York | 74-A, 76-D |
| Armstrong, John | N | Kingsbridge | 75-T |
| Armstrong, John | N | New York | 76-I |
| Armstrong, —— Mrs. | N | Walton's Wharf | 75-T2, 4/6 |
| Armstrong, William | N | New York | 74-A |
| Arnell, Valentine | N | New York | 76-L |
| Arnold, John | S | Brookhaven | 75-B1, 75-B7 |
| Arnold, Thomas | S | Southold | 76:1.0.0.2.0 |
| Arnold, Valentine | N | New York | 74-A |
| Arnold, William, Ensign | N | New York | 75-A |
| Arnott, Michael | N | New York | 76-A |
| Arrell, Peter | N | New York | 76-A |
| Arrison, Ann | N | Peck's slip | 76-H |

| | | | |
|---|---|---|---|
| Arthart, George | N | New York | 76-L |
| Arthur, Jesse | S | Smithtown | 75-L |
| Arthur, Jesse | S | Smithtown | 76:0.2.0.1.0 |
| Arthur, John | N | New York | 74-A |
| Arthur, John, storekeepr | N | New York | 74-T2, 5/19 |
| Arthur, Platt | S | Smithtown | 75-L |
| Arthur, Reuben | S | Huntington | 76-H3 |
| Arthur, Reuben | S | Smithtown | 76:0.1.4.0.2 |
| Arthur, William | S | Smithtown | 76:0.2.3.1.2.2.0 |
| Arwin, Jacob | N | New York | 74-A |
| Ash, Catherine | N | New York | 76-I |
| Ash, Gilbert | N | New York | 76-A |
| Ash, Gilbert, cabinetmaker | N | William Street | 75-D1, D2 |
| Ash, John, taylor | N | Georges Street | 75-D1, D2 |
| Ash, Thomas | N | New York | 74-A, 75-D2 |
| Ash, Thomas | N | New York | 76-N |
| Ash, Thomas, chairmaker | N | New York | 74-T2, 2/17 |
| Ash, William | N | New York | 74-A |
| Ash, William | N | Vesey street | 76-I |
| Ash, William, chairmaker | N | Broadway | 75-D2 |
| Ashe, Wm | N | Veese's street | 76-H |
| Ashfield, Catherine | N | New York | 76-K |
| Ashfield, John, baker | N | Division Street | 75-D1, D2 |
| Ashfield, V. Pearse | N | New York | 75-F |
| Ashfield, V. Pierce | N | New York | 76-A |
| Ashfield, Vincent Pearce | N | Cruger's Wharf | 74-T2, 4/28 |
| Ashton, Joseph, shoemaker | N | at T. Meredith's | 75-D2 |
| Aspinwall, John | N | New York | 74-A |
| Aspinwall, John Esq. | N | New York | 74-V |
| Atkins, Robert | N | New York | 76-A |
| Atkinson, Thomas | N | New York | 76-A |
| Atwell, Mary | N | rem. to Bedford | 76-J |
| Atwood, Thomas B. | N | New York | 75-F |
| Atwood, Thomas Bridgen | N | New York | 74-T2, 8/25 |
| Atwood, Thos. Bridgen | N | New York | 74-A |
| Aubergh, Earnest | N | New York | 74-A |
| Auchmuty, James | N | to Westchester Co | 76-P |
| Auchmuty, Richard | N | New York | 76-A |
| Auchmuty, Robert N. | N | New York | 76-A |
| Auchmuty, Samuel | N | New York | 76-A |

| | | | |
|---|---|---|---|
| Austin, Thos. | N | New York | 74-A |
| Avery, Humphery Jun. | S | Brookhaven | 75-B6 |
| Avery, Humphrey | S | Brookhaven | 75-B6 |
| Avery, Humphrey | S | Brookhaven | 76:1.2.0.1.0 |
| Avery, Nathan | S | Brookhaven | 75-B6 |
| Avery, Roger | S | Brookhaven | 75-B6 |
| Avery, Samuel | N | New York | 75-T |
| Avery, Thomas | S | Brookhaven | 75-B3, 75-B6 |
| Avery, Thomas | S | Brookhaven | 76:0.1.1.0.0 |
| Awlsorth, Samuel | N | New York | 74-A |
| Axtell, William | N | New York | 76-A |
| Aymar, Daniel | N | New York | 74-A |
| Aymar, Daniel [2] | N | New York | [on] 76-A |
| Aymar, James, 1st Lieut. | N | New York | 76-Y |
| Aymar, John | N | New York | 74-A |
| Aymer, William | N | New York | 76-A |
| Babcock, Bethiah | S | Southampton | 76:0.0.0.1.0 |
| Babcock, Simeon | S | Southampton | 76:0.1.2.1.2 |
| Baccus, John, cordwainer | N | nr. Sugar House | 75-D2 |
| Bache, Theophilact | N | New York | 75-F |
| Bache, Theophylact | N | New York | 76-A |
| Backer, Albart | N | removed upstate | 76-P |
| Backer, Sara | N | removed upstate | 76-P |
| Backhouse, John, merchant | N | Wall Street | 75-T2, 2/23 |
| Backhouse, Wm | N | New York | 76-A |
| Backhouse, Wm., merchant | N | Wall Street | 74-T2, 4/28 |
| Badger, John | N | New York | 76-A |
| Badkin, Richard | N | New York | 74-A |
| Bagley, Joseph | N | New York | 76-A |
| Baierd, Robert | N | New York | 74-A |
| Bailey, Daniel | Q | ........ | 76-E |
| Bailey, Elias | N | New York | 74-A, 76-A |
| Bailey, John | N | New York | 74-A |
| Bailey, John, carman | N | Ann Street | 75-D2 |
| Bailey, John, store | N | op. Coffee House | 74-T2, 10/20 |
| Bailey, Nath'n | Q | Newtown | 75-G |
| Bailey, William | N | New York | 76-A |
| Bailey; see also Baley, Bayley | | | |
| Baker, Abraham | S | ........ | 75-R |
| Baker, Abraham | S | Easthampton | 75-E |

| Baker, Abraham | S | Easthampton | 76:0.2.2.2.3 |
| Baker, Daniel | S | Easthampton | 75-E |
| Baker, David | S | Easthampton | 75-E |
| Baker, David | S | Easthampton | 76:0.1.2.2.2 |
| Baker, Jacob | S | Brookhaven | 75-B6 |
| Baker, Jacob | S | Islip | 75-I |
| Baker, Jacob | S | Islip | 76:0.1.0.1.1 |
| Baker, John | Q | ........ | 76-E |
| Baker, Jona^th Jun^r | S | Brookhaven | 75-B6 |
| Baker, Jonathan | S | Brookhaven | 76:1.0.0.1.0 |
| Baker, Jonathan Juner | S | Brookhaven | 76:0.1.3.1.3 |
| Baker, Leonard | N | New York | 74-T insolvent |
| Baker, Mehitable, Mrs. | S | Easthampton | 76:0.0.1.1.1 |
| Baker, Nathaniel | S | Easthampton | 76:0.1.3.1.4 |
| Baker, Nath^l | S | Easthampton | 75-E |
| Baker, Sam^ll | S | Easthampton | 75-E |
| Baker, Samuel | S | Easthampton | 76:0.1.2.3.1 |
| Baker, T. | Q | ........ | 76-E |
| Baker, Thomas | S | Easthampton | 75-E |
| Baker, Thomas, Lt. | S | Easthampton | 76:0.2.1.1.2 |
| Baker, Willem | S | Brookhaven | 76:0.1.1.1.2 |
| Baker, William | S | Brookhaven | 75-B3, 75-B6 |
| Balden, Abraham | Q | ........ | 75-A, 75-I, 76-E |
| Balden, George | Q | ........ | 75-A, 75-I |
| Balden, Henry | Q | ........ | 75-A |
| Balden, James | Q | ........ | 75-A |
| Balden, Jonathan | Q | ........ | 75-A |
| Balden, Stephen | Q | ........ | 75-A, 76-E |
| Balden, Thos | Q | ........ | 75-A |
| Balden; see also Baudin | | | |
| Balding, Abel | Q | ........ | 76-E |
| Balding, Samuel [2] | Q | ........ | [on] 76-E |
| Baldwin, Amos | S | Huntington | 75-H |
| Baldwin, George | Q | ........ | 76-E |
| Baldwin, James | Q | ........ | 76-B |
| Baldwin, Jesse | S | Huntington | 75-H non-signer |
| Baldwin, Joseph | N | New York | 74-A, 76-L |
| Baldwin, Joseph, tallowchdr | N | North River | 75-D2 |
| Baldwin, Samuel | N | New York | 76-A |
| Baldwin, Samuel [2] | N | New York | [on] 74-A |

| | | | |
|---|---|---|---|
| Baldwin, Tramor | N | New York | 74-A |
| Baldwin, Triamor, carpenter | N | Frankford Street | 75-D1, D2 |
| Balfour, Wm | N | New York | 76-A |
| Ball, George | N | New York | 76-F |
| Ball, George, china & glass | N | Bayard Street | 74-T2, 1/6 |
| Ball, George, merchant | N | New York | 76-V |
| Ball, Isaac | N | New York | 76-A, 76-L |
| Ball, Peter | N | New York | 74-A |
| Ball, Titus | N | New York | 76-A |
| Ball, William, Sergt. | N | New York | 76-G |
| Ballard, William | N | New York | 74-A |
| Bancker, Aaron | N | New York | 76-L |
| Bancker, Abraham B. | N | New York | 75-B |
| Bancker, Abraham P., Lieu' | N | New York | 76-C |
| Bancker, Aron | N | New York | 74-A |
| Bancker, Christ. | N | New York | 74-A |
| Bancker, Evert Jr. | N | New York | 74-A, 76-A |
| Bancker, Evert Jr. | N | New York | 75-R juror |
| Bancker, John | N | New York | 74-A, 75-B |
| Bancker, John, Lieut. | N | New York | 76-C |
| Bandon, Charles P. | N | New York | 76-I |
| Bankear, Abraham | N | New York | 74-A |
| Banker, Evert | N | New York | 75-T2, 5/4 |
| Banker, _____ Mrs. | N | Hanover Square | 75-D2 |
| Banker, Richard, merchant | N | Hanover Square | 75-T, 75-V |
| Banker, Sarah | N | New York | 75-V |
| Banks, James | N | New York | 76-I |
| Banks, Josiah, Capt., innkpr | N | Little Dock Street | 75-E |
| Bannot, Peter | N | New York | 76-A |
| Banta, Darius | N | New York | 74-A |
| Banta, Jacob | N | New York | 76-I |
| Banta, Paules | N | New York | 75-T |
| Banta, Paulus | N | New York | 74-A, 76-A |
| Banta, Weart, hse carpenter | N | nr Swamp Church | 75-D1, D2 |
| Banyar, Goldsbrow | N | New York | 76-F |
| Baragin, Luke | Q | Jamaica | 75-C |
| Barclay, Andrew | N | New York | 76-R juror |
| Barclay, Andrew D. | N | New York | 75-F |
| Barclay, Andrew, merchant | N | Wall Street | 74-V |
| Barclay, David | N | New York | 75-D2 |

| | | | |
|---|---|---|---|
| Barclay, David, peruke mkr | N | Peck Slip | 75-D1, D2 |
| Barclay, James | N | New York | 74-A |
| Barclay, Thomas, Ensign | N | New York | 75-A |
| Bard, Fredrick | N | New York | 76-L |
| Bard, Samuel, Dr. | N | New York | 74-T, 75-T |
| Bard; see also Beard | | | |
| Barden, Edward | N | New York | 76-A |
| Bardin, Edward, innholder | N | Chapel Street | 75-E |
| Bardin, Edward, innkeeper | N | New York | 74-R Freeman |
| Bardin, Edward, tavernkpr | N | in the Fields | 74-T |
| Bargen, Luke | Q | ........ | 76-B2 |
| Barits, Carman | Q | Hempstead | 76-D |
| Barke, George | N | New York | 76-A |
| Barker, Benjamin | Q | ........ | 76-E |
| Barkley, David | N | New York | 76-R |
| Barley, John | N | New York | 75-D1 |
| Barnby, Jonathan | S | Easthampton | 75-E |
| Barnes, Isaac | S | Shelter Island | 75-K |
| Barnes, Jeremiah | S | Easthampton | 75-E |
| Barnes, Matthew | S | Easthampton | 75-E |
| Barnes, Nathaniel | S | Easthampton | 76:0.1.1.1.1 |
| Barnes, Noah | S | Easthampton | 75-E |
| Barnes, Noah | S | Easthampton | 76:1.3.0.1.1.1.2 |
| Barnes, Thomas | N | New York | 76-A |
| Barnes, William | S | Easthampton | 75-E |
| Barns, Abraham | S | Easthampton | 75-E |
| Barns, John | N | New York | 76-M |
| Barns, Matthew | S | Easthampton | 76:0.1.2.3.1 |
| Barns, Seth | S | Easthampton | 75-E |
| Barns, William | S | Easthampton | 76:1.2.1.1.0 |
| Barr, Henrich | N | New York | 76-A |
| Barraga, Derick | Q | ........ | 76-B2 |
| Barran, Andrew | S | Brookhaven | 76:0.1.3.2.2.0.1 |
| Barrea, Francis | N | New York | 74-A |
| Barrea, John | N | New York | 74-A |
| Barrin, Garrit | N | New York | 76-H |
| Barrow, James | N | New York | 76-L |
| Barrow, John | N | New York | 74-A, 76-L |
| Barrow, Thomas | N | Broad Street | 75-T |
| Barrow, Thomas | N | New York | 74-A, 76-L |

| | | | |
|---|---|---|---|
| Barruck, Judah | N | New York | 74-V |
| Barry, Robt. | N | New York | 74-A, 76-D |
| Barry, Thomas | N | New York | 74-R |
| Barry, Thomas, merchant | N | New York | 74-T2, 5/26 |
| Bartelet, Peter | N | New York | 74-R apprentice |
| Barterm, Jasper B. | N | New York | 74-A |
| Bartlee, W$^m$ | S | Brookhaven | 76:0.1.2.1.1 |
| Bartlet, William | S | Brookhaven | 75-B7 |
| Bartley, David | N | New York | 74-A |
| Bartley, Elizabeth | N | to Westchester Co | 76-P |
| Bartman, Jacob | N | New York | 76-R |
| Barton, Elijah | Q | ........ | 75-A, 76-B |
| Barton, Thomas Jr., 2d Lt. | N | New York | 76-Y |
| Bartow, Obadiah | S | Huntington | 75-H |
| Bartow, Reuben | S | Huntington | 75-H |
| Bartow, Silas | S | Huntington | 75-H |
| Bartow, Thos. | N | New York | 74-A |
| Barwick/Berwick, John | N | New York | 76-R |
| Barwick, John | N | New York | 76-A |
| Barwick, Robert, taylor | N | St. James Street | 75-D1, D2 |
| Barwick, William | N | New York | 74-R |
| Bashford, John | Q | ........ | 76-E |
| Basset, Francis | N | New York | 74-T2, 11/24 |
| Basset, Frederick, juror | N | New York | 74-R, 75-R |
| Bassett, Francis | N | New York | 76-L |
| Bassett, Frederick | N | New York | 74-A, 75-F |
| Bassett, Frederick | N | New York | 76-G, 76-N |
| Bassett, William | S | Easthampton | 75-E |
| Bastion, Antoni | S | Brookhaven | 75-B10 |
| Bate, James | N | New York | 76-N |
| Bateman, William | N | New York | 75-V runaway |
| Bateman, William, engraver | N | Fair Street | 74-T2, 10/20 |
| Bates, Alexander | N | New York | 75-T |
| Bates, Daniel | N | New York | 75-D3 |
| Bates, George | Q | Jamaica | 75-C |
| Bates, James | S | Brookhaven | 75-B6 |
| Bates, James | S | Brookhaven | 76:0.1.1.1.0 |
| Bates, James, clark | N | Queen Street | 75-D1, D2 |
| Bates, James, Corp'l | N | New York | 75-D3 |
| Bates, Sam'l | N | New York | 76-A |

| | | | |
|---|---|---|---|
| Battine, David | Q | ........ | 75-A |
| Batty, David | Q | Hempstead | 76-D |
| Baudin, Wm. Jno. | Q | Jamaica | 75-H |
| Bauman, Sabast'n | N | New York | 74-A, 75-B, 76-C |
| Bauman, Sebastian | N | New York | 76-N |
| Bauman, William | N | New York | 76-A |
| Bausher, Peter | N | Fresh Water | 75-T2, 2/16 |
| Bawne, Joseph | Q | ........ | 75-A associator |
| Baxter, Israel | Q | ........ | 76-E |
| Bayard, Lawe | N | New York | 76-A |
| Bayard, Robert | N | New York | 76-A |
| Bayard, Sam'l Sr. | N | New York | 74-A |
| Bayard, Samuel | N | New York | 76-A |
| Bayard, Samuel Jr. | N | New York | 74-T |
| Bayard, William | N | Greenwich | 75-T |
| Bayard, William | N | New York | 76-A, 76-F |
| Bayley, Benjamin | S | Southold | 76:1.1.0.2.0 |
| Bayley, Benj$^m$ | S | ........ | 75-R |
| Bayley, Benj$^n$ | S | ........ | 75-R |
| Bayley, Daniel | Q | Jamaica | 75-D associator |
| Bayley, Elias | Q | Jamaica | 75-D associator |
| Bayley, Ephraim | Q | Jamaica | 75-A associator |
| Bayley, Ephraim | Q | Jamaica | 75-D associator |
| Bayley, Ephraim Esq. | Q | Jamaica | 76-C |
| Bayley, Gamaliel | S | ........ | 75-R |
| Bayley, Gamaliel | S | Southold | 76:0.1.2.1.0 |
| Bayley, Gam$^{ll}$ | S | ........ | 75-R |
| Bayley, George | Q | ........ | 76-E |
| Bayley, Isaac | Q | Jamaica | 75-D associator |
| Bayley, John | S | Huntington | 76-H3 |
| Bayley, Jona$^{th}$ | S | ........ | 75-R |
| Bayley, Jonathan | S | Southold | 76:0.1.0.1.2.1.0 |
| Bayley, Phillip | S | Huntington | 76-H3 |
| Bayley, Richard | N | New York | 74-A |
| Bayley, Stephen | S | ........ | 75-R |
| Bayley, Stephen | S | Southold | 76:0.1.1.2.6 |
| Bayley, William | N | New York | 74-A, 76-A |
| Bayley, William, hardware | N | Beaver Street | 74-T2, 5/19 |
| Bayley, Wm | Q | Newtown | 75-G |
| Baylies, Nathanael | S | Brookhaven | 75-B11 n.s. |

| Baylis, Daniel | Q | Jamaica | 75-A associator |
|---|---|---|---|
| Baylis, Daniel | Q | Jamaica | 75-E |
| Baylis, Daniel | S | Brookhaven | 75-B2 |
| Baylis, Elias | Q | ........ | 75-A associator |
| Baylis, Elijah | S | Brookhaven | 75-B10 |
| Baylis, Elijah | S | Brookhaven | 75-B11 n.s. |
| Baylis, Ephraim | Q | ........ | 75-A associator |
| Baylis, Ephraim, Captain | Q | Jamaica | 76-C |
| Baylis, George | Q | ........ | 76-E |
| Baylis, Isaac | Q | Jamaica | 75-A associator |
| Baylis, Isaac | Q | Jamaica | 75-E |
| Baylis, Jacob | S | Smithtown | 76:0.2.0.0.1 |
| Baylis, John | Q | Jamaica | 75-E |
| Baylis, John | S | Brookhaven | 75-B11 n.s. |
| Baylis, John | S | Brookhaven | 76:0.1.3.2.1 |
| Baylis, John | S | Brookhaven | 76:1.2.3.3.2.1.1 |
| Baylis, John, Junior | S | Brookhaven | 75-B8 |
| Baylis, John, Senior | S | Brookhaven | 75-B8 |
| Baylis, Nathanael | S | Brookhaven | 75-B10 |
| Baylis, Nathaniel | S | Brookhaven | 76:2.0.1.2.0 |
| Baylis, Nehemiah C. | Q | Jamaica | 75-E |
| Baylis, Thomas | S | Brookhaven | 75-B2 |
| Baylis, Thomas | S | Brookhaven | 76:1.1.0.4.3 |
| Bayliss, John, blacksmith | S | Brookhaven | 75-B10 |
| Bazly, Joseph | Q | ........ | 75-A associator |
| Bazly; see also Bezly | | | |
| Beadle, Michael | S | Huntington | 75-H |
| Beagle, Elijah | Q | ........ | 76-B2 |
| Beagle, Jacob | S | Huntington | 75-H |
| Beagle, Joseph | Q | ........ | 75-H |
| Beagle, Sylvanus | Q | ........ | 76-B |
| Beal, James | Q | ........ | 76-B |
| Beal, Matthew | S | Brookhaven | 76:1.0.1.3.0 |
| Beale, George | S | Huntington | 76-H3 |
| Beale, Mathew | S | Huntington | 76-H3 |
| Beale, Matthew | S | Brookhaven | 75-B3 |
| Bean, Jno. | N | New York | 74-A |
| Bean, Thomas | N | New York | 76-A |
| Beard/Bard, Robert | N | New York | 75-D1, D2 |
| Beard, Victor | N | New York | 74-V runaway |

| | | | |
|---|---|---|---|
| Beattie, David | Q | Hempstead | 75-H |
| Beaty, Edward, shoemaker | N | Little Queen St. | 75-D1, D2 |
| Beck, John | N | Fly Market | 76-H, 76-I |
| Beck, Jos. | N | New York | 75-D2 |
| Becke, John | N | New York | 74-R |
| Becker, Cornelius, Serg't | N | New York | 76-C |
| Becket, Jedediah | N | New York | 74-R witness |
| Beckitt, John, cordwainer | N | New York | 75-D1, D2 |
| Beckwith, Phineas | S | Southold | 76:0.2.2.2.3 |
| Beckwith, Phinehas | S | Brookhaven | 75-B10 |
| Bedell, Abijah | Q | ........ | 75-A, 76-B |
| Bedell, Benajah | Q | ........ | 76-B, 76-E |
| Bedell, Benj'n | Q | ........ | 75-A |
| Bedell, Benjah | Q | ........ | 75-A |
| Bedell, David | Q | ........ | 75-A |
| Bedell, David | Q | ........ | 76-B, 76-E |
| Bedell, Doremus | Q | ........ | 76-B |
| Bedell, Jacamiah | Q | ........ | 76-E |
| Bedell, Jacob [2] | Q | ........ | [on] 75-A |
| Bedell, Jacob [2] | Q | ........ | [on] 76-B |
| Bedell, Jeremiah | Q | ........ | 75-A |
| Bedell, Joseph | Q | ........ | 75-A, 76-A |
| Bedell, Joseph | Q | ........ | 76-B, 76-E |
| Bedell, Joseph 3d | Q | ........ | 75-A |
| Bedell, Joseph Sr. | Q | ........ | 75-A |
| Bedell, Silvanus | Q | ........ | 76-B |
| Bedell, Silvanus | Q | Hempstead | 76-D |
| Bedell, Silvanus Esq. | Q | ........ | 75-A |
| Bedell, Silvanus Esq. | Q | ........ | 75-A |
| Bedell, Silvester | Q | ........ | 76-B |
| Bedell, Sylvanus | Q | ........ | 76-E |
| Bedell, Sylvester | Q | ........ | 76-E |
| Bedell, Timothy | Q | ........ | 75-A |
| Bedell, Uriah | Q | ........ | 76-B |
| Bedell; see also Beedle, Beldel | | | |
| Bedlow, William | N | New York | 75-F |
| Bedlow, William, Capt. | N | New York | 75-T2, 10/5 |
| Beebee, Lester | S | ........ | 75-R |
| Beebee, Lester | S | Southold | 76:0.1.0.1.0 |
| Beebee, Samuel | S | ........ | 75-R |

| | | | |
|---|---|---|---|
| Beebee, Samuell | S | Southold | 76:0.1.2.2.5 |
| Beedle, Mordecai | Q | ........ | 76-E |
| Beekman, David, merchant | N | New York | 74-T, 74-V |
| Beekman, Garret | N | New York | 76-G |
| Beekman, George, butcher | N | at Jacob Harding's | 75-D1, D2 |
| Beekman, Gerard G. | N | New York | 74-A |
| Beekman, Gerard J. | N | New York | 75-B |
| Beekman, Gerardus | N | New York | 75-R |
| Beekman, Gerardus, 1st Lt. | N | New York | 76-C |
| Beekman, Gerarᵈ, 1st Lieut. | N | New York | 75-A |
| Beekman, Gerrard William | N | New York | 75-F |
| Beekman, Henry | N | New York | 76-N |
| Beekman, Henry W. | N | peruke maker | 75-D2 |
| Beekman, James | N | New York | 74-A |
| Beekman, James | N | New York | 75-T2, 5/4 |
| Beekman, John | N | New York | 74-A |
| Beekman, John, butcher | N | nr. Sugar House | 75-D1, D2 |
| Beekman, John, butcher | N | op. New Goal | 75-D1, D2 |
| Beekman, John Jr. | N | New York | 75-D3 |
| Beekman, John, merchant | N | Maiden Lane | 74-V |
| Beekman, Magnus | N | New York | 74-A |
| Beekman, ---- Mrs. | N | New York | 76-I |
| Beekman, Thomas | N | New York | 75-B |
| Beekman, Thomas | N | New York | 75-D3 |
| Beekman, Thoˢ | N | New York | 75-B |
| Beekman, William | N | New York | 74-A |
| Beekman, William | N | New York | 75-T merchant |
| Beesley, Joseph | Q | ........ | 76-E |
| Beets, John | N | Broadway | 76-I |
| Begly, Timothy | S | ........ | 75-R |
| Beitturner, Jacob | N | New York | 76-A |
| Beldel, Jacob | Q | ........ | 76-E |
| Belitha, John, Ensign | N | New York | 75-A |
| Belithy, John | N | New York | 74-A |
| Bell, Andrew | N | New York | 74-A, 76-L |
| Bell, George | N | New York | 74-A |
| Bell, George | N | New York | 74-T2, 7/28 |
| Bell, George | N | New York | 76-F, 76-I |
| Bell, James | N | New York | 76-A |
| Bell, Jane | N | removed upstate | 76-P |

| | | | |
|---|---|---|---|
| Bell, Joseph | N | New York | 76-A |
| Bell, Joseph, blacksmith | N | Cherry Street | 75-D1, D2 |
| Bell, Joseph, leather | N | Vanderwater St. | 75-T2, 2/2 |
| Bell, Robert, taylor | N | nr. City Hall | 75-D1, D2 |
| Bell, Samuel | N | New York | 74-A |
| Bell, Samuel Jr. | N | New York | 76-A |
| Bell, William | N | New York | 76-A |
| Bell, William, breechesmkr | N | New York | 74-R Freeman |
| Bellows, Eleazer | S | Brookhaven | 75-B1, 75-B6 |
| Bellows, Elezer | S | Brookhaven | 76:0.1.0.1.2 |
| Belos, John & Zopher | S | Brookhaven | 76:0.2.1.2.2 |
| Beman, Con⁸ | Q | Newtown | 75-G |
| Bend, Grove | N | New York | 74-A, 76-A |
| Bend, Grove, storekeeper | N | Smith Street | 75-T |
| Bender, Mathew | N | New York | 74-A |
| Bengston, John | N | New York | 76-A |
| Benham, Alley, wf of James | N | New York | 75-R |
| Benham, James | N | New York | 74-A, 75-R |
| Benham, James, shoemaker | N | William Street | 75-D1, D2 |
| Benham, Jas. | N | New York | 75-D3 |
| Benjamans, Jonathan | S | Brookhaven | 76:1.0.0.2.1 |
| Benjamin, Amesiah | S | Southold | 76:0.1.2.1.2 |
| Benjamin, Ammaziah | S | Brookhaven | 75-B10 |
| Benjamin, Benjamin | S | Brookhaven | 75-B10 |
| Benjamin, Benjamin | S | Southold | 76:0.1.2.1.1 |
| Benjamin, James | S | Brookhaven | 75-B10 |
| Benjamin, James | S | Southold | 76:0.1.1.1.1 |
| Benjamin, John | S | Southold | 75-N |
| Benjamin, John | S | Southold | 76:0.1.1.3.3.0.1 |
| Benjamin, Jonathan | S | Brookhaven | 75-B1 |
| Benjamin, Jonathan | S | Brookhaven | 75-B6, 75-B7 |
| Benjamin, Joshua | S | Brookhaven | 75-B10 |
| Benjamin, Nathan | S | Southold | 76:0.2.2.2.2 |
| Benjamin, Nathan, Lieut. | S | Southold | 75-N |
| Benjamin, Richard | S | Brookhaven | 75-B10 |
| Benjamin, Richard | S | Southold | 76:0.2.4.1.2 |
| Benjamin, Richard Jr. | S | Brookhaven | 75-B10 |
| Benjamin, Samuel | S | Brookhaven | 75-B10 |
| Benjamin, Samuell | S | Southold | 76:0.1.3.1.3 |
| Benjamin, Tho. | S | Southold | 76:0.1.1.1.2 |

| | | | |
|---|---|---|---|
| Benjamin, William | S | Southold | 75-N non-signer |
| Benjamin, William | S | Southold | 76:0.4.0.1.4 |
| Benjamins, Joshua | S | Southold | 76:0.1.1.2.0.2.2 |
| Bennen, Thomas | Q | ........ | 76-E |
| Bennet, Chris'r | N | New York | 74-A |
| Bennet, Cornelius | N | New York | 74-A |
| Bennet, Cornelius | Q | ........ | 75-A, 76-E |
| Bennet, Cornelius | Q | Jamaica | 75-C, 75-D |
| Bennet, Cornelus | N | New York | 76-L |
| Bennet, Edward | S | Easthampton | 75-E |
| Bennet, Garret | Q | ........ | 76-E |
| Bennet, George | Q | ........ | 76-E |
| Bennet, George | Q | Oyster Bay | 75-A associator |
| Bennet, George | Q | Oyster Bay | 75-F |
| Bennet, Isaac | Q | ........ | 76-B |
| Bennet, Isaac | Q | Jamaica | 75-C |
| Bennet, Israel | S | Brookhaven | 75-B10 |
| Bennet, Israel | S | Brookhaven | 76:1.0.1.2.1.1.0 |
| Bennet, Jacob | Q | ........ | 76-E |
| Bennet, James | Q | ........ | 76-E |
| Bennet, Jeremiah | S | Easthampton | 75-E |
| Bennet, Jeromus Sr. | Q | ........ | 76-E |
| Bennet, Jeromus [2] | Q | ........ | [on] 76-E |
| Bennet, John | N | New York | 76-A |
| Bennet, John | N | to Dutchess Co. | 76-P |
| Bennet, John | Q | ........ | 76-B |
| Bennet, John | Q | Jamaica | 75-C, 75-D |
| Bennet, John | S | Brookhaven | 75-B10 |
| Bennet, John | S | Brookhaven | 75-B11 n.s. |
| Bennet, John | S | Brookhaven | 76:0.1.1.2.1 |
| Bennet, John Jr. | Q | ........ | 76-E |
| Bennet, John Sr. | Q | ........ | 76-E |
| Bennet, John [2] | Q | ........ | [on] 75-A |
| Bennet, John [2] | Q | ........ | [on] 76-E |
| Bennet, Nicholas | Q | ........ | 76-E |
| Bennet, W. | Q | ........ | 76-E |
| Bennet, W. | Q | ........ | 76-E |
| Bennet, William | Q | ........ | 76-E |
| Bennett, Israel | S | Brookhaven | 75-B11 n.s. |
| Bennett, John, fifer | S | Huntington | 76-H2 |

| | | | |
|---|---|---|---|
| Bennett, William | N | New York | 74-A |
| Bennett, Wm, constable | N | New York | 74-R to 76-R |
| Bennett, Zebulon | S | Easthampton | 76:1.0.1.2.1 |
| Bennit, Edward | S | Easthampton | 76:0.1.4.1.1 |
| Bennit, Gamaliel | S | Easthampton | 76:0.1.1.1.0 |
| Bennit, Jeremiah | S | Easthampton | 76:0.2.1.1.0 |
| Bennit, Joseph | S | Huntington | 75-H |
| Benson, Christopher | N | New York | 74-A, 74-V |
| Benson, Christopher | N | New York | 74-R, 76-R juror |
| Benson, Christopher | N | New York | 76-A |
| Benson, Christopher | N | New York | 76-F, 76-I |
| Benson, Christopher, Capt. | N | New York | 76-Y |
| Benson, Robert | N | New York | 74-T2, 11/24 |
| Benson, Robert | N | North Ward | 75-R overseer |
| Benson, Robert, Lieut. | N | New York | 75-A |
| Benzokan, Eleazar | N | New York | 74-A |
| Beou, Rene | N | New York | 74-A |
| Bergaw, Richard | Q | ........ | 76-B2 |
| Bergen, Derrick | Q | ........ | 75-A, 76-E |
| Bergen, Derrick | Q | Jamaica | 75-C, 75-D |
| Bergen, Jacob | Q | ........ | 76-E |
| Bergen, Jacob | Q | Jamaica | 75-C, 75-D |
| Bergen, Jacob Jr. | Q | Jamaica | 75-C |
| Bergen, Johannes | Q | ........ | 76-E |
| Bergen, John | Q | Jamaica | 75-C, 75-D |
| Bergen, John Jr. | Q | Jamaica | 75-C |
| Bergen, Lucas | Q | Jamaica | 75-D |
| Bergen, Luke | Q | ........ | 75-A, 76-E |
| Bergen, Luke | Q | ........ | 76-B |
| Bergen, Teunis/Tunis | Q | ........ | 75-A, 76-E |
| Bergen, Tunis | Q | ........ | 76-B |
| Bergen, Tunis | Q | Jamaica | 75-C, 75-D |
| Berger, Derrick | Q | ........ | 76-B |
| Berger, Jacob | N | New York | 76-A |
| Bermot, Gemelielle | S | Easthampton | 75-E |
| Bernt, Henry | N | New York | 76-A |
| Berrian, John | N | New York | 74-T2, 11/24 |
| Berrian, Peter | N | New York | 76-R |
| Berrien, Abraham | Q | ........ | 76-E |
| Berrien, John | N | New York | 75-B |

| | | | |
|---|---|---|---|
| Berrien, Peter | N | New York | 74-A |
| Berrien, Richard | Q | ........ | 75-A associator |
| Berry, Charles | N | New York | 76-I |
| Berry, Charles | S | Huntington | 75-H |
| Berry, James | S | Huntington | 75-H |
| Berry, Joseph | S | Brookhaven | 75-B10 |
| Berry, Robert | N | New York | 76-L |
| Berry, Robert | S | ........ | 75-R |
| Bertine, John, carpenter | N | Barclay Street | 75-D1, D2 |
| Berton, Peter | N | New York | 74-A, 76-A |
| Berton, Peter, Capt. | N | New York | 75-A, 75-T |
| Bertoon, Peter | N | North Ward | 75-R overseer |
| Berwick/Barwick, John | N | New York | 76-R |
| Berzley, Joseph | Q | ........ | 75-I |
| Besset, Cornelius | S | Easthampton | 75-E |
| Bessonet, John | N | New York | 74-A |
| Betts, Aaron | N | New York | 76-B |
| Betts, Ath'r | Q | Newtown | 75-G |
| Betts, Augustin | Q | ........ | 75-A associator |
| Betts, Augustine | Q | Jamaica | 76-C |
| Betts, Azor, Doctor | N | St. James Street | 75-D1, D2 |
| Betts, Jas. | Q | Newtown | 75-G |
| Betts, John | N | New York | 74-A, 74-R |
| Betts, John | N | White Hall Slip | 76-H |
| Betts, John, cabinetmaker | N | New York | 74-R Freeman |
| Betts, Nathaniel | N | New York | 74-A |
| Betts, Rich'd | N | New York | 75-D3 |
| Betts, Rich'd | Q | Newtown | 75-G |
| Betts, Richard | Q | ........ | 76-E |
| Betts, Richard | Q | Jamaica | 75-C, 75-E |
| Betts, Richard | Q | N.J. | 75-A associator |
| Betts, Richard, Capt. | Q | ........ | 75-A |
| Betts, Richard, Capt. | Q | Jamaica | 75-D |
| Betts, Robert | Q | Jamaica | 75-E |
| Betts, Thomas | Q | ........ | 76-E |
| Betts, Thomas | Q | Jamaica | 75-D |
| Betts, Thos. | Q | Newtown | 75-G |
| Betts, Wm. | Q | ........ | 75-A associator |
| Betts, Wm. | Q | Newtown | 75-G |
| Betty, _____ Mrs. | N | rem to Ulster Co. | 76-P |

| | | | |
|---|---|---|---|
| Betty, Nichols | Q | ........ | 76-E |
| Bevans, Thomas | N | New York | 76-I |
| Bever, Henry | N | New York | 75-R |
| Bever, Martilane | N | New York | 75-R |
| Bezly, James | Q | ........ | 75-A |
| Bezly, see also Bazly | | | |
| Bicker, Cornelius | N | New York | 74-A |
| Bicker, Cornelius | N | New York | 76-D, 76-N |
| Bicker, Fred'k | N | New York | 76-A |
| Bicker, Henry | N | New York | 75-A |
| Bicker, John | N | New York | 76-I |
| Bicker, Nicholas | N | New York | 74-A |
| Bicker, Victor | N | New York | 74-A |
| Bicker, Victor | N | New York | 74-T2, 11/24 |
| Bicker, Victor Jr. | N | New York | 74-A |
| Bicker, Walter | N | New York | 74-A |
| Bicker, Walter, hatter | N | Broadway | 75-D1, D2 |
| Bickers, _____ | N | New York | 75-D3 |
| Bickers, Cornelus, Lieut. | N | New York | 76-L |
| Bickers, Victor, Lieut. | N | New York | 76-L |
| Biferi, Nicholas, teacher | N | New York | 74-T2, 5/5 |
| Bigelow, John | N | to Dutchess Co. | 76-P |
| Bigelow; see also Biglou | | | |
| Biges, Marak | S | Brookhaven | 76:0.0.1.6.1 |
| Biggs, Abell | S | Brookhaven | 75-B11 n.s. |
| Biggs, David | S | Brookhaven | 75-B11 n.s. |
| Biggs, Isaac | S | Brookhaven | 75-B10 |
| Biggs, Isaac | S | Brookhaven | 75-B11 n.s. |
| Biggs, Isaac | S | Brookhaven | 76:0.1.1.1.2.1.1 |
| Biggs, Jacob | S | Brookhaven | 75-B11 n.s. |
| Biggs, Jacob | S | Brookhaven | 76:1.0.1.1.2 |
| Biggs, John | S | Brookhaven | 75-B10 |
| Biggs, John | S | Brookhaven | 75-B11 n.s. |
| Biggs, Mary | S | Smithtown | 76:0.0.0.2.2 |
| Biggs, Nathanel | S | Brookhaven | 75-B8 |
| Biggs, Silas | S | Brookhaven | 75-B10 |
| Biggs, Silas | S | Huntington | 76-H3 |
| Biggs, Silas | S | Smithtown | 75-L recusant |
| Biggs, Silas | S | Smithtown | 76:0.1.1.1.0 |
| Biggs, ---- Widow | S | Islip | 76:0.1.0.1.1 |

| | | | |
|---|---|---|---|
| Biggs, William | S | Brookhaven | 75-B10 |
| Biggs, William | S | Brookhaven | 75-B10 |
| Biggs, William | S | Brookhaven | 75-B11 n.s. |
| Biggs, William | S | Smithtown | 76:0.2.1.1.0 |
| Biglou, John | N | to Westchester Co | 76-P |
| Biglou, Marah | N | to Westchester Co | 76-P |
| Biglou, Sarah | N | to Westchester Co | 76-P |
| Billard, Joshua | S | Southold | 76:1.1.5.1.0 |
| Billed, Joshua | S | ........ | 75-R |
| Binches, John | N | New York | 76-A |
| Bingham, James | N | New York | 75-D1 |
| Bingham, James, merchant | N | William Street | 75-D1, D2 |
| Bingham, John | N | New York | 74-A |
| Bingham, John Jr. coachm'r | N | William Street | 75-D2 |
| Bingham, Moses | N | New York | 76-A |
| Biniger, Jos., shoemaker | N | William Street | 75-D2 |
| Binkes, John, 1st Lieut. | N | New York | 76-Y |
| Binner, William & Brown | S | Brookhaven | 76:1.2.3.3.2 |
| Bino, Peter | N | New York | 76-I |
| Birch, Jonathan | S | Islip | 75-I |
| Birdsall, Benjamin | Q | ........ | 75-A associator |
| Birdsall, Benjamin | Q | Oyster Bay | 75-F |
| Birdsall, Daniel | Q | ........ | 76-E |
| Birdsall, James | Q | ........ | 76-B, 76-E |
| Birdsall, James | Q | Hempstead | 76-D |
| Birdsall, James [2] | Q | ........ | [on] 75-A |
| Birdsall, Jo's | Q | ........ | 76-E |
| Birdsall, John | Q | ........ | 76-B, 76-E |
| Birdsall, John | Q | Hempstead | 76-D |
| Birdsall, Joseph | Q | ........ | 75-I, 76-B |
| Birdsall, Joseph | Q | Hempstead | 76-D |
| Birdsall, Joshua | Q | ........ | 75-A, 76-B |
| Birdsall, ____ Jr. | Q | ........ | 76-E |
| Birdsall, Oliver | Q | ........ | 75-A |
| Birdsall, Oliver | Q | ........ | 76-B, 76-E |
| Birdsall, Oliver | Q | Hempstead | 76-D |
| Birdsall, Samuel | Q | ........ | 75-A |
| Birdsall, Samuel | Q | ........ | 76-B, 76-E |
| Birdsall, Somick | Q | ........ | 76-E |
| Birdsall, Thomas | Q | ........ | 75-A, 76-B |

| | | | |
|---|---|---|---|
| Birmingham, James | N | George Street | 76-I |
| Birmingham, James | N | in ye fields | 76-H |
| Birtts, Robert | S | Southold | 76:1.1.0.3.0 |
| Bish, John | N | New York | 74-A, 76-I |
| Bishop, Armstrong | S | ........ | 75-R |
| Bishop, Daniell | S | Southampton | 76:1.0.1.2.1 |
| Bishop, Enas | S | Huntington | 76-H2 |
| Bishop, Enes | S | Brookhaven | 76:0.1.3.1.0 |
| Bishop, Enos | S | Brookhaven | 75-B1, 75-B7 |
| Bishop, James | S | Brookhaven | 75-B1 n.s. |
| Bishop, James | S | Brookhaven | 75-B7 n.s. |
| Bishop, James | S | Brookhaven | 76:0.1.3.2.2 |
| Bishop, James | S | Southampton | 76:0.2.2.1.0 |
| Bishop, John | N | New York | 76-A |
| Bishop, John | S | Southampton | 76:0.1.1.1.2 |
| Bishop, John | S | Southampton | 76:1.1.1.1.0 |
| Bishop, John Jun$^r$ | S | ........ | 75-R |
| Bishop, John Jun$^r$ | S | Southampton | 76:0.1.1.1.2 |
| Bishop, Sam$^{ll}$ Jun$^r$ | S | ........ | 75-R |
| Bishop, Samuel | S | Southampton | 76:1.0.0.1.0 |
| Bishop, Stephen | S | ........ | 75-R |
| Bishop, Timothy | S | Southampton | 76:0.1.1.1.0 |
| Bisnet, John, bricklayer | N | New York | 74-T2, 7/28 |
| Bixton, James, servant | N | New York | 76-V runaway |
| Blaau, Waldrom | N | New York | 74-R juror |
| Blaau, Waldron | N | New York | 74-A, 76-A |
| Blaau, Waldron, 1st Lieut. | N | New York | 76-Y |
| Black, Jas. | N | New York | 76-N |
| Black, Jonathan, Lieut. | N | New York | 76-L |
| Black, Mary, Mrs. | N | to Dutchess Co. | 76-P |
| Black, Peter | N | New York | 75-D2 |
| Black, Richard | N | New York | 76-A |
| Black, Susannah, widow | N | removed upstate | 76-P |
| Blackare, John | N | New York | 76-A |
| Blackburn, Francis | Q | ........ | 76-E |
| Blackburne, Ashton Esq. | N | New York | 74-T |
| Blackie, Francis | N | New York | 74-A |
| Blackler, John | N | New York | 76-B |
| Blackney, Thomas | N | New York | 74-A |
| Blackwell, Jacob | Q | Newtown | 75-G |

| | | | |
|---|---|---|---|
| Blackwell, Jacob, Col. | Q | ........ | 75-D1 |
| Blagg, Edward, Coroner | N | New York | 74-R to 76-R |
| Blagg, John | N | New York | 75-D2 |
| Blagge, John | N | New York | 75-F |
| Blair, John | N | New York | 74-A |
| Blake, Jonathan | N | New York | 76-N |
| Blake, Jonathan [2] | N | New York | [on] 74-A |
| Blanchard, James | N | New York | 74-A |
| Blancheville, Patrick | N | New York | 76-A |
| Blanchwell, Patrick | N | New York | 76-I |
| Blanck, Isaac | N | New York | 74-A, 76-A |
| Blanck, Jacob | N | New York | 74-A |
| Blanck, Jeremiah | N | New York | 74-A, 76-A |
| Blanck, Paul | N | New York | 74-A |
| Blank, Cath., wf of Jacob | N | New York | 75-R |
| Blank, Jasper, apprentice | N | New York | 74-R |
| Blatsly, Benjamin | S | Huntington | 75-H |
| Blatsly, Daniel | S | Huntington | 75-H |
| Blatsly, Daniel Jr. | S | Huntington | 75-H |
| Bleak, J. | N | John Street | 75-D2 |
| Bleecker, Anthony L. | N | New York | 75-F |
| Bleecker, Rutger, innholder | N | Chapple Street | 75-D1, D2 |
| Blockley, Thomas | Q | ........ | 76-E |
| Blockley, Thomas, brass fdr | N | Hanover Square | 75-D1, D2 |
| Blockley, Thomas, engraver | N | Hanover Square | 75-T |
| Blockner, Daniel | N | New York | 76-A |
| Blonsher, Francis | N | New York | 74-A |
| Bloodgood, ____ | N | New York | 75-D2 |
| Bloodgood, Pepperel | Q | ........ | 75-A associator |
| Bloodgood, Pepperel | Q | ........ | 76-E |
| Bloom, B. | Q | Newtown | 75-B |
| Bloom, Barnabas | Q | ........ | 75-I |
| Bloom, Barnardus | Q | ........ | 75-A, 76-E |
| Bloom, Christian | N | New York | 76-A |
| Bloomer, Josh., Rev. | Q | ........ | 76-E |
| Bloore, Joshua, merchant | N | New York | 74-T2, 5/26 |
| Blouin, Daniel | N | New York | 75-R |
| Blundell, Archibald | N | New York | 76-A |
| Blundell, Christopher | N | New York | 76-A |
| Blydenburg, Samuel | S | Smithtown | 75-L |

| | | | |
|---|---|---|---|
| Blydenburgh, Benjamin | S | Smithtown | 75-L |
| Blydenburgh, Joseph | S | Islip | 76:1.1.2.2.0 |
| Blydenburgh, Joseph | S | Smithtown | 75-L |
| Blydenburgh, Joseph Jun^r | S | Islip | 76:0.2.3.1.2 |
| Blydenburgh, Ruth | S | Smithtown | 76:0.0.3.2.2.3.0 |
| Blydenburgh, Samuel | S | Smithtown | 76:0.1.0.1.2 |
| Board, James | N | New York | 74-A, 76-A |
| Board, see also Bord | | | |
| Bockay, William | N | New York | 76-L |
| Bockea, Isaac | N | New York | 76-L |
| Bockeay, Abram | N | New York | 76-L |
| Bockee, William | N | New York | 74-A |
| Boel, Henry | N | New York | 76-A |
| Boelen, Jacob | N | New York | 76-A |
| Boerum, Arree | Q | ........ | 75-A |
| Boerum, Aury | Q | ........ | 76-B, 76-E |
| Boerum, Aury | Q | Jamaica | 75-C |
| Boerum, Charles | Q | ........ | 75-A associator |
| Boerum, Charles | Q | Newtown | 75-G |
| Boerum, Jacob | Q | Newtown | 75-G |
| Boerum, John | Q | ........ | 76-B, 76-E |
| Bogardus, Cornelius | N | New York | 76-I |
| Bogardus, Cornelius C. | N | New York | 75-R |
| Bogart, Abraham | N | New York | 74-A |
| Bogart/Bogert; see also Outenbogart | | | |
| Bogart, Brache, Mrs. | N | to Dutchess Co. | 76-P |
| Bogart, Cornelius | N | New York | 74-V |
| Bogart, Elisabeth | N | removed upstate | 76-P |
| Bogart, Henry | N | at Curtenius' | 75-D2 |
| Bogart, Henry | N | New York | 75-C |
| Bogart, Henry C. | N | Smith Street | 74-T, 74-V |
| Bogart, Henry Jr. | N | New York | 75-D1 |
| Bogart, Isaac | N | New York | 74-A |
| Bogart, Isaac | Q | Oyster Bay | 75-F |
| Bogart, Jacob | N | New York | 74-A |
| Bogart, Jacob, cartman | N | Leary Street | 75-D1, D2 |
| Bogart, John | N | New York | 74-A |
| Bogart, John, merchant | N | New York | 75-V |
| Bogart, Nicholas | N | New York | 75-F |
| Bogart, Nicholas C. | N | New York | 74-V, 75-F |

| | | | |
|---|---|---|---|
| Bogart, Nicholas J. | N | New York | 74-A, 76-A |
| Bogart, Nichᵉ | N | New York | 75-D3 |
| Bogart, Nichᵉ H. | N | New York | 75-B |
| Bogart, Nichᵉ J., Doctor | N | in The Fly | 75-D1, D2 |
| Bogart, Peter | N | New York | 76-A |
| Bogert, Albert | N | New York | 76-L |
| Bogert, Cornelius | N | New York | 74-A |
| Bogert, Cornelius | Q | ........ | 75-A, 76-E |
| Bogert, Cornelius J. | N | New York | 75-B |
| Bogert, Hendrick | N | New York | 74-T insolvent |
| Bogert, Henry | N | New York | 76-L |
| Bogert, Jacobus | N | New York | 74-A, 76-L |
| Bogert, Jacobus N. | N | New York | 74-A |
| Bogert, John | N | New York | 74-A, 75-T |
| Bogert, John | N | New York | 76-L |
| Bogert, John Esq., merchant | N | New York | 74-T |
| Bogert, John J. | N | New York | 74-A |
| Bogert, Nicholas | N | Broadway | 75-T2, 5/4 |
| Bogert, Nicholas | N | New York | 74-A |
| Bogert, Nicholas N. | N | New York | 74-A |
| Bogert, Nichᵉ P. | N | New York | 74-A |
| Bogert, Peter | N | Burnet's Street | 74-T2, 10/13 |
| Bogert, Peter | N | New York | 74-A, 76-L |
| Bogert, Thomas | N | Ann als Scotch st | 74-T |
| Boggs, James, Ensign | N | New York | 75-A |
| Boggs, Rachel, Mrs. | N | rem to Ulster Co. | 76-P |
| Bollmain, Christian | N | New York | 76-A |
| Bolmer, Peter | N | New York | 74-A |
| Bolton, Anthony | N | New York | 74-A, 76-A |
| Bond, Abraham | N | Roosevelt's Slip | 76-H, 76-I |
| Bond, Jacob | Q | ........ | 75-A, 76-B |
| Bond, Peter | Q | ........ | 76-B |
| Bond, Peter [2] | Q | ........ | [on] 75-A |
| Bongarten, see Garten | | | |
| Bonham, James, shoemaker | N | at Relays | 75-D2 |
| Bonner, Daniel | N | New York | 74-A |
| Boos, Wendel | N | New York | 74-A |
| Booth, Benjamin, merchant | N | New York | 74-T2, 4/21 |
| Booth, Daniel | S | ........ | 75-R |
| Booth, Daniel | S | Southold | 76:0.2.4.2.3 |

| Booth, Daniel Jun$^r$ | S | ........ | 75-R |
|---|---|---|---|
| Booth, Daniel Jun$^r$. | S | ........ | 75-R |
| Booth, Ja: Whelock | S | ........ | 75-R |
| Booth, James Whe$^k$ | S | ........ | 75-R |
| Booth, James Whelock | S | Southold | 76:0.1.3.2.2 |
| Booth, Joseph | S | ........ | 75-R |
| Booth, Joseph | S | Southold | 76:0.2.3.1.1.2.1 |
| Booth, Samuel Jr. | S | Shelter Island | 75-K |
| Booth, Sml. | S | Southold | 76:1.1.0.1.1.0.1 |
| Booth, ---- Wid. | S | Southold | 76:0.0.0.2.2 |
| Bord, Samuel | N | New York | 74-A |
| Bord, see also Board | | | |
| Borrowe, John | N | New York | 74-T |
| Bortine, John | N | New York | 76-L |
| Boshart, Jacob | N | New York | 74-A |
| Boshart, Jacob, hse carp'r | N | Broadway | 75-D1, D2 |
| Boshea, John | S | Southold | 76:0.3.3.1.3 |
| Bosher, Jacob | N | New York | 76-A |
| Boslin, Jacob | N | New York | 74-A |
| Boss, Anne | N | to Dutchess Co. | 76-P |
| Boss, Joseph | Q | Newtown | 75-G |
| Boss, Leah | N | to Dutchess Co. | 76-P |
| Boss, Sam$^l$ | N | to Dutchess Co. | 76-P |
| Bost, David | N | New York | 75-D1 |
| Bostin, Antony | S | Brookhaven | 76:0.1.2.2.1 |
| Boston, Antony | S | Brookhaven | 75-B11 n.s. |
| Botticher, Fred. | N | New York | 76-A |
| Bousseau, John | S | ........ | 75-R |
| Bousseau, Nathaniel | S | ........ | 75-R |
| Bousseau, Nath$^l$ | S | ........ | 75-R |
| Bowden, Thomas | N | New York | 74-A, 76-I |
| Bowditch, Joel | S | Shelter Island | 75-K |
| Bowditch, Joel | S | Shelter Island | 76:1.0.1.1.0 |
| Bowditch, John | S | Shelter Island | 76:0.1.1.1.1 |
| Bowditch, Sarah, Wid. | S | Southampton | 76:0.0.0.1.2 |
| Bowditch, William | S | Shelter Island | 75-K |
| Bowen, Prentice | N | New York | 76-N |
| Bower, Abra'm, taylor | N | Cortland Street | 75-D2 |
| Bower, Ebenezer | S | Islip | 76:0.1.0.2.0 |
| Bower, Grant | S | Southampton | 76:0.1.2.1.5 |

| | | | |
|---|---|---|---|
| Bower, Hezekiah | S | ........ | 75-R |
| Bower, Hezekiah | S | Southampton | 76:0.1.1.2.2 |
| Bower, Jeremiah Jun. | S | ........ | 75-R |
| Bower, Jonah | S | Southampton | 76:1.0.0.1.0 |
| Bower, Patrick, ship captain | N | New York | 74-T2, 8/25 |
| Bower, William | S | Brookhaven | 75-B6 |
| Bower, William | S | Meritches | 76:0.1.3.2.2 |
| Bowler, Jacob | N | New York | 76-L |
| Bowles, John | N | New York | 76-A |
| Bowman, Elizabeth | N | to Westchester Co | 76-P |
| Bowne, Geo. | N | New York | 74-A |
| Bowne, James | N | New York | 75-F |
| Bowne, James | N | Queen Street | 75-D2 |
| Bowne, Matthew | N | New York | 74-A |
| Bowne, Robt. | N | New York | 74-A |
| Bowne, Samuel | N | New York | 74-A, 75-F |
| Bowne, Samuel | N | New York | 76-A |
| Box, Nathaniel | Q | Jamaica | 75-D associator |
| Box, Nathaniel | Q | Jamaica | 76-C |
| Box, Nath¹ | Q | ........ | 75-A associator |
| Boyar, see Keen | | | |
| Boyd, Jo. | N | New York | 74-A |
| Boyer, Samuel | N | New York | 76-A |
| Braambos, W. | Q | ........ | 76-E |
| Braan, Hugh | N | New York | 76-H |
| Brace, Robert, baker | N | Maiden Lane | 75-T |
| Brackman, Henry | N | New York | 74-A |
| Brackman, Samuel | N | New York | 74-A |
| Bradburn, Alex. | N | New York | 74-A |
| Bradford, Cornelius | N | New York | 74-A |
| Brady, Joseph | N | New York | 74-A |
| Bragaw, Isaac | Q | ........ | 76-E |
| Bragaw, J. | Q | Newtown | 75-B |
| Bragaw, John | Q | ........ | 76-E |
| Bragaw, Peter | Q | ........ | 76-E |
| Bragaw, Peter Sr. | Q | Newtown | 75-B |
| Bragaw, Richard | Q | Newtown | 75-B |
| Braine, Thomas | N | New York | 76-A |
| Braley, Jerry | N | removed upstate | 76-P |
| Bramar, David | N | New York | 76-A |

| | | | |
|---|---|---|---|
| Bramwell, George, saddler | N | Dock Street | 74-T2, 3/17 |
| Brandin, John | N | in the fields | 76-H |
| Brandon, John | N | near the Bridewell | 76-I |
| Brandon, John | N | New York | 74-A |
| Brandt, Christina wf John | N | New York | 74-V |
| Brandt, John | N | New York | 74-A |
| Brandt, John, baker | N | New York | 74-V |
| Brannon, Charles John | N | New York | 74-A, 76-A |
| Brasher, Abraham | N | New York | 74-T2, 11/24 |
| Brasher, Abraham | N | New York | 76-C Grenadier |
| Brasher, Abram A. | N | New York | 74-A |
| Brasher, Baker | N | New York | 75-D1 |
| Brasher, Baker, hatter | N | Dock Street | 75-D1, D2 |
| Brasher, E., Lieut. | N | New York | 76-C |
| Brasher, Ephraim | N | New York | 76-N |
| Brasher, Ephr^m | N | New York | 74-A, 75-B |
| Brasher, Henry | N | New York | 74-R juror |
| Brasher, Henry | N | New York | 75-D3, 76-N |
| Brasher, Henry, Lieut. | N | New York | 75-A, 76-C |
| Brasher, Isaac | N | New York | 76-A |
| Brasher, Jane | N | removed upstate | 76-P |
| Brasher, Meads, Ensign | N | New York | 76-S |
| Brasher, Philip | N | New York | 74-A, 75-F |
| Brasher, Philip, Adjutant | N | New York | 76-C, 76-L |
| Brasier, Isaac | N | nr the Shipyards | 74-T |
| Brass, ——— widow | N | Golden Hill | 74-T |
| Bratt, Isaac | N | New York | 74-R, 76-A |
| Breasted, Andrew | N | New York | 74-A |
| Breasted, Simon | N | New York | 74-A, 76-A |
| Breath, John | N | New York | 74-A |
| Breested, And. | N | New York | 74-A |
| Brehdegam, Frederick | N | New York | 74-A |
| Bremner, John | Q | ........ | 76-E |
| Bremner, John | Q | Jamaica | 75-D associator |
| Bremner, John | Q | Jamaica | 75-E |
| Bremner, see also Brimer | | | |
| Brevoort, Abraham, baker | N | Bowery Lane | 75-D1, D2 |
| Brevoort, Elias | N | New York | 76-A |
| Brevoort, Elias, blacksmith | N | Bowery Lane | 75-D1, D2 |
| Brevoort, Elias Jr. | N | New York | 74-A |

| | | | |
|---|---|---|---|
| Brevoort, Henry | N | New York | 76-A |
| Brevoort, John | N | New York | 74-R |
| Brevoort, John, baker | N | Rutgers Street | 75-D1, D2 |
| Brevort, Abraham | N | New York | 75-R |
| Brevort, Elias | N | Maiden Lane | 75-V |
| Brevorte, Abraham | N | New York | 76-D |
| Brewer, Abraham, Ensign | N | New York | 76-G |
| Brewer, Jacob, Ensign | N | New York | 75-A |
| Brewer, Jno. | Q | ........ | 75-A |
| Brewer, Richard | Q | ........ | 75-A, 76-B |
| Brewer, Richard | Q | ........ | 76-E |
| Brewerton, Geo. Jr., Judge | N | New York | 74-R to 76-R |
| Brewerton, George | N | New York | 74-A, 76-A |
| Brewerton, George | N | New York | 75-T2, 3/9 |
| Brewerton, George, Col. | N | New York | 76-Y |
| Brewerton, George Jr. Esq. | N | New York | 74-T |
| Brewerton, Jacob | N | New York | 74-A, 76-A |
| Brewerton, Jacob Jr., Lieut. | N | New York | 76-G |
| Brewster, Benjamen | S | Brookhaven | 76:1.2.0.4.1.1.0 |
| Brewster, Benjamin | S | Brookhaven | 75-B11 n.s. |
| Brewster, Benjamin | S | Smithtown | 75-L |
| Brewster, Benjamin Juner | S | Brookhaven | 75-B11 n.s. |
| Brewster, Benj$^m$ | S | Brookhaven | 75-B10 |
| Brewster, Benj$^m$ Junor | S | Brookhaven | 75-B10 |
| Brewster, Caleb | S | Brookhaven | 75-B4, 75-B8 |
| Brewster, Daniel | S | Southampton | 76:1.1.2.1.1 |
| Brewster, James | N | New York | 74-A, 76-A |
| Brewster, James | S | Southampton | 76:0.1.0.1.0 |
| Brewster, James, shipwright | N | New York | 74-V |
| Brewster, Jefery | S | Brookhaven | 76:0.1.0.2.1 |
| Brewster, Jeffrey | S | Brookhaven | 75-B3, 75-B6 |
| Brewster, John | S | Brookhaven | 75-B6, 75-B7 |
| Brewster, Joseph | S | Brookhaven | 75-B10 |
| Brewster, Joseph | S | Brookhaven | 75-B11 n.s. |
| Brewster, Joseph | S | Brookhaven | 76:0.1.4.3.2.1.0 |
| Brewster, Mary wf of James | N | New York | 74-V |
| Brewster, Nathaniel | S | Brookhaven | 75-B3, 75-B6 |
| Brewster, Nathaniel | S | Brookhaven | 76:0.1.0.1.2.0.1 |
| Brewster, Ruth | S | Brookhaven | 76:0.0.0.1.0 |
| Brewster, William | S | Brookhaven | 75-B6, 75-B7 |

| | | | |
|---|---|---|---|
| Brewster, William | S | Brookhaven | 76:0.3.1.1.3 |
| Brewster, William, Capt. | S | Brookhaven | 75-B7 |
| Brewster, William Jr. | S | Brookhaven | 75-B1, 75-B6 |
| Brewster, William, Lieut. | S | Brookhaven | 75-B1 |
| Brian, Fanny, schoolteacher | N | Golden Hill | 74-T |
| Brichet, Luke | S | Brookhaven | 76:1.0.0.1.0 |
| Bridge, Samuel | N | New York | 74-T2, 5/26 |
| Bridges, Alexander | N | New York | 76-A |
| Bridgewater, John | N | New York | 74-A |
| Bridgewater, John | N | New York | 76-A, 76-I |
| Briggard, Thomas | S | Brookhaven | 75-B10 |
| Briley, Jane Br [sic] | N | to Dutchess Co. | 76-P |
| Brill, David | N | New York | 76-A |
| Brim, Michael | N | at Mrs. Banker's | 75-D1, D2 |
| Brimer, Jno. | Q | ........ | 75-A associator |
| Brimer, see also Bremner | | | |
| Brinckerhoff, A., Jr. | Q | ........ | 76-E |
| Brinckerhoff, Ab'm | Q | ........ | 76-E |
| Brinckerhoff, Abr'm | Q | ........ | 75-A associator |
| Brinckerhoff, Abr'm | Q | Newtown | 75-G |
| Brinckerhoff, Abr'm Jr. | Q | ........ | 75-A |
| Brinckerhoff, Abraham | N | New York | 75-T2, 5/4 |
| Brinckerhoff, Abrm. | N | New York | 74-A |
| Brinckerhoff, Al. | Q | ........ | 76-E |
| Brinckerhoff, Albert | Q | Newtown | 75-B |
| Brinckerhoff, Daniel | Q | ........ | 75-A, 76-E |
| Brinckerhoff, Dirck | N | New York | 75-V |
| Brinckerhoff, Dirck | N | to Fish Kills | 74-T |
| Brinckerhoff, Elbert | Q | ........ | 75-A, 76-E |
| Brinckerhoff, Geo. 3d | Q | ........ | 76-E |
| Brinckerhoff, Geo. Jr. | Q | Newtown | 75-G |
| Brinckerhoff, George | Q | ........ | 75-A, 76-B |
| Brinckerhoff, George | Q | ........ | 75-A associator |
| Brinckerhoff, George [2] | Q | ........ | [on] 76-E |
| Brinckerhoff, Hend., J.P. | Q | Newtown | 75-B |
| Brinckerhoff, Hendk. | Q | ........ | 76-E |
| Brinckerhoff, Henry | N | New York | 74-A |
| Brinckerhoff, Isaac | Q | ........ | 76-E |
| Brinckerhoff, Jores | Q | ........ | 76-E |
| Brinckerhoff, Teunis [3] | Q | ........ | [on] 76-E |

| | | | |
|---|---|---|---|
| Brinckerhoff, Tunis | Q | ........ | 75-A |
| Brinckerhoff, Tunis | Q | Newtown | 75-B |
| Brinckerhoof, Abraham | N | New York | 75-R juror |
| Brinckle, Thomas, taylor | N | Peck's Slip | 75-D1, D2 |
| Brinckle, Thomas, taylor | N | Pecks Slip | 75-D2 |
| Brinckley, Thomas | N | New York | 75-D1 |
| Brismou, Gottfried | N | New York | 74-A |
| Britton, Major | N | New York | 74-A |
| Broadbolt, Henry | N | New York | 75-D3 |
| Broadwell, Henry, sadler | N | Bowry Lane | 75-D1, D2 |
| Brock, _____ Mrs., tearoom | N | New York | 74-T2, 5/26 |
| Brock, Sarah | N | New York | 76-I |
| Brockes, Thomas | N | New York | 74-A |
| Brookman, Thos. | N | New York | 74-A |
| Brooks, David, Dr. | Q | ........ | 75-A |
| Brooks, David, Dr. | Q | Oyster Bay | 75-H |
| Brooks, George | N | New York | 74-V |
| Brooks, Jas. | N | New York | 74-A |
| Brooks, John | N | New York | 76-A |
| Brooks, Philip, bookbinder | N | Dock Street | 75-T2, 10/12 |
| Broom, John | N | New York | 75-T2, 5/4 |
| Broome, John, merchant | N | New York | 74-T |
| Broome, Samuel | N | New York | 74-A |
| Broome, Samuel | N | New York | 75-T2, 5/4 |
| Broome, Samuel & Co. | N | New York | 74-T2, 11/17 |
| Broome, Samuel, Capt. | N | New York | 75-E |
| Broome, Samuel, merchant | N | Dock Street | 75-D2 |
| Brothers, Jacob | N | New York | 76-I |
| Broune, John | N | removed upstate | 76-P |
| Brouwer, Abraham | N | New York | 75-D1 |
| Brouwer, Abraham [2] | N | New York | [on] 74-A |
| Brouwer, Ann | N | removed upstate | 76-P |
| Brouwer, Daniel | N | New York | 75-D1 |
| Brouwer, Everardus | N | New York | 74-A |
| Brouwer, Garret | N | New York | 74-A |
| Brouwer, Jacob Jr. | N | New York | 74-A |
| Brouwer, Jacob S. | N | New York | 74-A |
| Brouwer, Jacob [2] | N | New York | [on] 74-A |
| Brouwer, John | N | New York | 75-D1 |
| Brouwer, John Jr. | N | New York | 74-A, 76-D |

| | | | |
|---|---|---|---|
| Brouwer, William | N | New York | 74-A |
| Brower, Abraham | N | New York | 74-A, 76-A |
| Brower, Abraham, Ensign | N | New York | 76-S |
| Brower, Abram | N | New York | 76-L |
| Brower, Catharine | N | rem to Ulster Co. | 76-P |
| Brower, Daniel | N | New York | 74-A |
| Brower, Jacob | N | New York | 76-D |
| Brower, Jacob, hatter | N | Leary Street | 75-D1, D2 |
| Brower, Jacob Jr., 1st Lt. | N | New York | 76-S |
| Brower, Jacob [2] | N | New York | [on] 76-L |
| Brower, Jeremiah | N | New York | 74-A |
| Brower, Jeremiah, merchant | N | New York | 74-T2, 3/3 |
| Brower, Jeremiah, merchant | N | New York | 76-V |
| Brower, John [2] | N | New York | [on] 76-L |
| Brower, Mary | N | to Dutchess Co. | 76-P |
| Brower, Nich[e] | N | New York | 74-A |
| Brower, Sam[l] | N | to Dutchess Co. | 76-P |
| Brower, Sebtent | N | New York | 76-A |
| Brown, Absalom | S | Southold | 75-N non-signer |
| Brown, Absalom, Sgt. | S | Southold | 75-N |
| Brown, Absolom | S | Southold | 76:0.1.0.1.2 |
| Brown, Anne, Mrs. | N | rem to Ulster Co. | 76-P |
| Brown, Asa | S | Southold | 75-N non-signer |
| Brown, Assa Jun[r] | S | Southold | 76:0.1.0.1.1 |
| Brown, Benjamin | N | New York | 76-D |
| Brown, Caleb | S | ........ | 75-R |
| Brown, Cath. | N | New York | 75-R |
| Brown, Charles | N | New York | 74-A |
| Brown, Charles | N | New York | 76-A, 76-I |
| Brown, Christopher | S | ........ | 75-R |
| Brown, Christopher | S | Southold | 76:0.1.1.1.2 |
| Brown, Danel | S | Meritches | 76:0.1.0.1.0 |
| Brown, Danial | S | Southold | 76:1.1.1.3.0 |
| Brown, Daniel | N | New York | 75-R |
| Brown, Daniel | S | Brookhaven | 75-B6 |
| Brown, Daniel | S | Shelter Island | 75-K |
| Brown, Daniel | S | Shelter Island | 76:1.1.0.1.0.1.1 |
| Brown, Daniel | S | Southampton | 76:0.2.2.1.5 |
| Brown, Daniel, carpenter | N | Cortland's Street | 75-D2 |
| Brown, Daniel [2] | S | ........ | [on] 75-R |

| | | | |
|---|---|---|---|
| Brown, David | S | Brookhaven | 75-B10 |
| Brown, Edward | S | Brookhaven | 76:1.0.0.0.0 |
| Brown, Elizabeth | N | New York | 74-T |
| Brown, Ephraim | S | Southold | 76:1.0.5.4.1 |
| Brown, Garshem | S | Brookhaven | 76:0.2.1.2.3 |
| Brown, George | S | ........ | 75-R |
| Brown, Gershom | S | Brookhaven | 75-B6, 75-B7 |
| Brown, Greshom | S | Brookhaven | 75-B1 |
| Brown, Henery | S | Brookhaven | 75-B10 |
| Brown, Hennery | S | Southold | 76:1.2.0.1.0 |
| Brown, Hennery Junr. | S | Southold | 76:0.1.0.1.5 |
| Brown, Henry | S | Southampton | 75-M |
| Brown, Henry | S | Southampton | 76:0.1.0.0.4 |
| Brown, Henry Juner | S | Brookhaven | 75-B10 |
| Brown, Isaiah | S | ........ | 75-R |
| Brown, Jacobus | N | New York | 74-A |
| Brown, James | N | New York | 76-R |
| Brown, James | S | ........ | 75-R |
| Brown, James | S | Southold | 76:1.1.0.3.1 |
| Brown, James, Rev[d] | S | Southampton | 76:1.0.1.4.1.1.2 |
| Brown, Jane | N | New York | 75-R |
| Brown, John | N | New York | 74-A |
| Brown, John, hse carpenter | N | Cortland Street | 75-D2 |
| Brown, John, shoemaker | N | Wall Street | 74-T |
| Brown, Jonathan, carpenter | N | Beaver Street | 75-D2 |
| Brown, Jonathan [2] | N | New York | [on] 74-A |
| Brown, Joseph | S | Brookhaven | 75-B2 |
| Brown, Joseph | S | Brookhaven | 76:0.2.7.3.2 |
| Brown, Joseph, alias Hayes | N | New York | 75-R |
| Brown, Joseph Jr. | S | Brookhaven | 75-B2 |
| Brown, Margaret | N | to Dutchess Co. | 76-P |
| Brown, Margert | N | rem. to Bedford | 76-J |
| Brown, Martha, Wid[w] | S | Southampton | 76:0.1.0.4.0 |
| Brown, Martin | S | Brookhaven | 75-B2 |
| Brown, Mary | N | rem to Ulster Co. | 76-P |
| Brown, ____ Mr. | N | rem to Ulster Co. | 76-P |
| Brown, Nathanil | S | Brookhaven | 75-B6 |
| Brown, Peter | S | Brookhaven | 75-B10 |
| Brown, Reuben | S | Brookhaven | 75-B10 |
| Brown, Richard | S | Southold | 76:3.0.2.4.4 |

| | | | |
|---|---|---|---|
| Brown, Richard [2] | S | Brookhaven | [on] 75-B10 |
| Brown, Roben | S | Southold | 76:0.1.1.1.1 |
| Brown, Ruth, Mrs. | N | to Westchester Co | 76-P |
| Brown, Samuel | S | Southampton | 75-M |
| Brown, Samuel | S | Southold | 75-N |
| Brown, Samuel [2] | N | New York | [on] 74-A |
| Brown, Samuell | S | Southold | 76:1.1.2.2.0.1 |
| Brown, ---- see Binner, Wm | | | |
| Brown, Selah | S | Brookhaven | 75-B1 |
| Brown, Selah | S | Brookhaven | 75-B6, 75-B7 |
| Brown, Selah | S | Brookhaven | 76:0.1.2.1.2 |
| Brown, Silvanus | S | Brookhaven | 75-B10 |
| Brown, Sylvanus | S | Southold | 76:0.1.3.2.2 |
| Brown, Thanel | S | Meritches | 76:1.1.0.1.3 |
| Brown, Thebe | S | Meritches | 76:0.0.0.1.0 |
| Brown, Thomas | N | New York | 74-A |
| Brown, Thomas | N | New York | 75-D2 |
| Brown, Thomas, pilot | N | Golden Hill | 75-D1, D2 |
| Brown, Thos. | N | New York | 74-A |
| Brown, ____ widow | N | rem to Ulster Co. | 76-P |
| Brown, William | N | New York | 74-A |
| Brown, William | N | New York | 76-A, 76-R |
| Brown, William | S | Brookhaven | 75-B10 |
| Brown, William | S | Shelter Island | 75-K |
| Brown, William | S | Shelter Island | 76:0.1.0.1.0 |
| Brown, William | S | Southold | 76:0.2.2.3.2 |
| Brown, William, Capt. | N | Smith Street | 74-T, 74-V |
| Brown, William, chairmaker | N | Broad Street | 75-D1, D2 |
| Brown, William Jr. | N | New York | 74-A, 75-D1 |
| Brown, Wm | S | Brookhaven | 75-B10 |
| Browne, James | N | New York | 76-A |
| Browne, James, Capt. | N | New York | 75-A |
| Browne, John | N | New York | 74-A, 76-A |
| Brownejohn, Samuel | N | New York | 74-A |
| Brownejohn, Thomas | N | New York | 74-A |
| Brownejohn, Thomas | N | New York | 76-A, 76-F |
| Brownejohn, Thomas, Capt. | N | New York | 76-Y |
| Brownejohn, Wm | N | New York | 74-A |
| Brownejohn, Wm., druggist | N | New York | 74-T |
| Browning, Joseph | N | New York | 76-A |

| | | | |
|---|---|---|---|
| Brownson, John | N | removed upstate | 76-P |
| Bruff, C.O., silversmith | N | Maiden Lane | 74-T |
| Brunsen, Elizabeth | N | New York | 76-R |
| Brunson, Robert | N | New York | 76-A |
| Brush, Ananias | S | Huntington | 75-H |
| Brush, Benj^m | S | Huntington | 75-H |
| Brush, Daniel | S | Smithtown | 75-L |
| Brush, Daniel | S | Smithtown | 76:0.0.1.1.2 |
| Brush, Edward | N | New York | 74-A |
| Brush, Elephalet | S | Huntington | 75-H |
| Brush, Eliakim | S | Huntington | 75-H |
| Brush, Eliphalet, clark | N | Queen Street | 75-D2 |
| Brush, Ezekiel | S | Huntington | 75-H |
| Brush, Gilbert | S | Huntington | 76-H2 |
| Brush, Jacamiah | S | Huntington | 75-H |
| Brush, Jacob | S | Huntington | 75-H |
| Brush, James | S | Huntington | 76-H2 |
| Brush, Jesse | S | Huntington | 75-H |
| Brush, Jesse, Capt. | S | Huntington | 75-H1 |
| Brush, Jesse Jr. | S | Huntington | 75-H |
| Brush, Jno. | Q | ........ | 75-A associator |
| Brush, John | Q | ........ | 76-E |
| Brush, John | Q | Jamaica | 75-D associator |
| Brush, John | S | Huntington | 75-H1 |
| Brush, John Jr. | S | Huntington | 75-H |
| Brush, Joshua | S | Huntington | 75-H |
| Brush, Nath^l | S | Huntington | 75-H |
| Brush, Nehemiah | S | Huntington | 76-H3 |
| Brush, Platt | S | Huntington | 75-H |
| Brush, Robert | S | Huntington | 75-H |
| Brush, Robert | S | Huntington | 76-H2 |
| Brush, Samuel | S | Huntington | 75-H |
| Brush, Smith | Q | Hempstead | 76-D |
| Brush, Thomas | S | Huntington | 75-H |
| Brush, Thomas, 1st Lieut. | S | Huntington | 76-H2 |
| Brush, Thomas Jr. | S | Huntington | 75-H |
| Brush, Thomas Jr. | S | Huntington | 75-H1, 76-H1 |
| Brush, Tredwell | S | Huntington | 75-H |
| Brush, Zophar | S | Huntington | 75-H |
| Bryad, James | N | New York | 76-A |

| | | | |
|---|---|---|---|
| Bryan, Augustin | S | Huntington | 75-H |
| Bryan, Augustine | S | Huntington | 75-H1 |
| Bryan, Epenetus | S | Huntington | 75-H |
| Bryan, Gilbert | S | Huntington | 75-H |
| Bryan, James | S | Huntington | 75-H |
| Bryan, Jesse | S | Huntington | 75-H |
| Bryan, Jesse | S | Huntington | 76-H3 |
| Bryan, Lemuel | S | Huntington | 75-H |
| Bryan, Lemuel | S | Huntington | 75-H |
| Bryan, Lemuel | S | Huntington | 75-H1 |
| Bryan, Melancthon | S | Huntington | 75-H |
| Bryan, Stratton | S | Huntington | 75-H |
| Bryant, Alexander | S | Huntington | 76-H2 |
| Buchanan, Benjamin | S | Brookhaven | 75-B11 n.s. |
| Buchanan, John | N | New York | 76-N |
| Buchanan, John, Capt. | N | New York | 76-G |
| Buchanan, Samuel | S | Smithtown | 75-L |
| Buchanan, Thomas | N | New York | 76-A |
| Buchanan, W. | N | New York | 74-A |
| Buchanan, Walter & Thos. | N | Queen Street | 74-T2, 5/12 |
| Buchanan, William | S | Brookhaven | 75-B10 |
| Buchanan, William | S | Brookhaven | 75-B11 n.s. |
| Buchanan, William | S | Brookhaven | 76:0.1.3.1.0 |
| Buchannan, John | N | New York | 76-I |
| Buchannan, John, Lieut. | N | New York | 75-A |
| Buchannan, Thomas | N | New York | 75-T2, 5/4 |
| Buckhouse/Buckhout, Peter | N | Water st., taylor | 75-D1, D2 |
| Budd, Joshua | S | ........ | 75-R |
| Budd, Joshua | S | Southampton | 76:0.1.3.1.3 |
| Budd, Thomas | N | New York | 76-G |
| Budd, William [2] | S | ........ | [on] 75-R |
| Buell, Samuel | S | Easthampton | 75-E |
| Buell, Samuel, Mr. | S | Easthampton | 76:1.0.2.1.1.2.1 |
| Buffet, Jesse | S | Huntington | 75-H non-signer |
| Buffet, John | S | Huntington | 75-H |
| Buffet, Joseph Jr. | S | Huntington | 75-H |
| Buffet, Joshua | S | Islip | 76:0.1.0.1.0.1.0 |
| Buffet, Zebulon | S | Huntington | 75-H |
| Buffett, John | S | Huntington | 75-H1 |
| Buffett, Nath'l Jr., Ensign | S | Huntington | 75-H1 |

| | | | |
|---|---|---|---|
| Buhler, Andries | N | New York | 76-A |
| Bulgin, John | N | New York | 75-D3 |
| Bulgine, John | N | New York | 75-D2 |
| Bull, Joseph | N | New York | 74-T2, 11/24 |
| Bull, William | N | near Lispenardes | 76-H, 76-I |
| Bull, William | N | New York | 76-A |
| Bumstead, Jacob | Q | ........ | 76-E |
| Bunce, Edmund | S | Huntington | 75-H |
| Bunce, Isaac Jr. | S | Huntington | 75-H non-signer |
| Bunce, Isaac Sen$^r$ | S | Huntington | 75-H |
| Bunce, Jesse, Sergt. | S | Huntington | 76-H3 |
| Bunce, John | S | Huntington | 75-H |
| Bunce, Joshua | S | Huntington | 75-H non-signer |
| Bunce, Joshua | S | Huntington | 75-H1 |
| Bunce, Lemuel | N | New York | 74-A, 76-N |
| Bunce, Matthew | S | Huntington | 75-H |
| Bunce, Sam$^l$ | S | Huntington | 75-H non-signer |
| Bunce, Samuel, joiner | N | Ship Yards | 75-D1, D2 |
| Bunce, Zebadiah | S | Huntington | 75-H non-signer |
| Bunyan, Primus | N | New York | 75-R |
| Burch, James | Q | Hempstead | 76-D |
| Burch, Jonathan | S | Huntington | 75-H |
| Burch, Jonathan | S | Islip | 76:1.0.0.1.0 |
| Burch, Will$^m$ | S | Huntington | 75-H |
| Burchel, Henry | N | New York | 76-I |
| Burdenham, Margrit | N | removed upstate | 76-P |
| Burell, W. | Q | ........ | 76-E |
| Burgan, Peter | Q | ........ | 76-B |
| Burgan, Richard | Q | ........ | 76-B |
| Burgaw, Peter | Q | ........ | 75-A |
| Burgaw, Rich'd | Q | ........ | 75-A |
| Burger, Daniel, blockmaker | N | New York | 75-D1, D2 |
| Burger, Dan$^l$ | N | New York | 74-A |
| Burger, David, measurer | N | Partition Street | 75-D1, D2 |
| Burger, Gerardus | N | New York | 76-L |
| Burger, Gerardus, blksmith | N | Bayard Street | 75-D1, D2 |
| Burger, Jane, widow | N | removed upstate | 76-P |
| Burger, Jno. | N | New York | 74-A, 75-D1 |
| Burger, John | N | New York | 76-N |
| Burger, John, goldsmith | N | Maiden Lane | 75-D1, D2 |

| Burger, John, hatter | N | in The Swamp | 75-D1, D2 |
|---|---|---|---|
| Burger, Manus | N | New York | 74-A |
| Burger, Manus, constable | N | New York | 74-R to 76-R |
| Burgess, Olive | N | New York | 76-A |
| Burk, Daniel | N | New York | 74-A, 76-H |
| Burke, Daniel | N | New York | 76-I |
| Burling, Edward | N | New York | 74-A |
| Burling, Edward | Q | ........ | 76-E |
| Burling, James | Q | ........ | 75-A associator |
| Burling, Joseph | Q | ........ | 76-E |
| Burling, Joseph | Q | Jamaica | 75-C |
| Burling, Lancaster | N | New York | 74-A, 76-L |
| Burling, Lancaster | N | New York | 74-T2, 11/24 |
| Burling, Samuel | N | New York | 74-A, 75-T |
| Burling, Thomas | N | New York | 75-F, 76-L |
| Burling, Thomas, chairmkr | N | Beekman Street | 74-T2, 8/25 |
| Burling, Thos., cabinetmkr | N | Chapel Street | 74-T2, 3/17 |
| Burlingham, Burne, Capt. | N | New York | 76-S |
| Burlingham, Jardon | N | New York | 74-A |
| Burlingham, Pardon | N | New York | 74-R, 75-R |
| Burlingham, Pardon, Capt. | N | New York | 76-G |
| Burlingham, Pardon J. | N | Fresh Water | 75-D2 |
| Burlingham, Pardon, Lieut. | N | New York | 75-A |
| Burnet, David | S | Southampton | 76:0.1.2.3.1 |
| Burnet, Joseph | S | Southampton | 76:0.1.1.1.1 |
| Burnet, Stephen | S | Easthampton | 75-E |
| Burnet, Stephen | S | Easthampton | 76:0.1.0.2.2 |
| Burnett, Charles | Q | ........ | 76-E |
| Burnham, Robert, ae c.15 | N | New York | 75-T runaway |
| Burns, Francis Jr. | S | Brookhaven | 75-B3 |
| Burns, John | N | New York | 76-A, 76-L |
| Burns, Margaret | N | New York | 74-R witness |
| Burns, Michael | Q | ........ | 75-A, 76-B |
| Burns, Robert, wheelwright | N | New York | 75-D1, D2 |
| Burns, Thomas | N | New York | 76-L |
| Burns, William | Q | ........ | 75-A, 76-E |
| Buroton, Thomas | N | New York | 76-A |
| Burr, Daniel | Q | ........ | 75-A associator |
| Burr, Daniel | Q | ........ | 76-E |
| Burr, Daniel Jr. | Q | ........ | 76-E |

| | | | |
|---|---|---|---|
| Burr, Isaac | S | Huntington | 75-H, 75-H1 |
| Burr, Samuel | Q | ........ | 75-A associator |
| Burr, Samuel | Q | ........ | 76-E |
| Burras, Benjamin | N | New York | 74-A, 75-R |
| Burras, Benjamin | N | New York | 76-D |
| Burras, John | N | New York | 74-A |
| Burrell, see Burell | | | |
| Burress, Benjamin | N | New York | 75-D2 |
| Burris, Benjamin, Corp'l | N | New York | 76-C |
| Burris, James | Q | Newtown | 75-G |
| Burris, John | Q | Newtown | 75-G |
| Burris, Rich'd | Q | Newtown | 75-G |
| Burris, Ths. | Q | Newtown | 75-G |
| Burroughs, Benjamin | N | removed upstate | 76-P |
| Burroughs, Jno., Ensign | N | New York | 75-A |
| Burroughs, John | Q | ........ | 75-A associator |
| Burroughs, John | Q | ........ | 76-E |
| Burroughs, Joseph | Q | ........ | 76-E |
| Burroughs, Joseph | Q | Newtown | 75-B |
| Burroughs, Thomas | Q | ........ | 75-A associator |
| Burroughs, Thomas | Q | ........ | 76-E |
| Burrow, Mary | N | New York | 76-K |
| Burrow, ____ Mrs. | N | removed upstate | 76-P |
| Burrowe, John | N | New York | 76-A |
| Burrows, Benjamin | N | New York | 75-D3 |
| Burrows, John, 2d Lieut. | N | New York | 76-S |
| Burrows, Lawrence | N | New York | 74-R marshall |
| Burt, Francis | S | Brookhaven | 75-B6 |
| Burtis, Aaron | Q | ........ | 75-A |
| Burtis, After/Aster | Q | ........ | 75-A, 75-I |
| Burtis, Benjamin | Q | ........ | 75-A, 76-B |
| Burtis, Carman | Q | ........ | 76-E |
| Burtis, Dan'l | Q | Newtown | 75-G |
| Burtis, Elias | Q | ........ | 75-A, 76-E |
| Burtis, Elizabeth | N | New York | 76-I |
| Burtis, Fordham | Q | ........ | 75-A associator |
| Burtis, James | Q | ........ | 75-A |
| Burtis, James | Q | ........ | 76-B, 76-E |
| Burtis, Jamª Jr. | Q | ........ | 75-A |
| Burtis, Jno. | Q | ........ | 75-A associator |

| | | | |
|---|---|---|---|
| Burtis, Jno., miller | Q | ........ | 75-A |
| Burtis, John | Q | ........ | 75-A associator |
| Burtis, John | Q | ........ | 75-A associator |
| Burtis, John | Q | Newtown | 75-G |
| Burtis, John [4 of the name] | Q | ........ | [on] 76-E |
| Burtis, Sam'l | Q | Newtown | 75-G |
| Burtis, William | Q | ........ | 75-A, 76-B2 |
| Burto, Frances | S | Brookhaven | 76:1.2.0.2.0 |
| Burton, William | N | New York | 74-A |
| Burton, Wm | N | New York | 74-A |
| Burton, Wm | N | New York | 76-A |
| Burtsell, Henry | N | New York | 74-R |
| Burwick, John | N | New York | 74-A |
| Bush, Charles | N | New York | 76-A |
| Bush, Evert | N | New York | 74-A |
| Bush, Helena | N | removed upstate | 76-P |
| Bush, James | N | New York | 76-A |
| Bush, Samuel | N | to Dutchess Co. | 76-P |
| Buskirk, John | N | New York | 74-A |
| Bussing, Abraham | N | New York | 74-A |
| Bussing, Isaac | N | New York | 74-A |
| Butler, Edmund | N | New York | 74-A |
| Butler, John | Q | ........ | 76-E |
| Butler, John Jr. | Q | ........ | 76-E |
| Butler, Michael | Q | ........ | 75-A, 76-E |
| Butler, Sarah | N | New York | 75-V |
| Butler, William | N | New York | 74-T |
| Butler, William | Q | ........ | 76-E |
| Butler, William, merchant | N | New York | 75-V |
| Butler, Wm | N | New York | 74-A |
| Button, William | S | ........ | 75-R |
| Button, William | S | Southampton | 76:0.1.3.3.1 |
| Buxton, John | N | New York | 74-A, 76-A |
| Bydebuck, Godfrey | N | New York | 76-A |
| Byerley, Thomas, teacher | N | Maiden Lane | 74-T |
| Byers, James | N | New York | 74-A, 75-B |
| Byers, James | N | New York | 75-F, 76-N |
| Byers, James, brass founder | N | Wall Street | 75-D1, D2 |
| Byrn, Garrard | N | New York | 76-A |
| Byron, Thomas | Q | ........ | 76-A |

| | | | |
|---|---|---|---|
| Byvanck, Anth. | N | New York | 75-D3 |
| Byvanck, Anthony | N | New York | 74-A |
| Byvanck, Anthony Jr. | N | New York | 76-D |
| Byvanck, Cathar'e, widow | N | to Dutchess Co. | 76-P |
| Byvanck, Evert | N | New York | 74-A |
| Byvanck, Evert Jr. | N | New York | 74-A |
| Byvanck, Isaac Jr. | N | New York | 75-R juror |
| Byvanck, John | N | New York | 74-A |
| Byvanck, John | N | New York | 74-R juror |
| Byvanck, John | N | New York | 75-F, 76-G |
| Byvanck, Peter, Lieut. | N | New York | 75-A |
| Byvanck, Petrus | N | New York | 74-A |
| Byvanck, Petrus | N | New York | 75-T2, 5/4 |
| Cadel, Joseph | Q | ........ | 75-A |
| Cadles, Joseph | Q | ........ | 76-E |
| Cain/Cairn, Edward, taylor | N | Broadway | 75-D1, D2 |
| Cain, see also Kain | | | |
| Calder, John | N | New York | 74-A, 76-A |
| Caldwell, William | N | New York | 76-A |
| Calican, Edward | N | to Westchester Co | 76-P |
| Callahan, Daniel | N | New York | 75-R |
| Callas, Stephen | Q | ........ | 75-A |
| Callas, Stephen | Q | ........ | 76-B, 76-E |
| Calwell, Harvy | Q | ........ | 75-A |
| Cameron, Hugh | N | New York | 75-D3 |
| Camfield, Samuel | N | New York | 76-A |
| Campbel, John | N | New York | 76-M |
| Campbel, John | Q | ........ | 76-A |
| Campbell, D. | N | New York | 76-A |
| Campbell, Daniel | N | Corles Hook | 76-I |
| Campbell, Daniel | N | New York | 76-A |
| Campbell, Daniel | N | Ogelsvies place | 76-H |
| Campbell, Duncan | N | New York | 76-A, 76-I |
| Campbell, Elenor | N | removed upstate | 76-P |
| Campbell, George | N | New York | 74-R juror |
| Campbell, George | N | New York | 76-A, 76-I |
| Campbell, George, cordwnr | N | Water Street | 75-D1, D2 |
| Campbell, James | N | New York | 74-A |
| Campbell, James, butcher | N | New York | 75-R |
| Campbell, James, shoemkr | N | Queen Street | 75-D2 |

| | | | |
|---|---|---|---|
| Campbell, James, shoemkr | N | Queen Street | 75-D2 |
| Campbell, Jane | N | removed upstate | 76-P |
| Campbell, John | N | New York | 76-N |
| Campbell, John, juror | N | New York | 74-R, 75-R |
| Campbell, John, potter | N | Broadway | 74-T2, 5/19 |
| Campbell, John, tailor | N | New York | 74-T |
| Campbell, John [2] | N | New York | [on] 76-A |
| Campbell, Margrit | N | removed upstate | 76-P |
| Campbell, Robert | N | New York | 76-N |
| Campbell, Robt. | N | New York | 76-I |
| Campbell, Sarah | N | removed upstate | 76-P |
| Campbell, Stephen | N | New York | 74-A |
| Campbell, Thomas | N | New York | 74-A |
| Campbell, Thomas, Ensign | N | New York | 75-A |
| Campbell, Thomas, potter | N | Great George St. | 75-D1, D2 |
| Campbell, Will'm | N | New York | 74-A |
| Campbell, Wm, house crptr | N | St. James Street | 75-D2 |
| Campble,_____ | N | removed upstate | 76-P |
| Campble, Eleanor | N | New York | 74-R |
| Campble, Fiby | N | removed upstate | 76-P |
| Canady, Sarah | N | removed upstate | 76-P |
| Canile, Peter | Q | Jamaica | 75-E |
| Cannon, Abraham | N | New York | 74-A, 76-I |
| Cannon, Abraham, shoemkr | N | Beekman Street | 75-D1, D2 |
| Cannon, Arent | N | Cowfoot Hill | 74-T2, 2/3 |
| Cannon, Arnout | N | New York | 74-A |
| Cannon, Arnout, constable | N | New York | 74-R to 76-R |
| Cannon, John | N | nr Powder House | 75-D1, D2 |
| Cannon, Josiah | N | New York | 76-A |
| Cannon, Peter, apprentice | N | New York | 74-R |
| Cannon, Peter, cooper | N | Cherry Street | 75-D1, D2 |
| Car, Wm | N | New York | 74-A |
| Caraens, Catherien | N | removed upstate | 76-P |
| Carbee, Wm | N | New York | 76-H |
| Carby, William | N | New York | 76-M |
| Carey, Daniel | N | New York | 74-R |
| Carey, Josiah | S | Easthampton | 76:0.1.0.1.2 |
| Cargell, John | N | near Pecks slip | 76-H, 76-I |
| Cargill, John | N | New York | 74-A |
| Caril, James | N | to Westchester Co | 76-P |

| | | | |
|---|---|---|---|
| Carle, John | Q | ........ | 76-E |
| Carleton, Dennis | N | New York | 76-A |
| Carll, Ananias | S | Huntington | 75-H |
| Carll, David | S | Huntington | 75-H |
| Carll, Gilbert | S | Huntington | 75-H |
| Carll, Jesse | S | Huntington | 75-H |
| Carll, John, Sergt. | S | Huntington | 76-H3 |
| Carll, Lemuel | S | Huntington | 75-H |
| Carll, Platt | S | Huntington | 75-H |
| Carll, Scudd | S | Huntington | 76-H3 |
| Carll, Selah | S | Huntington | 75-H, 75-H1 |
| Carll, Silas | S | Huntington | 75-H |
| Carll, Timothy, Capt. | S | Huntington | 75-H1 |
| Carll, Timothy Jr. | S | Huntington | 75-H |
| Carlton, Dennis | N | New York | 76-F |
| Carman, Adam | Q | ........ | 75-A |
| Carman, Benjamin | Q | ........ | 75-A, 76-E |
| Carman, C. | Q | ........ | 76-B |
| Carman, Israel | Q | ........ | 76-B |
| Carman, John | Q | ........ | 75-A |
| Carman, John | Q | ........ | 76-A, 76-B |
| Carman, Sam'l | Q | Oyster Bay | 75-A |
| Carman, Sam'l 3d | Q | ........ | 75-A [correct] |
| Carman, Sam'l 3d | Q | ........ | 75-A [correct] |
| Carman, Sam'l, Capt. | Q | ........ | 75-A |
| Carman, Sam'l Jr. | Q | ........ | 75-A |
| Carman, Samuel | S | Huntington | 75-H |
| Carman, Samuel [3] | Q | ........ | [on] 76-E |
| Carman, Samuel [4] | Q | ........ | [on] 76-B |
| Carman, Silas | Q | ........ | 76-E |
| Carman, Silas | Q | Hempstead | 76-D |
| Carman, Stephen | Q | ........ | 75-A |
| Carman, William | N | New York | 75-D2, 76-L |
| Carmer, Henry | N | New York | 74-A |
| Carmer, Nicholas | N | New York | 74-A |
| Carmer, Nicholas, hardware | N | Maiden Lane | 74-T2, 2/17 |
| Carmer, Nicholas, juror | N | New York | 74-R, 75-R |
| Carmer, Nicholas, Lieut. | N | New York | 75-A |
| Carmon, John | S | Huntington | 75-H |
| Carmon, Samuel | S | Islip | 76:0.1.2.1.1 |

| | | | |
|---|---|---|---|
| Carmour, Samuel | Q | ........ | 76-B2 |
| Carns, John | N | New York | 74-A |
| Carpenter, Benj., hse crptr | N | William Street | 75-D1, D2 |
| Carpenter, Benjamin | N | New York | 76-L |
| Carpenter, Benjamin | Q | Jamaica | 75-C |
| Carpenter, Benj$^n$, Capt. | N | New York | 75-A |
| Carpenter, Coles | Q | ........ | 76-E |
| Carpenter, Elizabeth, Mrs. | N | New York | 76-V |
| Carpenter, George | N | New York | 74-R |
| Carpenter, Increase | Q | Jamaica | 75-D associator |
| Carpenter, Increase | Q | Jamaica | 75-D associator |
| Carpenter, Increase Jr. | Q | ........ | 75-A associator |
| Carpenter, Increase, Lieut. | Q | Jamaica | 76-C |
| Carpenter, Isaac | Q | ........ | 76-E |
| Carpenter, Jacob | N | New York | 75-D1 |
| Carpenter, Jacob | Q | ........ | 75-A associator |
| Carpenter, Jacob | Q | Jamaica | 75-D associator |
| Carpenter, Jacob, ship crptr | N | Cherry Street | 75-D1, D2 |
| Carpenter, Jacob, ship crptr | N | Cherry Street | 75-D1, D2 |
| Carpenter, Jacob [2] | Q | ........ | [on] 76-E |
| Carpenter, James | N | New York | 74-A |
| Carpenter, James | Q | ........ | 75-A |
| Carpenter, James | Q | ........ | 76-B, 76-E |
| Carpenter, James, taylor | N | Cowfit Hill | 75-D1, D2 |
| Carpenter, John | Q | Oyster Bay | 75-F |
| Carpenter, John [3 John's] | Q | ........ | [on] 76-E |
| Carpenter, Joseph | Q | ........ | 76-E |
| Carpenter, Joseph | Q | Hempstead | 76-D |
| Carpenter, Joseph | Q | Oyster Bay | 75-F |
| Carpenter, Joshua | Q | ........ | 76-E |
| Carpenter, Joshua | Q | Jamaica | 75-D associator |
| Carpenter, Nehemiah | Q | ........ | 75-D associator |
| Carpenter, Nehemiah | Q | ........ | 75-D associator |
| Carpenter, Nehemiah | Q | ........ | 76-E |
| Carpenter, Nehemiah | Q | Jamaica | 75-C, 75-D |
| Carpenter, Nehemiah [3] | Q | ........ | [on] 76-C |
| Carpenter, Wil$^m$ | S | Huntington | 75-H |
| Carr, Adam | N | New York | 76-A |
| Carr, Anthony | N | New York | 76-A |
| Carr, James | N | New York | 74-A |

| | | | |
|---|---|---|---|
| Carr, Joseph | N | New York | 75-D1 |
| Carr, Joseph | N | New York | 76-N |
| Carr, Joseph, currier | N | in the Swamp | 75-D1, D2 |
| Carr, Josiah, clark | N | Queen Street | 75-D2 |
| Carr/Karr, William, taylor | N | Beekman Street | 75-D1, D2 |
| Carr, Robert | N | King George St. | 74-T2, 12/22 |
| Carr, Robert | N | New York | 74-A, 76-A |
| Carr, see also Car | | | |
| Carrow, John | N | New York | 76-H |
| Carrow, John, shoemaker | N | Chatham Street | 75-D1, D2 |
| Carsln, Daniel | N | New York | 75-B |
| Carstang, Gideon | N | New York | 76-A |
| Carter, Daniel | N | New York | 74-A |
| Carter, Dannel | N | New York | 74-A |
| Carter, Elizabeth | N | to Dutchess Co. | 76-P |
| Carter, Enoch | N | New York | 74-A |
| Carter, Hannah, Mrs. | N | to Dutchess Co. | 76-P |
| Carter, James | N | New York | 76-I |
| Carter, James | N | to Dutchess Co. | 76-P |
| Carter, John | N | to Dutchess Co. | 76-P |
| Carter, Mary | N | to Dutchess Co. | 76-P |
| Carter, Rachel | N | to Dutchess Co. | 76-P |
| Carter, Robert, Ensign | N | New York | 75-B |
| Carter, Thomas | N | New York | 76-A |
| Carter, Vincent | N | to Dutchess Co. | 76-P |
| Carter, Vincent, carman | N | Nassau Street | 75-D2 |
| Carter, William | N | to Dutchess Co. | 76-P |
| Cary, Elias | S | Brookhaven | 76:1.1.1.2.1 |
| Cary, Mary | N | removed upstate | 76-P |
| Case, Benj. | S | Southold | 76:1.0.2.7.0 |
| Case, Benj. Junʳ | S | Southold | 76:0.1.3.1.0 |
| Case, Dibbull | S | ........ | 75-R |
| Case, Echabod | S | Southold | 76:0.1.1.1.1 |
| Case, Gershom | S | Southold | 76:0.1.1.1.1 |
| Case, Gilbert | S | Southold | 76:0.1.1.1.1 |
| Case, Isaac ye 3ᵈ | S | ........ | 75-R |
| Case, Israel | S | Southold | 76:0.1.1.1.2 |
| Case, John | S | Southold | 75-N |
| Case, John | S | Southold | 76:0.1.1.2.1 |
| Case, Joseph | S | Shelter Island | 75-K |

| | | | |
|---|---|---|---|
| Case, Joshua | S | Southold | 76:1.0.1.2.0 |
| Case, Moses | S | ........ | 75-R |
| Case, Moses | S | Southold | 76:1.0.2.1.0.2.4 |
| Case, Samuel | S | Shelter Island | 75-K |
| Case, Samuel | S | Shelter Island | 76:1.1.0.3.0 |
| Case, Samuel Jr. | S | Shelter Island | 75-K |
| Case, Samuel Jr. | S | Shelter Island | 76:0.1.0.1.3 |
| Case, William | S | Southold | 76:1.1.1.1.0 |
| Case, William [2] | S | ........ | [on] 75-R |
| Casey, Sam[l] | N | New York | 74-A |
| Cashow, see Kashow | | | |
| Casseboom, David | Q | ........ | 75-A; 76-B, B2 |
| Cassel, David | Q | Hempstead | 76-D |
| Cassey, Samuel Sr. | N | New York | 74-A |
| Castellane, Daniel | N | New York | 74-R |
| Castle, Mary | N | removed upstate | 76-P |
| Cater, Thomas | N | New York | 76-A |
| Catlin, Wm | N | New York | 74-A |
| Cavenagh, Henry | N | New York | 74-R |
| Cavenagh, Hen[y] | N | New York | 74-A |
| Cavenaugh, Henry | N | New York | 76-R |
| Caverly, Peter | Q | Jamaica | 75-C |
| Caviller, Charles | N | New York | 74-A |
| Caviller, Peter | N | New York | 74-A |
| Cay, Robert | N | Bowery | 74-T2, 4/7 |
| Cayhterry, Richard | N | New York | 76-A |
| Cebra, William | Q | Jamaica | 75-E |
| Chace, Philip | S | ........ | 75-R |
| Chadne, Mary | N | removed upstate | 76-P |
| Chadoyne, David | Q | ........ | 76-E |
| Chadoyne, Elias | Q | ........ | 76-E |
| Chadwick, Tadmas | N | New York | 76-A |
| Chadwick, Thos. | N | New York | 74-A |
| Chamberland, Uriah | N | New York | 76-I |
| Chambers, Anne | N | New York | 74-T |
| Chambers, Maria | N | removed upstate | 76-P |
| Chanery, George | N | New York | 75-R |
| Chanery, Mary | N | New York | 75-R |
| Chapin, Benj., Doct[r] | S | Southampton | 76:0.1.2.1.3 |
| Chapman, Jno. | N | New York | 76-A |

| | | | |
|---|---|---|---|
| Chappel, Benjamin | S | ........ | 75-R |
| Chappel, Benjamin | S | Southampton | 76:0.1.1.1.1 |
| Chapple, Thomas | N | New York | 74-A |
| Chapple, Thomas, carpenter | N | with J. Bleak | 75-D1, D2 |
| Chapples, Peter | N | New York | 76-L |
| Chardavoyne, Abraham | N | crpntr, Cortland st | 75-D1, D2 |
| Chardavoyne, Elias | N | New York | 74-V |
| Chardavoyne, Isaac | N | New York | 74-V |
| Chardavoyne, William | N | New York | 74-V |
| Chardvayne, Lewis, taylor | N | Fair Street | 75-D2 |
| Charlot, James | N | to Dutchess Co. | 76-P |
| Charlot, Mary | N | to Dutchess Co. | 76-P |
| Charlot, Samuel | N | New York | 74-A |
| Charlot, Samuel | N | to Dutchess Co. | 76-P |
| Charlton, ____ Dr. | N | Broadway | 75-T2, 2/16 |
| Charlton, John | Q | ........ | 76-E |
| Charter, Joseph | N | New York | 74-A |
| Chase, Benjamin | S | ........ | 75-R |
| Chase, Benjamin | S | Southampton | 76:0.1.2.1.1 |
| Chase, Catharine | N | New York | 75-R |
| Chase, Catharine, Mrs. | N | to Dutchess Co. | 76-P |
| Chase, Charles | S | Southold | 76:1.0.0.1.2 |
| Chase, Mr. | Q | Jamaica | 75-H |
| Chatelain, John Francis | S | Easthampton | 75-E |
| Chatfield, Henry | S | Easthampton | 75-E |
| Chatfield, John | S | Easthampton | 75-E |
| Chatfield, John Esq' | S | Easthampton | 76:1.1.0.2.2 |
| Chatfield, Lewis | S | Easthampton | 75-E |
| Chattalin, Francis | S | Easthampton | 76:0.1.1.3.2 |
| Cheeseman, Jacob | N | New York | 74-R |
| Cheeseman, Joseph | N | New York | 74-A, 76-I |
| Cheeseman, Robert | N | New York | 74-A |
| Cheeseman, Robert | N | New York | 76-A, 76-I |
| Cheeseman, Thomas | N | New York | 74-R ship bldr |
| Cheesman, Benjamin | Q | ........ | 76-E |
| Cheesman, Jacob | N | New York | 74-R |
| Cheesman, Jacob, Capt. | N | New York | 75-E |
| Cheesman, Joseph | N | New York | 76-N |
| Cheshire, Benjamin | Q | ........ | 76-E |
| Cheshire, Jeremiah | Q | ........ | 76-E |

| | | | |
|---|---|---|---|
| Cheshire, Samuel | Q | ........ | 76-E |
| Cheshire, Thomas | Q | ........ | 76-E |
| Cheshire, William | Q | ........ | 76-E |
| Chew, Elizabeth | N | to Westchester Co | 76-P |
| Chew, Joseph | N | New York | 76-A |
| Chew, Richard | N | to Westchester Co | 76-P |
| Chichester, Eben$^r$ | S | Huntington | 75-H |
| Chichester, Eliphelet | S | Huntington | 75-H, 76-H2 |
| Chichester, Sylvanus | S | Huntington | 75-H |
| Chichester, Tim$^y$ | S | Huntington | 75-H |
| Child, Peter | N | New York | 75-D2 |
| Childs, Joseph | N | New York | 76-I |
| Chiser, John | Q | ........ | 76-E |
| Chorberker, Johannis | N | New York | 76-A |
| Christainse, Angeltue | N | removed upstate | 76-P |
| Christie, Elisabeth | N | removed upstate | 76-P |
| Christie, George | N | New York | 74-T2, 7/21 |
| Christie, Ralph | N | New York | 74-T2, 7/21 |
| Christopher, Barent | N | New York | 76-L |
| Christopher, Barnt | N | New York | 74-A |
| Chubb, John | N | New York | 74-R |
| Clark, Alexander | N | New York | 74-A |
| Clark, Alexander | N | New York | 76-A, 76-I |
| Clark, Archibald | N | New York | 74-A, 76-A |
| Clark, Benjman | S | Brookhaven | 76:0.1.0.1.3 |
| Clark, Daniel | N | New York | 76-A |
| Clark, Douglas, harnessmkr | N | Dey Street | 75-D1, D2 |
| Clark, Elisha | S | ........ | 75-R |
| Clark, Elisha | S | Southampton | 76:0.1.0.1.1 |
| Clark, Elisha | S | Southampton | 76:0.1.0.1.2 |
| Clark, James, ae 23, b Scot | N | runaway | 74-T |
| Clark, John | N | in the Fly | 74-T |
| Clark, John | N | New York | 75-D1, 76-A |
| Clark, John | S | Southold | 75-N |
| Clark, John | S | Southold | 76:0.1.0.1.3 |
| Clark, John | S | Southold | 76:0.1.1.2.4 |
| Clark, John | S | Southold | 76:1.0.0.2.2 |
| Clark, John, measurer | N | nr. City Hall | 75-D1, D2 |
| Clark, John [2] | N | New York | [on] 74-A |
| Clark, Joshua | S | Brookhaven | 75-B10 |

| | | | |
|---|---|---|---|
| Clark, Joshua | S | Southold | 76:1.0.0.2.0.2.0 |
| Clark, Ludlo | S | Brookhaven | 76:0.1.3.1.1 |
| Clark, Mathew | S | Brookhaven | 76:1.1.1.3.0 |
| Clark, Nathan | S | Southampton | 76:1.0.1.2.3 |
| Clark, Rich[d] | N | New York | 76-I |
| Clark, Samuel | S | Southampton | 76:1.0.1.2.0 |
| Clark, Samuell | S | Southampton | 76:1.1.2.2.1 |
| Clark, Scott | N | New York | 74-A |
| Clark, Scott L. | N | New York | 76-A |
| Clark, Thomas [2] | N | New York | [on] 74-A |
| Clark, William | N | to Westchester Co | 76-P |
| Clark, William | S | Brookhaven | 75-B6 |
| Clark, William Jr. | S | Brookhaven | 75-B1, 75-B6 |
| Clark, W[m] | S | Brookhaven | 76:1.1.0.2.1.2.2 |
| Clarke, Anthony | N | New York | 76-M |
| Clarke, Benjamin | N | New York | 74-R |
| Clarke, Clement Cooke | N | New York | 76-A |
| Clarke, John | N | New York | 74-R, 76-A |
| Clarke, John | N | New York | 76-F, 76-I |
| Clarke, John | N | New York | 76-M |
| Clarke, Ludley | S | Brookhaven | 75-B1 |
| Clarke, Ludlo | S | Brookhaven | 75-B7 |
| Clarke, Thomas | N | New York | 75-T |
| Clarke, William | N | New York | 74-A |
| Clarke, William | S | Brookhaven | 75-B1 |
| Clarke, William, Corporal | S | Brookhaven | 75-B7 |
| Clarkson, David | N | New York | 75-T2, 5/4 |
| Clarkson, Thomas | N | New York | 75-R |
| Clary, Justice | Q | ........ | 75-H |
| Class, John | N | New York | 74-A, 76-L |
| Class, John, hse carpenter | N | Nassau Street | 75-D1, D2 |
| Clatworth, Margaret | N | to Dutchess Co. | 76-P |
| Clayton, Samuel | N | New York | 76-A |
| Cleathen, Thomas | N | New York | 76-A |
| Cleeveland, Ichabod | S | Southold | 76:0.1.4.2.0.1.1 |
| Cleeves, Biah | S | Southold | 76:0.1.2.1.2 |
| Cleeves, David | S | Southold | 76:0.1.2.1.1 |
| Cleeves, Jeddediah | S | Southold | 76:1.0.0.1.0 |
| Cleeves, Joshua | S | Southold | 76:0.2.1.2.3 |
| Clegroe, William | N | New York | 74-A |

| | | | |
|---|---|---|---|
| Clem, John | N | New York | 74-A |
| Clem, Mary | N | Batton Street | 76-H |
| Clem, Mary | N | Deys street | 76-I |
| Clement, Daniel | Q | ........ | 76-E |
| Clement, John | Q | ........ | 76-E |
| Clement, Joseph Jr. | Q | ........ | 76-E |
| Clement, Samuel | Q | ........ | 76-E |
| Clement, Stephen | Q | ........ | 75-A, 76-B |
| Clement, Stephen | Q | Jamaica | 75-D |
| Clerk, Cornelius | S | Brookhaven | 75-B8 |
| Cleveland, Ichabod | S | ........ | 75-R |
| Cleveland, Joseph | S | ........ | 75-R |
| Cleveland, Joseph | S | Southold | 76:0.2.2.2.2 |
| Cleves, Benaiah Moore | S | Brookhaven | 75-B10 |
| Cleves, David | S | Brookhaven | 75-B10 |
| Cleves, Jedediah | S | Brookhaven | 75-B10 |
| Cleves, Joshua | S | Brookhaven | 75-B10 |
| Cleves, Joshua Jr. | S | Brookhaven | 75-B10 |
| Clevland, Ichabod | S | ........ | 75-R |
| Clevland, Joseph | S | ........ | 75-R |
| Clock, Jacob, Lieut. | N | New York | 75-A |
| Clopper, Cornelius | N | New York | 75-T2, 5/4 |
| Clopper, Peter | N | New York | 74-A |
| Cloquadeu, Cornelis | N | New York | 74-A |
| Closworthy, William | N | New York | 76-A |
| Clowes, Gerardus | Q | ........ | 75-A, 76-E |
| Clowes, Joseph | Q | ........ | 76-E |
| Clowes, S. | Q | ........ | 76-E |
| Clowes, Sam^l Esq. | Q | ........ | 75-A |
| Clowes, Samuel, Justice | Q | Hempstead | 75-H |
| Clowes, Thomas | Q | ........ | 75-A, 76-E |
| Clowes, Timothy | Q | ........ | 75-A, 76-E |
| Cobham, James | N | New Albany Dock | 74-T2, 9/2 |
| Cobham, James | N | New York | 74-A |
| Cobham, James | N | New York | 76-I, 76-V |
| Cochran, Daniel | N | New York | 75-D3 |
| Cochran, William | N | New York | 76-A, 76-I |
| Cock, Ann, boarding house | N | rem to Albany | 74-T |
| Cock, Ann, wid. of Abr^m | N | New York | 74-T |
| Cock, Benjamin | Q | ........ | 76-E |

| | | | |
|---|---|---|---|
| Cock, Clark | Q | ........ | 76-E |
| Cock, Daniel | Q | ........ | 75-A, 76-E |
| Cock, Daniel Jr. | Q | ........ | 76-E |
| Cock, Elijah | N | New York | 75-F |
| Cock, Elijah | Q | ........ | 76-E |
| Cock, G., Corp'l | N | New York | 75-D3 |
| Cock, Gabriel | Q | ........ | 76-E |
| Cock, John | Q | ........ | 75-A |
| Cock, John | Q | ........ | 76-B, 76-E |
| Cock, Levi | Q | ........ | 75-A |
| Cock, Levi | Q | ........ | 76-B, 76-E |
| Cock, Penn | Q | ........ | 76-E |
| Cock, Penn | Q | Jamaica | 75-A, 75-I |
| Cock, Peter | Q | ........ | 76-E |
| Cock, Stephen | Q | ........ | 75-A, 76-B |
| Cock, Thomas | Q | ........ | 75-A |
| Cock, Thomas | Q | ........ | 76-B, 76-E |
| Cock, W. | Q | ........ | 76-E |
| Cock, William, Lieut. | N | New York | 75-A |
| Cock, Wm. | Q | ........ | 75-A, 76-B |
| Cockcroft, Wm | N | New York | 74-A |
| Cockie, John | N | New York | 74-V |
| Cockle, John | N | New York | 74-T |
| Cockle, John | Q | ........ | 75-A associator |
| Cockle, John | Q | Jamaica | 75-D associator |
| Cockle, John Jr. | N | New York | 74-A |
| Cockram, Daniel | N | New York | 75-D1 |
| Cockram, Daniel, carpenter | N | Cortland Street | 75-D1, D2 |
| Cockram, Thomas, carpntr | N | Leary Street | 75-D1, D2 |
| Cockrem, Philip | N | New York | 76-A |
| Cockroft, Wm | N | New York | 76-A |
| Cocks, Robt | N | New York | 74-A |
| Codwise, Christopher | N | New York | 76-N |
| Codwise, Sarah, Mrs. | N | removed upstate | 76-P |
| Coe, Benj. | Q | Newtown | 75-G |
| Coe, Benjamin | Q | ........ | 75-A associator |
| Coe, Benjamin | Q | Newtown | 75-G |
| Coe, Jo. | Q | ........ | 76-E |
| Coe, John | Q | ........ | 75-A associator |
| Coe, John | Q | Newtown | 75-G |

| | | | |
|---|---|---|---|
| Coe, Jonathan | Q | ........ | 75-A associator |
| Coe, Jonathan | Q | Newtown | 75-G |
| Coe, Nehemiah | Q | ........ | 76-E |
| Coe, Robert | Q | ........ | 75-A associator |
| Coe, Robert | Q | ........ | 76-E |
| Coe, Robert | Q | Newtown | 75-G |
| Coe, Robert Jr. | Q | ........ | 76-E |
| Coe, Sam. | Q | Newtown | 75-G |
| Coff, Joseph | N | New York | 76-A |
| Coggeshall, James | N | New York | 76-A |
| Cohan, Solomon | N | New York | 74-R |
| Cohen, Sol'n Myers | N | New York | 74-A |
| Cohn, Aaron | N | New York | 76-A |
| Colbourn, Charles | N | New York | 76-A |
| Colden, David Esq. | Q | ........ | 76-B, 76-E |
| Colden, David Esq. | Q | Flushing | 75-A, 75-H |
| Colden, Justice | M | removed upstate | 76-P |
| Colden, Richard | Q | Flushing | 75-H |
| Cole, Aron | N | New York | 75-D2 |
| Cole, Ichabod | S | ........ | 75-R |
| Cole, John | N | New York | 76-A |
| Cole, Thaddeas | S | Brookhaven | 76:0.1.1.1.5 |
| Cole, Thaddeus | S | Brookhaven | 75-B3, 75-B6 |
| Colegrove, Francis, carman | N | Battoe Street | 75-D2 |
| Coleman, Benjamin | S | Southampton | 76:0.1.2.1.1 |
| Coleman, Patrick, servant | N | New York | 74-V |
| Coles, Albert | Q | ........ | 76-E |
| Coles, Benjamin | Q | ........ | 76-E |
| Coles, Daniel | Q | ........ | 76-E |
| Coles, Hubert | Q | ........ | 76-B |
| Coles, Jarvis | Q | ........ | 76-E |
| Coles, Jordan | Q | ........ | 76-E |
| Coles, Jos. | Q | ........ | 75-A associator |
| Coles, Joseph | Q | ........ | 76-E |
| Coles, Joseph | Q | Oyster Bay | 75-F |
| Coles, Nathaniel | Q | ........ | 76-E |
| Coles, Robt. | Q | ........ | 75-A |
| Coles, W. | Q | ........ | 76-E |
| Coley, William | N | New York | 74-A |
| Coley; see also Colly | | | |

| | | | |
|---|---|---|---|
| Colgan, Fleming | N | New York | 74-A |
| Colgan, Thomas | N | New York | 76-F |
| Colgen, Mary, Mrs. | Q | Jamaica | 76-V |
| Colister, Thomas | N | New York | 76-L |
| Collen, Pat'k, alias Smith | N | New York | 74-R |
| Collester, Thomas | N | New York | 74-A |
| Collier, Jacobus | Q | ........ | 76-E |
| Collier, Peter | S | Huntington | 75-H n.s. |
| Collines, Joseph | N | New York | 76-A |
| Collings, Joseph, apprentice | Q | Newtown | 75-V runaway |
| Collins, John | N | New York | 74-A |
| Collins, John, veterinarian | N | Leary Street | 74-T2, 4/21 |
| Collins, Joseph | N | New York | 75-R |
| Collins, Nehemiah | Q | ........ | 76-B |
| Collins, Robert T. | Q | ........ | 76-E |
| Collis, John, hairdresser | N | Broadway | 74-T2, 11/24 |
| Collis, Nehamiah | Q | ........ | 76-B2 |
| Collister, Thomas | N | New York | 74-R juror |
| Collister, Thomas | N | New York | 76-A |
| Collit, Jacob | N | New York | 76-G |
| Collord, Edward | N | New York | 76-N |
| Colly, Joseph | N | New York | 74-A |
| Colly, Joseph | N | New York | 74-R juror |
| Colly, see also Coley | | | |
| Colvell, Harvey | Q | ........ | 75-I |
| Colvin, James | N | New York | 76-N |
| Colwell, Edward | Q | ........ | 76-E |
| Colwell, Hervey | Q | ........ | 76-B, 76-E |
| Colwell, Robert [2] | Q | ........ | [on] 76-E |
| Colwell, Thomas | Q | ........ | 76-E |
| Colwell, Tillot | Q | ........ | 76-E |
| Colwell, William | N | New York | 74-R |
| Colyer, Ab. | Q | Jamaica | 75-C |
| Colyer, Abraham | Q | ........ | 76-E |
| Colyer, Abraham | Q | Jamaica | 76-C |
| Combes, Gilbert | Q | Jamaica | 75-C |
| Combs, Henry | S | Huntington | 75-H |
| Combs, John | Q | ........ | 76-B |
| Combs, Noah | Q | ........ | 76-E |
| Combs, Samuel | Q | ........ | 76-E |

Combs; see also Coombes, Coomes

| | | | |
|---|---|---|---|
| Compton, Mathias | N | New York | 76-A |
| Concklin, Jacob | S | Smithtown | 75-L |
| Conckling, Nathan | S | Easthampton | 75-E |
| Conckling, William | S | Easthampton | 75-E |
| Cone, Edward | N | New York | 75-R |
| Conery, Nicholas | N | New York | 76-M |
| Conger, David | N | New York | 74-A |
| Conger, Jeremiah, tanner | N | Heas[?] Street | 75-D1, D2 |
| Congor, Jeremiah | N | New York | 75-D1 |
| Conihane, Francis | Q | ........ | 76-E |
| Conking, David | S | Shelter Island | 76:0.1.0.1.1 |
| Conklan, Joseph | S | Meritches | 76:1.0.0.0.0.2.3 |
| Conklin, Elias | S | Easthampton | 75-E |
| Conklin, Elkanah | S | Huntington | 75-H |
| Conklin, Epenetus, 1st Lt. | S | Huntington | 75-H1 |
| Conklin, Gamaliel | S | Smithtown | 75-L |
| Conklin, Jeremiah | S | Easthampton | 75-E |
| Conklin, Jesse | S | Huntington | 75-H |
| Conklin, Joseph | S | Huntington | 76-H1 |
| Conklin, Philip, 2d Lt. | S | Huntington | 75-H1 |
| Conkline, John | S | ........ | 75-R |
| Conkling, Abraham | S | Easthampton | 75-E |
| Conkling, Abraham | S | Easthampton | 76:0.1.1.1.1 |
| Conkling, Alex$^r$ | S | Huntington | 75-H |
| Conkling, Ananias | S | ........ | 75-R |
| Conkling, Ananias | S | Easthampton | 76:0.1.1.1.1 |
| Conkling, Ananias | S | Huntington | 75-H |
| Conkling, Ananias Ju$^r$ | S | ........ | 75-R |
| Conkling, Benjamin | S | Brookhaven | 75-B10 |
| Conkling, Benjamin | S | Easthampton | 75-E |
| Conkling, Benjamin | S | Southold | 76:0.1.1.1.2.1.0 |
| Conkling, Benj$^m$ | S | Huntington | 75-H |
| Conkling, Cornelius | S | Huntington | 75-H |
| Conkling, Cornelius Jr. | S | Huntington | 75-H |
| Conkling, Daniel | S | Easthampton | 75-E |
| Conkling, Daniel | S | Easthampton | 76:0.3.3.1.3 |
| Conkling, Daniel | S | Southold | 76:1.2.1.4.2.0.1 |
| Conkling, Daniel [2] | S | ........ | [on] 75-R |
| Conkling, David | S | ........ | 75-R |

| | | | |
|---|---|---|---|
| Conkling, David | S | Huntington | 75-H |
| Conkling, David | S | Southold | 76:0.1.1.1.1 |
| Conkling, David Jun' | S | ........ | 75-R |
| Conkling, David junr. | S | ........ | 75-R |
| Conkling, Eben' | S | Huntington | 75-H |
| Conkling, Edward | S | ........ | 75-R |
| Conkling, Edward | S | Easthampton | 75-E |
| Conkling, Edward | S | Easthampton | 76:0.1.1.2.2 |
| Conkling, Edward | S | Southampton | 76:0.1.2.3.3 |
| Conkling, Eleazer | S | Easthampton | 75-E |
| Conkling, Eleazor | S | Easthampton | 76:0.1.2.1.3 |
| Conkling, Elias | S | Easthampton | 76:1.0.0.2.0 |
| Conkling, Elisha | S | Easthampton | 75-E |
| Conkling, Elisha | S | Easthampton | 76:1.0.2.2.2.1.0 |
| Conkling, Elkanah, Capt. | S | Huntington | 75-H1, 76-H1 |
| Conkling, Ezekiel | S | Huntington | 75-H |
| Conkling, Ezekiel | S | Huntington | 75-H1, 76-H1 |
| Conkling, Ezra | S | Huntington | 75-H |
| Conkling, Ezra, Corp'l | S | Huntington | 76-H2 |
| Conkling, Gamaliel | S | Smithtown | 76:0.1.2.1.2 |
| Conkling, Hubbart | S | Huntington | 75-H |
| Conkling, Isaac | S | Easthampton | 75-E |
| Conkling, Isaac | S | Huntington | 75-H |
| Conkling, Israel | S | Huntington | 75-H, 75-H1 |
| Conkling, Jacob | S | Easthampton | 75-E |
| Conkling, Jacob | S | Huntington | 75-H |
| Conkling, Jacob | S | Southold | 76:0.1.5.1.1 |
| Conkling, Jacob Jr. | S | Easthampton | 75-E |
| Conkling, Jacob [2] | S | ........ | [on] 75-R |
| Conkling, Jacobus | S | Easthampton | 76:0.2.5.2.1 |
| Conkling, Jedediah | S | Easthampton | 75-E |
| Conkling, Jedediah | S | Easthampton | 76:0.1.1.2.2 |
| Conkling, Jerem: | S | Easthampton | 75-E |
| Conkling, Jeremiah | S | Easthampton | 75-E |
| Conkling, Jeremiah | S | Easthampton | 75-E |
| Conkling, Jeremiah | S | Easthampton | 76:0.1.0.2.0 |
| Conkling, Jeremiah | S | Easthampton | 76:0.1.2.1.0 |
| Conkling, Jeremiah | S | Easthampton | 76:1.1.0.1.1.1.0 |
| Conkling, Jeremiah | S | Smithtown | 76:1.1.2.2.1 |
| Conkling, Jeremiah 3d | S | Easthampton | 76:0.2.0.3.0 |

| Conkling, Jesse | S | Huntington | 75-H1, 76-H1 |
|---|---|---|---|
| Conkling, Joel | S | Brookhaven | 75-B1 n.s. |
| Conkling, Joel | S | Brookhaven | 75-B7 n.s. |
| Conkling, John | S | Brookhaven | 75-B10 |
| Conkling, John | S | Huntington | 75-H |
| Conkling, John | S | Southold | 76:0.1.1.3.3.1.1 |
| Conkling, John | S | Southold | 76:1.1.0.4.0 |
| Conkling, John Jun$^r$ | S | ........ | 75-R |
| Conkling, John Junr. | S | Southold | 76:0.1.1.2.4.3.0 |
| Conkling, John [2] | S | ........ | [on] 75-R |
| Conkling, Jonah | S | Huntington | 75-H |
| Conkling, Jonathan | S | Southampton | 76:0.1.2.1.3 |
| Conkling, Jonathan | S | Southold | 76:1.2.0.2.1 |
| Conkling, Jonathan J$^r$. | S | ........ | 75-R |
| Conkling, Jonathan Jun$^r$ | S | ........ | 75-R |
| Conkling, Jonathan Junr. | S | Southold | 76:0.1.1.1.2.1.2 |
| Conkling, Joseph | S | Brookhaven | 75-B10 |
| Conkling, Joseph | S | Easthampton | 76:1.1.2.2.4.1.1 |
| Conkling, Joseph | S | Huntington | 75-H |
| Conkling, Joseph | S | Huntington | 75-H1, 76-H2 |
| Conkling, Joseph | S | Southold | 76:1.0.0.5.1 |
| Conkling, Joseph Jun$^r$ | S | Easthampton | 76:0.2.1.2.3 |
| Conkling, Joseph Ju$^r$. | S | ........ | 75-R |
| Conkling, Joseph [2] | S | ........ | [on] 75-R |
| Conkling, Mulford | S | Easthampton | 75-E |
| Conkling, Mulford | S | Easthampton | 76:0.2.1.2.2 |
| Conkling, Mulford Jr. | S | Easthampton | 75-E |
| Conkling, Nathan | S | Easthampton | 76:1.1.0.4.0 |
| Conkling, Nathan, 3 | S | Easthampton | 76:0.1.2.1.1 |
| Conkling, Nathan Jr. | S | Easthampton | 75-E |
| Conkling, Nathan Junr. | S | Easthampton | 75-E |
| Conkling, Nathan ye third | S | Easthampton | 75-E |
| Conkling, Nathanael | S | Southold | 76:0.1.4.2.1 |
| Conkling, Nathaniel | S | Brookhaven | 75-B10 |
| Conkling, Philip | S | Huntington | 75-H |
| Conkling, Platt | S | Huntington | 75-H |
| Conkling, Platt, Col. | S | Huntington | 75-H1 |
| Conkling, Richard Jr. | S | Huntington | 75-H |
| Conkling, Ruth, Wido | S | Easthampton | 76:0.0.0.2.1 |
| Conkling, Samuel | S | Brookhaven | 75-B1 n.s. |

| | | | |
|---|---|---|---|
| Conkling, Samuel | S | Brookhaven | 75-B7 n.s. |
| Conkling, Samuel | S | Brookhaven | 76:1.1.0.1.0 |
| Conkling, Samuel, Lt. | S | Easthampton | 76:0.1.2.2.3 |
| Conkling, Samuel [2] | S | Easthampton | [on] 75-E |
| Conkling, Selah | S | Huntington | 75-H |
| Conkling, Shadrach | S | Shelter Island | 75-K |
| Conkling, Silvanus | S | ........ | 75-R |
| Conkling, Sineus | S | Easthampton | 75-E |
| Conkling, Sineus | S | Easthampton | 76:1.2.2.3.3 |
| Conkling, Thomas | S | Brookhaven | 75-B10 |
| Conkling, Thomas | S | Huntington | 76-H2 |
| Conkling, Thomas | S | Shelter Island | 76:1.1.0.1.0 |
| Conkling, Thomas | S | Southold | 76:1.1.0.3.1.2.2 |
| Conkling, Thomas Jr. | S | Shelter Island | 75-K |
| Conkling, Thomas Jr. | S | Shelter Island | 76:0.1.4.1.2 |
| Conkling, Tho' | S | Huntington | 75-H |
| Conkling, Thos., G.S. | S | Huntington | 75-H |
| Conkling, Timothy | S | Huntington | 75-H |
| Conkling, Timothy | S | Huntington | 75-H1, 76-H1 |
| Conkling, Timothy Jr. | S | Huntington | 75-H |
| Conkling, William | S | Easthampton | 76:1.2.0.1.2 |
| Conkling, William Jr. | S | Easthampton | 75-E |
| Conkling, Zebulon | S | Easthampton | 75-E |
| Conkling, Zebulon | S | Easthampton | 76:0.1.1.1.4 |
| Conkling, Zephaniah | S | Brookhaven | 75-B7 n.s. |
| Conkling, Zepheniah | S | Brookhaven | 76:0.1.0.1.1 |
| Conn, William | S | ........ | 75-R |
| Conner, Elizabeth | N | New York | 75-R |
| Conner, Samuel | N | New York | 76-I |
| Conners, Jediah | S | Brookhaven | 75-B10 |
| Connery, Ann | N | New York | 76-R |
| Connery, Nicholas | N | Chapel Street | 74-T |
| Connery, Nicholas | N | New York | 76-A |
| Connery, Nicholas, Sergt. | N | New York | 76-G |
| Connery, Sam' | N | New York | 76-G |
| Conniham, Francis | N | New York | 76-G |
| Connor, Bryan | N | New York | 76-I, 76-R |
| Conoroy, Darlin | N | New York | 74-A |
| Conrad, Peter | N | New York | 74-A |
| Conrad, Peter, joiner | N | Maiden Lane | 75-D1, D2 |

| | | | |
|---|---|---|---|
| Conrey, Jonathan | N | New York | 74-A |
| Conway, Nicholas | N | New York | 76-I |
| Coo, John | N | New York | 74-A |
| Cooder, John | N | New York | 76-A |
| Cook, Abraham | S | Southampton | 76:1.0.1.1.1 |
| Cook, Abraham [2] | S | Southampton | [on] 75-M |
| Cook, Burnet | S | Southampton | 75-M |
| Cook, Calvin | S | Southampton | 76:0.1.0.0.0 |
| Cook, David | S | ........ | 75-R |
| Cook, David | S | Southampton | 76:1.1.3.2.0 |
| Cook, Elias | S | Southampton | 75-M |
| Cook, Elias | S | Southampton | 76:1.1.0.2.0.1.1 |
| Cook, Elias Junior | S | Southampton | 75-M |
| Cook, Elias Jun' | S | Southampton | 76:0.1.3.1.0 |
| Cook, George | N | New York | 74-A |
| Cook, George | N | New York | 76-A, 76-L |
| Cook, George, sadler | N | Broadway | 74-T |
| Cook, James | S | Southampton | 75-M |
| Cook, James | S | Southampton | 76:0.1.2.1.3 |
| Cook, John | S | Southampton | 75-M non-signer |
| Cook, John | S | Southampton | 76:1.1.0.1.2.3.0 |
| Cook, John Jun' | S | Southampton | 75-M |
| Cook, Jonathan | S | Southampton | 75-M |
| Cook, Jonathan | S | Southampton | 76:0.1.3.1.2.1.0 |
| Cook, Mary | S | Easthampton | 76:0.0.0.1.1 |
| Cook, Mitchel | S | Southampton | 76:0.1.0.1.1 |
| Cook, Mitchell | S | Southampton | 75-M |
| Cook, Silas [2] | S | ........ | [on] 75-R |
| Cook, Stephen | S | Southampton | 75-M |
| Cook, Sylvanus | S | ........ | 75-R |
| Cook, William | N | New York | 76-A |
| Cooke, George | N | New York | 75-D3 |
| Cooke, John Clarke | N | New York | 76-A |
| Cooley, Francis | N | Gold Street | 76-I |
| Cooley, Francis | N | Golden Hill | 76-H |
| Cooley, Francis | N | New York | 74-A; 74-R juror |
| Cooley, William | N | New York | 76-I |
| Cooly, Nathaniel | N | New York | 74-R |
| Coombes, Nathaniel | Q | ........ | 76-B |
| Coombes, Samuel | Q | ........ | 76-B |

| | | | |
|---|---|---|---|
| Coombes, Thomas | Q | ........ | 76-B |
| Coomes, John | Q | ........ | 75-A |
| Coomes, John | Q | Oyster Bay | 75-I |
| Coomes, Nath'l | Q | ........ | 75-A |
| Coomes, Thos. | Q | ........ | 75-A |
| Coomes, Wm. | Q | ........ | 75-A |
| Coomes; see also Combs | | | |
| Coon, Godfrey | N | New York | 75-R |
| Coon, Michael | N | New York | 76-A |
| Coon, see also Coun | | | |
| Coone, Hannah | N | New York | 75-R |
| Coons, Henry | N | New York | 76-A |
| Cooper, Abraham | S | ........ | 75-R |
| Cooper, Abraham | S | Southampton | 76:1.1.3.1.3 |
| Cooper, Ananias | S | Southampton | 76:1.1.1.3.0 |
| Cooper, Annanias | S | ........ | 75-R |
| Cooper, Anne, servant, 23 | N | New York | 75-V |
| Cooper, Benjamin | S | ........ | 75-R |
| Cooper, Benjamin | S | Southampton | 76:0.1.1.1.0 |
| Cooper, Caleb | S | ........ | 75-R |
| Cooper, Caleb | S | Southampton | 76:0.1.0.0.1 |
| Cooper, David | S | ........ | 75-R |
| Cooper, David | S | Southampton | 76:1.1.0.1.0 |
| Cooper, David Jun' | S | ........ | 75-R |
| Cooper, Elias | S | ........ | 75-R |
| Cooper, Elias | S | Southampton | 76:0.2.3.1.2.1.1 |
| Cooper, Joseph | Q | ........ | 76-E |
| Cooper, Joseph Jr. | Q | ........ | 76-E |
| Cooper, Josiah | S | ........ | 75-R |
| Cooper, Josiah | S | Southampton | 76:0.1.2.1.3 |
| Cooper, Sam^ll | S | ........ | 75-R |
| Cooper, Samuell | S | Southampton | 76:1.0.0.2.0.0.1 |
| Cooper, Samuell Jun' | S | Southampton | 76:0.1.2.1.1.1.1 |
| Cooper, Silas | S | ........ | 75-R |
| Cooper, Silas | S | Southampton | 76:0.1.1.1.0 |
| Cooper, Stephen | S | Easthampton | 76:1.0.2.1.3 |
| Cooper, Stephen Jr. | S | Easthampton | 75-E |
| Cooper, Stephen Junr. | S | Easthampton | 76:0.1.3.1.0 |
| Cooper, Thomas | S | Southampton | 75-M |
| Cooper, Thomas | S | Southampton | 76:1.0.0.1.0.2.1 |

| | | | |
|---|---|---|---|
| Cooper, Thomas Esqʳ | S | Southampton | 76:1.1.1.1.1 |
| Cooper, Thomˢ Junʳ | S | ........ | 75-R |
| Cooper, William | S | ........ | 75-R |
| Cooper, Zebulon | S | ........ | 75-R |
| Cooper, Zebulon | S | Southampton | 76:1.0.4.2.2 |
| Cooper, Zophar | S | ........ | 75-R |
| Cooper, Zopher | S | Southampton | 76:0.1.2.1.3 |
| Coot, Charles | N | New York | 74-A |
| Coper, Matthew | S | ........ | 75-R |
| Copp, John, Capt-Lieut. | N | New York | 75-E |
| Copper, Cornelius | N | New York | 75-F |
| Copperthwait, ____ | N | Vesey Street | 75-D2 |
| Corby, William | N | New York | 76-A |
| Corby; see also Korby | | | |
| Corcelius, George | N | New York | 74-A |
| Corcillius, Wm | N | New York | 74-A |
| Corcillus, John | N | New York | 74-A |
| Corcillus; see also Corselius | | | |
| Corey, Abijah | S | Southold | 76:1.0.2.2.2 |
| Corey, Abijah [2] | S | ........ | [on] 75-R |
| Corey, Abraham | S | ........ | 75-R |
| Corey, Braddock | S | ........ | 75-R |
| Corey, Jasper | S | Southold | 76:0.1.1.1.2 |
| Corey, Jessher | S | Brookhaven | 75-B10 |
| Corey; see also Courie | | | |
| Corichane, Frs. | N | New York | 74-A |
| Corin, Isaac | N | New York | 74-A |
| Corin, James | N | New York | 76-A |
| Cornelius, Evert | N | rem. to Bedford | 76-J |
| Cornelius, Jonathan | Q | ........ | 75-A |
| Cornelius, Jonathan | Q | ........ | 76-B, 76-E |
| Cornelius, Moses | Q | ........ | 75-A, 76-B |
| Cornell, Baruch | Q | ........ | 76-E |
| Cornell, Benj'n | Q | ........ | 75-A |
| Cornell, Caleb | Q | ........ | 76-E |
| Cornell, Charles | Q | ........ | 75-A, 76-B |
| Cornell, Charles [2] | Q | ........ | [on] 76-E |
| Cornell, Comfort | Q | ........ | 76-E |
| Cornell, Edward | Q | ........ | 75-A |
| Cornell, Elijah | Q | ........ | 75-A, 76-B |

| | | | |
|---|---|---|---|
| Cornell, Gilbert | Q | ........ | 76-E |
| Cornell, Gilliam | N | New York | 74-A |
| Cornell, Gilliam | Q | ........ | 75-A associator |
| Cornell, Jam's | Q | ........ | 75-A |
| Cornell, Johannes | Q | Newtown | 75-G |
| Cornell, John | N | removed upstate | 76-P |
| Cornell, John | Q | ........ | 75-A |
| Cornell, Oliver | Q | ........ | 76-E |
| Cornell, Sam'l Mott | Q | ........ | 75-A, 76-E |
| Cornell, Sam'l, son of Jos. | Q | ........ | 75-A |
| Cornell, Samuel [2] | Q | ........ | [on] 76-E |
| Cornell, Stephen | Q | ........ | 75-A associator |
| Cornell, Sylvester | Q | ........ | 76-B, 76-E |
| Cornell, Thomas | Q | ........ | 76-E |
| Cornell, Thomas, Rockaway | Q | Hempstead | 75-H |
| Cornell, Thomas [2] | Q | ........ | [on] 75-A |
| Cornell, Thomas [2] | Q | ........ | [on] 76-B |
| Cornell, Timothy | Q | ........ | 75-A, 76-B |
| Cornell, Timothy | Q | Jamaica | 75-D |
| Cornell, W. | Q | ........ | 76-E |
| Cornell, W. | Q | Newtown | 75-B |
| Cornell, Whitehead | Q | ........ | 75-A |
| Cornell, Will'm, son of Jos. | Q | ........ | 75-A |
| Cornell, William | Q | ........ | 75-A |
| Cornell, William | Q | Jamaica | 75-C |
| Cornell, Wm. 3d | Q | ........ | 75-A |
| Cornell, Wm. [2] | Q | ........ | [on] 76-B |
| Cornish, Benjamin | Q | ........ | 75-A associator |
| Cornish, Benjamin | Q | Newtown | 75-G |
| Cornish, Richard | N | New York | 74-R witness |
| Cornish, Richard | N | New York | 76-H |
| Cornwall, John | Q | ........ | 76-E |
| Cornwall, William | Q | Jamaica | 75-C |
| Cornwell, Charles | Q | ........ | 76-E |
| Cornwell, Cornelius | Q | ........ | 76-E |
| Cornwell, Daniel | Q | ........ | 76-E |
| Cornwell, George | Q | ........ | 76-E |
| Cornwell, James | Q | ........ | 76-E |
| Cornwell, Obadiah | Q | ........ | 76-E |
| Cornwell, S., Jr. | Q | ........ | 76-E |

| Cornwell, Sam'l son of Jos. | Q | ........ | 76-I |
| Cornwell, W. | Q | ........ | 76-E |
| Cornwell, Wm | Q | ........ | 76-B |
| Correy, Braddock | S | Southampton | 76:0.1.4.2.1 |
| Corry, Abra^m | S | ........ | 75-R |
| Corselius, George | N | New York | 76-A |
| Corselius, William | N | New York | 76-A |
| Corselius; see also Corcelius | | | |
| Corson, Jacob | N | New York | 74-A |
| Cortwright, Lawrence | N | New York | 74-T |
| Corvis, Richard J. | N | New York | 74-A |
| Corwin, Daniel | S | Brookhaven | 75-B10 |
| Corwin, Daniel | S | Southold | 76:1.0.1.4.3 |
| Corwin, David | S | Southold | 75-N |
| Corwin, David | S | Southold | 76:0.1.3.2.1 |
| Corwin, David | S | Southold | 76:1.1.0.1.0 |
| Corwin, David juner | S | Southold | 75-N |
| Corwin, Ely | S | Brookhaven | 75-B10 |
| Corwin, Henery | S | Brookhaven | 75-B10 |
| Corwin, Hennery | S | Southold | 76:0.1.1.1.1 |
| Corwin, Jacob | S | Brookhaven | 75-B10 |
| Corwin, James | S | Southold | 76:0.1.0.1.2 |
| Corwin, James [2] | S | ........ | [on] 75-R |
| Corwin, Jedediah | S | Southold | 76:0.2.1.2.4 |
| Corwin, Jeremiah | S | Brookhaven | 75-B10 |
| Corwin, Jeremiah | S | Southold | 76:0.1.3.3.1 |
| Corwin, John | S | Southold | 75-N |
| Corwin, John | S | Southold | 76:0.2.2.2.1.1.0 |
| Corwin, Jonathan | S | Southold | 75-N |
| Corwin, Jonathan | S | Southold | 76:0.1.0.2.0 |
| Corwin, Jonathan | S | Southold | 76:1.2.0.2.1 |
| Corwin, Joseph | S | Southold | 76:0.1.1.1.3 |
| Corwin, Joshua | S | Brookhaven | 75-B10 |
| Corwin, Joshua | S | Southold | 76:0.2.3.1.2 |
| Corwin, Mathias | S | Southold | 76:1.1.1.1.0 |
| Corwin, Matthias Jun^r | S | Southold | 76:0.1.0.1.1 |
| Corwin, Methias | S | Brookhaven | 75-B10 |
| Corwin, Methias | S | Southold | 75-N |
| Corwin, Nathan | S | Brookhaven | 75-B10 |
| Corwin, Nathan | S | Southold | 76:0.1.1.2.2 |

| | | | |
|---|---|---|---|
| Corwin, Nathanael | S | Southold | 76:0.1.1.1.2 |
| Corwin, Nathaniel | S | ........ | 75-R |
| Corwin, Peter, or Prance | S | Southold | 76:0.1.2.1.3 |
| Corwin, Richard | S | Brookhaven | 75-B10 |
| Corwin, Samuel | S | ........ | 75-R |
| Corwin, Samuel | S | Southold | 76:1.1.1.1.5 |
| Corwin, Samuel Jun. | S | ........ | 75-R |
| Corwin, Silas | S | Brookhaven | 75-B10 |
| Corwin, Silas | S | Southold | 76:0.3.3.1.2 |
| Corwin, Silas Jr. | S | Brookhaven | 75-B10 |
| Corwin, Stephen | S | ........ | 75-R |
| Corwin, Timothy | S | Brookhaven | 75-B10 |
| Corwin, Timothy | S | Southold | 76:1.2.2.2.0 |
| Corwin, Timothy Juner | S | Brookhaven | 75-B10 |
| Corwin, ---- Wid. | S | Southold | 76:0.1.0.3.0 |
| Corwithe, Burnet | S | Southampton | 76:0.1.0.1.1 |
| Corwithe, Burnett | S | ........ | 75-R |
| Corwithe, David | S | ........ | 75-R |
| Corwithe, David | S | Southampton | 76:1.1.2.2.2 |
| Corwithe, John | S | Southampton | 76:0.1.1.1.1 |
| Cosine, Walter | N | New York | 74-A |
| Cosk, Joseph | N | removed upstate | 76-P |
| Cott, Gabriel | Q | ........ | 75-A |
| Cott, Nicholas Jr. | Q | ........ | 75-A |
| Cotterill, Sarah | N | New York | 75-R apprentice |
| Coughlan, Andrew | N | New York | 76-A |
| Coun, Conrad | N | New York | 76-A |
| Courie, John | N | New York | 74-A |
| Cousins, Elizabeth | N | rem to Ulster Co. | 76-P |
| Coutant, Henry, carpenter | N | St. James Street | 75-D1, D2 |
| Couty, Jonathan, carpenter | N | King Street | 75-D2 |
| Covenhoven, Francis | N | Scotch st, painter | 75-D1, D2 |
| Covenhoven, Peter | N | New York | 76-A |
| Coverd, John | N | removed upstate | 76-P |
| Covert, Honse | Q | ........ | 75-A |
| Covert, Isaac | Q | ........ | 76-E |
| Covert, Johanas | Q | Hempstead | 76-D |
| Covert, Johannes | Q | ........ | 76-B, 76-E |
| Covert, Richard | Q | Jamaica | 75-C |
| Covert, Teunis Jr. | Q | ........ | 76-E |

| | | | |
|---|---|---|---|
| Covert, Tunis | Q | ........ | 75-A, 76-B |
| Covert, Tunis | Q | Jamaica | 75-C, 75-D |
| Covert, Tunis 3d | Q | ........ | 75-A |
| Covert, Tunis Jr. | Q | ........ | 75-A |
| Covert, Tunis Jr. | Q | Jamaica | 75-A, 75-C |
| Covert, Tunis [2] | Q | ........ | [on] 76-E |
| Covert, Walter | Q | ........ | 76-E |
| Covert, Wat | Q | ........ | 75-A |
| Covert, William | Q | Hempstead | 76-D |
| Covert, Wm | Q | ........ | 75-A, 76-B |
| Cowdrey, Jonathan Jr. | N | New York | 75-D1 |
| Cowdrey, Jonathan [2] | N | New York | [on] 74-A |
| Cowdry, Jonathan | N | New York | 75-D3 |
| Cowell, William | N | New York | 74-R, 75-R |
| Cowley, Francis | N | New York | 76-A |
| Cowley, Rebecca | N | New York | 76-I |
| Cowley, William | N | New York | 74-T2, 4/21 |
| Cowperthwait, Samuel | N | New York | 74-T2, 4/28 |
| Cox, Gabriel, coachmaker | N | Great George St. | 74-T2, 4/14 |
| Cox, John | N | New York | 76-A |
| Cox, Joseph | N | New York | 74-A, 76-L |
| Cox, Joseph, Lieut. | N | New York | 75-A |
| Cox, Ludwig | N | New York | 76-A |
| Cox, Nicholas | N | New York | 74-A |
| Cox, Nicholas, hatter | N | Nassau Street | 75-D1, D2 |
| Cox, Samuel | S | Brookhaven | 75-B10 |
| Cox, Sm$^l$ | S | Southold | 76:1.2.0.2.0 |
| Cox, Thomas | N | New York | 74-A |
| Cox, William | Q | ........ | 76-E |
| Cox; see also Cocks | | | |
| Coxetter, Bartholemeu | N | New York | 76-A |
| Coyl, Dennis | N | New York | 76-A |
| Coyle, Denis | N | New York | 74-A |
| Coyle, Patrick | N | New York | 76-A |
| Cozani, Joseph, teacher | N | New York | 74-T2, 5/5 |
| Cozani, ____ Mrs., school | N | Wall Street | 74-T2, 7-21 |
| Cozine, Walter | N | New York | 74-R |
| Crabb, Thomas | N | New York | 74-A, 75-F |
| Crabb, Thomas | N | New York | 74-T insolvent |
| Crabb, Thomas | N | New York | 75-R juror |

| | | | |
|---|---|---|---|
| Craft, James | Q | ........ | 76-E |
| Craft, Solomon | Q | ........ | 76-E |
| Crane, Rufus | N | New York | 75-D1 |
| Crane, Rufus, blacksmith | N | Lumber Street | 75-D1, D2 |
| Crane, Uzal | N | New York | 74-A |
| Craning, Effee | N | rem to Ulster Co. | 76-P |
| Crannell, Robert | N | New York | 76-A |
| Crawford, John | N | New York | 76-A |
| Crawley, John | N | New York | 76-A |
| Creamer, Balthazar | N | New York | 74-R, 75-R |
| Creamer, Belshazer | N | New York | 74-A |
| Creamer, Belthar | N | New York | 76-A |
| Creamer, Lud. | N | New York | 76-A |
| Cree, David, Grenadier | N | New York | 76-C |
| Creed, Benjamin | Q | ........ | 76-E |
| Creed, Benjamin | Q | Jamaica | 75-D associator |
| Creed, W., Sr. | Q | ........ | 76-E |
| Creed, William Jr. | Q | ........ | 75-A associator |
| Creed, William Jr. | Q | ........ | 76-E |
| Creed, William Jr. | Q | Jamaica | 75-D associator |
| Creed, William Sr. | Q | ........ | 75-A associator |
| Creed, William Sr. | Q | Jamaica | 75-D associator |
| Cregier, John | N | Murray's street | 76-I |
| Cregier, John | N | near the College | 76-H |
| Cregier, Martin | N | Nassau St. | 76-H, 76-I |
| Cregier, Martin | N | New York | 74-A |
| Cregier, see also Crygier | | | |
| Creiger, Martin | N | New York | 76-A |
| Creighton, James Sr. | N | New York | 76-V |
| Creighton, Mary | N | New York | 75-R |
| Cresun, Joshua | N | New York | 74-A |
| Crillen, William | N | New York | 76-I |
| Crocheron, Nicholas | N | New York | 74-R apprentice |
| Crocker, Andrew | N | removed upstate | 76-P |
| Croes, Geo. | N | New York | 75-D1 |
| Croger, George | N | New York | 76-A |
| Crolius, George | N | New York | 74-A |
| Crolius, John | N | New York | 74-A |
| Crolius, John Jr. | N | New York | 74-A |
| Crolius, Peter | N | New York | 74-A |

| | | | |
|---|---|---|---|
| Crolius, William | N | New York | 76-L |
| Crolius, William, Lieut. | N | New York | 75-A |
| Crolius, William Sr. | N | New York | 74-A |
| Crolius, William [2] | N | New York | [on] 74-A |
| Crommelin, Charles, Mrs. | Q | Hempstead Plains | 75-T |
| Crommelin, Robt | N | New York | 74-A |
| Crommeline, Robert | Q | ........ | 76-E |
| Cromwell, Benjamin | Q | Hempstead | 76-D |
| Cronin, Patrick | N | New York | 74-A |
| Crook, Benjamin | S | ........ | 75-R |
| Crook, Benjamin | S | Southampton | 76:0.1.4.2.1 |
| Crooker, James | Q | ........ | 76-E |
| Crooker, Samson | Q | ........ | 75-A associator |
| Crooker, Samson | Q | ........ | 76-E |
| Crooker, Samson | Q | Oyster Bay | 75-F |
| Crooker, W. | Q | ........ | 76-E |
| Crookshank, Alex | N | New York | 75-D1 |
| Crookshank, Alex'r, taylor | N | Little Dock Street | 75-D1, D2 |
| Crookshank, George | N | New York | 74-A, 76-I |
| Crosfill, Stephen | N | New York | 74-A |
| Cross, John | N | New York | 76-R |
| Cross, Sarah, wf of Harman | N | New York | 74-R |
| Crossfield, Stephen | N | New York | 76-F |
| Crossley, George | N | New York | 74-A, 75-R |
| Crossley, William | N | New York | 74-A |
| Crouscoup, John Ludtz | N | New York | 76-A |
| Crow, Bety | N | rem to Ulster Co. | 76-P |
| Crow, Henry | N | to Dutchess Co. | 76-P |
| Crow, Henry | N | to Westchester Co | 76-P |
| Crow, Lenah | N | to Dutchess Co. | 76-P |
| Crowder, Pietor | N | New York | 76-A |
| Cruees, Caleb | Q | ........ | 76-E |
| Cruffte, Peter | N | New York | 74-A |
| Cruger, Jno. Harris | N | New York | 76-A |
| Cruickshank, George | N | New York | 75-T2, 10/19 |
| Cryble, Daniel | N | New York | 76-N |
| Crygier, Simon | N | New York | 74-A |
| Crygier; see also Cregier | | | |
| Crystall, William | Q | ........ | 76-E |
| Cullen, James, servant, 21 | N | New York | 74-V runaway |

| | | | |
|---|---|---|---|
| Cullen, William | N | New York | 76-A |
| Cullen; see also Kulen | | | |
| Culver, Ebnezer | S | Southampton | 76:1.0.2.3.1 |
| Culver, Gersham, ae. 86 | S | ........ | 75-R |
| Culver, Gershon | S | Southampton | 76:1.0.0.0.0 |
| Culver, Gershon Ju[r] | S | Southampton | 76:1.0.0.5.0 |
| Culver, James | S | ........ | 75-R |
| Culver, James | S | Southampton | 76:0.1.2.1.5 |
| Culver, Jeremiah | S | Southampton | 76:1.1.2.3.2 |
| Culver, Jeremiah Ju[r] | S | Southampton | 76:0.1.1.2.2 |
| Culver, Jess | S | Southampton | 76:1.0.0.3.0 |
| Culver, John | Q | Newtown | 75-G |
| Culver, Moses | S | Southampton | 76:0.1.0.1.2 |
| Culver, William | S | Southampton | 76:0.1.1.1.0 |
| Culver, Zephniah | S | Southampton | 76:0.2.0.3.0 |
| Culvers, Jemima, Wid[w] | S | Southampton | 76:0.2.0.2.0 |
| Cumberson, Thos. | Q | Newtown | 75-G |
| Cumming, George, hairdrsr | N | Wall Street | 74-T |
| Cummings, George | N | New York | 74-A |
| Cummings, George | N | New York | 75-T2, 3/23 |
| Cummings, George | N | New York | 76-A |
| Cummings, George, hairdsr | N | New York | 74-T2, 3/17 |
| Cummins, Luke | Q | ........ | 75-A, 76-E |
| Cunningham, Ann | N | New York | 75-R |
| Cunningham, William | N | New York | 74-A, 74-R |
| Cunningham, William | N | New York | 75-T |
| Cunningham, Wm, blacksm. | N | Broadway | 75-D1, D2 |
| Cure, Walter[?] | N | New York | 76-N |
| Currey, Ann | N | New York | 75-R |
| Currie, Archibald | N | New York | 75-F |
| Currie, David | N | New York | 76-N |
| Curry, Ann | N | rem to Ulster Co. | 76-P |
| Curry, John | N | New York | 74-A |
| Curry, Joseph | N | New York | 74-A |
| Curson, Richard, merchant | N | New York | 74-T |
| Curtenius, _____ | N | Air Furnace | 75-D2 |
| Curtenius, Peter | N | New York | 74-A |
| Curtenius, Peter T. | N | New York | 74-R |
| Curtenius, Peter T. | N | New York | 74-T2, 11/24 |
| Curtenius, Peter T. | N | New York | 75-F |

| | | | |
|---|---|---|---|
| Curtis, Benj., med. student | N | at Dr. Treat's | 75-D1, D2 |
| Curtis, Jarel | Q | ........ | 76-E |
| Curtis, John | Q | ........ | 76-E |
| Curtis, Wm. | Q | ........ | 76-B |
| Cushing, Matthew | N | New York | 76-A |
| Cutler, Henry | N | New York | 75-D2 |
| Cutler, John | N | New York | 75-D2 |
| Cuttent, Zachrias | N | New York | 74-A |
| Cutter, Zeanos | N | New York | 74-A |
| Cutting, Leo'd, Rev. | Q | ........ | 76-E |
| Cuyler, Henry Esq. | N | New York | 74-T |
| Dagget, Micajah | N | New York | 74-R witness |
| Dailey, John | Q | ........ | 75-I |
| Dailsy, John | N | to Dutchess Co. | 76-P |
| Dains, Ebenezer | S | Southampton | 76:1.0.0.1.1 |
| Dains, John | S | ........ | 75-R |
| Dains, Paul | S | ........ | 75-R |
| Dains, Paul | S | Southampton | 76:0.1.0.1.1 |
| Dains, Peter | S | Southold | 76:0.3.0.5.3 |
| Dainse, Peter | S | ........ | 75-R |
| Dale, Robert, storekeeper | N | New York | 74-T2, 4/21 |
| Dallas, Charles | N | New York | 74-A |
| Dalley, John | N | New York | 74-A |
| Dallze, George | N | New York | 74-A |
| Dalon, Benj. | Q | ........ | 76-B |
| Dalton, Walter | Q | ........ | 75-A associator |
| Damilt, Obadiah | Q | ........ | 75-A associator |
| Damlong, John | N | New York | 76-A |
| Danelson, John | N | New York | 76-G |
| Danes, Peter | S | ........ | 75-R |
| Daniel, Mathew | N | New York | 74-A |
| Dankly, Jos. | N | New York | 74-A |
| Darbey, William, apprentice | N | New York | 74-R |
| Darg, John | N | New York | 74-R juror |
| Darg, John | N | New York | 76-A |
| Darius, Squire | N | New York | 74-A |
| Darling, Hamble | S | Smithtown | 76:0.1.1.1.0 |
| Darly, John | N | New York | 75-D3 |
| Daronen, Benjamin | Q | ........ | 75-I |
| Darrow, John | S | Southold | 76:0.1.2.1.4 |

| Name | | Place | Reference |
|---|---|---|---|
| Darrow, John [2] | S | ........ | [on] 75-R |
| Dash, Baltus | N | New York | 76-F, 76-L |
| Dash, Jno. Baltis Sr. | N | New York | 76-A |
| Dash, John B. Jr. | N | New York | 76-A |
| Dash, John Balthas | N | New York | 74-A |
| Dash, John Baltus, Ensign | N | New York | 76-Y |
| Dassigney, Benjamin | N | New York | 74-A, 76-A |
| Dassigny, Benj., shoemkr | N | Batteau Street | 75-D2 |
| Dassigny, Stephen | N | New York | 75-D1 |
| Daval, George | S | Shelter Island | 76:1.0.0.0.1 |
| Daval, John | S | Shelter Island | 76:1.0.0.1.0 |
| Davall, Benjamin | S | Shelter Island | 75-K |
| Davall, John | S | Shelter Island | 75-K |
| Davall, Samuel | S | ........ | 75-R |
| Davall, William | S | ........ | 75-R |
| Davall, William | S | Southampton | 76:1.2.2.4.0 |
| Davan, John | N | New York | 75-B, 76-A |
| Davan, John Jr. | N | New York | 74-A, 76-A |
| Davan, John, leather | N | Queen Street | 74-T2, 11/17 |
| Davas, John | N | New York | 74-A |
| Davenport, Francis | Q | ........ | 75-A |
| Davenport, Francis | Q | ........ | 76-B, 76-E |
| Davenport, John | S | Southold | 75-N |
| Davenport, John | S | Southold | 76: 0.1.0.2.2 |
| Davenport, Lewis | Q | ........ | 75-A |
| Davenport, Lewis | Q | ........ | 76-B, 76-E |
| Davenport, Newb'y | Q | ........ | 76-E |
| Davenport, S. H. | Q | ........ | 76-E |
| Davenport, Samuel | Q | ........ | 75-A, 76-B |
| Davey, William | N | New York | 75-D1 |
| Davids, Abraham | S | Southold | 76:1.0.1.1.0.5.2 |
| Davies, Benjamin | N | Coenties Market | 75-T2, 4/6 |
| Davies, Benjamin, storekpr | N | Broad Street | 74-T |
| Davies, Eliakim | S | Brookhaven | 75-B9 |
| Davies, Isaac | S | Brookhaven | 75-B6 |
| Davies, William | S | Huntington | 75-H |
| Davis, Benjamin | N | New York | 74-R juror; 75-R |
| Davis, Benj[n] | N | New York | 74-A |
| Davis, Benj[n], Sergt. | N | New York | 76-C |
| Davis, Caleb | S | Brookhaven | 75-B8 |

| | | | |
|---|---|---|---|
| Davis, Chapmyn | S | Brookhaven | 75-B2 |
| Davis, Daniel | S | Brookhaven | 75-B6, 75-B7 |
| Davis, Daniel | S | Brookhaven | 76:1.0.2.2.1 |
| Davis, Daniel & Osband | S | Brookhaven | 76:0.2.4.2.4 |
| Davis, Daniel Jr. | S | Brookhaven | 75-B1, 75-B7 |
| Davis, Daniel, third | S | Brookhaven | 75-B7 |
| Davis, David | S | Brookhaven | 76:0.1.2.1.3 |
| Davis, David, Sgt. | S | Brookhaven | 75-B2 |
| Davis, Ebenezer | S | Brookhaven | 75-B7 |
| Davis, Elicurn | S | Brookhaven | 76:1.0.2.2.4 |
| Davis, Elijah | S | Brookhaven | 75-B6 |
| Davis, Elijah | S | Brookhaven | 76:0.1.1.2.1 |
| Davis, Elijah Qrtrmaster | S | Brookhaven | 75-B1, 75-B7 |
| Davis, Elisha | S | Brookhaven | 75-B2 |
| Davis, Elisha | S | Easthampton | 75-E |
| Davis, Elisha | S | Easthampton | 76:1.0.0.0.0 |
| Davis, Elnathan | S | Brookhaven | 76:0.2.2.1.2 |
| Davis, Elnathan, Drumer | S | Brookhaven | 75-B7 |
| Davis, ---- Ensign | S | Brookhaven | 75-B2 |
| Davis, Eve | N | removed upstate | 76-P |
| Davis, George | S | Brookhaven | 75-B8 |
| Davis, Gilbert | S | Brookhaven | 75-B2 |
| Davis, Gillam | S | Brookhaven | 75-B7 |
| Davis, Gillum | S | Brookhaven | 75-B1, 75-B6 |
| Davis, Goldsmith | S | Brookhaven | 75-B1 |
| Davis, Goldsmith | S | Brookhaven | 75-B6, 75-B7 |
| Davis, Gorge | S | Brookhaven | 76:1.0.2.2.3 |
| Davis, Henry | S | Brookhaven | 75-B10 |
| Davis, Henry | S | Brookhaven | 75-B11 n.s. |
| Davis, Henry | S | Brookhaven | 76:0.1.1.1.1 |
| Davis, Isaac | N | New York | 74-A |
| Davis, Isaac | S | Brookhaven | 75-B1, 75-B4 |
| Davis, Isaac | S | Brookhaven | 75-B8 |
| Davis, Isaac | S | Southold | 76:0.1.0.1.0 |
| Davis, Isaac, carpenter | N | Rutgers Street | 75-D2 |
| Davis, Isaac, Lieut. | S | Brookhaven | 75-B7 |
| Davis, Israal | S | Brookhaven | 76:0.1.3.2.1 |
| Davis, Israel | S | Brookhaven | 75-B2 |
| Davis, James | N | New York | 75-R |
| Davis, James | N | New York | 76-A |

| | | | |
|---|---|---|---|
| Davis, James | S | Southold | 76:1.0.2.1.2 |
| Davis, James [2] | S | ........ | [on] 75-R |
| Davis, Jemes | S | Brookhaven | 76:0.1.2.2.2 |
| Davis, John | S | Brookhaven | 75-B7 |
| Davis, John | S | Easthampton | 75-E |
| Davis, John Cap$^t$ | S | Easthampton | 76:0.1.1.1.1 |
| Davis, Jonas | S | Brookhaven | 75-B8 |
| Davis, Joseph | S | Brookhaven | 75-B2, 75-B8 |
| Davis, Joseph | S | Brookhaven | 76:1.2.1.2.2 |
| Davis, Joseph Jr. | S | Brookhaven | 75-B9 |
| Davis, Joshua | S | Brookhaven | 75-B2 |
| Davis, Mary | N | New York | 75-R |
| Davis, Matthew | S | Easthampton | 76:0.1.1.1.0 |
| Davis, Nathan | S | Brookhaven | 75-B1, 75-B7 |
| Davis, Nathan | S | Brookhaven | 75-B10 |
| Davis, Nathaniel | S | Brookhaven | 75-B10 |
| Davis, Nathaniel | S | Brookhaven | 76:1.2.1.1.1 |
| Davis, Obediah | S | Brookhaven | 75-B8 |
| Davis, Obidiah | S | Brookhaven | 76:1.1.0.2.2 |
| Davis, Pheneas Juner | S | Brookhaven | 75-B11 n.s. |
| Davis, Phineus | S | Brookhaven | 76:1.0.4.1.1 |
| Davis Phineus Juner | S | Brookhaven | 76:0.1.1.1.1 |
| Davis, Richard | N | New York | 74-A |
| Davis, Richard | S | Brookhaven | 75-B2 |
| Davis, Richard, carver | N | William Street | 75-D1, D2 |
| Davis, Samual & his Son | S | Brookhaven | 76:1.1.4.2.1.1.1 |
| Davis, Samuel | S | Brookhaven | 75-B4, 75-B8 |
| Davis, Samuel, Juner | S | Brookhaven | 75-B8 |
| Davis, Silas | S | Brookhaven | 75-B2 |
| Davis, Silas | S | Brookhaven | 76:0.1.1.2.1 |
| Davis, Solomon | S | Brookhaven | 75-B9 n.s. |
| Davis, Solomon | S | Brookhaven | 76:1.0.0.1.0.2.0 |
| Davis, Spicer | S | Brookhaven | 75-B2 |
| Davis, Stephen | S | Brookhaven | 75-B10 |
| Davis, Stephen | S | Brookhaven | 75-B11 n.s. |
| Davis, Sylvanus | S | Southold | 76:1.1.0.0.0.0.1 |
| Davis, Thomas | N | New York | 74-T2, 12/29 |
| Davis, Thomas, carman | N | New York | 74-T2, 3/17 |
| Davis, Timothy | S | Brookhaven | 75-B2 |
| Davis, William | S | Brookhaven | 75-B1 |

| | | | |
|---|---|---|---|
| Davis, William | S | Brookhaven | 75-B6, 75-B7 |
| Davis, William | S | Brookhaven | 75-B9 |
| Davis, William | S | Brookhaven | 76:0.3.2.2.2 |
| Davis, Zophar | S | Brookhaven | 75-B7 |
| Davis, Zopher | S | Brookhaven | 75-B1 |
| Davis, Zopher & William | S | Brookhaven | 76:0.2.1.2.2 |
| Davison, Joshua | N | New York | 75-R apprentice |
| Davison, William | N | New York | 75-R |
| Dawkins, Henry | N | New York | 76-M |
| Day, _____, Mr., hairdrsr | N | Broad Street | 75-T2, 5/4 |
| Day, Cornelius, Ensign | N | New York | 75-A |
| Day, Edey | N | New York | 74-A |
| Day, Elias | N | New York | 76-H |
| Day, Isaac | N | New York | 75-V |
| Day, John | N | New York | 74-A |
| Day, John, constable | N | New York | 74-R to 76-R |
| Day, Josiah, teacher | N | Maiden Lane | 74-T |
| Day, Wiliiam | N | New York | 74-A, 76-A |
| Day, William | N | Warren Street | 76-H, 76-I |
| Day, William, constable | N | New York | 75-R |
| Dayley, John | N | rem to Ulster Co. | 76-P |
| Dayton, ----- | S | Meritches | 76:......... |
| Dayton, Abigail, M$^{rs}$ | S | Easthampton | 76:0.0.0.1.0 |
| Dayton, Bennet | S | Brookhaven | 76:0.1.1.1.0 |
| Dayton, Bennit | S | Brookhaven | 75-B1, 75-B7 |
| Dayton, Beriah | S | Southampton | 76:1.1.1.2.0 |
| Dayton, Daniel | S | Easthampton | 76:1.2.2.2.0.1.0 |
| Dayton, David | S | Brookhaven | 76:0.1.2.1.3 |
| Dayton, David | S | Easthampton | 75-E |
| Dayton, Ebenezer | S | Brookhaven | 75-B1, 75-B6 |
| Dayton, Ebenezer | S | Brookhaven | 76:0.1.1.1.2 |
| Dayton, Ebenezer, Clerk | S | Brookhaven | 75-B7 |
| Dayton, Henry | S | Easthampton | 75-E |
| Dayton, Henry | S | Easthampton | 76:1.1.1.2.0.1.0 |
| Dayton, Jacob | S | Easthampton | 75-E |
| Dayton, Jeremiah | S | Easthampton | 76:1.2.1.1.1.1.0 |
| Dayton, Jeremiah [2] | S | Easthampton | [on] 75-E |
| Dayton, Jesse | S | Easthampton | 75-E |
| Dayton, Jesse | S | Easthampton | 76:0.2.1.2.1 |
| Dayton, John | S | Brookhaven | 75-B6 |

| | | | |
|---|---|---|---|
| Dayton, John | S | Brookhaven | 76:0.1.2.1.1 |
| Dayton, John, Cap$^t$ | S | Easthampton | 76:0.3.1.2.3.1.0 |
| Dayton, John [2] | S | Easthampton | [on] 75-E |
| Dayton, Nathan | S | Easthampton | 76:0.1.0.0.0 |
| Dayton, Samuel | S | Brookhaven | 75-B3, 75-B6 |
| Dayton, Samuel | S | Brookhaven | 76:0.1.1.2.1 |
| Dayton, Samuel | S | Brookhaven | 76:1.1.0.1.3 |
| Dayton, Samuel | S | Easthampton | 75-E |
| Dayton, Samuel, third | S | Brookhaven | 75-B9 |
| Dayton, Spanear | S | Meritches | 76:1.1.1.1.1 |
| Dayton, Spencer | S | Southold | 75-N |
| Dayton, Tuthill | S | Southold | 75-N |
| Dayton, Tuttol | S | Meritches | 76:0.1.3.1.1 |
| Dayton, Willem | S | Brookhaven | 76:0.1.1.1.1 |
| De Saint Pry, _____ | N | New York | 75-T2, 4/13 |
| Deadloaf, see Detloff | | | |
| Deale, Robert, merchant | N | New York | 74-T |
| Dealing, John | N | New York | 74-A |
| Deall, Sam'l | N | New York | 74-A |
| Deall, Samuel, storekeeper | N | Broad Street | 74-T2, 1/27 |
| Deall, William | N | New York | 76-A, 76-I |
| Dean, Barnabas, pot baker | N | liv.w/ Jno Campbell | 75-D2 |
| Dean, Gilbert | N | New York | 76-N |
| Dean, Jacob | Q | ........ | 75-A, 76-B |
| Dean, Jacob | Q | Jamaica | 75-C |
| Dean, James | N | New York | 76-A |
| Dean, John | Q | Jamaica | 75-C |
| Dean, Thomas | Q | Hempstead | 76-D |
| Dean, Wm, cooper | N | St. James Street | 75-D2 |
| Deane, Alkey | N | New York | 76-I |
| Deane, Betsy | N | removed upstate | 76-P |
| Deane, Elk. | N | New York | 76-A |
| Deane, Nesbit, feltmaker | N | New York | 75-R |
| Deane, Nesbit, hatter | N | New York | 74-T2, 5/19 |
| Deane, Nesbitt | N | New York | 74-A |
| Deane, Richard | N | New York | 74-R juror |
| Deane, Richard | N | New York | 75-B, 75-F |
| Deane, Richard, distiller | N | Murray's Street | 74-T2, 6/2 |
| Deane, Richard, distiller | N | North River | 75-T |
| Deane, Samuel | N | New York | 74-A |

| | | | |
|---|---|---|---|
| Deane, Samuel, coachmaker | N | Batteau Street | 75-D1, D2 |
| Deane, William | N | New York | 74-A |
| Deas, James | N | New York | 76-A, 76-F |
| DeBevoise, Charles | Q | ........ | 76-E |
| DeBevoise, Charles | Q | Newtown | 75-B |
| DeBevoise, Daniel | Q | ........ | 76-E |
| DeBevoise, George | Q | ........ | 76-E |
| DeBevoise, John | Q | ........ | 76-E |
| DeBevoise, John | Q | Newtown | 75-B |
| DeBevoise, John Jr. | Q | ........ | 76-E |
| DeBoos, Wendel | N | New York | 76-L |
| Debow, Garret | N | New York | 74-A |
| Debow, Garrit | N | New York | 75-D1 |
| Debow, John | N | New York | 74-A |
| Debow, John | N | New York | 74-R, 76-R juror |
| DeBowe, John Jr. | N | New York | 74-A |
| DeClermon, Jean Salce | N | New York | 74-T |
| DeClermon, Mary, wf J.S. | N | New York | 74-T |
| DeClue, John | N | New York | 74-A, 76-A |
| Deforest, Theodorus | N | New York | 74-A, 76-N |
| DeForest, John | N | New York | 74-A, 76-A |
| Deforrest, Henry | N | New York | 75-D2, 75-D3 |
| DeForrest, Garret | N | New York | 76-I |
| DeForrest, Gerardus | N | New York | 74-A, 74-T |
| Degrawe, Walter, joiner | N | Maiden Lane | 75-D1, D2 |
| Degray, John | N | New York | 75-D2 |
| DeGray, Johon | N | New York | 75-D1 |
| DeGrey, John Junr. | N | New York | 75-D3 |
| Degroat, Garret | S | Brookhaven | 76:0.1.1.1.2 |
| Degroot, John | N | New York | 74-A |
| Degroot, Joseph | N | New York | 74-A |
| Degroot, Joseph Sr. | N | New York | 76-A |
| DeGroot, Peter | N | Monthuyl Street | 74-R |
| Degrote, Garrot | S | Brookhaven | 75-B6 |
| Degrove, Adolph [2] | N | New York | [on] 74-A |
| DeGrove, Adolph | N | New York | 76-N |
| DeGrove, Adolph jun. | N | New York | 75-A, Ensign |
| DeGrove, Adolph Jun' | N | New York | 76-G, 1st Lieut. |
| Degroy, John | N | New York | 74-A |
| DeGrusha, Thomas | N | New York | 75-R |

| | | | |
|---|---|---|---|
| DeGrushe, A. | N | New York | 74-A |
| DeGrushe, Elias | N | New York | 75-T, 76-L |
| DeGrushe, Elias, ropemaker | N | New York | 74-T2, 2/10 |
| DeLamate, Isaac | N | New York | 76-A |
| Delamater, Isaac | N | New York | 74-A |
| DeLamontagnie, Abraham | N | New York | 74-A |
| DeLamontanie, Catharine | N | Bowry Lane | 76-H |
| DeLamontanie, Mary | N | in ye fields | 76-H |
| Delancey, Jno. Jr. | N | New York | 76-A |
| Delancey, John | N | New York | 74-A, 76-A |
| DeLancey, John | N | New York | 74-T2, 11/24 |
| Delancy, Oliver | N | New York | 76-A |
| Delano, Jonathan | N | New York | 76-A |
| Delanois, John, clark | N | William Street | 75-D2 |
| Delanoy, Abraham | N | Horse & Cart St. | 74-T2, 6/16 |
| Delanoy, John | N | removed upstate | 76-P |
| Delanoy, John Jr. | N | New York | 75-D1 |
| DeLanoy, Abm. | N | New York | 74-A |
| DeLanoy, Abr$^m$ | N | New York | 76-N |
| DeLanoy, John | N | New York | 74-A |
| DeLaNoy, Wm | N | New York | 76-I |
| Delaplaine, Sam'l | N | New York | 74-A |
| DeLaPlaine, Joshua | N | New York | 74-A |
| Delaroche, Francis Humbert | N | New York | 76-A |
| DeLaRoche, G. | N | New York | 74-R |
| Delessy, Thomas | N | New York | 76-N |
| Demaray, Cristoffer | N | New York | 74-A |
| Demaray, Daved | N | New York | 74-A |
| Demarest, Jacob | N | New York | 74-A |
| Demaryee, David, cartman | N | New York | 75-D2 |
| Demasney, James | N | New York | 76-A |
| Demei, Jacob | N | New York | 74-A |
| Demilt, Peter | N | New York | 74-A |
| Demilt, see also Damilt | | | |
| DeMilt, Isaac | N | New York | 74-R |
| Deming, William, Lieut. | N | New York | 75-A |
| Demott, Abraham | Q | ........ | 75-A |
| Demott, Abraham | Q | ........ | 76-B, 76-E |
| Demott, Anthony | Q | ........ | 75-A |
| Demott, David | Q | ........ | 75-A |

| | | | |
|---|---|---|---|
| Demott, Jacobus | Q | ........ | 75-A |
| Demott, John | Q | ........ | 75-I, 76-E |
| Demott, Michael | Q | ........ | 76-B, 76-E |
| Demott, Michael [2] | Q | ........ | [on] 75-A |
| Demott, Samuel | Q | ........ | 76-E |
| Denie, Robert, merchant | N | New York | 74-V |
| Denise, John Jr. | Q | ........ | 76-E |
| Denmark, Henry | N | New York | 74-A |
| Denmark, Rachel | N | removed upstate | 76-P |
| Denney, Jacob | N | Scotch Street | 74-T |
| Denning, William | N | New York | 74-T2, 11/24 |
| Denning, William | N | New York | 75-F; 75-T2, 5/4 |
| Dennis, Thomas | S | Huntington | 75-H |
| Denny, Michael | N | New York | 76-A |
| Denton, Alex' | S | Huntington | 75-H |
| Denton, Amos | Q | ........ | 75-A associator |
| Denton, Amos | Q | ........ | 76-E |
| Denton, Amos | Q | Jamaica | 75-D associator |
| Denton, Amos Jr. | Q | ........ | 76-E |
| Denton, Amos Jr. | Q | Jamaica | 76-C |
| Denton, Benjamin | S | Huntington | 75-H, 76-H2 |
| Denton, Elizebeth | S | Brookhaven | 76:0.0.2.1.2 |
| Denton, Isaa [sic] | Q | ........ | 76-B2 |
| Denton, Isaac | Q | ........ | 76-B, 76-E |
| Denton, Isaac Jr. | Q | ........ | 75-A |
| Denton, Isaac [2] | Q | ........ | [on] 75-A |
| Denton, James | Q | ........ | 75-A |
| Denton, John | S | Huntington | 75-H |
| Denton, Joseph | S | Brookhaven | 75-B11 n.s. |
| Denton, Joseph [2] | Q | ........ | [on] 76-E |
| Denton, Nathaniel | Q | ........ | 76-E |
| Denton, Nathaniel, cooper | N | North River | 75-D2 |
| Denton, Nehemiah | N | New York | 74-A |
| Denton, Nehemiah, cooper | N | Roosevelt's Slip | 75-D1, D2 |
| Denton, Robert | Q | ........ | 75-A associator |
| Denton, Robert | Q | Jamaica | 75-D associator |
| Denton, Samuel | Q | ........ | 75-A |
| Denton, Samuel | Q | ........ | 75-A associator |
| Denton, Samuel | Q | ........ | 76-B, 76-E |
| Denton, Stephen | Q | ........ | 76-E |

| | | | |
|---|---|---|---|
| Denton, Stephen | Q | Hempstead | 76-D |
| Denton, Thomas | Q | ........ | 75-A associator |
| Denton, Thomas | Q | ........ | 76-E |
| Denton, Thomas | Q | Jamaica | 75-D associator |
| Denton, Timothy | Q | Jamaica | 76-C |
| Deoson, George | N | removed upstate | 76-P |
| Depeyster, Abm$^n$ W. | N | New York | 75-A: 2d Lieut. |
| Depeyster, William W. | N | New York | 76-N |
| Depeyster, Will$^m$ | N | New York | 75-A: Capt. |
| DePeyster, Abr. W. | N | New York | 74-A |
| DePeyster, Gerard | N | New York | 74-A |
| DePeyster, J. | N | New York | 74-A |
| DePeyster, J. | Q | ........ | 76-E |
| DePeyster, James, merchant | N | New York | 75-T |
| DePeyster, John Jr. | N | New York | 74-A |
| DePeyster, Joseph Reade | N | New York | 75-T |
| DePeyster, N. | N | New York | 75-F |
| DePeyster, Nicholas | N | Dock Ward | 75-R overseer |
| DePeyster, William | N | New York | 75-F |
| DePeyster, Will$^m$ Jun. | N | New York | 74-A, 75-B |
| Deravire, Abram | N | New York | 76-L |
| DeRett, John | N | removed upstate | 76-P |
| DeRevier, Abraham | N | New York | 74-A |
| DeRiemer, Nicholas, hatter | N | King George St. | 75-D1, D2 |
| Dering, Sylvester | S | Shelter Island | 75-K |
| Dering, Thomas | S | Shelter Island | 76:1.2.1.2.1.4.1 |
| Dering, Thom' | S | Shelter Island | 75-K |
| Dermott, Jno. | Q | ........ | 75-A |
| Desbrosses, Elias | N | New York | 74-A, 76-A |
| Desbrosses, James | N | New York | 74-A, 76-A |
| Desbrosses, James | N | New York | 75-T2, 5/4 |
| Desbrosses, James Jr. | N | New York | 74-A, 76-A |
| Desbrosses, James Jr. | N | New York | 75-F, 75-V |
| Designey, Benjamin | N | New York | 75-R |
| Desiortor, Jane | N | removed upstate | 76-P |
| DeSt.Croix, Joshua | N | New York | 74-A |
| Detloff, Henry | N | New York | 76-A |
| Detloff [Deadloaf], Hendrik | N | New York | 74-A |
| Detloff [Didwhoof], Henry | N | Barclay Street | 76-I |
| Detrich, John | N | New York | 76-A |

| | | | |
|---|---|---|---|
| Devan, John, juror | N | New York | 74-R, 75-R |
| Devanport, see Davanport | | | |
| Devereaux, John | N | New York | 74-A |
| Devereaux, Will'm | N | New York | 76-A |
| Deveriks, Robert | N | to Westchester Co | 76-P |
| Devine, Abraham | Q | ........ | 76-E |
| Devine, Ass'r | Q | Newtown | 75-G |
| Devoe, ____ Mrs. | N | removed upstate | 76-P |
| DeVoe, Frederick | N | New York | 74-A |
| Devois, Richard | N | New York | 74-T insolvent |
| Devoor, David | N | New York | 76-H |
| Devoore, David | N | New York | 76-A |
| Dewick, Richard | S | Brookhaven | 75-B10 |
| DeWiley, Jno. | N | New York | 75-D3 |
| Dewint, Gerret S., Capt. | N | New York | 75-A |
| Dewint, Guert Sp. | N | New York | 75-F |
| DeWint, Garret Sprs., Capt. | N | New York | 76-Y |
| DeWint, Guert Sp' | N | New York | 76-A |
| DeWintys, Guertspt. | N | New York | 74-A |
| Dewitt, Wm., Capt. | N | New York | 76-N |
| Dey, Philip | N | New York | 75-D3 |
| Dey, William, peace officer | N | New York | 75-T |
| Diamond, Abraham | S | Easthampton | 76:0.1.3.1.0 |
| Diamond, Isaac | S | Easthampton | 76:0.1.3.1.2 |
| Diamond; see also Dimon | | | |
| Dibbel, Lineus | S | Easthampton | 75-E |
| Dibble, Christ | S | Easthampton | 75-E |
| Dibble, Christopher | S | Easthampton | 76:0.2.2.1.3 |
| Dibble, Sineus | S | Easthampton | 76:0.1.3.1.0 |
| Dibble, Tho. | S | Easthampton | 75-E |
| Dibble, Thomas | S | Easthampton | 76:1.0.1.1.0 |
| Dickeman, John | N | New York | 75-T2, 10/5 |
| Dickenson, Benjamin | S | Southold | 75-N |
| Dickenson, Henry | Q | ........ | 76-E |
| Dickenson, ---- Lieut. | N | New York | 76-C |
| Dickenson, Towns'd | Q | ........ | 76-E |
| Dickerson, John | S | Southold | 76:0.1.2.1.3 |
| Dickerson, John [2] | S | ........ | [on] 75-R |
| Dickerson, Jonathan | S | Brookhaven | 75-B8 |
| Dickerson, Selah | S | ........ | 75-R |

| | | | |
|---|---|---|---|
| Dickerson, Selah | S | Southold | 76:0.2.2.2.1 |
| Dickerson, William | S | Southold | 76:1.1.2.1.1 |
| Dicking, Christopher | N | New York | 76-L |
| Dickinson, Abraham | S | ........ | 75-R |
| Dickinson, Charles | N | New York | 75-B |
| Dickinson, Jonathan | N | New York | 74-A |
| Dickinson, Silvanus | N | New York | 76-G |
| Dickson, Anne | N | to Westchester Co | 76-P |
| Dickson, David | N | New York | 74-A, 76-N |
| Dickson, David, Capt. | N | New York | 76-N |
| Dickson, David Jun' | N | New York | 75-B |
| Dickson, John, carpenter | N | Prince Street | 75-D2 |
| Dickson, Jonathan | S | Brookhaven | 76:0.1.3.2.2 |
| Dickson, ---- Lieut. | N | New York | 76-C |
| Dickson, Samuel | N | to Westchester Co | 76-P |
| Dif, John | N | New York | 74-A |
| Dikeman, John | N | New York | 76-A |
| Dikeman, John, Capt. | N | New York | 76-Y |
| Dikeman, John, Judge | N | New York | 74-R, 75-R |
| Dill, Barnard | N | New York | 75-D1 |
| Dill, Barnnae | N | New York | 76-A |
| Dillingham, Jacob | Q | ........ | 76-E |
| Dillingham, Silvanus | N | New York | 76-A |
| Dimon, Abraham | S | Easthampton | 75-E |
| Dimon, Isaak | S | Easthampton | 75-E |
| Dimon, Jonathan | S | Southold | 76:0.1.0.2.0 |
| Dimon; see also Diamond | | | |
| Dingee, Arthur | S | Huntington | 75-H |
| Dingee, ----- Capt. | S | Huntington | 75-H1 |
| Ditmars, Abraham | Q | ........ | 76-E |
| Ditmars, Abraham | Q | Jamaica | 75-D |
| Ditmars, Douw/Douwe | Q | ........ | 76-B, 76-E |
| Ditmars, Dow | Q | ........ | 75-A |
| Ditmars, Dow | Q | Jamaica | 75-D |
| Ditmars, Dow Jr. | Q | Jamaica | 75-C |
| Ditmars, Garret | Q | ........ | 76-E |
| Ditmars, Isaac | Q | ........ | 75-A |
| Ditmars, Isaac | Q | ........ | 76-B, 76-E |
| Ditmars, Isaac | Q | Jamaica | 75-C |
| Ditmars, John | Q | ........ | 76-E |

| | | | |
|---|---|---|---|
| Dixon, John | N | New York | 75-D1 |
| Dixon, Jonathan | S | Brookhaven | 75-B10 |
| Dixon, Robert | N | New York | 74-A |
| Dixon, Robert | Q | ........ | 76-E |
| Dobbins, Samuel | N | New York | 74-R |
| Dobbs, Adam | N | New York | 76-I |
| Dobson, Thomas | N | New York | 75-F |
| Docherty, Catharine, Mrs. | N | rem to Ulster Co. | 76-P |
| Docherty, Martha, Mrs. | N | rem to Ulster Co. | 76-P |
| Dod, Elias | N | New York | 74-A |
| Dodane, Anthony | N | New York | 76-A |
| Dodds, Thomas, cordwainer | N | William Street | 75-D2 |
| Dodge, Amos | N | New York | 74-A, 76-A |
| Dodge, Daniel | N | New York | 74-A |
| Dodge, Daniel | Q | ........ | 76-E |
| Dodge, John | N | New York | 74-A |
| Dodge, Joseph | Q | ........ | 75-A, 76-B |
| Dodge, Thomas | N | New York | 76-A |
| Dodge, Thomas | Q | ........ | 75-A associator |
| Dodge, Thomas | Q | ........ | 76-E |
| Dodge, Tristam | Q | ........ | 76-E |
| Dollison, Mary | N | New York | 76-R |
| Dolmage, Ad$^m$ | N | New York | 76-D |
| Dolmage, see also Dulmadge | | | |
| Dolmidge, Adam | N | New York | 76-A |
| Domini, Catharine, widow | S | Easthampton | 76:0.0.0.1.0 |
| Domini, Nathaniel | S | Easthampton | 76:1.0.1.1.1 |
| Dominick, Francis | N | New York | 74-A, 76-L |
| Dominick, Francis | N | New York | 74-T2, 1/13 |
| Dominick, George | N | New York | 74-A |
| Dominick, George, Capt. | N | New York | 75-A |
| Dominy, Henry | S | Easthampton | 75-E |
| Dominy, Henry | S | Easthampton | 76:0.1.1.1.0 |
| Dominy, Nathaniel Jun$^r$ | S | Easthampton | 76:0.1.1.1.4 |
| Dommoney, Nathaniel | S | Easthampton | 75-E |
| Domony, Nathaniel | S | Easthampton | 75-E |
| Donaldson, Erick | N | New York | 74-A |
| Donelson, John | N | New York | 76-G |
| Donkirz, Robert | N | New York | 76-A |
| Donnaldson, Archibald | N | New York | 76-A |

| | | | |
|---|---|---|---|
| Donnoly, William | N | New York | 75-R |
| Doran, ____ Capt. | N | New York | 74-T |
| Doran, Thomas | N | De Peyster Street | 74-T2, 10/13 |
| Dorin, Thomas | N | New York | 76-I |
| Dorlan, John | Q | ........ | 76-E |
| Dorlan, Joseph | Q | ........ | 76-B |
| Dorland, Benj. Jr. | Q | ........ | 76-E |
| Dorland, Benjamin | Q | ........ | 76-E |
| Dorland, Garret | Q | ........ | 75-A, 76-B |
| Dorland, Thomas | Q | ........ | 76-B, 76-E |
| Dorlen, Joseph | Q | ........ | 76-E |
| Dorlin, Elias | Q | ........ | 76-B |
| Dorlon, Benjamin | Q | ........ | 76-E |
| Dorlon, David | Q | ........ | 76-E |
| Dorlon, Elias 3d | Q | ........ | 76-E |
| Dorlon, Joseph | Q | ........ | 76-A |
| Dorlon, Samuel | Q | ........ | 76-E |
| Dorlon, Thomas | Q | ........ | 76-E |
| Dorman, Thomas | N | New York | 76-A |
| Dorry, Peter | N | New York | 76-A |
| Doty, Jabez | N | New York | 74-A |
| Doty, John | Q | ........ | 75-A |
| Doty, John | Q | ........ | 76-B, 76-E |
| Doty, Joseph | Q | ........ | 76-B2 |
| Doty, Joseph | Q | Oyster Bay | 75-F |
| Doty, Samuel | Q | ........ | 75-A, 76-B |
| Doty, Zebulon | Q | ........ | 76-E |
| Dougall, Walter | N | New York | 76-A |
| Dougan, John | N | New York | 76-A |
| Dougherty, Elisabeth | N | removed upstate | 76-P |
| Dougherty, Elizabeth | N | New York | 76-K |
| Doughty, Benjamin | Q | Jamaica | 75-D |
| Doughty, Charles | Q | ........ | 75-A |
| Doughty, Edward | N | New York | 74-A, 76-A |
| Doughty, Edward | N | New York | 76-F, 76-I |
| Doughty, Edward Jr. | N | New York | 74-A |
| Doughty, Edward Sr. | N | New York | 76-L |
| Doughty, George | Q | ........ | 75-A |
| Doughty, Isaiah | Q | ........ | 75-A |
| Doughty, Jacob | Q | ........ | 76-E |

| | | | |
|---|---|---|---|
| Doughty, James | Q | ........ | 75-A associator |
| Doughty, John | Q | ........ | 75-A |
| Doughty, John | Q | Jamaica | 75-C, 75-D |
| Doughty, Philip | N | New York | 74-R juror |
| Doughty, Robert | Q | ........ | 75-A, 76-E |
| Doughty, Samuel | N | New York | 74-A |
| Doughty, Samuel | Q | ........ | 75-H |
| Doughty, Samuel | Q | Jamaica | 75-C, 75-D |
| Doughty, Samuel Jr. | Q | Jamaica | 75-C |
| Doughty, Thomas Jr. | N | New York | 75-F |
| Doughty, Thomas, store | N | Dock Street | 74-T2, 10/27 |
| Douglas & Van Tuyl | N | New York | 76-I |
| Douglas, Agnes | N | upper Barracks | 76-H |
| Douglas, Ben$^n$ | N | New York | 75-D2 |
| Douglas, William and James | N | New York | 75-F |
| Douglass, Agnes | N | near the Barracks | 76-I |
| Douglass, Eleanor Campble | N | New York | 74-R, 75-R |
| Douglass, Elenor | N | removed upstate | 76-P |
| Douglass, Lemuel | S | Huntington | 75-H |
| Douglass, Matthew | N | New York | 76-A |
| Douglass, _____ Mr. | N | removed upstate | 76-P |
| Douglass, Richard Jr. | N | son of Richard | 74-R |
| Douglass, William | N | Murray's Street | 76-I |
| Douglass, William | N | New York | 75-R |
| Douglass, William | N | to Dutchess Co. | 76-P |
| Douglass, William & James | N | Queen Street | 74-T2, 11/10 |
| Dover, John | N | New York | 74-A |
| Dow, Jacob | S | Huntington | 75-H |
| Dow, Jacob | S | Islip | 76:0.1.4.1.0 |
| Dowers, John | N | New York | 75-R, 76-A |
| Downe, James | S | Southold | 76:0.1.1.2.2 |
| Downes, James | N | New York | 76-A, 76-F |
| Downes, Susana | N | removed upstate | 76-P |
| Downing, Annanias | Q | ........ | 76-E |
| Downing, Benjamin | Q | ........ | 75-A, 76-B |
| Downing, Benjamin [2] | Q | ........ | [on] 76-E |
| Downing, George [2] | Q | ........ | [on] 76-E |
| Downing, Jacob | Q | ........ | 76-E |
| Downs, Daniel | S | Meritches | 76:0.2.4.4.0 |
| Downs, Daniell | S | Brookhaven | 75-B6 |

| | | | |
|---|---|---|---|
| Downs, David | S | Southold | 76:0.1.2.3.4 |
| Downs, Peter | S | Brookhaven | 75-B10 |
| Downs, Peter | S | Southold | 76:0.1.1.3.0 |
| Downs, William | S | Brookhaven | 75-B10 |
| Downs, William | S | Southold | 76:0.1.3.2.3.0.1 |
| Doxe, Archel's | Q | ........ | 75-A |
| Doxe, Archibald | Q | ........ | 75-I |
| Doxsee, Jacob | Q | ........ | 76-B, 76-E |
| Doxy, Gabriel | Q | ........ | 75-A, 75-I |
| Doxy, Solomon | Q | ........ | 75-A, 75-I |
| Doxy, Solomon | Q | ........ | 76-E |
| Doyel, Darby | Q | ........ | 76-E |
| Drake, Geraudeus | S | Southampton | 76:1.1.1.3.0 |
| Drake, Jasper | N | New York | 76-I |
| Drake, Jesper | N | New York | 74-A |
| Drake, John | N | to Westchester Co | 76-P |
| Drake, John | S | ........ | 75-R |
| Drake, John | S | Southold | 76:0.2.0.3.0 |
| Drake, Moses | S | ........ | 75-R |
| Drauntman, Peggy, wf Geo. | N | New York | 74-T |
| Drawash(?), Ab'm | Q | ........ | 75-A |
| Drawman, see Van Nostrand, Aaron | | | |
| Drummond, John | N | New York | 76-A |
| Drury, Edward | N | New York | 76-A |
| Druyer, Cornelius | N | New York | 76-A |
| Duane, James | N | New York | 74-T2, 11/24 |
| Duane, James Esq. | N | New York | 74-V |
| Dubois, Lewis, carpenter | N | Ann Street | 75-D2 |
| Duboys, Cornelius J. | N | New York | 76-N |
| Dudley, Elizabeth | N | New York | 74-T |
| Dudley, Francis, hsecrpntr | N | New York | 74-T |
| Dudley, John | N | New York | 76-A |
| Dudley, William | N | New York | 74-T |
| Dudley, Wm | N | New York | 74-A |
| Duff, Alexander | N | removed upstate | 76-P |
| Dugan, Alexander | N | Warren Street | 76-H, 76-I |
| Dugan, Christopher | N | New York | 76-A |
| Duis, see Wells, Joseph | | | |
| Dukely, Robely | N | New York | 76-A |
| Duley, Nicholas | N | New York | 76-A |

| | | | |
|---|---|---|---|
| Dulin, Benj. | Q | ........ | 76-B |
| Dullman, Lewis Marin | N | New York | 74-R |
| Dulmadge, Jacob | N | New York | 76-A |
| Dulmadge, see also Dolmage | | | |
| Duly, John | N | New York | 76-A |
| Dumont, John | N | New York | 76-A |
| Dumont, John, 1st Lieut. | N | New York | 76-Y |
| Dunbar, Andrew | N | to Dutchess Co. | 76-P |
| Dunbar, George | Q | Jamaica | 75-D |
| Dunbar, James Jr. | Q | ........ | 75-A |
| Dunbar, John | N | New York | 74-A |
| Dunbar, John | Q | ........ | 76-B |
| Dunbar, Joseph | Q | ........ | 75-A, 76-B |
| Dunbar, Joseph Jr. | Q | ........ | 75-I |
| Dunbar, Joseph Sr. | Q | Jamaica | 75-C |
| Duncan, George | N | New York | 74-A |
| Dunham, Elijah | N | New York | 74-A |
| Dunlap, John | N | New York | 74-A |
| Dunman, Joseph | N | New York | 74-A |
| Dunn, Cary | N | New York | 76-N |
| Dunn, Cary, Ensign | N | New York | 75-A |
| Dunn, Cary Jr. | N | New York | 75-D3 |
| Dunn, Cary, silversmith | N | Crown Street | 74-T |
| Dunn, James | N | New York | 75-R |
| Dunn, Jane | N | New York | 74-R, 75-R |
| Dunn, Samuel | S | Brookhaven | 75-B8 |
| Dunner, Cary | N | New York | 74-A |
| Dunscomb, Dan | N | New York | 74-T2, 11/24 |
| Dunscomb, Daniel | N | New York | 74-A |
| Dunscomb, Daniel | N | New York | 75-F; 75-T2, 5/4 |
| Dunscomb, Daniel Jr. | N | New York | 74-A |
| Dunscomb, Edward | N | New York | 76-C Fuziliers |
| Dunscomb, James, cooper | N | Crown Street | 75-D1, D2 |
| Dunscomb, John | N | New York | 74-A |
| Dunscomb, Mary, Mrs. | N | rem to Ulster Co. | 76-P |
| Dunscomb, Sam'l | N | New York | 74-A |
| Durand, James | N | New York | 74-A, 76-G |
| Durand, Peter | N | New York | 74-A |
| Durborow, Joseph | N | New York | 74-A, 76-A |
| Durell, Jonathan | N | New York | 74-A, 76-N |

| | | | |
|---|---|---|---|
| Durell, Jonathan, pot baker | N | Chatham Street | 75-D1, D2 |
| Durham, Jane | N | Maiden Lane | 74-T |
| Durje, Jacob | N | New York | 76-A |
| Durke, John | S | ........ | 75-R |
| Durland, Garret Jr. | Q | Jamaica | 75-D |
| Durland, Garret Sr. | Q | Jamaica | 75-D |
| Durlin, Benj[n] | Q | ........ | [2 on] 75-A |
| Durlin, Benj[n] Jr. | Q | ........ | 75-A |
| Durlin, Daniel | Q | ........ | 75-A |
| Durlin, Elias | Q | ........ | 75-A |
| Durlin, Elias 3d | Q | ........ | 75-A |
| Durlin, Ja[*] | Q | ........ | 75-A |
| Durlin, Jno. | Q | ........ | 75-A |
| Durlin, Joseph | Q | ........ | 75-I |
| Durlin, Sam[l] | Q | ........ | 75-A |
| Durlin, Thos. | Q | ........ | [2 on] 75-A |
| Durling, Benjamin | Q | ........ | 76-B2 |
| Durling, Garret | Q | Jamaica | 75-C |
| Durye, John Jr. | N | New York | 74-A |
| Durye, Rulef | Q | ........ | 76-B |
| Duryea, Joost | Q | ........ | 76-E |
| Duryee, Aaron | Q | ........ | 76-E |
| Duryee, Ab. | N | New York | 74-A |
| Duryee, Abraham | N | New York | 74-T2, 11/24 |
| Duryee, Abraham | N | New York | 75-F |
| Duryee, Abraham | Q | ........ | 76-E |
| Duryee, Abraham, storekpr | N | New York | 74-T2, 5/26 |
| Duryee, Charles | N | New York | 74-A, 76-G |
| Duryee, Charles | S | Huntington | 75-H |
| Duryee, Charles, Ensign | N | New York | 75-A |
| Duryee, Chas. | N | New York | 75-D1 |
| Duryee, Daniel | Q | ........ | [2 on] 76-E |
| Duryee, Derick | N | New York | 74-A, 76-A |
| Duryee, Gabriel | Q | ........ | 76-E |
| Duryee, Garret | Q | ........ | 76-E |
| Duryee, George | Q | ........ | 75-A |
| Duryee, George | Q | ........ | 76-B, 76-E |
| Duryee, Jacob | N | New York | 75-D3 |
| Duryee, Jacob | Q | ........ | [2 on] 76-E |
| Duryee, Jacob | Q | Jamaica | 75-D associator |

| Duryee, Jacob | Q | Jamaica South | 75-V |
|---|---|---|---|
| Duryee, Jacob C. | N | New York | 74-A |
| Duryee, Jacob, juror | N | New York | 74-R, 75-R |
| Duryee, Jacob K. | N | New York | 74-A, 76-N |
| Duryee, Jacob K. | N | New York | 75-D1 |
| Duryee, Jacob K. | N | New York | 75-D3 |
| Duryee, Jacob K., shopkpr | N | Pecks Slip | 75-D1, D2 |
| Duryee, Job | Q | ........ | 76-E |
| Duryee, Johannes | N | New York | 74-T |
| Duryee, Johannes, baker | N | Golden Hill | 74-T2, 3/24 |
| Duryee, John | N | New York | 74-A, 75-F |
| Duryee, John | Q | ........ | 75-A |
| Duryee, John | Q | ........ | 76-B, 76-E |
| Duryee, Jorst | Q | Jamaica South | 75-V |
| Duryee, Ruliff | Q | ........ | 75-A, 76-E |
| Duryee, Ruliff/Rueloff | Q | Jamaica | 75-C, 75-D |
| Dusick, Richard | S | Brookhaven | 75-B11 n.s. |
| Duvrek, Richard & Satterly | S | Brookhaven | 76:0.2.2.2.2 |
| Duyckinck, Christopher | N | sailmkr, Crown St | 75-D2 |
| Duyckinck, Gerardus | N | New York | 75-T2, 5/4 |
| Duyckinck, Gerardus Jr. | N | New York | 75-V merchant |
| Duyckinck, Ger⁴ Jun. | N | New York | 75-B |
| Duyckinck, ---- Lieut. | N | New York | 76-C |
| Dwight, Stephen | N | New York | 74-A, 74-T |
| Dyckman, Jacob | N | Harlem | 74-T, 74-V |
| Dyckman, Jas. | N | New York | 74-A |
| Eagles, John | Q | ........ | 75-A associator |
| Eagles, ____ Mr. | N | removed upstate | 76-P |
| Eagles, William | N | New York | 76-L |
| Eames, William | N | New York | 76-A |
| Earl, Morris | N | New York | 74-A |
| Earl, Morris | N | New York | 76-G, 76-I |
| Earle, Abigail | N | New York | 74-R |
| Earle, Marmaduke | N | New York | 74-A |
| Earle, Moris | N | New York | 76-L |
| Eastburn, John, boat builder | N | James Street | 75-D1, D2 |
| Easterly, Thomas, apprentice | N | New York | 75-D1, D2 |
| Eastman, Edward | N | New York | 76-A |
| Eaton, Jacob | S | Brookhaven | 75-B2 |
| Eaton, Jacob & Hubburt | S | Brookhaven | 76:0.3.4.3.2 |

| | | | |
|---|---|---|---|
| Ebbets, Daniel | N | New York | 74-A |
| Ebbets, Daniel | N | New York | 76-A, 76-F |
| Ebbets, Daniel Jr., Ensign | N | New York | 76-Y |
| Ebbets, Richard | N | New York | 74-A |
| Ebert, Barnet, shoemaker | N | Ferry Street | 75-D1, D2 |
| Ebert, John | N | New York | 74-R juror |
| Ebert, John | N | New York | 75-B |
| Ebert, John | N | op. Fly Market | 76-I |
| Ebert, see also Everts | | | |
| Eckerts, Frederick | N | New York | 74-A |
| Eden, Medcalf | N | New York | 74-R |
| Eden, Medeiff | N | New York | 76-I |
| Edmond, Sam'l | N | New York | 74-A |
| Edmonds, Samuel | N | New York | 74-A |
| Edoll, Joseph | Q | ........ | 76-E |
| Edsall, Philip | Q | ........ | 75-A associator |
| Edsall, Philip Jr. | Q | ........ | 75-A associator |
| Edsall, Philip Jr. | Q | Newtown | 75-G |
| Edsall, Sam¹ | Q | ........ | 75-A associator |
| Edsall, Sam¹ | Q | Newtown | 75-G |
| Edsall, Samuel | N | New York | 74-A |
| Edsill, Edw. Esq. | Q | Newtown | 75-G |
| Edward, John | S | Islip | 76:0.1.2.1.3 |
| Edwards, Abra: | S | Easthampton | 75-E |
| Edwards, Abraham | S | Easthampton | 76:0.1.1.1.2 |
| Edwards, Benajah | S | Brookhaven | 75-B9 n.s. |
| Edwards, Bennaiah | S | Brookhaven | 76:1.0.2.2.0 |
| Edwards, Daniel | S | Southold | 75-N |
| Edwards, Daniel | S | Southold | 76:0.1.2.1.2 |
| Edwards, Daniel Jr. | S | Easthampton | 75-E |
| Edwards, David | S | Easthampton | 75-E |
| Edwards, David | S | Easthampton | 76:1.0.1.1.0 |
| Edwards, David Jr. | S | Easthampton | 75-E |
| Edwards, Ebenezear | S | ........ | 75-R |
| Edwards, Ebenezer | S | Southampton | 76:0.1.0.1.1 |
| Edwards, Gershom, Sgt. | S | Southold | 75-N |
| Edwards, Gorshom | S | Southold | 76:1.1.1.2.1 |
| Edwards, Henry | N | New York | 74-A |
| Edwards, Henry | S | ........ | 75-R |
| Edwards, John | S | ........ | 75-R |

| | | | |
|---|---|---|---|
| Edwards, John | S | Islip | 75-I |
| Edwards, John | S | Smithtown | 75-L recusant |
| Edwards, John | S | Southampton | 76:1.2.1.5.2 |
| Edwards, John | S | Southold | 75-N |
| Edwards, John Ju$^r$ | S | ........ | 75-R |
| Edwards, Jonathan | S | Brookhaven | 76:1.2.0.4.0 |
| Edwards, Jonathan | S | Easthampton | 75-E |
| Edwards, Jonathan | S | Easthampton | 76:0.1.2.1.1 |
| Edwards, Jonathan, Corp'l | S | Brookhaven | 75-B7 |
| Edwards, Joseph | S | Easthampton | 76:1.2.1.1.1 |
| Edwards, Richard | N | New York | 76-L |
| Edwards, Silas | S | ........ | 75-R |
| Edwards, Stephen | S | Easthampton | 76:0.1.4.1.1 |
| Edwards, Thomas | S | Easthampton | 75-E |
| Edwards, Thomas | S | Easthampton | 76:1.2.3.4.2 |
| Edwards, Thomas Jr. | S | Easthampton | 76:0.1.0.1.0 |
| Edwards, Thom$^s$ Jr. | S | Easthampton | 75-E |
| Edwards, Timothy | S | Southampton | 76:0.1.1.1.1 |
| Edwards, William | S | Brookhaven | 75-B1, 75-B6 |
| Edwards, W$^m$ | S | Brookhaven | 75-B7 |
| Egan, Timothy | N | to Dutchess Co. | 76-P |
| Egbert, Benjamin | N | New York | 76-I |
| Egbert, Benjamin, Capt. | N | New York | 76-G |
| Egberts, Abraham | N | New York | 74-A |
| Egberts, Benjamin | N | New York | 75-R |
| Eggert, Christian | N | New York | 76-A |
| Elderd, James | Q | ........ | 76-B2 |
| Elderd, Lucas | Q | Jamaica | 75-D |
| Eldert, Hendrick | Q | ........ | 76-E |
| Eldert, Israel | Q | ........ | 75-A, 76-B |
| Eldert, James | Q | ........ | 75-A |
| Eldert, Johannes | Q | Jamaica | 75-D |
| Eldert, Johannis, Capt. | Q | ........ | 75-A |
| Eldert, Luke | Q | ........ | 75-A |
| Eldert, Luke | Q | ........ | 76-B, 76-E |
| Eldred, James | Q | ........ | 76-B |
| Eldrid, Israel | Q | Hempstead | 76-D |
| Eldrif, Luke | Q | Jamaica | 75-C |
| Elison, Rob$^t$ | N | Cop. Street [sic] | 76-I |
| Elless, Garrit, hse carpenter | N | Beekman Street | 75-D1, D2 |

| | | | |
|---|---|---|---|
| Elliot, John | N | New York | 74-A |
| Elliot, John, Ensign | N | New York | 76-G |
| Elliot, William, weaver | N | New York | 74-T2, 5/26 |
| Elliott, Adom | N | New York | 74-A |
| Elliott, David | N | Broad Street | 75-D1, D2 |
| Elliott, John, juror | N | New York | 75-R, 76-R |
| Ellis, Charles | N | New York | 74-A |
| Ellis, Charles | N | New York | 74-T insolvent |
| Ellis, Jno. | N | New York | 76-N |
| Ellis, John | N | New York | 74-A |
| Ellis, Robert | N | Pearle Street | 76-H |
| Ellis, Samuel | N | New York | 74-A |
| Ellis, Samuel | N | nr Bear Market | 75-T2, 6/29 |
| Ellis, Samuel [2] | N | New York | [on] 76-A |
| Ellis, William | N | New York | 74-A |
| Ellison, John | N | New York | 74-A |
| Ellison, Mary, wid. of Robt | N | Kingsbridge | 75-T |
| Ellison, Thomas | Q | ........ | 76-B |
| Ellison, Thos. Jr., merchant | N | New York | 75-T2, 1/5 |
| Ellison, Timothy | Q | ........ | 76-E |
| Ellison, William | N | New York | 74-A, 76-A |
| Elliston, Mary wid. of Robt | N | Kingsbridge | 75-V |
| Ellsworth, John | Q | ........ | 75-A, 76-B |
| Elphinston, W., teacher | N | New York | 75-T |
| Elsworth, Ann | N | New York | 75-R |
| Elsworth, Francis | N | New York | 74-A, 76-A |
| Elsworth, Jane | N | removed upstate | 76-P |
| Elsworth, John | Q | Hempstead | 76-D |
| Elsworth, John, hatter | N | Golden Hill | 75-D1, D2 |
| Elsworth, Theop's | N | New York | 74-A |
| Elsworth, Will'm I. | N | New York | 74-A |
| Elsworth, William | N | New York | 76-L |
| Elsworth, William J. | N | New York | 76-L |
| Elsworth, William, Lieut. | N | New York | 75-A |
| Elsworth, William [2] | N | New York | [on] 74-A |
| Elting, Peter | N | New York | 75-F |
| Elting, Peter, Capt. | N | New York | 75-A |
| Elting, Peter, store | N | New Albany Pier | 75-T2, 1/12 |
| Eltring, Peter, flour | N | New Albany Dock | 74-T2, 9/2 |
| Ely, Abraham | N | New York | 74-A |

| | | | |
|---|---|---|---|
| Embree, John | Q | ........ | 76-E |
| Embree, Lawrence | N | New York | 74-A |
| Embree, Lawrence | N | New York | 74-T2, 11/24 |
| Embrie, Effingham | N | New York | 76-G |
| Emery, James, weaver, 22 | N | New York | 74-V runaway |
| Emery, William | N | Golden Hill | 74-T2, 5/5 |
| Emmens, Hendrick | Q | ........ | 75-A, 76-E |
| Emmens, Hendrick | Q | Jamaica | 75-D |
| Emmens, Hendrick Jr. | Q | ........ | 76-E |
| Emmens, Hendrick Jr. | Q | Jamaica | 75-C |
| Emmens, Hendrick Sr. | Q | Jamaica | 75-C |
| Emmens, James | N | New York | 76-L |
| Emmons, Benj. | S | Southold | 76:1.0.1.1.0.1.0 |
| Emmons, Benjamin Jun. | S | Southold | 75-N non-signer |
| Emmons, Benjamin Jun$^r$ | S | Southold | 76:0.3.3.1.0 |
| Emmons, Benjamin ye third | S | Southold | 75-N non-signer |
| Emmons, Hendrick | Q | ........ | 76-B |
| Englar, Adam, Capt. | N | New York | 74-V |
| English, Benj$^n$ | N | New York | 76-A |
| English, Hudson, cordwnr | N | Chappel Street | 75-D2 |
| English, James | N | New York | 75-D3 |
| Ennis, Sarah | N | removed upstate | 76-P |
| Enslee, Daniel, butcher | N | Fly Market | 76-V |
| Ensley, Daniel, butcher | N | New York | 74-V |
| Erhatt, George | N | De Peyster Street | 74-T2, 10/13 |
| Erlin, Margrit | N | removed upstate | 76-P |
| Ernest, Mattheus | N | New York | 74-A |
| Ernest, Matthew | N | New York | 74-T, 76-I |
| Ernest, Matthew, storekpr | N | New York | 74-T2, 7/28 |
| Erskine, Robert | N | New York | 75-F |
| Ervin, Jacob, cordwainer | N | Broadway | 75-D1, D2 |
| Ervin, Thomas | N | New York | 75-D1 |
| Erving, Jacob | N | New York | 75-D1 |
| Erwin, Alex'r | N | New York | 74-A |
| Esterly, see Easterly | | | |
| Ettridge, James | N | New York | 74-A, 76-A |
| Evens, Ann | N | removed upstate | 76-P |
| Everet, James | Q | Jamaica | 75-C |
| Everett, James | Q | ........ | 76-E |
| Everit, George | S | Huntington | 76-H2 |

| | | | |
|---|---|---|---|
| Everitt, Benjamin | Q | ........ | 75-A associator |
| Everitt, Benjamin | Q | ........ | [2 on] 76-E |
| Everitt, Benjamin | Q | Jamaica | 75-D associator |
| Everitt, Benjamin | Q | Jamaica | 75-E |
| Everitt, Daniel | Q | ........ | 75-A associator |
| Everitt, Daniel | Q | ........ | 76-E |
| Everitt, Daniel | Q | Jamaica | 75-D associator |
| Everitt, Nehemiah | Q | ........ | 75-A associator |
| Everitt, Nehemiah | Q | Jamaica | 75-D associaotr |
| Everitt, Nehemiah | Q | Jamaica | 75-E |
| Everitt, Nicholas | Q | ........ | 75-A associator |
| Everitt, Nicholas | Q | ........ | 76-E |
| Everitt, Nicholas | Q | Jamaica | 75-D associator |
| Everitt, Nicholas, 2d Lieut. | Q | Jamaica | 75-E |
| Everts, John | N | Fly Market | 76-H |
| Everts, see also Ebert | | | |
| Eyre, Benjamin | S | Easthampton | 76:1.1.0.2.1 |
| Eyre, William | S | Easthampton | 76:0.1.0.0.0 |
| Fach, George | N | New York | 76-A |
| Fach, Michael | N | New York | 74-A, 75-D3 |
| Faesh, Michael, mason | N | St. George's St. | 75-D2 |
| Fagenham, Christopher | N | shopkeeper | 74-R Freeman |
| Fagenham, Crist'r | N | New York | 76-I |
| Fairley, David, carman | N | New York | 75-T |
| Fairlie, Alex' | N | New York | 76-A |
| Fairlie, James | N | li w/ Eleazor Miller | 75-D1, D2 |
| Falkenhan, Samuel | N | New York | 74-A |
| Falkenhau, Samuel | N | New York | 76-A |
| Fall, John | N | New York | 76-I |
| Fall, Robert | N | New York | 76-R |
| Faning, David | S | Brookhaven | 76:0.1.2.2.1.0.1 |
| Faning, James | S | Southold | 76:0.1.1.1.1 |
| Faning, James | S | Southold | 76:1.0.0.0.0.2.0 |
| Faning, Phineas | S | Southold | 76:1.1.2.1.1.3.1 |
| Fanning, David | S | Brookhaven | 75-B6 |
| Fanning, Edmund | N | New York | 76-A |
| Fanning, James | S | Southampton | 76:1.1.2.2.1 |
| Fanning, Nath¹ | S | Brookhaven | 75-B10 |
| Fanning, Phineas | S | Brookhaven | 75-B10 |
| Fanning, Ph' | S | Southold | 75-N |

| | | | |
|---|---|---|---|
| Fanning, Thomas | S | Brookhaven | 75-B9 |
| Fanning, Thomas | S | Brookhaven | 76:1.1.0.1.1 |
| Fanool, Christian, baker | N | Division Street | 75-D2 |
| Fardon, Abraham | N | New York | 74-A |
| Fardon, Isaac | N | New York | 74-A |
| Fardon, Margrit | N | removed upstate | 76-P |
| Farley, James | Q | Oyster Bay | 75-F |
| Farmington, Benjamin | Q | ........ | 75-A associator |
| Farquhar, ____ Dr. | N | Smith Street | 75-T2, 2/23 |
| Farquhar, James, Capt. | N | New York | 74-T |
| Farquharson, Martin | N | New York | 75-D3 |
| Farral, Michael | N | New York | 74-A |
| Farrara, ---- Mrs. | N | New York | 76-I |
| Farrel, Martin | N | New York | 75-R |
| Farrell, John | N | New York | 76-C Fuziliers |
| Farrell, John, taylor | N | at Benn Douglas's | 75-D2 |
| Farrington, Benj. | Q | ........ | 76-E |
| Faulkner, ____ Capt. | N | New York | 74-T |
| Faulkner, John | N | New York | 74-A |
| Faulkner, John | N | New York | 76-A, 76-F |
| Faulkner, John, constable | N | New York | 74-R to 76-R |
| Faulkner, Will. D. | N | New York | 74-A |
| Faulkner, William | N | New York | 76-N |
| Fay, Jacob | N | New York | 76-L |
| Fay, John | N | New York | 74-A |
| Fee, Nicholas | N | New York | 74-R witness |
| Feeke, Daniel | Q | ........ | 76-E |
| Feke, Charles | Q | ........ | 76-E |
| Felliger, Christopher | N | New York | 76-R |
| Felthausen, John | N | New York | 74-A |
| Fenton, David | N | New York | 76-A |
| Fenton, Robert | N | New York | 76-A |
| Fenton, Robert, cooper | N | Stone Street | 75-D1, D2 |
| Fenton, Thomas, cordwnr | N | Division Street | 75-D2 |
| Ferdon, Abraham | N | New York | 74-T insolvent |
| Ferdon, Thomas | N | New York | 75-D1 |
| Ferguson, Dennis | N | New York | 76-A |
| Ferguson, Duncan | N | New York | 76-A |
| Ferguson, James | N | New York | 76-A |
| Ferrell, Mich'l | N | New York | 75-D3 |

| | | | |
|---|---|---|---|
| Ferrey, Joseph | S | Brookhaven | 76:0.1.1.1.3 |
| Ferribe, W. | Q | ........ | 76-E |
| Ferris, Josiah | N | New York | 74-A |
| Ferry, Joseph | S | Brookhaven | 75-B3 |
| Fetherby, John | Q | ........ | 75-A, 76-E |
| Fetherby, Thomas | Q | ........ | 75-A |
| Fetherby, Thomas | Q | ........ | 76-B, 76-E |
| Fetherby, Wm | Q | ........ | 75-A |
| Field, Benjamin | Q | ........ | 75-A associator |
| Field, Benjamin | Q | ........ | [2 on] 76-E |
| Field, Benjamin | Q | Newtown | 75-G |
| Field, Benjamin Jr. | Q | ........ | 75-A associator |
| Field, Benjamin Jr. | Q | Newtown | 75-G |
| Field, Da. | Q | ........ | 76-E |
| Field, Francis | N | New York | 75-T insolvent |
| Field, Gilbert | Q | ........ | 76-E |
| Field, Jacob | Q | ........ | 75-E |
| Field, James | Q | ........ | 75-A, 76-E |
| Field, James | S | Easthampton | 75-E |
| Field, James | S | Easthampton | 76:0.1.1.1.0 |
| Field, John | Q | Flushing | 75-V |
| Field, John | S | Easthampton | 76:0.1.0.1.0 |
| Field, Joseph | Q | ........ | 76-B, 76-E |
| Field, Peter | N | New York | 74-A |
| Field, Philip | Q | ........ | 76-E |
| Field, Robert | Q | ........ | 75-A associator |
| Field, Robert | Q | ........ | 76-E |
| Field, Robert | Q | Newtown | 75-G |
| Field, Stephen | Q | ........ | 75-A associator |
| Field, Stephen | Q | Newtown | 75-G |
| Field, Whit. | Q | ........ | 76-E |
| Field, Whitehead | Q | ........ | 75-A, 76-B |
| Field, William | N | New York | 74-A |
| Field, William | N | to Westchester Co | 76-P |
| Filer, Thomas | S | Easthampton | 75-E |
| Filer, Thomas | S | Easthampton | 76:0.1.2.1.3 |
| Filkin, Francis, Judge | N | New York | 74-R to 76-R |
| Filkins, Fras. | N | New York | 74-A |
| Filor, Benjamin, Capt. | S | Brookhaven | 75-B11 n.s. |
| Finch, Jno. Adam [2] | N | New York | [on] 76-A |

| | | | |
|---|---|---|---|
| Finch, John | S | Brookhaven | 76:1.1.1.1.0 |
| Finch, Nathaniel | S | Brookhaven | 75-B3, 75-B6 |
| Finch, Reynold | S | Brookhaven | 75-B3, 75-B6 |
| Fine, Frederick | N | B: Slip | 75-D2 |
| Fine, Frederick | N | New York | 74-A |
| Fine. Grant & Fine | N | New York | 74-A |
| Fink, Alexander | N | New York | 76-F |
| Finsher, Ann | N | removed upstate | 76-P |
| Finsher, Hanah | N | removed upstate | 76-P |
| Fish, Ambrose | Q | ........ | 76-E |
| Fish, Benjamin | Q | ........ | 75-A, 76-B2 |
| Fish, Jesse | Q | ........ | 76-E |
| Fish, John | N | New York | 74-A |
| Fish, John | N | New York | 76-L, 76-N |
| Fish, John | Q | ........ | 75-A associator |
| Fish, John | Q | ........ | 76-E |
| Fish, John | Q | Newtown | 75-G |
| Fish, Jonathan | Q | ........ | 75-A, 76-B |
| Fish, Jonathan | Q | ........ | [2 on] 76-E |
| Fish, Jonathan | Q | Newtown | 75-G |
| Fish, Lawrance | Q | Hempstead | 76-D |
| Fish, Lawrence | Q | ........ | 75-A |
| Fish, Lawrence | Q | ........ | 76-B, 76-E |
| Fish, Nathan | N | New York | 74-A, 76-I |
| Fish, Nathan | N | New York | 76-L, 76-N |
| Fish, Nicholas | N | New York | 76-N |
| Fish, Nicholas, Lieut. | N | New York | 76-C |
| Fish, Nich[s] | N | New York | 75-D3 |
| Fish, Sam. T. | Q | Newtown | 75-G |
| Fish, Samuel | Q | ........ | [2 on] 76-E |
| Fisher, Barth[w], baker | N | Cherry Street | 75-D1, D2 |
| Fisher, Donald | N | New York | 74-A |
| Fisher, George | N | Cherry Street | 75-T |
| Fisher, George | N | New York | 76-L |
| Fisher, George, for Barth[w] | N | New York | 75-D1, D2 |
| Fisher, Hend'k Jr. | N | New York | 74-A |
| Fisher, John | N | New York | 74-A, 76-G |
| Fisher, John, sadler | N | Broadway | 75-D2 |
| Fisher, Leonard | N | New York | 74-A, 76-D |
| Fisher, Thomas, store | N | Maiden Lane | 75-T2, 3/30 |

| | | | |
|---|---|---|---|
| Fitch, James | S | Brookhaven | 75-B7 |
| Fitch, Joseph | N | New York | 74-A |
| Fithian, Aaron | S | Easthampton | 75-E |
| Fithian, Aaron | S | Easthampton | 76:0.1.1.1.0 |
| Fithian, David | S | Easthampton | 75-E |
| Fithian, David, Capt. | S | Easthampton | 76:0.1.2.3.1.1.0 |
| Fitzgerald, Catherine | N | New York | 74-T2, 11/10 |
| FitzGerald, Walter | N | New York | 76-A |
| Fitzpatrick, James | N | New York | 74-A |
| Fiva, Anthony, languages | N | Crown Street | 74-T2, 12/15 |
| Fives, George | Q | ........ | 76-B |
| Fleet, Alexander | S | Huntington | 76-H3 |
| Fleet, Alexʳ | S | Huntington | 75-H |
| Fleet, Arnold | Q | ........ | 76-E |
| Fleet, Gilbert | S | Huntington | 75-H |
| Fleet, Gilbert, 1st Lt. | S | Huntington | 75-H1 |
| Fleet, Jesse | S | Huntington | 75-H Quaker |
| Fleet, John | Q | ........ | 75-A, 76-A |
| Fleet, John | Q | ........ | 76-B, 76-E |
| Fleet, Luke | Q | ........ | 76-E |
| Fleet, Luke | Q | Hempstead | 76-D |
| Fleet, Parrott | S | Huntington | 75-H Quaker |
| Fleet, Simon Jr. | S | Huntington | 75-H |
| Fleet, Simon Sr. | S | Huntington | 75-H |
| Fleet, Thomas | Q | ........ | 75-A |
| Fleet, Thomas | Q | ........ | 76-B, 76-E |
| Fleet, Thomˢ | S | Huntington | 75-H |
| Fleming, John [3] | N | New York | [on] 76-A |
| Fleming, Samuel | N | New York | 76-N |
| Fleming, Samuel, shoemkr | N | Hanover Square | 75-D1, D2 |
| Flemming, Edward | N | New York | 74-A |
| Flemming, Edward | N | New York | 74-T2, 11/24 |
| Fletcher, James | N | New York | 76-A |
| Fletcher, Richard | N | New York | 75-V, 76-I |
| Fletcher, Richard, Capt. | N | New York | 75-A |
| Flinn, Michael | N | New York | 76-A |
| Flint, Ammy | S | ........ | 75-R |
| Flint, Benoni | S | ........ | 75-R |
| Flint, Benoni | S | Southampton | 76:0.1.3.3.1 |
| Flint, Catharine | N | to Westchester Co | 76-P |

| | | | |
|---|---|---|---|
| Flint, Nathan | S | ........ | 75-R |
| Flint, Nathan | S | Southampton | 76:0.1.0.2.1 |
| Flood, Elenor | N | removed upstate | 76-P |
| Flower, Harman | Q | ........ | 75-A |
| Flower, Jno. | Q | ........ | 75-A |
| Flower, Mich'l | Q | ........ | 75-A |
| Flower, Timothy | Q | ........ | 75-A, 76-B |
| Flowers, Michael | Q | ........ | 76-E |
| Floyd, Benjamen | S | Brookhaven | 76:0.1.3.2.0.4.0 |
| Floyd, Benjamin | S | Brookhaven | 75-B10 |
| Floyd, Benjamin, Major | S | Brookhaven | 75-B11 n.s. |
| Floyd, Margaret | S | Smithtown | 76:0.1.2.2.2.4.3 |
| Floyd, Richard | S | Meritches | 76:0.2.1.2.1.5.7 |
| Floyd, Richard, Major | S | Brookhaven | 75-B12 n.s. |
| Floyd, William | S | Meritches | 76:0.2.1.3.2.10.2 |
| Flynn, James | N | New York | 76-A |
| Fober, Elizabeth | N | Partition Street | 76-I |
| Folliot, George | N | New York | 76-A |
| Folliot, George & Co. | N | New York | 74-T2, 10/6 |
| Forbes, Alexander, taylor | N | New York | 75-D1, D2 |
| Forbes, Alexander [2] | N | New York | [on] 74-A |
| Forbes, Alex' | N | New York | 76-A |
| Forbes, Duncan | N | to Dutchess Co. | 76-P |
| Forbes, Gilbert | N | New York | 74-A |
| Forbes, Gilbert, Sergt. | N | New York | 75-D3 |
| Forbes, James | N | New York | 74-A, 75-D1 |
| Forbes, James | N | New York | 76-I |
| Forbes, John | N | New York | 74-A |
| Forbes, John, juror | N | New York | 75-R, 76-R |
| Forbes, Joseph | N | New York | 74-A |
| Forbes, Joseph, housecrpntr | N | New York | 75-T |
| Forbes, William | Q | Jamaica | 76-C |
| Forbes, William A. | N | New York | 74-A, 75-D1 |
| Forbes, William, Corp'l | N | New York | 75-D3 |
| Forbes, William G. | N | New York | 74-A, 75-D3 |
| Forbes, William T. | N | New York | 74-A |
| Forbis, William | N | New York | 76-C Light Horse |
| Forbis, William, cordwainer | N | New York | 75-D2 |
| Forbis, William, sadler | N | Broadway | 75-D2 |
| Forbus, Mary | N | removed upstate | 76-P |

| | | | |
|---|---|---|---|
| Forbus, William | Q | ........ | 75-A associator |
| Forbus, William | Q | ........ | 76-E |
| Ford, Anthony | N | New York | 74-T |
| Ford, Anthony | N | New York | 74-T2, 3/17 |
| Ford, Anthony, Ensign | N | New York | 76-G, 76-S |
| Ford, Bartholomew | N | New York | 74-A |
| Ford, James | N | New York | 74-A |
| Ford, James, carpenter | N | Vesey Street | 75-D1, D2 |
| Ford, Sufy, widow | N | removed upstate | 76-P |
| Ford, Thomas | N | New York | 74-A |
| Ford, Timothy | N | New York | 74-R witness |
| Ford, William | N | New York | 74-A |
| Fordham, Ab$^m$ Jun$^r$ | S | ........ | 75-R |
| Fordham, Daniel | S | ........ | 75-R |
| Fordham, Daniel | S | Southampton | 76:0.2.5.2.1.1.0 |
| Fordham, Eaphraim | S | Southampton | 76:0.1.4.1.2 |
| Fordham, Ephraim | S | ........ | 75-R |
| Fordham, George | S | Southampton | 75-M |
| Fordham, George | S | Southampton | 76:0.1.4.3.3 |
| Fordham, John N. | S | ........ | 75-R |
| Fordham, Nathan | S | ........ | 75-R |
| Fordham, Nathan Esq$^r$ | S | Southampton | 76:1.1.0.2.1.2.0 |
| Fordham, Nathan Ju$^r$ | S | ........ | 75-R |
| Fordham, Robert | N | New York | 74-A, 76-A |
| Fordom, Abraham | S | Southampton | 76:1.2.1.3.1 |
| Fordom, Gidion | S | Southampton | 76:0.1.3.1.2 |
| Fordom, Phinaus | S | Southampton | 76:0.1.0.1.0 |
| Fordom, Stephen | S | Southampton | 76:0.1.1.1.1 |
| Fordon, Abraham | N | to Dutchess Co. | 76-P |
| Fordon, Adriantis | N | to Dutchess Co. | 76-P |
| Fordon, Altice | N | to Dutchess Co. | 76-P |
| Fordon, Cady | N | to Dutchess Co. | 76-P |
| Fordon, Cornelia | N | to Dutchess Co. | 76-P |
| Fordon, Elizabeth | N | to Dutchess Co. | 76-P |
| Fordon, Phebe | N | to Dutchess Co. | 76-P |
| Fordon, Samuel | N | to Dutchess Co. | 76-P |
| Forman, Lewis | N | New York | 74-A |
| Forman, Margret | N | removed upstate | 76-P |
| Forneir, Frances | S | Southold | 76:1.0.4.2.1 |
| Forschee, Daniel | N | New York | 76-A |

| | | | |
|---|---|---|---|
| Forsdal, Samuel | Q | ........ | 76-B2 |
| Forster, Henry | N | New York | 76-A |
| Forster, Jacob | Q | Jamaica | 75-D associator |
| Forster, John | Q | Jamaica | 75-D |
| Forster, Marm. | N | New York | 74-A |
| Forster, Marmaduke | N | New York | 75-R |
| Forster, Samuel | Q | Jamaica | 75-D |
| Forsyth, John | N | New York | 74-A, 76-A |
| Fort, Martin | N | New York | 75-R |
| Fortescue, William | N | New York | 74-A |
| Fortune, Alexander | N | New York | 76-A |
| Fortune, Alex$^r$ | N | New York | 76-N |
| Fortune, ____ Capt. | N | Nassau Street | 74-T |
| Fortune, William | N | New York | 76-A |
| Fortunne, Joseph, Sgt. | N | New York | 76-C |
| Fosdick, Samuel | Q | ........ | 75-A, 76-E |
| Foster, Benjamin | S | Southampton | 76:0.1.0.1.1 |
| Foster, Bethiah, widow | S | Southampton | 76:0.1.1.2.2 |
| Foster, Christofor | S | Southampton | 76:0.1.5.2.0 |
| Foster, Daniel | S | Southampton | 76:1.0.2.2.2.1.0 |
| Foster, David Hayns | S | Southampton | 76:0.1.3.3.2 |
| Foster, Elias | S | Southampton | 76:0.2.1.1.0 |
| Foster, Ephraim | S | ........ | 75-R |
| Foster, Jedidiah | S | ........ | 75-R |
| Foster, Jn° Jun. | S | ........ | 75-R |
| Foster, John | Q | ........ | 75-A |
| Foster, John | Q | ........ | 76-B, 76-E |
| Foster, John | S | ........ | 75-R |
| Foster, John | S | Southampton | 76:1.1.4.3.2.2.0 |
| Foster, Jonas | S | Southampton | 76:1.2.0.1.0 |
| Foster, Josiah | S | Southampton | 76:0.1.3.1.1 |
| Foster, Mama$^k$, Lieut. | N | New York | 75-A |
| Foster, Nathan | S | Southampton | 76:1.1.1.3.0 |
| Foster, Nath$^n$ Jun$^r$ | S | ........ | 75-R |
| Foster, Prudance | S | Southampton | 76:0.0.0.2.0 |
| Foster, Sam$^l$ | Q | ........ | 75-A |
| Foster, Sarah | N | to Westchester Co | 76-P |
| Foster, Stephen | S | ........ | 75-R |
| Foster, Stephen | S | Southampton | 76:1.1.1.2.0 |
| Foster, Stephen Jun$^r$ | S | Southampton | 76:0.1.1.1.1 |

| | | | |
|---|---|---|---|
| Foster, Temprance, Wid. | S | Southampton | 76:0.2.1.1.3 |
| Foster, Thomas | Q | ........ | 76-E |
| Foster, Wakeman | S | ........ | 75-R |
| Foster, William | N | to Westchester Co | 76-P |
| Foster, William | S | Southampton | 76:1.1.1.2.1.1.0 |
| Foster, Will^m | S | Huntington | 75-H |
| Foster, Zedediah | S | Southampton | 76:0.1.3.1.3 |
| Foucht, George, shoemaker | N | at John Lasher's | 75-D2 |
| Fought, George | N | New York | 75-D1 |
| Fountain, Stephen | S | Brookhaven | 75-B6 |
| Founten, Stephen | S | Brookhaven | 76:0.1.0.1.1 |
| Fourniers, François | S | Brookhaven | 75-B10 |
| Fowlar, John | S | Southampton | 76:1.1.1.1.1 |
| Fowle, Isaac | N | New York | 74-A, 75-D1 |
| Fowler, Anthony | N | New York | 74-T insolvent |
| Fowler, Catharine | N | removed upstate | 76-P |
| Fowler, David | Q | ........ | 76-E |
| Fowler, Felix | Q | ........ | 75-A, 76-B |
| Fowler, Frederick | N | New York | 74-A |
| Fowler, George | N | New York | 76-A |
| Fowler, George | Q | Jamaica | 75-C |
| Fowler, Isaac, turner | N | John Street | 75-D2 |
| Fowler, John | N | New York | 76-A, 76-R |
| Fowler, John | N | Plough & Harrow | 74-T |
| Fowler, John | Q | ........ | 75-A, 76-E |
| Fowler, John, 1st Lieut. | N | New York | 76-Y |
| Fowler, John, Capt. | S | ........ | 75-R |
| Fowler, John, innkeeper | N | Fresh Water | 75-T |
| Fowler, Theodosius | N | Great George St. | 74-T2, 6/2 |
| Fowler, Theodosius | N | New York | 76-N |
| Fowler, Thomas | Q | ........ | [2 on] 76-E |
| Foy, John | N | to Dutchess Co. | 76-P |
| Foy, Martin | N | New York | 75-R |
| Foy, Martin, currier | N | at N.N. Anthony's | 75-D2 |
| Fraiser, Joseph | S | ........ | 75-R |
| Francis, C., widow | N | removed upstate | 76-P |
| Francis, Samuel | N | nr. the Exchange | 76-H, 76-I |
| Franke, John | S | Southold | 76:0.1.0.1.1 |
| Franklin, George | N | New York | 75-F |
| Franklin, Henry | N | New York | 74-A, 75-F |

| | | | |
|---|---|---|---|
| Franklin, James | N | New York | 74-A |
| Franklin, John | N | Elbow Street | 74-T |
| Franklin, John | N | New York | 74-R |
| Franklin, Samuel | N | New York | 75-F, 76-A |
| Franklin, Samuel, merchant | N | New York | 75-T2, 1/5 |
| Franklin, Thomas | N | New York | 74-A, 75-F |
| Franklin, Walter | N | New York | 75-T2, 5/4 |
| Franklin, Walter | N | New York | 76-A |
| Franklin, Walter, merchant | N | New York | 74-T, 74-V |
| Franks, Jnº [2] | S | ........ | [on] 75-R |
| Fraser, Alexander | N | New York | 76-A |
| Frasher, John | N | removed upstate | 76-P |
| Fraunces, Samuel | N | New York | 74-T |
| Frauzers, Lovis | N | New York | 76-A |
| Frazer, Alexander, heelmkr | N | Broad Street | 75-D2 |
| Frazer, Cath. | N | New York | 76-I |
| Frazer, Walter | N | New York | 76-A |
| Frazer, William | N | New York | 75-D2 |
| Fream, James | N | New York | 75-D2 |
| Fredericks, Jonas | Q | ........ | 75-A associator |
| Fredrick, Jonas | Q | Jamaica | 75-D associator |
| Fredrick, Peter Jr. | Q | Jamaica | 76-C |
| Freeborn, John | N | New York | 74-A |
| Freeman, Asra | N | removed upstate | 76-P |
| Freeman, James | N | Monthuyl Street | 74-R |
| Freidental, Fridris | N | New York | 74-A |
| French, J., Esq. | Q | Jamaica | 75-D |
| French, Jemes | S | Brookhaven | 76:0.1.1.1.2 |
| French, Joseph Esq. | Q | Jamaica | 75-D1, 75-H |
| French, Margaret, Mrs. | N | to Dutchess Co. | 76-P |
| French, Othnel, shipwright | N | Shipyard | 75-D2 |
| Freytag, George | N | New York | 74-A |
| Frigenheim, Christopher | N | New York | 74-A |
| Frinch, Nathaniel | S | Brookhaven | 76:0.1.3.1.0 |
| Frost, Charles | Q | ........ | 76-E |
| Frost, Nathaniel | Q | ........ | 75-A |
| Frost, Penn | Q | ........ | 76-E |
| Frost, Stephen | Q | ........ | 76-E |
| Frost, Thomas | Q | ........ | 75-A, 76-E |
| Frost, W. | Q | ........ | [2 on] 76-E |

| | | | |
|---|---|---|---|
| Frost, Wm | Q | ........ | 75-A, 76-B |
| Fruge, Ab'm | N | New York | 76-A |
| Fry, Jacob | N | New York | 74-A |
| Fry, Millicent, Mrs. | N | to Dutchess Co. | 76-P |
| Fueter, Daniel | N | New York | 76-A |
| Fueter, Lewis, silversmith | N | Queen Street | 74-T |
| Fuhrle, David | N | New York | 76-A |
| Fuller, Richard | Q | ........ | 76-E |
| Fullerton, Alexander | N | removed upstate | 76-P |
| Funck, Eliz[th] | N | New York | 76-H |
| Funck, see also Vonck | | | |
| Fung, Michael | N | New York | 76-A |
| Furlong, George | N | New York | 74-T |
| Furman, Ab[m] | Q | ........ | 75-A |
| Furman, Ab[m] Jr. | Q | ........ | 75-A |
| Furman, Ezek[l] | Q | Newtown | 75-G |
| Furman, Gabriel | Q | ........ | 75-A associator |
| Furman, Gabriel | Q | ........ | 76-E |
| Furman, Gabriel | Q | Newtown | 75-G |
| Furman, Howard | Q | ........ | 75-A associator |
| Furman, Howard | Q | ........ | 76-E |
| Furman, Howard | Q | Newtown | 75-G |
| Furman, Jonathan | Q | ........ | 76-E |
| Furman, Jonathan | Q | Newtown | 75-G |
| Furman, Joseph | Q | Jamaica | 75-C |
| Furman, Thomas | Q | ........ | 76-E |
| Furman, W. | Q | ........ | 76-E |
| Furman, William | Q | ........ | 75-A associator |
| Furman, William | Q | Newtown | 75-G |
| Furness, Richard | N | New York | 74-R |
| Gabble, Christian | N | New York | 76-A |
| Gabell, Morrice | N | New York | 74-T insolvent |
| Gaine, Hugh | N | New York | 75-F |
| Galbraith, Thos. | N | New York | 74-A |
| Galbreath, Alex[r] | N | New York | 76-A |
| Galbreath, Thomas | N | New York | 75-F |
| Galbreath, Thomas | N | nr Fly Market | 75-D2 |
| Galbreath, Thos., merchant | N | New York | 75-T |
| Galer, Adam | N | New York | 74-A, 75-D1 |
| Galer, Adam, chairmaker | N | Little Queen St. | 74-T2, 8/25 |

| | | | |
|---|---|---|---|
| Galer/Gayler, Adam | N | New York | 75-D1, D2 |
| Galer, see also Geler | | | |
| Gallalant, Elisabeth | N | removed upstate | 76-P |
| Gallaudet, Elisha | N | New York | 74-A |
| Gallaudett, John | N | New York | 76-A |
| Galloway, John | N | New York | 75-R |
| Gamble, Samuel, ae c.33 | N | New York | 74-V runaway |
| Gann, John | S | Easthampton | 76:0.1.1.1.1 |
| Ganner, David | N | New York | 76-A |
| Gantz, Francis | N | New York | 76-A |
| Gardener, Harmanes | N | New York | 74-A |
| Gardinear, Jacob | N | New York | 74-R |
| Gardiner, Abraham | S | Easthampton | 75-E |
| Gardiner, Abraham Esq. | S | Easthampton | 76:1.1.1.2.1.4.1 |
| Gardiner, David | S | Southold | 76:0.1.0.2.3 |
| Gardiner, David | S | Southold | 76:0.1.1.1.1 |
| Gardiner, Jeremiah | S | Easthampton | 75-E |
| Gardiner, Jeremiah | S | Easthampton | 76:0.2.4.1.0 |
| Gardiner, Jeremiah | S | Southampton | 76:0.1.1.1.0 |
| Gardiner, Jerusha, Mrs. | S | Easthampton | 76:0.0.2.1.0.1.0 |
| Gardiner, John | S | Easthampton | 75-E |
| Gardiner, John | S | Southold | 75-N |
| Gardiner, John | S | Southold | 76:0.3.2.2.1.1.0 |
| Gardiner, John Esq$^r$ | S | Easthampton | 76:1.1.0.1.1 |
| Gardiner, John Jnr. | S | Easthampton | 76:0.1.0.1.0 |
| Gardiner, John Jr. | S | Easthampton | 75-E |
| Gardiner, Joseph | S | Southold | 75-N |
| Gardiner, Joseph | S | Southold | 76:0.1.2.1.2 |
| Gardiner, Lion | S | ........ | 75-R |
| Gardiner, Lion | S | Easthampton | 76:1.0.0.1.0 |
| Gardiner, Lion | S | Southold | 76:0.1.4.1.3 |
| Gardiner, Nancy | S | Easthampton | 76:0.0.1.1.1 |
| Gardiner, Na$^{th}$ | S | ........ | 75-R |
| Gardiner, Richard | Q | ........ | 76-E |
| Gardiner, Samuel | S | Easthampton | 75-E |
| Gardiner, Thomas | N | New York | 75-F |
| Gardner, Charles | N | New York | 74-A, 74-R |
| Gardner, Charles | N | New York | 76-I |
| Gardner, David | S | Southold | 75-N |
| Gardner, David | S | Southold | 75-N non-signer |

| | | | |
|---|---|---|---|
| Gardner, Thos. | N | New York | 74-A |
| Gareson, Mary | N | removed upstate | 76-P |
| Garit, Michal | N | New York | 76-L |
| Garland, ____ Mrs., ae 87 | N | New York | 74-T midwife |
| Garnier, Isaac | N | New York | 74-A |
| Garrabrance, Peter | N | New York | 74-A |
| Garrabrance, Peter Jr. | N | New York | 75-D1 |
| Garrabrance, Peter Jr. | N | New York | 76-A |
| Garrabrance, Peter, turner | N | John Street | 75-D2 |
| Garrabrants, Petter | N | New York | 74-A |
| Garrebrants, ____ widow | N | removed upstate | 76-P |
| Garret, Cath. wf of Daniel | N | New York | 74-R |
| Garret, Magnis | N | New York | 76-I |
| Garrison, Benjamin | N | New York | 74-A; 75-R juror |
| Garrison, Samuel, carpenter | N | William Street | 75-D2 |
| Garrison, see also Gerritsen | | | |
| Garrot, Benjaman | S | Brookhaven | 76:0.1.2.1.1 |
| Garson, Peter, shopkeeper | N | Broadway | 75-D2 |
| Garten, Frederick Bonn | N | New York | 76-A |
| Gaskin, Matthew | N | New York | 76-A |
| Gasley, Henry | N | removed upstate | 76-P |
| Gasner, John | N | New York | 76-L |
| Gass, Andreas | N | New York | 74-A |
| Gassner, John | N | New York | 74-A |
| Gates, William | S | Huntington | 75-H |
| Gates, William | S | Huntington | 76-H3 |
| Gatfield, Archibald | N | New York | 76-A, 76-I |
| Gatfield, Benjamin | N | New York | 76-A |
| Gatfield, Rachel | N | New York | 76-V |
| Gaub, Nicholaus | N | New York | 76-A |
| Gauchay, Andrew | N | New York | 75-D3 |
| Gault, Robert | N | New York | 74-A |
| Gautier, Andrew | N | New York | 76-A |
| Gautier, Andrew Esq. | N | New York | 75-T2, 2/23 |
| Gautier, Andrew, Judge | N | New York | 74-R to 76-R |
| Gautier, Lewis | N | New York | 76-I |
| Gavett, John | S | Easthampton | 76:0.1.1.1.0 |
| Gay, Charles | N | New York | 74-A |
| Gay, Robert | N | The Bowery | 75-T2, 3/23 |
| Gayler, see Galer, Geler | | | |

| | | | |
|---|---|---|---|
| Geffers, John | N | removed upstate | 76-P |
| Geffrey, James | N | New York | 74-A |
| Geler, David | N | New York | 76-A |
| Gelston, David | S | Southampton | 75-M |
| Gelston, David Esq. | S | Southampton | 76:0.1.1.1.1.2.2 |
| Gelston, Hugh | S | Southampton | 76:0.1.0.1.1 |
| Gelston, Hugh 3d | S | ........ | 75-R |
| Gelston, John | S | ........ | 75-R |
| Gelston, John | S | Southampton | 76:0.1.0.1.1 |
| Gelston, John, hse carpenter | N | Division Street | 75-D2 |
| Gelston, Maltby | S | Southampton | 75-M |
| Gelston, Maltby Esqʳ | S | Southampton | 76:1.1.0.3.1.1.0 |
| Gelston, Thomas | S | Southampton | 75-M |
| Gelston, Thomas | S | Southampton | 76:0.1.0.1.1 |
| Gelston, William | S | Southampton | 75-M |
| Gemble, Munya | N | removed upstate | 76-P |
| Genevele, Samuel, taylor | N | at Mr. Cocks | 75-D2 |
| Gerard, Benjamin | S | Brookhaven | 75-B7 |
| Gerard, Francois | N | New York | 76-A |
| Gerard, Nathaniel | S | Brookhaven | 76:1.0.0.2.1 |
| Gerard, Zophar | S | Brookhaven | 76:0.1.3.1.2 |
| Germand, William | N | New York | 75-R apprentice |
| Germond/Garmond, William | N | Ferry st., cooper | 75-D1, D2 |
| Gerow, Dan'l | N | New York | 75-D2 |
| Gerrard, Azel | S | Brookhaven | 76:0.1.3.1.3 |
| Gerrard, Benjamin | S | Brookhaven | 75-B1 |
| Gerrard, Benjamin | S | Smithtown | 75-L |
| Gerrard, Elias | S | Smithtown | 75-L |
| Gerrard, Isaac | S | Smithtown | 76:1.4.0.2.1 |
| Gerrard, John | S | Smithtown | 75-L |
| Gerrard, Joseph | S | Brookhaven | 75-B1, 75-B7 |
| Gerrard, Joseph | S | Brookhaven | 76:1.1.2.1.1.0.1 |
| Gerrard, Nathanael | S | Smithtown | 75-L |
| Gerrard, Nathˡ | S | Smithtown | 76:0.2.3.1.3 |
| Gerrard, William | S | Smithtown | 75-L |
| Gerrard, William Jr. | S | Brookhaven | 75-B1, 75-B7 |
| Gerrard, Wᵐ | S | Brookhaven | 76:0.1.1.2.6 |
| Gerrard, Zophar | S | Brookhaven | 75-B1 n.s. |
| Gerrard, Zopher | S | Brookhaven | 75-B7 |
| Gerritsen, Samuel | N | New York | 74-A, 75-D1 |

Gerritsen, see also Garrison

| | | | |
|---|---|---|---|
| Gibbons, —— Mr. | N | rem to Ulster Co. | 76-P |
| Gibbons, —— Mrs. | N | removed upstate | 76-P |
| Gibbons, Richard | N | New York | 74-R |
| Gibbs, Joseph | S | Southampton | 76:1.1.0.2.1 |
| Giffing, William | N | New York | 74-T, 76-A |
| Gilbert, Aaron | N | New York | 74-A, 76-N |
| Gilbert, Aaron, juror | N | New York | 74-R, 75-R |
| Gilbert, Eliner | S | Brookhaven | 76:0.1.1.1.0 |
| Gilbert, Elmer | S | Brookhaven | 75-B6 |
| Gilbert, John | N | New York | 74-A, 76-N |
| Gilbert, John | N | Queen Street | 75-D2 |
| Gilbert, ---- Lieut. | N | New York | 76-C |
| Gilbert, Thaddeus | S | Brookhaven | 75-B6 |
| Gilbert, William | N | New York | 74-A |
| Gilbert, William Jr. | N | New York | 74-A |
| Gilbert, William, juror | N | New York | 75-R, 76-R |
| Gilbert, William W. | N | New York | 74-A, 75-B |
| Gilbert, William W. | N | New York | 74-T2, 11/24 |
| Gilbert, Yellis | N | New York | 75-D3 |
| Gilburd, Samul | S | Meritches | 76:0.1.3.1.2 |
| Gilchrist, Adam | N | New York | 74-A |
| Gilchrist, Adam, juror | N | New York | 74-R, 75-R |
| Gildersleeve, Benjamin | S | Huntington | 75-H |
| Gildersleeve, Finch | S | Huntington | 75-H |
| Gildersleeve, John | S | Huntington | 75-H |
| Gildersleeve, Jonathan | Q | ........ | 75-A, 76-E |
| Gildersleeve, Obadiah | S | ........ | 75-R |
| Gildersleeve, Obadiah | S | Southampton | 76:0.3.2.3.1 |
| Gildersleeve, Philip | S | ........ | 75-R |
| Gildersleeve, Richard | Q | ........ | 75-E |
| Gildersleeve, Richard | Q | ........ | 76-B, 76-E |
| Gildersleeve, Stephen | S | Huntington | 75-H, 75-H1 |
| Gildersleeve, Whitehead | S | Huntington | 75-H |
| Gildersleve, John | S | Huntington | 76-H3 |
| Gildert, Leonard, | N | New York | 76-A |
| Giles, Gilbert | N | New York | 74-A, 76-G |
| Giles, Gilbert Jr. | N | New York | 76-G |
| Gillas, William | N | New York | 76-I |
| Gillespie, Thomas | N | New York | 76-A |

| | | | |
|---|---|---|---|
| Gillespy, John | N | New York | 76-N |
| Gillet, Paul | S | Smithtown | 75-L |
| Gillett, see Jillett | | | |
| Gillihen, James | N | New York | 74-A |
| Gillilan, John | N | New York | 76-L |
| Gilliland, James | N | New York | 74-A, 75-D1 |
| Gilliland, James, school | N | Broad Street | 75-T2, 1/5 |
| Gilliland, John | N | New York | 74-R |
| Gilliland, see also Gallalant; Gyllylen | | | |
| Ginavelay, Sam¹ | N | New York | 75-D3 |
| Giraud, Peter | N | New York | 74-A |
| Gladden, George | S | Easthampton | 75-E |
| Glass, Ann, midwife | N | Elbow Street | 74-T |
| Gleam, James | N | New York | 75-D3 |
| Glean, Anthony | N | New York | 74-A, 76-N |
| Glean, Anthony, son of Jas. | N | Ship Yards | 75-D1, D2 |
| Glean, James | N | New York | 74-A |
| Glean, Oliver | N | New York | 76-N |
| Glean, Oliver, clark | N | New York | 75-D1, D2 |
| Glean, Wm | Q | ........ | 75-A associator |
| Glean, Wm | Q | ........ | 76-E |
| Glebets, Richard | N | New York | 76-A |
| Glover, David | S | Southold | 75-N |
| Glover, Ezekial | S | ........ | 75-R |
| Glover, Ezekiel | S | Southold | 76:1.1.1.1.1 |
| Glover, Ezekiel Jr. | S | ........ | 75-R |
| Glover, Grover | S | ........ | 75-R |
| Glover, Grover | S | Southold | 76:1.1.1.1.0.2.4 |
| Glover, Hezekel | S | ........ | 75-R |
| Glover, James | S | Southold | 75-N |
| Glover, John | N | New York | 74-A, 76-A |
| Glover, Samuel | S | Southold | 75-N |
| Gobert, Peter | N | to Westchester Co | 76-P |
| Goddington, William | N | New York | 76-A |
| Godley, William | N | New York | 74-A |
| Godwin, William | N | New York | 75-D1 |
| Goelet, Peter | N | New York | 74-A |
| Goelet, Peter | N | New York | 75-T2, 5/4 |
| Goelet, Peter, merchant | N | New York | 74-T, 76-V |
| Goforth, William | N | New York | 74-A, 76-N |

| | | | |
|---|---|---|---|
| Goforth, William | N | New York | 74-R juror |
| Goforth, William | N | New York | 74-T2, 11/24 |
| Goforth, William, Capt. | N | New York | 75-E |
| Goforth, Wm., cordwainer | N | New York | 76-R |
| Gold, David | S | Brookhaven | 75-B11 n.s. |
| Gold, John | S | ........ | 75-R |
| Golden, Elizabeth | N | to Dutchess Co. | 76-P |
| Golden, Jno. | Q | ........ | 75-A |
| Golden, Joseph | Q | Jamaica | 75-C |
| Golden, William | Q | Jamaica | 75-D |
| Golden, Wm | Q | ........ | 75-A |
| Golder, Garret | Q | ........ | 75-A, 76-E |
| Golder, Jacob | Q | ........ | 76-B |
| Golder, James | Q | ........ | 75-A |
| Golder, Joseph | Q | ........ | [2 on] 76-B |
| Golder, Joseph | Q | Jamaica | 75-D, 75-E |
| Golder, Michael | Q | ........ | 75-A, 76-B |
| Golder, William | Q | ........ | 75-A, 76-E |
| Golder, William | Q | ........ | [2 on] 76-B |
| Goldin, Thorn | Q | ........ | 76-E |
| Golding, John | Q | ........ | 76-E |
| Goldsmith, Benjamin | S | Brookhaven | 75-B10 |
| Goldsmith, Benjamin | S | Southold | 76:0.2.2.3.2.1.0 |
| Goldsmith, ---- Capt. | S | Southold | 75-N |
| Goldsmith, Dan'l, Constable | N | New York | 75-D1, D2 |
| Goldsmith, Daniel | N | New York | 74-R to 76-R |
| Goldsmith, David | S | Brookhaven | 75-B10 |
| Goldsmith, David | S | Southold | 76:0.2.4.1.3 |
| Goldsmith, Jeremiah | N | New York | 74-R |
| Goldsmith, Jeremiah | N | New York | 75-D1 |
| Goldsmith, Jeremiah, joiner | N | Batteau Street | 75-D1, D2 |
| Goldsmith, John | S | ........ | 75-R |
| Goldsmith, John | S | Brookhaven | 75-B10 |
| Goldsmith, John | S | Southold | 76:1.0.0.2.1.0.1 |
| Goldsmith, John Junior | S | ........ | 75-R |
| Goldsmith, John Jun^r | S | Southold | 76:0.2.3.2.4 |
| Goldsmith, Jos. | S | ........ | 75-R |
| Goldsmith, Joseph | S | Southampton | 76:0.1.1.2.2 |
| Goldsmith, Joshua | S | Brookhaven | 75-B10 |
| Goldsmith, Joshua | S | Southold | 76:0.1.4.1.4 |

| | | | |
|---|---|---|---|
| Goldsmith, Joshua | S | Southold | 76:0.2.1.2.1 |
| Goldsmith, Joshua Jr. | S | Brookhaven | 75-B10 |
| Goldsmith, Nathan | S | Brookhaven | 75-B10 |
| Goldsmith, Nathan | S | Southold | 76:0.1.2.3.0 |
| Goldsmith, Nathaniel | S | ........ | 75-R |
| Goldsmith, Nath[l] | S | Southold | 76:0.2.2.2.2 |
| Goldsmith, Thomas | S | Southold | 76:1.1.1.2.2 |
| Goldsmith, ____ Wid. | S | Southold | 76:0.0.1.2.0 |
| Goldsmith, Willmot | S | Southold | 76:0.1.2.1.1 |
| Goldsmith, Wilmot | S | Southold | 75-N |
| Goldsmith, Zacheus | S | Southold | 76:1.0.0.1.0.2.0 |
| Gomez, Ab[m] | N | New York | 76-A |
| Gomez, Daniel | N | New York | 74-A |
| Gomez, Mattathias | N | New York | 74-A |
| Gomez, Mattathias, storekpr | N | Queen Street | 74-T2, 3/3 |
| Gomez, Moses | N | New York | 74-A |
| Gomez, Moses Jr. | N | New York | 74-A, 76-A |
| Gominell, James | N | New York | 74-A |
| Goodale, Joseph | S | ........ | 75-R |
| Goodberlat, John | N | New York | 74-A |
| Goodeerlet, John, taylor | N | Broadway | 74-T2, 11/24 |
| Goodel, Joseph | S | Southampton | 76:0.1.4.1.2 |
| Goodel, Josiah | S | Southampton | 76:1.2.0.2.1 |
| Goodman, Peter | N | New York | 76-A |
| Goodwely, Joseph | N | New York | 74-A |
| Goodwin, Joseph | N | New York | 74-A, 75-C |
| Goold, Edward, merchant | N | New York | 74-T, 74-V |
| Goold, Patrick | S | Easthampton | 75-E |
| Goold, Patrick | S | Easthampton | 76:0.1.0.1.0 |
| Gorbett, Peter | N | to Westchester Co | 76-P |
| Gorden, Elisabeth | N | removed upstate | 76-P |
| Gorden, Lieus | S | Brookhaven | 76:0.1.2.1.1 |
| Gordon, George | N | Maiden Lane | 74-T |
| Gordon, Ruth | N | removed upstate | 76-P |
| Gorham, Jonathan | Q | ........ | 75-A |
| Gorham, Jonathan | Q | ........ | 76-B, 76-E |
| Gorsline, John | Q | ........ | 76-E |
| Gorsline, Joseph | Q | ........ | 76-E |
| Gorsling, Jacob | Q | ........ | 76-E |
| Gosline, Jas. | Q | Newtown | 75-G |

| | | | |
|---|---|---|---|
| Gosline, John | Q | Newtown | 75-G |
| Gotterton, James | N | to Westchester Co | 76-P |
| Gouer, Erfie | N | New York | 74-A |
| Gould, Benjamin | S | Smithtown | 76:1.0.3.3.3 |
| Gould, Ebenezer | S | Huntington | 75-H |
| Gould, John | S | Huntington | 75-H |
| Gould, Joseph Jun′ | S | Smithtown | 75-L recusant |
| Gould, Joseph Jun′ | S | Smithtown | 76:0.1.0.1.1 |
| Gould, Joseph Sen′ | S | Smithtown | 76:1.1.3.2.1 |
| Gould, Samuel | S | Brookhaven | 76:1.0.0.2.0 |
| Goulden, Benjamin | N | removed upstate | 76-P |
| Gouldsbury, Joseph | N | Chapel Street | 74-T |
| Gounzer, Ludwig | N | New York | 76-A |
| Gouverneur, Abrah. N. | N | New York | 74-A |
| Gouverneur, Abraham | N | New York | 76-A |
| Gouverneur, Isaac | N | New York | 74-A |
| Govers, James | N | New York | 74-A, 76-A |
| Graff, Peter | N | New York | 76-A |
| Graham, Catharine | N | to Dutchess Co. | 76-P |
| Graham, Cathrin | N | rem. to Bedford | 76-J |
| Graham, Elienor | N | rem. to Bedford | 76-J |
| Graham, Ellinor | N | to Dutchess Co. | 76-P |
| Graham, Ennis | N | New York | 74-A |
| Graham, Ennis, juror | N | New York | 75-R, 76-R |
| Graham, Ennis, taylor | N | Wall Street | 74-T2, 4/28 |
| Graham, Esther, Mrs. | N | rem to Ulster Co. | 76-P |
| Graham, George | N | New York | 76-N |
| Graham, John | N | New York | 75-T |
| Graham, John | N | removed upstate | 76-P |
| Graham, Phebe, Mrs. | N | rem to Ulster Co. | 76-P |
| Graham, Thomas | N | rem. to Bedford | 76-J |
| Graham, Thomas | N | to Dutchess Co. | 76-P |
| Graham, _____ widow | N | to Dutchess Co. | 76-P |
| Graham, William | N | removed upstate | 76-P |
| Grant & Fine | N | New York | 74-A |
| Grant, Edward | N | New York | 76-A |
| Grant, Hannah | N | New York | 76-K |
| Grant, Jacob | N | New York | 74-A |
| Grant, John | Q | Jamaica | 75-C |
| Grant, John, apprentice | N | New York | 75-R |

| Grant, John [2] | N | New York | [on] 76-A |
|---|---|---|---|
| Grant, Mary | N | removed upstate | 76-P |
| Graves, Thomas | N | New York | 76-A |
| Gray, Andrew | N | New York | 76-A |
| Gray, Ann | N | removed upstate | 76-P |
| Gray, David | S | Brookhaven | 75-B11 n.s. |
| Gray, Hugh | N | New York | 74-A |
| Gray, John | N | New York | 74-A, 76-A |
| Gray, Wm | N | New York | 76-A |
| Greatoak, Jno. | Q | ........ | 75-A |
| Green, Ann | N | New York | 74-R, 75-R |
| Green, Ann | N | removed upstate | 76-P |
| Green, Daniel | N | New York | 76-N |
| Green, Daniel, shoemaker | N | Fly Market | 75-D2 |
| Green, Daniel, shoemaker | N | New York | 76-V |
| Green, Edward, shoemaker | N | Broadway | 75-D2 |
| Green, James, taylor | N | Beekman's Slip | 75-D2 |
| Green, John | S | Islip | 76:0.1.1.1.1 |
| Green, Morris | Q | ........ | 76-E |
| Green, _____ Mrs. | N | removed upstate | 76-P |
| Green, Obediah | S | Islip | 75-I Quaker |
| Green, Obediah | S | Islip | 76:1.0.1.2.0 |
| Green, Paul | N | New York | 74-R |
| Green, Richard | Q | ........ | 75-A |
| Green, Richard | Q | ........ | 76-B, 76-E |
| Green, Samuel | Q | ........ | 75-A, 76-E |
| Green, William | N | New York | 76-M |
| Green, William, books | N | New York | 75-T2, 4/13 |
| Greenoak, John | Q | ........ | 76-E |
| Greenoak, John Jr. | Q | ........ | 76-E |
| Gregg, David | N | New York | 74-A, 76-A |
| Gremmel, James | N | New York | 76-I |
| Grenell, John | S | Huntington | 75-H |
| Gressand, Ican George | N | New York | 76-A |
| Grierson, John | N | New York | 76-A |
| Grifdall, Thos. | N | New York | 74-A |
| Griffen, Joseph | Q | ........ | 76-E |
| Griffin, Jacob | Q | ........ | 76-E |
| Griffin, Jeremiah | N | New York | 74-A, 75-D1 |
| Griffin, Jno., carpenter | N | liv. w/Bloodgood | 75-D2 |

| | | | |
|---|---|---|---|
| Griffing, Daniel | S | Southold | 76:0.1.4.3.0 |
| Griffing, Daniel [2] | S | ........ | [on] 75-R |
| Griffing, James | S | ........ | 75-R |
| Griffing, James | S | Brookhaven | 75-B10 |
| Griffing, James | S | Southold | 76:0.1.2.1.2 |
| Griffing, James | S | Southold | 76:0.1.4.1.3 |
| Griffing, John | S | Brookhaven | 75-B10 |
| Griffing, John | S | Southold | 76:1.3.3.3.1 |
| Griffing, John Jr. | S | Brookhaven | 75-B10 |
| Griffing, Joseph | S | Brookhaven | 75-B10 |
| Griffing, Nathaniel | S | Brookhaven | 75-B10 |
| Griffing, Peter | S | ........ | 75-R |
| Griffing, Peter | S | Southold | 76:0.1.3.1.2 |
| Griffing, Samuel | S | Southold | 76:1.0.2.3.0 |
| Griffing, Samuel [2] | S | ........ | [on] 75-R |
| Griffing, Stephen | S | Brookhaven | 75-B10 |
| Griffis, James | S | Huntington | 76-H3 |
| Griffis, Sarah | N | to Westchester Co | 76-P |
| Griffis, Susanah | N | to Westchester Co | 76-P |
| Griffith, Benj. | N | New York | 74-A, 76-D |
| Griffith, Elisabeth | N | removed upstate | 76-P |
| Griffith, Robert | N | New York | 76-A |
| Griffiths, Anthony | N | New York | 74-R juror |
| Griffiths, Benjamin, Corp'l | N | New York | 75-D3 |
| Grifintz, John | N | New York | 75-D1 |
| Grigg, David | N | New York | 76-I |
| Grigg, Henry | N | in the Slote | 76-H |
| Grigg, John | N | New York | 76-A |
| Grigg, John | N | Sloat Alley | 76-I |
| Grigg, John, 1st Lieut. | N | New York | 76-Y |
| Grigg, Thomas | N | New York | 74-A, 76-A |
| Grigg, William | N | New York | 74-A |
| Grigg, William, Ensign | N | New York | 76-Y |
| Grim, David | N | New York | 74-A |
| Grim, David | N | New York | 76-A, 76-I |
| Grim, George, taylor | N | Fair Street | 75-D2 |
| Grim, Jacob | N | New York | 76-A |
| Grim, Peter | N | New York | 74-A, 76-A |
| Grim, Peter, 2d Lieut. | N | New York | 76-Y |
| Grim, Peter Jr. | N | New York | 75-B |

| | | | |
|---|---|---|---|
| Grimesly, Charles | N | New York | 74-A, 76-A |
| Grimsley, Char's | N | New York | 75-D1 |
| Grimsley, Charles, shoemkr | N | Broadway | 75-D1, D2 |
| Grindlemyer, Jacob | N | New York | 76-A |
| Grisdall, Thomas | N | New York | 76-A |
| Gritman, William | Q | ........ | 75-A, |
| Gritman, William | Q | ........ | 76-B2, 76-E |
| Groen, Silvester Mar. | N | New York | 74-A |
| Grommel, James | N | New York | 74-R juror |
| Groome, Francis | N | New York | 76-F |
| Grover, Eliakim | S | ........ | 75-R |
| Grub, Nicholas | N | New York | 74-A |
| Grumly, John | N | New York | 74-T, 74-V |
| Guest, John | N | New York | 74-T insolvent |
| Guest, William, blacksmith | N | Maiden Lane | 75-D1, D2 |
| Guion, Isaac | N | New York | 75-D2 |
| Gulick, Hendrick | N | New York | 76-A |
| Gulliver, Charles | Q | ........ | 76-E |
| Gumersall, Tho. | N | New York | 74-A |
| Gunn, George | N | removed upstate | 76-P |
| Gutrey, John | N | removed upstate | 76-P |
| Gutrey, Samuel | N | removed upstate | 76-P |
| Guyer, Luke | N | New York | 74-A |
| Gyer, Nathan | S | Brookhaven | 76:0.2.0.2.2 |
| Gyllylen, Wm., Sergt. | N | New York | 75-D3 |
| Haas, Frederick | N | New York | 76-A |
| Haassis, George | N | New York | 76-A |
| Hackstaf, Ludiwick | S | Brookhaven | 76:1.0.0.1.0 |
| Hackstaff, Luddewick | S | Brookhaven | 75-B10 |
| Hackstaff, Ludewick | S | Brookhaven | 75-B11 n.s. |
| Hackstaff, Ludewick Junior | S | Brookhaven | 75-B10 |
| Hacstaff, Ludewick | S | Brookhaven | 75-B11 n.s. |
| Hadden, Abram Smith | N | New York | 76-N |
| Haerlman, Mathias | N | New York | 76-A |
| Haff, Isaac | S | Huntington | 76-H3 |
| Haff, James | S | Huntington | 76-H3 |
| Haff, John | S | Huntington | 75-H |
| Haff, Simeon | S | Huntington | 75-H |
| Hagat, Joseph | N | New York | 74-A |
| Hageman, see Hegeman | | | |

| | | | |
|---|---|---|---|
| Hagner, Hendrick | Q | ........ | 75-A |
| Haight, Jacob | N | New York | 74-A |
| Haight, Thom[s] | S | Huntington | 75-H |
| Haines, Nathain | S | ........ | 75-R |
| Haines, Nathan | S | ........ | 75-R |
| Haines, Nathan | S | Southold | 76:1.1.1.1.1 |
| Hains, Daniel | S | Southampton | 75-M |
| Hains, Daniel | S | Southampton | 76:0.1.3.1.2.1.0 |
| Hains, David | S | ........ | 75-R |
| Hains, David | S | Southampton | 76:0.1.1.1.0 |
| Hains, Henry | N | to Westchester Co | 76-P |
| Hains, James, Dea[n] | S | Southampton | 76:1.0.0.1.0 |
| Hains, James Jun[r] | S | Southampton | 76:0.1.2.3.5 |
| Hains, James [2] | S | ........ | [on] 75-R |
| Hains, Samuel | S | ........ | 75-R |
| Hains, Samuel | S | Southampton | 76:0.1.2.1.0.1.0 |
| Hake, Samuel, merchant | N | New York | 74-T |
| Haldan, John | N | New York | 74-A, 76-A |
| Halden, James | N | New York | 76-F |
| Hall, Daniel | Q | ........ | 75-A, 76-E |
| Hall, Edward | N | New York | 76-A |
| Hall, Henry | N | New York | 74-A, 76-A |
| Hall, Henry, cordwainer | N | Chapel Street | 75-D1, D2 |
| Hall, John | Q | ........ | 75-A, 76-E |
| Hall, John Jr. | Q | ........ | 76-E |
| Hall, Joseph | Q | ........ | 76-E |
| Hall, Joseph | Q | ........ | [2 on] 75-A |
| Hall, Joseph | Q | ........ | [2 on] 76-B |
| Hall, Joseph Jr. | Q | ........ | 76-B |
| Hall, ____ Mrs. | N | removed upstate | 76-P |
| Hall, Peter | N | New York | 74-A, 74-V |
| Hall, Peter | N | New York | 76-A, 76-I |
| Hall, Robert | Q | ........ | 76-E |
| Hall, Rubin | Q | ........ | 75-A |
| Hall, William | Q | ........ | 75-A |
| Hall, William | Q | ........ | 76-B, 76-E |
| Hall, Wm. Reuben | Q | ........ | 76-E |
| Hallack, Daniel | S | Brookhaven | 76:1.1.3.1.1 |
| Halleck, Zebulon | S | ........ | 75-R |
| Halled, Thos | Q | ........ | 75-A |

| | | | |
|---|---|---|---|
| Halled; see also Hollowed | | | |
| Hallet, James | N | New York | 76-L |
| Hallet, Joseph | N | Hanover Square | 76-V |
| Hallet, Joseph | N | New York | 74-T2, 11/24 |
| Hallett, David | Q | ........ | 76-E |
| Hallett, George | Q | ........ | 76-E |
| Hallett, Jacob Jr. | Q | ........ | 76-E |
| Hallett, Jacob Jr. | Q | Newtown | 75-G |
| Hallett, James | N | New York | 74-A, 76-A |
| Hallett, James | Q | ........ | 75-A, 76-E |
| Hallett, James | Q | Newtown | 75-B |
| Hallett, Jonah | Q | ........ | 75-A associator |
| Hallett, Richard | Q | ........ | 75-A, 76-E |
| Hallett, Richard, | Q | Newtown | 75-B |
| Hallett, Sam'l, Capt. | Q | ........ | 75-A |
| Hallett, Samuel | N | New York | 74-A, 76-A |
| Hallett, Samuel | Q | Newtown | 75-G |
| Hallett, Samuel, Capt. | Q | Newtown | 75-H |
| Hallett, Thomas | Q | ........ | 76-B, 76-E |
| Hallett, W. | Q | ........ | [2 on] 76-E |
| Hallett, W., Jr. | Q | Newtown | 75-B |
| Halliock, Daniel | S | Brookhaven | 75-B10 |
| Halliock, James | S | Brookhaven | 75-B10 |
| Halliock, Richard | S | Brookhaven | 75-B10 |
| Halliock, William | S | Brookhaven | 75-B10 |
| Halliock, Zacharias | S | Brookhaven | 75-B10 |
| Halliock, Zerubbabel | S | Brookhaven | 75-B10 |
| Halliock, Zerubbabel Jr. | S | Brookhaven | 75-B10 |
| Halliok, Israel | S | Southold | 76:0.3.4.2.1 |
| Halliok, John | S | Southold | 76:1.0.2.3.4 |
| Halliok, Joseph | S | Southold | 76:0.1.5.2.2 |
| Halliok, Peter | S | Southold | 76:1.3.2.3.2.1.3 |
| Halliok, Richard | S | Southold | 76:0.1.2.1.1 |
| Halliok, --- Wid. | S | Southold | 76:0.0.4.1.3 |
| Halliok, William | S | Southold | 76:0.2.2.1.2.0.1 |
| Halliok, Zebolon | S | Southold | 76:0.1.2.3.3 |
| Halliok, Zebulon | S | Southold | 76:1.1.1.2.0 |
| Halliok, Zerobabell Jun' | S | Southold | 76:0.1.3.1.1 |
| Halliok, Zerobbabell | S | Southold | 76:1.2.0.2.4.0.1 |
| Hallit, Francis | S | Brookhaven | 75-B1, 75-B7 |

| | | | |
|---|---|---|---|
| Hallock, Caleb | S | Brookhaven | 75-B10 |
| Hallock, ---- Capt. | S | Southold | 75-N |
| Hallock, David | S | Brookhaven | 75-B11 n.s. |
| Hallock, David | S | Brookhaven | 75-B6 |
| Hallock, David | S | Meritches | 76:0.1.1.3.6.1.0 |
| Hallock, Henry | S | Brookhaven | 75-B11 n.s. |
| Hallock, Israel | S | Southold | 75-N |
| Hallock, John | S | ........ | 75-R |
| Hallock, John | S | ........ | 75-R |
| Hallock, Jonathan | S | Brookhaven | 76:1.2.1.2.2 |
| Hallock, Jonathan Juner | S | Brookhaven | 75-B11 n.s. |
| Hallock, Joseph [2] | S | ........ | [on] 75-R |
| Hallock, Josiah | S | Brookhaven | 75-B2 |
| Hallock, Josiah, & Davis | S | Brookhaven | 76:0.2.2.2.2 |
| Hallock, Noah | S | Brookhaven | 76:0.2.3.2.2.1.4 |
| Hallock, Noah Jr. | S | Brookhaven | 75-B2 |
| Hallock, Noah, Sgt. | S | Brookhaven | 75-B2 |
| Hallock, Peter | S | Southold | 75-N not at home |
| Hallock, Peter Jun[r] | S | Southold | 75-N |
| Hallock, Petter Juner | S | Brookhaven | 75-B10 |
| Hallock, Richard, Quaker | S | Brookhaven | 75-B11 n.s. |
| Hallock, Robt. | N | New York | 74-A |
| Hallock, Thomas | N | New York | 74-A |
| Hallock, Thomas | N | New York | 74-R juror |
| Hallock, William | S | ........ | 75-R |
| Hallock, William | S | Southampton | 76:0.1.2.1.0 |
| Hallock, Zebulon | S | ........ | 75-R |
| Hallock, Zebulon | S | Southold | 75-N |
| Hallok, Richard | S | Brookhaven | 76:1.1.1.2.4.0.1 |
| Hallot, Franses | S | Brookhaven | 76:1.0.1.1.2 |
| Halloway, Sarah | N | New York | 76-K |
| Hallsey, David | S | Southampton | 76:0.1.3.1.6.1.0 |
| Hallsey, Elias | S | Southampton | 76:0.1.2.1.1 |
| Hallsey, Hanah, widow | S | Southampton | 76:0.2.0.2.1 |
| Hallsey, Hanah, widow | S | Southampton | 76:0.3.0.4.1 |
| Hallsey, Henry | S | Southampton | 76:0.1.0.1.0 |
| Hallsey, Isaiah | S | ........ | 75-R |
| Hallsey, Jeremiah | S | Southampton | 76:0.1.3.1.3.1.0 |
| Hallsey, John | S | ........ | 75-R |
| Hallsey, John | S | Southampton | 76:0.1.0.1.0.0.1 |

| | | | |
|---|---|---|---|
| Hallsey, Jonathan | S | ........ | 75-R |
| Hallsey, Joshua | S | ........ | 75-R |
| Hallsey, Josiah | S | Southampton | 76:0.1.3.1.1.1.1 |
| Hallsey, Lemuel | S | ........ | 75-R |
| Hallsey, Mary, Wid[w] | S | Southampton | 76:0.1.2.2.2 |
| Hallsey, Matthew | S | Southampton | 76:1.2.5.4.3 |
| Hallsey, Moses Jun. | S | ........ | 75-R |
| Hallsey, Paul | S | ........ | 75-R |
| Hallsey, Paul | S | Southampton | 76:0.1.2.1.3.0.1 |
| Hallsey, Phebe, Widow | S | Southampton | 76:0.1.1.3.0 |
| Hallsey, Silas | S | ........ | 75-R |
| Hallsey, Stephen | S | ........ | 75-R |
| Hallsey, Stephen | S | Southampton | 76:0.2.2.3.2 |
| Hallsey, Stephen, Doctor | S | Southampton | 76:0.1.2.1.4 |
| Hallsey, Theophilus | S | Southampton | 76:0.1.0.1.2 |
| Hallsey, Timothy | S | Southampton | 76:0.3.4.3.1.0.1 |
| Hallsey, Wilmur | S | Southampton | 76:0.1.0.1.1.0.2 |
| Hallsey, Zeb. Jun[r] | S | ........ | 75-R |
| Halsey, Abraham | S | Southampton | 75-M |
| Halsey, Cornelius | S | Southampton | 76:1.2.3.4.3.0.1 |
| Halsey, Daniel | S | Southampton | 75-M |
| Halsey, David Fithian | S | ........ | 75-R |
| Halsey, Elisha | S | ........ | 75-R |
| Halsey, Elisha | S | Southampton | 76:0.1.0.3.0 |
| Halsey, Ethan | S | ........ | 75-R |
| Halsey, Hannah, widow | S | Southampton | 76:0.1.0.3.0 |
| Halsey, Henry | S | ........ | 75-R |
| Halsey, Isaac | S | Southampton | 76:0.1.0.1.1 |
| Halsey, Isaiah | S | Southampton | 76:0.1.0.0.0 |
| Halsey, James | S | Southampton | 76:0.1.0.1.1 |
| Halsey, Jeremiah | S | Southampton | 75-M |
| Halsey, Jesse, Lieut. | S | ........ | 75-R |
| Halsey, John | S | Southampton | 76:1.0.0.1.0.2.0 |
| Halsey, Jonah | S | Southampton | 76:1.1.1.2.3 |
| Halsey, Jonathan | S | Southampton | 76:0.2.5.1.3 |
| Halsey, Joshua | S | Southampton | 76:0.1.4.1.3 |
| Halsey, Josiah | S | ........ | 75-R |
| Halsey, Lemuel | S | Southampton | 76:0.1.1.1.3 |
| Halsey, Matthew [2] | S | Southampton | [on] 75-M |
| Halsey, Moses | S | Southampton | 76:0.1.2.1.2 |

| Halsey, Paul | S | Southampton | 75-M |
|---|---|---|---|
| Halsey, Samuel | S | Southampton | 76:1.1.1.2.1 |
| Halsey, Silas | S | ........ | 75-R |
| Halsey, Silas | S | Southampton | 76:1.1.0.1.1.1.2 |
| Halsey, Silas, Doc. | S | Southampton | 76:0.1.3.1.1 |
| Halsey, Silvanus | S | Southampton | 75-M |
| Halsey, Stephen Jun' | S | ........ | 75-R |
| Halsey, Stephen [2] | S | Southampton | [on] 75-M |
| Halsey, Theophilus | S | Southampton | 75-M |
| Halsey, Thomas | S | ........ | 75-R |
| Halsey, Timothy | S | Southampton | 75-M |
| Halsey, William Rogers | S | ........ | 75-R |
| Halsey, Willman | S | ........ | 75-R |
| Halsey, Zebulon | S | Southampton | 76:0.3.2.1.0.0.1 |
| Halstead, Chas. | N | New York | 75-D1 |
| Halstead, Christopher | N | carpntr, Wm St. | 75-D1, D2 |
| Halstead, Pearsean | N | New York | 74-A |
| Halstead, Pearson | N | Pearl Street | 74-T |
| Halsted, Daniel | N | New York | 76-A |
| Halsted, Elisabeth | N | removed upstate | 76-P |
| Halsted, Phebe | N | removed upstate | 76-P |
| Halsted. Pelsue & Halsted | N | New York | 76-I |
| Ham, Coenradt | N | New York | 74-R juror |
| Ham, Conrad W. | N | New York | 74-A |
| Ham, Conrad W., Lieut. | N | New York | 75-A |
| Ham, Edward | N | to Dutchess Co. | 76-P |
| Ham, _____ widow | N | to Dutchess Co. | 76-P |
| Hamersley, Andrew, sadlery | N | New York | 74-T2, 5/5 |
| Hamersly, Andrew | N | New York | 75-R juror |
| Hamilton, Archibald | Q | ........ | 75-A |
| Hamilton, Archibald, Capt. | Q | Flushing | 75-H |
| Hamilton, Henry, executed | N | New York | 74-T, 74-V |
| Hamilton, James | N | New York | 76-I |
| Hamilton, John | N | New York | 74-A |
| Hamilton, John | N | New York | 76-N |
| Hamilton, John [2] | N | New York | [on] 76-A |
| Hamilton, Lewis | N | New York | 74-A |
| Hamlet, Richard | N | New York | 74-R |
| Hammon, Henry | N | New York | 75-D1 |
| Hammond, Daniel | S | Brookhaven | 75-B9 |

| | | | |
|---|---|---|---|
| Hammond, Joshua | Q | ........ | 76-E |
| Hamon, Elisha H. & Overton | S | Brookhaven | 76:0.2.2.2.3 |
| Hampton, Jonathan | N | New York | 74-A |
| Hampton, Jonathan, lumber | N | Beekman Street | 74-T2, 12/22 |
| Hanagers, Adam | N | New York | 74-A |
| Hand, Abigail | S | Easthampton | 76:0.0.0.1.0 |
| Hand, Abraham | S | Easthampton | 75-E |
| Hand, Abraham | S | Easthampton | 76:0.1.2.1.1 |
| Hand, Asher | S | ........ | 75-R |
| Hand, Daniel | S | Easthampton | 75-E |
| Hand, David | S | ........ | 75-R |
| Hand, David | S | Southampton | 76:0.3.3.4.0.1.1 |
| Hand, Elias | S | Easthampton | 75-E |
| Hand, Elias | S | Easthampton | 76:0.1.1.2.0 |
| Hand, Experience, W[idow] | S | Easthampton | 76:0.0.2.2.3 |
| Hand, Ezekeil | S | Easthampton | 76:1.0.0.1.1 |
| Hand, Ezekiel | S | Easthampton | 75-E |
| Hand, Gideon | S | ........ | 75-R |
| Hand, Jacob | S | Easthampton | 76:1.2.3.3.3 |
| Hand, James | S | Easthampton | 75-E |
| Hand, James | S | Easthampton | 76:0.2.4.1.1 |
| Hand, Jeremiah | S | Easthampton | 75-E |
| Hand, Jeremiah | S | Easthampton | 76:0.1.0.1.0 |
| Hand, John | S | Easthampton | 76:0.3.4.2.3 |
| Hand, Joseph | S | ........ | 75-R |
| Hand, Nathan | S | Easthampton | 76:0.1.2.1.2 |
| Hand, Nathan | S | Shelter Island | 75-K |
| Hand, Nathaniel | S | Easthampton | 76:0.2.2.1.3 |
| Hand, Nath[ll] | S | Easthampton | 75-E |
| Handford, Joseph | N | New York | 76-M |
| Handforth, Joseph | N | New York | 76-A |
| Hands, Ezekiel | S | Brookhaven | 76:0.1.2.1.2 |
| Hangworth, Ab[m] | N | New York | 76-A |
| Haning, Jos. | N | New York | 75-D2 |
| Hanley, Edward | N | Murray's Street | 76-I |
| Hanley, Mathew | N | Barrack Street | 76-I |
| Hanley, Robert | S | ........ | 75-R |
| Hanna, Wil'm | Q | ........ | 76-A |
| Hanna, William | N | New York | 76-A |
| Hannah, Mary | N | New York | 74-R |

| | | | |
|---|---|---|---|
| Hanning, Jno., baker | N | Colledge | 75-D2 |
| Hanning, Joseph | N | New York | 75-D3 |
| Hanrahan, James | Q | ........ | 76-E |
| Hans, Gost. | N | New York | 76-A |
| Hansen, Mecil | N | New York | 76-A |
| Hanshee, Martin | N | New York | 76-A |
| Hanson, Robert | S | Brookhaven | 75-B6 |
| Harback, John | N | New York | 75-B |
| Harbell, Johannes | N | New York | 76-A |
| Hardenberg, Hen'k | Q | ........ | 76-E |
| Hardenberg, Rem | Q | ........ | 76-E |
| Hardenbergh, John | N | New York | 74-A, 76-A |
| Hardenbergh, Joh* | N | New York | 76-N |
| Hardenbroeck, Able | N | New York | 76-L |
| Hardenbroeck, Theop* | N | New York | 76-L |
| Hardenbroeck, William | N | New York | 76-L |
| Hardenbrook, Abel | N | New York | 74-A |
| Hardenbrook, Abel | N | New York | 75-R juror |
| Hardenbrook, Abel N. | N | New York | 74-A |
| Hardenbrook, Edw'd, Capt. | N | New York | 76-Y |
| Hardenbrook, Ger. | N | New York | 76-N |
| Hardenbrook, Wm | N | New York | 74-A |
| Hardin, Jacob | N | Frankfort Street | 74-T2, 12/22 |
| Hardinbergh, John | N | New York | 74-R juror |
| Harding, Jacob, butcher | N | Frankfort Street | 75-D2 |
| Harding, Robert | N | New York | 74-A |
| Hardley, David | N | New York | 76-A |
| Hardman, Lawrence | N | New York | 76-A, 76-R |
| Hare, Gilbert | Q | Oyster Bay | 75-F |
| Hare, Sam'l Jr. | Q | Oyster Bay | 75-E |
| Hare, Samuel Jr. | Q | ........ | 76-E |
| Hare, Samuel Sr. | Q | ....... | 76-E |
| Harley, Robert | S | Southold | 76:0.1.1.3.3 |
| Harley, Thom* | S | Shelter Island | 75-K |
| Harlow, Thomas | S | Shelter Island | 76:0.1.1.1.1. |
| Harnit, John | N | New York | 76-R |
| Harper, James | Q | ........ | 76-E |
| Harper, Robert | N | New York | 75-D1 |
| Harper, Robert, carpenter | N | Partition Street | 75-D1, D2 |
| Harrin, David | N | to Westchester Co | 76-P |

| | | | |
|---|---|---|---|
| Harring, David | N | rem. to Bedford | 76-J |
| Harris, Daniell | S | Southampton | 76:0.1.2.1.0 |
| Harris, George | S | Southampton | 76:0.1.1.2.2 |
| Harris, Hennery | S | Southampton | 76:1.0.0.1.0 |
| Harris, Hennery Jnr. | S | Southampton | 76:0.2.2.3.2 |
| Harris, John | N | New York | 74-A, 76-A |
| Harris, John | N | to Dutchess Co. | 76-P |
| Harris, John | S | ........ | 75-R |
| Harris, John | S | Southampton | 76:0.2.0.1.2 |
| Harris, Richard [2] | N | New York | [on] 76-A |
| Harris, Stephen | N | New York | 74-A |
| Harris, ____ widow | N | to Dutchess Co. | 76-P |
| Harrison, Jane, Mrs. | N | New York | 74-T |
| Harrison, Nath[l] | S | Huntington | 75-H |
| Harrison, Richard, attorney | N | New York | 74-T |
| Harrison, Thomas | N | New York | 76-A |
| Harrison, Thos., coachman | N | liv. w/Dr Jones | 75-D1, D2 |
| Harrison, Wm | N | New York | 74-A |
| Harsen, Garret, juror | N | New York | 74-R to 76-R |
| Harsen, George, Sergt. | N | New York | 76-C |
| Harsin, Aaron | N | New York | 75-D3 |
| Harsin, Arent, taylor | N | Princes Street | 75-D2 |
| Harsin, Garret | N | New York | 74-A |
| Harsin, George | N | New York | 74-A |
| Harsin; see also Horsen | | | |
| Hart, Andrew | S | Brookhaven | 75-B10 |
| Hart, Andrew | S | Southold | 76:0.1.1.2.3 |
| Hart, Charles | N | New York | 76-A |
| Hart, Cornelius | Q | ........ | 75-A, 76-B |
| Hart, John | S | Huntington | 75-H |
| Hart, John, Corp'l | S | Huntington | 76-H3 |
| Hart, Micah | S | Easthampton | 75-E |
| Hart, Nehemiah | S | Huntington | 76-H3 |
| Hart, Samuel | S | Huntington | 76-H2 |
| Hartley, Thomas, staymaker | N | New York | 74-T2, 4/21 |
| Hartly, Frederick | N | New York | 75-R |
| Hartman, George | N | New York | 76-A |
| Hartt, Daniel | S | Huntington | 75-H |
| Hartt, Joshua | S | Smithtown | 76:0.1.0.2.2.0.1 |
| Hartt, Micah | S | Huntington | 75-H |

| | | | |
|---|---|---|---|
| Hartt, Nehemiah | S | Huntington | 75-H |
| Hartt, Nehemiah Jr. | S | Huntington | 75-H |
| Hartt, Sam[l] | S | Huntington | 75-H |
| Hartwick, Lawrence | N | New York | 74-A |
| Hartwick, Lawrence | N | New York | 76-A, 76-L |
| Hartwick, Thomas, cooper | N | Dock Street | 75-D2 |
| Hartz, see Heartz | | | |
| Harve, ---- Wid. | S | Southold | 76:0.0.1.2.1 |
| Harvey, James | N | New York | 76-L |
| Harvey, Mary | N | New York | 75-R |
| Harway, James | N | New York | 74-A |
| Hatfield, _____ Mr. | N | rem to Ulster Co. | 76-P |
| Haucks, John | S | Easthampton | 76:1.1.1.2.1 |
| Haugewort, Leffert | Q | ........ | 76-E |
| Haus, Charles | N | New York | 76-A |
| Hause, Peletiah, cooper | N | New York | 75-R |
| Hautzman, Thomas | N | New York | 76-A |
| Haven, Nathanel | S | Brookhaven | 75-B6 |
| Haven, W[m] Lieut. | S | Southampton | 76:0.1.2.3.1 |
| Havens, Benj. | S | Brookhaven | 75-B6 |
| Havens, Benj. | S | Meritches | 76:1.2.2.2.1.2.1 |
| Havens, Constant | S | ........ | 75-R |
| Havens, Constant | S | Southampton | 76:0.1.5.2.2.1.0 |
| Havens, Daniel | S | Southampton | 76:0.1.2.1.0 |
| Havens, Ebenezer | S | Shelter Island | 75-K |
| Havens, George | S | Southampton | 76:1.2.1.2.1 |
| Havens, Hanery | S | Meritches | 76:1.1.1.2.2.1.0 |
| Havens, James | S | Shelter Island | 75-K |
| Havens, James | S | Shelter Island | 76:0.2.4.1.3 |
| Havens, Jeremiah | S | Southold | 75-N |
| Havens, John | S | Brookhaven | 76:1.0.0.1.2.1.0 |
| Havens, John | S | Meritches | 76:0.1.2.1.1 |
| Havens, John | S | Shelter Island | 75-K |
| Havens, John Jr. | S | Brookhaven | 75-B6 |
| Havens, John Jr. | S | Shelter Island | 75-K |
| Havens, John Jun[r] | S | Meritches | 76:0.1.2.1.4.0.1 |
| Havens, John, third | S | Brookhaven | 75-B6 |
| Havens, Jonathan | S | ........ | 75-R |
| Havens, Jonathan, Doc[r] | S | Southampton | 76:0.1.5.1.2.2.0 |
| Havens, Jonathan N. | S | Shelter Island | 75-K |

| | | | |
|---|---|---|---|
| Havens, Joseph | S | Shelter Island | 75-K |
| Havens, Joseph | S | Southampton | 76:0.1.3.0.1 |
| Havens, Joseph Jr. | S | Shelter Island | 75-K |
| Havens, Joseph Jur. | S | ........ | 75-R |
| Havens, Nathaniel | S | Brookhaven | 75-B6 |
| Havens, Nicoll | S | Shelter Island | 76:0.1.1.5.4.8.6 |
| Havens, Obadiah | S | Shelter Island | 75-K |
| Havens, Obediah | S | Shelter Island | 76:0.4.0.3.3.1.1 |
| Havens, Peter | S | Shelter Island | 75-K |
| Havens, Samuel | S | Southampton | 76:0.1.2.1.0 |
| Havens, Selah | S | Brookhaven | 75-B6 |
| Havens, Waller | S | Shelter Island | 75-K |
| Havens, Walter | S | Shelter Island | 76:0.1.2.1.2 |
| Havens, William | S | ........ | 75-R |
| Havens, William | S | Shelter Island | 75-K |
| Havens, William | S | Shelter Island | 76:1.2.1.1.1 |
| Havens, William Jr. | S | Shelter Island | 75-K |
| Havens, William Jr. | S | Shelter Island | 76:0.1.1.1.1 |
| Haviland, Benjamin | Q | ........ | 75-A |
| Haviland, Benjn. | N | New York | 74-A |
| Haviland, Eb. and Thomas | N | New York | 75-F |
| Haviland, John | Q | ........ | 75-A, 76-B |
| Haviland, John | S | Huntington | 75-H |
| Haviland, Jos. | Q | ........ | 75-A |
| Haviland, Jos. Jr. | Q | ........ | 76-E |
| Haviland, Joseph | N | New York | 75-T, 76-A |
| Haviland, Luke | Q | ........ | 75-A |
| Haviland, Sam[l] | N | New York | 76-G |
| Haviland, Thomas | N | New York | 74-A |
| Haviland, Will[m] | S | Huntington | 75-H |
| Hawk, Jno., carman | N | Lake's Wharf | 75-D2 |
| Hawk, John | N | New York | 74-A |
| Hawkings, Alex[r] | S | Brookhaven | 75-B8 |
| Hawkings, Alex[r] iuner | S | Brookhaven | 75-B8 |
| Hawkings, Gersum | S | Meritches | 76:0.1.1.2.6 |
| Hawkings, Jacob | S | Brookhaven | 75-B8 |
| Hawkings, Joseph | S | Brookhaven | 75-B8 |
| Hawkings, Nathaniel | S | Brookhaven | 75-B7 non-signer |
| Hawkings, Robert | S | Brookhaven | 75-B6 |
| Hawkings, Zachariah | S | Brookhaven | 75-B7 |

| | | | |
|---|---|---|---|
| Hawkings, Zackariah | S | Meritches | 76:1.1.0.3.1 |
| Hawkings, Zofar | Q | Hempstead | 76-D |
| Hawkins, Alexander | S | Brookhaven | 76:1.4.1.4.3.0.2 |
| Hawkins, Alexander [2] | S | Brookhaven | [on] 75-B4 |
| Hawkins, Benjamen | S | Brookhaven | 76:0.2.1.3.3 |
| Hawkins, Benjamin Junior | S | Brookhaven | 75-B8 |
| Hawkins, Caleb | S | Brookhaven | 75-B11 n.s. |
| Hawkins, Calop | S | Brookhaven | 76:0.3.3.1.1 |
| Hawkins, David | S | Brookhaven | 75-B4, 75-B8 |
| Hawkins, David | S | Brookhaven | 76:1.0.1.1.0 |
| Hawkins, Elazer | S | Brookhaven | 76:0.1.1.1.2.0.1 |
| Hawkins, Elazer Juner | S | Brookhaven | 75-B10 |
| Hawkins, Eleazer Senior | S | Brookhaven | 75-B8 |
| Hawkins, Elezer | S | Brookhaven | 76:1.1.1.3.1.1.4 |
| Hawkins, Gershom | S | Brookhaven | 75-B6 |
| Hawkins, Havens | S | Brookhaven | 75-B8 |
| Hawkins, Isaac | S | Brookhaven | 76:1.0.1.2.1 |
| Hawkins, Isaac Juner | S | Brookhaven | 75-B8 |
| Hawkins, Isaac Senior | S | Brookhaven | 75-B8 |
| Hawkins, Israel | S | Brookhaven | 75-B8 |
| Hawkins, Israel | S | Brookhaven | 76:0.1.1.1.2.2.3 |
| Hawkins, Jacob | S | Brookhaven | 75-B4 |
| Hawkins, John | S | Brookhaven | 75-B8 |
| Hawkins, Jonas | S | Brookhaven | 75-B8 |
| Hawkins, Jorg | S | Brookhaven | 76:0.1.2.1.1.0.1 |
| Hawkins, Joseph | N | New York | 76-M |
| Hawkins, Joseph | S | Brookhaven | 75-B4 |
| Hawkins, Nathaniel | S | Brookhaven | 75-B1 non-signer |
| Hawkins, Nathaniel | S | Brookhaven | 76:0.1.0.1.2 |
| Hawkins, Robbard | S | Brookhaven | 76:0.1.2.1.6 |
| Hawkins, Robert | S | Brookhaven | 75-B3 |
| Hawkins, Samuel | S | Brookhaven | 75-B8 |
| Hawkins, Samuel | S | Brookhaven | 76:1.2.2.3.0.0.1 |
| Hawkins, Sarah | N | New York | 76-I |
| Hawkins, Semeon | S | Brookhaven | 75-B4 |
| Hawkins, Simeon | S | Brookhaven | 75-B8 |
| Hawkins, Timothy | S | Brookhaven | 75-B8 |
| Hawkins, Timothy | S | Brookhaven | 76:0.1.2.1.2 |
| Hawkins, Zaceriah | S | Brookhaven | 76:0.1.1.1.1 |
| Hawkins, Zachariah | S | Brookhaven | 75-B10 |

| | | | |
|---|---|---|---|
| Hawkins, Zachariah Jr. | S | Brookhaven | 75-B1 n.s. |
| Hawkins, Zachariah Jr. | S | Middle Island Co. | 75-B5 neutral |
| Hawkins, Zacheriah | S | Brookhaven | 75-B11 n.s. |
| Hawkins, Zechariah | S | Brookhaven | 75-B6 |
| Hawkins, Zopar | S | Brookhaven | 75-B8 |
| Hawkins, Zophar | Q | ........ | 76-E |
| Haws, Peletiah H. | N | New York | 75-R |
| Hawxhurst, Henry | Q | ........ | 76-E |
| Hawxhurst, John | Q | ........ | 75-A |
| Hawxhurst, John | Q | ........ | 76-B, 76-E |
| Hawxhurst, Joseph | Q | ........ | 76-E |
| Hawxhurst, Samuel | Q | ........ | 76-E |
| Hawxhurst, Simeon | Q | ........ | 75-A, 76-E |
| Hawxhurst, Simon | Q | ........ | 76-B |
| Hawxhurst, W. | Q | ........ | 76-E |
| Hawxhurst, William | N | New York | 74-A, 76-A |
| Hay, Jane | N | removed upstate | 76-P |
| Hay, Solomon | N | New York | 74-A |
| Hay, William | N | New York | 76-A |
| Haydock, Henry | N | New York | 74-A |
| Haydock, John, tailor | N | New York | 74-T2, 6/30 |
| Hayes, Barack, Lieut. | N | New York | 76-G |
| Hayes, Hette, pickled foods | N | Stone Street | 74-T2, 8/18 |
| Hayes, Joseph, alias Brown | N | New York | 75-R |
| Hayes, Michael Solomon | N | New York | 75-T |
| Hayley, John | N | New York | 75-R |
| Hayne, Anthony | S | Southampton | 76:1.2.3.3.4 |
| Hayns, John | S | Southampton | 76:1.0.0.3.2 |
| Hays, Barach, Lieut. | N | New York | 75-A |
| Hays, Barrack | N | New York | 74-R, 76-A |
| Hays, David | N | New York | 76-A |
| Hays, Hugh | N | New York | 74-R |
| Hays, John | N | New York | 74-A |
| Hays, Michael S. | N | New York | 74-A |
| Hays, Michael S., constable | N | New York | 74-R to 76-R |
| Hays, Moses | N | New York | 74-R |
| Hays, William | N | New York | 75-R |
| Haywood, Thomas | N | New York | 74-A, 76-A |
| Hazard, Ebenezer | N | New York | 74-V, 76-N |
| Hazard, Morris | Q | ........ | 75-A associator |

| | | | |
|---|---|---|---|
| Hazard, Morris | Q | Newtown | 75-G |
| Hazard, Polly, Miss | N | New York | 74-T |
| Hazard, Richard Tole | N | New York | 74-A, 76-D |
| Hazard, Samuel | S | Smithtown | 75-L |
| Hazard, Thomas | N | New York | 74-A |
| Hazard, Thomas | N | New York | 75-F |
| Hazard, Thomas, merchant | N | New York | 74-T2, 5/26 |
| Hazard, Thos. | N | New York | 74-A |
| Hazen, see Heazen | | | |
| Heartz, Jacob | N | New York | 76-A |
| Heartz, John Jacob | N | New York | 74-A |
| Heath, Geo. | N | New York | 76-A |
| Heath, John | N | New York | 74-A |
| Heath, John | N | New York | 74-R juror |
| Heaton, Robert | N | New York | 76-R |
| Heazen, Ezekiel | N | New York | 74-A |
| Hecht, Fred. Wm. | N | New York | 74-A Capt., G.S. |
| Hecht, Fred. Wm. | N | New York | 76-A |
| Hedger, David Jun. | S | Brookhaven | 75-B10 |
| Hedges, Abraham | S | Easthampton | 75-E |
| Hedges, Abraham | S | Easthampton | 76:1.1.1.2.0 |
| Hedges, Benjamin | S | Easthampton | 75-E |
| Hedges, Benjamin | S | Easthampton | 76:1.0.1.1.1 |
| Hedges, Daniel | S | ........ | 75-R |
| Hedges, Daniel | S | Easthampton | 75-E |
| Hedges, Daniel | S | Easthampton | 76:0.1.2.1.2 |
| Hedges, Daniel, Lieut. | S | Southampton | 76:0.2.3.1.2.2.0 |
| Hedges, David | S | ........ | 75-R |
| Hedges, David | S | Southold | 76:1.1.0.4.0 |
| Hedges, David, Deac$^n$ | S | Southampton | 76:0.2.5.1.1.4.0 |
| Hedges, David Ju$^r$ | S | Southold | 76:0.1.2.1.2 |
| Hedges, Ebenezer | S | Easthampton | 76:0.1.1.3.1 |
| Hedges, Elezer | S | Easthampton | 75-E |
| Hedges, Elias | S | ........ | 75-R |
| Hedges, Ezekel | S | Brookhaven | 76:1.0.2.1.0.1.1 |
| Hedges, Ezekel Juner | S | Brookhaven | 76:0.1.0.1.1 |
| Hedges, Ezekiel | S | Brookhaven | 75-B3 |
| Hedges, Ezekiel Jur. | S | Brookhaven | 75-B6 |
| Hedges, Hannah, Wido | S | Easthampton | 76:0.0.0.2.0 |
| Hedges, Isaac | N | New York | 76-A |

| | | | |
|---|---|---|---|
| Hedges, Jacob | S | Easthampton | 75-E |
| Hedges, Jacob | S | Easthampton | 76:0.1.0.1.0 |
| Hedges, Jeremiah | S | Easthampton | 75-E |
| Hedges, Job | S | ........ | 75-R |
| Hedges, John | S | Easthampton | 75-E |
| Hedges, John | S | Easthampton | 76:1.1.1.2.2.2.0 |
| Hedges, Jonathan | S | ........ | 75-R |
| Hedges, Jonathan, Colo[l] | S | Southampton | 76:1.2.3.3.2 |
| Hedges, Jonathan, the 2[d] | S | ........ | 75-R |
| Hedges, Jonathon Jun[r] | S | Southampton | 76:0.1.1.1.0 |
| Hedges, Mathew | S | Southold | 76:0.1.3.1.4 |
| Hedges, Matthew | S | Southold | 75-N |
| Hedges, Nathan | S | Easthampton | 76:0.1.1.1.1 |
| Hedges, Philep | S | Easthampton | 76:0.1.0.1.0 |
| Hedges, Philip | S | Easthampton | 75-E |
| Hedges, Stephen | S | ........ | 75-R |
| Hedges, Stephen | S | Easthampton | 75-E |
| Hedges, Stephen | S | Easthampton | 76:1.2.2.2.0.1.2 |
| Hedges, Stephen | S | Southampton | 76:0.1.3.1.2.2.1 |
| Hedges, Thomas | S | Easthampton | 75-E |
| Hedges, Timothy | S | Southampton | 76:0.2.2.2.2 |
| Hedges, William | S | Easthampton | 75-E |
| Hedges, William | S | Easthampton | 76:0.1.0.1.2 |
| Hedges, William Jr. | S | Easthampton | 75-E |
| Hefner, Valten | N | New York | 76-A |
| Hegeman, Albert Jr. | Q | ........ | 75-A associator |
| Hegeman, Albert Sr. | Q | ........ | 75-A associator |
| Hegeman, Andries | Q | ........ | 76-E |
| Hegeman, Andries Jr. | Q | ........ | 75-A associator |
| Hegeman, Andries Jr. | Q | ........ | 76-E |
| Hegeman, Andries Sr. | Q | ........ | 75-A associator |
| Hegeman, Benj. | Q | ........ | 75-A, 76-B |
| Hegeman, Elbert | Q | ........ | 76-E |
| Hegeman, Elbert Jr. | Q | ........ | 76-E |
| Hegeman, John | Q | ........ | 76-B, 76-E |
| Hegeman, John | Q | ........ | [2 on] 75-A |
| Hegeman, Joseph | Q | ........ | 76-E |
| Hegeman, Peter | Q | ........ | 76-E |
| Hegeman, Peter | Q | Oyster Bay | 75-F |
| Hegeman, Rem | Q | ........ | 75-A associator |

| | | | |
|---|---|---|---|
| Hegeman, Rem | Q | ........ | 76-E |
| Hegeman, Rem | Q | Oyster Bay | 75-F |
| Heirs, Ludlam | Q | Newtown | 75-G |
| Heister, Andrew | N | New York | 76-A |
| Helme, Ants | S | Brookhaven | 75-B8 |
| Helme, Benjamin | N | New York | 75-T2, 5/4 |
| Helme, Thomas | S | Brookhaven | 76:0.2.1.2.1.2.1 |
| Helme, Thomas Esqʳ | S | Brookhaven | 75-B9 |
| Helme, Thomas Junʳ | S | Brookhaven | 75-B9 |
| Helme, William | S | Brookhaven | 75-B9 |
| Hempstead, Thomas | S | Southold | 76:0.2.2.2.3.0.2 |
| Hempsted, Robert | S | Southold | 76:1.0.0.1.1.2.1 |
| Hempsted, Robᵗ | S | ........ | 75-R |
| Hempsted, Thomas | S | ........ | 75-R |
| Hempsted, Thoˢ | S | ........ | 75-R |
| Hemsted, Robᵗ | S | ........ | 75-R |
| Henderson, Alex | N | New York | 75-D1 |
| Henderson, Ann | N | removed upstate | 76-P |
| Henderson, David | N | New York | 74-A |
| Henderson, John | N | New York | 76-A |
| Henderson, John | Q | ........ | 76-E |
| Henderson, Thomas | N | New York | 76-N |
| Henderson, Thomas, juror | N | New York | 74-R to 76-R |
| Henderson, Thos. | N | New York | 74-A |
| Hendrick, John, shoemaker | N | Fair Street | 75-D2 |
| Hendricks, Hester wf Uriah | N | New York | 75-T |
| Hendricks, John | N | New York | 74-A |
| Hendricks, Peter | N | New York | 74-A |
| Hendricks, Uriah | N | New York | 74-A, 76-A |
| Hendricks, Uriah, merchant | N | Broad Street | 74-T2, 5/12 |
| Hendricks, Uziah | N | Broad Street | 74-T2, 11/24 |
| Hendrickson, A. | Q | Jamaica | 75-D associator |
| Hendrickson, Aaron | Q | ........ | 75-A associator |
| Hendrickson, Aaron | Q | ........ | 76-E |
| Hendrickson, Aaron | Q | Jamaica | 75-D associator |
| Hendrickson, Aaron | Q | Jamaica | 75-E |
| Hendrickson, Abm. | Q | ........ | 76-E |
| Hendrickson, Abraham | Q | Jamaica | 75-E |
| Hendrickson, Albert | Q | Jamaica | 76-C |
| Hendrickson, Albt. | Q | ........ | 76-E |

| | | | | |
|---|---|---|---|---|
| Hendrickson, Barnar. | Q | ........ | 76-E | |
| Hendrickson, Daniel | Q | ........ | 75-A | |
| Hendrickson, Daniel | Q | ........ | 76-B, 76-E | |
| Hendrickson, H. Jr. | Q | Jamaica | 75-D associator | |
| Hendrickson, H. Sr. | Q | Jamaica | 75-D associator | |
| Hendrickson, Harman | Q | ........ | 75-A, 76-E | |
| Hendrickson, Hendrick | Q | ........ | 75-A | |
| Hendrickson, Hendrick | Q | ........ | 75-A associator | |
| Hendrickson, Hendrick | Q | ........ | 76-B, 76-E | |
| Hendrickson, Hendrick | Q | Hempstead | 76-D | |
| Hendrickson, Hendrick | Q | Jamaica | 75-E | |
| Hendrickson, Hendrick | Q | Jamaica | 76-C blacksmith | |
| Hendrickson, Hendrick Jr. | Q | ........ | 75-A associator | |
| Hendrickson, Isaac | Q | Jamaica | 75-D associator | |
| Hendrickson, Isaac [2] | Q | ........ | 75-A associators | |
| Hendrickson, J., Jr. | Q | Jamaica | 75-D associator | |
| Hendrickson, John | Q | ........ | 75-A associator | |
| Hendrickson, John | Q | ........ | 76-E | |
| Hendrickson, Stephen | Q | ........ | 75-A | |
| Hendrickson, Stephen | Q | ........ | 76-B, 76-E | |
| Hendrickson, Thomas | Q | ........ | 75-A, 76-B | |
| Hendrickson, Thos. Jr. | Q | ........ | 75-A | |
| Hendrickson, Wm | Q | ........ | 76-E | |
| Hendrie, Wm. | N | New York | 74-A | |
| Heniger, Christopher | N | New York | 76-L | |
| Henly, Eleanor | N | New York | 76-R | |
| Hennigar, Michael | N | New York | 74-A | |
| Henning, Joseph S. | N | New York | 74-A | |
| Henry, Hugh, tavernkeeper | N | Little Dock Street | 74-T | |
| Henry, James | N | near the College | 76-H | |
| Henry, John, merchant | N | New York | 75-T2, 1/5 | |
| Henry, Margaret | N | New York | 75-R | |
| Henry, Robert | N | Fresh Water Hill | 76-I | |
| Henry, Thomas Jr. | S | ........ | 75-R | |
| Hepborn, Thomas, storekpr | N | Dock Street | 76-V | |
| Herbeck, ---- Lieut. | N | New York | 76-C | |
| Herbert, Richard, constable | N | New York | 74-R, 75-R | |
| Herbert, Thomas | N | New York | 74-A | |
| Heron, Isaac | N | New York | 74-A, 76-F | |
| Heron, Isaac, Capt. | N | New York | 76-Y | |

| | | | |
|---|---|---|---|
| Heron, Isaac, watchmaker | N | New York | 75-T |
| Herrick, Ashbel | S | ........ | 75-R |
| Herrick, George, Maj. | S | Southampton | 76:0.1.2.1.0.0.1 |
| Herrick, Hennery | S | Southampton | 76:0.2.1.1.1 |
| Herrick, Michaiah | S | Southampton | 76:0.1.3.3.1.1.1 |
| Herrick, Nathan | S | Southampton | 76:1.1.1.1.1.1.2 |
| Herring, David | N | to Dutchess Co. | 76-P |
| Herring, David Jr. | N | to Dutchess Co. | 76-P |
| Herring, Hercules | N | New York | 76-R |
| Herring, John | N | to Dutchess Co. | 76-P |
| Hervey, William | N | New York | 76-A |
| Hesse, Sarah | N | New York | 76-K |
| Hetzell, John Jacob | N | New York | 76-A |
| Heurstin, William | N | New York | 74-A |
| Heustis, Charles | N | New York | 74-A |
| Heustis, Charles, carpenter | N | Queen Street | 75-D1, D2 |
| Hewett, James | N | New York | 76-A |
| Hewett; see also Huet | | | |
| Hewlett, Benj. | Q | ........ | [2 on] 76-B |
| Hewlett, Benj'n | Q | ........ | 75-A |
| Hewlett, Benj'n Jr. | Q | ........ | 75-A |
| Hewlett, Chas | Q | ........ | 75-A |
| Hewlett, Dan'l Jr. | Q | ........ | 75-A, 76-E |
| Hewlett, Daniel | Q | ........ | 75-A, 76-B |
| Hewlett, Daniel Sr. | Q | ........ | 76-E |
| Hewlett, George | Q | ........ | 75-A, 76-B |
| Hewlett, George Sr. | Q | N. Side | 75-A |
| Hewlett, James | Q | ........ | 76-E |
| Hewlett, Jno., Capt. | Q | ........ | 75-A |
| Hewlett, Jno. Jr. | Q | ........ | 75-A |
| Hewlett, John | Q | ........ | [2 on] 76-B |
| Hewlett, John | Q | ........ | [2 on] 76-E |
| Hewlett, John Esq. | Q | ........ | 75-A |
| Hewlett, John, Justice | Q | Oyster Bay | 75-H |
| Hewlett, John Sr. | Q | ........ | 76-E |
| Hewlett, John Sr. | Q | N. Side | 76-I |
| Hewlett, Joseph | Q | ........ | 75-A |
| Hewlett, Joseph | Q | ........ | 76-B, 76-E |
| Hewlett, Lawrence | Q | ........ | 75-A |
| Hewlett, Rich'd Esq. | Q | ........ | 75-A |

| | | | |
|---|---|---|---|
| Hewlett, Richard | Q | ........ | 75-A, 76-E |
| Hewlett, Richard | Q | Hempstead | 75-H |
| Hewlett, Samuel | Q | ........ | 76-E |
| Hewlett, Stephen | Q | ........ | 75-A, 75-H |
| Hewlett, Stephen | Q | ........ | 76-E |
| Hewlett, Thos | Q | ........ | 75-A |
| Hewlett, Townsend | Q | ........ | 75-A |
| Hewlett, W. | Q | ........ | 76-E |
| Hewlett, Wm. | Q | ........ | [2 on] 75-A |
| Heyer, Garrit | N | New York | 76-A |
| Heyer, Richard | N | New York | 76-L |
| Heyer, Walter Jr. | N | New York | 74-A |
| Heyer, William | N | New York | 76-R juror |
| Heyer, Wm., Col° | N | New York | 76-G |
| Heyr, Walter | N | New York | 76-L |
| Hick, Daniel | N | New York | 76-A |
| Hickey, Catharine | N | to Westchester Co | 76-P |
| Hickey, John | N | to Westchester Co | 76-P |
| Hicks, Austin | Q | ........ | 75-A |
| Hicks, Benjamin | Q | ........ | 76-E |
| Hicks, Bethiah | S | Easthampton | 76:0.0.0.2.0 |
| Hicks, Charles | Q | ........ | 76-B |
| Hicks, Charles | Q | ........ | [2 on] 76-E |
| Hicks, Charles, Capt. | Q | ........ | 75-A |
| Hicks, Charles, Capt. | Q | Hempstead | 75-H |
| Hicks, Charles Jr. | Q | ........ | 76-E |
| Hicks, Chas., Lieut. | Q | ........ | 75-A associator |
| Hicks, Edward | Q | ........ | 76-E |
| Hicks, Eliz., Wid. | S | Southampton | 76:0.0.2.1.1 |
| Hicks, George | Q | ........ | 76-E |
| Hicks, Gilbert | Q | ........ | 75-A associator |
| Hicks, Jacob | Q | ........ | 75-A |
| Hicks, Jacob Jr. | Q | ........ | 75-A |
| Hicks, James | Q | ........ | 75-A |
| Hicks, Joseph | S | Easthampton | 75-E |
| Hicks, Joseph | S | Easthampton | 76:1.3.1.3.2 |
| Hicks, Js. | Q | ........ | 75-A associator |
| Hicks, Paul | N | New York | 74-A |
| Hicks, Silas | Q | ........ | 75-A |
| Hicks, Stephen | Q | ........ | 75-A |

| | | | |
|---|---|---|---|
| Hicks, Thomas | Q | ........ | 75-A, 75-D |
| Hicks, Thomas | Q | ........ | [2 on] 76-E |
| Hicks, Thomas Esq. | Q | ........ | 75-D1 |
| Hicks, V. | Q | ........ | 76-E |
| Hicks, Whitehead | N | New York | 76-A |
| Hicks, Whitehead, Judge | N | New York | 74-R, 75-R |
| Hicks, Zeek: | S | Easthampton | 75-E |
| Higba, Joseph | S | Huntington | 75-H |
| Higbe, Daniel | Q | Jamaica | 75-E |
| Higbee, Jonas | S | Huntington | 76-H2 |
| Higbee, Nathaniel | Q | ........ | 76-E |
| Higbee, Samuel | Q | ........ | 75-E |
| Higbee, Stephen | S | Huntington | 75-H1 |
| Higby, Aaron | S | Huntington | 75-H |
| Higby, Henry | Q | ........ | 76-B, 76-E |
| Higby, Henry | Q | Jamaica | 75-C, 75-D |
| Higby, John | Q | ........ | 75-A, 76-B |
| Higby, Joseph | Q | ........ | 75-A associator |
| Higby, Joseph | Q | Jamaica | 75-D associator |
| Higby, Joseph | Q | Jamaica | 75-E |
| Higby, Moses | Q | ........ | 76-E |
| Higby, Moses | Q | Jamaica | 75-D associator |
| Higby, Nathaniel | Q | ........ | 75-A |
| Higby, Nathaniel | Q | Jamaica | 75-C, 75-D |
| Higby, Nehemiah | Q | Jamaica | 76-C |
| Higby, Sam'l, cooper | Q | Jamaica | 75-D associator |
| Higby, Samuel | Q | ........ | 76-E |
| Higby, Samuel | Q | Jamaica | 75-E |
| Higby, Samuel Jr. | Q | Jamaica | 75-D associator |
| Higby, Seth | Q | Jamaica | 75-C |
| Higby, Stephen | Q | ........ | 75-A, 76-B |
| Higby, Stephen | Q | Jamaica | 75-D |
| Higby, Thomas | Q | ........ | 76-E |
| Higby, Thomas | Q | Jamaica | 75-E |
| Higgins, Benj., cabinetmkr | N | Cortland Street | 75-D2 |
| Higgins, Benjamin | N | New York | 74-A |
| Higgins, Patrick | N | New York | 76-I |
| Higgins, Patrick, tavernkpr | N | Murray Street | 75-D1, D2 |
| Higgins, Patrick, tavernkpr | N | New York | 75-R |
| Higlay, Christopher | S | Huntington | 75-H |

| | | | |
|---|---|---|---|
| Higley, Moses | Q | ........ | 75-A associator |
| Higley, Sam'l Jr. | Q | ........ | 75-A associator |
| Higley, Sam'l Sr. | Q | ........ | 75-A associator |
| Hildref, Daniel | S | Southampton | 76:0.2.2.1.3 |
| Hildref, Joseph | S | Southampton | 76:0.1.0.1.2.0.1 |
| Hildreth, Benjamin, distiller | N | St. James Street | 74-T |
| Hildreth, Benjn. Jr. | N | New York | 74-A |
| Hildreth, Daniel | S | ........ | 75-R |
| Hildreth, Daniel Jun' | S | ........ | 75-R |
| Hildreth, Isaac | S | Southampton | 75-M |
| Hildreth, James | S | Southampton | 75-M |
| Hildreth, James | S | Southampton | 76:1.1.1.2.2.1.0 |
| Hildreth, James Jun. | S | Southampton | 75-M |
| Hildreth, John | S | Southampton | 75-M |
| Hildreth, John | S | Southampton | 76:0.3.2.3.3.0.1 |
| Hildreth, Joseph | S | ........ | 75-R |
| Hildreth, Joseph Jun' | S | ........ | 75-R |
| Hildreth, Joshua | S | Southampton | 75-M |
| Hildreth, Joshua | S | Southampton | 76:0.1.0.1.1 |
| Hildreth, Luther | S | Southampton | 75-M |
| Hildreth, Noah | S | Southampton | 75-M |
| Hildreth, Peter | S | Southampton | 76:1.1.0.4.0 |
| Hildreth, Peter, the 2nd | S | ........ | 75-R |
| Hildreth, Shadrach | S | ........ | 75-R |
| Hildrith, Joseph | N | New York | 76-A |
| Hildrith, Peter | S | ........ | 75-R |
| Hildrith, Peter Jun' | S | Southampton | 76:0.1.1.1.1 |
| Hill, Deborah | N | removed upstate | 76-P |
| Hill, Eliphelet | S | Huntington | 76-H3 |
| Hill, George, hse carpenter | N | at Mr. Nevins | 75-D1, D2 |
| Hill, James | N | Broadway | 76-H |
| Hill, James | N | New York | 74-A |
| Hill, John | N | New York | 74-A |
| Hill, John | S | Southampton | 75-M |
| Hill, John | S | Southampton | 76:1.0.0.1.0 |
| Hill, John, restauranteer | N | Rotten Row | 74-T |
| Hill, Jonathan | S | ........ | 75-R |
| Hill, Jonathan | S | Southampton | 76:0.1.1.2.4 |
| Hill, Thomas | N | New York | 74-A |
| Hill, Wm | S | ........ | 75-R |

| | | | |
|---|---|---|---|
| Hillam, Thomas, merchant | N | New York | 75-T2, 1/5 |
| Hilliard, see Hylyard | | | |
| Hillman, John | N | New York | 76-A |
| Hills, John | N | removed upstate | 76-P |
| Hillsteam, Michael | N | New York | 76-A |
| Hillyer, John | N | New York | 74-A, 76-A |
| Hillyer, Simon | N | New York | 74-A |
| Hilman, Henry | N | to Westchester Co | 76-P |
| Hinchman, Benjamin | Q | ........ | 75-A associator |
| Hinchman, James | Q | ........ | 75-A associator |
| Hinchman, James | Q | Jamaica | 75-E |
| Hinchman, John | Q | ........ | 76-E |
| Hinchman, Obadiah | Q | ........ | 75-A |
| Hinchman, Obadiah | Q | ........ | 76-B, 76-E |
| Hinchman, Robert | S | Brookhaven | 75-B10 |
| Hinchman, Robert | S | Southold | 76:0.1.1.1.0 |
| Hinchman, Robt. | Q | ........ | 75-A associator |
| Hinchman, Thomas | Q | ........ | 76-E |
| Hinchman, ---- Wid. | S | Southold | 76:0.0.5.3.1 |
| Hinckman, Benj. | Q | Jamaica | 75-D Associator |
| Hinckman, Obadiah | Q | Jamaica | 75-C, 75-D |
| Hinckman, Robert | Q | Jamaica | 75-D associator |
| Hinde, John, dry goods | N | Water Street | 74-T2, 6/16 |
| Hinds, Elizabeth | N | to Dutchess Co. | 76-P |
| Hinksman, John | Q | Jamaica | 75-C |
| Hinshaw, Samuel, mariner | N | William Street | 75-D1, D2 |
| Hinsler, Lodowick | N | New York | 74-A |
| Hitchcock, Daniel | N | New York | 74-A |
| Hitchcock, Daniel | Q | ........ | 75-A associator |
| Hitchcock, Daniel | Q | ........ | 76-E |
| Hitchcock, Joseph | N | New York | 76-A |
| Hitchcock, Miles | N | New York | 74-A |
| Hitchcock, Stephen | N | New York | 74-A |
| Hitchin, Mary | N | to Dutchess Co. | 76-P |
| Hitchings, Rich'd | N | New York | 74-A |
| Hoagland, Albert | Q | ........ | 75-A |
| Hoagland, Corn. Jr. | Q | ........ | 76-E |
| Hoagland, Cornelius | Q | ........ | 75-A |
| Hoagland, Cornelius | Q | ........ | 76-B, 76-E |
| Hoagland, Elbert | Q | ........ | 76-B, 76-E |

| | | | |
|---|---|---|---|
| Hoagland, Tunis | Q | ........ | 76-E |
| Hoagland, William | Q | ........ | 76-B, 76-E |
| Hoagland, Wm | Q | ........ | 75-A |
| Hobard, John | S | Brookhaven | 75-B10 |
| Hobard, Richard S. | S | Brookhaven | 75-B10 |
| Hobart, John Sloss | S | Huntington | 75-H, 75-H1 |
| Hobart, Joshua | S | Brookhaven | 75-B10 |
| Hobart, Joshua | S | Southold | 76:1.0.0.2.1 |
| Hobby, Caleb | N | New York | 76-N |
| Hodge & Shober | N | New York | 74-A |
| Hodge, Robert, Lieut. | N | New York | 75-A |
| Hodsden, John Esq. | N | New York | 76-V |
| Hoff, ____ Mr. | N | removed upstate | 76-P |
| Hoff, Peter | S | Huntington | 75-H |
| Hoffman, Johannis | N | New York | 76-A |
| Hoffman, Michael | N | New York | 76-A |
| Hoffman, Michael, storekpr | N | Broadway | 74-T2, 7/14 |
| Hoffman, Nicholas | N | New York | 74-T2, 11/24 |
| Hoffman, Nicholas | N | New York | 75-F |
| Hoghland, Benjamin | N | New York | 74-A, 76-N |
| Hoghlandt, Benj[n] | N | Fly Market | 76-I |
| Hogin, Bridget | N | New York | 75-R |
| Hogin, Roger | N | New York | 75-R |
| Hogland, Adrian | N | Bloomingdale | 75-V |
| Hogland, Benjamin | N | New York | 75-V |
| Hogland, William | N | New York | 75-V |
| Hojer, Peter C. | N | New York | 74-A |
| Holaway, Lewis | N | to Westchester Co | 76-P |
| Holden, James | N | New York | 74-A, 76-A |
| Holden, James | N | nr. the Barracks | 76-I |
| Holdin, John | N | upper Barracks | 76-H |
| Holdsworth, John, cutler | N | New York | 74-T |
| Holdsworth, Mary, wf John | N | New York | 74-T |
| Holladay, Ellenor | N | Barrack Street | 76-H |
| Hollowed, Thomas | Q | ........ | 76-E |
| Hollowed; see also Halled | | | |
| Holmes, Hugh | Q | ........ | 75-A, 76-B |
| Holmes, Jacob | N | New York | 74-A |
| Holmes, Jane | N | rem. to Bedford | 76-J |
| Holmes, Joel | N | New York | 74-A |

| | | | |
|---|---|---|---|
| Holmes, Joel, taylor | N | Oswego Market | 74-T |
| Holmes, John | Q | ........ | 75-A, 76-B |
| Holmes, Jonathan, coachmkr | N | French Church St | 75-D1, D2 |
| Holmes, Josiah | N | New York | 74-A |
| Holmes, Peter | N | New York | 76-A |
| Holmes, Sarah | N | New York | 74-V |
| Holmes, Sarah | N | to Dutchess Co. | 76-P |
| Holmes, Thomas, ae c.37 | N | New York | 75-V runaway |
| Holt, John | N | New York | 75-D2, 76-N |
| Homan, Daniel | S | Brookhaven | 76:0.1.0.1.2 |
| Homan, Ebenezer | S | Brookhaven | 75-B3, 75-B6 |
| Homan, Ebenezer | S | Brookhaven | 76:1.1.2.2.3 |
| Homan, Ebenezer, Jr. | S | Brookhaven | 75-B3, 75-B6 |
| Homan, Ezekel | S | Brookhaven | 76:1.1.0.2.0 |
| Homan, Ezekiel | S | Brookhaven | 75-B3, 75-B6 |
| Homan, Jeremiah | S | Islip | 75-I non-signer |
| Homan, Jeremiah | S | Southampton | 76:0.1.2.1.3 |
| Homan, John | S | Brookhaven | 75-B1 n.s. |
| Homan, John | S | Brookhaven | 76:0.2.4.1.0.0.1 |
| Homan, John | S | Brookhaven | 76:1.0.0.2.0 |
| Homan, John, Sergt. | S | Brookhaven | 75-B7 n.s. |
| Homan, John, Sgt. | S | Middle Island Co. | 75-B5 neutral |
| Homan, Joseph | S | Brookhaven | 75-B1 n.s. |
| Homan, Joseph | S | Brookhaven | 75-B3, 75-B6 |
| Homan, Joseph | S | Brookhaven | 75-B7 n.s. |
| Homan, Mordecai | S | Brookhaven | 75-B1, 75-B3 |
| Homan, Mordecai | S | Brookhaven | 75-B7 |
| Homan, Mordecai | S | Brookhaven | 76:0.1.1.1.0 |
| Homan, Mordecai | S | Brookhaven | 76:0.3.5.1.2 |
| Homan, Mordecai 3d | S | Brookhaven | 75-B3, 75-B6 |
| Homan, Mordecai, Jr. | S | Brookhaven | 75-B3 |
| Homan, Mordecai [2] | S | Brookhaven | [on] 75-B6 |
| Homan, Robbard | S | Brookhaven | 76:0.1.1.1.2.0.2 |
| Homan, Robert | S | Brookhaven | 75-B7 |
| Homan, Zebulon | S | Islip | 76:0.1.3.1.1 |
| Homon, Phenes | S | ........ | 75-R |
| Hone, Philip | N | New York | 74-A |
| Honmer, John | N | New York | 74-A |
| Hoog, Thomas Andrew | N | Broadway | 75-T2, 6/22 |
| Hoog, Thos. Andw. | N | New York | 74-A |

| | | | |
|---|---|---|---|
| Hoogeland, John | N | New York | 76-L |
| Hoogland, _____ | N | New York | 75-D2 |
| Hooker, Cloye | N | rem. to Bedford | 76-J |
| Hope, James | N | New York | 76-A |
| Hopkins, Daniel | Q | ........ | 76-E |
| Hopkins, Samuel | S | Brookhaven | 75-B9 |
| Hopkins, Samuel | S | Brookhaven | 76:1.1.1.3.2 |
| Hopkins, Samuel Jr. | S | Brookhaven | 75-B9 |
| Hopkins, Thomas | Q | ........ | 76-E |
| Hopkins, W., Jr. | Q | ........ | 76-E |
| Hopkins, William | Q | Oyster Bay | 75-F |
| Hopper, Andrew | N | at Spring Gardin | 76-H |
| Hopper, Andrew | N | head of Broadway | 76-I |
| Hopper, Andrew | N | New York | 74-A |
| Hopper, John, 2d Lieut. | N | New York | 76-Y |
| Hopper, Matthew [2] | N | New York | [on] 74-A |
| Hopper, Powles | N | New York | 74-A |
| Hopper, Rinier | N | New York | 74-A, 76-A |
| Hopper, Yalless | N | New York | 76-A |
| Hopping, Benjamin | S | Easthampton | 75-E |
| Hopping, Benjamin | S | Easthampton | 76:1.1.1.2.1 |
| Hopping, Henry | S | Easthampton | 75-E |
| Hopping, Henry | S | Easthampton | 75-E |
| Hopping, Henry | S | Easthampton | 76:1.1.1.2.1 |
| Hopping, Henry Jun[r] | S | Easthampton | 76:0.1.1.1.0 |
| Hopping, Joseph | S | Easthampton | 75-E |
| Hopson, George | N | New York | 74-A |
| Hopwood, Thomas | N | New York | 76-A |
| Horn, Harcull | N | New York | 75-D1 |
| Horne, Robert | N | New York | 74-A, 76-A |
| Horner, James | N | French Ch. St. | 76-I |
| Horner, James | N | New York | 74-A, 76-A |
| Horner, Sarah | N | New York | 74-R |
| Horsen, Jacob | N | New York | 75-V |
| Horsen, John | N | Bloomingdale | 75-V |
| Horsfield, Thomas | N | New York | 76-A |
| Horsmanden, Daniel | N | New York | 76-A |
| Horton, Ambrose | S | Southold | 76:0.2.1.1.0 |
| Horton, Ambrous | S | Southold | 75-N |
| Horton, Barnabas | S | Southold | 76:1.1.2.2.1 |

| | | | |
|---|---|---|---|
| Horton, Barnabas Jun. | S | ........ | 75-R |
| Horton, Barna' | S | ........ | 75-R |
| Horton, Barnbass | S | Southold | 76:1.1.1.2.1.1.2 |
| Horton, Benjamin | S | ........ | 75-R |
| Horton, Calvin | S | Southold | 76:0.1.0.1.1 |
| Horton, ---- Capt. | S | Southold | 75-N |
| Horton, David | S | Southold | 76:0.1.0.1.0 |
| Horton, David | S | Southold | 76:0.1.3.1.2 |
| Horton, David | S | Southold | 76:1.1.0.0.0 |
| Horton, David [2] | S | Brookhaven | [on] 75-B10 |
| Horton, James | S | ........ | 75-R |
| Horton, John | S | Southold | 76:1.2.2.0.0 |
| Horton, Jonathan | S | Brookhaven | 75-B10 |
| Horton, Jonathan | S | Southold | 76:0.1.2.0.2.0.1 |
| Horton, Jonathan | S | Southold | 76:0.1.2.1.1 |
| Horton, Joseph | S | ........ | 75-R |
| Horton, Joseph | S | Southold | 75-N |
| Horton, Joseph | S | Southold | 76:0.2.2.2.3 |
| Horton, Joseph | S | Southold | 76:1.1.1.3.2 |
| Horton, Joshua | S | Shelter Island | 75-K |
| Horton, Joshua | S | Southold | 76:0.1.3.3.2 |
| Horton, Micah | S | Southold | 76:1.1.2.2.1 |
| Horton, Moses | S | Shelter Island | 75-K |
| Horton, Moses | S | Shelter Island | 76:1.0.1.1.2 |
| Horton, Nathan | N | New York | 76-L |
| Horton, Nathan | Q | ........ | 76-E |
| Horton, Nathen | N | New York | 74-A |
| Horton, Simon | Q | ........ | 75-A associator |
| Horton, Simon | Q | Newtown | 75-G |
| Horton, ---- Wid: | S | Southold | 76:0.0.0.2.3.2.1 |
| Horton, William | S | ........ | 75-R |
| Horton, William | S | Southold | 76:1.0.1.0.0 |
| Horton, William Juner | S | ........ | 75-R |
| Horton, William Jun' | S | ........ | 75-R |
| Horton, William Junr. | S | Southold | 76:0.1.0.1.0.0.2 |
| Hortz, Jacob | N | New York | 76-A |
| Hosack, Alexander | N | New York | 74-A, 76-A |
| Hosmer, John | N | New York | 74-V |
| Hossick, Alex' | N | Deys Street | 76-H, 76-I |
| Houghsher, Christopher | N | New York | 74-A |

| | | | |
|---|---|---|---|
| Hounam, James | N | New York | 74-A |
| House, John P. | N | New York | 75-T |
| Houseal, Bernard Mich[l] | N | New York | 76-A |
| Houseman, Abraham | N | New York | 76-I |
| Houseman, Aurt | N | New York | 74-A |
| Houseman, John | N | New York | 74-A |
| Houseman, William, Ensign | N | New York | 76-G |
| Houser, Jacob | N | New York | 74-A |
| Houston, John | N | New York | 75-D3 |
| How, Henry, taylor | N | William Street | 75-D2 |
| How, John | S | Easthampton | 75-E |
| Howard, Edw. | Q | Newtown | 75-G |
| Howard, James | Q | ........ | 76-E |
| Howard, Mary | N | removed upstate | 76-P |
| Howard, Robert | N | New York | 76-A |
| Howard, Sheffield | N | Great George St. | 74-T2, 6/16 |
| Howard, Thomas | N | New York | 74-A |
| Howard, William | Q | ........ | 76-E |
| Howard, Wm | N | New York | 75-D3 |
| Howard, Wm | Q | ........ | 75-A associator |
| Howard, Wm | Q | Newtown | 75-G |
| Howe, Jonathan | S | Brookhaven | 75-B10 |
| Howe; see also How | | | |
| Howel, John | S | Brookhaven | 75-B1, 75-B7 |
| Howel, John | S | Brookhaven | 76:0.2.1.1.1 |
| Howel, Phenehas | S | Brookhaven | 75-B10 |
| Howel, Richard | S | Southold | 75-N non-signer |
| Howel, Stephen | N | New York | 76-N |
| Howell, Ab[m] | S | ........ | 75-R |
| Howell, Abraham | S | ........ | 75-R |
| Howell, Abraham | S | Southampton | 76:0.1.2.1.1.2.4 |
| Howell, Charles | S | ........ | 75-R |
| Howell, Daniel | S | ........ | 75-R |
| Howell, Daniel | S | Brookhaven | 75-B10 |
| Howell, Daniel | S | Southold | 76:1.2.2.3.1.0.2 |
| Howell, Daniel, Chairman | S | Southampton | 75-M Committee |
| Howell, Daniel Esq. | S | Southampton | 76:1.2.2.2.1 |
| Howell, David | S | Brookhaven | 75-B6 |
| Howell, David | S | Meritches | 76:1.0.1.3.3.3.2 |
| Howell, David | S | Southampton | 75-M |

| | | | |
|---|---|---|---|
| Howell, David | S | Southampton | 76:0.1.0.2.2.1.0 |
| Howell, David | S | Southampton | 76:1.2.0.2.0.2.0 |
| Howell, David, Capt. | S | ........ | 75-R |
| Howell, David, Capt. | S | Southampton | 76:0.2.3.1.2.0.1 |
| Howell, David Jun' | S | Southampton | 76:0.1.1.2.0 |
| Howell, Ebenezer | S | Southampton | 76:0.2.0.1.0 |
| Howell, Edmund | S | Southold | 75-N |
| Howell, Edward | S | ........ | 75-R |
| Howell, Elias | S | ........ | 75-R |
| Howell, Elias | S | Southampton | 76:1.0.0.1.1.1.0 |
| Howell, Elias Jun' | S | Southampton | 76:0.1.0.1.2 |
| Howell, Elisha | S | Southampton | 76:1.1.0.3.0 |
| Howell, Ephraim | S | ........ | 75-R |
| Howell, Eunice, widow | S | Southampton | 76:0.0.0.1.0 |
| Howell, Ezekiel | S | Southampton | 76:1.1.1.3.0 |
| Howell, Ezekiel [2] | S | ........ | [on] 75-R |
| Howell, Frederack & Sister | S | Southampton | 76:0.1.0.1.0 |
| Howell, Henry | S | Southampton | 75-M |
| Howell, Henry | S | Southampton | 76:0.1.0.1.3.1.0 |
| Howell, Isaac | S | ........ | 75-R |
| Howell, Isaac | S | Southampton | 76:0.1.3.1.4 |
| Howell, Israel | S | Islip | 75-I |
| Howell, Israel | S | Islip | 76:1.2.3.5.1 |
| Howell, Israel Jun' | S | Southold | 75-N |
| Howell, Israel Jun'. | S | Islip | 75-I non-signer |
| Howell, Isrel | S | Southold | 76:1.0.1.1.0 |
| Howell, Jabesh | S | ........ | 75-R |
| Howell, James | S | ........ | 75-R |
| Howell, James | S | Southampton | 76:0.1.1.1.4 |
| Howell, Jediah | S | Southampton | 76:1.1.0.4.3.1.0 |
| Howell, Jehiel | S | ........ | 75-R |
| Howell, Jeremiah | S | Southampton | 75-M |
| Howell, Jeremiah | S | Southampton | 76:0.1.1.1.5 |
| Howell, John | S | Southampton | 76:0.1.1.1.3 |
| Howell, John | S | Southampton | 76:1.3.1.2.0 |
| Howell, John, Capt. | S | ........ | 75-R |
| Howell, John Jun' | S | ........ | 75-R |
| Howell, John ye third | S | Southampton | 76:0.1.1.1.2 |
| Howell, Jonah | S | ........ | 75-R |
| Howell, Jonah | S | Southampton | 76:0.1.3.2.2 |

| Howell, Jonah | S | Southampton | 76:1.0.0.1.0 |
|---|---|---|---|
| Howell, Jonah Jun[r] | S | ........ | 75-R |
| Howell, Jonathan | S | Shelter Island | 75-K |
| Howell, Jonathan | S | Southold | 76:1.1.1.3.0 |
| Howell, Jonathon | S | Southampton | 76:0.1.0.4.0 |
| Howell, Joseph | S | Brookhaven | 75-B10 |
| Howell, Joshua | S | Brookhaven | 75-B10 |
| Howell, Joshua | S | Southampton | 76:1.2.0.1.1 |
| Howell, Joshua | S | Southold | 76:0.1.1.1.4 |
| Howell, Josiah, Cap[t] | S | Southampton | 76:0.2.2.1.1.0.1 |
| Howell, Josua | S | Southampton | 75-M |
| Howell, Lemuel | S | Southampton | 75-M |
| Howell, Lemuel | S | Southampton | 76:0.1.0.1.0 |
| Howell, Lemuel | S | Southampton | 76:1.2.0.3.0.2.4 |
| Howell, Luess | S | Southampton | 76:0.1.1.1.0 |
| Howell, Matthew | S | ........ | 75-R |
| Howell, Matthew | S | Southampton | 76:0.1.0.1.4 |
| Howell, Mica | S | Southold | 75-N |
| Howell, Micah | S | Southold | 76:1.0.0.1.0.2.0 |
| Howell, Micah Juner | S | Southold | 75-N |
| Howell, Micah Jun[r] | S | Southold | 76:0.1.0.1.2 |
| Howell, Moses | S | Southampton | 75-M |
| Howell, Nathaniell | S | Southampton | 76:1.2.0.1.0 |
| Howell, Obadiah | S | Southampton | 76:1.1.0.0.0 |
| Howell, Philip | S | Southampton | 75-M |
| Howell, Philip | S | Southampton | 76:0.1.2.2.2 |
| Howell, Phineas | S | Southampton | 75-M |
| Howell, Phineas | S | Southampton | 76:0.1.0.1.1 |
| Howell, Phineas | S | Southold | 76:0.1.2.1.0 |
| Howell, Price | S | ........ | 75-R |
| Howell, Recompence | S | Southold | 75-N |
| Howell, Reeves | S | Brookhaven | 75-B6 |
| Howell, Reivs | S | Brookhaven | 76:0.2.3.1.2 |
| Howell, Reve | S | Brookhaven | 75-B7 |
| Howell, Richard | S | Southold | 76:0.1.1.1.1 |
| Howell, Richard | S | Southold | 76:1.1.0.4.0.1.0 |
| Howell, Richard | S | Southold | 76:1.3.0.3.2.3.6 |
| Howell, Robert | Q | Jamaica | 75-C |
| Howell, Roke | S | Southold | 76:0.2.0.1.1 |
| Howell, Ryal | S | Southampton | 76:0.2.2.2.3 |

| | | | |
|---|---|---|---|
| Howell, Ryall | S | ........ | 75-R |
| Howell, Sam<sup>ll</sup> | S | ........ | 75-R |
| Howell, Samuel | S | Southampton | 76:0.1.3.1.0.0.1 |
| Howell, Samuel, Corporal | S | Southold | 75-N |
| Howell, Samuel the 3<sup>d</sup> | S | Southampton | 75-M |
| Howell, Samuell | S | Southampton | 76:1.1.1.2.0 |
| Howell, Samuell Ju<sup>r</sup> | S | Southampton | 76:1.0.0.1.0.0.1 |
| Howell, Seth | S | Southampton | 75-M |
| Howell, Seth | S | Southampton | 76:0.1.1.1.1 |
| Howell, Silas | S | ........ | 75-R |
| Howell, Silas | S | Brookhaven | 75-B10 |
| Howell, Silas | S | Southampton | 76:1.0.1.2.0.1.1 |
| Howell, Silas | S | Southold | 75-N |
| Howell, Silvanus | S | Southampton | 76:0.1.1.1.1 |
| Howell, Sm<sup>l</sup> | S | Southold | 76:0.1.0.1.1.1.0 |
| Howell, Stephen | S | Southampton | 76:0.1.2.1.0 |
| Howell, Stephen Jr. | S | ........ | 75-R |
| Howell, Stephen [2] | S | ........ | [on] 75-R |
| Howell, Thomas | S | Southampton | 75-M |
| Howell, Timothy | S | Southampton | 76:1.0.1.1.1 |
| Howell, Walter | S | Southampton | 75-M |
| Howell, Walter | S | Southampton | 76:0.1.2.1.0 |
| Howell, William | S | Brookhaven | 75-B10 |
| Howell, William | S | Southold | 76:0.1.0.2.2 |
| Howell, Zebulon | S | Southampton | 76:1.0.2.2.1 |
| Howes, John, wheelwright | N | at Hallitts, B'way | 75-D1, D2 |
| Howser, Elizabeth | N | to Westchester Co | 76-P |
| Howser, Jacob | N | to Westchester Co | 76-P |
| Howser, Mattis | N | to Westchester Co | 76-P |
| Howspers, Polabot | N | New York | 74-A |
| Hoy, James | N | New York | 76-A |
| Hubbard, Benajah | S | Brookhaven | 75-B3, 75-B6 |
| Hubbard, Jacob | N | New York | 74-A |
| Hubbard, R. Steers | S | Southold | 76:1.1.2.4.0 |
| Hubbard, Richard S. Jr. | S | Brookhaven | 75-B10 |
| Hubbard, Rosel | S | Brookhaven | 75-B2 |
| Hubbard, ---- Wid. | S | Southold | 76:0.0.2.1.1.0.1 |
| Hubbard, ---- Wid. | S | Southold | 76:0.0.2.2.0 |
| Hubbel, Isaac, cabinetmaker | N | Little Dock St. | 74-T2, 9/15 |
| Hubbell, Isaac | N | New York | 74-A |

| | | | |
|---|---|---|---|
| Hubbell, Jehiel | N | New York | 74-A |
| Hubbell, Jekiel | N | New York | 75-D1 |
| Hubble, James | S | Huntington | 76-H3 |
| Hubble, Josiah, hse carpntr | N | gone to Boston | 75-D2 |
| Hubbs, Catherine | N | Golden Hill St. | 74-T2, 9/15 |
| Hubbs, Jacobus | S | Smithtown | 75-L |
| Hubbs, James, Corp'l | S | Huntington | 76-H3 |
| Hubbs, Selah | S | Smithtown | 75-L |
| Hubert, Frydrik | N | New York | 74-A |
| Hubnors, George | N | New York | 76-A |
| Huburt, Jeremiah | S | Brookhaven | 76:1.1.1.2.1 |
| Hudson, ---- Capt. | S | Southold | 75-N |
| Hudson, Frederick | S | Southold | 75-N |
| Hudson, Frederick | S | Southold | 76:0.1.1.2.2.3.2 |
| Hudson, Frederick Esq$^r$ | S | Brookhaven | 75-B9 |
| Hudson, Hennery | S | Southold | 76:0.1.4.1.2 |
| Hudson, Henry | S | ........ | 75-R |
| Hudson, Henry | S | Brookhaven | 75-B10 |
| Hudson, John | S | ........ | 75-R |
| Hudson, John | S | Easthampton | 75-E |
| Hudson, John | S | Islip | 75-I |
| Hudson, John | S | Islip | 76:1.0.5.1.0 |
| Hudson, John | S | Southampton | 76:0.2.1.1.0 |
| Hudson, John | S | Southampton | 76:1.1.1.2.0 |
| Hudson, John Jun. | S | ........ | 75-R |
| Hudson, Nathaniel | S | Brookhaven | 75-B10 |
| Hudson, Nath$^l$ | S | Southold | 76:0.1.4.1.2 |
| Hudson, Obadiah | S | Brookhaven | 75-B10 |
| Hudson, Obediah | S | Southold | 76:1.2.2.1.2 |
| Hudson, Richard | S | Southold | 76:1.0.1.1.4 |
| Hudson, Samuel | S | Southold | 76:1.0.0.2.0.2.0 |
| Hudson, Samuell Jun$^r$ | S | Southold | 76:0.1.2.1.3 |
| Hudson, Timothy | S | Southold | 75-N |
| Hudson, Timothy | S | Southold | 76:1.1.0.2.0.0.1 |
| Huet, Charles, breechesmkr | N | New York | 74-R |
| Huggit, Benjamin | N | Nassau Street | 74-T |
| Huggit, Benjamin | N | New York | 75-T2, 10/5 |
| Huggit, Benjamin | N | New York | 76-A, 76-F |
| Hugh, Mary | N | removed upstate | 76-P |
| Hugh, Sarah | N | removed upstate | 76-P |

| | | | |
|---|---|---|---|
| Hughes, Hugh | N | New York | 74-A, 76-N |
| Hughes, Hugh, schoolmastr | N | gone to Boston | 75-D2 |
| Hughes, John | Q | ........ | 75-A, 76-B |
| Hughes, Miles | N | New York | 75-D3 |
| Hughes, Richard | N | New York | 76-A |
| Hughes, Thomas | N | New York | 76-A |
| Hughes, Timothy | N | New York | 74-A |
| Hughes, Timothy, carpenter | N | Barclay Street | 75-D2 |
| Hughston, James | Q | ........ | 76-E |
| Huht, Fred'k Wm., Capt. | N | New York | 76-Y |
| Hulbert, John | S | Southampton | 75-M |
| Hulbert, John Colo[l] | S | Southampton | 76:0.1.0.3.0 |
| Hulet, William, Ensign | N | New York | 76-Y |
| Hulett, William Charles | N | Broad Street | 75-T2, 1/12 |
| Hulick, Peter, staymaker | N | Hanover Square | 74-T |
| Hulick, Peter, staymaker | N | William Street | 75-D1, D2 |
| Hull, George | N | New York | 74-A |
| Hull, Itelle | N | New York | 74-A |
| Hull, Robert | N | Broadway | 75-T, 76-H |
| Hull, Robert | N | New York | 74-A, 76-A |
| Hull, Robert | N | New York | 76-F |
| Hull, Robert, innkeeper | N | Broadway | 74-T2, 3/10 |
| Hull, Stephen | N | New York | 75-D2 |
| Hull, Tiddeman | N | New York | 74-T, 75-F |
| Hullit, Peter, staymaker | N | William Street | 75-D2 |
| Huls, Gildart | S | Brookhaven | 76:0.1.2.2.2 |
| Huls, Jesse | S | Brookhaven | 76:0.1.4.3.4 |
| Huls, Paul | S | Brookhaven | 76:1.0.1.3.0 |
| Huls, Peter & Wilm Took | S | Brookhaven | 76:0.2.0.1.0 |
| Huls, Thomas | S | Brookhaven | 76:0.2.2.4.2 |
| Huls, Zoper | S | Meritches | 76:0.1.1.2.4 |
| Hulse, Caleb | S | Southold | 75-N |
| Hulse, David | S | Brookhaven | 75-B8 |
| Hulse, Flower | Q | ........ | 75-A, 76-B |
| Hulse, Gilbert | S | Brookhaven | 75-B10 |
| Hulse, Gilbert | S | Brookhaven | 75-B11 n.s. |
| Hulse, Henry | S | Brookhaven | 75-B6 |
| Hulse, Isaac | S | Brookhaven | 75-B6, 75-B7 |
| Hulse, Jesse | S | Brookhaven | 75-B10 |
| Hulse, Jesse | S | Brookhaven | 75-B11 n.s. |

| | | | |
|---|---|---|---|
| Hulse, Jno. | Q | ........ | 75A |
| Hulse, John | S | Brookhaven | 75-B1 non-signer |
| Hulse, John | S | Brookhaven | 75-B7 non-singer |
| Hulse, John | S | Easthampton | 75-E |
| Hulse, Jonah | S | Brookhaven | 75-B6 |
| Hulse, Nehemiah | S | Brookhaven | 75-B1, 75-B7 |
| Hulse, Paul | S | Brookhaven | 75-B1, 75-B6 |
| Hulse, Paul, Deacon | S | Brookhaven | 75-B7 |
| Hulse, Richard | S | Brookhaven | 75-B3, 75-B6 |
| Hulse, Selah | S | Brookhaven | 75-B11 n.s. |
| Hults, Abagail | S | Brookhaven | 76:0.0.1.3.0 |
| Hults, Anthony | N | to Dutchess Co. | 76-P |
| Hults, Henery | S | Brookhaven | 76:1.2.3.2.2 |
| Hults, John | S | Brookhaven | 76:0.1.3.1.1 |
| Hults, Nehemiah | S | Brookhaven | 76:0.2.2.1.2 |
| Humphreys, Jas. Jr, books | N | New York | 75-T2, 11/23 |
| Humphry, Thos., runaway | N | New York | 74-T2, 11/10 |
| Hunt, Alsop | N | New York | 74-A, 74-T |
| Hunt, Benjamin | S | Southampton | 76:0.1.0.0.1 |
| Hunt, Catharine | N | New York | 75-R |
| Hunt, Catharine | N | rem to Ulster Co. | 76-P |
| Hunt, Cosby | N | New York | 76-G |
| Hunt, Hannah | N | to Westchester Co | 76-P |
| Hunt, Jesse, ship captain | N | New York | 74-T2, 7/28 |
| Hunt, John | N | New York | 75-F |
| Hunt, John, store | N | Hanover Square | 74-T2, 11/10 |
| Hunt, Joseph | N | New York | 76-A |
| Hunt, Joseph | N | rem to Ulster Co. | 76-P |
| Hunt, Joseph | N | Vesey Street | 75-D1, D2 |
| Hunt, Lake | N | New York | 75-D2 |
| Hunt, Leake | N | New York | 74-A |
| Hunt, Nathaniel | Q | ........ | 76-E |
| Hunt, Samuel | S | Easthampton | 75-E |
| Hunt, Thomas | Q | ........ | 76-E |
| Hunt, Thos. | N | New York | 74-A |
| Hunt, Ward | N | New York | 74-A, 76-N |
| Hunt, Ward, joiner | N | Dock Street | 74-T |
| Hunt, William, saddler | N | Wall Street | 75-T2, 9/28 |
| Hunter, Ann | N | removed upstate | 76-P |
| Hunter, George | N | New York | 74-A |

| | | | |
|---|---|---|---|
| Hunter, John | N | New York | 76-N |
| Hunter, Margaret | N | New York | 75-R |
| Huntill, Fred | N | New York | 76-A |
| Hunting, Zeruiah, widow | S | Southampton | 76:0.1.0.2.1.1.0 |
| Huntting, Benjamin | S | ........ | 75-R |
| Huntting, Isaac | S | Easthampton | 76:0.1.2.2.0 |
| Huntting, Isaac Mulford | S | Easthampton | 75-E |
| Huntting, John | S | Easthampton | 75-E |
| Huntting, Mary, M$^{rs}$ | S | Easthampton | 76:0.0.0.1.0 |
| Huntting, Nath'el | S | Easthampton | 75-E |
| Huntting, Nathaniel | S | Easthampton | 76:0.2.2.3.2 |
| Huntting, Sarah, widow | S | Easthampton | 76:0.0.1.1.2 |
| Huntting, William | S | Easthampton | 75-E |
| Huntting, William | S | Easthampton | 76:0.1.1.1.0.0.1 |
| Hurrelston, Elizabeth | N | removed upstate | 76-P |
| Hurst, Charles | N | Turtle Bay | 74-T |
| Hurst, Timothy | N | New York | 74-T |
| Hurtin, William, watchmkr | N | William Street | 75-D1, D2 |
| Hustice, John | N | New York | 75-R |
| Huston, Ann | N | Albany Peer | 76-I |
| Hutchens, Thos. | Q | ........ | 75-A |
| Hutching, Jeremiah | Q | ........ | 76-B |
| Hutchings, Jacamiah | Q | ........ | 75-A, 76-B2 |
| Hutchings, Jacob | N | New York | 74-A |
| Hutchings, John Nathn. | N | New York | 74-A |
| Hutchings, Samuel | Q | ........ | 76-E |
| Hutchings, William | Q | ........ | 76-E |
| Hutchins, Jacob | N | Water Street | 76-I |
| Hutchins, John | Q | Jamaica | 75-C |
| Hutchins, John Nathan | N | Cortlandt Street | 74-T2, 3/31 |
| Hutchins, Jona. | Q | ........ | 76-E |
| Hutchins, Jonathan | N | New York | 76-G |
| Hutchins, Thomas | Q | ........ | 76-B, 76-E |
| Hutchinson, Andrew | N | New York | 74-A |
| Hutchinson, Andrew | N | New York | 74-T insolvent |
| Hutchinson, Benjamin | S | Southold | 75-N Ensign |
| Hutchinson, Benjamin | S | Southold | 75-V |
| Hutchinson, Benjamin | S | Southold | 76:0.1.2.1.0.1.1 |
| Hutchinson, Sam$^l$ | S | Easthampton | 75-E |
| Hutchinson, Samuel, Doc$^{tr}$ | S | Easthampton | 76:0.1.3.3.2.1.0 |

| | | | |
|---|---|---|---|
| Hutchinson, Thomas | S | ........ | 75-R |
| Hutchinson, Thomas | S | Southold | 76:0.1.1.3.1.0.1 |
| Hutt, John, engraver | N | Dock Street | 74-T2, 6/9 |
| Hutten, Christopher | N | New York | 76-D |
| Hyatt, Asa | S | ........ | 75-R |
| Hyatt, John | N | New York | 76-N |
| Hyatt, ___ Mrs. | N | Kingsbridge | 75-T |
| Hyatt, Thomas | N | New York | 76-A, 76-I |
| Hyer, Cornelius | N | New Street | 74-V |
| Hyer, Diederick | N | New York | 76-A |
| Hyer, Walter | N | New York | 74-A |
| Hyer, William | N | Smith Street | 74-V |
| Hyer, William [2] | N | New York | [on] 74-A |
| Hylton, William, merchant | N | New York | 74-T2, 9/2 |
| Hylyard, Samuel | N | New York | 76-I |
| Hyne, Elizabeth | N | rem to Ulster Co. | 76-P |
| Hynes, Mary | N | rem to Ulster Co. | 76-P |
| Hynshaw, ___ Capt. | N | Golden Hill | 74-T |
| Hyslop, Robert, store | N | New York | 75-T2, 9/21 |
| Hyslop, Robt. | N | New York | 74-A |
| Idemyer, John | N | New York | 74-A |
| Imbrie, James | N | New York | 76-A |
| Imlay, John | N | New York | 75-T2, 5/4; 5/25 |
| Imlay, John and William | N | New York | 75-F |
| Inglis, Charles | N | New York | 76-A |
| Inglis, Hudson | N | New York | 75-D1 |
| Inglis/Inglish, James, taylor | N | Chappel Street | 75-D1, D2 |
| Inglis, M. | N | New York | 75-D1 |
| Inglis, Thomas | N | New York | 74-A |
| Inglish, Wm, mason | N | Partition Street | 75-D2 |
| Ingliss, James | N | New York | 76-R |
| Ingram, John | S | Southold | 76:0.1.1.1.1 |
| Ingram, William | N | New York | 74-A |
| Innes, John | Q | Jamaica | 75-E |
| Innes, John Sr. | Q | Jamaica | 75-D associator |
| Innis, George | N | New York | 75-R |
| Innous, William | N | New York | 74-A |
| Ireland, Daniel | Q | ........ | 76-E |
| Ireland, Daniel | S | Huntington | 75-H |
| Ireland, Jacob | S | Huntington | 75-H |

| | | | |
|---|---|---|---|
| Ireland, John | S | Huntington | 75-H non-signer |
| Ireland, Joseph | S | Huntington | 75-H, 76-H2 |
| Ireland, Thomas | Q | ........ | 76-E |
| Ireland, Thomᵉ | S | Huntington | 75-H |
| Irvin, Elizabeth | N | New York | 74-T, 75-R |
| Isaacs, Aaron | S | Easthampton | 75-E |
| Isaacs, Aaron | S | Easthampton | 76:1.1.2.1.3 |
| Isaacs, Aaron Jr. | S | Easthampton | 75-E |
| Isaacs, Aaron Juner | S | Easthampton | 76:0.1.0.1.0 |
| Isaacs, Abraham | N | New York | 74-A |
| Israel, Levy | N | New York | 76-A |
| Israel, Samuel | N | Little Dock St. | 74-T |
| Ivers, John | N | New York | 74-A |
| Ivers, Thomas | N | New York | 74-T2, 11/24 |
| Ivers, Thos. | N | New York | 74-A |
| Jackson, Benjamin | Q | ........ | 76-E |
| Jackson, Cornelius | Q | ........ | 75-A, 76-B |
| Jackson, David | Q | ........ | 75-A |
| Jackson, David | Q | ........ | 76-B, 76-E |
| Jackson, David | S | Huntington | 75-H |
| Jackson, Hanna | N | removed upstate | 76-P |
| Jackson, Henry | Q | ........ | 75-A, 76-B |
| Jackson, Isaac | Q | ........ | 76-E |
| Jackson, Jacob | Q | ........ | 75-A |
| Jackson, Jacob | Q | ........ | 76-B, 76-E |
| Jackson, Jacob | Q | Hempstead | 76-D |
| Jackson, John | N | New York | 76-N |
| Jackson, John | Q | ........ | 76-B |
| Jackson, John Jr. | Q | ........ | 75-A, 76-E |
| Jackson, John [3] | Q | ........ | [on] 76-E |
| Jackson, Obadiah | Q | ........ | 76-E |
| Jackson, Obadiah | Q | Hempstead | 76-D |
| Jackson, Parmenus | Q | ........ | 75-A |
| Jackson, Parmenus | Q | ........ | 76-B, 76-E |
| Jackson, Rich'd | Q | Hempstead | 76-D |
| Jackson, Rich'd Jr. | Q | Hempstead | 76-D |
| Jackson, Richard Jr. | Q | ........ | 76-E |
| Jackson, Richard [2] | Q | ........ | [on] 76-E |
| Jackson, Robert | Q | ........ | 75-A, 76-B |
| Jackson, Robert Jr. | Q | ........ | 76-E |

| | | | |
|---|---|---|---|
| Jackson, Robert [2] | Q | ........ | [on] 76-E |
| Jackson, Sa. the 3d | Q | ........ | 76-E |
| Jackson, Sam<sup>l</sup> | S | Huntington | 75-H |
| Jackson, Samuel | Q | ........ | 75-A, 76-B |
| Jackson, Samuel | Q | Hempstead | 76-D |
| Jackson, Samuel [2] | Q | ........ | [on] 76-E |
| Jackson, Thomas | Q | ........ | 76-B |
| Jackson, Thomas [2] | Q | ........ | [on] 75-A |
| Jackson, Thomas [2] | Q | ........ | [on] 76-E |
| Jackson, Townsend | Q | ........ | 75-A |
| Jackson, Townsend | Q | ........ | 76-B, 76-E |
| Jacobs, Abraham R. | N | New York | 74-A |
| Jacobs, Abraham, shoemkr | N | Vesey Street | 75-D1, D2 |
| Jacobs, ____ Capt. | N | New York | 75-T |
| Jacobs, Daniel | N | New York | 76-A |
| Jacobs, Eleanor, widow | S | Southampton | 76:0.0.2.1.2 |
| Jacobs, Filera | N | New York | 75-R |
| Jacobs, Hendrick | Q | ........ | 76-E |
| Jacobs, Hendrick | Q | Newtown | 75-B |
| Jacobs, Moses, drugs | N | New York | 75-T2, 1/19 |
| Jacobs, Philip | N | New York | 74-A |
| Jacobs, Sarah | N | New York | 75-R |
| Jacobs, Tunes | N | New York | 74-A |
| Jacobs, Tunis, carpenter | N | Crown Street | 75-D1, D2 |
| Jacobs, William | N | New York | 74-A |
| Jacobs, Wm, son of Sarah | N | New York | 75-R apprentice |
| Jadvin, Joseph | N | New York | 74-A |
| Jadwin, Joseph | N | New York | 74-T |
| Jager, Ebenezer | S | Southampton | 76:0.2.0.1.0 |
| Jager, James | S | Southampton | 76:0.1.1.1.0 |
| Jager, Jeremiah | S | Southampton | 76:1.1.2.0.3 |
| Jager, Jeremiah Jun<sup>r</sup> | S | Southampton | 76:0.1.3.1.2 |
| Jager, John | S | Southampton | 76:2.0.0.2.0 |
| Jager, Joseph | S | Southampton | 76:0.1.1.1.1 |
| Jager, Josiah | S | Southampton | 76:0.1.2.1.0 |
| Jager, Nathan Jur. | S | Southampton | 76:1.1.2.3.0 |
| Jager, Nathaniel | S | Southampton | 76:1.0.2.2.0 |
| Jager, Samuell | S | Southampton | 76:1.0.1.1.0 |
| Jager, Samuell Jun<sup>r</sup> | S | Southampton | 76:1.0.0.1.1 |
| Jager, Stephen Esq<sup>r</sup> | S | Southampton | 76:1.0.5.4.2.3.2 |

| | | | |
|---|---|---|---|
| Jager, Stephen Jun' | S | Southampton | 76:0.1.0.1.0 |
| Jager, William | S | Southampton | 76:1.0.0.2.0 |
| Jaggar, Hezekiah | S | ........ | 75-R |
| Jagger, Abraham | S | ........ | 75-R |
| Jagger, Josiah | S | ........ | 75-R |
| Jagger, Matthew | S | ........ | 75-R |
| Jagger, Matthew | S | Southampton | 76:1.1.0.2.1.1.0 |
| Jagger, William | S | Easthampton | 76:0.1.2.1.1 |
| James, Abel Esq. | N | New York | 75-T |
| James, Ben. | N | New York | 74-A |
| James, Benjamin, Capt. | N | New York | 75-A, 76-S |
| James, Benjamin, store | N | New York | 74-T2, 11/3 |
| Jane, James | S | Smithtown | 76:0.1.4.1.0 |
| Jane, Joseph | S | Smithtown | 76:0.2.1.2.4.0.1 |
| Jane, Micajah | S | Brookhaven | 75-B3 |
| Jane, Micajah | S | Brookhaven | 75-B6 |
| Jane, William | S | Brookhaven | 75-B9 |
| Janeway, George | N | New York | 74-A |
| Janeway, George | N | New York | 75-T2, 5/4 |
| Janeway, George, Capt. | N | New York | 75-A |
| January, George, Capt. | N | New York | 76-L |
| Jarrett, Azel | S | Brookhaven | 75-B2 |
| Jarvis, Abraham Jr. | S | Huntington | 75-H, 75-H1 |
| Jarvis, Arthur | N | New York | 74-A |
| Jarvis, Arthur, merchant | N | Queen Street | 75-D1, D2 |
| Jarvis, Austin | S | Huntington | 75-H |
| Jarvis, Eliphalet | S | Huntington | 75-H, 75-H1 |
| Jarvis, Henry | S | Huntington | 75-H, 75-H1 |
| Jarvis, Ichabod | S | Huntington | 75-H non-signer |
| Jarvis, Isaiah | S | Huntington | 76-H2 |
| Jarvis, James | N | New York | 74-R juror |
| Jarvis, James, hatter | N | New York | 74-V |
| Jarvis, Jonathan | S | Huntington | 75-H, 75-H1 |
| Jarvis, Joseph | S | Huntington | 75-H, 76-H2 |
| Jarvis, Moses | S | Huntington | 75-H |
| Jarvis, Nathaniel | S | Huntington | 75-H, 76-H2 |
| Jarvis, Philip | S | Huntington | 75-H |
| Jarvis, Robert | S | Huntington | 75-H, 75-H1 |
| Jarvis, Sam$^{el}$ | S | Huntington | 75-H |
| Jarvis, Seth | S | Huntington | 75-H, 76-H3 |

| | | | |
|---|---|---|---|
| Jauncey, James | N | New York | 75-T |
| Jauncey, Joseph, Capt. | N | Wyncoop Street | 74-T2, 6/16 |
| Jauncey, Margaret | N | New York | 74-T |
| Jay, Frederick | N | New York | 74-T2, 11/24 |
| Jay, John | N | New York | 74-T2, 11/24 |
| Jayne, Jams | S | Brookhaven | 76:1.1.2.1.0 |
| Jayne, Joseph Juner | S | Brookhaven | 75-B11 n.s. |
| Jayne, Jotham | S | Brookhaven | 75-B8 |
| Jayne, Matthias | S | Brookhaven | 76:1.2.1.2.1 |
| Jayne, Robbart | S | Brookhaven | 76:0.1.3.3.0 |
| Jayne, Robert | S | Brookhaven | 75-B10 |
| Jayne, Robert | S | Brookhaven | 75-B11 n.s. |
| Jayne, Robert Juner | S | Brookhaven | 75-B11 n.s. |
| Jayne, Samual | S | Brookhaven | 76:0.1.3.1.1.0.1 |
| Jayne, Samuel | S | Brookhaven | 75-B10 |
| Jayne, Samuel | S | Brookhaven | 75-B11 n.s. |
| Jayne, Stephen | S | Brookhaven | 75-B11 n.s. |
| Jayne, Stephen | S | Brookhaven | 76:1.3.0.5.1 |
| Jayne, William | S | Brookhaven | 75-B10 |
| Jayne, William | S | Brookhaven | 75-B11 n.s. |
| Jayne, William Juner | S | Brookhaven | 75-B11 n.s. |
| Jeacock, Thomas | N | New York | 74-T insolvent |
| Jeanes, Shadrach | S | Brookhaven | 75-B6 |
| Jeanneret, John, tavern | N | Peck's Slip | 74-T |
| Jeffers, see Geffers | | | |
| Jeffray, James, nailmaker | N | New York | 75-T runaway |
| Jeffrey, see Geffrey | | | |
| Jemison, Elinor | N | to Dutchess Co. | 76-P |
| Jenings, Ebenezar | S | Southold | 76:0.2.2.2.2 |
| Jenings, Hezekiah | S | Southold | 76:0.1.1.1.2 |
| Jenings, John | S | Southold | 76:0.2.2.1.0 |
| Jenings, Lemuel | S | ........ | 75-R |
| Jenkins, see Jinkins | | | |
| Jennigs, William | S | Southampton | 76:1.0.0.1.1 |
| Jennings, Ebenezer | S | ........ | 75-R |
| Jennings, Eben' | S | ........ | 75-R |
| Jennings, Elias | S | ........ | 75-R |
| Jennings, Elias | S | Southampton | 76:0.1.0.1.0 |
| Jennings, Elnathan | S | ........ | 75-R |
| Jennings, Hezekiah | S | ........ | 75-R |

| | | | |
|---|---|---|---|
| Jennings, James | S | ........ | 75-R |
| Jennings, James | S | Southampton | 76:0.1.0.1.2 |
| Jennings, Jonathan | S | Southold | 76:0.1.0.1.1 |
| Jennings, Lemuel | S | Southampton | 76:0.1.1.2.1 |
| Jennings, Sam[ll] | S | ........ | 75-R |
| Jennings, Samuel | S | Southampton | 76:1.0.1.1.0 |
| Jennings, Samuel Jnr. | S | Southampton | 76:0.1.0.1.1 |
| Jennings, Silvanus | S | Southampton | 76:0.1.3.2.1 |
| Jennings, Stephen | S | Southampton | 76:0.1.4.2.2 |
| Jennings, Zebulon | S | Southampton | 76:0.1.1.1.0 |
| Jessop, Silas | S | ........ | 75-R |
| Jessup, Hennery | S | Southampton | 76:0.1.1.1.2 |
| Jessup, Isaac | S | Southampton | 75-M |
| Jessup, Isaac | S | Southampton | 76:0.1.2.1.1 |
| Jessup, John | S | Southampton | 76:1.0.0.1.0 |
| Jessup, John Jun[r] | S | Southampton | 76:0.3.0.1.6 |
| Jessup, Nathaniel | S | Southampton | 75-M |
| Jessup, Nathaniel | S | Southampton | 76:1.1.0.1.0.1.0 |
| Jessup, Silas | S | Southampton | 76:0.1.3.1.2.0.1 |
| Jessup, Stephen | S | Southampton | 75-M |
| Jessup, Stephen | S | Southampton | 76:0.1.0.1.2.0.1 |
| Jessup, Thomas Jun[r] | S | Southampton | 76:0.1.1.1.1 |
| Jessup, Zeb. | S | ........ | 75-R |
| Jesup, Thomas | S | Southampton | 76:1.0.2.3.0 |
| Jillett, Wm | Q | ........ | 75-A |
| Jillit, Elisha | S | Smithtown | 76:1.0.1.2.1 |
| Jinkins, Jerrey | N | New York | 76-I |
| Job, John, apprentice | N | New York | 74-R |
| Job, Samuel | N | New York | 74-A |
| Jobs, John, shoemaker | N | Smith Street | 75-D1, D2 |
| Johnes, Jonathan | S | Brookhaven | 75-B1 |
| Johnes, Obadiah | S | ........ | 75-R |
| Johnes, Thomas | S | ........ | 75-R |
| Johnson, ---- Capt. | N | New York | 76-E |
| Johnson, Catherine | N | New York | 76-I |
| Johnson, David | N | New York | 74-A |
| Johnson, David | N | New York | 75-T2, 5/4 |
| Johnson, Elenor, Mrs. | N | to Dutchess Co. | 76-P |
| Johnson, Isaac | N | New York | 74-A |
| Johnson, Isaac, Sec[y] | N | New York | 75-D2 |

| | | | |
|---|---|---|---|
| Johnson, Jabez, Capt. | N | King Street | 74-T2, 6/16 |
| Johnson, Jacob | Q | ........ | 75-A associator |
| Johnson, Jacques | Q | ........ | 76-E |
| Johnson, Jacques | Q | Jamaica | 75-D associator |
| Johnson, James | N | New York | 74-A, 76-M |
| Johnson, James, Ensign | N | New York | 75-A |
| Johnson, John | N | New York | 74-R |
| Johnson, John | N | New York | 76-A |
| Johnson, John | S | Huntington | 75-H |
| Johnson, John, Capt. | N | New York | 75-E |
| Johnson, John, chairmaker | N | Broadway | 75-D1, D2 |
| Johnson, John, hse carpntr | N | Beekman Street | 75-D1, D2 |
| Johnson, John, Lieut. | N | New York | 75-B, 76-C |
| Johnson, John [2] | N | New York | [on] 74-A |
| Johnson, Margaret | N | New York | 74-R |
| Johnson, Martin | Q | ........ | 76-E |
| Johnson, Martin | Q | Jamaica | 75-C |
| Johnson, Reuben | S | Huntington | 75-H, 76-H1 |
| Johnson, Robert | N | New York | 76-I |
| Johnson, Robert, taylor | N | Broad Street | 75-D2 |
| Johnson, Sam'l | N | New York | 74-A |
| Johnson, Samuel | N | New York | 76-N |
| Johnson, Samuel | N | West Ward | 75-R overseer |
| Johnson, Samuel | Q | ........ | 75-A, 76-B |
| Johnson, Samuel, ae c.19 | N | New York | 76-V runaway |
| Johnson, Samuel, Capt. | N | New York | 75-A |
| Johnson, William | N | New York | 74-T insolvent |
| Johnson, William Jr. | S | Huntington | 75-H |
| Johnson, Will^m | S | Huntington | 75-H |
| Johnson, Wm | Q | ........ | 75-A, 76-B |
| Johnston, David | N | New York | 74-T2, 11/24 |
| Johnston, David | N | South Street | 74-T |
| Johnston, David Esq. | N | New York | 75-T, 75-V |
| Johnston, John | Q | Jamaica | 75-C |
| Johnston, Robert | N | New York | 76-A |
| Johnston, Robert, shoemkr | N | Peck Slip | 75-D1, D2 |
| Johnston, William, shoemkr | N | William Street | 75-D1, D2 |
| Johnston, Wm | N | New York | 75-D2 |
| Jonas, Lyon, furrier | N | Little Dock Street | 74-T2, 11/24 |
| Jones, Benjamen | S | Brookhaven | 75-B10 |

| | | | |
|---|---|---|---|
| Jones, Benjamin | N | New York | 76-N |
| Jones, Benjamin | S | Brookhaven | 75-B11 n.s. |
| Jones, Cave | N | Learys Street | 76-H |
| Jones, Daniel | S | Brookhaven | 75-B3, 75-B6 |
| Jones, Daniel | S | Brookhaven | 76:0.1.4.1.3 |
| Jones, Daniel Juner | S | Brookhaven | 75-B11 n.s. |
| Jones, David | N | New York | 74-A, 76-A |
| Jones, David | Q | ........ | 76-E |
| Jones, David, ale | N | Broadway | 74-T2, 8/18 |
| Jones, ____ Dr. | N | New York | 75-D2 |
| Jones, Ebbenezer, Capt. | S | Brookhaven | 75-B11 n.s. |
| Jones, Ebenezer | S | Brookhaven | 75-B10 |
| Jones, Ebenezer | S | Brookhaven | 76:1.3.1.2.3 |
| Jones, Edward | S | Easthampton | 76:0.1.2.2.3 |
| Jones, Eliakim | S | Brookhaven | 75-B6 |
| Jones, Elisha | S | Easthampton | 75-E |
| Jones, Elisha | S | Easthampton | 76:0.1.0.1.1 |
| Jones, Ezekeil | S | Easthampton | 76:1.1.1.1.0 |
| Jones, Ezekeil Jun' | S | Easthampton | 76:0.1.1.1.2 |
| Jones, Ezekiel | S | Easthampton | 75-E |
| Jones, Ezekiel Jr. | S | Easthampton | 75-E |
| Jones, George | N | rem. to Bedford | 76-J |
| Jones, Gilbert | Q | Hempstead | 76-D |
| Jones, Isaac | S | Brookhaven | 75-B6 |
| Jones, James | N | New York | 74-A |
| Jones, James | N | New York | 74-R, 75-R |
| Jones, Jeremiah | S | Easthampton | 75-E |
| Jones, John | N | Learys Street | 76-I |
| Jones, John | N | New York | 74-A |
| Jones, John | Q | ........ | 76-E |
| Jones, John | Q | Hempstead | 76-D |
| Jones, John | S | Brookhaven | 76:1.3.0.1.1 |
| Jones, John, Dr. | N | New York | 74-T |
| Jones, John, tavernkeeper | N | New York | 74-T |
| Jones, John [2] | N | New York | [on] 76-A |
| Jones, Jonathan | S | Brookhaven | 75-B1, 75-B6 |
| Jones, Jonathan | S | Brookhaven | 75-B7 |
| Jones, Jonathan | S | Brookhaven | 76:1.1.1.2.0 |
| Jones, Joseph | S | Brookhaven | 75-B6 |
| Jones, Nicholas | Q | ........ | 76-E |

| | | | |
|---|---|---|---|
| Jones, Nicholas | Q | Jamaica | 75-C, 75-D |
| Jones, Obadiah | S | Southampton | 76:1.3.0.2.1 |
| Jones, Paul | S | ........ | 75-R |
| Jones, Peter | Q | ........ | 75-A |
| Jones, Peter | Q | ........ | 76-B, 76-E |
| Jones, Sam$^{ll}$ | S | ........ | 75-R |
| Jones, Samuel | N | New York | 74-T2, 11/24 |
| Jones, Samuel | N | New York | 76-A |
| Jones, Samuel | Q | ........ | 76-E |
| Jones, Samuell | S | Southampton | 76:0.1.2.1.2 |
| Jones, Stephen | S | Brookhaven | 75-B11 n.s. |
| Jones, Stephen | S | Brookhaven | 76:0.1.0.1.1 |
| Jones, Steven | S | Brookhaven | 75-B10 |
| Jones, Thomas | S | Easthampton | 75-E |
| Jones, Thomas | S | Southampton | 76:0.1.1.1.0 |
| Jones, Thomas, Judge | Q | ........ | 75-H |
| Jones, Vincent | S | Brookhaven | 75-B10 |
| Jones, Vincent | S | Brookhaven | 75-B11 n.s. |
| Jones, Walter | Q | ........ | 76-E |
| Jones, William | N | New York | 76-A |
| Jones, William | Q | ........ | 76-E |
| Jones, William | S | Southampton | 76:1.1.2.2.3.2.0 |
| Jones, W$^m$ | Q | Hempstead | 76-D |
| Jones, W$^m$ Jun$^r$ | S | ........ | 75-R |
| Jordan, Abigail | N | removed upstate | 76-P |
| Jordan, Peter | N | removed upstate | 76-P |
| Josephsen, Manuel | N | New York | 76-F |
| Judah, Barruck, Mrs. | N | New York | 74-T |
| Judah, Samuel | N | New York | 74-V, 75-F |
| Judah, Samuel, merchant | N | Wall Street | 74-T2, 5/26 |
| Justis, Hannah | N | to Westchester Co | 76-P |
| Justus, Charles | Q | ........ | 76-E |
| Kain, Arter | N | to Westchester Co | 76-P |
| Kain, Arthur | N | to Dutchess Co. | 76-P |
| Kann, John | N | New York | 74-R |
| Kashaw, Andries | Q | ........ | 76-E |
| Kashaw, John | Q | ........ | 76-E |
| Kashaw, Moury | Q | ........ | 76-E |
| Kashow, Jacob | Q | ........ | 76-E |
| Kashow, Johan$^s$ | Q | ........ | 75-A |

| | | | |
|---|---|---|---|
| Kashow, John, minor | Q | ........ | 76-E |
| Kauff, Christian | N | New York | 76-A |
| Kay, William | N | New York | 74-A |
| Keacham, Thomas | Q | ........ | 76-B2 |
| Kearns, John | Q | ........ | 76-E |
| Kearns, Margaret | N | New York | 75-T |
| Keating, John | N | New York | 74-T, 76-N |
| Keating, John, paper mfr | N | New York | 74-T2, 6/30 |
| Kedore, George | N | New York | 74-A |
| Keen & Boyar | N | New York | 74-A |
| Keen, Isaac | Q | ........ | 76-E |
| Keen, John | N | New York | 76-A |
| Keene, Jonathan | S | Southold | 76:0.1.1.1.1.1.0 |
| Keer, Andrew | N | New York | 76-A |
| Keily, John | N | New York | 74-A, 76-N |
| Keith, or Kilty, Timothy | N | New York | 74-T2, 11/10 |
| Kelcy, Nath[l] | S | Huntington | 75-H non-signer |
| Keley, John | S | Huntington | 75-H |
| Keley, Jonathan | S | Huntington | 75-H |
| Keley, Platt | S | Huntington | 75-H |
| Keley, Stephen | S | Huntington | 75-H |
| Kellam, Thomas | S | Huntington | 75-H1 |
| Kellcy, Stephen, Corp'l | S | Huntington | 76-H2 |
| Kellcy, Stephen, trustee | S | Huntington | 75-H1 |
| Kelley, John | N | New York | 74-A |
| Kellum, Ebenezer | S | Huntington | 75-H |
| Kellum, Obadiah | S | Huntington | 75-H, 76-H2 |
| Kellum, Obid | S | Huntington | 75-H |
| Kellum, Phillip | S | Huntington | 75-H |
| Kellum, Robert | S | Huntington | 75-H |
| Kelly, Anthony, shoemaker | N | Coffee House | 75-D2 |
| Kelly, Craig, shoemaker | N | Cowfit Hill | 75-D1, D2 |
| Kelly, David | S | Huntington | 75-H |
| Kelly, Elizabeth | N | removed upstate | 76-P |
| Kelly, John | N | New York | 74-R |
| Kelly, Mick | N | New York | 76-E |
| Kelly, Robert | S | Huntington | 75-H |
| Kelso, John, chairmaker | N | Broad Street | 75-D1, D2 |
| Kelso, John, chairmaker | N | New York | 74-R Freeman |
| Kemble, Lawrence | N | New York | 74-A |

| | | | |
|---|---|---|---|
| Kemmenay, Engelbart | N | New York | 76-N |
| Kempe, Jno. T. | N | New York | 76-A |
| Kemper, Jacob | N | New York | 75-D3 |
| Kemper, Jacob Jr. | N | New York | 74-A |
| Kemper, Jacob Jr. | N | New York | 75-D1 |
| Kemper, Jacob, wheelwright | N | Old Slip Market | 75-D2 |
| Kendal, John, Capt. | Q | Flushing | 75-H |
| Kendrick, John | N | New York | 74-A, 75-D1 |
| Kenneday, John | N | New York | 74-A |
| Kennedy, Bridgit | N | New York | 74-R |
| Kennedy, John | N | New York | 74-R, 75-R |
| Kennedy, John | N | New York | 76-A |
| Kennedy, Sarah | N | New York | 74-R |
| Kenney, John | S | ........ | 75-R |
| Kenny, John | S | Southampton | 76:0.2.2.1.1 |
| Kershow, Isaac | N | New York | 74-A |
| Keser, Johannis | N | New York | 76-A |
| Kesler, Jacob | N | New York | 74-A |
| Ketcham, Abijah | S | Huntington | 75-H |
| Ketcham, Abijah | S | Huntington | 75-H1, 76-H1 |
| Ketcham, Alexander | S | Huntington | 75-H |
| Ketcham, Caleb | S | Huntington | 75-H |
| Ketcham, Daniel | S | Huntington | 75-H |
| Ketcham, David | S | Huntington | 75-H Quaker |
| Ketcham, Ezekiel | S | Huntington | 75-H |
| Ketcham, Isaac | N | New York | 76-M |
| Ketcham, Isaac | S | Huntington | 75-H |
| Ketcham, Isaac Carll | S | Huntington | 75-H |
| Ketcham, Isaac, Cold Sr. | S | Huntington | 75-H |
| Ketcham, Isaac Sr. | S | Huntington | 75-H |
| Ketcham, Israel | S | Huntington | 75-H |
| Ketcham, Israel | S | Huntington | 75-H Quaker |
| Ketcham, Jacob | S | Huntington | 75-H |
| Ketcham, James | N | New York | 74-A |
| Ketcham, Jesse | S | Huntington | 75-H |
| Ketcham, Jesse, Sergt. | S | Huntington | 76-H2 |
| Ketcham, John | S | Huntington | 75-H |
| Ketcham, John Jr. | Q | ........ | 76-E |
| Ketcham, Joseph | S | Huntington | 75-H |
| Ketcham, Joshua | S | Huntington | 75-H |

| | | | |
|---|---|---|---|
| Ketcham, Joshua | S | Huntington | 75-H1, 76-H1 |
| Ketcham, Nathan[1] | S | Huntington | 75-H |
| Ketcham, Nath[1] Jr. | S | Huntington | 75-H non-signer |
| Ketcham, Philip | S | Huntington | 75-H |
| Ketcham, Phillip | S | Huntington | 75-H |
| Ketcham, Reuben | S | Huntington | 75-H |
| Ketcham, Samuel | S | Huntington | 75-H |
| Ketcham, Samuel | S | Smithtown | 76:0.1.2.1.2 |
| Ketcham, Solomon | S | Huntington | 75-H, 75-H1 |
| Ketcham, Stephen | S | Huntington | 75-H, 75-H1 |
| Ketcham, Timothy | S | Huntington | 75-H |
| Ketcham, William | N | New York | 74-A |
| Ketcham, Zebulon | S | Huntington | 75-H, 75-H1 |
| Ketcham, Zophar | S | Huntington | 75-H |
| Ketchum, Joshua | S | Huntington | 75-H |
| Ketchum, Nathaniel | N | New York | 76-N |
| Keteltas, Abraham | Q | ........ | 75-A associator |
| Keteltas, Abraham | Q | Jamaica | 75-D associator |
| Keteltas, Garret | N | New York | 75-T2, 5/4 |
| Keteltas, Peter Jr. | N | New York | 75-B |
| Keteltas, Wydert, Capt. | N | New York | 76-S |
| Keteltas, Wynandt | N | New York | 75-B |
| Keteltas, Wynandt, Capt. | N | New York | 76-G |
| Keteltas, Wyn[dt] | N | New York | 76-N |
| Ketteltas, Viner, Lieut. | N | New York | 75-A |
| Ketteltas, W. | N | New York | 75-D3 |
| Kettletas, Peter | N | New York | 75-F |
| Keyser, ___ | N | to Dutchess Co. | 76-P |
| Keyser, Aaron | N | New York | 76-A |
| Keyser, Andrew | N | New York | 74-A, 74-R |
| Keyser, Michael | N | New York | 76-I |
| Kibble, Stephen | N | New York | 74-A, 76-A |
| Kibble, Stephen | N | New York | 76-F |
| Kidder, John, wife of, | N | New York | 76-K |
| Kierstead, Luke, juror | N | New York | 74-R, 75-R |
| Kiersted, John | N | New York | 74-A |
| Kiersted, Luke [2] | N | New York | [on] 74-A |
| Kilburn, Judith wid of Law[∞] | N | New York | 75-T |
| Killbrun, Judith | N | New York | 75-V |
| Killmaster, James | N | New York | 76-A |

| | | | |
|---|---|---|---|
| Killpatrick, Samuel | N | New York | 74-R |
| Kilty, or Keith, Timothy | N | New York | 74-T2, 11/10 |
| King, Abraham | S | Brookhaven | 75-B10 |
| King, Abraham | S | Southold | 76:0.1.4.1.1 |
| King, Alexander | S | ........ | 75-R |
| King, Alexander | S | Southampton | 76:1.0.1.4.0 |
| King, Alexander Jun<sup>r</sup> | S | Southampton | 76:0.1.2.1.1 |
| King, Alexander Ju<sup>r</sup> | S | ........ | 75-R |
| King, Ann | N | removed upstate | 76-P |
| King, Anthony | N | New York | 76-L |
| King, Asa | S | ........ | 75-R |
| King, Assa | S | Southold | 76:1.1.0.1.1 |
| King, Benj<sup>a</sup> | S | ........ | 75-R |
| King, Benjamin | S | Southampton | 76:0.1.1.1.1 |
| King, Benjamin | S | Southold | 76:1.1.1.2.0 |
| King, ---- Capt. | S | Southold | 75-N |
| King, Daniel | S | Easthampton | 75-E |
| King, Daniel | S | Easthampton | 76:0.3.3.2.1 |
| King, Edward | N | New York | 74-A |
| King, Elenor | N | removed upstate | 76-P |
| King, Ephraim | S | ........ | 75-R |
| King, Ephraim | S | Southold | 76:1.3.0.2.0 |
| King, Ephraim Junr. | S | Southold | 76:0.1.2.1.0 |
| King, Henry | N | New York | 75-R |
| King, James | S | Southold | 76:1.0.1.2.3 |
| King, Jeremiah | S | ........ | 75-R |
| King, Jeremiah | S | Southold | 76:0.1.6.3.0.0.1 |
| King, Joel | S | ........ | 75-R |
| King, John | N | Broad Street | 75-T |
| King, John | N | New York | 74-A |
| King, John | N | New York | 76-F, 76-I |
| King, John | S | ........ | 75-R |
| King, John | S | Brookhaven | 75-B6 |
| King, John | S | Easthampton | 75-E |
| King, John | S | Southold | 76:1.1.2.1.3 |
| King, John Jr. | S | ........ | 75-R |
| King, John, juror | N | New York | 74-R, 75-R |
| King, John, Lieut. | N | New York | 75-A |
| King, John, mason | N | Barclay Street | 75-D1, D2 |
| King, Jonathan | S | ........ | 75-R |

| | | | |
|---|---|---|---|
| King, Jonathan | S | Brookhaven | 75-B6 |
| King, Jonathan | S | Southold | 76:0.2.3.2.2 |
| King, Jonathan Juner | S | ........ | 75-R |
| King, Joseph | S | ........ | 75-R |
| King, Joseph | S | Southold | 76:0.1.3.3.0 |
| King, Jothen | S | Meritches | 76:0.1.1.1.2 |
| King, Linus | N | New York | 76-A |
| King, Nathaniel | S | ........ | 75-R |
| King, Nathaniel | S | Southold | 76:1.1.2.3.3 |
| King, Peter | S | ........ | 75-R |
| King, Peter | S | Southampton | 76:0.1.1.1.4 |
| King, Richard | S | Easthampton | 75-E |
| King, Richard | S | Easthampton | 76:0.1.1.1.0 |
| King, Sam$^l$ | S | ........ | 75-R |
| King, Samuel | S | Southampton | 76:0.1.2.1.2 |
| King, William | S | Southold | 76:1.1.1.2.1 |
| King, William Jun$^r$ | S | Southold | 76:0.1.2.1.3 |
| King, William [2] | S | ........ | [on] 75-R |
| King, Zebulon | S | Southold | 76:1.0.1.1.0 |
| Kingsbury, Asa | N | New York | 76-V |
| Kingsland, Aaron | N | New York | 75-D2 |
| Kingston, John | N | New York | 76-A |
| Kingston, Rachel | N | to Dutchess Co. | 76-P |
| Kingston, Rachel, Mrs. | N | rem to Ulster Co. | 76-P |
| Kinnan, Thos. | N | New York | 74-A |
| Kinner, Jerimiah | S | Brookhaven | 75-B9 |
| Kinner, William | S | Brookhaven | 75-B9 |
| Kinster, Sam'l | N | New York | 74-A |
| Kip, Abraham | N | New York | 74-A |
| Kip, Abraham | N | New York | 75-R juror |
| Kip, Elezabeth | N | New York | 76-K |
| Kip, Elizabeth, Mrs. | N | to Dutchess Co. | 76-P |
| Kip, Garret | N | New York | 76-D, 76-N |
| Kip, Garritt, measurer | N | Leary Street | 75-D2 |
| Kip, Henry H., brass fndr | N | Broadway | 75-D1, D2 |
| Kip, Henry H. | N | New York | 74-A, 76-N |
| Kip, Henry [2] | N | New York | [on] 74-A |
| Kip, Isaac | N | New York | 74-R juror |
| Kip, Isaac | N | New York | 75-F |
| Kip, Jacob | N | New York | 74-A |

| | | | |
|---|---|---|---|
| Kip, James | N | New York | 76-L |
| Kip, John H. | N | New York | 74-A |
| Kip, John H., merchant | N | New York | 74-T2, 4/28 |
| Kip, John H., Lieut. | N | New York | 75-A |
| Kip, Leonard | N | New York | 74-A |
| Kip, Leonard, store | N | Dock Street | 74-T2, 12/22 |
| Kip, Rich'd Jr. | N | New York | 74-A |
| Kip, Richard | N | New York | 74-A |
| Kip, Richard | N | New York | 74-R juror |
| Kipp, Catherien | N | removed upstate | 76-P |
| Kipp, Jacob | N | to Dutchess Co. | 76-P |
| Kipp, Jane | N | removed upstate | 76-P |
| Kipp, Joanna | N | to Dutchess Co. | 76-P |
| Kipp, Sarah | N | removed upstate | 76-P |
| Kipp, Thomas | Q | ........ | 75-A, 76-E |
| Kippin, William | N | New York | 74-A |
| Kirbaker, John | N | New York | 76-I |
| Kirby, Daniel | Q | ........ | 75-A |
| Kirby, Daniel | Q | ........ | 76-B, 76-E |
| Kirby, John | N | New York | 74-A, 76-I |
| Kirby, Joseph | N | New York | 76-A |
| Kirby, Peter | N | New York | 74-A |
| Kirby, Thomas | Q | ........ | 76-E |
| Kirk, John | N | removed upstate | 76-P |
| Kirk, John, apprentice | N | New York | 74-V runaway |
| Kirk, Richard | Q | ........ | 76-E |
| Kirkland, William | N | New York | 74-A |
| Kirkwood, John | N | New York | 74-A |
| Kisaam, Dan'l W. | Q | ........ | 75-A associator |
| Kissam, Benj. | Q | ........ | 75-A |
| Kissam, Benjamin | N | New York | 74-T, 76-A |
| Kissam, D.W. | Q | ........ | 76-E |
| Kissam, Daniel | Q | ........ | 76-E |
| Kissam, Daniel 3d | Q | ........ | 76-E |
| Kissam, Daniel Esq. | Q | ........ | 75-A |
| Kissam, Daniel Esq. | Q | Cowneck | 75-H |
| Kissam, John | Q | ........ | 75-A, 76-E |
| Kissam, Joseph | Q | ........ | 75-A |
| Kissam, Joseph | Q | ........ | 76-B, 76-E |
| Kissam, Peter, Ensign | N | New York | 75-A |

| | | | |
|---|---|---|---|
| Kissick, John | N | New York | 76-I |
| Kissick, Philip | N | New York | 74-A, 76-A |
| Kissick, Philip | N | New York | 76-V |
| Kissick, Philip, distiller | N | Queen Street | 74-T2, 3/24 |
| Kissick, Philip, juror | N | New York | 74-R to 76-R |
| Klein, George | N | New York | 76-A |
| Klein, Johannes | N | New York | 74-A |
| Klein, John | N | New York | 76-A |
| Klein, John, baker | N | Sloat Alley | 75-T |
| Klinck, Jacob | N | New York | 74-A, 76-A |
| Kline, John | N | New York | 74-A |
| Klyne, John, baker | N | Duke Street | 75-T |
| Knapp, J.C., attorney | N | New York | 74-T2, 1/6 |
| Knapp, John C. | N | Broad Street | 74-V |
| Knapp, John Cogghill | N | New York | 76-A |
| Kneht, Jacob | N | New York | 76-A |
| Knell, Peter | N | New York | 74-A |
| Knickerbacker, Ab'm | N | New York | 76-A |
| Knickerbocker, Abraham | N | New York | 74-R |
| Knight, Robert | S | ........ | 75-R |
| Knoblock, John | N | New York | 76-A |
| Knott, James | N | New York | 74-A |
| Knowdell, Conrad | N | New York | 74-A |
| Knox, George | N | New York | 76-N |
| Knox, Nicholas | N | New York | 74-A |
| Knox, Robert | N | New York | 74-A, 76-A |
| Komodanga, Lodowick | N | New York | 76-I |
| Korby, William | N | New York | 76-I |
| Kortright, ____ Mrs. | N | to Dutchess Co. | 76-P |
| Kortwright, Lawrence Esq. | N | New York | 75-V |
| Kortwright, Sally dau Law<sup>ce</sup> | N | New York | 75-T |
| Kulen, Joseph | S | Brookhaven | 76:1.3.0.1.4 |
| Kuortzinger, Matteis | N | New York | 74-A |
| L'Homedieu, Benjamin | S | Southold | 75-N non-signer |
| L'Homedieu, Constant | S | ........ | 75-R |
| L'Homedieu, Ephraim Jun<sup>r</sup> | S | ........ | 75-R |
| L'Homedieu, James | S | Smithtown | 75-L |
| L'Homedieu, John | S | Smithtown | 75-L |
| L'Homedieu, Jonathan | S | Smithtown | 75-L recusant |
| L'Homedieu, Sylvester | S | ........ | 75-R |

| | | | |
|---|---|---|---|
| L'Homedue, Joseph | S | Southampton | 76:1.1.0.2.0 |
| L'hommedieu, John | S | Smithtown | 75-L |
| L'Hommedieu, Benj. | S | Southold | 76:0.2.2.1.3 |
| L'Hommedieu, Constant | S | Southold | 76:0.3.1.2.4 |
| L'Hommedieu, Ezra | S | Southold | 76:0.1.0.2.0.3.4 |
| L'Hommedieu, Ezra [2] | S | ........ | [on] 75-R |
| L'Hommedieu, Grover | S | ........ | 75-R |
| L'Hommedieu, Grover | S | Southampton | 76:0.2.2.1.4 |
| L'Hommedieu, Hennery | S | Southold | 76:0.1.6.1.2 |
| L'Hommedieu, Henry | S | Brookhaven | 75-B10 |
| L'Hommedieu, John | S | Brookhaven | 75-B10 |
| L'Hommedieu, John | S | Southold | 76:1.0.0.1.1 |
| L'Hommedieu, Sam[l] | S | ........ | 75-R |
| L'Hommedieu, Sam[l] Capt[n] | S | Southampton | 76:0.1.1.1.0 |
| L'Hommedieu, Sylvester | S | Southold | 76:1.0.0.2.0 |
| L'Hommedue, James | S | Smithtown | 76:0.1.1.1.2 |
| L'Hommedue, John | S | Smithtown | 76:1.0.4.2.1 |
| L'Hommedue, Jonathan | S | Smithtown | 76:0.1.1.1.1 |
| L'Humedy, Jonathan | S | Brookhaven | 75-B10 |
| Laane, Tise | Q | Hempstead | 76-D |
| Labagh, Isaac | N | New York | 74-A, 76-L |
| Laboyteaux, John | N | New York | 74-A |
| Laboyteaux, John | N | New York | 75-R juror |
| Laboyteaux, John, taylor | N | Beekman's Slip | 74-T2, 5/5 |
| Lachman, Jost | N | New York | 76-A |
| Lackman, Nicholas | N | New York | 76-A |
| LaCroix, William | N | New York | 76-A |
| Ladlam, Stephen | N | New York | 76-A |
| Lafoy, Arreietta | N | Broadway | 76-H |
| Lafoy, Ereetty | N | head of Broadway | 76-I |
| Lagear, John | N | New York | 76-A |
| LaGrange, Sarah, Mrs. | N | to Dutchess Co. | 76-P |
| Lahriwick, Thomas | N | New York | 76-A |
| Laight, Edward | N | New York | 74-A, 76-F |
| Laight, Edward | N | New York | 74-T2, 11/24 |
| Laight, Edward | N | New York | 76-R juror |
| Laight, Edward & William | N | New York | 74-T2, 8/25 |
| Laight, Edward & William | N | New York | 75-F |
| Laight, William | N | New York | 74-A |
| Laight, William | N | New York | 75-T2, 5/4 |

| | | | |
|---|---|---|---|
| Lain, Josiah | N | to Westchester Co | 76-P |
| Lain, William | N | to Westchester Co | 76-P |
| Lake, _____ Mrs. | N | to Dutchess Co. | 76-P |
| Lakerman, Catheren | N | removed upstate | 76-P |
| Lakerman, Richard | N | New York | 74-A |
| Lam, Eunice | S | Easthampton | 76:0.0.0.1.2 |
| Lamasney, James | N | near the Hospital | 76-I |
| Lamasney, James | N | New York | 76-F |
| Lamasney, see also Lemasney | | | |
| Lamasny, James | N | nr New Hospital | 76-H |
| Lamb, Alexander | N | New York | 74-A, 76-L |
| Lamb, John | N | New York | 74-A |
| Lamb, John | N | New York | 75-T2, 5/4 |
| Lamb, Thomas | N | New York | 76-A |
| Lambert, Daniel | N | New York | 75-R |
| Lambert, John, Mrs. | N | New York | 74-T, 74-V |
| Lambertson, Bernardus | Q | Jamaica | 76-C |
| Lambertson, Cornelius | Q | Jamaica | 75-C, 76-C |
| Lambertson, David | Q | ........ | 75-A associator |
| Lambertson, David | Q | ........ | 76-E |
| Lambertson, David | Q | Jamaica | 75-D associator |
| Lambertson, David | Q | Jamaica | 75-E |
| Lambertson, Jacob | Q | ........ | 75-A |
| Lambertson, Jacob | Q | ........ | 76-A, 76-B |
| Lambertson, John | Q | ........ | 75-A, 76-E |
| Lambertson, John | Q | Jamaica | 75-C, 75-D |
| Lambertson, John Jr. | Q | ........ | 76-B |
| Lambertson, John Jr. | Q | Jamaica | 75-C |
| Lambertson, John Sr. | Q | ........ | 76-B |
| Lambertson, Matthias | Q | ........ | 75-A, 76-B |
| Lambertson, Matthias | Q | Jamaica | 75-C, 75-D |
| Lambertson, Nicholas | Q | ........ | 75-A, 76-B |
| Lambertson, Nicholas | Q | Jamaica | 75-C, 75-D |
| Lambertson, Nicholas | Q | Jamaica | 76-C |
| Lambertson, Nicholas Jr. | Q | Jamaica | 75-C, 76-C |
| Lambertson, Simon | N | New York | 75-D1 |
| Lambertson, Simon | Q | ........ | 75-A |
| Lambertson, Simon | Q | ........ | 76-B, 76-E |
| Lambertson, Simon | Q | Jamaica | 75-D |
| Lambertson, Tunis | Q | Jamaica | 75-C |

| | | | |
|---|---|---|---|
| Lambertson, Waters | Q | ........ | 76-E |
| Lambertson, Waters | Q | Jamaica | 75-C, 75-E |
| Lamkin, Albert | N | New York | 76-A |
| Lampley, Jacob | N | New York | 75-R |
| Lamply, Jacob, innkeeper | N | New York | 74-R Freeman |
| Landon, Jared | S | ........ | 75-R |
| Landon, Sam^el | S | ........ | 75-R |
| Landon, Sam^ll J^r | S | ........ | 75-R |
| Landon, Samuel | S | ........ | 75-R |
| Landon, Samuell | S | Southold | 76:1.2.2.1.2.3.2 |
| Landon, William | S | ........ | 75-R |
| Landon, William | S | Southold | 76:0.1.1.1.3 |
| Landon, Wm | Q | ........ | 76-B |
| Lane, Billy | N | to Dutchess Co. | 76-P |
| Lane, Doxse | S | Brookhaven | 75-B6 |
| Lane, Joseph | S | Brookhaven | 75-B6 |
| Lane, Mary | N | to Westchester Co | 76-P |
| Lane, Sarah | N | to Dutchess Co. | 76-P |
| Lane, Tice | Q | ........ | 75-A, 76-E |
| Lane, Timethy | S | Brookhaven | 76:0.1.3.1.0 |
| Lane, Timothy | S | Brookhaven | 75-B7 |
| Lane, Timothy | S | Middle Island Co. | 75-B5 neutral |
| Lane; see also Laane | | | |
| Langden, John, age 16 | N | New York | 76-V runaway |
| Langdon, Arch'l | Q | ........ | 75-A |
| Langdon, Archibald | Q | ........ | 76-B |
| Langdon, James | Q | ........ | 76-E |
| Langdon, James [2] | Q | ........ | [on] 75-A |
| Langdon, Jas., hatter | Q | ........ | 75-A |
| Langdon, Joseph | Q | ........ | 75-H |
| Langdon, Joseph, hatter | Q | ........ | 75-I |
| Langdon, Pearson | Q | ........ | 75-A, 76-B |
| Langdon, Richard | Q | ........ | 75-A, 76-E |
| Langdon, Samuel | Q | ........ | 76-B, 76-E |
| Langdon, Samuel [2] | Q | ........ | [on] 75-A |
| Langdon, William | Q | ........ | 76-B2 |
| Langdon, William [2] | Q | ........ | [on] 75-A |
| Langdon, William [2] | Q | ........ | [on] 76-E |
| Lapreice/Lapris, Charles | N | New York | 74-R |
| Larew, William | N | New York | 76-I |

| | | | |
|---|---|---|---|
| Larkin, Jushua | S | Easthampton | 76:0.1.3.1.2 |
| Larzelore, Nicholas, shoem'r | N | Batteau Street | 75-D2 |
| Lashear/Loshiear, Abraham | N | mason, Moereoit St | 75-D1, D2 |
| Lasher, Frederick, constable | N | New York | 74-R to 76-R |
| Lasher, Fredk. | N | New York | 74-A |
| Lasher, John | N | New York | 74-T2, 11/24 |
| Lasher, John | N | New York | 75-B |
| Lasher, John | N | New York | 75-R juror |
| Lasher, John, Col. | N | New York | 76-C |
| Lasher, John, shoemaker | N | Broadway | 75-D2 |
| Lasher, John [2] | N | New York | [on] 74-A |
| Lashly, Elizabeth | N | to Dutchess Co. | 76-P |
| Lashly, Mary | N | to Dutchess Co. | 76-P |
| Lasiere, Ann | N | removed upstate | 76-P |
| Lassells, Ralph | N | New York | 74-A |
| Latham,      Dr. | Q | ........ | 75-A associator |
| Latham, Hanah, Wid. | S | Southampton | 76:0.0.0.1.1 |
| Latham, Hubbard | S | Southampton | 76:0.1.3.1.3 |
| Latham, John | N | New York | 75-D1 |
| Latham, Joseph | N | New York | 74-A |
| Latham, Joseph | Q | ........ | 76-E |
| Latham, Joseph Jr. | N | New York | 74-A |
| Latham, Joseph Ju', Ensign | N | New York | 76-G |
| Latham, Samuel | Q | ........ | 76-E |
| Laton, David | Q | ........ | 75-A associator |
| Laton, David | Q | ........ | 76-E |
| Laton, David | Q | Oyster Bay | 75-F |
| Laton, John | Q | ........ | 76-E |
| Laton, W. | Q | ........ | 76-E |
| Laton, William | Q | Oyster Bay | 75-F |
| Laton, William Jr. | Q | Oyster Bay | 75-F |
| Latten, Daniel | Q | ........ | 76-E |
| Latten, Garret | Q | Jamaica | 75-C |
| Latten, Isaac | Q | ........ | 76-B |
| Latten, Josiah | Q | ........ | 76-B |
| Latten, Josias | Q | ........ | 76-E |
| Latten, Sias | Q | ........ | 75-A |
| Lattimore, Margaret, Mrs. | N | rem to Ulster Co. | 76-P |
| Lattin, Isaac | Q | ........ | 75-A |
| Lattin, Josiah | Q | Oyster Bay | 75-F |

| | | | |
|---|---|---|---|
| Lattin, Richard | Q | ........ | 76-E |
| Latting, Benj. Jr. | Q | ........ | 76-E |
| Latting, Benjamin | Q | ........ | 76-E |
| Latting, Benjamin | Q | Oyster Bay | 75-F |
| Latting, Garret | Q | ........ | 75-A |
| Latting, Garret | Q | Jamaica | 75-D |
| Latting, William | Q | ........ | 76-E |
| Latting, William | Q | Oyster Bay | 75-F |
| Lattouch, Js. | N | New York | 74-A |
| Laurence, Jacobus | Q | ........ | 75-A |
| Laurilliard, see Lorrilliard | | | |
| Law, Andrew, Ensign | N | New York | 76-Y |
| Law, Henry | N | New York | 74-A, 76-A, 76-F |
| Law, Henry, sloop owner | N | Beekman Street | 74-T2, 9/22 |
| Lawn, George | N | New York | 74-A |
| Lawrance, Jacob | N | New York | 76-N |
| Lawrance, John | N | New York | 76-A |
| Lawrence, Abraham | Q | ........ | 75-A, 76-B2 |
| Lawrence, Abraham | Q | Flushing | 75-V |
| Lawrence, Abraham [2] | Q | ........ | [on] 76-E |
| Lawrence, Adam | Q | ........ | 75-A |
| Lawrence, Adam | Q | Jamaica | 75-D |
| Lawrence, Caleb | N | New York | 74-A |
| Lawrence, Caleb | Q | ........ | 76-E |
| Lawrence, Clarke | Q | ........ | 76-E |
| Lawrence, D. | Q | ........ | 76-B |
| Lawrence, Dan'l, Dr. | Q | ........ | 75-A |
| Lawrence, Daniel | Q | ........ | 75-A associator |
| Lawrence, Daniel | Q | ........ | 76-E |
| Lawrence, Daniel | Q | Jamaica | 75-D |
| Lawrence, Daniel | Q | Newtown | 75-G |
| Lawrence, Isaac | Q | ........ | 76-E |
| Lawrence, Jacobus | Q | ........ | 76-E |
| Lawrence, John | N | New York | 75-F |
| Lawrence, John | Q | ........ | 76-E |
| Lawrence, John, Lieut. | N | New York | 75-A |
| Lawrence, John [2] | N | New York | [on] 74-A |
| Lawrence, Jonathan | N | New York | 74-A |
| Lawrence, Jonathan | Q | ........ | 75-A, 75-D1 |
| Lawrence, Jonathan, Capt. | Q | Newtown | 75-G |

| | | | |
|---|---|---|---|
| Lawrence, Jordan | Q | ........ | 76-E |
| Lawrence, Jo⁶ | Q | ........ | 76-E |
| Lawrence, Joseph | N | New York | 74-A, 75-F |
| Lawrence, Joseph | Q | ........ | 76-E |
| Lawrence, Joseph | Q | Newtown | 75-G |
| Lawrence, Leonard | N | New York | 74-A |
| Lawrence, Leonard | Q | ........ | 76-E |
| Lawrence,        Mr. | Q | ........ | 76-E |
| Lawrence, Nicholas, shoem'r | N | William Street | 75-D1, D2 |
| Lawrence, Obadiah | Q | ........ | 75-A |
| Lawrence, Obadiah | Q | ........ | 76-B, 76-E |
| Lawrence, Richard | Q | ........ | 75-A associator |
| Lawrence, Richard | Q | Newtown | 75-G |
| Lawrence, Robert | Q | ........ | 76-B, 76-E |
| Lawrence, Sam'l | Q | ........ | 75-A associator |
| Lawrence, Sam'l | Q | Newtown | 75-G |
| Lawrence, Silas | Q | ........ | 76-E |
| Lawrence, Somerset | Q | ........ | 76-E |
| Lawrence, Steph. Jr. | Q | ........ | 76-E |
| Lawrence, Stephen | Q | ........ | 76-E |
| Lawrence, Stephen | Q | Flushing | 75-T |
| Lawrence, Thomas | N | New York | 74-A, 76-I |
| Lawrence, Thomas | N | New York | 76-L, 76-N |
| Lawrence, Thomas | Q | ........ | 75-A associator |
| Lawrence, Thomas | Q | ........ | 76-E |
| Lawrence, Thomas, Capt. | Q | Newtown | 75-G |
| Lawrence, William, ae 20 | N | New York | 74-T runaway |
| Lawrence, William Jr. | Q | ........ | 76-E |
| Lawrence, Wm | Q | Newtown | 75-G |
| Lawson, Thomas | Q | ........ | 76-E |
| Lawson, William | N | in the Fly | 74-T |
| Lawson, William | N | New York | 74-A |
| Lawson, William, shoemkr | N | Beekman Street | 75-D1, D2 |
| Leach, Charity wf Stephen | N | New York | 75-T |
| Leach, Johnson | S | Shelter Island | 75-K |
| Leach, Stephen | N | New York | 75-R, 76-A |
| Leadbelter, James | N | New York | 76-A |
| Leady, Theady | N | New York | 76-E |
| Leak, John | S | Brookhaven | 76:0.1.1.1.2 |
| Leak, Philep | S | Brookhaven | 76:1.0.0.1.0 |

| | | | |
|---|---|---|---|
| Leake, Ann | N | New York | 74-T |
| Leake, John | N | New York | 76-A |
| Leake, John G. | N | New York | 74-T |
| Leake, —— Mrs. | N | removed upstate | 76-P |
| Leary, James | N | New York | 74-A |
| Leary, Jno. | N | Broadway | 75-D2 |
| Leary, John | N | New York | 76-F |
| Leary, John Junʳ | N | New York | 75-B |
| Leary, John, son of James | N | New York | 74-R |
| Leary, ---- widow | N | New York | 76-I |
| Leary, Wm. | N | New York | 74-A |
| Leary, Wm., Town Major | N | New York | 76-S |
| Leaviz, Benjn. | N | New York | 74-A |
| Leaycraft, Richard | N | New York | 76-N |
| Leaycraft, Robert, baker | N | Golden Hill | 75-D1, D2, D3 |
| Ledru, Harman | N | New York | 74-A |
| Ledyard, Benja. | N | New York | 74-A |
| Ledyard, ---- Capt. | N | New York | 76-B |
| Ledyard, Isaac, med student | N | Broad Street | 75-D1, D2 |
| Lee, John | N | New York | 74-A, 76-I |
| Lee, Joseph | N | New York | 76-A |
| Lee, Joseph | S | ........ | 75-R |
| Leek, Abra: | S | Easthampton | 75-E |
| Leek, Benjamin | S | Easthampton | 76:1.0.0.1.0 |
| Leek, David | S | Easthampton | 75-E |
| Leek, David | S | Easthampton | 76:0.1.4.1.1.1.0 |
| Leek, John | S | Brookhaven | 75-B1 |
| Leek, John | S | Brookhaven | 75-B6 |
| Leek, John, Corporal | S | Brookhaven | 75-B7 |
| Leek, Phillip | S | Brookhaven | 75-B6 |
| Leeke, Benjamin | S | Easthampton | 75-E |
| LeFever, Andrias | N | rem to Ulster Co. | 76-P |
| Leffert, Isaac | Q | Jamaica | 75-D |
| Lefferts, Derrick | N | New York | 75-T |
| Lefferts, Isaac | Q | ........ | 76-E |
| Lefferts, Jacobus | N | New York | 75-T2, 5/4 |
| Lefferts, Jacobus Esq. | N | New York | 74-T |
| Lefferts, Jacobus, Judge | N | New York | 74-R |
| Lefferts, Jo. | Q | ........ | 76-E |
| Lefferts, Leffert | Q | ........ | 75-A, 76-B |

| | | | |
|---|---|---|---|
| Lefoy, Thomas | N | New York | 74-A |
| Lefoy, Thomas | N | New York | 75-D1 |
| Lefoy, Thomas, hatter | N | Cortland Street | 75-D1, D2 |
| Leg, Elizabeth | N | to Westchester Co | 76-P |
| Legang, ——— Mrs. | N | removed upstate | 76-P |
| Legar, John | N | New York | 76-A |
| Legg, Elizabeth | N | to Dutchess Co. | 76-P |
| Legross, John | Q | ........ | 75-A |
| Legross, John | Q | ........ | 76-B, 76-E |
| Lehys, William | N | removed upstate | 76-P |
| Leister, see Luyster | | | |
| Lell, John | N | New York | 76-A |
| Lelond, Hanomon | Q | ........ | 76-E |
| Lemasney, John | N | New York | 74-A |
| Lemasney, see also Lamasney | | | |
| Lenght, James Jr. | N | New York | 76-I |
| Lent, Garret | N | New York | 76-A |
| Lent, Hallul | N | removed upstate | 76-P |
| Lent, Jac. | Q | Newtown | 75-B |
| Lent, see also Lint | | | |
| Lenthwaite, William, innkpr | N | Chatham Street | 75-D1, D2 |
| Lenzi, P., confectioner | N | Dock Street | 74-T2, 6/22 |
| Leonard, George | N | New York | 76-R |
| Leonard, Jacob | N | New York | 74-A |
| Leonard, James | N | New York | 76-A |
| Leonard, James, 2d Lieut. | N | New York | 76-Y |
| Leonard, Jeffery | N | New York | 75-D1 |
| Leonard, Jesse, mariner | N | Batteau Street | 75-D2 |
| Leonard, ---- Lieut. | N | New York | 76-C |
| Leonard, Robert | N | New York | 74-A |
| Leonard, Robert | N | New York | 76-A |
| Leonard, Robt. | N | New York | 74-A |
| Leonard, Thos. | N | New York | 74-A |
| Leonard, William | N | New York | 75-B, 76-I |
| Lepol, Michael | N | New York | 74-A |
| LeRoome, John | N | New York | 74-A |
| Leroy, Jacob | N | New York | 75-V |
| Leslie, Alexander | N | New York | 74-A, 76-A |
| Leslie, Alexander | N | New York | 76-F, 76-I |
| Leslie, James | N | New York | 74-A |

| | | | |
|---|---|---|---|
| Lesly, James | N | New York | 76-A |
| Lessler, Michael | N | New York | 76-A |
| Lesslie, Alexander, shoemkr | N | Chatham Street | 75-D1, D2 |
| Lessly, Alexander | N | New York | 74-R |
| Lester, Benjamin | Q | ........ | 75-A |
| Lester, Benjamin | Q | ........ | 76-B, 76-E |
| Lester, Jacob | N | New York | 74-T |
| Lester, John | S | Easthampton | 76:0.1.4.1.1 |
| Lester, Syl. | S | ........ | 75-R |
| Lester, Sylvester | S | Southold | 76:0.1.0.1.2.0.2 |
| Lester, Thomas | N | New York | 75-D1 |
| Lester, Thomas | S | Southold | 76:0.1.0.2.3 |
| Lester; see also Lister | | | |
| Leverage, John | N | New York | 76-V runaway |
| Leveret, Elithan | Q | Newtown | 75-G |
| Leverich, John | Q | ........ | 76-E |
| Leverich, John Jr. | Q | Newtown | 75-G |
| Leverich, W. | Q | ........ | 76-E |
| Levison, Christ. | N | New York | 74-A |
| Levison, David | N | New York | 74-A, 76-A |
| Levissen, Christopher | N | New York | 76-A |
| Levy, Hayman, storekeeper | N | Bayard Street | 74-T2, 8/25 |
| Lewis, Foster | N | New York | 74-A |
| Lewis, Foster | N | New York | 76-H, 76-I |
| Lewis, Foster | N | New York | 76-N |
| Lewis, Foster, innholder | N | New York | 75-E |
| Lewis, Foster, innkeeper | N | Dock Street | 75-D1, D2 |
| Lewis, Francis | N | New York | 74-T2, 8/18 |
| Lewis, Francis & Son, store | N | Fly Market | 75-T2, 3/30 |
| Lewis, Francis Jr. | N | New York | 75-B |
| Lewis, Harman | N | New York | 74-A |
| Lewis, Henry | N | New York | 74-A, 75-D3 |
| Lewis, James | Q | ........ | 75-A, 76-E |
| Lewis, John | N | New York | 74-A |
| Lewis, John | Q | Hempstead | 76-D |
| Lewis, John | S | Islip | 75-I |
| Lewis, John, Capt. | N | New York | 76-Y |
| Lewis, John Jr., 2d Lieut. | N | New York | 76-Y |
| Lewis, John Jun. | S | Islip | 75-I |
| Lewis, John [2] | N | New York | [on] 76-A |

| | | | |
|---|---|---|---|
| Lewis, Joseph, Mr. | S | Huntington | 76-H1 |
| Lewis, Morgan | N | New York | 75-D3 |
| Lewis, Sam[l] | S | Huntington | 75-H |
| Lewis, Scudder | S | Huntington | 75-H |
| Lewis, Thomas | Q | ........ | 76-E |
| Lewis, William | N | New York | 76-R |
| Lewis, William | N | to Dutchess Co. | 76-P |
| Leyburn, Patrick | N | New York | 76-A |
| Lhommedieu, see L'Hommedieu | | | |
| Lickletter, James | N | New York | 76-L |
| Liester, see Luyster | | | |
| Lifford, James | Q | ........ | 76-E |
| Light, James | N | New York | 74-A, 74-R |
| Light, Mary | N | removed upstate | 76-P |
| Lightbourn, Benj. | N | New York | 76-N |
| Lightfoot, Daniel | N | New York | 74-A, 76-A |
| Limbeck, David | N | New York | 74-A |
| Lin, Barnard | N | New York | 76-A |
| Linch, Jane | N | removed upstate | 76-P |
| Linch, Margrit | N | removed upstate | 76-P |
| Linck, Mary | N | New York | 76-K |
| Lincoln, Stroud Cotton | N | New York | 74-A, 76-A |
| Lindaman, Charles | N | New York | 76-A |
| Lindner, Johannis | N | New York | 76-A |
| Lindsay, Edmund | Q | ........ | 76-E |
| Lindsay, George | N | New York | 74-A |
| Lindsey, Abraham | N | New York | 74-R |
| Lindsey, Mary | N | to Dutchess Co. | 76-P |
| Lindsey, Mary, Mrs. | N | rem to Ulster Co. | 76-P |
| Lindsey; see also Linzie | | | |
| Ling, John B. | N | New York | 76-F |
| Ling, John Burt, juror | N | New York | 74-R, 75-R |
| Linkenson, Hossey | N | New York | 74-R |
| Linklete, James | N | New York | 74-A |
| Linn, see Lin | | | |
| Lint, Abraham | Q | ........ | 76-E |
| Lint, Daniel | Q | ........ | 76-E |
| Lint, Jacobus | Q | ........ | 76-E |
| Lint; see also Lent | | | |
| Lintenau, Catherien | N | removed upstate | 76-P |

| Lintener, Jacob | N | near ye Barracks | 76-H |
|---|---|---|---|
| Lintner, Jacob | N | near the Barracks | 76-I |
| Lintworth, William | N | New York | 76-I |
| Lintwright, Grace | N | New York | 75-R |
| Linzie, Philip | N | New York | 76-A |
| Lions, Jemes | S | Brookhaven | 76:2.2.0.3.0 |
| Lisaight, William | S | Huntington | 75-H |
| Lishier, Oliver | N | New York | 74-T insolvent |
| Liskom, Isaac | S | Southampton | 76:1.0.1.1.1 |
| Lispenard, Anthony, Capt. | N | New York | 75-A |
| Lispenard, Leonard | N | New York | 74-T2, 11/24 |
| Lispenard, Leonard | N | New York | 76-A |
| Lissner, Wm, perukemaker | N | New York | 74-R |
| Lister, Thomas, ship carpntr | N | Ship Yards | 75-D2 |
| Lister; see also Lester | | | |
| Litch, William | N | New York | 76-A |
| Litchfield, John Esq. | N | New York | 75-T, 75-V |
| Littel/Little, Eleazer, crptr | N | Hague Street | 75-D1, D2 |
| Littell, Eleazer | N | New York | 74-A |
| Little, George | N | New York | 76-A |
| Little, Henry | N | New York | 74-A |
| Little, Robert | N | New York | 74-A |
| Livingston, Abraham | N | New York | 75-F |
| Livingston, Alexander | N | New York | 74-T insolvent |
| Livingston, Henry, Capt. | N | New York | 76-C |
| Livingston, Henry G. | N | New York | 75-B, 75-D3 |
| Livingston, Jno. | Q | ........ | 75-A |
| Livingston, John, merchant | N | New York | 75-V |
| Livingston, Peter Van B. | N | New York | 74-T2, 11/24 |
| Livingston, Philip | N | New York | 74-T2, 11/24 |
| Livingston, Philip Esq. | N | New York | 74-V merchant |
| Livingston, Richard | N | New York | 75-R, 76-N |
| Livingston, Robert R. | N | New York | 74-R Judge |
| Livingston, W., Lieut. | N | New York | 76-C |
| Livingston, Wm. S. | N | New York | 76-N |
| Lockhart, John | N | New York | 74-R juror |
| Lockhart, John | N | New York | 75-F |
| Lockhart, John | N | New York | 76-A, 76-G |
| Lockman, John | N | New York | 76-A |
| Lockwood, Eliphalet | N | New York | 75-D1 |

| | | | |
|---|---|---|---|
| Lockwood, Eliphalet, crpntr | N | gone to Boston | 75-D1, D2 |
| Lockwood, Ephraim | N | New York | 76-N |
| Lockwood, John | S | Huntington | 75-H |
| Lod, Caspar | N | New York | 74-A |
| Lodge, Catharine, Miss | N | New York | 74-T, 74-V |
| Loftus, Willoughby | N | New York | 74-A, 76-I |
| Logan, Abigail | N | removed upstate | 76-P |
| Logan, John | N | New York | 74-R, 75-R |
| Logan, John | N | New York | 76-A |
| Login, Robert | N | to Westchester Co | 76-P |
| Long, Christopher | N | New York | 76-A |
| Long, James | N | New York | 76-A, 76-F |
| Long, John | N | New York | 74-A, 76-A |
| Long, William, dry goods | N | Great George St. | 74-T2, 7/7 |
| Long, Wm & Sarah, school | N | Broadway | 74-T |
| Long, Wm & Sarah, school | N | New York | 75-T2, 11/2 |
| Longbotham, Samuel | S | Brookhaven | 75-B11 n.s. |
| Longbotham, William | S | Brookhaven | 75-B10 |
| Longbotham, William | S | Brookhaven | 75-B11 n.s. |
| Longbothom, Nathanael | S | Brookhaven | 75-B8 |
| Longbothom, Samu. | S | Brookhaven | 75-B10 |
| Longbotom, Nathaniel | S | Brookhaven | 76:0.1.0.1.1.0.1 |
| Longbottom, David | S | Brookhaven | 76:0.1.0.1.2 |
| Longbottom, Jacob | S | Smithtown | 76:1.1.2.2.1 |
| Longbottom, Jacob [2] | S | Smithtown | [on] 75-L |
| Longbottom, Joshu | S | Brookhaven | 76:1.0.1.1.0 |
| Longbottom, Joshua | S | Brookhaven | 75-B8 |
| Longbottom, Nathanael | S | Middle Island Co. | 75-B5 neutral |
| Longbottom, Nath[l] | S | Brookhaven | 75-B7 |
| Longbottom, Wm & Sam'l | S | Brookhaven | 76:0.2.2.3.2 |
| Longley, John | N | New York | 74-A |
| Longley, Thomas | N | New York | 74-A |
| Longmore, Elen | N | New York | 76-I |
| Loper, Abra: | S | Easthampton | 75-E |
| Loper, Abraham | S | Easthampton | 76:0.1.3.1.0 |
| Loper, Amos | S | Easthampton | 76:0.1.1.1.2 |
| Loper, Daniel | S | Easthampton | 75-E |
| Loper, David | S | Easthampton | 75-E |
| Loper, Isaac | S | ........ | 75-R |
| Loper, Isaac | S | Southampton | 76:0.1.3.3.0 |

| Loper, James | S | ........ | 75-R |
|---|---|---|---|
| Loper, James | S | Easthampton | 75-E |
| Loper, James | S | Easthampton | 76:1.0.0.1.1 |
| Loper, James | S | Southampton | 76:0.1.1.1.3 |
| Loper, John | S | ........ | 75-R |
| Loper, John | S | Southampton | 76:0.1.1.1.1 |
| Loper, William | S | Easthampton | 76:0.1.3.1.1 |
| Lorilliard, Peter | N | above New Gaol | 76-H |
| Lorilliard, Peter A. | N | Chathem Street | 76-I |
| Lorrilliard, Charles | N | New York | 76-A |
| Lorrilliard, Peter | N | New York | 74-A |
| Losee, Andrew, Lieut. | N | New York | 75-A |
| Losee, Cornelius | Q | ........ | 75-A associator |
| Losee, Cornelius | Q | ........ | 76-E |
| Losee, Cornelius | Q | Jamaica | 75-D associator |
| Losee, Isaac | S | Huntington | 75-H |
| Losee, John | Q | ........ | 76-E |
| Losee, John | Q | Jamaica | 76-C |
| Losee, Nicholas | Q | Jamaica | 75-C |
| Losee, Peter | Q | ........ | 75-A |
| Losee, Peter | Q | ........ | 76-B, 76-E |
| Losee, Simon | Q | ........ | 75-A, 76-B |
| Losey, Peter | N | rem. to Bedford | 76-J |
| Losey, Simon | N | New York | 75-R apprentice |
| Loshee, Peter, mason | N | Partition Street | 75-D1, D2 |
| Loshiear, see Lashear | | | |
| Losie, Peter | N | to Dutchess Co. | 76-P |
| Losije, Lambert | N | New York | 76-A |
| Losijes, Andrew | N | New York | 74-A |
| Lott, Ab$^m$ P. | N | New York | 74-A, 75-B |
| Lott, Ab$^m$ P. | N | New York | 76-N |
| Lott, Abm. | N | New York | 75-D3 |
| Lott, Abraham | Q | ........ | 76-E |
| Lott, Abraham | Q | Jamaica | 75-C |
| Lott, Abraham E., merchant | N | New York | 74-T, 74-V |
| Lott, Abraham E. | N | New York | 75-F |
| Lott, Abraham Esq. | N | New York | 75-T |
| Lott, Abraham P. | N | New York | 74-T2, 11/24 |
| Lott, Abraham P. | N | New York | 75-F |
| Lott, And. | N | New York | 75-B |

| | | | |
|---|---|---|---|
| Lott, Andrew | N | New York | 75-D3 |
| Lott, Jacob | Q | ........ | 76-E |
| Lott, Jacob | Q | Jamaica | 75-C, 75-D |
| Lott, Johannes | Q | Jamaica | 75-C, 75-D |
| Lott, Johannes H. | Q | ........ | 76-E |
| Lott, Maurice | Q | ........ | 75-A |
| Lott, Stephen | Q | ........ | 76-E |
| Lott, Stephen | Q | Jamaica | 75-C, 75-D |
| Louden, Sam'l | N | New York | 74-A |
| Loudon, Richard | Q | ........ | 76-E |
| Loudon, Samuel, books | N | New York | 74-T2, 6/2 |
| Loudon, Samuel, juror | N | New York | 75-R, 76-R |
| Loudon, Samuel, shipchndlr | N | New York | 75-T |
| Lough, James | N | New York | 74-A |
| Loughead, William | N | New York | 76-A |
| Lounds, Wm | N | New York | 76-H |
| Lounds; see also Lowndes | | | |
| Love, James | N | New York | 76-A |
| Low, Charles, shoemaker | N | Broadway | 75-D1, D2 |
| Low, Cornelius P. | N | New York | 75-F |
| Low, Elezar | S | Southold | 76:0.1.4.3.2 |
| Low, Isaac | N | New York | 74-T2, 11/24 |
| Low, Isaac | N | New York | 75-F |
| Low, John | N | New York | 76-I |
| Low, Marenus | N | New York | 76-I |
| Low, Marinus | N | New York | 74-R witness |
| Low, Nicholas, Capt. | N | New York | 75-A |
| Low, Peter | N | New York | 74-A |
| Low, Peter | N | New York | 74-R juror |
| Low, Peter | N | New York | 75-D3 |
| Low, Peter Jr., cabinetmkr | N | Leary Street | 75-D2 |
| Low, Peter Junr. | N | New York | 75-D3 |
| Low, Thomas | N | New York | 74-R |
| Lowden, Richard | Q | ........ | 76-E |
| Lowe, Jacob, at Getfield's | N | Queen Street | 75-D2 |
| Lower, Henry | N | New York | 75-D2, D3 |
| Lower, Herwy | N | New York | 76-K |
| Lower, Jacob | N | New York | 75-D3 |
| Lower, John, baker | N | Golden Hill | 75-D1, D2 |
| Lower, Valentine | N | New York | 74-A |

| | | | |
|---|---|---|---|
| Lowere, Henry | Q | ........ | 76-E |
| Lowere, William | Q | ........ | 76-E |
| Loweree, Thomas | Q | ........ | 76-E |
| Lowerree, Edward | N | New York | 74-A |
| Lowery, Henry, apprentice | N | New York | 74-T |
| Lowge, Peter | Q | ........ | 76-E |
| Lowndes, William | N | New York | 76-A |
| Lowndes; see also Lounds | | | |
| Lowrey, Michael | N | New York | 76-I |
| Lowrey, Thomas | N | New York | 74-A, 76-A |
| Lowrey, Thomas | N | nr Oswego Mart. | 76-I |
| Lowrie, William | N | New York | 76-A |
| Lowry, Thomas | N | New York | 74-R juror |
| Lowry, Thomas | N | nr Oswego Mart. | 76-H |
| Lowther, William | N | New York | 75-F |
| Lowther, William | N | Queen Street | 74-T2, 11/24 |
| Lowther, Wm | N | New York | 74-A |
| Lucaim, John Andries | N | New York | 76-A |
| Lucam, Andreas [2] | N | New York | [on] 74-A |
| Lucas, Sebastian | N | New York | 76-F |
| Lucom, George | N | New York | 76-C Grenadier |
| Ludlam, Anthony | S | ........ | 75-R |
| Ludlam, Daniel | Q | ........ | 75-A associator |
| Ludlam, Daniel | Q | ........ | 76-E |
| Ludlam, Daniel | Q | Jamaica | 75-D associator |
| Ludlam, Daniel | Q | Jamaica | 76-C |
| Ludlam, David | Q | ........ | 75-A |
| Ludlam, Ephraim | Q | ........ | 75-C |
| Ludlam, Henery | S | Southampton | 76:0.2.2.1.2 |
| Ludlam, Henry | N | New York | 74-A, 76-A |
| Ludlam, Henry | Q | ........ | 75-A |
| Ludlam, Henry | Q | ........ | 76-B, 76-E |
| Ludlam, Henry Jr. | Q | ........ | 75-A |
| Ludlam, Henry Jr. | Q | ........ | 76-B, 76-E |
| Ludlam, Jas. | Q | ........ | 75-A |
| Ludlam, Jeremiah | S | ........ | 75-R |
| Ludlam, Joseph | Q | ........ | 76-B, 76-E |
| Ludlam, Nathaniel | Q | Jamaica | 75-E |
| Ludlam, Nehemiah | Q | Jamaica | 75-E |
| Ludlam, Nicholas | Q | ........ | 75-A |

| | | | |
|---|---|---|---|
| Ludlam, Nicholas | Q | ........ | 76-B, 76-E |
| Ludlam, Nicholas | Q | Jamaica | 75-C, 75-D |
| Ludlam, Silas | S | Southampton | 76:0.1.3.1.2 |
| Ludlam, Thomas | Q | ........ | 75-A |
| Ludlam, Thomas | Q | ........ | 76-B2, 76-E |
| Ludlam, William | Q | ........ | 75-A |
| Ludlam, William | Q | ........ | 76-B, 76-E |
| Ludlam, William | Q | Jamaica | 75-A associator |
| Ludlam, William | Q | Jamaica | 75-E |
| Ludlam, William Jr. | Q | ........ | 75-A associator |
| Ludlam, W$^m$ | S | ........ | 75-R |
| Ludlam, Wm., Sr. | Q | ........ | 75-A associator |
| Ludlam, Wm., Sr. | Q | ........ | 76-E |
| Ludlam; see also Ladlam | | | |
| Ludlom, Anthony | S | Southampton | 76:0.1.0.1.3.1.0 |
| Ludlom, Jeremiah | S | Southampton | 76:0.1.0.1.4 |
| Ludlom, W$^m$ | S | Southampton | 76:1.0.0.4.0 |
| Ludlow, Carey Esq. | N | New York | 74-T |
| Ludlow, D. | N | New York | 74-A |
| Ludlow, Daniel | N | New York | 76-A |
| Ludlow, Daniel, storekeeper | N | New York | 74-T2, 3/10 |
| Ludlow, David | Q | ........ | 76-B |
| Ludlow, Ephraim | Q | ........ | 76-E |
| Ludlow, G.G., Col. | Q | ........ | 76-E |
| Ludlow, Gabriel G. | Q | ........ | 75-A |
| Ludlow, Gabriel G. | Q | Hempstead | 75-H |
| Ludlow, Gabriel W. | N | New York | 74-T2, 11/24 |
| Ludlow, Geo. D. | N | New York | 76-A |
| Ludlow, George and Wm | N | New York | 75-F |
| Ludlow, George D. | Q | ........ | 76-E |
| Ludlow, Judge | Q | Plains | 75-H |
| Ludlow, William W. | N | New York | 74-T2, 11/24 |
| Luebe, Thomas Grey | N | New York | 76-A |
| Lugrin, Simeon | Q | ........ | 76-E |
| Lugrin, Simeon & Catherine | N | French Church St | 74-T |
| Lum, John | S | Southampton | 76:1.1.0.2.1 |
| Lummis, Nehemiah | Q | ........ | 76-B |
| Lupton, Christopher | S | Southampton | 76:0.1.0.3.0 |
| Lupton, David | S | ........ | 75-R |
| Lupton, David | S | Southampton | 76:1.1.0.2.1 |

| | | | |
|---|---|---|---|
| Lupton, James | S | Brookhaven | 75-B9 |
| Lupton, James | S | Southold | 76:0.1.1.2.3 |
| Lupton, James Jun. | S | Southold | 75-N non-signer |
| Lupton, James, Sgt. | S | Southold | 75-N |
| Lupton, Josiah | S | Southold | 76:0.2.0.1.1 |
| Lupton, Josiah, Capt. | S | Southold | 75-N |
| Lupton, Thomas | N | New York | 76-A |
| Lupton, William | N | New York | 74-A |
| Luse, Eleaser | S | Brookhaven | 75-B10 |
| Luyster, Daniel | Q | ........ | 76-E |
| Luyster, Daniel | Q | Newtown | 75-B |
| Luyster, Garret | Q | ........ | 76-E |
| Luyster, Garret | Q | Newtown | 75-B |
| Luyster, Jacob | Q | ........ | 75-A associator |
| Luyster, Jacobus | Q | ........ | 76-E |
| Luyster, Jacobus | Q | Oyster Bay | 75-F |
| Luyster, Jeromus | Q | ........ | 75-A, 76-E |
| Luyster, John | Q | ........ | 75-A associator |
| Luyster, John | Q | ........ | 76-E |
| Luyster, John | Q | Oyster Bay | 75-F |
| Luyster, Peter | Q | ........ | 76-E |
| Luyster, Peter Jr. | Q | ........ | 76-E |
| Lydeback, Godfried, baker | N | New York | 74-R |
| Lydig, Philip | N | New York | 74-A, 76-A |
| Lyell, Sarah | N | removed upstate | 76-P |
| Lynch, Michael | N | New York | 76-M |
| Lynch, Philip | N | New York | 76-I |
| Lynch, Thomas | N | New York | 76-A |
| Lynch, Thomas, store | N | Broad Street | 74-T2, 11/10 |
| Lyng, John Burt, goldsmith | N | Great Dock St. | 74-T |
| Lyng, John Burt, goldsmith | N | Great George St. | 74-T2, 4/28 |
| Lyng, John Burt | N | New York | 74-A |
| Lynn, Aaron | N | New York | 74-A |
| Lynsen, Daniel, weaver | N | New York | 75-D1, D2 |
| Lyon, James, Reverend | S | Brookhaven | 75-B11 n.s. |
| Lyon, John | S | Brookhaven | 75-B10 |
| Lyons, Henry | S | Brookhaven | 75-B11 n.s. |
| Lyons, John | S | Brookhaven | 75-B11 n.s. |
| Mabee, Abraham | N | New York | 75-R |
| Mabye, Petr. | N | New York | 74-A |

| | | | |
|---|---|---|---|
| Macarty, Mary | N | rem. to Bedford | 76-J |
| MacGowin, ____ Mrs. | N | New York | 74-T, 74-V |
| Machet, John | N | New York | 76-A |
| Machet/Meshet, Peter | N | coppersmith | 75-D1, D2 |
| Machet, Peter | N | New York | 76-A |
| Machett, John Jr. | N | New York | 74-A |
| Mackee, David | S | Southampton | 76:0.1.1.0.0.2.0 |
| Mackee, George | S | Southampton | 76:0.1.0.1.2 |
| Mackfarling, David | S | Southold | 76:0.1.0.2.0 |
| Mackie, Geo. | S | ........ | 75-R |
| Mackrell, James | N | New York | 74-A |
| Maclore, James | S | Southold | 76:0.2.1.2.2 |
| Madison, Benjamin | S | ........ | 75-R |
| Maffet, John | N | New York | 76-A |
| Magans, Jude, Mrs. | N | rem to Ulster Co. | 76-P |
| Magee, James | S | Huntington | 75-H |
| Magee, James, seaman | N | New York | 74-T |
| Maghee, Samuel | N | New York | 74-A |
| Magra, James, Dr. | N | New York | 74-T |
| Magra, ____ Mrs. | N | Stone Street | 75-T2, 2/2 |
| Maguire, Elisabeth | N | rem. to Bedford | 76-J |
| Mahan, Thomas | N | New York | 74-A, 76-A |
| Mahoney, Cornelius | N | New York | 74-A |
| Mahoney, John | N | New York | 74-R |
| Mahony, John, runaway | N | New York | 74-T2, 11/10 |
| Mahony, Mary | N | New York | 74-R |
| Main, William, servant | N | New York | 74-V runaway |
| Main; see also Mane | | | |
| Malcolm, William | N | New York | 74-T2, 6/16 |
| Maldrem, see Mildrum | | | |
| Male, Jacob | N | New York | 76-I |
| Mallos, David | N | New York | 76-I |
| Mallos, David Henry | N | New York | 76-Y 2d Lieut. |
| Mallows, David Henry | N | New York | 76-L |
| Malone, John, cordwainer | N | liv at Lake Hunts | 75-D1, D2 |
| Maltby, Burtis | S | Huntington | 75-H |
| Malunar, Abraham | N | New York | 76-A |
| Man, Adam | N | New York | 74-A |
| Man, David, butcher | N | Bowery Lane | 75-D1, D2 |
| Man, James | Q | ........ | 75-A |

| | | | |
|---|---|---|---|
| Manchester, John | N | New York | 74-A |
| Mandevel, David | N | New York | 74-A |
| Mandeville, Yellis, shoemkr | N | Maiden Lane | 75-D1, D2 |
| Mandeville, Yellis, silversm. | N | with Jno. Leary | 75-D1, D2 |
| Mandivell, Yellis Jr. | N | New York | 76-D |
| Mane, John | N | New York | 74-A |
| Mange, Peter | N | New York | 76-A |
| Mangel, Johannis | N | removed upstate | 76-P |
| Manley, Robert | N | New York | 76-N |
| Manley, Robert, wheelwrt | N | Great George St. | 75-D1, D2 |
| Manley, Robt. | N | New York | 74-A |
| Manly, Sarah | N | New York | 75-R |
| Mann, see Man | | | |
| Manneree, Abr'm | Q | ........ | 75-A |
| Mansen, Abraham | N | New York | 76-I |
| Manx, Henry | N | New York | 74-A |
| Manx, see also Marx | | | |
| Mapes, Benj: | S | Meritches | 76:1.0.1.0.0 |
| Mapes, James | S | Southold | 75-N |
| Mapes, James | S | Southold | 76:0.1.2.1.0.1.0 |
| Mapes, Joseph | S | Southold | 75-N |
| Mapes, Joseph | S | Southold | 76:1.0.0.2.0.2.3 |
| Mapes, Joseph Jr. | S | Southold | 75-N |
| Mapes, Joseph Jun' | S | Southold | 76:0.1.3.1.1.1.0 |
| Mapes, Joseph ye 3d | S | Southold | 75-N |
| Mapes, Lemuel | S | Southampton | 76:1.0.0.1.0 |
| Mapes, Thomas | S | Southold | 76:0.1.2.1.2 |
| Marcelles, Isaac | N | New York | 74-A |
| March, Abr'm | Q | Newtown | 75-G |
| March, Jona'n | Q | Newtown | 75-G |
| Marchall, Abram | N | removed upstate | 76-P |
| Marchant, Mary, widow | N | to Dutchess Co. | 76-P |
| Marchant, Shubal | S | Smithtown | 76:1.1.0.4.1 |
| Marden, Moses | N | New York | 76-A, 76-I |
| Margeron, John | N | New York | 74-A |
| Maridet, Thomas | N | New York | 76-L |
| Mariner, Joshua, hse crpntr | N | Baptizt Street | 75-D2 |
| Mariner, Wm., innholder | N | Horse & Cart St. | 75-E |
| Marius, Jacob | N | New York | 74-A |
| Marle, Jones | N | New York | 76-A |

| | | | |
|---|---|---|---|
| Marlin, Lester | N | Leary Slip | 76-I |
| Marr, James | Q | ........ | 76-B, 76-E |
| Marr, Joakim | N | New York | 76-A |
| Marrener, William | N | William Street | 76-I |
| Marriner, Wm | N | Oyster house | 76-H |
| Marschalck, Cornelius | N | bolter, Dey Street | 75-D2 |
| Marschalck, Cornelus | N | New York | 76-L |
| Marschalk, Abraham | N | New York | 74-A |
| Marschalk, Abraham | N | removed upstate | 76-P |
| Marschalk, And'w | N | New York | 74-A |
| Marschalk, Cornelius | N | New York | 74-A |
| Marschalk, Francis | N | New York | 76-V |
| Marschalk, George | N | New York | 74-A |
| Marschalk, Isaac | N | New York | 74-A |
| Marschalk, Isaac, baker | N | Broad Street | 75-D1, D2 |
| Marschalk, Joseph | N | New York | 74-A |
| Marselus, Andrew | N | New York | 74-A |
| Marsh, Daniel | N | New York | 74-A |
| Marsh, Daniel, Lieut. | N | New York | 75-A |
| Marsh, Margaret | N | Pecks Slip | 76-H, 76-I |
| Marsh, Mephibosheth | N | New York | 74-A |
| Marshalck, Isaac | N | New York | 76-L |
| Marshall, John | N | New York | 76-I |
| Marshall, John [2] | N | New York | [on] 76-A |
| Marshel, Joseph | S | Southampton | 76:0.1.1.2.1 |
| Marston, Cornelia wf Thos. | N | New York | 75-T |
| Marston, Ephraim | Q | ........ | 75-A associator |
| Marston, Ephraim | Q | Jamaica | 75-D associator |
| Marston, Ephraim, Ensign | Q | Jamaica | 75-E |
| Marston, Francis | Q | ........ | 76-E |
| Marston, John | N | New York | 75-T2, 5/4 |
| Marston, John | Q | ........ | 76-E |
| Marston, John Esq. | N | New York | 75-T |
| Marston, Lawrence | Q | ........ | 76-E |
| Marston, Nathan | N | New York | 75-T |
| Marston, Nathaniel | N | New York | 76-A |
| Marston, Nathaniel | N | Wall Street | 74-T2, 4/14 |
| Marston, Nathaniel Esq. | N | New York | 75-V |
| Marston, Thomas | N | New York | 75-T2, 5/4 |
| Martaen, Mary | N | removed upstate | 76-P |

| Marten, Hugh | N | removed upstate | 76-P |
|---|---|---|---|
| Marten, John | N | removed upstate | 76-P |
| Marthers, Ebenezer | S | Brookhaven | 75-B10 |
| Marthers, Ebenezer Jr. | S | Brookhaven | 75-B10 |
| Marthers, Edward | S | Southold | . 76:0.3.3.3.4 |
| Martin,         Dr. | Q | Hempstead | 75-H |
| Martin, Enoch | Q | ........ | 76-E |
| Martin, John | N | New York | 74-A |
| Martin, John | Q | ........ | 75-A |
| Martin, John | Q | ........ | 76-B, 76-E |
| Martin, John, constable | N | New York | 75-R, 76-R |
| Martin, Samuel | Q | ........ | 75-H |
| Martin, Thomas | Q | ........ | 76-E |
| Martlin, Hester | N | North River | 76-H |
| Marvin, Benja. | S | Brookhaven | 75-B6 |
| Marvin, Benjman | S | Brookhaven | 76:0.2.2.2.6 |
| Marvin, Elihu | S | Brookhaven | 75-B6 |
| Marvin, Ephraim | S | Brookhaven | 75-B6 |
| Marvin, Ephraim | S | Brookhaven | 76:0.1.2.1.2 |
| Marvin, Jedediah | S | Brookhaven | 75-B3, 75-B6 |
| Marvin, Jedediah | S | Brookhaven | 76:0.1.1.1.1 |
| Marvin, John | Q | ........ | 75-A |
| Marvin, John | Q | ........ | 76-B, 76-E |
| Marvin, John | S | Brookhaven | 75-B3, 75-B6 |
| Marvin, John | S | Brookhaven | 76:0.1.2.1.3 |
| Marvin, John Jun. | S | Brookhaven | 75-B6 |
| Marvin, Matthew | S | Brookhaven | 75-B3, 75-B6 |
| Marvin, Moses | S | Brookhaven | 75-B6 |
| Marvin, Seth | S | Brookhaven | 76:0.3.0.1.0 |
| Marvin, Seth [2] | S | Brookhaven | [on] 75-B6 |
| Marx, Henry | N | New York | 76-A |
| Marx; see also Manx | | | |
| Masavei, George | N | New York | 76-C Grenadier |
| Mash, Elisabeth, widow | N | removed upstate | 76-P |
| Maskelyn, John | N | New York | 76-A |
| Mason, James | N | New York | 76-M |
| Mason, Jared | N | New York | 74-A |
| Mason, Mary, Mrs. | N | to Westchester Co | 76-P |
| Mason, Richard | Q | ........ | 75-A, 76-B |
| Mason, Thomas | N | New York | 76-A, 76-I |

| | | | |
|---|---|---|---|
| Mass, Margaret | N | removed upstate | 76-P |
| Masterton, David | N | New York | 74-A |
| Matheson, Robert, servant | N | New York | 75-T runaway |
| Mathews, David, Judge | N | New York | 74-R to 76-R |
| Mathews, Timothy | S | Southampton | 75-M |
| Matlack, White | N | New York | 74-A, 75-F |
| Matlack, White | N | New York | 76-G |
| Matlack, Wm | N | New York | 76-G |
| Matsteller, Conrad | N | New York | 74-A |
| Matten, John | N | removed upstate | 76-P |
| Matthew, Elias | S | ........ | 75-R |
| Matthews, David Esq. | N | New York | 74-T |
| Matthews, Ezekiel | Q | ........ | 75-A, 76-B |
| Matthews, Mary, Mrs. | N | rem to Ulster Co. | 76-P |
| Matthews, Richard | Q | ........ | 75-A, 76-B |
| Matthews, Timothy | S | Southampton | 76:1.1.0.2.1 |
| Maugere, Matthew | N | New York | 76-A |
| Maunsell, _____ Col. | N | Greenwich | 75-T |
| Maverick, Peter Rushton | N | New York | 75-D1 |
| Maverick, Peter, silversmith | N | Batteau Street | 75-D2 |
| Maxfield, _____ Mrs. | N | to Dutchess Co. | 76-P |
| Maxwell, Abigail | N | to Dutchess Co. | 76-P |
| Maxwell, Anthony | N | to Dutchess Co. | 76-P |
| Maxwell, Enoch, cordwnr | N | Broadway | 75-D1, D2 |
| Maxwell, James | N | New York | 76-A |
| Maxwell, John | N | to Dutchess Co. | 76-P |
| Maxwell, Joseph | N | to Dutchess Co. | 76-P |
| Maxwell, William | N | to Dutchess Co. | 76-P |
| Maxwell, William | N | Wall Street | 76-V |
| May, George | N | New York | 74-A, 76-B |
| May, John | N | New York | 76-B |
| May, Tulip | N | New York | 74-A |
| Maybe, see Mabye | | | |
| McAdam, _____ , wharf | N | New York | 75-T2, 8/31 |
| McAdam, William | N | New York | 74-T merchant |
| McAdams, John, 1st Lieut. | N | New York | 76-Y |
| McAdom, Wm, shoemaker | N | Crown Street | 75-D2 |
| McAkroy, James | N | New York | 75-R |
| McAlpaen, Catherien | N | removed upstate | 76-P |
| McAlpine, Robt. [2] | N | New York | [on] 74-A |

| | | | |
|---|---|---|---|
| McAnulty, John | N | New York | 75-D1 |
| McArthur, John | N | New York | 76-N |
| McAtee, James | N | New York | 74-A |
| McAtee, James | N | Rosevelts Slip | 76-I |
| McAtill, James, Ensign | N | New York | 75-A |
| McAttee, James | N | Roosevelt's | 76-H |
| McBain, John | N | New York | 75-D3 |
| McBride, William | N | New York | 76-A, 76-I |
| McCallem, Edward | N | New York | 75-R |
| McCallum, Duncan | S | Southampton | 76:0.3.3.2.1 |
| McCalpin, Andrew | N | near Greenwich | 76-I |
| McCandess, James | N | New York | 76-A |
| McCandless, James | N | New York | 74-A |
| McCann, Gilbert | Q | ........ | 75-A |
| McCann, Hugh, ae c.19 | N | New York | 74-V runaway |
| McCant, Michael, mason | N | Bowery Lane | 75-D1, D2 |
| McCarte, Thomas | N | to Westchester Co | 76-P |
| McCarter, Sarah | N | removed upstate | 76-P |
| McCarthy/McCarty, Judith | N | New York | 74-R, 75-R |
| McCartney, Edward | N | New York | 74-A |
| McCarty, Thomas | N | New York | 76-A |
| McClaughan, James | N | New York | 74-R |
| McClaughan, Thomas | N | New York | 74-R |
| McClean, Donald, Ensign | N | New York | 76-Y |
| McClean, Thomas | N | New York | 75-D2 |
| McClelan, Hugh Steward | N | William Street | 75-D1, D2 |
| McClelan, Thos. Esq. | N | New York | 74-A |
| McClosky, Alexander | N | to Dutchess Co. | 76-P |
| McClosky, Margaret, Mrs. | N | to Dutchess Co. | 76-P |
| McCloud, John | N | New York | 75-R |
| McCluar, James | N | New York | 74-A |
| McClure, James, shoemaker | N | Broadway | 75-D2 |
| McClure, Moses | N | New York | 75-C |
| McCollom, Edward | N | New York | 76-A |
| McCollom, Edward [2] | N | New York | [on] 74-A |
| McComb, John | N | New York | 74-A |
| McComb, John, Lieut. | N | New York | 76-G |
| McComb, William | N | New York | 76-I |
| McConnegall, Patrick | N | New York | 76-A |
| McConnell, John | Q | Newtown | 75-B |

| | | | |
|---|---|---|---|
| McConnighy, David | N | New York | 75-R |
| McCormick, Daniel | N | New York | 74-T2, 6/9 |
| McCormick, Daniel | N | New York | 75-F, 75-V |
| McCormick, Daniel, 1st Lt. | N | New York | 76-S |
| McCormick, Daniel, Lieut. | N | New York | 75-A, 76-G |
| McCormick, John | N | New York | 76-A |
| McCorpin, Dougle | N | to Westchester Co | 76-P |
| McCoun, Augustine | Q | ........ | 76-B, 76-E |
| McCoun, Gilbert | Q | ........ | 76-B, 76-E |
| McCoun, Justus | Q | ........ | 76-B |
| McCoun, Procolus | Q | ........ | 76-B, B2; 76-E |
| McCoun, Richard | Q | ........ | 75-A, 76-B |
| McCoun, W. | Q | ........ | 76-E |
| McCoun, William | Q | ........ | 76-A, 76-B |
| McCoy, Ananias | N | New York | 74-R |
| McCoy, Annanias, currier | N | Ferry Street | 75-D1, D2 |
| McCoy, James, cordwainer | N | Chappel Street | 75-D1, D2 |
| McCoy, John, breechesmkr | N | Georges Street | 75-D1, D2 |
| McCready, James | N | New York | 74-A |
| McCready, John, ae c.30 | N | New York | 74-V runaway |
| McCreddie, Jane, servant | N | New York | 75-T runaway |
| McCullen, James | N | New York | 76-L |
| McCullum, Ann, wf Hugh | N | New York | 74-T |
| McCullum, Hugh, soldier | N | New York | 74-T |
| McDanel, Thomas | N | New York | 74-A, 76-A |
| McDaniel, Hannah | N | removed upstate | 76-P |
| McDavitt, Eve | N | removed upstate | 76-P |
| McDavitt, P. | N | New York | 74-A |
| McDavitt, P., vendue store | N | New York | 74-T2, 9/29 |
| McDavitt, Patrick, store | N | Queen Street | 75-T2, 5/18 |
| McDonald, Alex'r Jr. | N | New York | 74-A |
| McDonald, Alexander | N | to Westchester Co | 76-P |
| McDonald, Angus | N | New York | 74-A |
| McDonald, Ann | N | New York | 75-R |
| McDonald, Archibald | N | New York | 75-R |
| McDonald, Archibald | N | New York | 76-A, 76-I |
| McDonald, David | N | New York | 75-D1 |
| McDonald, Francis | N | New York | 76-B |
| McDonald, John | N | New York | 74-A |
| McDonald, Niell | N | New York | 74-A |

| | | | |
|---|---|---|---|
| McDonald, Sarah | N | removed upstate | 76-P |
| McDonald, Walter, teacher | N | rem. to Bedford | 76-J |
| McDonell, Hugh | N | New York | 74-A |
| McDonnald, John | N | New York | 76-A |
| McDonnaugh, John | Q | ........ | 76-E |
| McDonnaugh, John Jr. | Q | Newtown | 75-B |
| McDonnaugh, John Sr. | Q | Newtown | 75-B, 75-G |
| McDougal, Duncan | N | New York | 74-R juror |
| McDougal, Duncan, innkpr | N | Elbow Street | 75-D2 |
| McDougall, Alexander | N | New York | 74-T2, 11/24 |
| McDougall, Allan | N | New York | 74-A |
| McDougall, John, mariner | N | Crumlines Wharf | 75-D1, D2 |
| McDougall, Stephen | N | Crumlines Wharf | 75-D1, D2 |
| McDougall, Stephen | N | New York | 75-D1 |
| McDougall, Will'm | N | New York | 74-A |
| McDowal, Benjamin | N | New York | 76-A |
| McDowall, John | N | New York | 74-A |
| McDowell, Benjamin | N | shoemkr, Broad St | 75-D1, D2 |
| McDowll, Hugh | N | New York | 76-A |
| McDurcan, Patrick, ae c.15 | N | New York | 74-V runaway |
| McEntass, Sarah | N | removed upstate | 76-P |
| McEuen, Malcom | N | New York | 76-N |
| McEuen, Malcom, plumber | N | New Burling Slip | 75-D1, D2 |
| McEvers, Charles | N | New York | 76-A |
| McEvers, Charles | Q | ........ | 76-E |
| McEvers, Charles and Co. | N | New York | 75-F |
| McEvers, Charles Esq. | N | Hanover Square | 74-T2, 3/17 |
| McEwen, March | Q | ........ | 76-E |
| McFall, John | N | New York | 76-A |
| McFarland, Daniel | N | New York | 76-G |
| McFarlane, Dougall | N | New York | 76-A |
| McFarran, Thos. | N | New York | 74-A |
| McFarthing, Neal | N | rem to Ulster Co. | 76-P |
| McGear, John | S | Huntington | 76-H2 |
| McGibbons, John, publisher | N | New York | 74-T2, 9/22 |
| McGillaray, John | N | New York | 76-A |
| McGillbraw, John | N | New York | 76-I |
| McGillvray, John | N | New York | 74-A |
| McGinnis, Robert | N | New York | 74-T2, 9/2 |
| McGlathry, Thomas, sales | N | New York | 75-T2, 4/6 |

| | | | |
|---|---|---|---|
| McGogan, Lydia | N | to Westchester Co | 76-P |
| McGogan, Mary | N | to Westchester Co | 76-P |
| McGoun, Jeremiah | N | New York | 74-V runaway |
| McGraw, Alex' | N | New York | 76-I |
| McGurney, ____ widow | N | removed upstate | 76-P |
| McInter, Hugh | N | New York | 74-A |
| McIntire, Hugh | N | Leary Street | 74-T2, 4/21 |
| McIntire, Hugh | N | New York | 76-A |
| McIntosh, Catherine | N | New York | 76-K |
| McIntosh, John | Q | ........ | 75-A, 76-E |
| McIntosh, Phineas | N | New York | 74-A |
| McIntosh, Phineas | N | New York | 75-T2, 1/5 |
| McIntosh, William | N | Cowfoot Hill | 74-T |
| McKay, Ananias | N | New York | 74-R |
| McKay, Patrick | N | New York | 76-A |
| McKay; see also McKoy | | | |
| McKenny, James | N | New York | 74-A, 76-G |
| McKenzie, John | N | New York | 76-A, 76-V |
| McKinlay, John | N | New York | 76-A |
| McKinley, Nathaniel | N | New York | 74-A |
| McKinley, Nathaniel, taylor | N | Wall Street | 75-D1, D2 |
| McKinley, Samuel, merch't | N | liv w Th Galbreath | 75-D1, D2 |
| McKinley, William | N | New York | 74-A |
| McKinney, James, Sergt. | N | New York | 75-D3 |
| McKinney, John | N | New York | 74-A |
| McKisler, James | N | removed upstate | 76-P |
| McKoy, Annanias | N | New York | 75-D1 |
| McKoy; see also McKay | | | |
| McLane, Catharine | N | New York | 76-I |
| McLean, Donald | N | New York | 76-V |
| McLean, Donald, druggist | N | Water Street | 74-T2, 5/5 |
| McLean, Peter | N | New York | 76-A, 76-F |
| McLean, Thos. | N | New York | 75-D3 |
| McLeod, Neil | N | New York | 76-A |
| McLintock, John, servant | N | New York | 74-V runaway |
| McManis, Hugh | N | removed upstate | 76-P |
| McManomy, John | N | New York | 76-A |
| McMenomy, Eliz., Mrs. | N | to Dutchess Co. | 76-P |
| McMenomy, John | N | New York | 74-A |
| McMenomy, John | N | to Dutchess Co. | 76-P |

| | | | |
|---|---|---|---|
| McMenomy, Peggy | N | to Dutchess Co. | 76-P |
| McMicking, Patrick | N | New York | 74-V |
| McMillan, Alexander | N | New York | 74-A |
| McMullen, Alex'r | Q | ........ | 76-E |
| McMullen, Docea | N | New York | 76-K |
| McNabb, William | N | New York | 76-A |
| McNeal, Daniel | N | New York | 76-G |
| McNeill, Arthur | N | New York | 74-A |
| McNiel, Arthur | N | Chapel Street | 74-T2, 4/14 |
| McNight, Duncan | N | New York | 76-I |
| McOlnulty, Daniel | N | Queen Street | 76-I |
| McOnnully, Daniel | N | New York | 76-A |
| McOnulty, Daniel | N | New York | 74-A |
| McPharson, John | N | Broadway | 76-H |
| McPherson, Donald | N | New York | 76-A |
| McPherson, Donald, Ensign | N | New York | 76-Y |
| McPherson, Dougald | N | New York | 76-A |
| McPherson, Farquhar | N | barber, Broad St | 75-D1, D2 |
| McPherson, John | N | New York | 76-A |
| McPhey, Garrett | Q | Jamaica | 75-E |
| McQuarry, John | N | George Street | 74-T2, 12/22 |
| McQue, Patrick | N | New York | 76-I |
| McQueen, John | N | New York | 75-R juror |
| McReady, Dennis | N | Wall Street | 74-T2, 1/6; 75-F |
| McVichar, Archibald | N | New York | 74-A |
| McWilliam, Elizabeth | N | New York | 75-R |
| McWilliam, Thomas | N | New York | 75-R |
| McWilliams, Ann | N | George Street | 76-I |
| McWilliams, Ann | N | New York | 75-R |
| McWilliams, Thomas | N | Cortlands Street | 76-H |
| McWilliams, Thomas | N | New York | 76-A |
| Mead, Isaac | N | New York | 74-A |
| Meade, Joseph | N | New York | 74-R |
| Meads, Samuel, shoemaker | N | at Goforths | 75-D2 |
| Meatkers, James | N | New York | 74-A |
| Meed, Isaac | N | New York | 76-L |
| Meekin/Michan, Michael | N | New York | 75-D3 |
| Meeks, Edward | N | New York | 74-A, 76-N |
| Meeks, Edward, blacksmith | N | William Street | 75-D2 |
| Meeks, John, shoemaker | N | Hanover Square | 75-D2 |

| | | | |
|---|---|---|---|
| Meeks, Joseph | N | New York | 74-A |
| Meeks, Joseph | N | New York | 74-A, by mark |
| Meeks, Joseph, cordwainer | N | Maiden Lane | 75-D2 |
| Meeks, Joseph, shoemaker | N | William Street | 75-D1, D2 |
| Meharg, Alexander | Q | Newtown | 75-V |
| Meldrum, Robt. | N | New York | 74-A |
| Mercer and Schenck | N | New York | 75-F |
| Mercer, Isaac | N | New York | 74-R |
| Mercer, William | N | New York | 74-R juror |
| Mercier, Abraham | N | Cortlandt Street | 74-T merchant |
| Mercier, William | N | New York | 76-N |
| Meredith, Thomas | N | Broadway | 75-D2 |
| Meredith, Thos. | N | New York | 74-A |
| Merrit, Elizabeth | N | to Dutchess Co. | 76-P |
| Merrit, Sam'l | Q | Newtown | 75-G |
| Merritt, Elizabeth | N | to Westchester Co | 76-P |
| Mersereau, Samuel | N | at Mr. Broome's | 75-D1, D2 |
| Mersereau, Samuel | N | New York | 75-D1 |
| Mersereau, Samuel, Corp'l | N | New York | 75-D3 |
| Mersier, Peter | N | New York | 75-F |
| Merverick, Peter R., Ensign | N | New York | 75-A |
| Mesier, Abr'm | N | New York | 75-B |
| Mesier, Abraham, merchant | N | Cortlandt Street | 75-V |
| Mesier, Peter | N | West Ward | 75-R overseer |
| Mesnard, D. | N | New York | 74-A |
| Mesnard, Daniel | N | Duke Street | 75-T |
| Messenger, John | Q | Jamaica | 75-D associator |
| Messenger, Samuel | Q | ........ | 75-A associator |
| Messenger, Samuel | Q | ........ | 76-E |
| Messenger, Samuel | Q | Jamaica | 75-D associator |
| Messenger, Samuel | Q | Jamaica | 76-C |
| Messenger, William | Q | Jamaica | 75-D associator |
| Messier, Peter | N | New York | 74-A |
| Metcalf, William | N | New York | 75-D2 |
| Meusier, ---- Lieut. | N | New York | 76-C |
| Michael, Ezebel | N | to Westchester Co | 76-P |
| Michaelmas, John | N | New York | 75-R |
| Michaelsen, Johan | N | New York | 74-A |
| Michager, Jain | S | Brookhaven | 76:0.1.3.2.0 |
| Michalsal, John | N | New York | 76-A |

| | | | |
|---|---|---|---|
| Michan, see Meekin | | | |
| Michel, Susana | N | to Westchester Co | 76-P |
| Middlemass, John | N | New York | 76-A |
| Middleton, George | N | New York | 74-A |
| Middleton, Peter | N | New York | 76-A |
| Middleton, Peter, Dr. | N | New York | 74-T |
| Midky, Catharine | N | to Westchester Co | 76-P |
| Milbourn, William | Q | ........ | 76-E |
| Milbourn, Wm. | N | New York | 74-A |
| Milbourn, Wm., merchant | N | Dock Street | 74-T2, 4/28 |
| Mildebaeger, Oliver | N | New York | 75-B |
| Mildrum, James | N | New York | 76-A, 76-I |
| Mildrum, see also Meldrum | | | |
| Millar, David Henry | N | New York | 76-A |
| Millar, Wm | Q | ........ | 76-B |
| Milldoler, John | N | New York | 74-R juror |
| Milledeller, John | N | New York | 75-D1 |
| Miller, Abraham Esq$^r$ | S | Easthampton | 76:0.1.0.1.1 |
| Miller, Abr$^m$ | S | Easthampton | 75-E |
| Miller, Alex'dr Litch | N | New York | 74-A |
| Miller, Alexander Litch | N | New York | 75-D3 |
| Miller, Ananias | S | Easthampton | 75-E |
| Miller, Ananias | S | Easthampton | 76:0.1.3.1.3 |
| Miller, Andrew | N | New York | 76-I |
| Miller, Andrew | S | Brookhaven | 75-B2 |
| Miller, Andrew | S | Brookhaven | 76:0.1.3.5.4 |
| Miller, Andrew Jun$^r$ | S | Brookhaven | 75-B9 |
| Miller, Benj. | N | New York | 75-D3 |
| Miller, Burnet Esq. | S | Easthampton | 76:1.2.3.2.2.3.1 |
| Miller, Burnett | S | Easthampton | 75-E |
| Miller, Charles | N | New York | 74-A |
| Miller, Charles | N | New York | 76-A, 76-L |
| Miller, Christopher, carpets | N | New York | 74-T2, 9/15 |
| Miller, Cornelius | Q | ........ | 75-A, 76-B |
| Miller, David | S | Easthampton | 76:0.1.1.0.0 |
| Miller, David Jun$^r$ | S | Easthampton | 76:0.1.0.2.0 |
| Miller, David [2] | S | Easthampton | [on] 75-E |
| Miller, Dionisius | N | New York | 75-D2 |
| Miller, Ebenezer, Capt. | S | Brookhaven | 75-B2 |
| Miller, Eleazer | S | Easthampton | 75-E |

| Miller, Eleazer Esqʳ | S | Easthampton | 76:1.1.1.3.0.1.0 |
|---|---|---|---|
| Miller, Eleazer Jr. | N′ | New York | 74-T, 74-V |
| Miller, Eleazer Jr. | N | New York | 75-T2, 7/27; 75-F |
| Miller, Eleazor | N | Hanover Square | 75-D2 |
| Miller, Elisha | S | Easthampton | 75-E |
| Miller, Elisha | S | Easthampton | 76:0.1.0.1.1 |
| Miller, Ellick | N | New York | 76-L |
| Miller, Ezekiel | S | Easthampton | 75-E |
| Miller, Fredrick | N | New York | 75-D3 |
| Miller, George | S | Easthampton | 75-E |
| Miller, George | S | Easthampton | 76:0.1.3.1.3 |
| Miller, Gulielmus | S | Easthampton | 76:0.1.0.2.0 |
| Miller, Gurdon | S | Easthampton | 75-E |
| Miller, Hannah, Wido. | S | Easthampton | 76:0.0.1.3.1.1.0 |
| Miller, Hannah, Widw. | S | Easthampton | 76:0.1.2.1.0 |
| Miller, Henry | N | New York | 74-A |
| Miller, Henry | Q | ........ | 75-A, 76-E |
| Miller, Henry | S | Easthampton | 75-E |
| Miller, Hugh | N | New York | 76-A |
| Miller, Huntting | S | Easthampton | 75-E |
| Miller, Jacob | N | New York | 76-A |
| Miller, Jacob | S | Easthampton | 75-E |
| Miller, Jacob | S | Easthampton | 76:0.1.1.1.2 |
| Miller, Jason | S | Easthampton | 75-E |
| Miller, Jasper | N | New York | 76-I |
| Miller, Jeremiah | S | Easthampton | 75-E |
| Miller, Jeremiah | S | Easthampton | 76:0.2.0.1.1.3.1 |
| Miller, Jeremiah Jr. | S | Easthampton | 75-E |
| Miller, Jeremiah Junʳ | S | Easthampton | 76:0.1.0.1.3.0.1 |
| Miller, John | N | Hunter's Quay | 75-T2, 2/9 |
| Miller, John | N | New York | 76-A |
| Miller, John | Q | ........ | 76-E |
| Miller, John | S | Easthampton | 75-E |
| Miller, John | S | Easthampton | 76:1.0.3.1.2 |
| Miller, John Jr. | S | Easthampton | 75-E |
| Miller, John, Lieut. | S | Easthampton | 76:0.1.2.1.1 |
| Miller, Jonathan | S | Easthampton | 75-E |
| Miller, Joseph | S | Easthampton | 76:0.1.3.1.4 |
| Miller, Joshua | N | New York | 76-A |
| Miller, Mary | N | New York | 76-K |

| | | | |
|---|---|---|---|
| Miller, Mary | N | removed upstate | 76-P |
| Miller, Michael | N | New York | 76-A |
| Miller, Nathan | S | Easthampton | 75-E |
| Miller, Nathan | S | Easthampton | 76:0.1.0.1.1 |
| Miller, Nathan Jr. | S | Easthampton | 75-E |
| Miller, Nathaniel | S | Brookhaven | 75-B9 n.s. |
| Miller, Peleg | S | Easthampton | 75-E |
| Miller, Philip | N | New York | 76-A, 76-F |
| Miller, Richard | S | Brookhaven | 75-B9 n.s. |
| Miller, Richard | S | Brookhaven | 76:0.1.0.2.1.4.3 |
| Miller, Robert | N | New York | 76-A |
| Miller, Sarah, Wido | S | Easthampton | 76:0.0.0.2.0 |
| Miller, Thomas | N | New York | 76-A |
| Miller, Timothy | S | Brookhaven | 75-B9 n.s. |
| Miller, Timothy | S | Brookhaven | 76:1.1.3.3.1.1.0 |
| Miller, Timothy | S | Easthampton | 76:0.1.2.1.1 |
| Miller, Uriah | S | ........ | 75-R |
| Miller, Uriah | S | Easthampton | 75-E |
| Miller, Uriah | S | Easthampton | 76:1.1.1.2.0 |
| Miller, Uriah | S | Southampton | 76:0.2.2.1.1 |
| Miller, Will'm | Q | ........ | 75-A |
| Miller, William | N | New York | 74-A, 76-I |
| Miller, William | S | Brookhaven | 75-B2 |
| Miller, William | S | Brookhaven | 76:1.1.3.2.2.1.0 |
| Miller, Zeruiah, Wido | S | Easthampton | 76:0.0.1.1.1 |
| Milligan, Robert | S | Huntington | 75-H |
| Mills, Amos | Q | ........ | 76-E |
| Mills, Andrew | Q | Jamaica | 75-E |
| Mills, David | Q | Jamaica | 75-C |
| Mills, Hope | Q | ........ | 75-A, 76-B |
| Mills, Hope | Q | Jamaica | 75-D |
| Mills, Hope Jr. | Q | Jamaica | 75-C |
| Mills, Isaac | Q | ........ | 76-E |
| Mills, Isaac | Q | Jamaica | 75-D associator |
| Mills, Isaac | S | Smithtown | 75-L |
| Mills, Isaac | S | Smithtown | 76:0.3.3.1.3 |
| Mills, Israel [2] | S | Smithtown | [on] 75-L |
| Mills, Israll | S | Huntington | 76-H3 |
| Mills, Jacob | S | Smithtown | 75-H1 |
| Mills, Jacob | S | Smithtown | 75-L Committee |

| | | | |
|---|---|---|---|
| Mills, Jacob | S | Smithtown | 76:1.1.1.2.0.2.1 |
| Mills, Jedediah | S | Smithtown | 75-L |
| Mills, Jedediah, Corp'l | S | Huntington | 76-H3 |
| Mills, Jn° | Q | ........ | 75-A associator |
| Mills, John | N | New York | 75-D1 |
| Mills, John | Q | Jamaica | 75-C |
| Mills, John | Q | Jamaica | 75-D associator |
| Mills, John | S | ........ | 75-R |
| Mills, John Jr. | Q | Jamaica | 76-C |
| Mills, John, shoemaker | N | Broadway | 75-D1, D2 |
| Mills, Jonas | S | Smithtown | 75-H1 |
| Mills, Jonas | S | Smithtown | 76:1.2.1.2.0.2.2 |
| Mills, Jonas [2] | S | Smithtown | [on] 75-L |
| Mills, Jonathan | S | Smithtown | 75-L |
| Mills, Jonathan | S | Smithtown | 76:1.1.1.1.0.5.1 |
| Mills, Josh. | Q | ........ | 75-A |
| Mills, Joshua | N | New York | 74-A |
| Mills, Joshua | Q | ........ | 76-B |
| Mills, Mary | N | removed upstate | 76-P |
| Mills, Nathaniel | Q | ........ | 75-A |
| Mills, Nathaniel | Q | Jamaica | 75-C |
| Mills, Nathaniel Jr. | Q | ........ | 76-E |
| Mills, Nathaniel Jr. | Q | Jamaica | 75-C, 75-D |
| Mills, Nathaniel Sr. | Q | Jamaica | 75-D |
| Mills, Nathaniel [2] | Q | ........ | [on] 76-E |
| Mills, Obadiah | Q | ........ | 75-A |
| Mills, Obadiah | Q | ........ | 76-B, 76-E |
| Mills, Obadiah | Q | Jamaica | 75-C, 75-D |
| Mills, Peter | Q | ........ | 76-B |
| Mills, Samuel | Q | ........ | 76-B, 76-E |
| Mills, Samuel | Q | Jamaica | 75-C |
| Mills, Samuel | S | Smithtown | 75-L |
| Mills, Samuel | S | Smithtown | 76:0.1.1.1.0 |
| Mills, Thomas | N | New York | 74-A |
| Mills, Timothy | S | Smithtown | 75-L |
| Mills, Timothy | S | Smithtown | 76:0.1.1.2.0.0.1 |
| Mills, William | S | Huntington | 76-H3 |
| Mills, William | S | Smithtown | 75-L |
| Mills, Zophar | S | Smithtown | 75-L |
| Mills, Zophar | S | Smithtown | 76:0.1.4.2.1 |

| | | | |
|---|---|---|---|
| Millson, Sam'l | N | New York | 76-A |
| Milner, William | N | New York | 74-T2, 4/21 |
| Miltenburger, John | N | New York | 76-L |
| Minchull, John | N | New York | 74-T2, 12/15 |
| Minthorn, Mangle, Capt. | N | New York | 75-A |
| Minthorn, Nangle | N | New York | 76-I |
| Minuse, John | N | New York | 74-A |
| Minuss, John | N | New York | 76-A |
| Miserole, Isaac | Q | Newtown | 75-B |
| Mitchel, Isabel | N | rem. to Bedford | 76-J |
| Mitchel, Isabel | N | to Dutchess Co. | 76-P |
| Mitchel, Mehitabel, Wid$^w$ | S | Southampton | 76:0.0.2.1.0.1.0 |
| Mitchel, Robert | Q | ........ | 75-A associator |
| Mitchel, Susanah | N | rem. to Bedford | 76-J |
| Mitchel, Susannah | N | to Dutchess Co. | 76-P |
| Mitchel, William | N | rem. to Bedford | 76-J |
| Mitchell, Augustine | Q | ........ | 76-E |
| Mitchell, Henry | N | New York | 75-T2, 3/23 |
| Mitchell, Henry, 2d Lieut. | N | New York | 76-S |
| Mitchell, Henry, Ensign | N | New York | 75-A |
| Mitchell, Henry, Lieut. | N | New York | 76-G |
| Mitchell, Henry, spirits | N | New York | 74-T2, 7/28 |
| Mitchell, Isaac, post-rider | N | New York | 74-T |
| Mitchell, James | N | New York | 76-A, 76-G |
| Mitchell, John | Q | ........ | 75-A, 76-E |
| Mitchell, John Jr. [2] | Q | ........ | [on] 76-E |
| Mitchell, Robert | Q | ........ | 76-E |
| Mitchell, Thos. | Q | ........ | 75-A associator |
| Mitchell, Uriah | Q | ........ | 75-A associator |
| Mitchell, Viner | N | New York | 76-A |
| Mitchell, Viner, chairmaker | N | opposite St Paul's | 75-D1, D2 |
| Moell, Jacob | N | New York | 76-A |
| Moffatt, Walter | N | New York | 74-A |
| Moffatt, Walter | N | New York | 76-D, 76-N |
| Mogar, Christopher | S | Meritches | 76:0.1.3.3.6 |
| Moger, Arther | S | Brookhaven | 76:0.1.1.1.0 |
| Moger, Arthur | S | Brookhaven | 75-B1, 75-B7 |
| Moger, Christopher | S | Brookhaven | 75-B6 |
| Moger, Christopher, Ensign | S | Brookhaven | 75-B1, 75-B7 |
| Moger, Isaiah | S | Brookhaven | 75-B3, 75-B6 |

| | | | |
|---|---|---|---|
| Moger, Isaih | S | Brookhaven | 76:0.1.2.3.1 |
| Moger, James | S | Brookhaven | 75-B1, 75-B9 |
| Moger, John | S | Brookhaven | 75-B7 |
| Molley, —— Mrs. | N | rem to Ulster Co. | 76-P |
| Molloy, Mich'l | N | New York | 74-A |
| Molun, George | N | New York | 74-A |
| Monell, James | N | New York | 74-A |
| Money, Sam. | S | Huntington | 76-H1 |
| Money, Silas | S | Huntington | 75-H1, 76-H1 |
| Monfoort, Garret | Q | Hempstead | 76-D |
| Monfort, Cornelius | Q | ........ | 75-A |
| Monfort, Garret | Q | ........ | 76-E |
| Monfort, John | Q | ........ | 75-A, 76-E |
| Monfort, Peter [2] | Q | ........ | [on] 76-E |
| Monfort, W. | Q | ........ | 76-E |
| Monfort, Wm | Q | ........ | 75-A, 76-B |
| Monroe, David | S | Huntington | 76-H3 |
| Monroe, Hugh | N | removed upstate | 76-P |
| Monrow, David Jun' | S | Southampton | 76:0.1.2.1.3 |
| Montaine, John | Q | ........ | 75-A associator |
| Montania, Vincent | N | constable | 74-R to 76-R |
| Montanie, John | N | New York | 76-L |
| Montanye, Benjamin | N | New York | 74-A |
| Montanye, Benjamin, blks'th | N | Queen Street | 75-D1, D2 |
| Montanye, Isaac | N | New York | 74-A |
| Montanye, Isaac, hatter | N | Batteau Street | 75-D1, D2 |
| Montanye, John | N | New York | 74-A |
| Montanye, John | Q | ........ | 76-E |
| Montanye, John, hatter | N | New York | 75-D2 |
| Montanye, John Jr. | N | New York | 74-A |
| Montanye, John T., hatter | N | Broadway | 75-D1, D2 |
| Montanye, John T. | N | New York | 74-A |
| Montanye, Mary | N | Fresh Water | 76-I |
| Montanye, Peter | N | New York | 74-A |
| Montanye; see also DeLamontanie | | | |
| Montayne, Becka, Mrs. | N | to Dutchess Co. | 76-P |
| Montayne, Janitje | N | to Dutchess Co. | 76-P |
| Montayne, Rachel | N | to Dutchess Co. | 76-P |
| Montayne, Rachel | N | to Westchester Co | 76-P |
| Montgomery, Jemes | S | Brookhaven | 76:1.1.0.3.0 |

| | | | |
|---|---|---|---|
| Moody, Sarah, Mrs. | N | removed upstate | 76-P |
| Moody, see Mudy | | | |
| Mooer, Simon | S | ........ | 75-R |
| Mook, William | N | New York | 76-A |
| Moon, Joseph | N | New York | 76-A |
| Mooney, William | N | New York | 74-A |
| Moor, Ab'm | N | New York | 76-A |
| Moor, Blusty | N | New York | 76-A |
| Moor, Jacob | N | near Kings Bridge | 76-H |
| Moor, John | N | near Kings Bridge | 76-I |
| Moor, John | N | New York | 76-A |
| Moor, Mary | N | removed upstate | 76-P |
| Moore, Benj. | S | Southold | 76:0.1.0.1.3.0.1 |
| Moore, Benjamin | N | New York | 74-A, 76-A |
| Moore, Benjamin | Q | ........ | 75-A associator |
| Moore, Benjamin | Q | ........ | 76-E |
| Moore, Benjamin | S | Brookhaven | 75-B10 |
| Moore, Blasey | N | New York | 74-A |
| Moore, Boltis | N | New York | 76-A |
| Moore, Calvin | S | ........ | 75-R |
| Moore, Calvin | S | Southold | 76:0.1.2.4.3.0.1 |
| Moore, Daniel | S | Southampton | 75-M |
| Moore, Daniel | S | Southampton | 76:1.0.1.3.0 |
| Moore, David | Q | ........ | 76-E |
| Moore, Edward | N | to Dutchess Co. | 76-P |
| Moore, Francis | N | New York | 74-A |
| Moore, Henderson | N | New York | 74-A |
| Moore, Hennery | S | Southold | 76:1.3.0.1.0 |
| Moore, Henry | N | New York | 76-A |
| Moore, Henry | S | ........ | 75-R |
| Moore, Henry | S | Southampton | 76:0.1.1.1.2 |
| Moore, Henry Jr. | S | Brookhaven | 75-B10 |
| Moore, Isaac | N | New York | 75-R |
| Moore, Israel | S | Brookhaven | 75-B10 |
| Moore, J., Jr. | Q | Newtown | 75-B |
| Moore, Jacob | Q | ........ | 76-E |
| Moore, Jacob, tobacconist | N | Fair Street | 75-D2 |
| Moore, James | N | New York | 75-B, 75-D3 |
| Moore, James | N | New York | 76-A |
| Moore, James | Q | ........ | 76-E |

| | | | |
|---|---|---|---|
| Moore, James | S | Brookhaven | 75-B10 |
| Moore, Jeremiah | N | New York | 76-A |
| Moore, John | Q | ........ | 75-H, 76-E |
| Moore, John | Q | Newtown | 75-B |
| Moore, John | S | ........ | 75-R |
| Moore, John | S | Brookhaven | 75-B10 |
| Moore, John | S | Southold | 76:0.1.5.3.3.2.0 |
| Moore, John B. | N | New York | 74-A |
| Moore, John B. | N | New York | 74-T2, 11/24 |
| Moore, John B., 1st Lieut. | N | New York | 76-Y |
| Moore, John, bricklayer | N | John Street | 75-D2 |
| Moore, John Esq. | N | New York | 74-A |
| Moore, John Jr. | Q | ........ | 75-A, 76-E |
| Moore, John Jr. | Q | Newtown | 75-H |
| Moore, John Sr. | Q | ........ | 75-A |
| Moore, John Sr. | Q | Newtown | 75-H |
| Moore, John [2] | N | New York | [on] 76-A |
| Moore, Joseph | Q | ........ | 76-E |
| Moore, Joseph | S | Southampton | 75-M |
| Moore, Joseph | S | Southampton | 76:0.1.2.1.3 |
| Moore, Lambert | Q | ........ | 76-E |
| Moore, Lambert Esq. | N | New York | 74-V |
| Moore, Micah, Dr. | S | ........ | 75-R |
| Moore, Michael, shoemaker | N | liv w Jno Anthony | 75-D1, D2 |
| Moore, Nathaniel | Q | ........ | 75-A, 76-E |
| Moore, Nathaniel | Q | Newtown | 75-B, 75-H |
| Moore, Nathaniel Jr. | Q | ........ | 76-E |
| Moore, Nicholas, mason | N | Chappel Street | 75-D2 |
| Moore, Richard, schoolmstr | N | Barclay Street | 75-D1, D2 |
| Moore, Rich[d] | N | New York | 75-D1 |
| Moore, Robert | S | ........ | 75-R |
| Moore, Robert | S | Southampton | 75-M |
| Moore, Sam., Capt. | Q | Newtown | 75-G |
| Moore, Sam. Sr. | Q | Newtown | 75-B |
| Moore, Sam'l 3d | Q | ........ | 75-A |
| Moore, Sam'l 3d | Q | Newtown | 75-B |
| Moore, Sam'l, Capt. | Q | ........ | 75-A associator |
| Moore, Samuel | Q | ........ | 75-A |
| Moore, Samuel | Q | ........ | 76-B, 76-E |
| Moore, Samuel Sr. | Q | ........ | 76-E |

| Moore, Silas | S | Southold | 75-N |
|---|---|---|---|
| Moore, Silas | S | Southold | 76:1.1.1.2.1 |
| Moore, Simon | S | Southold | 75-N |
| Moore, Simon | S | Southold | 76:1.1.0.1.0 |
| Moore, Stephen | Q | ........ | 76-E |
| Moore, Tho | S | Southold | 76:0.3.2.1.4 |
| Moore, Thomas W., Capt. | N | New York | 75-A |
| Moore, Thomas William | N | New York | 74-T, 75-F |
| Moore, ---- Wid. | S | Southold | 76:0.0.0.1.0.1.1 |
| Moore, ---- Wid. | S | Southold | 76:0.0.0.2.4.1.1 |
| Moore, ---- Wid. | S | Southold | 76:0.0.0.4.0 |
| Moore, ---- Wid. | S | Southold | 76:0.0.2.3.0 |
| Moore, William | N | New York | 75-R |
| Moorse, Nicholas | N | New York | 74-A |
| Moran, James | N | New York | 76-A |
| More, Ann | N | to Westchester Co | 76-P |
| More, Catharine | N | to Westchester Co | 76-P |
| More, Edard | S | Brookhaven | 76:0.1.0.1.1 |
| More, Edward | S | Brookhaven | 75-B11 n.s. |
| More, Edward | S | Brookhaven | 75-B10 |
| More, James | N | New York | 74-A |
| More, John | N | New York | 74-A, 76-L |
| More, John | S | Brookhaven | 75-B8 |
| More, Phane | N | to Westchester Co | 76-P |
| More, Silas | S | Southold | 75-N non-signer |
| More, Thomas | S | Huntington | 76-H3 |
| Morehouse, John | S | ........ | 75-R |
| Morehouse, Phebe | S | Southampton | 76:0.0.0.1.1 |
| Morfett, Charles | N | rem. to Bedford | 76-J |
| Morgan, Jam. | N | New York | 76-E |
| Morgan, John | S | Huntington | 75-H |
| Morgan, Joseph, cutler | N | Duke Street | 75-D1, D2 |
| Morgan, Mary, Mrs. | N | to Dutchess Co. | 76-P |
| Morgan, Philip | N | New York | 76-A |
| Morgan, Richard | N | New York | 74-A |
| Morgan, Sarah wf of Philip | N | New York | 76-R |
| Moris, David | N | New York | 76-L |
| Moris, Jacob | N | New York | 76-L |
| Morison, James | S | Southold | 76:0.3.0.1.0.2.0 |
| Morlidge, Samuel | N | New York | 76-C Grenadier |

| | | | |
|---|---|---|---|
| Morrel, George | N | New York | 76-A |
| Morrel, John | Q | ........ | 75-A, 76-E |
| Morrell, Caleb | Q | ........ | 75-A, 76-E |
| Morrell, Daniel | N | New York | 75-D1, D2 |
| Morrell, James [2] | Q | ........ | [on] 76-E |
| Morrell, John Sr. | Q | Newtown | 75-B |
| Morrell, John [3] | Q | ........ | [on] 76-E |
| Morrell, Jonathan | Q | ........ | 76-E |
| Morrell, Joseph | Q | ........ | 76-E |
| Morrell, Richard | Q | ........ | 76-E |
| Morrell, Robert | Q | ........ | 75-A associator |
| Morrell, Robert | Q | ........ | 76-E |
| Morrell, Sam'l | Q | ........ | 75-A associator |
| Morrell, Thomas | Q | ........ | 75-A, 76-E |
| Morrell, William | N | removed upstate | 76-P |
| Morrill, Joseph | Q | Newtown | 75-G |
| Morris, David | N | New York | 74-A |
| Morris, David, house crpntr | N | Dey Street | 75-D2 |
| Morris, Jacob | N | New York | 74-A, 75-D3 |
| Morris, James | N | New York | 75-R |
| Morris, James | S | Islip pr order G.S. | 75-I |
| Morris, James | S | Islip | 76:1.0.1.1.1 |
| Morris, James Juner | S | Islip | 76:0.1.2.1.3 |
| Morris, James Jun'. | S | Islip | 75-I |
| Morris, Lewis | N | New York | 75-D3, 76-N |
| Morris, Martin | N | New York | 76-A |
| Morris, Mary | N | removed upstate | 76-P |
| Morris, William | S | Islip | 76:0.1.3.1.0 |
| Morrison, Daniel | N | to Dutchess Co. | 76-P |
| Morrison, David | N | New York | 76-G |
| Morse, Charles | N | New York | 74-A, 76-A |
| Morse; see also Moorse | | | |
| Morton, Hugh | N | New York | 74-A |
| Morton, James | N | New York | 75-D2 |
| Morton, James, merchant | N | Queen Street | 74-T2, 4/28; 75-F |
| Morton, John | N | New York | 75-F; 75-T2, 5/4 |
| Morton, Nathaniel, Sgt. | S | Brookhaven | 75-B1 |
| Morton, William, 2d Lieut. | N | New York | 76-Y |
| Morwood, R. | N | New York | 75-T2, 1/19 |
| Moses, Isaac | N | New York | 74-A |

| | | | |
|---|---|---|---|
| Moses, Isaac, merchant | N | New York | 74-T, 75-F |
| Mosure, Lemuel | S | Huntington | 75-H |
| Mott, Adam | Q | ........ | 75-A, 76-E |
| Mott, Adam | Q | Conn. [sic] | 75-A associator |
| Mott, Adam Sr. | Q | ........ | 76-E |
| Mott, Gershom | N | New York | 74-A, 76-N |
| Mott, Gershom, Capt. | N | New York | 75-E |
| Mott, Isaac | N | New York | 76-A |
| Mott, Jackson | Q | ........ | 75-A, 76-E |
| Mott, Jacob | Q | ........ | 75-A, 76-E |
| Mott, Jacob | Q | ........ | 75-A associator |
| Mott, Jacob, Capt. | Q | Hempstead | 75-H |
| Mott, Jacob Jr. | Q | ........ | 76-E |
| Mott, Jno. [2] | Q | ........ | [on] 75-A |
| Mott, John | N | Bowry Lane | 76-I |
| Mott, John | Q | ........ | 76-B, 76-E |
| Mott, John Jun$^r$ | N | Bowry Lane | 76-H |
| Mott, Noah Jr. | Q | ........ | 76-E |
| Mott, Richard | Q | ........ | 75-A, 76-E |
| Mott, Samuel | Q | ........ | 75-A |
| Mott, Samuel | Q | ........ | 76-B, 76-E |
| Mott, Samuel 3d | Q | ........ | 76-E |
| Mountain, Andrew | N | New York | 76-I |
| Mounton, Andrew | N | New York | 74-A |
| Mowatt, John | N | New York | 74-A |
| Mowberry, Anning | S | Huntington | 75-H |
| Mowbray, John | S | Islip | 75-I |
| Mowbray, John | S | Islip | 76:1.1.1.4.1.1.0 |
| Mucklevain, William | N | New York | 76-A |
| Muclebray, John | N | New York | 76-F |
| Mudge, Coles | Q | ........ | 76-E |
| Mudge, Michael | Q | ........ | 76-E |
| Mudge, William | Q | ........ | 76-E |
| Mudy, Samuel | Q | ........ | 76-E |
| Muffett, Robert, saddler | N | Wall Street | 75-T2, 9/28 |
| Muirson, Benj$^m$ W. | S | Brookhaven | 75-B10 |
| Mulford, Abra: Jr. | S | Easthampton | 75-E |
| Mulford, Abraham | S | Easthampton | 75-E |
| Mulford, Abraham | S | Easthampton | 76:1.0.2.2.1 |
| Mulford, Abraham Jun$^r$ | S | Easthampton | 76:0.1.0.1.2 |

| Mulford, Daniel | S | ........ | 75-R |
|---|---|---|---|
| Mulford, David | S | Brookhaven | 76:0.3.1.2.0.1.1 |
| Mulford, David, Capt. | S | Brookhaven | 75-B1 |
| Mulford, David, Col. | S | Easthampton | 76:1.2.1.3.1.4.4 |
| Mulford, David, Ensign | S | Brookhaven | 75-B7 |
| Mulford, David Jun. | S | Brookhaven | 75-B6 |
| Mulford, David [2] | S | Easthampton | [on] 75-E |
| Mulford, Elias | S | Easthampton | 75-E |
| Mulford, Eliast | S | Easthampton | 76:0.3.0.1.1 |
| Mulford, Elisha | S | Easthampton | 75-E |
| Mulford, Elisha | S | Easthampton | 76:1.1.1.2.0 |
| Mulford, Elisha Sr. | S | Easthampton | 75-E |
| Mulford, Ezekeil, Capt. | S | Easthampton | 76:0.1.3.3.2.1.0 |
| Mulford, Ezekiel | S | Easthampton | 75-E |
| Mulford, J. | S | Easthampton | 75-E |
| Mulford, Jeremiah | S | Brookhaven | 75-B7 |
| Mulford, Job | S | Brookhaven | 75-B1, 75-B6 |
| Mulford, Job, Sergt. | S | Brookhaven | 75-B7 n.s. |
| Mulford, John | S | Easthampton | 75-E |
| Mulford, John Esq. | S | Easthampton | 76:1.2.0.1.0.2.1 |
| Mulford, Jonathan | S | Easthampton | 75-E |
| Mulford, Josiah | S | Easthampton | 75-E |
| Mulford, Lemuel | S | Easthampton | 75-E |
| Mulford, Lemuel | S | Easthampton | 76:1.0.0.2.0 |
| Mulford, Matthew | S | Easthampton | 75-E |
| Mulford, Nathan | S | Easthampton | 75-E |
| Mulford, Nathan | S | Easthampton | 76:0.1.0.1.0 |
| Mulford, Samuel | S | Easthampton | 76:1.1.0.2.2.2.1 |
| Mulford, Samuel [2] | S | Easthampton | [on] 75-E |
| Mulford, William | S | Easthampton | 75-E |
| Mulford, William | S | Easthampton | 76:0.1.0.1.0.1.0 |
| Mullar, Jeremiah | N | New York | 76-A |
| Mullenar, Susanah | N | removed upstate | 76-P |
| Muller, Charles | N | New York | 76-A |
| Muller, Frederick | N | New York | 76-A |
| Muller, George | N | New York | 76-A |
| Muller, John God. | N | New York | 76-A |
| Muller, Joseph | S | Easthampton | 75-E |
| Mulligan, Cook, merchant | N | New York | 76-V |
| Mulligan, Hercules | N | New York | 74-T2, 11/24 |

| | | | |
|---|---|---|---|
| Mulligan, Hercules | N | New York | 74-V, 75-F |
| Mulligan, Hers. | N | New York | 74-A |
| Mullin, George | N | New York | 76-I |
| Mulliner, William | N | New York | 74-R, 75-R |
| Muncey, Isaac | S | Islip | 75-I |
| Muncey, Sam[l] | S | Huntington | 75-H |
| Muncil, Alexander | S | Smithtown | 76:0.1.7.2.1 |
| Munro, David | S | Brookhaven | 75-B7 |
| Munroe, David | S | Brookhaven | 76:1.1.2.3.0 |
| Munsee, Hendrick | Q | ........ | 75-A |
| Munsel, Alexander | S | Smithtown | 75-L recusant |
| Mure, John, servant | N | runaway | 74-T |
| Murgiffroyd, Samuel | N | New York | 76-A |
| Murison, Jorg, Docter | S | Brookhaven | 76:1.2.0.1.0.4.2 |
| Murphey, Garret | Q | Jamaica | 75-C |
| Murphy, Ann | N | New York | 74-R |
| Murphy, Garr't | Q | ........ | 75-A associator |
| Murphy, Philip | N | New York | 76-A |
| Murphy, Robert | N | New York | 74-A |
| Murray, Alexander | N | New York | 75-T2, 10/19 |
| Murray, Alletta | N | to Dutchess Co. | 76-P |
| Murray, Daniel | Q | ........ | 75-A |
| Murray, Daniel | Q | ........ | 76-B, 76-E |
| Murray, George | N | New York | 74-A |
| Murray, Hugh | N | New York | 74-R, 75-R |
| Murray, James | N | New York | 74-A |
| Murray, James, nailmaker | N | New York | 75-T runaway |
| Murray, John Jun. | N | New York | 76-A |
| Murray, John, merchant | N | New York | 75-T |
| Murray, Lindley | N | New York | 74-A |
| Murray, Lindley | N | New York | 74-T2, 11/24 |
| Murray, Lindley | N | New York | 76-A |
| Murray, Robert | N | New York | 76-A |
| Murray, Robert, merchant | N | New York | 75-T |
| Murry, Diana | N | to Dutchess Co. | 76-P |
| Murry, James | N | to Westchester Co | 76-P |
| Murry, John | N | to Dutchess Co. | 76-P |
| Murry, Lendly | S | Islip | 76:0.1.1.1.0 |
| Murry, Mary, Mrs. | N | to Dutchess Co. | 76-P |
| Murry, William | N | removed upstate | 76-P |

| | | | |
|---|---|---|---|
| Mussey, Samuel | S | Islip | 76:1.1.1.5.4 |
| Mutty, Peter | Q | Oyster Bay | 75-F |
| Myer, George [2] | N | New York | [on] 76-A |
| Myer, James | N | New York | 76-A |
| Myer, Mary | N | New York | 74-R |
| Myers, Abraham, constable | N | New York | 74-R to 76-R |
| Myers, Cornelius | N | New York | 76-I |
| Myers, Frederick | N | New York | 76-I |
| Myers, Gerardus | N | New York | 74-A |
| Myers, Jacobus, cartman | N | Nassau Street | 75-D1, D2 |
| Myers, James | N | New York | 74-A |
| Myers, John | N | New York | 74-A, 75-V |
| Myers, John J. | N | New York | 76-D |
| Myers, Manuel | N | New York | 74-R |
| Myers, Myer | N | New York | 74-A, 74-T |
| Myers, Peter | N | New York | 76-D |
| Myers, Samuel | N | New York | 76-A |
| Myford, J. | N | New York | 74-A |
| Myford, John, stores, &c. | N | New York | 74-T2, 4/14 |
| Myford, John, tavernkeeper | N | New York | 74-T, 75-T |
| Nack, Rinier | N | New York | 74-A |
| Nailor, Michael | N | New York | 76-A |
| Naroy, Samuel | N | New York | 76-A |
| Narrin, William | N | removed upstate | 76-P |
| Nash, Abigail, Mrs. | N | to Dutchess Co. | 76-P |
| Nash, Daniel | S | Brookhaven | 75-B6 |
| Nash, Daniel | S | Brookhaven | 76:0.1.2.1.0 |
| Nash, George | N | to Dutchess Co. | 76-P |
| Nash, James | N | New York | 76-M |
| Nash, John | N | New York | 76-I |
| Nathan, David | N | New York | 76-A |
| Navaro, David | N | New York | 76-A |
| Nearn, Mary | N | New York | 76-K |
| Neaven, James | N | New York | 76-A |
| Needham, John | Q | ........ | 76-E |
| Needham, John | S | Huntington | 75-H |
| Needham, John Jr. | Q | ........ | 76-E |
| Needham, William | N | New York | 74-A |
| Needham, William, cartman | N | liv w/ Copperthwait | 75-D1, D2 |
| Needham, William, Lieut. | N | New York | 75-A |

| | | | |
|---|---|---|---|
| Neil, Mary | N | removed upstate | 76-P |
| Neilson, William, store | N | New York | 74-T, 75-F |
| Nestel, Michael | N | New York | 74-A |
| Nestell, Jasper | N | New York | 74-V |
| Nestle, Caspar | N | New York | 76-A |
| Nevins, ____ Mr. | N | New York | 75-D2 |
| Newcark, Barney, shoemkr | N | Crown Street | 75-D1, D2 |
| Newhall, Thomas | N | New York | 74-A |
| Newkirk, Barne | N | New York | 74-A |
| Newman, William | S | Huntington | 75-H |
| Newman, Wm., drummer | S | Huntington | 76-H3 |
| Newten, Peter | N | New York | 74-A |
| Newton, Agnis | N | New York | 76-I |
| Newton, Benjamin | S | Brookhaven | 75-B10 |
| Newton, Benjamin | S | Smithtown | 76:1.0.1.3.0.0.1 |
| Newton, Caleb | S | Islip | 76:0.2.2.2.2.1.0 |
| Newton, Caleb | S | Smithtown | 75-L recusant |
| Newton, Calop | S | Brookhaven | 75-B10 |
| Newton, Isaac | S | Smithtown | 75-L recusant |
| Newton, Isac | S | Brookhaven | 75-B10 |
| Newton, Isac | S | Brookhaven | 76:0.1.3.1.3 |
| Newton, John | S | Brookhaven | 75-B10 |
| Newton, John | S | Brookhaven | 76:0.1.3.1.0 |
| Newton, John | S | Smithtown | 75-L recusant |
| Nexsen, Elias | N | New York | 74-A |
| Nexsen, Elias, hides | N | Burling's Slip | 74-T2, 7/7 |
| Nichelson, Sara | N | removed upstate | 76-P |
| Nicholl, Chas. Jr. | N | New York | 74-A |
| Nicholls, George | N | New York | 74-A, 76-I |
| Nicholls, Richard, attorney | N | New York | 75-T, 75-V |
| Nichols, John | N | New York | 74-A |
| Nichols, Lewis | N | New York | 74-A |
| Nichols, Samuel | N | New York | 76-A |
| Nichols, Samuel | Q | ........ | 76-E |
| Nicholson, Finnly | N | New York | 76-V |
| Nicholson, Jonathan, shoemr | N | at the Coffee House | 75-D1, D2 |
| Nickerson, William | S | Southampton | 76:1.0.1.2.0 |
| Nicol, William | S | Islip | 76:1.1.1.2.1.8.7 |
| Nicoll, Benjamin | S | Smithtown | 75-L |
| Nicoll, Benjamin | S | Smithtown | 76:0.4.6.2.2 |

| | | | |
|---|---|---|---|
| Nicoll, Charles | N | New York | 74-T2, 11/24 |
| Nicoll, Chas. | N | New York | 74-A |
| Nicoll, Edward | N | New York | 74-A |
| Nicoll, Edward | N | New York | 74-T2, 10/13 |
| Nicoll, Edward | N | New York | 76-A |
| Nicoll, Edward Jr., 2d Lt. | N | New York | 76-Y |
| Nicoll, Edward, juror | N | New York | 74-R, 75-R |
| Nicoll, Stephen | S | Smithtown | 75-L |
| Nicoll, W. | S | Islip | 75-I |
| Nicoll, William | S | Smithtown | 75-L |
| Nicoll, Will<sup>m</sup>, hatter | S | Huntington | 75-H |
| Nicoll, Wm. | S | Shelter Island | 76:0.1.1.1.0.7.3 |
| Nicolls, Charles | N | New York | 76-F |
| Nicolls, Richard Esq. | N | New York | 74-V |
| Nicolls, William Jun<sup>r</sup>. | S | Islip | 75-I |
| Nicols, Benjamin Jun<sup>r</sup> | S | Smithtown | 75-L |
| Niers, William | N | New York | 76-A |
| Niven, Daniel | N | New York | 74-A |
| Nixon, Elias | N | Burling's Slip | 74-T2, 3/17 |
| Nixon, John | N | New York | 74-A |
| Nixon, John | N | New York | 76-A, 76-R |
| Nixon, Thomas | N | Fly Market | 74-T2, 5/26 |
| Nixon, Thos. | N | New York | 74-A |
| Nixon, Wm. | N | New York | 74-A |
| Nixson, Elias, see Nexsen | | | |
| Noaks, Isaac | S | Huntington | 75-H |
| Noaks, Isaac | S | Islip | 76:0.1.3.1.2 |
| Noaks, Jacob | S | Huntington | 75-H1 |
| Noaks, Jacob Jr. | S | Huntington | 75-H |
| Noaks, Jacob Sr. | S | Huntington | 75-H |
| Noaks, Simon | S | Huntington | 75-H |
| Nobal, Gabriel | N | New York | 75-D1 |
| Noble, Elizabeth | N | New York | 75-R |
| Noble, John | N | nr ye Air Furnace | 76-H |
| Noblet, John | N | New York | 75-R, 76-R |
| Noblit, John | N | Chambers Street | 75-D1, D2 |
| Noblit, John | N | New York | 76-A |
| Noel and Hazard | N | New York | 75-F |
| Noonan, Robert, servant | N | New York | 75-V runaway |
| Norman, William | N | New York | 76-A |

| | | | |
|---|---|---|---|
| Norris, Henry | S | Southampton | 76:1.1.0.1.0 |
| Norris, Jacob | N | New York | 76-L |
| Norris, James | S | Southampton | 76:0.1.0.1.1 |
| Norris, John | N | New York | 74-A |
| Norris, John | S | ........ | 75-R |
| Norris, John | S | Southampton | 76:1.1.0.3.1 |
| Norris, John 2$^{nd}$ | S | ........ | 75-R |
| Norris, Nathan | S | Southampton | 75-M |
| Norris, Nathan | S | Southampton | 76:1.1.0.3.0 |
| Norris, Nathan Jun$^r$ | S | Southampton | 75-M |
| Norris, Nathan Jun$^r$ | S | Southampton | 76:0.1.1.1.1 |
| Norris, Oliver | S | Shelter Island | 75-K |
| Norris, Richard, staymaker | N | rem to Eliz., NJ | 75-R |
| Norris, Richard, staymaker | N | Smith Street | 74-T2, 2/3 |
| Norris, Silas | S | Southampton | 75-M |
| Norris, Silas | S | Southampton | 76:0.3.2.1.2 |
| Norris, Thomas | S | Southampton | 75-M non-signer |
| Norris, Thomas | S | Southampton | 76:1.0.0.1.1 |
| North, Benjamin | N | New York | 74-A |
| North, Benjamin | Q | ........ | 75-A associator |
| North, Benjamin | Q | Newtown | 75-G |
| North, Thomas | Q | ........ | 76-E |
| North, Thos. | Q | Newtown | 75-G |
| Norton, Benjamin | S | Brookhaven | 75-B7 |
| Norton, George | S | Brookhaven | 75-B9 |
| Norton, George | S | Huntington | 75-H |
| Norton, George | S | Huntington | 75-H1, 76-H1 |
| Norton, Jabish | S | Brookhaven | 75-B9 |
| Norton, Nathaniel | S | Brookhaven | 76:0.1.3.1.1 |
| Norton, Nath$^l$ | S | Brookhaven | 75-B7 |
| Norton, Timothy | S | Brookhaven | 75-B9 |
| Norton, Timothy | S | Brookhaven | 76:1.2.1.3.1 |
| Norton, Timothy Jr. | S | Brookhaven | 75-B2 |
| Norwood, Andrew | N | New York | 74-A |
| Norwood, Andrew, shoemkr | N | Broadway | 75-D1, D2 |
| Norwood, Benjamin | N | New York | 76-A |
| Norwood, John | N | New York | 74-A, 76-A |
| Norwood, Richard | N | New York | 74-A, 74-T |
| Norwood, Richard | N | New York | 75-R juror |
| Norwood, Richard | N | New York | 76-N |

| | | | |
|---|---|---|---|
| Norwood, Tobias | N | New York | 74-A |
| Norwood, Vanderclife | N | New York | 76-A |
| Nostran, Jacobus | S | Huntington | 75-H |
| Nostran, Jacobus, weaver | S | Huntington | 75-H1 |
| Nostran, Sam[l] | S | Huntington | 75-H |
| Nostran, Samuel | S | Huntington | 75-H1, 76-H2 |
| Nostrand, Ab'm | Q | ........ | 75-A |
| Nostrand, Albert | Q | ........ | 75-A associator |
| Nostrand, Daniel | Q | ........ | 76-B |
| Nostrand, Daniel | Q | Hempstead | 76-D |
| Nostrand, Daniel [2] | Q | ........ | [on] 75-A |
| Nostrand, Daniel [2] | Q | ........ | [on] 76-E |
| Nostrand, Frederick | Q | ........ | 75-A, 76-E |
| Nostrand, Frederick Jr. | Q | ........ | 75-A |
| Nostrand, G., Jr. | Q | ........ | 76-E |
| Nostrand, Garret | Q | ........ | 76-B |
| Nostrand, Garret | Q | Jamaica | 75-C, 75-D |
| Nostrand, Garret [2] | Q | ........ | [on] 75-A |
| Nostrand, Garret [2] | Q | ........ | [on] 76-E |
| Nostrand, Garrit | Q | O. [Oyster Bay] | 75-A |
| Nostrand, George | Q | ........ | 76-E |
| Nostrand, Jacob | Q | ........ | 75-A, 76-E |
| Nostrand, Jno. [2] | Q | ........ | [on] 75-A |
| Nostrand, John | Q | ........ | 76-B, 76-E |
| Nostrand, John | Q | Jamaica | 75-C, 75-D |
| Nostrand, Luke | Q | ........ | 75-A, 76-B |
| Nostrand, Pet. Jr. | Q | ........ | 76-E |
| Nostrand, Peter | Q | ........ | 76-B |
| Nostrand, Peter | Q | Jamaica | 75-D, 76-C |
| Nostrand, Peter [2] | Q | ........ | [on] 75-A |
| Nostrand, Peter [2] | Q | ........ | [on] 76-E |
| Nostrand, see also Van Nostrant | | | |
| Nostrans, James | S | Huntington | 75-H |
| Nowland, William, perukemkr | N | New York | 74-R |
| Nowlin, John | N | to Westchester Co | 76-P |
| Nox, Richard | N | removed upstate | 76-P |
| Nox, Sarah | N | removed upstate | 76-P |
| Nutter, Valentine | N | New York | 76-A |
| Nutter, Valentine, bookbndr | N | nr Coffee House | 74-T2, 9/22 |
| Nutter, Valentine, Ensign | N | New York | 76-Y |

| | | | |
|---|---|---|---|
| O'Briant, Henry | N | New York | 75-D3 |
| O'Brien, Henry | N | New York | 76-A |
| O'Brien, Henry, staymaker | N | Broadway | 74-T2, 9/22 |
| O'Brien, James | N | New York | 74-A |
| O'Bryan, Patt., b. Ireland | N | runaway | 74-T |
| O'Dear, Alexander | N | New York | 76-E |
| O'Donald, James | N | New York | 75-R |
| O'Donnel, James, taylor | N | New York | 74-T2, 5/19 |
| O'Donnell, James | N | New York | 75-R |
| O'Farel, Sarah | N | rem. to Bedford | 76-J |
| O'Farrell, Michael | N | New York | 75-D2 |
| O'Ham, James | N | New York | 75-R |
| O'Neal, Anne | N | to Dutchess Co. | 76-P |
| O'Neil, James | N | New York | 74-A |
| O'Neil, Robert | N | New York | 74-T |
| O'Neill, John | N | New York | 76-A |
| Oakes, Garret | N | New York | 74-A |
| Oakes, Simon | S | Huntington | 76-H3 |
| Oakes, Thom's | N | New York | 74-A |
| Oakes, Thomas | N | New York | 74-R juror |
| Oakley, Andrew | Q | ........ | 75-A associator |
| Oakley, Andrew | Q | ........ | 75-E |
| Oakley, Andrew | Q | Jamaica | 75-D associator |
| Oakley, Andrew | Q | Jamaica | 76-C |
| Oakley, Benj$^m$ | S | Huntington | 75-H |
| Oakley, Israel | Q | ........ | 76-E |
| Oakley, Israel | Q | Hempstead | 76-D |
| Oakley, James Jr. | S | Huntington | 75-H1 |
| Oakley, Jno. | Q | ........ | 75-A |
| Oakley, Nathaniel | S | Huntington | 75-H1, 76-H1 |
| Oakley, Nathaniel | S | Islip | 76:1.2.0.2.2 |
| Oakley, Samuel, trustee | S | Huntington | 75-H1 |
| Oakley, Stephen | N | New York | 76-N |
| Oakley, Willmoth | S | Huntington | 75-H1, 76-H1 |
| Oakly, Henry | S | Huntington | 75-H non-signer |
| Oakly, James Jr. | S | Huntington | 75-H Quaker |
| Oakly, Miles | S | Huntington | 75-H non-signer |
| Oakly, Nathaniel | S | Islip | 75-I |
| Oakly, Sam$^l$ [2] | S | Huntington | [on] 75-H |
| Oakly, Samuel | S | Islip | 75-I |

| | | | |
|---|---|---|---|
| Oakly, Wilmot | S | Huntington | 75-H |
| Oaks, Garret | N | Crugers Wharf | 76-I |
| Oaks, Garret | N | New York | 76-A |
| Oaks, Jacob | S | Huntington | 76-H1 |
| Oats, Elizabeth | N | removed upstate | 76-P |
| Ogden, Benjamin | N | New York | 74-A, 76-A |
| Ogden, Henry | N | New York | 74-A |
| Ogden, Henry | N | New York | 75-D1 |
| Ogden, Henry, taylor | N | Broadway | 75-D1, D2 |
| Ogden, Jacob | Q | ........ | 76-E |
| Ogden, John, hatter | N | French Church St | 75-D1, D2 |
| Ogden, Nathaniel, mason | N | John Street | 75-D1, D2 |
| Ogden, Nicholas | N | New York | 75-R |
| Ogden, Nichs. | N | New York | 74-A |
| Ogdon, Sarah | N | removed upstate | 76-P |
| Ogelve, John | N | New York | 75-D2 |
| Ogilvie, John | N | New York | 76-A |
| Ogilvie, Thos. | N | New York | 74-A |
| Ogilvie, William | N | New York | 74-A |
| Ogsbury, Alexander | N | New York | 76-A, 76-L |
| Ogsbury, Alexander [2] | N | New York | [on] 74-A |
| Oldfield, Joseph | Q | ........ | 75-A |
| Oldfield, Joseph | Q | ........ | 76-B, 76-E |
| Oldfield, Joseph | Q | Jamaica | 75-C, 75-D |
| Onderdonck, Adrian | Q | ........ | 75-A associator |
| Onderdonck, Adrian | Q | ........ | 76-E |
| Onderdonck, Hend'k | Q | ........ | 76-E |
| Onderdonck, Peter | Q | ........ | 75-A associator |
| Onderdonck, Peter | Q | ........ | 76-E |
| Oothout, John, juror | N | New York | 75-R, 76-R |
| Orchard, Joseph | N | New York | 75-T, 76-A |
| Orr, Ann | N | rem to Ulster Co. | 76-P |
| Orr, Hannah | N | removed upstate | 76-P |
| Orsborn, Jacob | S | Southampton | 76:0.1.0.1.2 |
| Orsborn, James | S | Brookhaven | 75-B1, 75-B7 |
| Orsborn, Thomas | S | Easthampton | 76:0.1.2.1.1 |
| Ortus, Edward | Q | ........ | 76-E |
| Osban, Ezekiel | S | Brookhaven | 76:0.1.2.1.1 |
| Osband, see Davis, Daniel | | | |
| Osborn, Abraham | S | Easthampton | 75-E |

| Osborn, Cornelius | S | Easthampton | 75-E |
| Osborn, Daniel | S | Brookhaven | 75-B10 |
| Osborn, Daniel | S | Easthampton | 75-E |
| Osborn, Daniel | S | Easthampton | 76:1.0.0.0.0 |
| Osborn, Daniel Jun. | S | Brookhaven | 75-B10 |
| Osborn, David | S | Easthampton | 75-E |
| Osborn, David | S | Easthampton | 76:0.1.2.1.4 |
| Osborn, Elisabeth, Mrs. | S | Easthampton | 76:0.0.0.1.0 |
| Osborn, Elisha | S | Easthampton | 75-E |
| Osborn, Elisha | S | Easthampton | 76:0.2.2.1.3 |
| Osborn, Jacob | S | Easthampton | 76:1.2.0.2.1 |
| Osborn, Jacob [2] | S | Easthampton | [on] 75-E |
| Osborn, Jedediah | S | Easthampton | 75-E |
| Osborn, Jedediah | S | Easthampton | 76:1.1.4.2.0 |
| Osborn, Jeremiah | S | Easthampton | 75-E |
| Osborn, Jeremiah | S | Easthampton | 76:0.1.0.2.0.1.0 |
| Osborn, Jeremiah Jr. | S | Easthampton | 75-E |
| Osborn, Jonathan | S | Easthampton | 75-E |
| Osborn, Jonathan | S | Southold | 75-N |
| Osborn, Jonathon | S | Easthampton | 76:1.2.2.1.0 |
| Osborn, Joseph | S | Easthampton | 76:1.0.0.1.1.0.1 |
| Osborn, Joseph Jr. | S | Easthampton | 75-E |
| Osborn, Joseph Jun' | S | Easthampton | 76:0.1.3.1.4 |
| Osborn, Joseph [2] | S | Easthampton | [on] 75-E |
| Osborn, Josiah | S | Easthampton | 75-E |
| Osborn, Lewis | S | Easthampton | 75-E |
| Osborn, Lewis | S | Easthampton | 76:0.2.1.1.0 |
| Osborn, Mary | S | Easthampton | 76:0.0.1.1.5 |
| Osborn, Mary, M" | S | Easthampton | 76:0.0.1.3.0.0.1 |
| Osborn, Matthew | S | Easthampton | 75-E |
| Osborn, Matthew | S | Easthampton | 76:0.1.1.1.2 |
| Osborn, Phyletous | S | Easthampton | 75-E |
| Osborn, Smith | S | Easthampton | 75-E |
| Osborn, Thomas | S | Easthampton | 75-E |
| Osborn, Zebedee | S | Easthampton | 75-E |
| Osborn, Zebedee | S | Easthampton | 76:0.2.1.2.1 |
| Osman, Adonijah | S | Southold | 76:1.1.1.4.0 |
| Osman, Adonijah Jr. | S | Brookhaven | 75-B10 |
| Osman, Adonijah Jun' | S | Southold | 76:0.1.2.1.1 |
| Osman, Daniel | S | Southold | 76:1.0.0.1.0.3.4 |

| | | | |
|---|---|---|---|
| Osman, Daniel Jun<sup>r</sup> | S | Southold | 76:0.1.4.1.1 |
| Osman, Jacob | S | Southold | 76:0.1.1.1.1 |
| Osman, Jonathan | S | Southold | 76:0.1.0.1.0 |
| Osman, Peter | S | Southold | 76:0.1.0.5.2 |
| Osman, ---- Wid. | S | Southold | 76:0.0.0.2.0 |
| Osman, Winds | S | Southold | 76:0.1.1.1.3.1.0 |
| Osmer, Marah | S | Brookhaven | 76:0.0.2.1.1.0.1 |
| Ostrander, Jacob | N | removed upstate | 76-P |
| Osward, Philip | N | New York | 76-A |
| Ott, Jacob | N | New York | 74-A, 76-A |
| Otterson, Andrew | N | New York | 75-D1 |
| Oudenaarde, Hendrick | N | New York | 75-F |
| Oughterson, Andrew | N | New York | 76-C Fuziliers |
| Oughterson, Andrew, taylor | N | Broad Street | 75-D1, D2 |
| Outenbergh, Henry | N | New York | 76-L |
| Outenbogart, Ab<sup>m</sup>, butcher | N | Queen Street | 75-D1, D2 |
| Outenbogart, Gilbert, crptr | N | Division Street | 75-D2 |
| Outenbogart, Joseph | N | New York | 74-A |
| Outenbogart, Richard | N | New York | 75-C |
| Outenbogart, Richard, brklyr | N | Division Street | 75-D1, D2 |
| Outenbogert, Gilbert | N | New York | 75-C |
| Outerkirk, Jane | N | New York | 75-R |
| Outhout, see Oothout | | | |
| Overton, Aaron | S | ........ | 75-R |
| Overton, Aron | S | ........ | 75-R |
| Overton, Benjamin | S | Brookhaven | 75-B7 |
| Overton, Benjman | S | Brookhaven | 76:0.1.0.1.0 |
| Overton, David | S | Brookhaven | 75-B7 |
| Overton, David | S | Brookhaven | 76:0.1.3.1.2 |
| Overton, David | S | Brookhaven | 76:1.3.0.3.1 |
| Overton, David | S | Middle Island Co. | 75-B5 neutral |
| Overton, David Jun<sup>r</sup> | S | Brookhaven | 75-B7 |
| Overton, Elten | S | ........ | 75-R |
| Overton, Elton | S | Southold | 76:0.3.3.2.3 |
| Overton, Isaac | S | ........ | 75-R |
| Overton, Isaac | S | Brookhaven | 75-B6 |
| Overton, Isaac | S | Southold | 76:0.1.1.1.4 |
| Overton, Isaac Esq<sup>r</sup> | S | Brookhaven | 75-B7 |
| Overton, Isac | S | Brookhaven | 76:0.1.3.1.1 |
| Overton, James | S | ........ | 75-R |

| | | | |
|---|---|---|---|
| Overton, James | S | Brookhaven | 75-B1, 75-B7 |
| Overton, James | S | Brookhaven | 76:0.1.1.1.0 |
| Overton, James | S | Southold | 76:0.1.1.1.0 |
| Overton, John | S | Brookhaven | 75-B7 |
| Overton, John | S | Southold | 76:1.2.2.0.0 |
| Overton, John Jun[r] | S | ........ | 75-R |
| Overton, John Jun[r] | S | Southold | 76:0.2.3.3.2 |
| Overton, John [2] | S | ........ | [on] 75-R |
| Overton, Joshua | S | ........ | 75-R |
| Overton, Joshua | S | Southold | 76:0.1.2.1.2 |
| Overton, Justus | S | Brookhaven | 75-B1, 75-B7 |
| Overton, Messenger | S | Brookhaven | 75-B1, 75-B7 |
| Overton, Moses | S | ........ | 75-R |
| Overton, Nath'l | S | Brookhaven | 75-B1 |
| Overton, Nathanael | S | Southold | 76:0.1.3.1.0 |
| Overton, Nathanael | S | Southold | 76:1.0.1.2.0 |
| Overton, Nathaniel Jun[r] | S | ........ | 75-R |
| Overton, Nathaniel [2] | S | ........ | [on] 75-R |
| Overton, Nathan[l] | S | Brookhaven | 75-B7 |
| Overton, Palmer | S | Brookhaven | 75-B1, 75-B7 |
| Overton, Thomas | S | Southold | 75-N non-signer |
| Overton, Thomas | S | Southold | 76:0.1.3.1.2 |
| Overton; see Haman, Elijah | | | |
| Owen, Abijah, Corporal | S | Southold | 75-N non-signer |
| Owen, James | S | Southold | 75-N non-signer |
| Owens, James | S | Southold | 76:1.1.1.2.0.1.0 |
| Owl, Joseph | N | New York | 76-A |
| Owl, Walter | N | New York | 76-A |
| Pack, see Park | | | |
| Packman, Aaron | N | New York | 76-A |
| Padgett, John | N | removed upstate | 76-P |
| Pagan, William | N | New York | 75-F, 76-A |
| Page, Esther | N | removed upstate | 76-P |
| Page, Hette, Mrs. | N | rem to Ulster Co. | 76-P |
| Page, Samuel | N | New York | 74-A |
| Pain, Allsup | S | Southold | 76:1.0.0.1.0 |
| Pain, Anne, Widow | S | Southampton | 76:0.0.0.1.0 |
| Pain, Benj. | S | Southold | 76:0.1.1.2.1.1.0 |
| Pain, Benjamin | S | ........ | 75-R |
| Pain, Benjamin | S | Brookhaven | 75-B10 |

| | | | |
|---|---|---|---|
| Pain, Benjamin | S | Southold | 75-N |
| Pain, Benjamin | S | Southold | 76:0.1.3.1.1 |
| Pain, Benjⁿ | S | ........ | 75-R |
| Pain, Cornelious | S | Easthampton | 75-E |
| Pain, Daniel | S | Southampton | 76:1.3.1.3.0 |
| Pain, Deliverance | S | Shelter Island | 76:0.0.1.3.0 |
| Pain, Elnathan | S | ........ | 75-R |
| Pain, Isaac | S | Easthampton | 75-E |
| Pain, John | S | Southampton | 76:0.2.2.3.4 |
| Pain, John | S | Southold | 75-N non-signer |
| Pain, John | S | Southold | 76:0.1.6.1.0 |
| Pain, John [3] | S | ........ | [on] 75-R |
| Pain, Jonathan | S | Southampton | 76:1.2.2.5.0 |
| Pain, Jonathan Jʳ | S | ........ | 75-R |
| Pain, Peter | S | ........ | 75-R |
| Pain, Peter | S | Southampton | 76:0.1.2.1.1 |
| Pain, Silas | S | ........ | 75-R |
| Pain, ____ widow | N | in the Meadows | 75-D2 |
| Pain, ____ widow | S | Southold | 76:0.1.0.1.0 |
| Pain, ____ widow | S | Southold | 76:0.1.1.1.0 |
| Pain, William | S | ........ | 75-R |
| Paine, Elisha | S | Shelter Island | 75-K |
| Paine, Elisha, Mr. | S | Southampton | 75-M non-signer |
| Paine, James | S | Smithtown | 75-L |
| Paine; see also Pane, Payne | | | |
| Pake, William | N | New York | 74-A |
| Palmater, Joshua | N | removed upstate | 76-P |
| Palmer, Ann | N | New York | 74-R |
| Palmer, Harrison | N | New York | 74-A, 75-F |
| Palmer, Jacob | Q | ........ | 76-E |
| Palmer, John | N | New York | 74-A |
| Palmer, William | N | New York | 76-I |
| Pane, Allsup [2] | S | ........ | [on] 75-R |
| Pane, George | N | New York | 74-A |
| Pannell, Hayes | N | New York | 76-A |
| Panton, Francis | N | New York | 74-A |
| Panton, Francis | N | New York | 76-A, 76-F |
| Panton, Francis, 1st Lieut. | N | New York | 76-Y |
| Parcells, William | N | New York | 76-A |
| Parfitt, Thos. | N | New York | 74-A |

| | | | |
|---|---|---|---|
| Parisien, Otto | N | New York | 74-A |
| Parisien, Otto, silversmith | N | Dock Street | 74-T |
| Parisien, Thomas | N | New York | 76-A |
| Park/Pack, Isaac, shoemkr | N | Upper Barracks | 75-D1, D2 |
| Parker, Abraham | S | Shelter Island | 75-K |
| Parker, Abraham | S | Shelter Island | 76:1.0.1.2.0 |
| Parker, Elizabeth | N | New York | 76-K |
| Parker, John | N | New York | 74-A |
| Parker, John | Q | ........ | 75-A associator |
| Parker, Phinehas | S | Shelter Island | 75-K |
| Parker, Phinehas | S | Shelter Island | 76:0.1.1.1.1 |
| Parker, Trustian | N | New York | 74-A |
| Parkinson, Martin, constable | N | New York | 74-R to 76-R |
| Parkinson, Martin, innkpr | N | Irish Street | 75-D1, D2 |
| Parmer, Philip | Q | ........ | 75-A |
| Parmyter, Par. | N | New York | 74-A |
| Parnal, Debroah, widow | S | Southampton | 76:0.0.0.2.0 |
| Parr, Else | N | to Westchester Co | 76-P |
| Parr, Haurich | N | New York | 74-A |
| Parr, Thomas, taylor | N | New York | 74-T2, 5/5 |
| Parsall, John | Q | ........ | 76-E |
| Parsall, John | Q | Newtown | 75-G |
| Parse, Jeremiah | S | Easthampton | 75-E |
| Parsel, Thomas | N | New York | 74-A |
| Parsel, Thomas, cordwainer | N | Fair Street | 75-D1, D2 |
| Parsell, Jacob | Q | Newtown | 75-G |
| Parsels, William | N | New York | 75-R |
| Parshall, David | S | Southold | 76:0.1.1.1.3 |
| Parshel, Lias | S | Southold | 76:0.3.2.2.2 |
| Parsill, Thomas, constable | N | New York | 74-R, 75-R |
| Parso, Thomas | N | New York | 74-A |
| Parson, John yᵉ 3d | S | Easthampton | 75-E |
| Parsons, Benj. | S | Easthampton | 75-E |
| Parsons, Benjamin | S | Easthampton | 76:0.1.1.1.1 |
| Parsons, Elnathan | S | Easthampton | 75-E |
| Parsons, Henry | S | Easthampton | 76:0.1.1.1.1 |
| Parsons, James | N | New York | 75-F |
| Parsons, Jeremiah | S | Easthampton | 76:0.1.3.1.0 |
| Parsons, John | S | Easthampton | 76:1.3.3.1.1.2.0 |
| Parsons, John 3ᵈ | S | Easthampton | 76:1.1.1.1.1 |

| | | | |
|---|---|---|---|
| Parsons, John 4th | S | Easthampton | 76:0.2.3.2.2 |
| Parsons, John 5th | S | Easthampton | 75-E |
| Parsons, John 5th | S | Easthampton | 76:0.1.0.1.1 |
| Parsons, John Jun' | S | Easthampton | 76:1.0.0.0.0 |
| Parsons, John ye 4 | S | Easthampton | 75-E |
| Parsons, John [2] | S | Easthampton | [on] 75-E |
| Parsons, Ludlam | S | Easthampton | 75-E |
| Parsons, Ludlam | S | Easthampton | 76:0.1.1.1.1 |
| Parsons, Merrey | S | Easthampton | 75-E |
| Parsons, Merrey | S | Easthampton | 76:0.1.0.1.1 |
| Parsons, Phebe, Mrs. | S | Easthampton | 76:0.0.0.1.1.1.0 |
| Parsons, Robert | S | Easthampton | 76:1.1.1.1.2 |
| Parsons, Samuel | S | Easthampton | 76:1.1.1.4.1 |
| Parsons, Samuel [2] | S | Easthampton | [on] 75-E |
| Parsons, Seth | S | Easthampton | 75-E |
| Parsons, William | N | Hunter's Quay | 74-T2, 5/12 |
| Parsons, William | S | Easthampton | 75-E |
| Parsons, William, store | N | Cruger's Wharf | 74-T2, 9/29 |
| Pasca, John | N | New York | 76-A |
| Patchen, Andrew | S | Brookhaven | 75-B6 |
| Patchen, Andrew | S | Brookhaven | 76:0.3.3.1.5 |
| Paterson, Robert | N | New York | 74-A |
| Patten/Pattent, John, butcher | N | New York | 75-D1, D2 |
| Patterson, George, servant | N | runaway | 74-T |
| Patterson, John | N | New York | 74-A |
| Pattey, Joseph | S | ........ | 75-R |
| Patton, James, tanner | N | at N.N. Anthony's | 75-D1, D2 |
| Patton, William | N | New York | 76-A |
| Patty, Ezekiel, a hipocrite | S | Brookhaven | 75-B10 |
| Patty, James | S | Brookhaven | 75-B10 |
| Pauck, Rachael | N | removed upstate | 76-P |
| Paul, John | N | New York | 74-A |
| Paul, Thomas | N | New York | 76-A |
| Paulding, Peter | N | New York | 74-A |
| Pava, James O | N | New York | 76-A |
| Pawel, Mary | N | New York | 75-R |
| Payn, Ezekeil | S | Easthampton | 76:0.1.1.1.0 |
| Payne, James | S | Smithtown | 76:0.1.2.2.3 |
| Peack, George | N | New York | 76-L |
| Peack, Jonathan | N | New York | 76-I |

Peack; see also Peeck

| | | | |
|---|---|---|---|
| Pearce, Ellis | N | New York | 75-R |
| Pears, William | N | New York | 76-L |
| Pearsall, D____ | Q | ........ | 76-B2 |
| Pearsall, Daniel | S | Huntington | 75-H |
| Pearsall, Hezekiah | Q | ........ | 75-A, 76-B |
| Pearsall, James | S | Huntington | 75-H |
| Pearsall, John | Q | Newtown | 75-B |
| Pearsall, Joseph | N | New York | 74-A |
| Pearsall, Joseph | Q | ........ | 75-A |
| Pearsall, Joseph, watchmkr | N | Hanover Square | 74-T |
| Pearsall, Thomas | N | New York | 75-F |
| Pearsall, Thomas | N | Queen Street | 75-D2 |
| Pearsall, Thomas | Q | ........ | 76-E |
| Pearsall, Thomas Jr. | N | New York | 74-A, 75-F |
| Pearsall, Thomas, watchmkr | N | New York | 74-T2, 2/3 |
| Pearsall, William | Q | ........ | 76-E |
| Pearsee, Jonath. | N | New York | 74-A |
| Pearsee, Jonathan | N | New York | 75-D3 |
| Pearson, Henry | Q | ........ | 75-A |
| Pearson, Jno. | Q | ........ | 75-A |
| Pearson, W. | N | New York | 74-A |
| Pearson, William, clocks | N | Hanover Square | 74-T2, 4/14 |
| Pearson, Wm | Q | ........ | 75-A |
| Pearss, William | N | New York | 74-A |
| Pease, Matthew | S | Brookhaven | 75-B10 |
| Peck, Augustus | S | ........ | 75-R |
| Peck, Augustus | S | Southold | 76:0.1.1.1.0 |
| Peck, George | N | New York | 74-A |
| Peck, Isaac | N | New York | 75-D3 |
| Peck, Jonathan, hse crpntr | N | Depeyster's Slip | 75-D1, D2 |
| Peck, Jonathan, Lieut. | N | New York | 76-G |
| Peck, Joseph | S | Southold | 76:0.2.1.2.4 |
| Peck, Joseph [2] | S | ........ | [on] 75-R |
| Peck, Phebe, Mrs. | N | rem to Ulster Co. | 76-P |
| Peck, William | N | rem to Ulster Co. | 76-P |
| Peck, William, mason | N | Georges Street | 75-D1, D2 |
| Peck, William, taylor | N | Wall Street | 75-D1, D2 |

Peck; see also Peack

| | | | |
|---|---|---|---|
| Peckwell, Henry | N | New York | 74-A |

| | | | |
|---|---|---|---|
| Pederick, John | S | Huntington | 75-H |
| Pederick, Josiah | S | Huntington | 75-H |
| Peeck, John | N | removed upstate | 76-P |
| Peeck; see also Peack | | | |
| Peel, Francis, shoemaker | N | George Street | 75-D2 |
| Peet, Thomas | N | New York | 75-D1 |
| Peirce, Abiah, widow | S | Southampton | 76:0.0.0.2.1 |
| Peirce, John | N | New York | 74-A |
| Peirce, see also Pearss | | | |
| Peirson, Abraham | S | Southampton | 76:1.0.0.1.0.2.0 |
| Peirson, Abraham [2] | S | ........ | [on] 75-R |
| Peirson, Daniel | S | ........ | 75-R |
| Peirson, Daniel | S | Southampton | 76:0.2.1.1.4 |
| Peirson, David | S | ........ | 75-R |
| Peirson, David Jun$^r$ | S | ........ | 75-R |
| Peirson, David Jun$^r$ | S | Southampton | 76:0.1.0.1.2 |
| Peirson, Henry | S | ........ | 75-R |
| Peirson, Isaac | S | ........ | 75-R |
| Peirson, Jedediah | S | ........ | 75-R |
| Peirson, Jedidiah | S | Southampton | 76:0.2.3.1.3.1.0 |
| Peirson, Jeremiah | S | ........ | 75-R |
| Peirson, Job | S | ........ | 75-R |
| Peirson, Job | S | Southampton | 76:1.0.0.1.0.2.0 |
| Peirson, John | S | ........ | 75-R |
| Peirson, Josiah | S | ........ | 75-R |
| Peirson, Josiah | S | Southampton | 76:1.0.1.1.2 |
| Peirson, Lemuel | S | ........ | 75-R |
| Peirson, Lemuel | S | Southampton | 76:1.1.1.2.2 |
| Peirson, Lemuel 3d | S | Southampton | 76:0.3.0.1.2.2.3 |
| Peirson, Lemuel Jun. | S | ........ | 75-R |
| Peirson, Lemuel Jun$^r$ | S | Southampton | 76:0.1.0.1.1.2.1 |
| Peirson, Lemuel the 3$^d$ | S | ........ | 75-R |
| Peirson, Matthew | S | ........ | 75-R |
| Peirson, Matthew | S | Southampton | 76:0.1.1.1.0 |
| Peirson, Matthew | S | Southampton | 76:1.1.0.1.0 |
| Peirson, Matthew 2$^d$ | S | ........ | 75-R |
| Peirson, Nathan | S | ........ | 75-R |
| Peirson, Nathan | S | Southampton | 76:1.1.0.1.1.1.1 |
| Peirson, Sam$^{ll}$ | S | ........ | 75-R |
| Peirson, Samuel | S | ........ | 75-R |

| | | | |
|---|---|---|---|
| Peirson, Silvanus | S | ........ | 75-R |
| Peirson, Silvanus | S | Southampton | 76:1.0.0.1.1 |
| Peirson, Stephen | S | ........ | 75-R |
| Peirson, Stephen | S | Southampton | 76:1.0.0.1.0 |
| Peirson, Theophilus | S | ........ | 75-R |
| Peirson, Theophilus | S | Southampton | 76:0.1.3.1.2 |
| Peirson, Timothy | S | ........ | 75-R |
| Peirson, Timothy | S | Southampton | 76:0.1.0.2.2 |
| Peirson, Timothy | S | Southampton | 76:0.1.3.3.3 |
| Peirson, William, Lieut. | N | New York | 75-A |
| Peirson, Zebulon | S | Southampton | 76:1.2.1.1.3.1.0 |
| Peirson, Zebulun | S | ........ | 75-R |
| Peirson, Zechariah | S | ........ | 75-R |
| Peirson, Zechariah | S | Southampton | 76:0.1.1.1.1 |
| Peirson; see also Pearson | | | |
| Peitsch, George | N | New York | 76-A |
| Pell, Gilbert | N | New York | 76-A |
| Pell, John | N | New York | 75-F |
| Pell, Josiah | N | New York | 74-A |
| Pell, Philip, coppersmith | N | in the Meadows | 75-D1, D2 |
| Pell, Robert | N | New York | 75-D2 |
| Pell, Thos. Wm. | N | New York | 75-D3 |
| Pelletreau, Elias | N | New York | 74-A, 76-N |
| Pelletreau, Elias | S | ........ | 75-R |
| Pelletreau, Elias | S | Southampton | 76:1.2.0.1.0.2.0 |
| Pelletreau, Elias, blockmkr | N | liv w/ Frdk Fine | 75-D1, D2 |
| Pelletreau, Elias Jr. | N | New York | 74-A |
| Pelletreau, John | S | ........ | 75-R |
| Pelsue & Halsted | N | New York | 76-I |
| Pelton, Benjamin, cabinetmkr | N | Ann Street | 75-D2 |
| Pelton, Benjn. | N | New York | 74-A |
| Pelton, Daniel, joiner | N | Dutch[?] Street | 75-D1, D2 |
| Pelton, William, shoemaker | N | Dutch Street | 75-D1, D2 |
| Peney, Edward | S | ........ | 75-R |
| Penfold, Edmond | Q | ........ | 76-E |
| Penney, Isaac | S | Southampton | 76:0.1.1.1.0 |
| Pennie, Edward | S | Southold | 76:0.1.3.1.2 |
| Pennie, Edward | S | Southold | 76:1.2.0.2.0.1.0 |
| Pennie, ---- Wid. | S | Southold | 76:0.0.2.2.2 |
| Pennie, William | S | Southold | 76:0.1.5.1.1 |

| | | | |
|---|---|---|---|
| Pennie, William | S | Southold | 76:1.0.1.1.0 |
| Penny, Charles | N | New York | 74-R |
| Penny, Ed. | Q | ........ | 76-E |
| Penny, Edward juner | S | Brookhaven | 75-B10 |
| Penny, Phaeby | N | New York | 74-R |
| Penny, Richard | N | New York | 76-A |
| Peppinger, Elizabeth, Mrs. | N | to Dutchess Co. | 76-P |
| Peppinger, Richard | N | to Dutchess Co. | 76-P |
| Percy, Nathan, post rider | N | New York | 74-T |
| Perkins, James | N | removed upstate | 76-P |
| Perrie, Eliakem | S | Southold | 76:0.2.2.1.1 |
| Perry, Edmund | S | ........ | 75-R |
| Perry, Eliakim | S | ........ | 75-R |
| Perry, Elia$^m$ | S | ........ | 75-R |
| Perry, Henry W. | N | New York | 76-A |
| Perry, John | N | New York | 74-T2, 11/10 |
| Perry, Mervin | N | New York | 76-A |
| Perry, Mervin | Q | Jamaica | 75-C |
| Perry, Ruth | N | New York | 74-V |
| Perry, Ruth, wid of Thomas | N | New York | 74-T |
| Perry, Thomas, watchmaker | N | New York | 74-T |
| Perry, ---- Wid. | S | Southold | 76:0.2.0.2.1.1.2 |
| Person, Joseph | N | New York | 76-L |
| Peter, John | N | New York | 76-I |
| Peters, Harry | N | New York | 76-A |
| Peters, Jacob | Q | ........ | 76-B2 |
| Peters, Jno. | Q | ........ | 75-A |
| Peters, Thomas Jr. | Q | ........ | 76-B |
| Peters, Valentine H., Esq. | Q | ........ | 75-A |
| Peters, Valentine H. | Q | ........ | 76-B, 76-E |
| Peters, Valentine H. | Q | Hempstead | 76-D |
| Peterson, David | Q | ........ | 75-A, 76-B |
| Peterson, Garret | N | New York | 74-A |
| Peterson, Gerit, Light Horse | N | New York | 76-L |
| Peterson, Jacob | Q | ........ | 75-A, 76-B |
| Pettie, Daniel | S | Brookhaven | 76:0.1.2.1.0 |
| Pettits, Thomas | N | New York | 74-A |
| Pettitt, Adam | Q | ........ | 75-A |
| Pettitt, Benjamin | Q | ........ | 75-A, 76-A |
| Pettitt, Increase | Q | ........ | 75-A, 76-E |

| | | | |
|---|---|---|---|
| Pettitt, Isaac | Q | ........ | 75-A |
| Pettitt, Isaac | Q | ........ | 76-B, 76-E |
| Pettitt, Isaac | Q | Jamaica | 75-C |
| Pettitt, James | Q | ........ | 75-A, 76-E |
| Pettitt, Jas. Jr. | Q | ........ | 75-A |
| Pettitt, John | Q | ........ | 75-A |
| Pettitt, John | Q | ........ | 75-A associator |
| Pettitt, John [2] | Q | ........ | [on] 76-E |
| Pettitt, Joseph | Q | ........ | 76-B |
| Pettitt, Joseph Jr. | Q | ........ | 76-E |
| Pettitt, Mich'l | Q | ........ | 75-A |
| Pettitt, Nat'l | Q | Newtown | 75-G |
| Pettitt, Obadiah | Q | ........ | 76-E |
| Pettitt, P. | Q | ........ | 76-E |
| Pettitt, Samuel [2] | Q | ........ | [on] 75-A |
| Pettitt, Samuel [2] | Q | ........ | [on] 76-B, 76-E |
| Pettitt, Stephen | Q | ........ | 75-A associator |
| Pettitt, Stephen | Q | Newtown | 75-G |
| Pettitt, W. | Q | ........ | 76-E |
| Pettitt, William | Q | Jamaica | 75-C, 75-D |
| Pettitt, Wm [2] | Q | ........ | [on] 75-A |
| Petty, Benjamin | S | Brookhaven | 75-B1 |
| Petty, Daniel | S | Brookhaven | 75-B6, 75-B7 |
| Petty, Ezekiel | S | Southold | 76:1.0.0.2.0 |
| Petty, Ezekiel Jr. | S | Southold | 75-N non-signer |
| Petty, Ezekiel Jun$^r$ | S | Southold | 76:0.1.1.1.2 |
| Petty, James | S | Southold | 75-N non-signer |
| Petty, James | S | Southold | 76:0.1.1.1.2 |
| Petty, James | S | Southold | 76:0.1.2.2.2 |
| Petty, James Jun. | S | Southold | 75-N non-signer |
| Petty, John | S | Southold | 76:1.1.0.2.0 |
| Petty, John Jun. | S | Southold | 75-N non-signer |
| Petty, Joseph | S | Southold | 76:1.0.4.4.1 |
| Petty, William, Corporal | S | Southold | 75-N |
| Pety, Daniel | S | Brookhaven | 75-B1 |
| Phenex, Philip | N | New York | 74-A |
| Phenix, Daniel, Capt. | N | New York | 75-A |
| Phenix, Philip | N | New York | 76-S |
| Phenix, Thomas | N | New York | 76-I |
| Phenix, Thomas, shoemaker | N | Dey Street | 75-D2 |

| | | | |
|---|---|---|---|
| Philips, Hugh | N | New York | 76-A |
| Philips, Joseph | S | Brookhaven | 76:0.1.1.1.0 |
| Philips, Samual | S | Brookhaven | 76:1.1.1.2.1 |
| Philips, Samuel | S | Smithtown | 75-L |
| Philips, Thomas | N | New York | 74-R |
| Philips, Thomas, lapidary | N | Golden Hill | 75-D1, D2 |
| Philips, William Esqʳ | S | Smithtown | 75-L |
| Philips, Zebulon | S | Smithtown | 75-L |
| Philipse, Adolph. | N | New York | 76-A |
| Philipse, Fred'k | N | New York | 76-A |
| Phillips, Charles | N | New York | 74-A, 76-L |
| Phillips, David | N | New York | 74-A, 76-I |
| Phillips, David, spirits | N | Horse & Cart St. | 74-T2, 3/31 |
| Phillips, Ebenezer | N | New York | 76-N |
| Phillips, Ebenezer | S | Smithtown | 75-L |
| Phillips, Ellerner | N | removed upstate | 76-P |
| Phillips, Joseph | S | Brookhaven | 75-B2 |
| Phillips, Mary, millinery | N | Smith Street | 74-T2, 4/28 |
| Phillips, Samuel | S | Brookhaven | 75-B9 |
| Phillips, Samuel | S | Smithtown | 75-H1 |
| Phillips, Samuel | S | Smithtown | 76:0.1.2.1.1.1.0 |
| Phillips, Samuel Jr. | S | Brookhaven | 75-B2 |
| Phillips, Theophelus, Dr. | S | Brookhaven | 75-B2 |
| Phillips, William | S | Brookhaven | 75-B2 |
| Phillips, William | S | Smithtown | 76:1.2.0.2.1 |
| Phillips, William | S | Southampton | 76:1.3.0.2.1 |
| Phillips, William Junʳ | S | Smithtown | 75-L |
| Phoenix, Daniel | N | New York | 75-F; 75-T2, 5/4 |
| Phuran, John | N | New York | 74-A |
| Pierce, John, joiner | N | Maiden Lane | 75-D1, D2 |
| Pierse, Jonathan | N | New York | 75-D3 |
| Pierson, David, Capt. | S | Southampton | 76:0.1.0.1.3.1.0 |
| Pierson, Elias | S | Southampton | 76:1.2.0.3.1 |
| Pierson, Job Junʳ | S | ........ | 75-R |
| Pierson, Timothy | S | ........ | 75-R |
| Pigeon, Wm | Q | ........ | 75-A, 76-B |
| Pike, Asher | N | New York | 74-A |
| Pike, Asher, mason | N | Fair Street | 75-D2 |
| Pike, Hennery | S | Southold | 76:1.0.1.1.1.0.1 |
| Pike, Henry | S | Southold | 75-N |

| | | | |
|---|---|---|---|
| Pike, Jonathan | S | Southold | 75-N |
| Pike, Jonathan | S | Southold | 76:0.1.2.1.1 |
| Pike, Selah | S | Easthampton | 75-E |
| Pike, Selah | S | Easthampton | 76:1.0.0.1.1 |
| Pine, Daniel | Q | ........ | 75-A, 76-B |
| Pine, James | Q | ........ | 76-B |
| Pine, James | Q | Hempstead | 76-D |
| Pine, James [2] | Q | ........ | [on] 75-A |
| Pine, James [2] | Q | ........ | [on] 76-E |
| Pine, ____ Mrs. | N | Maiden Lane | 75-T |
| Pine, Reuben | Q | ........ | 76-E |
| Pine, Richard | Q | ........ | 75-A, 76-E |
| Pine, Robert | N | New York | 76-R |
| Pine, William, painter | N | Gold Street | 75-D1, D2 |
| Pinfold, Edmond | Q | ........ | 75-A associator |
| Pinfold, William | Q | ........ | 75-A associator |
| Pinkerton, Elizabeth | N | New York | 75-R |
| Pinkney, William | N | New York | 74-A, 76-I |
| Pintard, Lewis | N | New York | 75-T2, 5/4 |
| Pintard, Lewis, merchant | N | New York | 74-V, 75-F |
| Pinto, Isaac | N | New York | 74-A, 76-N |
| Piper, Jacob | N | New York | 74-A |
| Piper, Jacob, shoemaker | N | Broadway | 75-D1, D2 |
| Pitcher, William | N | New York | 75-D1 |
| Pitt, Abm. | N | New York | 74-A |
| Pitt, Abraham | N | New York | 74-A |
| Pitt, William | Q | ........ | 76-B |
| Pitts, Elizabeth | N | New York | 75-R |
| Place, J., cordwainer | Q | ........ | 76-E |
| Place, James | Q | ........ | 75-A, 76-B |
| Place, Richard | Q | ........ | 75-A, 76-E |
| Place, Robert | N | New York | 74-A |
| Place, Samuel | Q | ........ | 76-B |
| Place, Thomas | Q | ........ | 75-A, 76-E |
| Place, Thomas | Q | Hempstead | 76-D |
| Planton, John | N | near Liberty Pole | 76-H |
| Planton, John | N | near the Bridewell | 76-I |
| Planton, John | N | New York | 74-A |
| Platt, Ebenezer | S | Huntington | 75-H, 75-H1 |
| Platt, Ebenezer Smith | N | New York | 74-T2, 5/26 |

| | | | |
|---|---|---|---|
| Platt, Epenetus | Q | ........ | 75-A, 76-E |
| Platt, Epenetus | Q | Hempstead Plains | 75-T |
| Platt, Jeremiah | N | New York | 76-N |
| Platt, Jeremiah, merchant | N | New York | 75-T, 75-V |
| Platt, Jno. | Q | ........ | 75-A |
| Platt, Jonas | S | Huntington | 75-H |
| Platt, Joseph | S | Smithtown | 75-L |
| Platt, Joseph | S | Smithtown | 76:0.2.0.1.2 |
| Platt, Nathan | S | Huntington | 75-H |
| Platt, Nathaniel | S | Smithtown | 75-L |
| Platt, Nathaniel, Capt. | S | Huntington | 76-H3 |
| Platt, Nath[l] | S | Smithtown | 76:0.1.1.2.1.2.1 |
| Platt, Obadiah | S | Huntington | 75-H |
| Platt, Philip | Q | ........ | 75-A, 76-B |
| Platt, Philip | Q | Jamaica | 75-D |
| Platt, Philip S. | Q | ........ | 76-E |
| Platt, Richard | S | Huntington | 75-H |
| Platt, Richard | S | Smithtown | 75-L |
| Platt, Uriah | Q | ........ | 75-A |
| Platt, Uriah | Q | ........ | 76-B, 76-E |
| Platt, Zebulon | S | Huntington | 75-H |
| Platt, Zephaniah | S | Smithtown | 75-L |
| Platt, Zephaniah | S | Smithtown | 76:1.1.1.3.2.4.2 |
| Platt, Zophar | S | Huntington | 75-H |
| Platt, Zophar, J.P. | S | Huntington | 76-H1 |
| Platt, Zophar Jr. | S | Huntington | 75-H, 76-H1 |
| Pleas, Wil[m] | S | Huntington | 75-H |
| Please, Freeman | Q | ........ | 76-E |
| Plenderleath, —— Mr. | N | New York | 74-T |
| Plumb, David | N | New York | 76-G |
| Polhemus, A., Jr. | Q | ........ | 76-E |
| Polhemus, Ab. Jr. | Q | Newtown | 75-B |
| Polhemus, Ab. Sr. | Q | Newtown | 75-B |
| Polhemus, Ab'm | Q | ........ | 76-E |
| Polhemus, Abraham | Q | Jamaica | 75-C |
| Polhemus, Johannes | Q | Jamaica | 75-H |
| Polhemus, Johannes [2] | Q | Jamaica | [on] 75-D |
| Polhemus, John | Q | ........ | 75-A |
| Polhemus, John | Q | ........ | 76-B, 76-E |
| Polhemus, John | Q | Jamaica | 75-C |

| | | | |
|---|---|---|---|
| Polk, John, chairmaker | N | Chatham Street | 75-D1, D2 |
| Polke, Jonathan | N | New York | 74-A |
| Polke, see also Poolk | | | |
| Pollen, Pat'k, als Collen | N | New York | 74-R |
| Polock, Issachar | N | New York | 74-T2, 11/17 |
| Polock, Issachar | Q | ........ | 76-E |
| Pool, Elizabeth | N | New York | 76-K |
| Pool, Jacob, chairmaker | N | Broad Street | 75-D1, D2 |
| Pool, Pearse | Q | ........ | 75-A |
| Pool, Solomon | Q | ........ | 76-B, 76-E |
| Pool, Solomon | Q | Hempstead | 76-D |
| Pool, W. | Q | ........ | 76-E |
| Pool; see also Powell | | | |
| Poole, William | N | New York | 76-A |
| Pooles, Thomas | N | New York | 74-A |
| Poolk, George | N | New York | 74-A |
| Porsonett, John | N | New York | 74-A |
| Port, Jeremiah | Q | ........ | 76-E |
| Port, Solomon | Q | ........ | 76-B2 |
| Porter, Andrew | N | New York | 74-R juror |
| Portugee, John, taylor | N | Chappel Street | 75-D2 |
| Post, Anthony | N | New York | 74-A, 76-L |
| Post, Francis | N | New York | 74-A, 76-L |
| Post, Hennery | S | Southampton | 76:0.2.0.1.5 |
| Post, Henry | S | ........ | 75-R |
| Post, Isaac | S | ........ | 75-R |
| Post, Isaac Esq' | S | Southampton | 76:1.1.0.3.2.1.0 |
| Post, Isaac Jun' | S | ........ | 75-R |
| Post, Jacob | N | New York | 74-A |
| Post, Jacob, chairmaker | N | Maiden Lane | 75-D1, D2 |
| Post, James | S | ........ | 75-R |
| Post, James | S | Southampton | 76:0.1.1.1.0 |
| Post, Jeremiah | S | ........ | 75-R |
| Post, Jeremiah | S | Southampton | 76:0.2.2.1.1 |
| Post, John | N | New York | 74-A, 75-F |
| Post, John | Q | ........ | 76-E |
| Post, John, Cap' | S | Southampton | 76:1.1.1.1.1 |
| Post, John Jun' | S | Southampton | 76:0.1.2.2.1 |
| Post, Joseph | S | Southampton | 76:1.0.0.1.0 |
| Post, Joseph Jun' | S | Southampton | 76:0.1.2.1.2 |

| | | | |
|---|---|---|---|
| Post, Nathan | S | Southampton | 76:0.1.0.1.1 |
| Post, Stephen | S | Southampton | 76:0.1.2.1.4 |
| Post, William | N | Fletcher Street | 74-T2, 10/13 |
| Post, William | N | New York | 74-A, 76-L |
| Pott, Jacob | N | New York | 76-H |
| Potter, Gilbert | S | Huntington | 75-H |
| Potter, Gilbert, Dr. | S | Huntington | 75-H1 |
| Potter, James | N | New York | 76-A |
| Poudy, William | N | removed upstate | 76-P |
| Poulsen, Dan. | N | New York | 74-A |
| Povey, Edmond Jun' | S | ........ | 75-R |
| Powell, Amos | Q | ........ | 75-A |
| Powell, Amos | Q | ........ | 76-B, 76-E |
| Powell, Henry | Q | ........ | 76-E |
| Powell, Solomon | Q | ........ | 76-B |
| Powell, Solomon [2] | Q | ........ | [on] 75-A |
| Powell, Stephen | Q | ........ | 75-A |
| Powell, Stephen | Q | ........ | 76-B, 76-E |
| Powell; see also Pool | | | |
| Powers, George, butcher | N | Fly Market | 74-T |
| Powers, Joseph | N | New York | 74-A |
| Pozer, Jacob | N | New York | 74-A |
| Pozer, Jacob | N | New York | 76-A, 76-I |
| Pozer, Jacob, baker | N | Bridge Street | 75-T |
| Pozer, Jacob, constable | N | New York | 75-R, 76-R |
| Pragret, Henry | Q | Hempstead | 76-D |
| Prance, see Corwin, Peter | | | |
| Pratt, John | Q | ........ | 76-B, 76-E |
| Pratt, Jonathan | Q | ........ | 75-A, 76-E |
| Pratt, Silas | Q | Newtown | 75-B |
| Pratt, Thomas | N | New York | 75-R, 76-N |
| Pratt, Thomas, clark | N | Little Queen St. | 75-D2 |
| Price, Benjamin | S | ........ | 75-R |
| Price, Benjamin | S | Southampton | 76:0.1.3.1.0 |
| Price, Catherien | N | removed upstate | 76-P |
| Price, John, schoolteacher | N | Golden Hill | 74-T |
| Price, Thomas | N | New York | 76-A |
| Prichit, John | N | New York | 74-A |
| Prickett, Richard | N | New York | 74-A |
| Priestley, John, joiner | N | Broadway | 75-D1, D2 |

| | | | |
|---|---|---|---|
| Prime, Benj^m Y. | S | Huntington | 75-H |
| Prince, John | S | Southold | 76:0.1.2.1.0 |
| Prince, John [2] | S | ........ | [on] 75-R |
| Prince, Joseph | S | Southold | 76:1.2.0.1.0 |
| Prince, Joseph [2] | S | ........ | [on] 75-R |
| Prince, Robert, joiner | N | William Street | 75-D1, D2 |
| Prince, Robert, joiner | N | William Street | 75-D1, D2 |
| Prince, Samuel | N | New York | 74-A |
| Prince, Samuel, cabinetmkr | N | Cart & Horse St. | 75-T |
| Prince, Samuel, juror | N | New York | 74-R, 75-R |
| Prince, Thomas [2] | S | ........ | [on] 75-R |
| Prince, William | Q | ........ | 76-E |
| Prince, William | Q | Flushing Landing | 75-T |
| Prince; see also Corwin, Peter | | | |
| Pringle, ---- | N | New York | 76-I |
| Pringle, Thos. | N | New York | 74-A |
| Pritchard, James | N | New York | 74-A |
| Pritchard, Luke | S | Brookhaven | 75-B1 |
| Probasco, John | Q | ........ | 76-E |
| Proctor, Johannes | N | New York | 74-A |
| Proctor, Will. | N | New York | 74-A |
| Proctor, William | N | New York | 74-R |
| Provoost, David | N | New York | 76-A |
| Provoost, Nathaniel | Q | ........ | 76-E |
| Provorst, Robert | N | New York | 74-A |
| Provost, David | N | New York | 76-A |
| Provost, Elisabeth | N | removed upstate | 76-P |
| Provost, Nathaniel | Q | Newtown | 75-B |
| Pryer, Capper | N | New York | 76-A |
| Pryor, Edward | N | New York | 74-A, 76-A |
| Pryor, Edward, Capt. | N | New York | 76-Y |
| Pulby, John David | N | New York | 74-V runaway |
| Pultow, John | S | Brookhaven | 75-B10 |
| Punderson, ---- Docter | S | Brookhaven | 76:0.1.3.2.2.1.0 |
| Puntglus, John Christian | N | New York | 74-A |
| Puntius, John C. | N | New York | 76-L |
| Puntzius, John Philip | N | New York | 76-A |
| Purcell, Henry, engraver | N | Broadway | 74-T |
| Quackenbos, John | N | New York | 75-D3 |
| Quackenbos, John, Capt. | N | New York | 75-E |

| | | | |
|---|---|---|---|
| Quackenbos, Nicholas | N | New York | 75-R juror |
| Quackenbos, Peter, baker | N | New York | 75-D1, D2 |
| Quackenbos, Walter | N | New York | 74-A |
| Quackenboss, Benjamin | N | New York | 76-A |
| Quackenbush, Ann | N | removed upstate | 76-P |
| Quackenbush, Benjamin Jr. | N | New York | 74-A |
| Quackenbush, James | N | New York | 74-A |
| Quackenbush, Jane | N | New York | 76-K |
| Quackenbush, Peter | N | New York | 74-A |
| Quain, John | N | New York | 76-R |
| Quan, Abraham | S | Easthampton | 75-E |
| Quay, William | N | New York | 74-A |
| Quelch, John | N | New York | 74-A |
| Quereau, Benjamin | N | New York | 76-N |
| Quick, Jacobus | N | New York | 74-A, 76-L |
| Quick, Luke | N | New York | 74-A |
| Quick, Luke C. | N | New York | 76-A |
| Quigley, Thomas | N | New York | 74-A |
| Quill, Thomas | N | New York | 76-A |
| Quinby & Pell | N | New York | 75-F |
| Quinby, Moses | N | New York | 74-A |
| Quithell, Eunice | S | Southampton | 76:0.0.1.1.3 |
| Rackett, Absolom | S | Southold | 76:0.1.3.1.1 |
| Rackett, Benjamin | S | ........ | 75-R |
| Rackett, Benjamin | S | Southold | 76:0.2.4.2.2 |
| Rackett, Daniel | S | Southold | 76:0.1.1.1.0 |
| Rackett, John | S | Southold | 76:0.1.0.1.0 |
| Rackett, John | S | Southold | 76:1.0.0.1.1 |
| Rackett, Jonathan | S | Southold | 76:1.1.2.2.3 |
| Rafter, Thos. | N | New York | 74-A |
| Rainer, Amos | Q | ........ | 75-A, 76-B |
| Rainer, Benj'n | Q | ........ | 75-A, 76-B |
| Rainer, Elijah | Q | ........ | 75-A |
| Rainer, Elijah | Q | ........ | 76-A, 76-B |
| Rainer, Ezekiel | Q | ........ | 75-A |
| Rainer, Henry | Q | ........ | 75-A |
| Rainer, Hugh | S | Southampton | 75-M non-signer |
| Rainer, Isaac | Q | ........ | 75-A, 76-B |
| Rainer, Jacob | Q | ........ | 75-A, 76-B |
| Rainer, Jas. | Q | ........ | 75-A |

| | | | |
|---|---|---|---|
| Rainer, Jno. | Q | ........ | 75-A |
| Rainer, Joel | Q | ........ | 75-A, 76-B |
| Rainer, John | Q | ........ | 75-A, 76-B |
| Rainer, Joseph | Q | ........ | 75-A, 76-B |
| Rainor, Adoniah | S | Southampton | 76:0.1.1.2.1 |
| Rainor, David | S | Southampton | 76:1.1.2.2.1 |
| Rainor, Willam | S | Southampton | 76:1.2.3.1.2 |
| Ramage, Smith | N | New York | 75-F |
| Ramage, Smith, Capt. | N | New York | 76-Y |
| Ramer, Martha | N | to Westchester Co | 76-P |
| Ramsay, John | N | New York | 74-A |
| Ramson, see Remsen | | | |
| Randal, Marian | N | New York | 76-I |
| Randal, Stephen | S | Brookhaven | 75-B6 |
| Randall, Robert, merchant | N | New York | 74-T2, 4/14 |
| Randall, Thomas | N | New York | 74-T2, 11/24 |
| Randall, Thomas | N | New York | 74-V, 75-F |
| Randel, Stephen | S | Brookhaven | 75-B1 |
| Randell, John | N | New York | 75-D3 |
| Randiker, John | N | New York | 76-A |
| Randol, Samuel | S | Brookhaven | 76:1.1.3.2.1 |
| Randol, Stephen | S | Brookhaven | 75-B7 |
| Ranger, Samuel | S | Easthampton | 76:0.1.3.1.2 |
| Ransier, Frederick | N | New York | 76-A |
| Ransier, Fredrick | N | New York | 74-A |
| Rapalje, Abra. | Q | ........ | 76-E |
| Rapalje, Abraham | Q | ........ | 75-A |
| Rapalje, Abraham | Q | Newtown | 75-B |
| Rapalje, Abraham J. | Q | ........ | 76-E |
| Rapalje, Abraham Jr. | Q | Newtown | 75-B |
| Rapalje, Bern's | Q | ........ | 76-E |
| Rapalje, Cornelius | Q | ........ | 76-B |
| Rapalje, Cornelius | Q | Newtown | 75-B |
| Rapalje, Cornelius [2] | Q | ........ | [on] 75-A |
| Rapalje, Cornelius [2] | Q | ........ | [on] 76-E |
| Rapalje, D. | Q | Newtown | 75-B |
| Rapalje, Dan'l Sr. | Q | ........ | 76-E |
| Rapalje, Daniel | Q | ........ | 75-A, 76-E |
| Rapalje, Daniel 4th | Q | Newtown | 75-B |
| Rapalje, Daniel Esq. | Q | ........ | 75-D1 |

| | | | |
|---|---|---|---|
| Rapalje, Daniel [2] | Q | Newtown | [on] 75-B |
| Rapalje, Garret | N | New York | 74-A |
| Rapalje, Geo. Jr. | Q | ........ | 76-E |
| Rapalje, George Jr. | Q | Newtown | 75-B |
| Rapalje, George [2] | Q | ........ | [on] 75-A |
| Rapalje, George [2] | Q | ........ | [on] 76-E |
| Rapalje, Isaac | Q | ........ | 75-A, 76-B |
| Rapalje, Jeromus | Q | Hempstead | 75-H |
| Rapalje, Jeromus [2] | Q | ........ | [on] 76-E |
| Rapalje, Jeronimus | Q | ........ | 75-A |
| Rapalje, Jeronimus | Q | Newtown | 75-B |
| Rapalje, John | Q | ........ | 76-E |
| Rapalje, Joris | Q | ........ | 76-E |
| Rapalje, Martin | Q | ........ | 75-A |
| Rapalje, Martin | Q | ........ | 76-B, 76-E |
| Rapalje, Martin | Q | Newtown | 75-B |
| Rapalje, Rem | N | New York | 76-F |
| Rapalje, Rich'd | Q | ........ | 75-A associator |
| Rapalje, Rich'd | Q | Newtown | 75-G |
| Rapalje, Richard | Q | ........ | 76-E |
| Rapalje, Stephen | N | New York | 74-A, 75-F |
| Rapalje, Stephen | Q | ........ | 75-A |
| Rapalyie, Abel, 2d Lieut. | N | New York | 76-Y |
| Rape, John | N | New York | 74-R |
| Rapelje, Rem | N | New York | 76-A |
| Rapp, John | N | New York | 76-A |
| Raven, John L. | N | New York | 74-A |
| Rawlin, Jonathan | Q | ........ | 75-A |
| Ray, Cornelius | N | New York | 75-D3 |
| Ray, John | N | New York | 74-A |
| Ray, John Jr. | N | New York | 74-A |
| Ray, Richard and Samuel | N | New York | 75-F; 75-T2, 1/5 |
| Ray, Robert | N | New York | 75-F; 75-T2, 5/4 |
| Ray, Robert, merchant | N | King Street | 75-T2, 8/31 |
| Raymond, Simeon | S | Brookhaven | 75-B6 |
| Rayner, David Jun' | S | ........ | 75-R |
| Rayner, Ebnezer | S | Meritches | 76:0.1.2.1.2 |
| Rayner, Elihu | S | Southampton | 76:0.1.1.4.0 |
| Rayner, Hugh | S | Southampton | 76:0.2.1.3.2 |
| Rayner, Ichabod | S | Easthampton | 75-E |

| | | | |
|---|---|---|---|
| Rayner, Jesse | S | Meritches | 76:0.1.1.1.3 |
| Rayner, Jessey | S | Brookhaven | 75-B6 |
| Rayner, Joseph | S | Brookhaven | 75-B6 |
| Rayner, Josepth | S | Meritches | 76:0.1.4.1.3 |
| Rayner, Josiah | S | Meritches | 76:1.1.0.2.2 |
| Rayner, Jos[ler] | S | Meritches | 76:0.1.5.1.0 |
| Raynor, Adonijah | S | ........ | 75-R |
| Raynor, Benjamin | S | Brookhaven | 75-B6 |
| Raynor, Ebenezer | S | Brookhaven | 75-B6 |
| Raynor, Josiah | S | Southampton | 75-M |
| Raynor, Stephen | S | Southampton | 76:0.1.1.2.0 |
| Rayour, Josepth | S | Meritches | 76:1.1.1.1.0 |
| Rea, William | N | rem to Ulster Co. | 76-P |
| Rea, William | N | to Dutchess Co. | 76-P |
| Read, John | N | New York | 76-R apprentice |
| Reade, John | N | East Ward | 75-R overseer |
| Reade, John | N | New York | 75-F; 75-T2, 5/4 |
| Reade, John, Lieut. | N | New York | 75-A |
| Reade, Lawrence, merchant | N | New York | 74-T |
| Reden, Henry | N | New York | 76-A |
| Reder, Matthew | N | New York | 74-A |
| Redett, Matthew | Q | ........ | 76-E |
| Redman, Bartholomew | S | Brookhaven | 76:0.1.0.3.2 |
| Redmond, Bar[th] | S | Brookhaven | 75-B8 |
| Reed, Catharine | N | to Dutchess Co. | 76-P |
| Reed, Dunkin | N | to Westchester Co | 76-P |
| Reed, Jacob | N | New York | 74-A |
| Reed, Jacob Jr., merchant | N | at Th Pearsall's | 75-D1, D2 |
| Reed, Joseph | Q | Jamaica | 76-C |
| Reed/Read, Thomas, clark | N | New York | 76-D1, D2 |
| Reed/Reid, Joseph, shoemkr | N | Bridge Street | 75-D1, D2 |
| Reeve, Barnabas | S | Brookhaven | 75-B8 |
| Reeve, ---- Capt. | S | Southold | 75-N |
| Reeve, Hezekiah | S | Brookhaven | 75-B10 |
| Reeve, Hezekieh | S | Southold | 76:0.1.1.1.1 |
| Reeve, Isaac | S | Southold | 75-N not at home |
| Reeve, Isaah | S | Meritches | 76:0.1.0.2.4 |
| Reeve, Ishamel | S | Southold | 76:1.1.1.2.2 |
| Reeve, Ishmael | S | Brookhaven | 75-B10 |
| Reeve, James | S | Brookhaven | 75-B10 |

| | | | |
|---|---|---|---|
| Reeve, James | S | Southold | 75-N |
| Reeve, James | S | Southold | 76:0.1.0.2.1 |
| Reeve, James | S | Southold | 76:1.0.1.2.0.3.0 |
| Reeve, James 3$^d$ | S | Brookhaven | 75-B10 |
| Reeve, James Junr. | S | Southold | 75-N |
| Reeve, Jonathan | S | Brookhaven | 75-B10 |
| Reeve, Joseph | S | Brookhaven | 75-B10 |
| Reeve, Joseph | S | Southold | 76:1.0.0.2.1 |
| Reeve, Paul | S | Brookhaven | 75-B10 |
| Reeve, Paul | S | Southold | 76:0.1.3.1.2 |
| Reeve, Perrier | S | Southold | 76:1.1.2.2.0 |
| Reeve, Peter | S | Southold | 75-N |
| Reeve, Selah | S | Brookhaven | 75-B10 |
| Reeve, Selah | S | Southold | 76:0.1.4.1.2.0.1 |
| Reeve, Silas | S | Southold | 76:0.1.0.1.3 |
| Reeve, Solomon & his Son | S | Brookhaven | 75-B9 n.s. |
| Reeve, Thomas | S | Southold | 75-N |
| Reeve, Thomas Jr. | S | Southold | 75-N |
| Reeve, Walter | S | Southold | 76:0.1.2.1.2 |
| Reeve, ____ Wid. | S | Southold | 76:0.1.0.1.0 |
| Reeve, Zadock | S | Southold | 75-N |
| Reeve; Whitehouse & Reeve | N | William Street | 74-T2, 9/29 |
| Reeves, Barnabus | S | Brookhaven | 76:0.1.1.2.0 |
| Reeves, Benjamin | N | to Westchester Co | 76-P |
| Reeves, Bethuel | S | Southampton | 76:0.2.3.2.1 |
| Reeves, David | S | Southampton | 76:0.1.1.1.2 |
| Reeves, Isaac | S | Southold | 76:0.2.1.1.3.1.1 |
| Reeves, Israel | S | Southold | 76:0.3.1.3.1 |
| Reeves, James Jun$^r$ | S | Southold | 76:0.2.3.1.2 |
| Reeves, James y$^e$ 4th | S | Southold | 75-N |
| Reeves, John | S | Southampton | 76:1.1.0.3.0 |
| Reeves, John Ju$^r$ | S | Southampton | 76:0.1.4.1.0 |
| Reeves, Jonathan | S | Southold | 76:0.1.2.1.1 |
| Reeves, Joshua | S | ........ | 75-R |
| Reeves, Joshua | S | Southold | 76:0.1.2.1.1 |
| Reeves, Nathan | S | Southampton | 76:0.1.1.2.5 |
| Reeves, Solomon | S | Brookhaven | 76:1.2.0.1.0 |
| Reeves, Solomon | S | Southold | 76:1.0.0.1.0 |
| Reeves, Stephen | N | New York | 76-A |
| Reeves, Stephen | Q | ........ | 76-A |

| | | | |
|---|---|---|---|
| Reeves, Stephen | S | Southampton | 76:1.0.0.1.0 |
| Reeves, Stephen Jur. | S | Southampton | 76:0.1.2.2.3 |
| Reeves, Thomas | S | Southold | 76:1.2.1.2.4 |
| Reeves, Thomas Jun' | S | Southold | 76:0.1.0.1.2 |
| Reeves, Zadock | S | Southold | 76:0.1.1.1.1 |
| Reevs, William | S | Meritches | 76:1.0.2.1.0 |
| Reger, Frederick | N | New York | 74-A |
| Reicble, George | N | New York | 76-A |
| Reid, William | Q | ........ | 76-E |
| Reilley, Jeremiah | N | New York | 74-A |
| Reily, Jeremiah, shoemaker | N | Battoe Street | 74-T |
| Reis, Peter | N | removed upstate | 76-P |
| Relay, Frances | N | New York | 75-R |
| Relay, Henry | N | New York | 76-L |
| Remend, Abram | N | New York | 74-A |
| Remind, Nich' | N | New York | 76-A |
| Remmey, John | N | New York | 74-A, 76-D |
| Remp, Michael | S | Huntington | 75-H |
| Remsen, Ab'm | Q | ........ | 75-A, 76-E |
| Remsen, Abraham | Q | ........ | 76-B |
| Remsen, Anthony | Q | Jamaica | 75-D |
| Remsen, Ares | Q | Jamaica | 75-C |
| Remsen, Aris | Q | ........ | 76-B |
| Remsen, Auris | Q | ........ | 75-A |
| Remsen, Aury | Q | Jamaica | 75-D |
| Remsen, Christopher | Q | ........ | 76-B, 76-E |
| Remsen, Christopher | Q | Newtown | 75-G |
| Remsen, Christopher [2] | Q | ........ | [on] 75-A |
| Remsen, Cornelius | Q | ........ | 76-E |
| Remsen, Daniel | Q | ........ | 75-A, 76-B |
| Remsen, Daniel | Q | Jamaica | 75-C, 75-D |
| Remsen, Geo. and Juos. A. | N | New York | 75-F |
| Remsen, George | N | New York | 76-A, 76-I |
| Remsen, Henry | N | New York | 74-T2, 11/24 |
| Remsen, Henry, Capt. | N | New York | 75-A |
| Remsen, Henry, merchant | N | New York | 75-T2, 1/5 |
| Remsen, Isaac | Q | ........ | 75-A |
| Remsen, Isaac | Q | ........ | 76-B, 76-E |
| Remsen, Isaac Jr. | Q | ........ | 76-E |
| Remsen, Jacob | N | New York | 74-A |

| | | | |
|---|---|---|---|
| Remsen, Jacob | N | South Ward | 75-R overseer |
| Remsen, Jacob | Q | ........ | 76-E |
| Remsen, Jacob Jr., Ensign | N | New York | 76-G |
| Remsen, Jacob, storekeepr | N | Whitehall | 75-T |
| Remsen, Jacob [2] | Q | Jamaica | [on] 75-C |
| Remsen, Jeremiah | Q | ........ | 76-E |
| Remsen, Jeromius | Q | Newtown | 75-B, 75-G |
| Remsen, Jeromus | Q | ........ | 76-E |
| Remsen, Jeronimus A. | N | New York | 76-R juror |
| Remsen, Jerormus Jr. | Q | Newtown | 75-G |
| Remsen, Jno. | Q | J. [Jamaica] | 75-A |
| Remsen, John | Q | ........ | 75-A |
| Remsen, John | Q | Jamaica | 75-D |
| Remsen, John A. | N | New York | 76-A |
| Remsen, John, Lieut. | N | New York | 75-A |
| Remsen, John Sr. | Q | Jamaica | 75-D |
| Remsen, John [2] | Q | Jamaica | [on] 75-C |
| Remsen, John [3] | Q | ........ | [on] 76-B |
| Remsen, John [4] | Q | ........ | [on] 76-E |
| Remsen, Joris | N | New York | 74-A |
| Remsen, Joris, juror | N | New York | 74-R, 76-R |
| Remsen, Luke | Q | ........ | 75-A associator |
| Remsen, Luke | Q | Newtown | 75-G |
| Remsen, Rem | Q | H. [Hempstead] | 75-A |
| Remsen, Rem | Q | Jamaica | 75-C, 75-D |
| Remsen, Rem | Q | N.J. [sic] | 75-A associator |
| Remsen, Rem | Q | Newtown | 75-G |
| Remsen, Rem Jr. | Q | Jamaica | 75-C |
| Remsen, Rem P. | Q | ........ | 76-E |
| Remsen, Rem Sr. | Q | Jamaica | 75-A, 75-C |
| Remsen, Rem [2] | Q | ........ | [on] 76-B |
| Remsen, Rem [2] | Q | ........ | [on] 76-E |
| Remsen, Simon | Q | ........ | 76-E |
| Remsen, William, Capt. | N | New York | 76-G |
| Remsen, William, Lieut. | N | New York | 75-A |
| Renan, Daniel | N | New York | 74-A |
| Renaudet, Adrian | N | Maiden Lane | 75-T |
| Renaudez, Adrn. | N | New York | 74-A |
| Renby, Catherien | N | removed upstate | 76-P |
| Rendriese, John | N | New York | 74-A |

| | | | |
|---|---|---|---|
| Renne, Samuel | Q | ........ | 76-E |
| Renney, Sam'l | Q | Newtown | 75-G |
| Rescorla, William | N | New York | 74-A |
| Resler, Jacob | N | New York | 76-A |
| Rete, Gregory | Q | ........ | 76-E |
| Revers, John | N | New York | 74-A |
| Reynolds, George, cooper | N | Henry Street | 75-D1, D2 |
| Reynolds, see also Runnals | | | |
| Reynolds, Timothy | S | Brookhaven | 75-B6 |
| Rhinehart, Jacob | Q | ........ | 75-A, 76-B |
| Rhinelander, Fred'k, Capt. | N | New York | 76-Y |
| Rhinelander, Frederick | N | New York | 75-R juror |
| Rhinelander, Fred[k] | N | New York | 74-A, 76-A |
| Rhinelander, Jac. | Q | ........ | 76-E |
| Rhinelander, Philip | N | New York | 75-F, 76-A |
| Rhinelander, Philip, Ensign | N | New York | 76-Y |
| Rhinelander, Philip Jr. | N | New York | 74-A |
| Rhinelander, Wm Jr. | N | New York | 74-A |
| Rhinelander, Wm., 2d Lt. | N | New York | 76-Y |
| Rhoades, Amadis | Q | ........ | 76-B |
| Rhoades, Amos | Q | ........ | 75-A, 76-B2 |
| Rhoades, Anthony | Q | ........ | 75-A |
| Rhoades, Anthony | Q | ........ | 76-B, 76-E |
| Rhoades, George | Q | ........ | 75-A, 76-B |
| Rhoades, Hope | Q | ........ | 75-A associator |
| Rhoades, Hope | Q | ........ | 76-E |
| Rhoades, Hope | Q | Jamaica | 75-D associator |
| Rhoades, Hope | Q | Jamaica | 75-E |
| Rhoades, Hope Jr. | Q | ........ | 75-A associator |
| Rhoades, Isaac | Q | ........ | 75-A associator |
| Rhoades, Isaac | Q | ........ | 76-E |
| Rhoades, Isaac | Q | Jamaica | 75-D associator |
| Rhoades, Isaac | Q | Jamaica | 76-C |
| Rhoades, John | Q | ........ | 75-A associator |
| Rhoades, John | Q | ........ | 76-E |
| Rhoades, John | Q | Jamaica | 75-D associator |
| Rhoades, Jonah | Q | ........ | 75-A associator |
| Rhoades, Jonah | Q | Jamaica | 75-D associator |
| Rhoades, Nathaniel | Q | Jamaica | 75-E |
| Rhoades, Richard | Q | ........ | 75-A |

| | | | |
|---|---|---|---|
| Rhoades, Richard | Q | ........ | 75-A associator |
| Rhoades, Richard | Q | Jamaica | 75-D associator |
| Rhoades, Richard | Q | Jamaica | 75-E |
| Rhoades, Richard [3] | Q | ........ | [on] 76-E |
| Rhoades, Timothy | Q | ........ | 75-A, 76-E |
| Rhodes, Thomas | S | Huntington | 75-H |
| Rice, John | Q | ........ | 76-E |
| Rice, Peter | N | removed upstate | 76-P |
| Richards, Eliz., wid of Paul | N | New York | 74-T |
| Richards, Rebecca | N | to Dutchess Co. | 76-P |
| Richards, Smith, merchant | N | Queen Street | 75-D2 |
| Richardson, Barnard | N | New York | 74-A |
| Richardson, John | N | New York | 76-F |
| Richets, William | N | to Westchester Co | 76-P |
| Ricker, Henry | N | New York | 74-A, 76-A |
| Ricker, Peter | N | New York | 74-A, 75-F |
| Ricks, John | N | New York | 76-E |
| Rider, Barnebus | S | Brookhaven | 76:1.2.2.3.1 |
| Rider, David | N | New York | 76-A |
| Rider, Eunes | S | Brookhaven | 76:0.0.0.2.1 |
| Rider; see also Ryder | | | |
| Ridgway, Christien | N | removed upstate | 76-P |
| Ridout, David, potter | N | New York | 75-D2 |
| Ridout, Peter | N | New York | 74-A |
| Riely, Thomas | N | New York | 76-E |
| Riese, John | N | removed upstate | 76-P |
| Rigby, Joseph | N | New York | 74-A |
| Rigby, Joseph | N | New York | 74-R juror |
| Rigby, Joseph, cordwainer | N | Little Queen St. | 75-D1, D2 |
| Rigger, Mary | N | removed upstate | 76-P |
| Riker, Ab'n | Q | Newtown | 75-G |
| Riker, Andrew | N | New York | 76-L |
| Riker, Andrew | Q | ........ | 76-E |
| Riker, Henry | N | New York | 76-L, 76-N |
| Riker, Jacobus | Q | ........ | 75-A |
| Riker, Jacobus | Q | ........ | 76-B, 76-E |
| Riker, Jacobus | Q | Newtown | 75-B |
| Riker, James | N | New York | 74-A, 76-N |
| Riker, John | Q | ........ | 75-A associator |
| Riker, John Jr. | N | New York | 76-N |

| | | | |
|---|---|---|---|
| Riker, John, juror | N | New York | 74-R, 75-R |
| Riker, Peter | Q | Newtown | 75-G |
| Riker, Samuel | Q | ........ | 75-A associator |
| Riker, Samuel | Q | Newtown | 75-G |
| Riley, Else | N | to Westchester Co | 76-P |
| Riley, James | N | to Westchester Co | 76-P |
| Rindollar, Emmanuel | N | New York | 74-A |
| Rinehart, see Rhinehart | | | |
| Riney, Elesabeth | N | removed upstate | 76-P |
| Ring, Linus | N | New York | 74-A |
| Ringdollar, Emanuel | N | New York | 75-R Freeman |
| Ripp, Thomas | Q | ........ | 76-B |
| Risler, John | N | New York | 76-A |
| Ritche, Catharine | N | to Dutchess Co. | 76-P |
| Ritche, Edward | N | to Dutchess Co. | 76-P |
| Ritche, George | N | to Dutchess Co. | 76-P |
| Ritche, John James | N | to Dutchess Co. | 76-P |
| Ritche, Margaret | N | to Dutchess Co. | 76-P |
| Ritche, Mary | N | to Dutchess Co. | 76-P |
| Ritche, Sarah | N | to Dutchess Co. | 76-P |
| Ritter, John | N | New York | 74-A, 76-A |
| Ritter, Michael | N | New York | 74-A, 76-I |
| Ritzma, Rodolphus | N | New York | 74-T2, 11/24 |
| Ritzome, Rud. | N | New York | 74-A |
| Rivington, James | N | New York | 74-A, 75-F |
| Roach, Elenor, runaway | N | New York | 74-T2, 11/10 |
| Roach, Thomas | N | New York | 76-M |
| Robb, Elizabeth | N | to Dutchess Co. | 76-P |
| Robb, James | N | to Dutchess Co. | 76-P |
| Robb, Jane | N | to Dutchess Co. | 76-P |
| Robb, Keturah, Mrs. | N | to Dutchess Co. | 76-P |
| Robb, Michael | N | to Dutchess Co. | 76-P |
| Robb, Nicholas | N | to Dutchess Co. | 76-P |
| Robbins, Daniel | S | Brookhaven | 75-B9 |
| Robbins, Henry | S | Brookhaven | 75-B9 |
| Robbins, Isaac | Q | ........ | 76-E |
| Robbins, Isaac | S | Brookhaven | 75-B12 n.s. |
| Robbins, Isaac | S | Brookhaven | 75-B3 |
| Robbins, Isaac | S | Brookhaven | 76:0.1.1.2.2 |
| Robbins, Jacob | Q | ........ | 76-E |

| | | | |
|---|---|---|---|
| Robbins, Jas. | Q | ........ | 75-A |
| Robbins, Jeremiah | Q | ........ | 75-A, 76-E |
| Robbins, John | Q | ........ | 76-E |
| Robbins, John Sr. | Q | ........ | 76-E |
| Robbins, Rich'd | Q | ........ | 75-A |
| Robbins, Samuel | Q | ........ | 76-E |
| Robbins, Stephen | Q | ........ | 75-A |
| Robbins, Stephen | Q | ........ | 76-B, 76-E |
| Robbins, Van Acarly | S | Huntington | 75-H |
| Robbins, Zebulon | S | Brookhaven | 75-B12 n.s. |
| Robbins, Zebulon | S | Brookhaven | 76:2.0.0.1.0 |
| Robboson, Edmond | S | Brookhaven | 76:0.1.2.1.1 |
| Roberson, Adam | N | removed upstate | 76-P |
| Robert, Christopher | Q | ........ | 75-A associator |
| Robert, Christopher | Q | ........ | 76-E |
| Roberts, Ezekiel, hatter | N | Gold Street | 75-D2 |
| Roberts, J. | N | New York | 76-A |
| Roberts, John | N | New York | 74-T insolvent |
| Roberts, John | S | Huntington | 75-H |
| Roberts, John, Sheriff | N | New York | 74-R to 76-R |
| Roberts, Jonathan | Q | ........ | 75-A associator |
| Roberts, Jonathan | Q | Newtown | 75-G |
| Roberts, Sam'l | N | New York | 74-A |
| Robertson, Alexander | N | New York | 74-A |
| Robertson, Alexander | N | New York | 74-V, 75-F |
| Robertson, Alexander & Co | N | Queen Street | 74-T2, 9/22 |
| Robertson, Arthur | N | New York | 75-D1 |
| Robertson, John | N | New York | 76-A |
| Robertson, Patrick Jr. | N | New York | 74-A |
| Robertson, Peter | N | New York | 74-A |
| Robeson, Abraham | Q | ........ | 76-E |
| Robeson, Robbard | S | Brookhaven | 76:1.0.1.0.0 |
| Robins, Ezekiel | N | New York | 75-D1, 76-A |
| Robins, Henry | S | Brookhaven | 76:1.2.0.2.3 |
| Robins, Henry Juner | S | Brookhaven | 75-B9 n.s. |
| Robins, Moses | N | New York | 74-A |
| Robinson, Arthur | N | New York | 75-D3 |
| Robinson, Christopher | S | Brookhaven | 75-B1 n.s. |
| Robinson, Christopher | S | Brookhaven | 75-B7 |
| Robinson, Daniel | S | Southold | 75-N |

| Robinson, Edmond | S | Brookhaven | 75-B2 |
|---|---|---|---|
| Robinson, George | N | New York | 74-A |
| Robinson, Isaac | S | Brookhaven | 75-B7, 75-B9 |
| Robinson, Isaac | S | Brookhaven | 76:2.0.0.0.0 |
| Robinson, Israel | S | Brookhaven | 75-B6, 75-B7 |
| Robinson, John | N | New York | 74-A |
| Robinson, John | S | Brookhaven | 75-B9 |
| Robinson, John | S | Brookhaven | 76:1.1.0.1.0.1.0 |
| Robinson, John, servant | N | New York | 74-V runaway |
| Robinson, Jonathan | S | Southold | 75-N non-signer |
| Robinson, Jonathan | S | Southold | 76:0.1.0.1.0 |
| Robinson, Joseph | N | New York | 74-A |
| Robinson, Joseph | Q | ........ | 75-A associator |
| Robinson, Joseph | Q | Jamaica | 75-E, 76-C |
| Robinson, Joseph, Deputy | Q | Jamaica | 75-D associator |
| Robinson, Richard | N | New York | 74-A |
| Robinson, Rukard, Sergt. | S | Brookhaven | 75-B9 |
| Robinson, Samuel | S | Brookhaven | 75-B6 |
| Robinson, Thomas | N | New York | 75-D1 |
| Robinson, Thomas | S | Brookhaven | 75-B2 |
| Robinson, ____ widow | N | removed upstate | 76-P |
| Robinson, William | N | New York | 74-A |
| Robison, Arthur, plummer | N | Dock Street | 75-D2 |
| Robison, James, Capt. | N | New York | 76-N |
| Robison, Thomas, hatter | N | New York | 75-D2 |
| Robison, Thomas, taylor | N | Elbow Lane | 75-D2 |
| Robson, Iserel | S | Brookhaven | 76:1.1.0.2.0 |
| Robson, Robert | N | New York | 76-I |
| Robson, Robert [2] | N | New York | [on] 74-A |
| Robson, Thomas | S | Brookhaven | 76:1.0.0.0.0 |
| Robsun, Daneil | S | Meritches | 76:0.1.5.1.1 |
| Robsun, David | S | Meritches | 76:0.1.2.1.1 |
| Robsun, Samuel | S | Meritches | 76:0.1.3.1.0 |
| Robsun, Stephen | S | Meritches | 76:1.0.1.2.2 |
| Rochar, Pierre | N | New York | 74-A |
| Rodman, John | Q | ........ | 76-E |
| Rodman, Thos. | Q | ........ | 75-A associator |
| Roe, Austin | S | Brookhaven | 75-B8 |
| Roe, Austin | S | Brookhaven | 76:0.2.2.1.1 |
| Roe, D., constable | Q | ........ | 76-E |

| | | | |
|---|---|---|---|
| Roe, Daniel | S | Brookhaven | 75-B1 |
| Roe, Daniel | S | Brookhaven | 76:0.0.3.2.5 |
| Roe, Daniel, Lieut. | S | Brookhaven | 75-B7 |
| Roe, Ezekiel | Q | ........ | 76-E |
| Roe, Isaac | S | Brookhaven | 75-B8 |
| Roe, John | Q | ........ | 76-E |
| Roe, John | S | Brookhaven | 75-B4 |
| Roe, John | S | Brookhaven | 76:1.2.1.2.2.1.1 |
| Roe, John Junor | S | Brookhaven | 75-B8 |
| Roe, John Senior | S | Brookhaven | 75-B8 |
| Roe, Justice | S | Brookhaven | 75-B8 |
| Roe, Nathanael Juner | S | Brookhaven | 75-B8 |
| Roe, Nathanael Senior | S | Brookhaven | 75-B8 |
| Roe, Nathaniel | S | Brookhaven | 75-B4 |
| Roe, Nathaniel | S | Brookhaven | 76:1.1.1.3.4 |
| Roe, Nathaniel Jr. | S | Brookhaven | 75-B4 |
| Roe, Phillip | S | Brookhaven | 75-B4 |
| Roe, Phillips | S | Brookhaven | 75-B8 |
| Roe, Phillips | S | Brookhaven | 76:0.2.3.1.3 |
| Roe, W. | Q | ........ | 76-E |
| Roebuck, Jarvis | N | New York | 74-A |
| Roebuck, Jarvis | N | New York | 74-R juror |
| Roebuck, Jarvis | N | New York | 76-A |
| Rogart, Jno. | N | New York | 75-D3 |
| Roger, Abraham | S | ........ | 75-R |
| Roger, Elisabeth | N | rem. to Bedford | 76-J |
| Rogers, Abraham | S | ........ | 75-R |
| Rogers, Alexander | S | Huntington | 75-H1 |
| Rogers, Alex' | S | Huntington | 75-H |
| Rogers, Caleb | S | Huntington | 76-H2 |
| Rogers, Daniel | S | Huntington | 75-H |
| Rogers, David | S | ........ | 75-R |
| Rogers, David | S | Southampton | 76:1.0.0.1.0 |
| Rogers, Israel | Q | ........ | 75-A, 76-B |
| Rogers, Jacamiah | S | Huntington | 75-H |
| Rogers, James | N | New York | 76-A |
| Rogers, James | N | New York | 76-G, 76-I |
| Rogers, James | S | Huntington | 75-H |
| Rogers, James | S | Southampton | 76:0.1.2.1.2 |
| Rogers, Jeremiah | S | Southampton | 76:0.1.2.1.2 |

| Rogers, Jesse | S | Islip | 75-I |
|---|---|---|---|
| Rogers, Jesse | S | Islip | 76:0.1.1.1.0 |
| Rogers, John | Q | ........ | 75-A associator |
| Rogers, John | S | ........ | 75-R |
| Rogers, John | S | Huntington | 75-H |
| Rogers, John | S | Islip | 75-I |
| Rogers, John | S | Southampton | 76:0.1.1.1.2.1 |
| Rogers, Jonas | S | Huntington | 75-H |
| Rogers, Jonathan | S | Southampton | 76:0.1.0.1.1.1.0 |
| Rogers, Jonathan | S | Southold | 76:0.1.1.1.5 |
| Rogers, Jonathan [2] | S | ........ | [on] 75-R |
| Rogers, Joseph | S | ........ | 75-R |
| Rogers, Joseph | S | Huntington | 75-H |
| Rogers, Joseph | S | Southampton | 76:0.2.2.2.2 |
| Rogers, Joshua | N | New York | 76-N |
| Rogers, Joshua | S | ........ | 75-R |
| Rogers, Joshua | S | Huntington | 75-H |
| Rogers, Joshua | S | Southampton | 76:0.2.2.1.2 |
| Rogers, Josiah | S | Huntington | 75-H, 75-H1 |
| Rogers, Lewis | N | New York | 76-G |
| Rogers, Michael | Q | ........ | 75-A, 76-E |
| Rogers, Moses | S | Huntington | 75-H |
| Rogers, Nathaniel | S | ........ | 75-R |
| Rogers, Nath¹ | S | Southampton | 76:0.2.1.1.3 |
| Rogers, Obadiah, Capᵗ | S | Southampton | 76:1.0.0.2.0.2.1 |
| Rogers, Otheniel | N | New York | 74-A |
| Rogers, Richard | S | Huntington | 75-H non-signer |
| Rogers, Sarah, Widow | S | Southampton | 76:0.0.2.3.1 |
| Rogers, Stephen | S | Smithtown | 75-L |
| Rogers, Stephen | S | Southampton | 76:1.0.2.2.2 |
| Rogers, Stephen | S | Southampton | 76:1.2.2.4.0.0.1 |
| Rogers, Topping | S | ........ | 75-R |
| Rogers, Uriah | S | ........ | 75-R |
| Rogers, Uriah, Mjr. | S | Southampton | 76:0.1.2.2.2 |
| Rogers, ____ Widow | S | Southampton | 76:0.1.0.1.4 |
| Rogers, William | S | Huntington | 75-H |
| Rogers, William | S | Southold | 76:0.1.2.2.1 |
| Rogers, William, Capt. | S | Southampton | 76:0.1.2.1.1.1.1 |
| Rogers, William Jun., Capt. | S | ........ | 75-R |
| Rogers, William [2] | S | ........ | [on] 75-R |

| | | | |
|---|---|---|---|
| Rogers, William's Widow | S | Southampton | 76:0.0.0.1.0.1.0 |
| Rogers, W<sup>m</sup> Jun<sup>r</sup> | S | ........ | 75-R |
| Rogers, Zachariah | S | Huntington | 75-H |
| Rogers, Zephniah | S | Southampton | 76:0.1.1.1.2 |
| Rogers, Zophar | S | Huntington | 75-H non-signer |
| Rogers, Zophar | S | Huntington | 75-H1 |
| Rolph, Benjamin | S | Huntington | 75-H |
| Rolph, Moses | S | Huntington | 75-H |
| Rolph, Reuben | S | Huntington | 75-H |
| Roltonour, Godfred | N | New York | 76-A |
| Romans, Bernard, maps | N | New York | 74-T2, 10/20 |
| Romine, John | N | New York | 74-A, 76-I |
| Romme, Cornelius | N | New York | 76-A |
| Romme, Luke | N | New York | 74-A |
| Roney, John | S | Huntington | 75-H |
| Ronold, James, joiner | N | George Street | 75-D2 |
| Room, Luke | N | Hanover Square | 74-T2, 11/3 |
| Roome, Henry | N | New York | 74-A |
| Roome, Jacob | N | New York | 74-A |
| Roome, Jacob, Capt. | N | New York | 74-T |
| Roome, Jn° L.C., Lieut. | N | New York | 75-A |
| Roome, John | N | New York | 74-T2, 11/24 |
| Roome, John, Capt. | N | New York | 75-A |
| Roome, John L.C. | N | New York | 74-T, 76-F |
| Roome, Peter | N | New York | 76-L |
| Roorbach, Fred'k | N | New York | 74-A |
| Roorback, Gar. | N | New York | 76-N |
| Roorback, Garret, juror | N | New York | 74-R, 75-R |
| Roorback, Gart. | N | New York | 74-A |
| Roosevelt, Isaac | N | New York | 74-T2, 11/24 |
| Roosevelt, Jacobus | N | New York | 76-V |
| Roosevelt, Jacobus Jr. | N | New York | 74-A |
| Roosevelt, John J. | N | New York | 75-B |
| Roosevelt, John, merchant | N | Maiden Lane | 75-D1, D2 |
| Roosevelt, John T. | N | New York | 75-D3 |
| Roosevelt, Nicholas | N | New York | 74-T2, 11/24 |
| Roosevelt, Nich<sup>s</sup>, Capt. | N | New York | 75-A |
| Roscron, Henry | S | Smithtown | 75-L |
| Rose, Abraham | S | ........ | 75-R |
| Rose, Abraham | S | Southampton | 76:0.1.3.2.0.1.1 |

| | | | |
|---|---|---|---|
| Rose, Daniel | S | Brookhaven | 75-B3, 75-B6 |
| Rose, Daniel | S | Brookhaven | 76:0.2.1.3.1.1.0 |
| Rose, David | S | ........ | 75-R |
| Rose, David | S | Brookhaven | 75-B6 |
| Rose, David | S | Southampton | 76:1.1.1.1.1 |
| Rose, David, L.D. | S | Brookhaven | 76:0.1.3.2.3 |
| Rose, Ezekeil | S | Southampton | 76:0.1.1.1.0 |
| Rose, Ezekiel | S | ........ | 75-R |
| Rose, James | N | New York | 74-A |
| Rose, Jane Bell, widow | S | Southampton | 76:0.0.1.4.1 |
| Rose, Jesse | S | Brookhaven | 75-B3, 75-B6 |
| Rose, Jesse | S | Brookhaven | 76:0.1.5.2.0.1.1 |
| Rose, Joseph | N | New York | 74-A |
| Rose, Lemuel | S | Huntington | 75-H, 76-H3 |
| Rose, Moses | S | ........ | 75-R |
| Rose, Moses | S | Southampton | 76:0.1.0.1.0 |
| Rose, Nathan | S | Brookhaven | 75-B6 |
| Rose, Nathan | S | Brookhaven | 76:0.1.0.1.0 |
| Rose, Nathan | S | Brookhaven | 76:0.1.4.1.3.1.0 |
| Rose, Nathan, Capt. | S | Brookhaven | 75-B3 |
| Rose, Nathan Jr. | S | Brookhaven | 75-B3, 75-B6 |
| Rose, Nicholas, wheelwrt | N | Fresh Water | 75-D1, D2 |
| Rose, Stephen | S | ........ | 75-R |
| Rose, Stephen | S | Southampton | 76:0.1.3.2.1 |
| Rose, Thomas | S | Brookhaven | 75-B6 |
| Rose, Thomas | S | Brookhaven | 76:0.1.2.3.2.1.0 |
| Rose, Thomas, Lieut. | S | Brookhaven | 75-B3 |
| Rosell, Jonathan | Q | ........ | 76-E |
| Ross, Alexander, servant | N | New York | 74-V runaway |
| Ross, Alexander [2] | N | New York | [on] 76-A |
| Ross, Benjamin | N | New York | 74-A |
| Ross, Daniel, oysterman | N | Lombart Street | 75-D2 |
| Ross, Hugh | N | New York | 76-I, 76-R |
| Ross, James | N | New York | 76-A |
| Ross, Levy, cooper | N | Battoe Street | 75-D2 |
| Ross, Robert | N | at North River | 74-T |
| Ross, Robert | N | New York | 74-A, 76-A |
| Rote, Philip, distiller | N | St James Street | 75-D1, D2 |
| Row, David Jun' | S | ........ | 75-R |
| Rowlan, John | Q | Jamaica | 75-D |

| | | | |
|---|---|---|---|
| Rowland, Jonathan | Q | ........ | 76-B, 76-E |
| Rubie, Edward | N | New York | 74-A |
| Ruckel, Daniel | N | New York | 75-D1 |
| Ruckel, Jasper | N | New York | 74-A |
| Ruckell, Daniel | N | New York | 74-A |
| Ruckell, Jasper | N | New York | 76-A |
| Ruckistire, John | N | New York | 74-A |
| Ruddle, William | N | New York | 76-A |
| Rudman, William | N | New York | 74-T |
| Rudyard, Thomas | S | Brookhaven | 76:1.0.2.1.3 |
| Rug, Joseph | S | Southampton | 76:0.1.1.2.4 |
| Ruger, Fred[k] | N | New York | 76-A |
| Rugg, Silas | S | ........ | 75-R |
| Ruggard, Thomas | S | Brookhaven | 75-B11 n.s. |
| Ruland, David | S | Huntington | 76-H2 |
| Ruland, Jeremiah | S | Huntington | 75-H |
| Ruland, John | S | Huntington | 75-H |
| Ruland, John | S | Huntington | 75-H non-signer |
| Ruland, Joseph | S | Brookhaven | 75-B7 |
| Ruland, Joseph Jun[r] | S | Brookhaven | 75-B7 |
| Ruland, Lake | S | Huntington | 76-H3 |
| Ruland, Luke Jr. | S | Huntington | 75-H |
| Ruland, Luke Sen[r] | S | Huntington | 75-H |
| Ruland, Peter | S | Huntington | 75-H non-signer |
| Ruland, Peter | S | Huntington | 75-H1 |
| Ruland, Peter Jr. | S | Huntington | 75-H |
| Ruland, Richard | S | Huntington | 75-H |
| Ruland, Thom[s] | S | Huntington | 75-H |
| Rumsey, James | N | New York | 76-N |
| Runnals, Enes | S | Brookhaven | 76:0.2.3.1.2 |
| Ruoiser, Jacob | N | New York | 76-A |
| Rurgers, Harman | N | New York | 74-R |
| Rusco, David | S | Huntington | 75-H |
| Rusco, David Jr. | S | Huntington | 75-H |
| Rusco, Nathaniel, Corp'l | S | Huntington | 76-H2 |
| Rusco, Nath[l] | S | Huntington | 75-H |
| Rushmore, Benjamin | Q | Oyster Bay | 75-F |
| Rushmore, Carman | Q | ........ | 75-A |
| Rushmore, Carman | Q | ........ | 76-B, 76-E |
| Rushmore, John | Q | ........ | 75-A, 76-B |

| | | | |
|---|---|---|---|
| Rushmore, Wm | Q | ........ | 75-A, 76-B |
| Rushton, Elizabeth | N | to Westchester Co | 76-P |
| Rusler, Sophia | N | Fly Ferry Stairs | 76-H |
| Rusler, Sophia | N | Fly Mart nr Stairs | 76-I |
| Russel, Abraham | N | New York | 75-T |
| Russel, David | S | Easthampton | 76:0.1.1.1.3 |
| Russel, John | N | New York | 76-D, 76-L |
| Russel, Jonathan | S | Southampton | 76:0.2.3.1.3 |
| Russel, Permelia, Wd. | S | Easthampton | 76:0.0.1.1.1 |
| Russel, Stephen | S | Easthampton | 75-E |
| Russel, Timothy | N | New York | 76-L |
| Russel, Wm | N | New York | 74-A |
| Russell, Abraham | N | New York | 74-A |
| Russell, Abram | N | New York | 76-L |
| Russell, Bartholomew | N | New York | 74-A |
| Russell, Caleb | S | ........ | 75-R |
| Russell, James | N | New York | 74-A |
| Russell, John | N | New York | 74-A |
| Russell, Jonathan | S | ........ | 75-R |
| Russell, Joseph | S | Southampton | 76:1.0.0.1.3 |
| Russell, Mary | N | removed upstate | 76-P |
| Russell, Solomon | N | New York | 75-D1 |
| Russell, Stephen | S | Easthampton | 76:0.1.2.1.1 |
| Rutgers, Adrian | N | New York | 74-T |
| Rutgers, Anth. | N | New York | 74-A |
| Rutgers, ___ Capt. | Q | Jamaica | 75-D associator |
| Rutgers, Harman | N | New York | 74-R |
| Rutgers, Henry Jr., Lieut. | N | New York | 76-G |
| Rutgers, Her's | N | New York | 75-D3 |
| Rutgers, John | N | New York | 76-G |
| Rutherford, Margaret | N | New York | 76-I |
| Rutler, Daniel, stone cutter | N | Cliff Street | 75-D2 |
| Rutter, John | N | Cherry Street | 75-E |
| Rutter, John | N | New York | 74-A |
| Rutter, John | N | New York | 76-I, 76-N |
| Rutter, John, oysters | N | Cherry Street | 74-T2, 10/6 |
| Ryan, Cornelius | N | New York | 74-A, 75-R |
| Ryan, Cornelius | N | New York | 76-A |
| Ryan, Isabel wf of Corn's | N | New York | 75-R |
| Ryan, John | N | New York | 74-A |

| | | | |
|---|---|---|---|
| Ryan, Mary | N | New York | 76-I |
| Ryan, Polly, wf of Lewis | N | New York | 76-V |
| Ryder, Bernardus | Q | Jamaica | 75-C, 75-D |
| Ryder, Bernardus Jr. | Q | Jamaica | 76-C |
| Ryder, Christopher | Q | ........ | 75-A associator |
| Ryder, Christopher | Q | Jamaica | 75-D associator |
| Ryder, Jacobus | Q | ........ | 76-E |
| Ryder, Jeames | Q | Hempstead | 76-D |
| Ryder, John | Q | ........ | 76-E |
| Ryder, Stephen | Q | ........ | 75-A associator |
| Ryder, Stephen | Q | Jamaica | 75-E |
| Ryder, Uriah | Q | ........ | 75-A associator |
| Ryder, Urias | Q | Jamaica | 75-E |
| Ryen, James | N | New York | 76-E |
| Ryerson, Cornelius | Q | ........ | 75-A |
| Ryerson, Cornelius | Q | ........ | 76-B, 76-E |
| Ryerson, George | Q | ........ | 75-A |
| Ryerson, George | Q | ........ | 76-B, 76-E |
| Ryerson, George | Q | Jamaica | 75-D |
| Ryerson, Martin | Q | ........ | 75-A, 76-B |
| Ryerson, Peter | Q | ........ | 75-A |
| Ryerson, Peter | Q | ........ | 76-B, 76-E |
| Rykeman, John | N | New York | 76-A |
| Rylee, Elizabeth | N | New York | 75-R |
| Rymmer, Mary | N | New York | 74-T insolvent |
| Ryne, Catheren | N | removed upstate | 76-P |
| Ryne, Christopher | N | removed upstate | 76-P |
| Sabaden, Charles | N | New York | 75-R, 76-I |
| Sabathin, Hannah wf of Chs | N | New York | 75-R |
| Sables, Jacob | N | New York | 76-L |
| Sackett, John | N | New York | 74-A, 76-A |
| Sackett, Sam'l | N | New York | 74-A |
| Sackett, Samuel | N | New York | 75-F, 76-V |
| Sackett, William | Q | ........ | 76-E |
| Sackett, Wm | Q | ........ | 75-A associator |
| Sackett, Wm | Q | Newtown | 75-G |
| Saddler, John | N | New York | 76-I |
| Salmon, Jonathan | S | Southold | 76:0.1.0.1.0 |
| Salmon, Joshua | S | ........ | 75-R |
| Salmon, Joshua | S | Southold | 76:1.2.0.2.0 |

| | | | |
|---|---|---|---|
| Salmon, Joshua Junʳ | S | ........ | 75-R |
| Salmon, Joshua Junʳ | S | Southold | 76:0.1.1.1.2 |
| Sals, John, Dr. | N | Fresh Water | 75-T2, 2/16 |
| Salter, Daniel, carman | N | Spring Garden | 75-D1, D2 |
| Salter, Manassa, juror | N | New York | 74-R, 75-R |
| Salter, Monasseh | N | New York | 74-A |
| Salts, Maurice | N | New York | 74-A |
| Samith, Daniel, carpenter | S | Brookhaven | 75-B8 |
| Samler, John | N | New York | 76-A |
| Sammis, Alexander | S | Huntington | 75-H |
| Sammis, David | Q | ........ | 76-E |
| Sammis, David | S | Huntington | 75-H |
| Sammis, Ebenezer | S | Huntington | 75-H, 76-H2 |
| Sammis, Henry | S | Huntington | 75-H |
| Sammis, Jesse | S | Huntington | 75-H |
| Sammis, Jesse | S | Huntington | 75-H1, 76-H1 |
| Sammis, Job | S | Huntington | 75-H |
| Sammis, John Jr. | S | Huntington | 75-H |
| Sammis, Jonas | S | Huntington | 75-H, 76-H2 |
| Sammis, Jonathan | S | Smithtown | 76:1.2.0.1.1 |
| Sammis, Jonathan Jr. | S | Huntington | 75-H |
| Sammis, Jonathan Senʳ | S | Smithtown | 75-L |
| Sammis, Joseph | S | Huntington | 75-H |
| Sammis, Nathanael | S | Smithtown | 75-L |
| Sammis, Nathaniel | S | Huntington | 76-H2, 76-H3 |
| Sammis, Nehemiah | Q | ........ | 76-B2, 76-E |
| Sammis, Phillip | S | Huntington | 76-H2 |
| Sammis, Platt | S | Huntington | 76-H2 |
| Sammis, Reuben | S | Huntington | 75-H |
| Sammis, Selah | S | Huntington | 75-H non-signer |
| Sammis, Silas Jr. | S | Huntington | 75-H |
| Sammis, Silas Sr. | S | Huntington | 75-H |
| Sammis, Timothy, Sergt. | S | Huntington | 76-H2 |
| Sammis, Timʸ | S | Huntington | 75-H |
| Sammis, William | S | Huntington | 75-H, 76-H2 |
| Sammis, Wm | S | Huntington | 75-H |
| Sammons, David | Q | ........ | 75-A |
| Sammons, Nehemiah | Q | ........ | 75-A |
| Sample, Thomas | N | New York | 76-A |
| Samuel, Sam. | N | New York | 76-A |

| | | | |
|---|---|---|---|
| Sandallan, William | N | New York | 74-A |
| Sanders, Abraham | N | New York | 74-A |
| Sandford, Abraham | S | Southampton | 75-M |
| Sandford, Benjamin | S | Southampton | 75-M |
| Sandford, Daniel Jun. | S | ........ | 75-R |
| Sandford, David | S | Southampton | 75-M |
| Sandford, David | S | Southampton | 76:1.4.0.4.1 |
| Sandford, David Jun' | S | Southampton | 75-M |
| Sandford, David, shoemaker | N | Moorefield Street | 75-D2 |
| Sandford, Elias | S | Southampton | 75-M |
| Sandford, Elias | S | Southampton | 76:0.1.4.1.2 |
| Sandford, Ezekeil H. | S | Southampton | 76:1.2.1.2.1 |
| Sandford, Ezekiel | S | Southampton | 75-M |
| Sandford, Ezekiel y$^e$ Third | S | Southampton | 75-M |
| Sandford, Henry | S | ........ | 75-R |
| Sandford, Henry | S | Southampton | 76:1.1.0.4.0 |
| Sandford, James | S | ........ | 75-R |
| Sandford, Joel | S | ........ | 75-R |
| Sandford, Joel | S | Southampton | 76:1.1.3.2.3 |
| Sandford, John | N | New York | 74-A |
| Sandford, John | S | Southampton | 75-M |
| Sandford, John, bricklayer | N | George Street | 75-D2 |
| Sandford, John, Capt. | S | Southampton | 76:1.1.3.4.3 |
| Sandford, Jonah | S | Southampton | 75-M |
| Sandford, Jonah | S | Southampton | 76:0.2.0.2.1 |
| Sandford, Josiah | S | Southampton | 75-M |
| Sandford, Lewis | S | Southampton | 75-M |
| Sandford, Nathan | S | Southampton | 75-M |
| Sandford, Silas | S | Southampton | 75-M |
| Sandford, Silas & Zephant' | S | Southampton | 76:0.2.0.0.0 |
| Sandford, Silvanus | S | ........ | 75-R |
| Sandford, Silvanus | S | Southampton | 76:0.1.0.1.0.0.1 |
| Sandford, Stephen | S | Southampton | 75-M |
| Sandford, Stephen | S | Southampton | 76:1.1.0.1.1 |
| Sandford, Thomas | S | Southampton | 75-M |
| Sandford, Thomas Esq. | S | Southampton | 75-M non-signer |
| Sandford, Thomas Esq. | S | Southampton | 76:1.1.0.2.1.1.0 |
| Sandford, William | S | Southampton | 75-M |
| Sandford, Zachariah | S | Southampton | 75-M |
| Sandford, Zecheriah | S | Southampton | 76:0.1.0.1.2 |

| Sands, Benjamin | Q | ........ | 75-A associator |
|---|---|---|---|
| Sands, Benjamin | Q | ........ | 76-E |
| Sands, Comfort | N | New York | 74-A |
| Sands, Comfort | N | New York | 74-T2, 11/24 |
| Sands, Cornwell | N | New York | 74-A |
| Sands, Edward | N | New York | 75-D3 |
| Sands, George | Q | ........ | 76-E |
| Sands, Henry | Q | ........ | 76-E |
| Sands, John | N | New York | 75-R |
| Sands, John | Q | ........ | 75-A associator |
| Sands, John | Q | ........ | 76-E |
| Sands, John Jr. | Q | ........ | 75-A, 76-B |
| Sands, Joshua | N | New York | 76-N |
| Sands, Pelham | Q | ........ | 75-A |
| Sands, Pelham | Q | ........ | 76-B, 76-E |
| Sands, Richard | N | New York | 76-N |
| Sands, Richardson | N | New York | 75-D3 |
| Sands, Samuel | Q | ........ | 76-E |
| Sands, Simon | Q | ........ | 75-A associator |
| Sands, Simon | Q | ........ | 76-E |
| Sands, Stephen | N | New York | 74-A |
| Sands, Stephen, clockmaker | N | New York | 74-T |
| Sands, Thom[s] | S | Huntington | 75-H |
| Sanfar, Jacob | N | New York | 76-A |
| Sanford, Abraham | S | Southampton | 76:0.1.1.1.3 |
| Sanford, Daniell | S | Southampton | 76:0.2.4.1.2 |
| Sargent, William | N | New York | 74-A |
| Sarly, Jacob, Capt. | N | New York | 76-V |
| Satterly, Daniel | S | Brookhaven | 75-B10 |
| Satterly, Daniel | S | Brookhaven | 75-B11 n.s. |
| Satterly, Daniel | S | Brookhaven | 76:0.1.1.2.0 |
| Satterly, Elnathan | S | Brookhaven | 75-B8 |
| Satterly, Elnathan & B | S | Brookhaven | 76:0.2.3.3.5 |
| Satterly, John | S | Brookhaven | 75-B10 |
| Satterly, John | S | Brookhaven | 75-B11 n.s. |
| Satterly, Mary, widdow | S | Brookhaven | 76:0.0.0.2.2 |
| Satterly, Richard | S | Brookhaven | 75-B8 |
| Satterly, Stephen | S | Brookhaven | 75-B3, 75-B6 |
| Saturly, Josiah | S | Brookhaven | 75-B7 |
| Saturly, Samuel | S | Brookhaven | 75-B1, 75-B7 |

| | | | |
|---|---|---|---|
| Saunders, Abraham | N | New York | 76-I |
| Saunders, Abraham, Capt. | N | New York | 74-V |
| Saunders, John | N | New York | 76-A |
| Sause, Richard | N | New York | 74-A |
| Sause, Richard, merchant | N | Fly Market | 74-T2, 5/26 |
| Savage, Barnt, Ensign | N | New York | 75-A |
| Savage, James | N | New York | 75-R |
| Sawyer, Benjamin | S | Shelter Island | 75-K |
| Sawyer, Benjamin | S | Shelter Island | 76:0.3.3.2.2 |
| Sawyer, Francis | N | New York | 76-L |
| Sawyer, Moses | S | Shelter Island | 75-K |
| Sawyer, Moses | S | Shelter Island | 76:0.1.2.2.2 |
| Sawyer, Moses Mable | S | Shelter Island | 75-K |
| Sawyer, Richard | S | Shelter Island | 75-K |
| Saxtan, Caleb | S | Islip | 75-I |
| Saxton, Caleb | S | Islip | 76:0.1.1.1.0 |
| Saxton, Isaac | S | Huntington | 75-H non-signer |
| Saxton, Isrel | S | Brookhaven | 76:1.0.2.4.0 |
| Saxton, W$^m$ | S | Brookhaven | 76:1.0.1.1.0.0.2 |
| Saxton, Zebulon | S | Islip | 76:0.1.2.4.1 |
| Sayer, Nehemiah | S | ........ | 75-R |
| Sayre, Benjamin | S | Southampton | 76:1.1.1.2.1 |
| Sayre, Benjamin 2$^d$ | S | ........ | 75-R |
| Sayre, Benjamin Jun$^r$ | S | Southampton | 76:0.1.0.2.0 |
| Sayre, David | S | Southampton | 76:0.2.2.1.1 |
| Sayre, David | S | Southampton | 76:0.3.1.1.1 |
| Sayre, David [2] | S | ........ | [on] 75-R |
| Sayre, Ichabod Jun$^r$ | S | ........ | 75-R |
| Sayre, James | S | ........ | 75-R |
| Sayre, John | S | ........ | 75-R |
| Sayres, Benjamin | S | ........ | 75-R |
| Sayres, Benjamin | S | Easthampton | 75-E |
| Sayrs, Abraham | S | Southampton | 76:0.1.3.1.1 |
| Sayrs, Ichabud Ju$^r$ | S | Southampton | 76:0.1.3.2.2 |
| Sayrs, Ickabud | S | Southampton | 76:1.1.0.2.0. |
| Sayrs, John | S | Southampton | 76:1.2.2.2.1 |
| Sayrs, Joseph | S | Southampton | 76:1.2.0.1.0 |
| Sayrs, Joshuah | S | Southampton | 76:0.1.6.1.0 |
| Sayrs, Mathew | S | Southampton | 76:0.1.5.3.1 |
| Sayrs, Nemiah | S | Southampton | 76:1.1.0.3.0 |

| | | | |
|---|---|---|---|
| Scande, Nicholas | N | New York | 76-A |
| Scandirith, Timothy | N | Fly Market | 76-H |
| Scandlin, John | N | New York | 74-T, 76-A |
| Scandlin, ____ Lieut. | N | New York | 74-T |
| Scandrett, Timothy | N | Fly Market | 76-I |
| Scandrett, Timothy | N | New York | 74-A |
| Scandrett, William | N | New York | 74-A, 76-I |
| Schart, Philip | N | New York | 74-A |
| Schaumburgh, Adam | N | Barrack Street | 76-H |
| Schaumburgh, Adam | N | Chathem Street | 76-I |
| Schaumburgh, Adam | N | New York | 74-A, 76-A |
| Schellenger, Abraham | S | Easthampton | 76:0.1.1.1.3 |
| Schellenger, Jonathan | S | Easthampton | 75-E |
| Schellenger, Jonathan | S | Easthampton | 76:0.2.2.2.3.1.0 |
| Schellenger, William | S | ........ | 75-R |
| Schellinger, Abra: | S | Easthampton | 75-E |
| Schellinger, Abraham | S | Southampton | 75-M |
| Schellinger, Daniel juner | S | Southampton | 75-M |
| Schellinger, Daniel [2] | S | Southampton | [on] 75-M |
| Schellinger, Isaac | S | Easthampton | 75-E |
| Schellinger, Isaac | S | Easthampton | 76:0.1.1.1.2 |
| Schellinger, Silas | S | Southampton | 76:0.1.0.1.1 |
| Schenck, Abraham | Q | ........ | 76-E |
| Schenck, Adrian | Q | ........ | 75-A, 76-B |
| Schenck, Jno. | Q | ........ | 75-A associator |
| Schenck, John | Q | ........ | 75-A, 76-B |
| Schenck, John | Q | Oyster Bay | 75-F |
| Schenck, John [2] | Q | ........ | [on] 76-E |
| Schenck, Martin | Q | ........ | 75-A associator |
| Schenck, Martin | Q | ........ | 76-E |
| Schenck, Martin Jr. | Q | ........ | 76-E |
| Schenck, Nicholas | Q | ........ | 75-A, 76-B |
| Schenck, Peter | Q | ........ | 76-E |
| Schenck. Mercer & Schenck | N | New York | 75-F |
| Schenk, Abrm. | N | New York | 74-A |
| Schenk, Peter A. | N | New York | 74-A |
| Schermerhorn, Peter, Lieut. | N | New York | 75-A |
| Schermerhorne, Peter | N | New York | 74-T2, 5/12 |
| Schiltz, Christian | N | New York | 74-A |
| Schoonmaker, Martinus | N | New York | 75-V |

| | | | |
|---|---|---|---|
| Schotler, Garret | N | New York | 74-A |
| Schultez, Coenradt | N | New York | 76-A |
| Schultz, Christian | N | New York | 76-A |
| Schultz, Christian, baker | N | New York | 74-V |
| Schurman, Garret | N | to Dutchess Co. | 76-P |
| Schutt, Johannes | N | to Dutchess Co. | 76-P |
| Schuyler, David | N | New York | 74-A |
| Schuyler, John | N | Dock Ward | 75-R overseer |
| Schuyler, John | N | New York | 74-A |
| Schuyler, John | N | New York | 75-F; 75-T2, 3/9 |
| Schuyler, Sam'l | N | New York | 74-A |
| Schuyler, Samuel | N | New York | 75-F |
| Schuyler, Samuel, storekpr | N | nr Fly Market | 74-T2, 5/19 |
| Scofel, Jonathan | S | Brookhaven | 76:0.1.1.1.1 |
| Scoot, Peter | Q | ........ | 76-B2 |
| Scorfield, Thomas | N | New York | 76-A, 76-H |
| Scott, Jackson Jun' | S | ........ | 75-R |
| Scott, Jacson | S | Southampton | 76:1.2.2.2.1.1.0 |
| Scott, Johan' | Q | ........ | 75-A |
| Scott, John Morin Esq. | N | Greenwich | 75-T |
| Scott, John Morin | N | New York | 74-T |
| Scott, Peter | Q | ........ | 75-A, 76-B |
| Scott, Peter R. | Q | ........ | 75-I |
| Scott, Robert | N | New York | 74-A |
| Scott, William | N | Fly Market | 76-H |
| Scott, William | N | New York | 76-A, 76-F |
| Scott, William, Broadway | N | nr Oswego Mart. | 76-I |
| Scribner, Ebenezer | S | Brookhaven | 75-B6 |
| Scribner, Joseph | S | Brookhaven | 76:1.0.2.1.1 |
| Scribner, Joseph Juner | S | Brookhaven | 76:0.1.0.1.0 |
| Scribner, Joseph Jun' | S | Brookhaven | 75-B6 |
| Scribner, Seth | S | Brookhaven | 75-B6 |
| Scribner, Seth | S | Brookhaven | 76:0.1.2.1.0 |
| Scudder, Benjamin | S | Huntington | 75-H1 |
| Scudder, Edmund | S | Huntington | 75-H |
| Scudder, Henry | S | Huntington | 75-H, 75-H1 |
| Scudder, Henry, 2d Lieut. | S | Huntington | 76-H3 |
| Scudder, Jacob, Sergt. | N | New York | 76-G |
| Scudder, Joel | S | Huntington | 75-H |
| Scudder, Joel, 2d Lt. | S | Huntington | 75-H1 |

| | | | |
|---|---|---|---|
| Scudder, John | S | Islip | 76:1.0.0.0.0.2.4 |
| Scudder, Jonah | S | Huntington | 75-H |
| Scudder, Jonathan | S | Huntington | 75-H, 75-H1 |
| Scudder, Moses | S | Huntington | 75-H1 |
| Scudder, Peter | S | Huntington | 75-H1 |
| Scudder, Samuel | N | New York | 74-A |
| Scudder, Thomas | S | Huntington | 76-H1 |
| Scudder, Thomas Jr. | S | Huntington | 75-H non-signer |
| Scudder, Thomas Jr. | S | Huntington | 75-H1 |
| Scudder, Timothy Jr. | S | Huntington | 75-H |
| Scudder, Timothy Sr. | S | Huntington | 75-H |
| Scudder, Will$^m$ | S | Huntington | 75-H |
| Scutler, Garrit, glazier | N | William Street | 75-D2 |
| Seabring, Frederick, blksm | N | at Fresh Water | 75-D1, D2 |
| Seabury, A. | Q | ........ | 76-B |
| Seabury, Adam | Q | ........ | 75-A |
| Seabury, David | N | New York | 74-A, 75-F |
| Seabury, David, merchant | N | Hanover Square | 74-T, 75-T |
| Seagroove, J. | N | New York | 76-A |
| Seagrove, P. | N | New York | 75-B |
| Sealy, Israel | Q | ........ | 75-A |
| Seaman, Abraham | Q | ........ | 76-E |
| Seaman, Ambrose | Q | ........ | 75-A, 76-E |
| Seaman, Benjamin | Q | Hempstead | 76-D |
| Seaman, David, distiller | N | New York | 74-T |
| Seaman, Edmund Esq. | N | New York | 74-T, 74-V |
| Seaman, Edmund Esq. | N | New York | 75-T merchant |
| Seaman, Eliz. (Zabriskie) | N | New York | 74-T |
| Seaman, Isaac | Q | ........ | 75-A |
| Seaman, Isaac | Q | ........ | 76-B, 76-E |
| Seaman, Israel | Q | ........ | 75-A, 76-E |
| Seaman, Jacob | Q | ........ | 76-E |
| Seaman, Jacob | Q | Hempstead | 76-D |
| Seaman, James, 1st Lieut. | N | New York | 76-Y |
| Seaman, Jno. William | Q | O. [Oyster Bay] | 75-A associator |
| Seaman, John | Q | ........ | 75-A, 76-B |
| Seaman, John | Q | Hempstead | 76-D |
| Seaman, John Wil$^{ms}$ | Q | Hempstead | 76-D |
| Seaman, Jonathan | Q | ........ | 76-E |
| Seaman, Joshua | N | New York | 76-A |

| Seaman, Obadiah | N | New York | 75-F |
|---|---|---|---|
| Seaman, Obadiah | Q | ........ | 76-E |
| Seaman, Obadiah | Q | Hempstead | 76-D |
| Seaman, Richd. | N | New York | 74-A |
| Seaman, Salomon | Q | ........ | 75-A |
| Seaman, Salomon | Q | Hempstead | 76-D |
| Seaman, Sam'l | Q | ........ | 75-A associator |
| Seaman, Sam'l, taylor | Q | ........ | 75-A |
| Seaman, Samuel | Q | ........ | 76-B, 76-E |
| Seaman, Samuel | Q | Hempstead | 76-D |
| Seaman, Solomon | Q | ........ | 76-E |
| Seaman, Stephen | N | New York | 74-A |
| Seaman, Th., cooper | Q | ........ | 76-E |
| Seaman, Thomas | Q | ........ | 76-B |
| Seaman, Thomas [2] | Q | ........ | [on] 75-A |
| Seaman, Thomas [2] | Q | ........ | [on] 76-E |
| Seaman, Willet | N | New York | 75-F |
| Seaman, William | Q | ........ | 75-A associator |
| Seaman, William | Q | Hempstead | 76-D |
| Seaman, Zeb. Jr. | Q | O. [Oyster Bay] | 75-A associator |
| Seaman, Zebulon | Q | ........ | 76-B |
| Seaman, Zebulum | Q | J. [Jerusalem] | 75-A |
| Seaman, Zebulun | Q | Hempstead | 76-D |
| Seamans, Israel | Q | ........ | 76-B |
| Seamans, James | N | New York | 76-A |
| Seamans, Levy | N | New York | 76-A |
| Seamors, Noah | Q | ........ | 76-E |
| Searing, Dan'l | Q | ........ | 75-A associator |
| Searing, Gilbert | Q | ........ | 75-A associator |
| Searing, Jacob | Q | ........ | 75-A associator |
| Searing, James | Q | ........ | 76-E |
| Searing, John | Q | ........ | 75-A associator |
| Searing, John [3] | Q | ........ | [on] 76-E |
| Searing, Jonathan | Q | ........ | 75-A, 76-E |
| Sears, Hester, dau Isaac | N | New York | 74-T |
| Sears, Isaac | N | New York | 74-A, 76-N |
| Sears, Isaac, merchant | N | Queen Street | 75-D2 |
| Seaton, Andrew | S | Brookhaven | 76:0.2.5.4.7 |
| Seaton, Rebecca wf of Wm | N | New York | 75-T |
| Seaton, William | N | New York | 75-T2, 5/4 |

| | | | |
|---|---|---|---|
| Seaton, William, merchant | N | New York | 75-T, 75-V |
| Sebring, Ab<sup>m</sup> | N | New York | 76-I |
| Sebring, Barent, juror | N | New York | 74-R, 75-R |
| Sebring, Barnet | N | New York | 74-A |
| Sebring, Cornelius | N | New York | 74-A |
| Sebring, Cornelius | N | New York | 74-T merchant |
| Sebring, Cornelius | N | New York | 76-N |
| Sebring, Cornelius, juror | N | New York | 75-R, 76-R |
| Sebring, Isaac | N | New York | 76-N |
| Sebring, John | N | New York | 75-F, 75-T |
| See, Paul | N | New York | 74-A |
| Seguin, James | N | New York | 74-A |
| Seixas, Benjamin | N | New York | 74-R, 75-B |
| Seixas, Benjamin, H.B. | N | New York | 74-A |
| Seixas, Gershom M. | N | New York | 74-A |
| Seixas, Isaac | N | New York | 74-A |
| Sell, Elizabeth | N | New York | 74-R |
| Sell, George, son of Eliz. | N | New York | 74-R apprentice |
| Sell, James | S | Brookhaven | 75-B1, 75-B7 |
| Sell, James Esq<sup>r</sup> | S | Brookhaven | 75-B9 |
| Sell, Jemes | S | Brookhaven | 76:0.1.2.2.3.2.2 |
| Sell, Wessel | S | Brookhaven | 75-B9 |
| Sell, Wessel, Clerk | S | Brookhaven | 75-B2 |
| Sell, Wessels | S | Brookhaven | 76:0.1.0.2.1.3.0 |
| Sells, James, 2<sup>d</sup> | S | Brookhaven | 75-B6 |
| Seloover, James | N | New York | 74-A |
| Semler, Casper | N | New York | 76-A |
| Senness, George | N | New York | 74-A |
| Sentis, Matthew | N | New York | 74-T |
| Serrain/Serren, Henry | N | New York | 75-D3 |
| Serrin, Jonathan | Q | ........ | 76-B |
| Servine, Thomas | N | New York | 76-B |
| Serwood, David | S | Brookhaven | 76:1.1.1.1.4 |
| Settle, James | N | New York | 74-A |
| Sexton, Israel | S | Brookhaven | 75-B10 |
| Sexton, William | S | Brookhaven | 75-B7 |
| Sexton, Zebulon | S | Islip | 75-I |
| Shadbolt, Embree | Q | Hempstead | 76-D |
| Shaddain, Henry | S | Huntington | 76-H3 |
| Shaddel, David | N | New York | 74-A, 75-D1 |

| | | | |
|---|---|---|---|
| Shadden, Henry | S | Smithtown | 76:0.2.2.1.2 |
| Shaden, Lewis, coachmaker | N | Broadway | 75-D2 |
| Shadford, Thomas | N | New York | 74-R |
| Shadwin, Lewis | N | New York | 75-D3 |
| Shafer, Jacob | N | New York | 76-A |
| Shaffer, Daniel | N | New York | 74-A |
| Shaffer, Jacob | N | New York | 75-D3 |
| Shaffer, Wm | N | New York | 74-A |
| Shaffers, Thomas | N | removed upstate | 76-P |
| Shannan, John | Q | Newtown | 75-G |
| Sharp, Richard | N | East Ward | 75-R overseer |
| Sharp, Richard | N | New York | 75-T2, 5/4 |
| Sharpe, Richard | N | New York | 74-T, 74-V |
| Sharpe, Richard, dry goods | N | New York | 75-F; 75-T2, 1/5 |
| Shatford, Wm | Q | ........ | 76-B |
| Shaver, Daniel | N | New York | 74-T insolvent |
| Shaver, Jacob, distiller | N | at Skinner's | 75-D2 |
| Shaw, Amos | Q | ........ | 75-A |
| Shaw, Charles | N | New York | 74-T2, 11/24 |
| Shaw, Daniel | N | New York | 76-N |
| Shaw, Daniel | N | New York | 76-R juror |
| Shaw, Daniel | S | Brookhaven | 75-B10 |
| Shaw, Daniel | S | Southold | 76:0.1.1.1.2.1.0 |
| Shaw, Daniel, Capt. | N | New York | 75-A |
| Shaw, George | N | New York | 76-A |
| Shaw, George, tanner | N | New York | 74-A |
| Shaw, Harman | Q | ........ | 75-A |
| Shaw, Henry | Q | ........ | 75-A, 76-E |
| Shaw, James | N | New York | 74-A, 76-A |
| Shaw, John | N | New York | 74-V |
| Shaw, John | N | New York | 76-A, 76-G |
| Shaw, Samuel | Q | ........ | 76-E |
| Sheafe, Henry | N | New York | 76-N |
| Shear, Moses | N | New York | 74-A |
| Sheen, Jacob | N | New York | 74-A |
| Sheen, John | N | New York | 74-A |
| Sheffield, Robert | S | ........ | 75-R |
| Sheffield, Robert | S | Easthampton | 76:0.2.1.0.0 |
| Sheir, Martin | N | New York | 76-I |
| Shemal, Valentine | N | New York | 74-R |

| | | | |
|---|---|---|---|
| Shepherd, Edward | N | New York | 74-A |
| Shepherd, Edward, barber | N | John Street | 75-D2 |
| Shepherd, Edward Jr. | N | New York | 75-D1 |
| Shepperd, Mary | N | removed upstate | 76-P |
| Sheppherd, John Jr. | N | New York | 76-A |
| Sherer, Wm | N | New York | 74-A |
| Sheril, Samuel Jr. | S | Easthampton | 75-E |
| Sherlott, Samuel | N | New York | 74-R |
| Sherman, Anthony | S | Southampton | 76:0.1.3.1.1 |
| Sherrel, Jacob | S | Easthampton | 75-E |
| Sherril, Abraham | S | Easthampton | 75-E |
| Sherril, Henry | S | Easthampton | 76:0.1.0.4.0 |
| Sherril, Jacobus | S | Easthampton | 76:1.2.4.2.1 |
| Sherril, Jeremiah | S | Easthampton | 75-E |
| Sherril, Recompens | S | Easthampton | 75-E |
| Sherril, Recompense | S | Easthampton | 76:1.2.0.2.0 |
| Sherril, Recompense Jr. | S | Easthampton | 75-E |
| Sherril, Recompense Jun$^r$ | S | Easthampton | 76:0.1.2.1.1 |
| Sherrill, Jeremiah | S | Easthampton | 76:0.1.1.1.1 |
| Sherrill, Jeremiah Jr. | S | Easthampton | 75-E |
| Sherrod, James | S | Brookhaven | 75-B6 |
| Sherwin, Joseph | N | New York | 74-R |
| Sherwood, ____ Lieut. | N | New York | 74-T |
| Sherwood, Moses | N | New York | 74-A, 76-I |
| Sherwood, Moses, constable | N | New York | 74-R to 76-R |
| Shewkirk, E. G. | N | New York | 76-A |
| Shields, William | N | New York | 75-R |
| Shier, Daniel | N | New York | 76-A |
| Shier, Henry | N | New York | 76-A |
| Shier, Martin | N | New York | 74-A, 76-A |
| Shingler, Henry | N | New York | 74-A |
| Shipten, William | N | New York | 76-F |
| Shoals, John | N | New York | 76-A |
| Shoals, John | Q | ........ | 75-A, 76-E |
| Shoals, John | Q | Hempstead | 75-H |
| Shoals, John | Q | Newtown | 75-B |
| Shober. Hodge & Shober | N | New York | 74-A |
| Shonnerd, Fred$^k$ | N | New York | 76-G |
| Shotwell, Abraham | N | New York | 76-A |
| Shotwell, Henry | N | New York | 74-A |

| | | | |
|---|---|---|---|
| Shouldis, John | N | New York | 76-A |
| Shuckburgh, ____ Mrs. | N | Broadway | 75-T2, 2/16 |
| Shundel, Christopher | N | New York | 76-A |
| Shurts, Aaron | N | to Dutchess Co. | 76-P |
| Shurts, Ann | N | to Dutchess Co. | 76-P |
| Shurts, Horatio Gates | N | to Dutchess Co. | 76-P |
| Shurts, Jacob | N | to Dutchess Co. | 76-P |
| Shurts, Jacob Jr. | N | to Dutchess Co. | 76-P |
| Shurts, John Washington | N | to Dutchess Co. | 76-P |
| Shurts, Margaret | N | to Dutchess Co. | 76-P |
| Shurts, Oliver | N | to Dutchess Co. | 76-P |
| Shurts, Susannah | N | to Dutchess Co. | 76-P |
| Shurts, William | N | to Dutchess Co. | 76-P |
| Shut, Henry, Light Horse | N | New York | 76-L |
| Shuts, Christopher | N | New York | 76-L |
| Sibley, Richard | N | New York | 74-A |
| Sibley, Richard | N | New York | 76-A, 76-F |
| Sickels, Ethan | N | New York | 76-N |
| Sickels, Ethan, leather | N | New York | 74-T2, 3/31 |
| Sickels, Henry [2] | N | New York | [on] 76-L |
| Sickles, Daniel | N | New York | 74-A, 76-V |
| Sickles, Daniel, hse crpntr | N | Broad Street | 75-D2 |
| Sickles, Michael, cooper | N | New York | 75-R |
| Sickles, Robert | N | New York | 74-A |
| Sickles, Zacharias | N | New York | 74-A |
| Sickles. Wickham & Sickles | N | New York | 75-F |
| Siegler, Goodheart | N | New York | 76-V |
| Siemon, John | N | New York | 74-A |
| Siemon, John, furrier | N | Hanover Square | 74-T |
| Sigler, Nathaniel | Q | ........ | 76-B |
| Silvester, Francis | N | New York | 74-A |
| Silvester, John | N | New York | 74-A |
| Silvester, John [2] | N | New York | [on] 76-L |
| Sim, Peter | N | New York | 76-N |
| Sime, Peter | N | New York | 74-A |
| Simm, Wm, b. Scot., ae 15 | N | New York | 74-T runaway |
| Simmerman, Henry | N | New York | 76-A |
| Simmons, John | N | opposite old mat$^y$ | 76-H |
| Simmons, John, innholder | N | New York | 75-T |
| Simmons, John, Wall Street | N | near City Hall | 76-I |

| | | | |
|---|---|---|---|
| Simmons, Joseph | N | New York | 76-A |
| Simmons, Joshua | N | New York | 74-R |
| Simmons, Samuel | Q | Jamaica | 75-C |
| Simnet, John, watchmaker | N | Murray's Wharf | 74-T2, 1/20 |
| Simon, Moses | S | Southold | 76:1.0.2.1.2 |
| Simons, Morice | N | New York | 74-T |
| Simons, Moses | S | Brookhaven | 75-B10 |
| Simons, Peter | S | Southold | 76:1.2.3.1.3 |
| Simons, Petter | S | Brookhaven | 75-B10 |
| Simonson, Aaron | Q | ........ | 76-E |
| Simonson, Charles | Q | ........ | 75-A, 76-E |
| Simonson, Jnº | Q | Hempstead | 76-D |
| Simonson, John | Q | ........ | 75-A, 76-B |
| Simonson, Mauris Jr. | Q | ........ | 75-A |
| Simonson, Mourris | Q | ........ | 76-E |
| Simonson, Simon | N | New York | 74-A |
| Simonson, Simon | Q | ........ | 76-E |
| Simpson, Catharine, widow | N | Nassau Street | 74-T |
| Simpson, George | N | New York | 76-A |
| Simpson, James | N | New York | 75-D2 |
| Simpson, Solomon | N | New York | 74-T2, 3/3 |
| Simson, Solomon | N | New York | 74-V |
| Sinclair, Jannett | N | New York | 75-V |
| Sinclair, Robert, merchant | N | New York | 75-V |
| Sinclair, Robt. | N | New York | 74-A |
| Sinclear, John | N | New York | 74-A |
| Sinerly, Dorothy | N | New York | 75-R |
| Sinklar, Yeofan | N | rem. to Bedford | 76-J |
| Sinnott, Thomas, cordwnr | N | Fresh Water St. | 75-D1, D2 |
| Sitcher, Wm, blacksmith | N | Maiden Lane | 75-D2 |
| Skaats, Bartholomew | N | silversm, Dey st | 75-D1, D2 |
| Skaats, Reynear, cartman | N | Dey Street | 75-D1, D2 |
| Skaats, Rinier | N | New York | 74-A |
| Skellhorn, Richard, brassfdr | N | Beaver Street | 75-T |
| Skellinger, Stephen | S | Southampton | 75-M |
| Skidmore, Daniel | Q | Jamaica | 75-E |
| Skidmore, Isaac | S | Huntington | 75-H, 75-H1 |
| Skidmore, Jno. Sr. | Q | ........ | 75-A associator |
| Skidmore, John | Q | ........ | 75-A associator |
| Skidmore, John | Q | Jamaica | 75-D associator |

| | | | |
|---|---|---|---|
| Skidmore, John Esq., Capt. | Q | Jamaica | 75-E |
| Skidmore, John J. | Q | ........ | 75-A associator |
| Skidmore, John J. | Q | Jamaica | 75-D associator |
| Skidmore, John Jr. | Q | Jamaica | 75-D associator |
| Skidmore, John [2] | Q | ........ | [on] 76-E |
| Skidmore, Jos. Sr. | Q | ........ | 76-E |
| Skidmore, Joseph | Q | ........ | 76-E |
| Skidmore, Joseph | S | Huntington | 76-H3 |
| Skidmore, Mica | S | Brookhaven | 75-B2 |
| Skidmore, Nathan | Q | ........ | 75-A, 76-E |
| Skidmore, Nathen | Q | Hempstead | 76-D |
| Skidmore, Peter | S | Brookhaven | 75-B9 |
| Skidmore, Peter | S | Brookhaven | 76:1.1.7.1.2.1.0 |
| Skidmore, Phillip | S | Huntington | 75-H |
| Skidmore, Sam[l] | S | Huntington | 75-H |
| Skidmore, Saml. Jr. | Q | ........ | 76-E |
| Skidmore, Samuel | Q | ........ | 76-E |
| Skidmore, Samuel | Q | Jamaica | 75-D associator |
| Skidmore, Samuel | S | Huntington | 75-H1 |
| Skidmore, Thomas | S | Huntington | 75-H non-signer |
| Skidmore, Thomas | S | Huntington | 75-H1 |
| Skidmore, Walter | Q | ........ | 76-E |
| Skidmore, Whitehead | Q | ........ | 75-A associator |
| Skidmore, Whitehead | Q | Jamaica | 75-D associator |
| Skidmore, Whithead | Q | ........ | 76-E |
| Skidmore, Zophar | S | Smithtown | 75-L recusant |
| Skidmore, Zophar | S | Smithtown | 76:0.1.1.1.3 |
| Skillin, John | N | New York | 75-D1 |
| Skillin, John, carrier | N | Ship Yards | 75-D1, D2 |
| Skinner, Jonathan Esq. | N | New York | 74-A |
| Skinner, S. Sp., distilller | N | New York | 74-T2, 3/17 |
| Skinner, Sam[l] Sp. | N | New York | 76-A |
| Skinner, Samuel S. | N | New York | 76-F |
| Slack, Forster | N | New York | 74-A, 75-D1 |
| Slack; see also Slight | | | |
| Sladdle, John, currier | N | Ferry Street | 75-D2 |
| Slayter, William | N | New York | 76-I |
| Slee, Nathaniel | N | Scotch Street | 74-T2, 5/12 |
| Slegel, John | N | New York | 75-D1 |
| Sleight, Matthew | N | New York | 74-T |

| | | | |
|---|---|---|---|
| Slidel, Mary | N | to Dutchess Co. | 76-P |
| Slidell, John | N | New York | 74-A, 76-A |
| Slidell, Joshua | N | New York | 76-A |
| Slidell, Michael | N | New York | 74-A |
| Slidle, Mary | N | to Westchester Co | 76-P |
| Slight, Forrester, sadler | N | at Stephen Hulls | 75-D2 |
| Sloan, John | N | New York | 76-A |
| Sloan, John, ship joiner | N | Queen Street | 75-D1, D2 |
| Slone, John | Q | ........ | 76-E |
| Sloo, Nathaniel | N | Scotch Street | 74-T |
| Sloson, Henry | N | New York | 76-N |
| Slover, Sarah | N | to Westchester Co | 76-P |
| Slow, William | N | New York | 76-I |
| Smalling, Chas. | Q | ........ | 75-A |
| Smalling, William | S | Huntington | 76-H3 |
| Smalling, William | S | Islip | 75-I |
| Smart, John | N | New York | 76-A |
| Smart, Thos. | N | New York | 74-A |
| Smealee, Walter | N | New York | 76-A |
| Smedes, Abraham | N | New York | 76-N |
| Smelzell, George | N | New York | 76-A |
| Smith, Aaron | S | Smithtown | 75-L |
| Smith, Aaron | S | Smithtown | 76:0.1.2.1.1.2.1 |
| Smith, Abner | S | Smithtown | 75-L |
| Smith, Abner | S | Smithtown | 76:0.1.1.1.3.0.3 |
| Smith, Albert | N | New York | 74-A, 76-A |
| Smith, Albert, Ensign | N | New York | 76-Y |
| Smith, Amos | Q | ........ | 75-A |
| Smith, Amos | Q | ........ | 76-B, 76-E |
| Smith, Amos | S | Brookhaven | 75-B10 |
| Smith, Amos | S | Brookhaven | 75-B11 n.s. |
| Smith, Amos | S | Huntington | 75-H |
| Smith, Ananias | S | Brookhaven | 75-B6 |
| Smith, Anenias | S | Brookhaven | 76:0.1.3.3.3 |
| Smith, Ann | N | removed upstate | 76-P |
| Smith, Annanias | S | Brookhaven | 75-B3 |
| Smith, Anthony, apprentice | N | New York | 74-R |
| Smith, Arthur | S | Brookhaven | 75-B10 |
| Smith, Arthur | S | Brookhaven | 75-B11 n.s. |
| Smith, Barnardus | N | New York | 74-A, 76-A |

| | | | |
|---|---|---|---|
| Smith, Benajah | S | Brookhaven | 75-B10 |
| Smith, Benajah | S | Brookhaven | 75-B11 n.s. |
| Smith, Benj. | Q | ........ | 76-E |
| Smith, Benj. [3] | Q | ........ | [on] 76-B |
| Smith, Benj'n | Q | ........ | 75-A |
| Smith, Benj'n | Q | Jamaica | 75-E |
| Smith, Benjamin | Q | R. [Rockaway] | 75-A, 76-E |
| Smith, Benjamin | S | Brookhaven | 75-B11 n.s. |
| Smith, Benjamin | S | Brookhaven | 75-B12 n.s. |
| Smith, Benjamin Jr. | Q | ........ | 76-E |
| Smith, Benjamin Juner | S | Brookhaven | 75-B11 n.s. |
| Smith, Benjamin [2] | S | Brookhaven | [on] 75-B10 |
| Smith, Benjmam | S | Brookhaven | 76:0.1.1.2.4 |
| Smith, Benjman | S | Brookhaven | 76:0.2.5.2.1 |
| Smith, Benj$^n$ | S | Meritches | 76:0.1.2.1.1 |
| Smith, Caleb | S | Smithtown | 75-L |
| Smith, Caleb | S | Smithtown | 76:1.1.1.1.1.2.2 |
| Smith, Catharine wid John | N | New York | 74-V |
| Smith, Charles | Q | ........ | 76-E |
| Smith, Charles | Q | Jamaica | 75-C |
| Smith, Charles | S | Brookhaven | 76:0.1.0.2.0.0.2 |
| Smith, Christopher | N | New York | 75-F, 76-A |
| Smith, Christopher | N | New York | 76-V merchant |
| Smith, Cornel | Q | ........ | 76-E |
| Smith, Cornell | Q | R. [Rockaway] | 75-A |
| Smith, Daniel | Q | ........ | 76-A |
| Smith, Daniel | Q | Jamaica | 75-D associator |
| Smith, Daniel | Q | Jamaica | 76-C |
| Smith, Daniel | Q | Rockaway | 76-B |
| Smith, Daniel | S | Brookhaven | 76:2.1.2.1.1.0.3 |
| Smith, Daniel | S | Huntington | 76-H3 |
| Smith, Daniel | S | Smithtown | 75-L Committee |
| Smith, Daniel | S | Smithtown | 75-H1 |
| Smith, Daniel | S | Smithtown | 76:1.0.0.2.2.6.0 |
| Smith, Daniel & Jemes | S | Brookhaven | 76:0.1.2.2.2 |
| Smith, Daniel Jr. | Q | ........ | 76-E |
| Smith, Daniel Juner | S | Brookhaven | 75-B11 n.s. |
| Smith, Daniel Junr. | S | Brookhaven | 75-B10 |
| Smith, Daniel [2] | Q | ........ | [on] 75-A |
| Smith, Daniel [2] | Q | ........ | [on] 76-E |

| Smith, Daniel [2] | S | Huntington | [on] 75-H |
| Smith, David | N | removed upstate | 76-P |
| Smith, David | S | Brookhaven | 75-B7 |
| Smith, David | S | Huntington | 75-H, 76-H3 |
| Smith, David | S | Smithtown | 75-L |
| Smith, Dayton | S | Southold | 76:1.0.1.2.1 |
| Smith, Dayton [2] | S | ........ | [on] 75-R |
| Smith, Ebenezer | S | Smithtown | 75-L |
| Smith, Ebenezer | S | Smithtown | 76:0.2.0.2.1.1.0 |
| Smith, Edmond | S | Brookhaven | 76:1.0.0.2.0.2.3 |
| Smith, Edmond Jun[r] | S | Smithtown | 76:0.1.0.0.0.7.5 |
| Smith, Edmund | S | Brookhaven | 75-B4, 75-B8 |
| Smith, Edmund | S | Smithtown | 75-H1 |
| Smith, Edmund Jun[r]. | S | Smithtown | 75-L Committee |
| Smith, Elemuel | S | Smithtown | 76:1.3.0.3.0.1.0 |
| Smith, Elemuel Sen[r] | S | Smithtown | 75-L |
| Smith, Elias | N | New York | 74-T2, 4/28 |
| Smith, Elias | Q | ........ | 75-A |
| Smith, Elifelat | S | Brookhaven | 76:0.1.1.1.1 |
| Smith, Elijah | Q | ........ | 76-B |
| Smith, Elijah | Q | Hempstead Plains | 75-T |
| Smith, Elijah | S | Brookhaven | 75-B10 |
| Smith, Elijah, blacksmith | S | Brookhaven | 75-B11 n.s. |
| Smith, Elijah R. | Q | ........ | 75-I |
| Smith, Elijah [2] | Q | ........ | [on] 75-A |
| Smith, Elnathan | S | Huntington | 75-H |
| Smith, Epenetus | S | Huntington | 75-H |
| Smith, Epenetus | S | Smithtown | 76:1.1.2.2.3.2.1 |
| Smith, Epenetus, Ch[m]. | S | Smithtown | 75-L Committee |
| Smith, Ephraim | S | Brookhaven | 75-B3, 75-B6 |
| Smith, Ephraim | S | Brookhaven | 76:0.1.2.1.1 |
| Smith, Floyd | S | Huntington | 76-H3 |
| Smith, Floyd | S | Smithtown | 75-L |
| Smith, Floyd | S | Smithtown | 75-L |
| Smith, Floyd | S | Smithtown | 76:1.1.0.3.1.2.4 |
| Smith, Gab'l | Q | ........ | 75-A associator |
| Smith, George | Q | ........ | 76-E |
| Smith, George | S | Islip | 75-I |
| Smith, Gerardus | N | New York | 76-L |
| Smith, Gerrard | N | New York | 74-A |

| | | | |
|---|---|---|---|
| Smith, Gersham | Q | Hempstead | 76-D |
| Smith, Gersham | S | Smithtown | 76:1.0.4.2.2 |
| Smith, Gershom | Q | ........ | 76-E |
| Smith, Gershom | S | Smithtown | 75-L recusant |
| Smith, Gilbart | S | Brookhaven | 76:1.1.2.2.2.1.0 |
| Smith, Gilbart Juner | S | Brookhaven | 76:0.1.4.1.2 |
| Smith, Gilbert | N | New York | 74-A, 75-D1 |
| Smith, Gilbert | S | Smithtown | 76:1.2.1.4.0 |
| Smith, Gilbert, Doctor | S | Brookhaven | 75-B11 n.s. |
| Smith, Gilbert Esq. | S | Brookhaven | 75-B10 |
| Smith, Gilbert Junior | S | Brookhaven | 75-B10 |
| Smith, Gilbor | S | Brookhaven | 75-B11 n.s. |
| Smith, Hannah, Widow | S | Southampton | 76:0.0.0.2.2 |
| Smith, Henery | S | Southampton | 76:0.1.0.1.1 |
| Smith, Henry | S | ........ | 75-R |
| Smith, Henry | S | Huntington | 75-H |
| Smith, Henry, scowerer | N | Great Dock Street | 74-T2, 12/8 |
| Smith, Hezekiah | S | Huntington | 76-H3 |
| Smith, Hezekiah [2] | S | Huntington | [on] 75-H |
| Smith, Hugh | S | Brookhaven | 75-B6 |
| Smith, Hugh | S | Meritches | 76:0.1.3.2.0.4.2 |
| Smith, Ichabod | S | Huntington | 75-H |
| Smith, Ichabod Jr. | S | Huntington | 75-H |
| Smith, Isaac | Q | ........ | 76-B |
| Smith, Isaac | Q | Hempstead Plains | 75-T |
| Smith, Isaac | S | Brookhaven | 75-B1, 75-B7 |
| Smith, Isaac | S | Brookhaven | 75-B10 |
| Smith, Isaac | S | Smithtown | 75-L |
| Smith, Isaac | S | Southampton | 76:0.1.1.1.0 |
| Smith, Isaac Esq. | Q | ........ | 75-A |
| Smith, Isaac Jr. | Q | ........ | 75-A |
| Smith, Isaac Jr. | S | Huntington | 75-H |
| Smith, Isaac Juner | S | Brookhaven | 75-B10 |
| Smith, Isaac Juner | S | Brookhaven | 75-B11 n.s. |
| Smith, Isaac Jun' | S | Brookhaven | 75-B7 n.s. |
| Smith, Isaac Jun' | S | Smithtown | 75-L |
| Smith, Isaac Sr. | S | Huntington | 75-H1 |
| Smith, Isaac [2] | Q | ........ | [on] 76-E |
| Smith, Isac | S | Brookhaven | 76:0.2.1.1.0 |
| Smith, Isac | S | Brookhaven | 76:1.1.2.2.2 |

| | | | |
|---|---|---|---|
| Smith, Isah | S | Brookhaven | 76:0.2.2.2.3 |
| Smith, Isaiah, Sergt. | S | Brookhaven | 75-B7 n.s. |
| Smith, Iserl | S | Brookhaven | 76:1.0.0.1.0.1.3 |
| Smith, Israel | Q | ........ | 76-B, 76-E |
| Smith, Israel | Q | Rockaway | 75-A |
| Smith, Israel | S | Brookhaven | 75-B10 |
| Smith, Israel | S | Huntington | 75-H |
| Smith, Jacob | N | New York | 76-L |
| Smith, Jacob | Q | ........ | 76-E |
| Smith, Jacob | S | Huntington | 75-H |
| Smith, Jacob | S | Smithtown | 75-L |
| Smith, Jacob | S | Smithtown | 76:0.1.2.3.2.1.2 |
| Smith, Jacob [2] | N | New York | [on] 74-A |
| Smith, James | N | New York | 75-T |
| Smith, James | N | New York | 76-R |
| Smith, James | Q | ........ | 76-B |
| Smith, James | Q | Rockaway | 75-A, 76-B |
| Smith, James | S | Brookhaven | 75-B10 |
| Smith, James | S | Brookhaven | 75-B7 Quaker |
| Smith, James | S | Huntington | 75-H, 76-H3 |
| Smith, James | S | Islip | 75-I |
| Smith, James | S | Islip | 76:0.2.2.2.1.2.0 |
| Smith, James | S | Smithtown | 75-L recusant |
| Smith, James Sr. | S | Huntington | 75-H |
| Smith, James [2] | N | New York | [on] 74-A |
| Smith, James [2] | N | New York | [on] 76-N |
| Smith, James [2] | Q | ........ | [on] 75-A |
| Smith, James [2] | Q | ........ | [on] 76-E |
| Smith, Jeffery | S | Smithtown | 75-H1 |
| Smith, Jeffery | S | Smithtown | 75-L |
| Smith, Jeffrey | S | Smithtown | 76:0.1.3.2.1.4.2 |
| Smith, Jemes | S | Brookhaven | 76:1.2.2.2.1 |
| Smith, Jerehmiah | S | Huntington | 75-H |
| Smith, Jesse | N | New York | 74-A, 76-G |
| Smith, Jesse | S | Huntington | 75-H, 76-H2 |
| Smith, Jesse | S | Smithtown | 75-L |
| Smith, Jesse, merchant | N | Dock Street | 75-D1, D2 |
| Smith, Jn° | Q | ........ | 75-A associator |
| Smith, Jno. | Q | Sp. [sic] | 75-A |
| Smith, Jno. Sam. | N | New York | 76-A |

| | | | |
|---|---|---|---|
| Smith, Jno., son of Sam. | Q | Rockaway | 75-A |
| Smith, Job | S | Huntington | 75-H, 76-H3 |
| Smith, Job | S | Smithtown | 75-L |
| Smith, Job | S | Smithtown | 76:1.1.3.1.1.5.4 |
| Smith, Job Jun‘ | S | Smithtown | 75-L |
| Smith, Joel | S | Huntington | 75-H |
| Smith, Johannis | N | New York | 76-A |
| Smith, John | N | New York | 74-R juror |
| Smith, John | N | New York | 76-A |
| Smith, John | N | New York | 76-F |
| Smith, John | N | to Dutchess Co. | 76-P |
| Smith, John | N | to Westchester Co | 76-P |
| Smith, John | Q | ........ | 75-A |
| Smith, John | Q | Jamaica | 75-C, 75-D |
| Smith, John | Q | Jamaica | 75-D associator |
| Smith, John | Q | Jamaica | 75-E, 76-C |
| Smith, John | Q | Rockaway | 75-A, 76-B |
| Smith, John | S | Brookhaven | 75-B11 n.s. |
| Smith, John | S | Brookhaven | 75-B3 |
| Smith, John | S | Brookhaven | 76:0.1.1.1.5 |
| Smith, John | S | Huntington | 75-H |
| Smith, John Juner | S | Brookhaven | 75-B11 n.s. |
| Smith, John W. | N | New York | 75-T |
| Smith, John [3] | N | New York | [on] 74-A |
| Smith, John [3] | S | Brookhaven | [on] 75-B6 |
| Smith, John [7 of the name] | Q | ........ | [on] 76-E |
| Smith, Jonathan | Q | ........ | 75-A |
| Smith, Jonathan | Q | ........ | 76-B2, 76-E |
| Smith, Jonathan | Q | Rockaway | 75-A |
| Smith, Jonathan | S | Brookhaven | 75-B10 |
| Smith, Jonathan | S | Brookhaven | 76:1.1.0.3.0.1.1 |
| Smith, Jonathan R. | Q | ........ | 76-I |
| Smith, Jos. Jr. | Q | Rockaway | 75-A |
| Smith, Joseph | N | New York | 76-N |
| Smith, Joseph | Q | ........ | 75-A, 76-E |
| Smith, Joseph | S | Huntington | 75-H |
| Smith, Joseph | S | Smithtown | 76:1.1.2.2.2 |
| Smith, Joseph Jur. | S | Smithtown | 75-L |
| Smith, Joseph R. | Q | ........ | 75-I |
| Smith, Joseph [2] | Q | Rockaway | [on] 75-A |

| Smith, Josh. | Q | Rockaway | 75-A |
|---|---|---|---|
| Smith, Joshua | Q | ........ | 76-B |
| Smith, Joshua | S | Smithtown | 75-L |
| Smith, Joshua | S | Smithtown | 76:0.1.2.1.2.2.0 |
| Smith, Josiah | S | Brookhaven | 75-B6 |
| Smith, Josiah | S | Huntington | 76-H2 |
| Smith, Josiah | S | Meritches | 76:1.0.1.3.0.7.0 |
| Smith, Josias, Capt. | N | New York | 74-T, 74-V |
| Smith, Jost Jr. | Q | Rockaway | 75-A |
| Smith, Jotham | S | Southampton | 76:0.2.0.1.2 |
| Smith, Lemuel | S | Huntington | 75-H |
| Smith, Lemuel Jun' | S | Smithtown | 75-L |
| Smith, Ludlam | Q | ........ | 75-A |
| Smith, Ludlam | Q | Jamaica | 75-C, 75-D |
| Smith, Ludlum | Q | ........ | 76-B |
| Smith, Margaret | S | Smithtown | 76:0.0.0.1.2.3.2 |
| Smith, Mary, Wid. | S | Southampton | 76:0.1.1.2.1 |
| Smith, Mathew | S | Huntington | 76-H3 |
| Smith, Mathew | S | Meritches | 76:1.0.2.3.1.4.3 |
| Smith, Matthew | S | Brookhaven | 75-B6 |
| Smith, Merrit | S | Smithtown | 76:0.1.0.1.1.0.1 |
| Smith, Micah | S | Smithtown | 75-L |
| Smith, Micah | S | Smithtown | 76:0.1.2.1.2.3.4 |
| Smith, Michael, chairmaker | N | Broad Street | 75-D1, D2 |
| Smith, Moses, merchant | N | Burling Slip | 75-D2 |
| Smith, Moubray | S | Islip | 76:0.2.6.2.2 |
| Smith, Mowbray | S | Islip | 75-I |
| Smith, Nanus | Q | Rockaway | 75-A |
| Smith, Nathan | S | Huntington | 76-H3 |
| Smith, Nathanael | S | Brookhaven | 75-B10 |
| Smith, Nathanael | S | Brookhaven | 75-B11 n.s. |
| Smith, Nathaniel | Q | ........ | 75-A, 76-A |
| Smith, Nathaniel | Q | ........ | 75-A associator |
| Smith, Nathaniel | Q | Jamaica | 75-D associator |
| Smith, Nathaniel | Q | Jamaica | 75-E |
| Smith, Nathaniel | S | Brookhaven | 75-B3, 75-B6 |
| Smith, Nathaniel | S | Brookhaven | 76:0.1.5.1.2 |
| Smith, Nathaniel | S | Brookhaven | 76:1.2.1.2.1.0.1 |
| Smith, Nathaniel | S | Huntington | 76-H3 |
| Smith, Nathaniel | S | Islip | 75-I non-signer |

| | | | |
|---|---|---|---|
| Smith, Nathaniel | S | Islip | 76:0.1.1.1.1 |
| Smith, Nathaniel | S | Smithtown | 75-L |
| Smith, Nathaniel | S | Smithtown | 76:0.2.1.1.3.1.0 |
| Smith, Nathaniel [2] | Q | ........ | [on] 76-E |
| Smith, Nath[l] | S | Huntington | 75-H |
| Smith, Nath[l] | S | Huntington | 75-H non-signer |
| Smith, Nehemiah | Q | Jamaica | 76-C |
| Smith, Nicholas | Q | ........ | 75-A associator |
| Smith, Nicholas | Q | ........ | 76-E |
| Smith, Nicholas | Q | Jamaica | 75-E |
| Smith, Nicholas Jr. | Q | ........ | 75-A associator |
| Smith, Nicholas Jr. | Q | Jamaica | 75-D associator |
| Smith, Nicholas Sr. | Q | Jamaica | 75-D associator |
| Smith, Noah | Q | ........ | 76-E |
| Smith, Noah | Q | Jamaica | 75-D associator |
| Smith, Noah Jr. | Q | ........ | 75-A associator |
| Smith, Noah Jr. | Q | Jamaica | 76-C |
| Smith, Noah Sr. | Q | ........ | 75-A associator |
| Smith, Obadiah | Q | ........ | 75-A, 76-B |
| Smith, Obadiah | Q | Jamaica | 75-D associator |
| Smith, Obadiah | Q | Jamaica | 75-E |
| Smith, Obadiah | S | Smithtown | 75-L |
| Smith, Obadiah Jun[r] | S | Smithtown | 76:1.1.1.2.1.2.5 |
| Smith, Obadiah Sen[r] | S | Smithtown | 76:1.3.0.1.0.1.5 |
| Smith, Obidiah | S | Smithtown | 75-L |
| Smith, Othniel | Q | ........ | 75-A associator |
| Smith, Othniel | Q | Jamaica | 75-D associator |
| Smith, Othniel, Ensign | Q | Jamaica | 76-C |
| Smith, Paschal Nelson | N | New York | 74-T |
| Smith, Patrick, als Pollen | N | New York | 74-R |
| Smith, Peleg | S | Huntington | 76-H2 |
| Smith, Peter | Q | ........ | 75-A associator |
| Smith, Peter | Q | Jamaica | 75-D associator |
| Smith, Peter | S | Smithtown | 75-L recusant |
| Smith, Peter Jr. | Q | ........ | 76-E |
| Smith, Peter Sr. | Q | ........ | 76-E |
| Smith, Phascal | N | New York | 75-D2 |
| Smith, Philetus | S | Smithtown | 75-H1 |
| Smith, Philetus | S | Smithtown | 75-L Committee |
| Smith, Philetus | S | Smithtown | 76:0.2.3.2.1.4.3 |

| | | | |
|---|---|---|---|
| Smith, Philip | S | Brookhaven | 75-B10 |
| Smith, Philip | S | Huntington | 75-H, 76-H1 |
| Smith, Phillip | S | Brookhaven | 75-B11 n.s. |
| Smith, Plat | S | Islip | 76:0.1.0.1.2 |
| Smith, Platt | Q | ........ | 75-A associator |
| Smith, Platt | Q | ........ | 76-E |
| Smith, Platt | Q | Jamaica | 76-C |
| Smith, Platt | S | Islip | 75-I non-signer |
| Smith, Richard | N | New York | 74-A, 76-A |
| Smith, Richard | Q | ........ | 76-A |
| Smith, Richard | Q | Hempstead | 76-D |
| Smith, Richard | Q | Jamaica | 75-E |
| Smith, Richard | S | Smithtown | 75-L |
| Smith, Richard | S | Smithtown | 76:0.1.3.1.1.4.3 |
| Smith, Richard, housecrpntr | N | New York | 75-T |
| Smith, Richard William | N | New York | 75-R apprentice |
| Smith, Richard [2] | Q | ........ | [on] 75-A |
| Smith, Richard [2] | Q | ........ | [on] 76-B |
| Smith, Richard [4] | Q | ........ | [on] 76-E |
| Smith, Robert | N | New York | 74-A, 76-A |
| Smith, Rock | Q | ........ | 76-B |
| Smith, Rock, Nanus' Rock | Q | ........ | 75-I |
| Smith, Roger | N | New York | 74-A |
| Smith, Ruth, widdow | S | Southampton | 76:0.0.1.1.1.1.1 |
| Smith, S. | Q | Rockaway | 75-I |
| Smith, Sam'l | Q | Jamaica | 75-A associator |
| Smith, Sam'l | Q | Jamaica | 75-D associator |
| Smith, Sam'l, taylor | Q | ........ | 75-A |
| Smith, Samuel | Q | ........ | 75-A, 76-B |
| Smith, Samuel | Q | Rockaway | 75-A |
| Smith, Samuel | S | Huntington | 75-H |
| Smith, Samuel | S | Smithtown | 75-L |
| Smith, Samuel, 1st Lieut. | S | Huntington | 76-H3 |
| Smith, Samuel Jr. | Q | ........ | 76-E |
| Smith, Samuel [3] | Q | ........ | [on] 76-E |
| Smith, Selah | S | Brookhaven | 75-B8 |
| Smith, Selah | S | Brookhaven | 76:0.1.0.1.0 |
| Smith, Shubal | S | Huntington | 75-H |
| Smith, Silas | Q | ........ | 76-E |
| Smith, Silas | S | Brookhaven | 75-B10 |

| | | | |
|---|---|---|---|
| Smith, Silas | S | Brookhaven | 75-B11 n.s. |
| Smith, Silas | S | Huntington | 75-H |
| Smith, Silas | S | Islip | 76:0.1.1.1.4.0 |
| Smith, Siloh | Q | ........ | 76-B |
| Smith, Silvester | Q | Jamaica | 75-E |
| Smith, Simeon | Q | Jamaica | 75-E |
| Smith, Solomon | S | Smithtown | 75-L |
| Smith, Solomon | S | Smithtown | 76:1.0.0.4.0.4.2 |
| Smith, Stephen | N | New York | 76-D |
| Smith, Stephen | Q | ........ | 75-A, 76-E |
| Smith, Stephen | S | Smithtown | 75-L recusant |
| Smith, Stephen | S | Smithtown | 76:1.0.1.1.0.1.0 |
| Smith, Stephen Sen' | S | Smithtown | 76:1.1.3.2.0.1.0 |
| Smith, Thaddeus | S | Huntington | 75-H |
| Smith, Thomas | N | Hanover Square | 74-T |
| Smith, Thomas | N | New York | 76-A |
| Smith, Thomas | N | removed upstate | 76-P |
| Smith, Thomas | S | Brookhaven | 75-B4, 75-B8 |
| Smith, Thomas | S | Brookhaven | 76:0.1.0.2.1 |
| Smith, Thomas | S | Islip | 75-I |
| Smith, Thomas Jr. | Q | ........ | 76-B, 76-E |
| Smith, Thomas [2] | Q | ........ | [on] 76-E |
| Smith, Thos. Esq. (Justice) | Q | Oyster Bay | 75-A, 75-H |
| Smith, Thos. Howell | Q | ........ | 76-E |
| Smith, Thos. Jr. | Q | Oyster Bay | 75-A |
| Smith, Timothy | Q | ........ | 76-E |
| Smith, Timothy | S | Brookhaven | 75-B10 |
| Smith, Timothy | S | Brookhaven | 75-B11 n.s. |
| Smith, Timothy | S | Huntington | 75-H |
| Smith, Timothy | S | Islip | 76:0.2.5.2.1.2.2 |
| Smith, Uriah | S | Brookhaven | 75-B7 |
| Smith, Uriah | S | Brookhaven | 76:0.2.1.2.1 |
| Smith, W. | N | New York | 75-D2 |
| Smith, W. | Q | Cow Neck | 76-E |
| Smith, W. Jr. [2] | Q | ........ | [on] 76-E |
| Smith, Wait | Q | ........ | 75-A associator |
| Smith, Wait | Q | Jamaica | 75-D associator |
| Smith, Walter | Q | ........ | 75-A associator |
| Smith, Walter | Q | ........ | 76-E |
| Smith, Walter | Q | Jamaica | 75-E |

| | | | |
|---|---|---|---|
| Smith, Waters | Q | Jamaica | 75-D associator |
| Smith, Waters | Q | Newtown | 76-V |
| Smith, Willaim | S | Smithtown | 75-L recusant |
| Smith, William | Q | ........ | 75-A |
| Smith, William | Q | Jamaica | 75-C |
| Smith, William | S | Brookhaven | 75-B6 |
| Smith, William | S | Brookhaven | 75-B8, B10 |
| Smith, William | S | Islip | 75-I |
| Smith, William | S | Islip | 76:1.2.2.3.3 |
| Smith, William | S | Meritches | 76:1.1.1.3.1.1.0 |
| Smith, William, blockmaker | N | William Street | 75-D1, D2 |
| Smith, William, Col. | S | Huntington | 75-H non-signer |
| Smith, William, Ensign | N | New York | 76-G, 76-S |
| Smith, William Juner | S | Islip | 75-I |
| Smith, William Jun' | S | Smithtown | 76:0.1.1.1.1 |
| Smith, William, juror | N | New York | 75-R, 76-R |
| Smith, William Sen' | S | Smithtown | 76:0.1.0.3.1 |
| Smith, William, whitesmith | N | Crown Street | 75-D1, D2 |
| Smith, William [2] | Q | ........ | [on] 76-E |
| Smith, William [3] | N | New York | [on] 76-A |
| Smith, William [4] | N | New York | [on] 74-A |
| Smith, Will$^m$ | N | New York | 75-D1 |
| Smith, W$^m$ | S | Meritches | 76:1.1.2.2.4.6.2 |
| Smith, Wm. | Q | Rockaway | 75-A, 76-B |
| Smith, Zadoc | S | Huntington | 75-H |
| Smith, Zeb. | Q | ........ | 76-E |
| Smith, Zeb. | Q | Rockaway | 75-A |
| Smith, Zebulon | Q | ........ | 76-B |
| Smith, Zebulon | S | Huntington | 75-H |
| Smith, Zebulon R. Jr. | Q | ........ | 75-I |
| Smith, Zepheniah | S | Brookhaven | 75-B11 n.s. |
| Smith, Zephinias | S | Brookhaven | 75-B10 |
| Smylie, John | N | to Dutchess Co. | 76-P |
| Smylie, Peggy, widow | N | to Dutchess Co. | 76-P |
| Snaith, Thomas, servant | N | New York | 74-V runaway |
| Snedecar, John | S | Huntington | 75-H |
| Snedeker, Abraham | Q | ........ | 76-E |
| Snedeker, Abraham | Q | Jamaica | 75-C |
| Snedeker, Albert | Q | ........ | 76-E |
| Snedeker, Barent | Q | ........ | 75-A, 76-B |

| | | | |
|---|---|---|---|
| Snedeker, Barent [2] | Q | ........ | [on] 76-E |
| Snedeker, Christian | Q | ........ | 75-A |
| Snedeker, Christian | Q | ........ | 76-B, 76-E |
| Snedeker, Garret | Q | ........ | 76-B2 |
| Snedeker, Garret | Q | Jamaica | 75-D |
| Snedeker, Gilbert | Q | ........ | 76-B |
| Snedeker, Gorce | Q | ........ | 76-E |
| Snedeker, Isaac | Q | ........ | 76-B |
| Snedeker, Jno. Jr. | Q | ........ | 75-A |
| Snedeker, Joha. | Q | ........ | 76-E |
| Snedeker, Johannes | Q | ........ | 75-A, 76-E |
| Snedeker, Johannes | Q | Jamaica | 75-C, 75-D |
| Snedeker, John | Q | ........ | 76-B, 76-E |
| Snedeker, John | Q | Jamaica | 75-C |
| Snedeker, Rem [2] | Q | Jamaica | [on] 75-C |
| Snedeker, W. | Q | ........ | 76-E |
| Sneed, Ezechl. | N | New York | 74-A |
| Sneed, Ezekiel | N | New York | 75-R |
| Snell, John | N | New York | 76-A, 76-I |
| Snider, Peter | N | New York | 75-R |
| Sniffen, Peter | Q | ........ | 76-E |
| Snoughte, Johonis | N | New York | 74-A |
| Snow, John | Q | ........ | 76-E |
| Snowden, Randolph | N | New York | 76-A |
| Snyder, John | S | Brookhaven | 75-B6 |
| Snyder, Simon | N | New York | 74-A |
| Snyder, Simon, stonecutter | N | at Mr. Suddeker | 75-D1, D2 |
| Snyder, William | N | New York | 74-A |
| Sobouvon, Henry | N | New York | 76-A |
| Sodi, Pietro, teacher | N | New York | 74-T2, 5/5 |
| Solomons, Isaac | N | New York | 76-A |
| Somandyke, John | N | Fresh Water | 76-I |
| Somerendike, Jacob | N | New York | 74-R |
| Somerendyke, Nicholas | N | chairmkr, Bowry | 75-D1, D2 |
| Somerindick, Teunis | N | New York | 74-A |
| Somerindicke, Teunis | N | New York | 76-A |
| Somerndyck, John | N | Bowry Lane | 76-H |
| Somerndyck, John | N | New York | 76-L Light Horse |
| Somkye, Leon | N | New York | 74-A |
| Soper, David | S | Easthampton | 75-E |

| | | | |
|---|---|---|---|
| Soper, Ebeneazer | S | Brookhaven | 75-B10 |
| Soper, Elemuel | S | Smithtown | 76:0.1.1.1.1 |
| Soper, Ephraim | S | Brookhaven | 75-B10 |
| Soper, John | S | Huntington | 75-H non-signer |
| Soper, Jonah | S | Smithtown | 76:0.1.2.1.1 |
| Soper, Josiah | S | Huntington | 75-H |
| Soper, Moses | S | Huntington | 75-H, 76-H3 |
| Soper, Samuel | S | Smithtown | 75-L |
| Soper, William | S | Huntington | 75-H |
| Sopers, Ebenezar | S | Southold | 76:1.1.2.2.2 |
| Southard, Abel | Q | ........ | 76-B |
| Southard, Annanias | Q | ........ | 75-A, 76-E |
| Southard, Caleb | Q | ........ | 76-B, 76-E |
| Southard, James | Q | ........ | 75-A, 76-B |
| Southard, John | Q | ........ | 75-A, 76-B |
| Southard, Rich'd | Q | ........ | 75-A |
| Southard, Silvanus | Q | ........ | 75-A |
| Southard, Solomon | Q | ........ | 76-B |
| Southard, Thomas | Q | ........ | 75-A, 76-B |
| Soward, Joseph | S | Brookhaven | 75-B6 |
| Soward, Joseph | S | Brookhaven | 76:1.1.1.2.0 |
| Soward, Joseph Jr. | S | Brookhaven | 75-B1 |
| Soward, Joseph Jr. | S | Brookhaven | 75-B6, 75-B7 |
| Sowers, Thomas Esq., Capt | N | New York | 74-T, 74-V |
| Spalden, Michael | N | New York | 76-I |
| Sparling, Peter | N | New York | 76-A |
| Speaight, Richard | N | New York | 74-A, 74-R |
| Speaight, Richard, druggist | N | New York | 74-T2, 5/5 |
| Speer, Barant | N | New York | 74-A |
| Spence, Richard, boat bldr | N | Cherry Street | 75-D2 |
| Spencer, Richard | N | New York | 75-D1 |
| Spenns, William | N | New York | 76-A |
| Spers, John | N | New York | 76-A |
| Spicer, Abigail | N | New York | 76-I |
| Spicer, Benj. | S | ........ | 75-R |
| Spicer, Benjamin | S | Southampton | 76:0.1.0.0.0 |
| Spier, Hugh | N | New York | 76-A |
| Spier, John | N | New York | 76-A |
| Spirck, Frederick | N | New York | 76-A |
| Spofford, George | N | New York | 74-A, 75-F |

| | | | |
|---|---|---|---|
| Spoke, Cathrine | N | to Westchester Co | 76-P |
| Spooner, Thomas | N | New York | 75-R |
| Spragg, Edward | Q | ........ | 75-A, 76-B |
| Spragg, Elijah | Q | ........ | 75-A |
| Spragg, Elijah | Q | ........ | 76-B, 76-E |
| Spragg, John | Q | ........ | 75-A, 76-B |
| Spragg, Samuel | Q | ........ | 76-E |
| Spragg, Wm | Q | ........ | 75-A, 76-B |
| Sprague, Gideon | N | New York | 74-A |
| Spranger, Henry | N | New York | 74-A |
| Spranger, Henry | N | New York | 75-D1 |
| Spranger, Henry, carpenter | N | nr Trinity Church | 75-D1, D2 |
| Spring, Anne | N | to Dutchess Co. | 76-P |
| Spring, Charity | N | to Dutchess Co. | 76-P |
| Spring, Elizabeth | N | to Dutchess Co. | 76-P |
| Spring, Jane, Mrs. | N | to Dutchess Co. | 76-P |
| Spring, Jeremiah | N | to Dutchess Co. | 76-P |
| Spring, Peter | N | to Dutchess Co. | 76-P |
| Springall, Gregory | N | New York | 76-A |
| Springall, Gregory, distiller | N | Chapel Street | 75-T2, 4/13 |
| Springall, Gregory [2] | N | New York | [on] 74-A |
| Springer, Martin | N | to Westchester Co | 76-P |
| Springsteen, Casper | Q | ........ | 75-A, 76-B |
| Springsteen Harmanus | N | to Dutchess Co. | 76-P |
| Sproat, Hugh | N | New York | 76-A |
| Sproat, Thomas | N | New York | 76-A |
| Sprong, Casper | Q | ........ | 76-E |
| Spury, Jacob | N | New York | 76-A |
| Squiar, Ellis | S | Southampton | 76:0.1.2.1.4 |
| Squier, Abraham | S | ........ | 75-R |
| Squier, John | S | Huntington | 75-H, 75-H1 |
| Squier, Jonathan | S | Easthampton | 75-E |
| Squier, Jonothan | S | Easthampton | 76:0.1.1.1.1 |
| Squiraman, Garret | N | rem. to Bedford | 76-J |
| Squire, Abraham | S | Southampton | 76:0.1.0.1.5 |
| Squire, Stephen | S | Southampton | 76:0.1.4.1.1 |
| Stackhouse, Stacy, chairmkr | N | Wall St & B'way | 75-D1, D2 |
| Stackhus, Stacy | N | New York | 74-A |
| Stag, —— Mr., baker | N | New York | 75-V |
| Stagg, John [2] | N | New York | [on] 74-A |

| | | | |
|---|---|---|---|
| Stagg, Thomas | N | New York | 74-A |
| Stagg, Thomas, constable | N | New York | 75-R, 76-R |
| Stahl, Melcher | N | New York | 76-A |
| Stakes, John | N | New York | 74-R |
| Stakes, Nicholas | N | New York | 74-R, 76-R |
| Stakes, William, butcher | N | at the sign Dove | 75-D2 |
| Stallmann, Daniel | N | New York | 76-A |
| Stambrough, David | S | Southampton | 76:0.1.1.3.0 |
| Stambrough, Davis | S | ........ | 75-R |
| Stambrough, Eleazor | S | Southampton | 76:1.1.0.2.0 |
| Stambrough, Josiah | S | Southampton | 76:1.0.0.0.0 |
| Stambrough, Josiah Jun' | S | Southampton | 76:0.1.1.1.1 |
| Stambrough, Lewis | S | Southampton | 76:0.1.1.1.0 |
| Stambrough, Stephen | S | ........ | 75-R |
| Stambrough, Stephen | S | Southampton | 76:0.1.0.1.1 |
| Stambrough, Thomas | S | Southampton | 76:0.1.0.1.2. |
| Stamler, Christian, habitmkr | N | Queen Street | 75-T |
| Stamler, Christian, tailor | N | New York | 74-T2, 2/24 |
| Stanbrough, Elisha | S | ........ | 75-R |
| Stanbrough, Ezra | S | ........ | 75-R |
| Stanbrough, Josiah | S | ........ | 75-R |
| Stanbrough, Luis | S | ........ | 75-R |
| Stanbrough, Thomas | S | ........ | 75-R |
| Stanten, George | N | New York | 76-L |
| Stanton, Barnabas | S | ........ | 75-R |
| Stanton, George | N | New York | 74-A |
| Stanton, George | N | New York | 76-A |
| Stanton, Henry | N | Warren Street | 76-H, 76-I |
| Stanton, John, coachmaker | N | Broadway | 75-D1, D2 |
| Stanton, John, sloop owner | N | New York | 74-T2, 5/12 |
| Staples, John | N | New York | 74-A, 76-I |
| Stark, Thomas | N | removed upstate | 76-P |
| Starkings, Joseph | Q | ........ | 76-E |
| Statia, Rebeca, widow | N | removed upstate | 76-P |
| Stavener, Michael | N | New York | 76-A |
| Stecklin, John | N | New York | 76-L |
| Steed, William | Q | ........ | 76-E |
| Steed, William | Q | Jamaica | 75-D associator |
| Steedford, Hannah | N | New York | 76-I |
| Steel, John | N | New York | 76-A |

| | | | |
|---|---|---|---|
| Steel, Robert | N | New York | 76-A |
| Steel, Stephen | N | New York | 74-A |
| Steele, Thomas | N | Beekman Street | 75-V |
| Steenback, Anthony, shoemr | N | Little Queen St. | 75-D1, D2 |
| Steenbergh, S. V. | N | New York | 74-A |
| Stegh, John, Lieut. | N | New York | 76-L |
| Steil, John, taylor | N | New York | 74-T2, 5/5 |
| Stephen, Thomas | S | Southampton | 76:1.1.0.2.0.2.1 |
| Stephen, Thomas Jur. | S | Southampton | 76:0.1.2.1.1 |
| Stephens, Edward | S | ........ | 75-R |
| Stephens, John | N | New York | 74-A |
| Stephens, Thomas | S | ........ | 75-R |
| Stephens, William | S | Southampton | 76:0.1.2.1.1 |
| Stepple, William | N | New York | 74-T2, 8/18 |
| Stevens, Jno. | Q | ........ | 75-A |
| Stevenson, Hanah | N | removed upstate | 76-P |
| Stevenson, Hugh | N | New York | 74-R |
| Stevenson, John, merchant | N | New York | 75-T2, 1/5 |
| Stevenson, John, shoemaker | N | Ship Yards | 75-D1, D2 |
| Stevenson, Polly, widow | N | to Dutchess Co. | 76-P |
| Stevenson, Thomas | N | New York | 76-R juror |
| Steward, John | S | Brookhaven | 75-B8 |
| Steward, Lodowick | N | New York | 75-R |
| Stewart, Alexander | N | New York | 74-T merchant |
| Stewart, Catharine | N | removed upstate | 76-P |
| Stewart, James | N | New York | 74-R, 76-R |
| Stewart, James & Alexander | N | Cruger's Wharf | 74-T2, 4/21 |
| Stewart, James, 1st Lieut. | N | New York | 76-Y |
| Stewart, Jane | N | New York | 74-R |
| Stewart, Lodowick | N | New York | 74-R |
| Stewart, Susanna, wf Alex. | N | New York | 74-T |
| Stewart, William | N | New York | 75-F |
| Stewart, William, druggist | N | nr. Fly Market | 74-T |
| Steynvelt, Christopher | N | New York | 74-A |
| Stiles, Dan'l | N | New York | 74-A |
| Stiles, James | N | New York | 74-A |
| Stiles, James, planemaker | N | Barclay Street | 75-D1, D2 |
| Stiles, John | N | New York | 76-A |
| Stiles, John, Ensign | N | New York | 75-A |
| Stiles, Wm | Q | ........ | 76-B |

| | | | |
|---|---|---|---|
| Still, William | S | Brookhaven | 75-B1, 75-B6 |
| Still, William | S | Brookhaven | 75-B7 |
| Still, William | S | Brookhaven | 76:0.1.1.1.0 |
| Stillwell, John | N | New York | 74-A |
| Stillwell, John, hse crpntr | N | Murray Street | 75-D1, D2 |
| Stilwell, Anthony | N | New York | 74-A |
| Stilwell, Elias | N | New York | 75-R |
| Stilwell, Thomas | N | New York | 76-A |
| Stilwell, William | Q | ........ | 76-E |
| Stilwill, Anthony | N | New York | 74-A |
| Stimusson, Cristoffil | Q | Hempstead | 76-D |
| Stin, John | Q | Jamaica | 75-E |
| Stin, William | Q | Jamaica | 75-E |
| Stine, William | Q | Jamaica | 76-C |
| Stites, John, storekeeper | N | New York | 74-T2, 5/12 |
| Stites, William | Q | ........ | 76-B2, 76-E |
| Stitts, Wm | Q | ........ | 75-A |
| Stivers, Benj'n | Q | ........ | 75-A |
| Stocker, Henry | Q | ........ | 75-A associator |
| Stocker, Henry | Q | ........ | 76-E |
| Stocker, Jno. | Q | ........ | 75-A |
| Stockford, Thos. | Q | ........ | 75-A |
| Stockholm, Aaron | N | New York | 74-A, 76-N |
| Stockholm, Andrew | N | New York | 75-B, 76-N |
| Stockholm, Jan. | N | New York | 76-A |
| Stockholm, _____ Maj' | N | New York | 76-C |
| Stockholm, _____ Mr. | N | New York | 75-D3 |
| Stockton, Ann, lodgings | N | Great George St. | 74-T2, 3/24 |
| Stompf, Nicholas | N | New York | 76-A |
| Stonestreet, Philip | N | New York | 74-R, 76-A |
| Storer, James | S | Southampton | 76:0.1.1.1.1 |
| Storer, Nehemiah | S | ........ | 75-R |
| Storet, Benj. Jr., 1st Lieut. | N | New York | 76-Y |
| Storm, David | N | New York | 74-A |
| Storm, John | N | New York | 74-A |
| Storrs, John | S | Southold | 76:0.1.3.1.2.1.0 |
| Storrs, John [2] | S | ........ | [on] 75-R |
| Stout, Abraham | N | New York | 74-R juror |
| Stout, Benjamin | N | New York | 74-A |
| Stout, Benjamin | N | New York | 76-A, 76-F |

| | | | |
|---|---|---|---|
| Stout, Benjamin Jr. | N | New York | 76-A |
| Stout, John | N | New York | 76-L, 76-N |
| Stout, John B. | N | New York | 74-A, 76-A |
| Stout, John, Lieut. | N | New York | 76-G |
| Stout, Richard | N | New York | 76-A |
| Stout, Robert | N | New York | 76-A |
| Stoutenburgh, Isaac | N | New York | 74-A |
| Stoutenburgh, Isaac | N | New York | 75-R juror |
| Stoutenburgh, Isaac G. | N | New York | 74-A |
| Stoutenburgh, Jacobus | N | New York | 75-T2, 10/5 |
| Stoutenburgh, Jacobus | N | New York | 76-L Engineer |
| Stoutenburgh, Peter | N | New York | 74-A |
| Stoutenburgh, Peter, Capt. | N | New York | 75-A |
| Stoutenburgh, Peter, juror | N | New York | 75-R, 76-R |
| Stoutenburgh, Tobias | N | New York | 74-A |
| Stover, James | S | ........ | 75-R |
| Stover, Margaret | N | George at Wm st | 74-T2, 12/22 |
| Strachan, William | N | New York | 74-A |
| Stratten, Daniel | S | ........ | 75-R |
| Stratten, Jeremiah | S | ........ | 75-R |
| Stratten, Stephen | S | Easthampton | 75-E |
| Stratton, Benjamin | S | Easthampton | 75-E |
| Stratton, Benjamin | S | Easthampton | 76:0.1.0.2.1.0.1 |
| Stratton, Eliphalet | S | Huntington | 75-H, 75-H1 |
| Stratton, Jeremiah | S | Southampton | 76:1.1.0.4.2 |
| Stratton, John | S | Easthampton | 76:1.1.0.1.0 |
| Stratton, John | S | Smithtown | 75-L |
| Stratton, John | S | Smithtown | 76:0.1.1.1.1 |
| Stratton, John, 1st Sergt. | S | Huntington | 76-H3 |
| Stratton, John [2] | S | Easthampton | [on] 75-E |
| Stratton, Jonathan | S | Huntington | 75-H |
| Stratton, Matthew | S | Easthampton | 75-E |
| Stratton, Matthew | S | Easthampton | 76:0.1.2.1.3 |
| Stratton, Sam[l] | S | Huntington | 75-H |
| Stratton, Samuel | S | Easthampton | 75-E |
| Stratton, Stephen | S | Easthampton | 76:1.0.1.2.1 |
| Stratton, Stephen | S | Huntington | 75-H, 76-H2 |
| Striker, James | N | New York | 76-A, 76-Y |
| Stringham, Jacob | Q | ........ | 75-A, 76-B |
| Stringham, S. | Q | ........ | 76-E |

| | | | |
|---|---|---|---|
| Stringham, Samuel | Q | ........ | 75-A, 76-B |
| Stringhans, Joseph | N | New York | 76-A |
| Strong, Benajah | S | Islip | 75-I |
| Strong, Benajah | S | Islip | 76:0.2.1.2.2.3.2 |
| Strong, George | S | Easthampton | 75-E |
| Strong, John | S | Easthampton | 75-E |
| Strong, John | S | Easthampton | 76:0.1.2.2.0 |
| Strong, Martha | S | Brookhaven | 76:0.1.0.2.0.0.1 |
| Strong, Selah | S | Brookhaven | 76:0.1.3.3.2.2.2 |
| Strong, Selah Esq[r] | S | Brookhaven | 75-B9 |
| Strong, Selah Jr. | S | Brookhaven | 75-B4, 75-B8 |
| Stronge, George | S | Easthampton | 76:0.1.1.2.0 |
| Stroutter, Johannis | N | New York | 76-A |
| Strut, Joycen Moreule | N | New York | 75-D1 |
| Stryker, Henry | N | New York | 74-A |
| Stryker, James | N | New York | 74-A |
| Stuard, James, free negro | N | New York | 74-R |
| Stuart, Ann | N | New York | 75-T |
| Stuart, Elisabeth | N | rem. to Bedford | 76-J |
| Stuart, Jacob | N | to Dutchess Co. | 76-P |
| Stuart, James | N | New York | 76-A |
| Stuart, John | N | rem. to Bedford | 76-J |
| Stuart, Silas | S | ........ | 75-R |
| Stuart, Silas | S | Southampton | 76:0.1.3.1.3 |
| Stuck, Francis | N | New York | 76-A |
| Studiford, ____ widow | N | removed upstate | 76-P |
| Stymes, Frederick, Sergt. | N | New York | 76-C |
| Stymest, Benjamin | Q | ........ | 76-B2 |
| Stymets, Benjamin | N | New York | 74-A |
| Stymets, Frederick | N | New York | 74-A, 74-R |
| Stymets, Frederick, baker | N | Nassau Street | 75-D1, D2 |
| Stymets, Garet | N | New York | 76-L |
| Stymets, Gasper, hse crpntr | N | Moscite[?] Street | 75-D1, D2 |
| Subner, John | N | New York | 74-A |
| Suddeker, ____ Mr. | N | New York | 75-D2 |
| Sullivan, John | N | to Westchester Co | 76-P |
| Sullivan, John, breechesmkr | N | New York | 75-R |
| Sumerix, Henry | S | Brookhaven | 75-B6 |
| Sumers, Henery | S | Brookhaven | 76:0.1.0.1.2 |
| Suppler, John | N | New York | 75-D2 |

| | | | |
|---|---|---|---|
| Sutton, Caleb | N | New York | 76-A |
| Sutton, Robert | Q | ........ | 75-A, 76-B |
| Sutton, William | N | New York | 76-A |
| Suydam, Cornelius | Q | ........ | 75-A, 76-E |
| Suydam, Farnan's | Q | ........ | 76-E |
| Suydam, Hendr'k | Q | ........ | 76-E |
| Suydam, Henry | Q | ........ | 75-A |
| Suydam, J. | Q | Newtown | 75-B |
| Suydam, Jacob [2] | Q | ........ | [on] 76-E |
| Suydam, Jacobus | Q | ........ | 76-E |
| Suydam, John | Q | ........ | 75-A, 76-B |
| Suydam, John | Q | Newtown | 75-G |
| Suydam, John [2] | Q | ........ | [on] 76-E |
| Swales, Bellow | N | to Westchester Co | 76-P |
| Swan, Godfred | N | New York | 76-A |
| Swansin, William | N | New York | 74-A |
| Swansir, Will'm | N | New York | 76-A |
| Swanzer, ____ | N | George Street | 74-T2, 12/22 |
| Swarthout, Cornelius | N | New York | 76-I |
| Swartwout, Cornelius | N | New York | 74-A, 76-L |
| Swasey, Richard | S | Southold | 76:1.0.0.1.0.2.0 |
| Swasey, Richard Jun' | S | Southold | 76:1.0.2.2.5 |
| Sweasy, Joseph | S | Brookhaven | 75-B3 |
| Sweazey, Joseph | S | Brookhaven | 75-B6 |
| Sweedland, Christopher | N | New York | 76-A |
| Sweedland, Christopher | N | White Hall | 75-T2, 3/16 |
| Sweeten, John | N | New York | 76-I |
| Sweezey, Isaac | S | Brookhaven | 75-B6 |
| Swere, John | N | New York | 76-A |
| Swese, Richard iuner | S | Brookhaven | 75-B10 |
| Swesey, Stephen | S | Brookhaven | 76:1.1.0.1.0 |
| Swesy, James Jun' | S | Brookhaven | 75-B6 |
| Swesy, Stephen, 3[d] | S | Brookhaven | 75-B6 |
| Swezey, Abel | S | Brookhaven | 75-B1 |
| Swezey, Abel & wid. | S | Brookhaven | 76:0.2.6.4.3 |
| Swezey, Christopher | S | Brookhaven | 75-B1, 75-B7 |
| Swezey, Daniel | S | Brookhaven | 75-B1, 75-B7 |
| Swezey, Enos | S | Brookhaven | 75-B1 non-signer |
| Swezey, Enos | S | Brookhaven | 75-B7 |
| Swezey, Isaac | S | Brookhaven | 75-B1, 75-B7 |

| | | | |
|---|---|---|---|
| Swezey, James | S | Brookhaven | 75-B1, 75-B7 |
| Swezey, James Jr. | S | Brookhaven | 75-B1, 75-B7 |
| Swezey, Jemes | S | Brookhaven | 76:1.2.0.2.1 |
| Swezey, Stephen | S | Brookhaven | 75-B7 |
| Swezey, Stephen & wid. | S | Brookhaven | 76:1.2.3.3.3 |
| Swezey, Stephen, third | S | Brookhaven | 75-B7 |
| Swezey, William | S | Brookhaven | 75-B1, 75-B6 |
| Swezey, William, Corporal | S | Brookhaven | 75-B7 |
| Swezy, Abel | S | Brookhaven | 75-B6 |
| Swezy, James | S | Brookhaven | 75-B6 |
| Swigar, Paul | N | New York | 76-E |
| Swigard, John | N | New York | 75-D3 |
| Swiggard, Jona'n, Lieut. | N | New York | 75-A |
| Sword, Samuel | N | New York | 76-F |
| Sydal, John, constable | N | New York | 75-R, 76-R |
| Sydel, John | N | New York | 74-A |
| Sykes, Philip | N | New York | 76-A |
| Symons, Bob | N | New York | 76-B |
| Symons, Solomon | Q | ........ | 76-B |
| Tabele, Jacob | N | New York | 74-A |
| Taber, Amon | S | Southold | 76:1.0.0.3.0 |
| Taber, Amon Jr. | S | ........ | 75-R |
| Taber, Amon Junr. | S | Southold | 76:0.1.0.1.2 |
| Taber, Frederick | S | ........ | 75-R |
| Taber, Frederick | S | Southold | 76:0.1.1.1.0 |
| Table, John | N | removed upstate | 76-P |
| Taffy, see Toffe | | | |
| Tailer, William | N | New York | 76-A |
| Tallcott, George | Q | ........ | 75-H |
| Talleball, Christopher | S | Southold | 75-N non-signer |
| Taller, Isaac | N | New York | 74-A |
| Tallmadge, Samuel | S | Brookhaven | 75-B7 |
| Tallmage, Elisha | S | Easthampton | 75-E |
| Tallmage, Sam'l | S | Brookhaven | 75-B1 |
| Tallman, Harmanus, crpntr | N | Kings Street | 75-D1, D2 |
| Tallman; see also Taulman | | | |
| Talmadge, Benjamen | S | Brookhaven | 76:1.1.1.1.0 |
| Talmadge, David | S | Easthampton | 75-E |
| Talmage, Daniel | S | Southampton | 76:1.2.0.1.0 |
| Talmage, David | S | Easthampton | 76:0.1.2.2.0 |

| Talmage, David Jr. | S | Easthampton | 75-E |
| Talmage, David Jun' | S | Easthampton | 76:0.2.0.1.0 |
| Talmage, Enos | S | Easthampton | 75-E |
| Talmage, Enos | S | Easthampton | 76:0.1.2.2.2 |
| Talmage, Enos Jr. | S | Easthampton | 75-E |
| Talmage, Jeremiah | S | Easthampton | 75-E |
| Talmage, Jeremiah | S | Easthampton | 76:0.1.1.2.4 |
| Talmage, John | S | Brookhaven | 75-B8 |
| Talmage, John | S | Easthampton | 75-E |
| Talmage, John | S | Easthampton | 76:1.2.1.2.0 |
| Talmage, Joseph | S | ........ | 75-R |
| Talmage, Nathaniel | S | Easthampton | 75-E |
| Talmage, Nathaniel | S | Easthampton | 76:1.0.0.3.0 |
| Talmage, Thomas | S | Easthampton | 75-E |
| Talmage, Thomas | S | Easthampton | 76:1.0.0.3.3 |
| Talman, John | Q | ........ | 75-A |
| Talman, John | Q | ........ | 76-B, 76-E |
| Talman, John Jr. | Q | ........ | 76-E |
| Talman, Oliver | Q | ........ | 76-E |
| Talman, William | Q | ........ | 76-E |
| Talman; see also Tallman, Taulman | | | |
| Tankard, James, servant | N | New York | 74-T runaway |
| Tanner, J. and M., school | N | New York | 74-T |
| Tanner, John | N | New York | 74-A |
| Tanner, John | N | Smith Street | 75-T |
| Tapp, William | N | New York | 76-N |
| Tarbell, David | S | ........ | 75-R |
| Tarbell, Jonah | S | ........ | 75-R |
| Tarbell, Jonah | S | Southampton | 75-M |
| Tarbell, Jonah | S | Southampton | 76:1.1.2.1.1 |
| Tarbell, Sarah, Wid. | S | Southampton | 76:0.0.0.2.0 |
| Tarbell; see also Talleball | | | |
| Targe, John | N | New York | 74-A |
| Tattersall, Richard | Q | ........ | 75-A |
| Taulman, Peter | N | New York | 76-D |
| Tayler, Catherine | N | New York | 76-K |
| Tayler, William | N | New York | 74-A |
| Taylor, Adam | N | New York | 74-R |
| Taylor, Betsy | N | removed upstate | 76-P |
| Taylor, Chaterin | N | removed upstate | 76-P |

| | | | |
|---|---|---|---|
| Taylor, Edmund | N | New York | 74-A |
| Taylor, Fortunatus | S | Brookhaven | 75-B2 |
| Taylor, Fortunatus | S | Brookhaven | 76:0.1.2.1.1 |
| Taylor, George | S | Southold | 75-N |
| Taylor, George | S | Southold | 76:0.1.1.1.1 |
| Taylor, George, ship joiner | N | Queen Street | 75-D1, D2 |
| Taylor, Henry | N | New York | 74-A |
| Taylor, James | N | New York | 76-A |
| Taylor, James, ship joiner | N | Queen Street | 75-D1, D2 |
| Taylor, John | N | Gardin Street | 76-H |
| Taylor, John | N | Governeiors wharf | 76-I |
| Taylor, John | N | in the fields | 76-H |
| Taylor, John | N | near the Bridewell | 76-I |
| Taylor, John | N | New York | 74-V, 75-R |
| Taylor, John | N | New York | 76-M |
| Taylor, John | S | Huntington | 75-H |
| Taylor, John [2] | N | New York | [on] 74-A |
| Taylor, Jordan | S | Huntington | 75-H non-signer |
| Taylor, Moses Jr. | N | New York | 74-A |
| Taylor, Moses, taylor | N | Leary Street | 75-D2 |
| Taylor, Nathaniel | S | Huntington | 76-H3 |
| Taylor, Nathaniel | S | Smithtown | 75-L |
| Taylor, Nathaniel | S | Smithtown | 76:0.1.1.1.0.1.1 |
| Taylor, Stephen | N | New York | 76-R apprentice |
| Taylor, Stephen, shoemaker | N | at Goforth's | 75-D1, D2 |
| Taylor, Tim[y] | S | Huntington | 75-H |
| Taylor, Willet | N | New York | 74-T, 76-A |
| Taylor, Willett | N | New York | 74-A |
| Taylor, William | N | New York | 76-A |
| Taylor, William | S | Huntington | 76-H3 |
| Taylor, William [3] | N | New York | [on] 74-A |
| Teale, Doxse | S | Meritches | 76:0.2.3.1.2 |
| Tear, Daniel | N | Scotch Street | 74-T2, 4/14 |
| Teff, Elizabeth | N | New York | 76-I |
| Teller, Isaac | N | New York | 74-A |
| Teller, ____ Mrs. | N | removed upstate | 76-P |
| Teller, William | N | removed upstate | 76-P |
| Templeton, Oliver | N | New York | 75-T2, 5/4 |
| Templeton, Oliver, merch't | N | New York | 74-T |
| TenBroeck, William | N | New York | 76-D |

| | | | |
|---|---|---|---|
| TenEyck, Abrm. | N | New York | 74-A |
| TenEyck, Andrew | N | New York | 74-A, 76-L |
| TenEyck, Daniel | N | New York | 74-A, 76-L |
| TenEyck, Richard | N | New York | 74-A, 76-L |
| TenEyck, Thomas, Ensign | N | New York | 75-A |
| Teppet, Stephen | N | New York | 74-A |
| Ter, Daniel | N | New York | 74-A |
| Tergay, John | N | New York | 76-L |
| Terhune, Stephen | N | New York | 74-A |
| Terhune, Stephen | N | New York | 75-T2, 10/5 |
| Terhune, Stephen, painter | N | Crown Street | 75-D1, D2 |
| Terrett, William | N | New York | 74-A |
| Terril, Barnabas | S | Southold | 76:1.0.0.1.0.3.0 |
| Terril, Richard | S | Brookhaven | 75-B10 |
| Terrill, Barnabus | S | Brookhaven | 75-B10 |
| Terrill, Richard | S | Brookhaven | 75-B11 n.s. |
| Terry, Brewster | S | Brookhaven | 75-B1, 75-B6 |
| Terry, Bruster | S | Brookhaven | 76:0.1.3.1.2 |
| Terry, Daniel | Q | ........ | 76-E |
| Terry, Daniel | S | ........ | 75-R |
| Terry, Daniel | S | Southold | 76:0.1.1.1.0 |
| Terry, Daniel | S | Southold | 76:0.2.2.2.3 |
| Terry, Daniel | S | Southold | 76:0.3.1.2.3 |
| Terry, Daniel, yuner | S | Brookhaven | 75-B10 |
| Terry, David | S | ........ | 75-R |
| Terry, David | S | Southold | 76:1.2.1.2.1 |
| Terry, David Jun. | S | Southold | 75-N |
| Terry, David Junr. | S | Southold | 76:0.1.2.1.3 |
| Terry, Elijah | S | Southold | 76:0.2.6.1.1 |
| Terry, Gershom | S | Brookhaven | 75-B1, 75-B6 |
| Terry, Gershom | S | Brookhaven | 75-B7, 75-B10 |
| Terry, Gershom | S | Brookhaven | 76:1.1.0.3.0 |
| Terry, Gorshom | S | Southold | 76:0.1.1.1.0.0.1 |
| Terry, Gorshom | S | Southold | 76:0.1.1.2.1 |
| Terry, Hennery | S | Southold | 76:0.1.3.1.1 |
| Terry, Henry | S | Brookhaven | 75-B10 |
| Terry, Isaiah, Corporal | S | Southold | 75-N non-signer |
| Terry, James | S | Southampton | 75-M |
| Terry, Jeremiah | S | Easthampton | 75-E |
| Terry, Jeremiah | S | Easthampton | 76:0.1.2.1.3 |

| | | | |
|---|---|---|---|
| Terry, Jeremiah | S | Islip | 75-I |
| Terry, Jeremiah | S | Islip | 76:0.1.3.1.3 |
| Terry, John | S | Southold | 76:0.1.2.1.2 |
| Terry, John | S | Southold | 76:1.1.0.2.1 |
| Terry, John, Bateing Hollow | S | Southold | 75-N |
| Terry, John Cleves | S | Brookhaven | 75-B10 |
| Terry, John Jun. | S | ........ | 75-R |
| Terry, John, Wading River | S | Southold | 75-N |
| Terry, Jonathan | S | Southold | 75-N non-signer |
| Terry, Jonathan | S | Southold | 76:0.1.2.1.2.0.1 |
| Terry, Jonathan | S | Southold | 76:0.3.0.2.3 |
| Terry, Jonathan [2] | S | ........ | [on] 75-R |
| Terry, Joseph | S | ........ | 75-R |
| Terry, Joseph | S | Brookhaven | 75-B1, 75-B7 |
| Terry, Joseph | S | Brookhaven | 76:0.1.3.1.1 |
| Terry, Joseph | S | Southold | 76:0.1.2.1.2 |
| Terry, Joseph [2] | S | Brookhaven | [on] 75-B6 |
| Terry, Joshua | S | Southold | 76:0.3.3.0.0 |
| Terry, Joshua [2] | S | ........ | [on] 75-R |
| Terry, Noah | S | ........ | 75-R |
| Terry, Noah | S | Shelter Island | 76:0.1.2.1.1 |
| Terry, Paul | S | Brookhaven | 75-B6, 75-B7 |
| Terry, Richard | S | Southold | 76:0.2.3.3.3 |
| Terry, Richard | S | Southold | 76:1.1.0.2.0 |
| Terry, Richard [2] | S | ........ | [on] 75-R |
| Terry, Robert | S | Southold | 76:1.1.0.1.0.0.1 |
| Terry, Samuel | S | Brookhaven | 75-B7 |
| Terry, Shadrach | S | Smithtown | 76:0.1.0.1.0 |
| Terry, Thomas | S | Southold | 76:0.3.4.3.1.0.2 |
| Terry, Thomas, third | S | ........ | 75-R |
| Terry, William | S | Islip | 75-I |
| Terry, William | S | Islip | 76:0.1.1.1.1 |
| Tetard, I. G. | N | Kingsbridge | 74-V |
| Tetard, J.D., Rev. | N | Kingsbridge | 75-T |
| Tetley, William Birchall | N | portrait painter | 74-T |
| Tettil, Joshua | Q | ........ | 76-E |
| Thacher, Edward | N | Broad Street | 75-T |
| Tharp, James Murphy | N | New York | 74-V |
| Thatford, William | Q | ........ | 75-A |
| Thatford, William | Q | Jamaica | 75-C, 75-D |

| | | | |
|---|---|---|---|
| Thecher, Edward | N | New York | 75-T2, 1/19 |
| Thecher, Mary, hairdresser | N | Broad Street | 74-T2, 10/27 |
| Theston, see Thurston | | | |
| Thew, Tunis, Capt, mariner | N | Partition Street | 75-D1, D2 |
| Thibou, Lewis | N | New York | 74-A |
| Thilman, Nicholas | N | New York | 76-I |
| Thomas, David | N | New York | 76-A |
| Thomas, Henry | N | New York | 76-A, 76-L |
| Thomas, John | N | New York | 76-N |
| Thomas, John | Q | ........ | 76-E |
| Thomas, John | S | Huntington | 75-H |
| Thomas, Mary | N | New York | 76-I |
| Thomas, Peter | Q | ........ | 75-A, 76-E |
| Thomas, Robert | N | New York | 74-A |
| Thomas, Walter | N | New York | 76-A |
| Thomas, William | N | to Westchester Co | 76-P |
| Thompson, Andrew | N | New York | 74-A |
| Thompson, Andrew | N | New York | 75-D2 |
| Thompson, Andrew, brklyr | N | Fresh Water | 75-D1, D2 |
| Thompson, Archibald | N | to Dutchess Co. | 76-P |
| Thompson, David | N | New York | 74-R juror |
| Thompson, David | N | New York | 76-A |
| Thompson, Elias | S | Brookhaven | 75-B8 |
| Thompson, George | N | New York | 74-A, 76-A |
| Thompson, Isaac | S | Islip | 75-I |
| Thompson, James | N | New York | 74-A |
| Thompson, James | N | New York | 74-T, 74-V |
| Thompson, James, barber | N | Beekman Slip | 75-D2 |
| Thompson, Jno. | N | New York | 74-A |
| Thompson, John | S | Brookhaven | 75-B6 |
| Thompson, John [2] | N | New York | [on] 76-A |
| Thompson, Jonathan | S | Brookhaven | 75-B8 |
| Thompson, Jonathan | S | Brookhaven | 76:1.1.0.2.1.2.1 |
| Thompson, Margaret | N | removed upstate | 76-P |
| Thompson, Mary | N | New York | 76-I |
| Thompson, Peter | N | New York | 76-A |
| Thompson, Peter, bricklayer | N | Ferry Street | 75-D1, D2 |
| Thompson, Philip | N | New York | 74-A, 74-R |
| Thompson, Sam[l] | N | New York | 76-A |
| Thompson, Samuel | S | Brookhaven | 75-B4, 75-B8 |

| | | | |
|---|---|---|---|
| Thompson, Samul | S | Meritches | 76:1.2.0.2.2 |
| Thompson, William | S | Brookhaven | 75-B6 |
| Thompson, William | S | Meritches | 76:0.1.1.1.1 |
| Thompson, William | S | Smithtown | 75-L recusant |
| Thompson, William | S | Smithtown | 76:0.1.1.1.3 |
| Thompson, William [3] | N | New York | [on] 74-A |
| Thompson, Wm., shopkpr | N | Beekman Slip | 75-D2 |
| Thomson, Benjamin | S | Brookhaven | 75-B6 |
| Thomson, Isaac | S | Islip | 76:0.1.1.1.0.2.3 |
| Thomson, Jonathan | S | Brookhaven | 75-B4, 75-B6 |
| Thomson, Mary | N | New York | 74-R |
| Thomson, ____ Mr. | N | removed upstate | 76-P |
| Thomson, Robert | N | New York | 74-A, 76-L |
| Thomson, Susannah | N | New York | 74-R |
| Thomson, Zeb: | S | ........ | 75-R |
| Thomson, Zebulon | S | Southampton | 76:0.1.2.1.0 |
| Thonnaird, Fred. | N | New York | 76-A |
| Thorn, Catharine | N | removed upstate | 76-P |
| Thorn, Charles | Q | ........ | 76-E |
| Thorn, Dan'l | Q | Flushing | 75-H |
| Thorn, Jno., tanner | N | N.N. Anthony | 75-D2 |
| Thorn, Samuel, taylor | N | Cherry Street | 75-D2 |
| Thorn, Stephen | Q | ........ | 76-E |
| Thorn, Thomas | Q | ........ | 76-B |
| Thorn, William | N | New York | 75-D1 |
| Thorne, Benj. Jr. | Q | ........ | 76-E |
| Thorne, Benjamin | Q | ........ | 76-E |
| Thorne, Charles | N | New York | 74-A |
| Thorne, Daniel | Q | ........ | 76-E |
| Thorne, Edward | Q | ........ | 76-E |
| Thorne, George | Q | ........ | 76-E |
| Thorne, Jas. | Q | ........ | 75-A |
| Thorne, John | Q | Flushing | 75-A associator |
| Thorne, John | Q | Hempstead | 75-A associator |
| Thorne, John [2] | Q | ........ | [on] 76-E |
| Thorne, Joseph | Q | ........ | 76-B |
| Thorne, Joseph [3] | Q | ........ | [on] 76-E |
| Thorne, Melanthon | Q | ........ | 76-E |
| Thorne, Oliver | Q | ........ | 76-E |
| Thorne, Philip | Q | ........ | 75-A, 76-B |

| | | | |
|---|---|---|---|
| Thorne, Philip [2] | Q | ........ | [on] 76-E |
| Thorne, Richard | Q | ........ | 76-E |
| Thorne, Richard, Capt. | Q | ........ | 75-D1 |
| Thorne, Samuel [3] | Q | ........ | [on] 76-E |
| Thorne, Stephen | Q | ........ | 76-E |
| Thorne, Stephen Jr. | Q | ........ | 76-E |
| Thorne, Thomas | Q | ........ | 75-A |
| Thorne, Thomas | Q | ........ | 75-A associator |
| Thorne, Thomas | Q | ........ | 76-E |
| Thorne, Thomas Jr. | Q | ........ | 76-E |
| Thorne, William | N | New York | 74-A |
| Thorne, William | Q | ........ | 75-A associator |
| Thorne, Wm., taylor, store | N | Smith's Fly | 74-T2, 12/1 |
| Thorneycraft, Benj. | Q | ........ | 76-E |
| Thorneycraft, Henry | Q | ........ | 76-E |
| Thorneycraft, Joseph | Q | ........ | 76-E |
| Thorneycraft, Joseph | Q | Oyster Bay | 75-F |
| Thorneycraft, Peter | Q | ........ | 76-E |
| Thorneycraft, Robt. | Q | ........ | 76-E |
| Thorneycraft, W. | Q | ........ | 76-E |
| Thornhill, Rich'd | N | New York | 74-A |
| Thorp, John | N | New York | 74-A |
| Thurman, John Jr. | N | Wall Street | 75-T |
| Thurman, Ralph | N | New York | 74-A |
| Thurston, Benjamin | Q | Jamaica | 75-E |
| Thurston, Daniel | Q | ........ | 75-A |
| Thurston, John | Q | ........ | 75-A |
| Thurston, John | Q | ........ | 75-A associator |
| Thurston, John | Q | ........ | 76-B |
| Thurston, John | Q | Jamaica | 75-D associator |
| Thurston, Jonathan | Q | ........ | 75-A associator |
| Thurston, Jonathan | Q | Jamaica | 75-D associator |
| Thurston, Jonathan | Q | Jamaica | 76-C |
| Thurston, W. | Q | ........ | 76-E |
| Thurston, William | N | New York | 74-A |
| Thurston, William | Q | ........ | 75-A, 76-B |
| Thurston, William | Q | Jamaica | 75-E |
| Thurston, William, wheelwt | N | Broadway | 75-D1, D2 |
| Tidd, William | N | to Westchester Co | 76-P |
| Tiebou, Lewis | N | New York | 76-L |

| | | | |
|---|---|---|---|
| Tiebout, Albertus | N | New York | 76-A |
| Tiebout, Catharine | N | New York | 74-R |
| Tiebout, Henry | N | New York | 74-A |
| Tiebout, Henry | N | New York | 74-R juror |
| Tiebout, Henry | N | New York | 75-B, 75-D2 |
| Tiebout, Henry | N | New York | 76-N |
| Tiebout, Henry, 1st Lieut. | N | New York | 76-C |
| Tiebout, Jones | N | New York | 74-A |
| Tiebout, Mary | N | New York | 74-T |
| Tiebout, Theunis, carpenter | N | Golden Hill | 75-D2 |
| Tiebout, Tunis | N | New York | 74-A |
| Tier, Mathias | N | New York | 76-L |
| Tiler, Benjamen | S | Brookhaven | 76:0.1.2.1.3 |
| Tiler, David | S | Brookhaven | 76:0.1.1.2.2 |
| Till, Robert | N | New York | 76-A |
| Tiller, Benjamin | S | Brookhaven | 75-B10 |
| Tillerson, Samuel | S | Southold | 76:0.1.3.2.0.1.0 |
| Tilletson, Samuel | S | Smithtown | 76:1.2.2.4.0 |
| Tilley, David | Q | ........ | 76-E |
| Tilley, John | Q | ........ | 76-E |
| Tillinghast, Joseph | S | Easthampton | 76:0.1.2.1.3 |
| Tillitson, Daniel | S | Smithtown | 76:0.3.2.1.2 |
| Tillitson, Nicholas | S | Smithtown | 75-L |
| Tillotson, Daniel | S | Smithtown | 75-L |
| Tillotson, Samuel Jun' | S | Smithtown | 75-L |
| Tillou, Peter | N | New York | 74-A |
| Tillyou, William | N | New York | 74-A |
| Tilou, William, turner | N | Maiden Lane | 75-T |
| Tilyou, John | N | New York | 75-D2 |
| Tilyou, Vincent | N | New York | 74-A |
| Tinney, Wm, shopkeeper | N | Queen Street | 75-D2 |
| Titlar, Valentine | N | New York | 74-A |
| Titus, Abial | S | Huntington | 75-H |
| Titus, Benjamin | S | Huntington | 75-H |
| Titus, Charles | Q | ........ | 76-E |
| Titus, Edmond | Q | ........ | 75-A |
| Titus, Edw'd | Q | Newtown | 75-G |
| Titus, Francis | Q | Newtown | 75-G |
| Titus, Henry | S | Huntington | 75-H, 75-H1 |
| Titus, Israel | S | Huntington | 75-H |

| | | | |
|---|---|---|---|
| Titus, John | Q | ........ | 75-A, 76-B |
| Titus, John | S | Huntington | 75-H |
| Titus, Jonathan Jr. [2] | S | Huntington | [on] 75-H |
| Titus, Jos., Ensign | S | Huntington | 75-H1 |
| Titus, Joseph | S | Huntington | 75-H |
| Titus, Peter | Q | ........ | 76-E |
| Titus, Peter Jr. | Q | ........ | 75-A |
| Titus, Peter Jr. | Q | ........ | 76-B, 76-E |
| Titus, Richard | Q | ........ | 75-A, 76-E |
| Titus, Samuel | Q | ........ | 75-A |
| Titus, Samuel [2] | Q | ........ | [on] 76-E |
| Titus, Tim | Q | ........ | 75-A |
| Titus, Timothy | Q | ........ | 76-B |
| Titus, Timothy | S | Huntington | 75-H |
| Titus, Zebulon | S | Huntington | 75-H |
| Tobe, Samuel | S | Brookhaven | 76:0.2.3.1.1 |
| Todd, James and William | N | New York | 75-V |
| Todd, ____ Mrs. | N | Broadway | 75-T2, 2/16 |
| Toffe/Taffy, John | Q | ........ | 75-A, 76-E |
| Toffie, James | N | New York | 76-A |
| Tolbert, James | N | New York | 74-A |
| Tolmie, ____ Dr. | N | Smith's Fly | 74-T2, 12/1 |
| Tolmie, Norman | N | New York | 76-L |
| Tolmie, Normand | N | New York | 74-A |
| Tolmie, Normand, Capt. | N | New York | 76-Y |
| Toltic[?], James | N | New York | 76-R |
| Tom, Nathaniel | Q | ........ | 75-A associator |
| Tom, Nathaniel | Q | ........ | 75-D1 |
| Tomkins, Nancy | N | removed upstate | 76-P |
| Tomlinson, James, joiner | N | William Street | 75-D2 |
| Tommelson, Ann | N | removed upstate | 76-P |
| Tongue, Dorothy, wf Wm | N | New York | 74-T |
| Tongue, William | N | New York | 76-A |
| Tongue, William, broker | N | nr the Exchange | 74-T2, 9/8 |
| Took, Wilm. see Huls, Peter | | | |
| Tooker, Abijah | S | Brookhaven | 75-B8 |
| Tooker, Charles | S | Brookhaven | 75-B10 |
| Tooker, Charles | S | Brookhaven | 75-B11 n.s. |
| Tooker, Charls | S | Brookhaven | 76:0.3.0.2.4 |
| Tooker, Daniel | N | New York | 74-A, 76-A |

| | | | |
|---|---|---|---|
| Tooker, Eliphat | S | Brookhaven | 76:1.0.3.2.2 |
| Tooker, Jemes | S | Brookhaven | 76:0.1.3.1.2 |
| Tooker, John | S | Brookhaven | 75-B9 |
| Tooker, Jonah | S | Brookhaven | 75-B6 |
| Tooker, Nathanael Junior | S | Brookhaven | 75-B8 |
| Tooker, Nathanael Senior | S | Brookhaven | 75-B8 |
| Tooker, Nathaniel | S | Brookhaven | 75-B9 |
| Tooker, Nathaniel | S | Brookhaven | 76:1.0.2.1.0.1.0 |
| Tooker, Nathaniel | S | Brookhaven | 76:1.1.2.1.2 |
| Tooker, Phillips | S | Brookhaven | 75-B8 |
| Tooker, Philps | S | Brookhaven | 76:0.2.3.1.2 |
| Tooker, Timothy | S | Brookhaven | 75-B10 |
| Tooker, Timothy | S | Brookhaven | 75-B11 n.s. |
| Tooker, Timothy | S | Brookhaven | 76:1.1.1.1.1 |
| Tooker, William | S | Brookhaven | 75-B10 |
| Topping, Charles | S | ........ | 75-R |
| Topping, Charles | S | Southampton | 76:0.1.0.1.2 |
| Topping, Daniel | S | ........ | 75-R |
| Topping, Daniel | S | Southampton | 76:1.1.3.2.3 |
| Topping, Daniel Jun$^r$ | S | Southampton | 76:0.1.2.1.1 |
| Topping, Daniel, the 2$^{nd}$ | S | ........ | 75-R |
| Topping, David | S | ........ | 75-R |
| Topping, David | S | Southampton | 76:1.2.0.2.1 |
| Topping, David Jr. | S | ........ | 75-R |
| Topping, Edward | S | Southampton | 75-M |
| Topping, Edward | S | Southampton | 76:0.1.2.3.4 |
| Topping, Elithan | S | Southampton | 76:0.1.4.3.3 |
| Topping, Ethan | S | ........ | 75-R |
| Topping, Ethan | S | Southampton | 76:0.1.1.1.0 |
| Topping, Henry | S | ........ | 75-R |
| Topping, Henry | S | Southampton | 76:0.1.0.1.1 |
| Topping, Jeremiah | S | ........ | 75-R |
| Topping, Joseph | S | ........ | 75-R |
| Topping, Joseph | S | Southampton | 76:0.1.1.1.0 |
| Topping, Matthew | S | ........ | 75-R |
| Topping, Seth | S | ........ | 75-R |
| Topping, Silas | S | ........ | 75-R |
| Topping, Silas | S | Southampton | 76:0.1.1.1.0 |
| Topping, Silvanus | S | ........ | 75-R |
| Topping, Silvanus | S | Southampton | 76:1.0.0.1.1 |

| | | | |
|---|---|---|---|
| Topping, Silvanus 2ᵈ | S | ........ | 75-R |
| Topping, Silvanus Junʳ | S | Southampton | 76:0.1.0.1.3 |
| Topping, Stephen | S | ........ | 75-R |
| Topping, Stephen | S | Southampton | 76:1.1.0.1.1.1.0 |
| Topping, Stephen Junʳ | S | ........ | 75-R |
| Topping, Stephen Junʳ | S | Southampton | 76:0.1.1.1.1.1.1 |
| Topping, Thomas | S | Southampton | 75-M |
| Topping, Thomas | S | Southampton | 7o:0.1.2.1.0 |
| Topping, Zephʳ | S | ........ | 75-R |
| Tothen, Thos. | N | New York | 76-G |
| Totten, Jacob | Q | Hempstead | 76-D |
| Totten, John | S | Huntington | 75-H |
| Totten, Joseph | N | New York | 74-A |
| Totten, Joseph | N | New York | 74-T2, 11/24 |
| Totten, Joseph | N | New York | 74-V, 75-F |
| Totten, Joseph | N | New York | 76-F |
| Totten, Joseph | Q | ........ | 75-A |
| Totten, Losee | S | Huntington | 75-H |
| Totten, Richard | Q | Hempstead | 76-D |
| Totten, Robert | N | New York | 74-A |
| Totten, Robert and James | N | New York | 75-F |
| Totten, Silas | N | New York | 74-A, 76-A |
| Totten, Simeon | S | Huntington | 75-H |
| Totten, Stephen | S | Huntington | 75-H non-signer |
| Totten, Thomas | S | Huntington | 76-H1 |
| Totton, Joseph, Capt. | N | New York | 76-Y |
| Totton, Peter, 2d Lieut. | N | New York | 76-Y |
| Towers, Joseph | N | New York | 74-R juror |
| Towle, Robert | N | New York | 74-A |
| Townsend, Ab. | Q | ........ | 75-A |
| Townsend, Absalom | Q | ........ | 76-B, 76-E |
| Townsend, Ben. | Q | Oyster Bay | 75-F |
| Townsend, Daniel | Q | ........ | 76-E |
| Townsend, ____ Dr. | Q | ........ | 75-A associator |
| Townsend, Geo. Jr. | Q | ........ | 76-E |
| Townsend, George | Q | ........ | 75-A associator |
| Townsend, George | Q | Oyster Bay | 75-F |
| Townsend, H., Jr. | Q | ........ | 76-E |
| Townsend, Henry [2] | Q | ........ | [on] 76-E |
| Townsend, Hewlett | Q | ........ | 75-A, 76-E |

| Townsend, James | N | New York | 74-A |
| Townsend, James | Q | Oyster Bay | 75-A associator |
| Townsend, James | Q | Oyster Bay | 75-F |
| Townsend, James Jr. | Q | Oyster Bay | 75-F |
| Townsend, Jas., Dr. | Q | ........ | 76-E |
| Townsend, Jas., Jr. | Q | ........ | 76-E |
| Townsend, Jno. | Q | ........ | 75-A |
| Townsend, Jno. | Q | Hempstead | 75-A |
| Townsend, Jno. Esq. | Q | ........ | 75-A |
| Townsend, Jno., Justice | Q | Oyster Bay | 75-H |
| Townsend, John | N | nr Coffee House | 76-H |
| Townsend, John | N | nr Coffee House | 76-I |
| Townsend, John Jr. | Q | ........ | 76-E |
| Townsend, John [2] | Q | ........ | [on] 76-E |
| Townsend, Jonathan | Q | ........ | 75-A associator |
| Townsend, Joseph | Q | ........ | 75-A |
| Townsend, Jotham | Q | ........ | 76-E |
| Townsend, Jotham | Q | Oyster Bay | 75-F |
| Townsend, Micajah | Q | ........ | 75-A associator |
| Townsend, Micajah | Q | ........ | 76-E |
| Townsend, Micajah | Q | Oyster Bay | 75-F |
| Townsend, Nathaniel | Q | ........ | 75-A, 76-B |
| Townsend, Nathaniel | Q | Jamaica | 75-C, 75-D |
| Townsend, Nicholas | Q | ........ | 75-A, 76-B |
| Townsend, Nicholas | Q | Jamaica | 75-C |
| Townsend, Prior | Q | ........ | 76-E |
| Townsend, Prior | Q | Oyster Bay | 75-F |
| Townsend, Rich'd Jr. | Q | ........ | 75-A, 76-E |
| Townsend, Richard | Q | ........ | 75-A, 76-B |
| Townsend, Richard [3] | Q | ........ | [on] 76-E |
| Townsend, Robert | Q | ........ | 76-E |
| Townsend, Sam[l] | S | Huntington | 75-H non-signer |
| Townsend, Samuel | Q | ........ | 76-B |
| Townsend, Samuel Esq. | Q | ........ | 75-D1 |
| Townsend, Samuel Jr. | Q | ........ | 76-B2 |
| Townsend, Samuel [3] | Q | ........ | [on] 76-E |
| Townsend, Solomon | N | ship captain | 75-T2, 3/23 |
| Townsend, Thos. | Q | ........ | 75-A |
| Townsend, Timothy | Q | ........ | 75-A, 76-E |
| Townsend, W. [2] | Q | ........ | [on] 76-E |

| | | | |
|---|---|---|---|
| Townsend, William | Q | Oyster Bay | 75-F |
| Trail, George | N | New York | 75-T2, 2/23 |
| Trail, George | N | New York | 76-A |
| Traile, George | N | New York | 76-N |
| Traves, Ruth | S | Smithtown | 76:0.0.2.1.0 |
| Treadwell, Benj., Dr. | Q | ........ | 76-E |
| Treadwell, Benj'n Jr. | Q | ........ | 75-A |
| Treadwell, Benjamin | Q | ........ | 75-A, 76-E |
| Treadwell, Benjamin | Q | Hempstead | 76-D |
| Treadwell, Benjamin [2] | Q | ........ | [on] 76-B |
| Treadwell, John | Q | ........ | 75-A |
| Treadwell, John | Q | ........ | 76-B, 76-E |
| Treadwell, Samuel | Q | ........ | 75-A |
| Treadwell, Samuel | Q | ........ | 76-B, 76-E |
| Treadwell, Thomas | Q | ........ | 75-A |
| Treadwell, Thomas | Q | ........ | 76-B, 76-E |
| Treadwell, Thomas | Q | Hempstead | 76-D |
| Treadwell, Thomas | S | Smithtown | 75-L Committee |
| Treadwell, Thomas | S | Smithtown | 76:0.1.2.2.4.6.6 |
| Treadwell, Thomas Esq. | S | Smithtown | 75-H1 |
| Treat, ____ Dr. | N | New York | 75-D2 |
| Treat, Malachy | N | New York | 74-A, 76-N |
| Treat, Malachy, Dr. | N | New York | 74-T |
| Treemain, Jonathan | N | New York | 76-A |
| Tremper, Michael | N | New York | 74-A |
| Trevillian, Francis | N | New York | 76-A, 76-I |
| Trigleth, Rich[d] | N | New York | 75-D3 |
| Triglith, Elezabeth | N | New York | 76-K |
| Trim, Tobias | N | New York | 76-A |
| Tripp, Henry D. | N | New York | 76-N |
| Troup, J.J. | Q | ........ | 76-E |
| Troup, Jno. | Q | ........ | 75-A |
| Troup, John | Q | Jamaica | 75-C, 75-D |
| Troup, John Esq. | Q | Jamaica | 75-T, 75-V |
| Troup, John I. | Q | Jamaica | 75-T |
| Troup, John J. | Q | ........ | 76-B2 |
| Troup, Robt. | N | New York | 76-N |
| Trouteman, George | N | New York | 74-A |
| Truman, Clark | S | ........ | 75-R |
| Truman, Clark | S | Easthampton | 76:0.1.1.1.0 |

| Truman, Elezar | S | Southold | 76:1.3.1.4.2 |
|---|---|---|---|
| Truman, William | S | Southold | 76:0.1.2.2.0 |
| Tucker, Daniel | N | New York | 76-F |
| Tucker, Frederick, carrier | N | Beekman Street | 75-D1, D2 |
| Tucker, James | N | New York | 76-A |
| Tucker, James | S | Brookhaven | 75-B1, 75-B6 |
| Tucker, James | S | Brookhaven | 75-B7 |
| Tucker, Jonah | S | Brookhaven | 75-B3 |
| Tucker, Jonah | S | Brookhaven | 76:0.1.4.1.2 |
| Tucker, Lifilet | S | Brookhaven | 75-B9 |
| Tucker, Thomas | N | New York | 74-A |
| Tucker, Thomas, Lieut. | N | New York | 75-A |
| Tucker, William | S | Brookhaven | 75-B11 n.s. |
| Tucker; see also Tooker | | | |
| Tuder, Mary wid. of John | N | New York | 76-V |
| Tuder, Sam[l] | N | New York | 75-B |
| Tufts, Nath'l | N | New York | 74-A |
| Tuner, Cornelius Turk | N | New York | 74-A |
| Turck, Ahasuerus | N | New York | 76-L |
| Turck, Cornelus | N | New York | 76-L |
| Turk, Ahars. | N | New York | 74-A |
| Turk, Cornelius | N | New York | 74-A |
| Turk, Cornelius Jr., baker | N | Broadway | 75-D2 |
| Turner, Henry | S | Brookhaven | 75-B7 |
| Turner, James | Q | ........ | 75-A |
| Turner, John | S | Brookhaven | 75-B1, 75-B6 |
| Turner, John | S | Brookhaven | 75-B7 |
| Turner, John | S | Brookhaven | 76:0.2.2.1.2 |
| Turner, John, 1st Lieut. | N | New York | 75-A, 76-S |
| Turner, John [2] | N | New York | [on] 74-A |
| Turner, Margrit | N | removed upstate | 76-P |
| Turner, Samuel | S | Brookhaven | 75-B7 |
| Turner, Samuel | S | Brookhaven | 76:0.2.1.3.0 |
| Turner, William | Q | Jamaica | 75-C |
| Turner, William | S | Brookhaven | 75-B7 |
| Turner, William | S | Brookhaven | 76:0.1.2.4.1 |
| Turner, William, 1st Lieut. | N | New York | 75-A |
| Turner, William [2] | N | New York | [on] 74-A |
| Tuthill, Azariah | S | ........ | 75-R |
| Tuthill, Azariah | S | Southold | 76:1.1.1.2.1 |

| | | | |
|---|---|---|---|
| Tuthill, Azariah Jr. | S | Southold | 76:0.1.0.1.1 |
| Tuthill, Barnabas | S | ........ | 75-R |
| Tuthill, Barnabass, Major | S | Southold | 76:0.2.5.2.3 |
| Tuthill, Benj. | S | Southold | 76:0.1.0.1.1.1.1 |
| Tuthill, Benjamin | S | Brookhaven | 75-B9 |
| Tuthill, Benjamin | S | Southold | 75-N |
| Tuthill, Christopher | S | ........ | 75-R |
| Tuthill, Christopher | S | Southold | 76:1.1.5.4.3 |
| Tuthill, Daniel | Q | Jamaica | 75-D associator |
| Tuthill, Daniel | Q | Jamaica | 76-C |
| Tuthill, Daniel | S | Brookhaven | 75-B10 |
| Tuthill, Daniel | S | Southold | 76:1.0.0.1.0 |
| Tuthill, Daniel | S | Southold | 76:1.2.1.2.0.2.0 |
| Tuthill, Daniel [2] | S | ........ | [on] 75-R |
| Tuthill, Hennery | S | Southold | 76:1.1.0.1.1 |
| Tuthill, Henry | S | Brookhaven | 75-B10 |
| Tuthill, Isaiah | S | Southold | 75-N non-signer |
| Tuthill, Isaiah | S | Southold | 76:0.1.1.1.3.0.1 |
| Tuthill, James | S | Southold | 75-N non-signer |
| Tuthill, James | S | Southold | 76:0.2.3.1.3 |
| Tuthill, Jeremiah | S | ........ | 75-R |
| Tuthill, Jeremiah | S | Southold | 76:1.1.1.4.1 |
| Tuthill, Jeremiah Jr. | S | ........ | 75-R |
| Tuthill, John | S | ........ | 75-R |
| Tuthill, John | S | Southold | 75-N |
| Tuthill, John | S | Southold | 76:0.1.4.1.2 |
| Tuthill, John | S | Southold | 76:0.3.1.1.0 |
| Tuthill, John | S | Southold | 76:1.0.1.2.2 |
| Tuthill, John | S | Southold | 76:1.3.3.3.2.2.1 |
| Tuthill, John Jun. | S | Southold | 75-N |
| Tuthill, John Junior | S | ........ | 75-R |
| Tuthill, John Jun' | S | ........ | 75-R |
| Tuthill, John Junr. | S | Southold | 76:0.1.3.1.0 |
| Tuthill, John Ju' | S | ........ | 75-R |
| Tuthill, Jonathan | S | ........ | 75-R |
| Tuthill, Jonathan | S | Southold | 76:0.1.1.3.1 |
| Tuthill, Joshua | S | Brookhaven | 75-B9 |
| Tuthill, Joshua | S | Southold | 76:2.0.1.3.0.0.1 |
| Tuthill, Mary, Wid^w | S | Southampton | 76:0.0.0.1.4 |
| Tuthill, Nathan | S | Brookhaven | 75-B10 |

| | | | |
|---|---|---|---|
| Tuthill, Nathan | S | Southold | 76:0.1.4.3.4 |
| Tuthill, Nathaniel | S | Shelter Island | 75-K |
| Tuthill, Peter | S | ........ | 75-R |
| Tuthill, Peter | S | Southold | 76:0.1.0.1.3.0.1 |
| Tuthill, Rofos | S | Southold | 76:0.2.1.2.2.0.1 |
| Tuthill, Rufus | S | ........ | 75-R |
| Tuthill, Sm[l] | S | Southold | 76:0.1.4.3.3 |
| Tutho, Jonathan | S | Easthampton | 75-E |
| Tuttel, John | S | Southampton | 76:0.2.5.2.1 |
| Tuttle, Benjamen | S | Brookhaven | 76:1.2.3.3.0 |
| Tuttle, Daniel | Q | ........ | 76-C |
| Tuttle, John | N | Learys Street | 76-I |
| Tuttle, John | N | North River | 76-H |
| Tuttle, Jonathan Jr. | S | ........ | 75-R |
| Twene, Jonathan | N | New York | 76-A |
| Tyler, Jacob | N | New York | 76-A |
| Tyler, James, 2d Lieut. | N | New York | 75-A |
| Tyler, John, sadler | N | liv w/Jas Hallitt | 75-D1, D2 |
| Tyler, Nath'l | N | New York | 74-A |
| Udall, Joseph | S | Islip | 75-I |
| Udall, Joseph | S | Islip | 76:1.1.1.3.2.5.3 |
| Udall, Nathaniel | S | Huntington | 76-H2 |
| Udall, Tho[s] | S | Islip | 75-I |
| Udle, Nath[l] | S | Huntington | 75-H |
| Uhnderel, see Vhnderel | | | |
| Uldrick, Catherine | N | New York | 74-R |
| Uldrick, George | N | New York | 74-R |
| Uncle, Thomas, saddler | N | Wall Street | 74-T2, 3/17 |
| Underhill, _____ , mills | Q | Flushing | 75-V |
| Underhill, Adonigah | S | Islip | 76:0.1.1.2.1.1.3 |
| Underhill, Adonijah | S | Islip | 75-I Quaker |
| Underhill, Amos | Q | ........ | 76-E |
| Underhill, Baruch | Q | ........ | 76-B, 76-E |
| Underhill, Benj[n] | N | New York | 74-A, 76-A |
| Underhill, Caleb | Q | ........ | 75-A |
| Underhill, Caleb | Q | ........ | 76-B, 76-E |
| Underhill, Daniel | Q | ........ | 75-A, 76-E |
| Underhill, George | Q | ........ | 76-E |
| Underhill, Isaac | Q | ........ | 76-E |
| Underhill, John | Q | ........ | 75-A, 76-B |

| | | | |
|---|---|---|---|
| Underhill, Peter | Q | ........ | 75-A |
| Underhill, Peter | Q | ........ | 76-B, 76-E |
| Underhill, Thomas | Q | ........ | 76-E |
| Ungerar, Nicodemus | N | New York | 76-A |
| Urmhauster, John Christopher | N | New York | 76-A |
| Urquhart, Walter | N | Wall Street | 76-V |
| Urst, George | N | New York | 76-A |
| Ustick, Henry | N | New York | 74-A, 76-A |
| Ustick, Henry | N | New York | 76-F, 76-I |
| Ustick, Henry | N | Smith Street | 75-T |
| Ustick, Henry, juror | N | New York | 74-R, 75-R |
| Ustick, Thomas | N | New York | 74-A |
| Ustick, William | N | New York | 74-T2, 11/24 |
| Ustick, William | N | New York | 75-R overseer |
| Ustick, William, storekpr | N | New York | 74-T2, 4/21, 75-F |
| Ustick, Wm | N | New York | 74-A, 76-A |
| Utt, Harman | N | New York | 76-A |
| Utt, Jacob | N | New York | 76-I |
| Vail, Abraham | S | ........ | 75-R |
| Vail, Abraham | S | Southold | 76:0.1.2.2.0 |
| Vail, Benj: | S | Southold | 76:0.2.4.2.3 |
| Vail, Daniel | S | Southold | 76:0.1.1.1.0 |
| Vail, David | S | Southold | 76:0.1.1.1.2 |
| Vail, Elisha | S | Southold | 76:0.1.1.1.2 |
| Vail, Elisha [2] | S | ........ | [on] 75-R |
| Vail, Jeremiah | S | ........ | 75-R |
| Vail, Jeremiah | S | Southold | 76:0.2.3.1.0 |
| Vail, Jeremiah Juner | S | ........ | 75-R |
| Vail, John | S | Huntington | 75-H |
| Vail, John | S | Southold | 76:1.0.0.1.1 |
| Vail, Jonathan | S | Southold | 76:0.2.3.2.2 |
| Vail, Micah | S | Huntington | 75-H |
| Vail, Moses | S | Huntington | 75-H |
| Vail, Obadiah | S | ........ | 75-R |
| Vail, Obediah | S | Southold | 76:1.1.1.3.1 |
| Vail, Peter | S | Southold | 76:1.2.2.3.0 |
| Vail, Peter Jr. | S | Brookhaven | 75-B10 |
| Vail, Platt | S | Huntington | 75-H |
| Vail, Samuel, Sergt. | S | Huntington | 76-H2 |
| Vail, Stephen | S | ........ | 75-R |

| | | | |
|---|---|---|---|
| Vail, Stephen | S | Southold | 76:0.1.2.1.5 |
| Vail, Stephen | S | Southold | 76:1.0.0.1.1.0.1 |
| Vail, Stephen Jun$^r$ | S | ........ | 75-R |
| Vail, Stephen Jun$^r$ | S | Southold | 76:0.1.1.1.2.0.1 |
| Vail, Thomas | S | ........ | 75-R |
| Vail, Thomas | S | Southold | 76:0.1.1.1.2 |
| Vaile, Daniel | S | ........ | 75-R |
| Vaile, Obadiah | S | ........ | 75-R |
| Vaill, John | S | ........ | 75-R |
| Vaill, Jonathan | S | Brookhaven | 75-B10 |
| Valentine, Caleb | Q | ........ | 76-E |
| Valentine, David | N | New York | 74-A |
| Valentine, David | Q | ........ | 76-E |
| Valentine, Jacamiah | Q | ........ | 75-A, 76-B |
| Valentine, Jacob | Q | ........ | 75-A associator |
| Valentine, Jacob [2] | Q | ........ | [on] 76-E |
| Valentine, Jeconiah | Q | Jamaica | 75-D |
| Valentine, Jeremiah | Q | Jamaica | 75-C |
| Valentine, Jona. | Q | ........ | 76-E |
| Valentine, Jonah | Q | ........ | 76-B |
| Valentine, Jonas | Q | ........ | 75-A |
| Valentine, Mary | N | New York | 74-T2, 4/14 |
| Valentine, Obadiah | Q | ........ | 75-A |
| Valentine, Obadiah | Q | ........ | 76-B, 76-E |
| Valentine, Philip | Q | ........ | 75-A associator |
| Valentine, Philip | Q | ........ | 76-E |
| Valentine, Richard | Q | ........ | 75-A associator |
| Valentine, Robert | Q | ........ | 75-A |
| Valentine, Robert | Q | ........ | 76-B, 76-E |
| Valentine, Thomas | Q | ........ | 76-E |
| Valentine, William | Q | ........ | 76-B, 76-E |
| Valentine, William | Q | Jamaica | 75-C |
| Valentine, Wm | N | New York | 74-A |
| Valentine, Wm | Q | ........ | 75-A |
| Valentine; see also Volentine | | | |
| Valleau, Fanconier | N | New York | 76-A |
| Valleau, Theodore [2] | N | New York | [on] 74-A |
| VanAllen, John | N | New York | 75-D1 |
| VanAllen, Peter | N | New York | 74-A |
| VanAlst, Bragraw | Q | Newtown | 75-B |

| | | | |
|---|---|---|---|
| VanAlst, G. | Q | Newtown | 75-B |
| VanAlst, Isaac | Q | Newtown | 75-B |
| VanAlst, John | Q | ........ | 76-E |
| VanAlst, John Jr. | Q | ........ | 76-E |
| VanAlst, John Jr. | Q | Newtown | 75-B |
| VanAlst, John Sr. | Q | Newtown | 75-B |
| VanAlstyne, Abraham | N | New York | 74-A |
| VanAntwerp, Jacobus | N | New York | 74-A |
| VanAntwerp, James Jr. | N | New York | 74-A |
| VanAntwerp, John | N | New York | 74-A |
| VanAntwerp, John, crpntr | N | Quaker Meet'g St | 75-D1, D2 |
| VanAntwerp, Nicholas | N | New York | 76-D |
| VanAntwerp, Simon | N | New York | 74-A, 74-T |
| VanAntwerp, Simon | N | New York | 76-I |
| Vanarden, David | N | New York | 74-A |
| Vanarden, Jacobus | N | New York | 74-A |
| Vanaron, Joslar S. | N | New York | 74-A |
| VanArsdalen, Nicholas | Q | ........ | 76-B, 76-E |
| Vanarsdalien, Nich'l | Q | ........ | 75-A |
| Vanarsdalle, Abram, 2d Lt. | Q | Jamaica | 76-C |
| VanAullen, Cornelius | N | New York | 75-D3 |
| Vanausdal, Abraham | Q | Jamaica | 75-C |
| Vanausdal, Isaac | Q | Jamaica | 75-C |
| Vanausdal, Nicholas | Q | Jamaica | 75-C, 75-D |
| VanAusdoll, Abram | Q | Jamaica | 76-C |
| VanAusdoll, Isaac | Q | Jamaica | 76-C |
| Vanbelt Jacob | S | Huntington | 75-H |
| Vanbelt, John | S | Huntington | 75-H |
| VanBenthuysen, Peter | N | New York | 74-A |
| VanBlake, Peter | N | New York | 75-C |
| VanBrackle, James | N | New York | 74-R, 75-R |
| VanBramer, Henry | N | New York | 74-R to 76-R |
| VanBrockle, James | N | New York | 74-A |
| Vanbrunt, Jacob | S | Brookhaven | 75-B8 |
| Vanbrunt, Jacob | S | Brookhaven | 76:0.1.2.2.0.2.4 |
| VanBrunt, Goort | Q | ........ | 75-I |
| VanBrunt, Joost | Q | ........ | 75-A, 76-B |
| VanBrunt, Joost | Q | Jamaica | 75-C |
| VanBrunt, Joseph | Q | Jamaica | 75-D |
| VanBueren, Beekman, Dr. | N | New York | 74-R witness |

| | | | |
|---|---|---|---|
| Vance, John | N | New York | 74-A |
| VanCortlandt, Aug[t] | N | New York | 76-A |
| VanCortlandt, Augustus | N | New York | 74-T |
| VanCortlandt, John | N | New York | 75-T2, 5/4 |
| VanCortlandt, Wm Rickets | N | New York | 75-R overseer |
| VanCot, Gabrel | Q | Hempstead | 76-D |
| VanCott, John | Q | ........ | 75-A, 76-B |
| VanCott, Nich. Jr. | Q | ........ | 76-E |
| VanCott, Nicholas | Q | ........ | 75-A |
| VanCott, Nicholas | Q | ........ | 76-B, 76-E |
| VanCott, Tunis | Q | ........ | 75-A, 76-B |
| VanCotts, James | Q | Hempstead | 76-D |
| VanCotts, Joh. Jr. | Q | ........ | 76-E |
| VanCotts, Johannes Jr. | Q | ........ | 76-B |
| VanCotts, see also VanScott | | | |
| Vandale, Francis, teacher | N | New York | 75-T |
| VanDalsen, John | N | New York | 74-A |
| VanDalsen, William | N | New York | 76-L |
| VanDalsom, John, pewterer | N | Cortland Street | 75-D2 |
| VanDam, Anthony | N | New York | 74-T2, 8/18 |
| VanDam, Anthony | N | New York | 75-F; 75-T2, 5/4 |
| VanDam, Nicholas | Q | ........ | 76-E |
| Vandebergh, Elizabeth | N | rem to Ulster Co. | 76-P |
| Vandebergh, Harmanus | N | rem to Ulster Co. | 76-P |
| Vandenbarck, Harman | N | New York | 75-C |
| Vandenbergh, Lucas | N | New York | 76-I |
| VanDenbergh, Adam Jr. | N | New York | 74-R |
| VanDenbergh, Harman | N | New York | 74-A |
| VanDenBergh, Corn[s] | N | New York | 76-A |
| VanDenBergh, Garret | N | New York | 74-A |
| Vandenham, Henry | N | New York | 76-I |
| VanDenHam, Henry Jr. | N | New York | 74-A |
| VanDerBelt, Hend. | Q | ........ | 76-E |
| Vanderberg, Garret, stables | N | New York | 74-T2, 12/22 |
| Vanderbilt, John | N | New York | 74-A |
| VanderFeeld, Elizabeth | N | New York | 76-K |
| Vanderhoef, Peter | N | New York | 74-A |
| VanDerHoef, Peter | N | New York | 76-L |
| Vanderhoff, Laranc | N | New York | 74-A |
| Vanderhoof, Agnes | N | New York | 76-I |

| | | | |
|---|---|---|---|
| VanderHoof, Lawrence | N | carman, Brdway | 75-D1, D2 |
| Vanderoof, Egbert | N | New York | 74-A |
| Vandersman, Adrianus | N | New York | 74-A |
| Vandervoort, Peter | N | New York | 74-A, 75-F |
| Vandervoort, Peter | N | New York | 76-N |
| VanDeursen, Isaac | N | New York | 76-L |
| VanDeusen, Gilbert | N | to Dutchess Co. | 76-P |
| VandeVoort, Peter | N | Queen Street | 75-D2 |
| Vandewater, Sarah | N | New York | 76-I |
| Vandewater, William | N | New York | 74-A |
| VandeWater, Alertus | N | New York | 74-A |
| VanDeWater, Wm, juror | N | New York | 75-R, 76-R |
| VanDine, Aras | Q | ........ | 76-E |
| VanDine, Denise | Q | Newtown | 75-G |
| VanDine, Domini[s] | Q | ........ | 76-E |
| VanDine, Douw | Q | ........ | 76-B, 76-E |
| VanDine, Dow | Q | Newtown | 75-B |
| VanDine, Dow, Capt. | Q | ........ | 75-A |
| VanDine, Wm | Q | Newtown | 75-G |
| VanDolsom, William | N | New York | 75-D1 |
| VanDooser, Gilbert | N | to Westchester Co | 76-P |
| VanDuersen, Abrm. | N | New York | 74-A |
| VanDuesen, Abraham, juror | N | New York | 74-R, 75-R |
| Vandusen, Abraham | N | tallow chandler | 75-D1, D2 |
| VanDusen, Abram | N | New York | 76-L |
| VanDusen, Andrew, butcher | N | Queen Street | 75-D1, D2 |
| VanDusen, Isaac | N | Ship Yards | 75-D2 |
| VanDusen, Wm. | N | tallow chandler | 75-D1, D2 |
| VanDyck, Abraham | N | New York | 74-A, 75-B |
| VanDyck, Abraham, innkpr | N | Broadway | 75-E |
| VanDyck, ____ Cap[n] | N | New York | 76-C |
| VanDyck, Mathias | Q | ........ | 75-A associator |
| VanDyck, Nicholas | N | New York | 74-A, 74-V |
| VanDyck, Nicholas | Q | ........ | 75-A associator |
| VanDycke, James | N | New York | 75-F |
| VanDycke, Nicholas | N | New York | 74-T |
| VanDyk, John | N | New York | 76-D |
| Vandyke, James | N | New York | 75-D3 |
| VanDyke, James | N | New York | 74-A |
| VanDyke, John | N | New York | 75-D1, D2 |

| | | | |
|---|---|---|---|
| VanDyke, Nicholas | Q | ........ | 76-E |
| VanEveren, Martha, Mrs. | N | removed upstate | 76-P |
| VanEvery, Mindert | N | New York | 74-A, 76-A |
| VanGeld, Abraham | N | New York | 74-A |
| Vangelder, Collin | N | New York | 74-A |
| VanGelder, Abra. | N | New York | 76-N |
| VanGelder, Abraham | N | constable | 74-R to 76-R |
| VanGelder, Elizabeth | N | removed upstate | 76-P |
| VanGelder, Gerret | N | New York | 74-A |
| VanGelder, James | N | New York | 74-A |
| VanGelder, James, crpntr | N | Division Street | 75-D2 |
| VanGelder, Walter | N | New York | 75-D3 |
| VanGelder, Walter, gunsm. | N | Queen Street | 75-D2 |
| VanHoeck, Cornelius | N | New York | 74-A |
| VanHook, Isaac Jr. | N | New York | 74-A |
| Vanhoose, Renear | S | Brookhaven | 75-B2 |
| Vanhorn, S. | N | New York | 75-D2 |
| VanHorn, Andrew, blksmith | N | Little Queen St. | 75-D1, D2 |
| VanHorne, Augustus | N | New York | 75-T2, 5/4 |
| VanHorne, D. | N | New York | 75-D3 |
| VanHorne, D., Junr. | N | New York | 75-D3 |
| VanHorne, David, merchant | N | New York | 75-T, 75-V |
| VanHorne, James | N | New York | 74-A |
| VanHouten, John | N | New York | 75-D1 |
| VanHul, see Van Zul | | | |
| VanKleeck, Ann Mariah | N | to Dutchess Co. | 76-P |
| VanKleeck, Baltus | Q | ........ | 76-E |
| VanKleeck, Braache | N | to Dutchess Co. | 76-P |
| VanKleeck, Catharine, wid. | N | to Dutchess Co. | 76-P |
| VanKleeck, James | N | New York | 74-R |
| VanKleeck, James, cartman | N | New York | 75-D1, D2 |
| VanKleeck, John | N | to Dutchess Co. | 76-P |
| VanKleeck, Peter, pewterer | N | Partition Street | 75-D1, D2 |
| VanKleek, Henry & Son | N | New York | 75-F |
| VanKurson, John | N | New York | 75-D3 |
| Vanlau, John | Q | ........ | 76-B |
| Vanleaw, Jno. | Q | Flushing | 75-A |
| Vanleaw, Jno. | Q | Jamaica | 75-A associator |
| VanLeew, John | Q | Jamaica | 75-D |
| VanLeew, John | Q | Jamaica | 75-D associator |

| | | | |
|---|---|---|---|
| VanLiew, John | Q | ........ | 76-E |
| VanMaple, Henry | N | New York | 74-A |
| VanNies, John | N | removed upstate | 76-P |
| VanNordan, Jacobus | N | New York | 76-A |
| VanNorden, Jacobus Jun. | N | New York | 76-A |
| VanNort, Catharine | N | to Westchester Co | 76-P |
| VanNort, Cornelius | N | to Westchester Co | 76-P |
| VanNort, Hester | N | to Dutchess Co. | 76-P |
| VanNort, Hester, Mrs. | N | rem to Ulster Co. | 76-P |
| VanNort, John | N | to Westchester Co | 76-P |
| VanNort, Mary | N | to Westchester Co | 76-P |
| VanNostrant, A. [2] | Q | Jamaica | [on] 75-D |
| VanNostrant, A. [3] | Q | ........ | [on] 76-E |
| VanNostrant, Aaron | Q | ........ | 75-A |
| VanNostrant, Aaron, | Q | (als. Drawman) | 75-A |
| VanNostrant, Aaron | Q | Hempstead | 75-A |
| VanNostrant, Aaron | Q | Jamaica | 75-C |
| VanNostrant, Aaron [2] | Q | ........ | [on] 76-B |
| VanNostrant, Abra. | Q | ........ | 76-B |
| VanNostrant, Albert | Q | ........ | 75-A, 76-B |
| VanNostrant, Albert | Q | Oyster Bay | 75-F |
| VanNostrant, C. | Q | ........ | 76-E |
| VanNostrant, Cornelius | Q | ........ | 75-A |
| VanNostrant, D., Jr. | Q | ........ | 76-E |
| VanNostrant, Garet | Q | Hempstead | 76-D |
| VanNostrant, Garret | Q | ........ | 76-B2 |
| VanNostrant, J. | Q | ........ | 76-B, 76-E |
| VanNostrant, J. [4] | Q | ........ | [on] 76-E |
| VanNostrant, Jacob | Q | ........ | 75-A, 76-B2 |
| VanNostrant, John | Q | ........ | 75-A, 76-B |
| VanNostrant, M. | Q | ........ | 76-E |
| VanNostrant, Martin | Q | ........ | 75-A |
| VanNostrant, Wm | Q | ........ | 75-A, 76-B |
| VanNostrant; see also Nostrand | | | |
| VanNouten, Roelof | N | New York | 74-A |
| VanOrden, Jacob | N | New York | 76-I |
| VanOrden, Minee | N | removed upstate | 76-P |
| VanOrden, Petrus | N | New York | 74-A |
| VanOrden, Wolvert | N | New York | 74-T insolvent |
| VanOuden, John, blksmith | N | at I. VanDusen's | 75-D2 |

| | | | |
|---|---|---|---|
| Vanpelt, Thos. | N | New York | 75-D3 |
| VanPelt, John | N | New York | 75-D2 |
| VanPelt, Joseph, 2d Lieut. | N | New York | 75-A |
| VanPelt, Thomas | N | New York | 74-A |
| VanPelt, Thomas, 2d Lieut. | N | New York | 76-G, 76-S |
| VanPelt, Thomas, Ensign | N | New York | 75-A |
| Vanphilt, Christian, baker | N | Partition Street | 75-D2 |
| VanRanst, Cornelius | N | New York | 75-F, 76-F |
| VanRanst, Hester dau Peter | N | New York | 75-T, 75-V |
| VanRanst, Peter | N | New York | 74-A |
| Vanreelred, W. | Q | ........ | 76-E |
| VanRyper, Herman, crpntr | N | Barclay Street | 75-D2 |
| VanSchaak, Peter | N | New York | 74-T2, 11/24 |
| VanSchifer, John | N | New York | 74-A |
| Vanscot, James | Q | ........ | 76-E |
| VanScots, Cornelius | Q | Hempstead | 76-D |
| Vanscott, Cornelius | Q | ........ | 76-E |
| Vanscott, see also VanCotts | | | |
| Vanscott, see also Scott | | | |
| Vanscoy, Isaac | S | Easthampton | 76:0.2.1.2.3 |
| VanScoye, Isaac | S | Easthampton | 75-E |
| VanScoye, Isaac Jr. | S | Easthampton | 75-E |
| VanSeringen, G. | N | New York | 74-A |
| VanSeys, James | N | New York | 76-L |
| VanSice, Johannes | N | New York | 74-A |
| VanSicklen, Minne | Q | ........ | 76-E |
| VanSteen, Mary | N | rem to Ulster Co. | 76-P |
| VanThul, Christian | N | New York | 75-D1 |
| VanTile, Ann | N | New York | 75-R |
| VanTile, Cornelius | N | New York | 74-R, 76-R |
| VanTorne, John | N | New York | 76-L |
| VanTuyl, Andrew | N | New York | 74-A, 76-A |
| VanTuyl. Douglas & — | N | New York | 76-I |
| VanValsen, James | Q | ........ | 76-B |
| VanValsom, Peter | Q | ........ | 76-B2 |
| VanVarck, Abram, Ensign | N | New York | 75-A |
| VanVarck, James | N | New York | 74-A |
| VanVarik, Abraham, Lieut. | N | New York | 76-G |
| Vanvelred, Daniel | Q | ........ | 76-E |
| VanVelser, Daniel | Q | ........ | 76-B |

| | | | |
|---|---|---|---|
| VanVelsor, William | Q | ........ | 76-B2 |
| VanVlaricum, Luke | N | New York | 75-R |
| VanVleck, Abraham H. | N | New York | 75-V |
| VanVleck, Abram. | N | New York | 74-A |
| VanVleck, Abrm. H. | N | New York | 74-A |
| VanVleck, Daniel | N | New York | 74-A |
| VanVleck, Henry & Son | N | New York | 74-T2, 9/15 |
| VanVleck, Isaac | N | New York | 74-A, 76-N |
| VanVleck, John | N | New York | 74-A |
| VanVleck, Samuel | N | New York | 74-A |
| VanVoorhees, Jacob | N | New York | 74-T2, 11/24 |
| VanVoorhis, Jacob | N | New York | 74-A, 75-F |
| VanVorhis, Jacob | N | New York | 74-R |
| VanVorst, John | N | New York | 74-A, 76-A |
| VanVorst, Peggy | N | removed upstate | 76-P |
| VanVredenburgh, John Wm | N | New York | 74-R, 75-R juror |
| VanWagenen, G. H. | N | New York | 74-A |
| VanWagenen, Garret | N | New York | 75-D1 |
| VanWagenen, Huybt. | N | New York | 74-A |
| VanWagenen, Jacob | N | New York | 74-A |
| VanWagener, G. H. | N | New York | 75-D3 |
| VanWaggener, Teunis | N | New York | 75-D3 |
| VanWagner, Garrit J., Dr. | N | Dock Street | 75-D2 |
| Vanwick, Ab'm | Q | ........ | 75-A |
| Vanwick, Barnt | Q | ........ | 75-A |
| VanWick, Eldert | Q | ........ | 75-A |
| VanWick, Gilb't | Q | ........ | 75-A |
| VanWick, Sam'l | Q | ........ | 75-A |
| VanWick, Thos. | Q | ........ | 75-A |
| VanWicke, Abraham, Capt. | N | New York | 76-C |
| VanWickel, David | Q | ........ | 76-E |
| VanWicklen, Abm. | Q | ........ | 76-E |
| VanWicklen, Evert Sr. | Q | Jamaica | 75-C |
| VanWicklen, G. | Q | ........ | 76-E |
| VanWicklen, Garret | Q | ........ | 76-E |
| VanWicklen, J. | Q | ........ | 76-E |
| VanWicklen, Jacob | Q | ........ | 76-E |
| VanWinckelen, Henry | N | New York | 76-L |
| VanWinkle, Jacob | N | New York | 74-A |
| VanWinkle, John, bricklyr | N | George Street | 75-D2 |

| | | | |
|---|---|---|---|
| VanWinkle, Simeon, bricklyr | N | Fresh Water | 75-D1, D2 |
| VanWormer, Catherine | N | New York | 74-T |
| VanWormer, Cornelius | N | New York | 74-T |
| VanWyck, _____ , Capt. | N | New York | 75-E |
| VanWyck, Ab'm | Q | ........ | 76-E |
| VanWyck, Ab^m A. | N | New York | 75-D3 |
| VanWyck, Ab^m, Corp'l | N | New York | 75-D3 |
| VanWyck, Abraham | N | New York | 74-A, 75-R |
| VanWyck, Abraham A. | N | New York | 75-B |
| VanWyck, Abraham, Capt. | N | New York | 76-G, 76-S |
| VanWyck, Abrm. A. | N | New York | 76-N |
| VanWyck, Cornelius | Q | ........ | 75-A associator |
| VanWyck, Gilbert | Q | ........ | 76-E |
| VanWyck, Gilbert, Justice | Q | Hempstead | 75-H |
| VanWyck, Samuel | Q | ........ | 76-B |
| VanWyck, Stephen | Q | ........ | 76-E |
| VanWyck, Theod. | N | New York | 74-A |
| VanWyck, Theodorus | Q | ........ | 75-A, 76-B |
| VanWyck, Thos. | Q | ........ | 76-E |
| VanWyck, W. | Q | ........ | 76-E |
| VanWycklen, Evert | Q | Jamaica | 75-C, 75-D |
| VanWycklen, Garret | Q | Jamaica | 75-C |
| VanZandt, _____ Dr. | N | New York | 75-D3 |
| VanZandt, Jacobus | N | New York | 74-A, 75-F |
| VanZandt, James | N | New York | 75-D3 |
| VanZandt, James [2] | N | New York | [on] 75-B |
| VanZandt, _____ Lieut. | N | New York | 76-C |
| VanZandt, Tobias, Lieut. | N | New York | 75-A |
| VanZandt, Viner | N | New York | 76-N |
| VanZandt, Wynandt | N | New York | 76-A |
| VanZandt, Wynant | N | New York | 74-A |
| VanZile, William [2] | N | New York | [on] 74-A |
| VanZul [or Hul], Samuel | N | New York | 74-A |
| VanZuyle, Abraham | N | New York | 74-A |
| VanZyle, Cornelius | N | New York | 74-A |
| Varbous, Isaac | N | New York | 75-D1 |
| Vardell, Thomas | N | New York | 74-A, 76-A |
| Vargoson, Mary | S | Smithtown | 76:0.0.0.2.0 |
| Varian, John | N | New York | 75-R |
| Varian, John, butcher | N | Bowery Lane | 75-D1, D2 |

| | | | |
|---|---|---|---|
| Varian, Joseph | N | Ann Street | 74-T |
| Varian, Joseph, butcher | N | Scotch Street | 75-D1, D2 |
| Varian, Richard | N | Fresh Water | 74-T |
| Varian, Richard | N | [Bulls Head] | 76-H, 76-I |
| Varian, Richard, butcher | N | Bowery Lane | 75-D1, D2 |
| Varick, Abraham | N | New York | 74-A |
| Varick, Guilliam | N | New York | 74-A, 76-L |
| Varick, Rich^d, Corp'l | N | New York | 75-D3 |
| Vassie, Thomas | N | New York | 76-A |
| Vavasor, Josiah S., dry gds | N | Maiden Lane | 74-T2, 5/26 |
| Vavasor, Josiah Short | N | New York | 74-T |
| Vavasor, Josias S. | N | Pot Baker's Hill | 75-T |
| Veal, ---- Capt. | S | Huntington | 75-H1 |
| Vedito, John | Q | ........ | 75-A |
| Vedito, John Ue | Q | ........ | 76-E |
| Vedito, Stephen | Q | ........ | 76-E |
| Velser, Dan'l | Q | ........ | 75-A |
| Velser, Jacob | Q | ........ | 75-A |
| Velser, Peter | Q | ........ | 75-A |
| Velser, Will'm | Q | ........ | 75-A |
| Velser, Wm | Q | ........ | 75-A |
| Veltbergh, Cornelius | N | removed upstate | 76-P |
| Venaler, Cornelius | N | Batteau Street | 75-D2 |
| Verburgh, William | N | New York | 74-A |
| Vergereau, Peter | N | New York | 76-N |
| Vergereau, Peter, gentleman | N | New York | 75-D1, D2 |
| Verholst, G. | N | New York | 75-D1 |
| Verity, James | Q | ........ | 75-A |
| Verity, James Jr. | Q | ........ | 75-A |
| Verity, James [2] | Q | ........ | [on] 76-B |
| Verity, John | Q | ........ | 76-E |
| Verity, Simmons/Symonds | Q | ........ | 75-A, 76-B |
| Verity, William | Q | ........ | 75-A |
| Vermillie, William | N | New York | 76-L |
| Vermilye, William | N | New York | 74-A, 76-A |
| Vermilyea, John | N | New York | 74-A |
| Vernam, Thomas | N | New York | 76-I |
| Verner, Philip | N | New York | 76-A |
| Vernon, Thomas, feltmaker | N | New York | 75-R |
| Verplanck, Samuel | N | New York | 75-T2, 5/4 |

| | | | |
|---|---|---|---|
| Vervalen, Jacob | N | New York | 76-L |
| Vhnderel, Willem | N | New York | 74-A |
| Vilkin, Christopher | N | New York | 74-A |
| Vine, Robert | N | removed upstate | 76-P |
| Vitita, see Vedito | | | |
| Vogel, Peggy | N | removed upstate | 76-P |
| Volentine, Nathan | S | Huntington | 75-H |
| Volentine, Richard | S | Huntington | 75-H |
| Vonck, Pieter | N | New York | 74-A |
| Vonck; see also Funck | | | |
| Voorhees, Reuliff | Q | ........ | 76-E |
| Voorhies, James | Q | ........ | 76-E |
| Voorhies, Jno. | Q | ........ | 75-A |
| Voorhies, John | Q | ........ | 76-E |
| Vorhis, Daniel | N | New York | 74-A |
| Voris, Simon | Q | ........ | 76-E |
| Voris, Stephen | Q | ........ | 76-E |
| Vredenbergh, John, Sergt. | N | New York | 76-C |
| Vredenbergh, John W. | N | New York | 76-F |
| Vredenburgh, Jacob | N | New York | 74-A |
| Vredenburgh, Jacob, barber | N | Cortland Street | 75-D1, D2 |
| Vredenburgh, John W. | N | New York | 74-A |
| Vredenburgh, John William | N | New York | 76-R juror |
| Vredenburgh, John [2] | N | New York | [on] 74-A |
| Vredenburgh, Matthias | N | New York | 74-A |
| Vredenburgh, William | N | New York | 74-A |
| Vredenburgh, Wm. Jr. | N | New York | 74-A |
| Vreedenburgh, Matice | N | New York | 76-L |
| Vroman, William | N | removed upstate | 76-P |
| Waag, Bm. | N | New York | 74-A |
| Waag; see also Wagg | | | |
| Waass, John | N | removed upstate | 76-P |
| Wachtel, George L. | N | New York | 74-A |
| Waddel, John | N | New York | 74-T |
| Waddel, William | N | New York | 74-T |
| Waddel, William Esq. | N | New York | 75-T2, 2/23 |
| Waddell, Henry | N | New York | 74-V |
| Waddell, Robert Ross | N | New York | 75-T2, 6/29 |
| Waddell, William | N | New York | 74-V |
| Waddell, William, Judge | N | New York | 74-R to 76-R |

| | | | |
|---|---|---|---|
| Waddell, William, Lt. Col. | N | New York | 76-Y |
| Waddell, Wm | N | New York | 76-A |
| Wade, Benjamin | S | Southampton | 76:0.1.0.1.1 |
| Wade, Ebenezar | S | Southold | 76:0.1.3.1.3 |
| Wadick, James | N | New York | 74-A |
| Wadick, Mary | N | New York | 76-I |
| Wadick, —— widow | N | rem to Ulster Co. | 76-P |
| Wagg, Ab$^m$ | N | New York | 76-A |
| Wagg; see also Waag | | | |
| Wagna, John | N | New York | 76-A |
| Wainwright, Samuel | Q | ........ | 76-E |
| Waldegrove, George Jr. | N | New York | 76-L |
| Waldron, Adolph, constable | N | New York | 74-R |
| Waldron, Daniel, merchant | N | New York | 75-D1, D2 |
| Waldron, Garret | N | New York | 74-A, 74-T |
| Waldron, Garret | N | New York | 76-L |
| Waldron, John | N | New York | 74-A |
| Waldron, John | N | New York | 76-C Grenadier |
| Waldron, John P. | N | New York | 74-A |
| Waldron, Oliver | N | New York | 74-A |
| Waldron, Peter | N | New York | 74-A |
| Waldron, Peter, blacksmith | N | at the Bear Mar't | 75-D1, D2 |
| Waldron, Peter G. | N | New York | 74-A, 76-L |
| Waldron, Richard | N | New York | 74-A, 75-V |
| Waldron, Samuel | Q | ........ | 75-A associator |
| Waldron, Samuel | Q | ........ | 76-E |
| Waldron, Samuel | Q | Newtown | 75-G |
| Walf, George | N | New York | 76-A |
| Walgrove, Garret | N | New York | 74-A |
| Walgrove, George | N | New York | 74-A, 76-F |
| Walgrove, George Jr. | N | New York | 74-A |
| Walker, Benjamin | N | New York | 75-R |
| Walker, John | N | Broadway | 76-H, 76-I |
| Walker, John [2] | N | New York | [on] 76-A |
| Walker, Mark | N | New York | 75-R |
| Walker, Thomas | N | New York | 74-A |
| Wall, George | N | New York | 76-A |
| Wallace, Alexander | N | New York | 74-A |
| Wallace, Hugh Esq. | Q | ........ | 75-H |
| Wallace, Jas. | N | New York | 74-A |

| | | | |
|---|---|---|---|
| Wallar, Peter, Capt. | N | New York | 75-T |
| Walmsley, John | N | New York | 76-A |
| Walmsley; see also Wamsley | | | |
| Walsh, ⸺ Capt. | N | New York | 74-T |
| Walsh, Hugh | N | New York | 74-A |
| Walsh, Hugh, tallow chndlr | N | Broad Street | 75-D1, D2 |
| Walsh, Patrick | N | High Constable | 74-R to 76-R |
| Walsh, Richard | N | New York | 75-R |
| Walter, Jno., Lieut. | N | New York | 75-A |
| Walter, John, Lieut. | N | New York | 76-L |
| Walters, Henry | Q | ........ | 76-B |
| Walters, Henry | Q | Hempstead | 76-D |
| Walters, James | Q | ........ | 76-B |
| Walters, John | Q | ........ | 76-E |
| Walters, Simeon | Q | ........ | 76-E |
| Walters, Willem | N | New York | 74-A |
| Walters, William | Q | ........ | 76-E |
| Walton, Abraham | N | New York | 74-T2, 11/24 |
| Walton, Abraham | Q | ........ | 76-E |
| Walton, Jacob | N | New York | 76-A |
| Walton, Jacob Esq. | N | New York | 74-T, 75-T |
| Walton, William | N | New York | 74-T2, 11/24 |
| Walton, Wm | N | New York | 76-G |
| Wamsley, William | N | New York | 74-A |
| Wandle, Abraham, shoemkr | N | Queen Street | 75-D1, D2 |
| Wands, Stephined | S | Easthampton | 75-E |
| Wanser, Abraham | Q | ........ | 75-A, 76-B2 |
| Wanser, Henry | Q | ........ | 75-A |
| Wanser, Henry Jr. | Q | ........ | 76-E |
| Wansor, Abraham | Q | ........ | 76-E |
| Wansor, Benjamin | Q | Hempstead | 76-D |
| Wansor, Jacob | Q | Hempstead | 76-D |
| Wansor, William | Q | Hempstead | 76-D |
| Ward, Abigail | S | Smithtown | 76:0.0.1.1.0 |
| Ward, Monson | N | New York | 74-A |
| Ward, Samuel | N | New York | 74-A |
| Ward, Sarah | N | to Dutchess Co. | 76-P |
| Ward, Thomas | N | New York | 74-R |
| Ward, William | S | Smithtown | 76:1.0.2.2.2 |
| Warnal, Peter Sr. | Q | ........ | 76-B |

| | | | |
|---|---|---|---|
| Warne, Robert | N | New York | 74-A |
| Warner, Abram | N | New York | 76-L |
| Warner, Charles, coachmkr | N | Broadway | 75-D1, D2 |
| Warner, Daniel | S | Southold | 76:0.1.3.2.2.1.3 |
| Warner, Elfelet | S | Brookhaven | 75-B10 |
| Warner, Eliphalet | S | Southold | 76:0.1.2.1.3 |
| Warner, Eve | N | to Westchester Co | 76-P |
| Warner, George | N | New York | 76-L |
| Warner, Jane, Mrs. | N | removed upstate | 76-P |
| Warner, John, Capt. | N | New York | 75-A |
| Warner, Matice | N | New York | 76-L |
| Warner, Matthis | N | New York | 74-A |
| Warner, Richard | N | New York | 74-A |
| Warner, Thomas | N | New York | 76-A, 76-F |
| Warner, Thomas | N | New York | 76-I, 76-L |
| Warner, Thomas Jr. | N | New York | 76-D |
| Warner, Thomas [2] | N | New York | [on] 74-A |
| Warner, —— widow | N | to Dutchess Co. | 76-P |
| Warner, William | N | New York | 74-A |
| Warner, William | N | New York | 74-A |
| Waterbury, James, shoemkr | N | at Goforths | 75-D1, D2 |
| Waterman, Margaret | N | New York | 74-R witness |
| Waterman, William | N | New York | 76-A |
| Waters, Benj. | Q | ........ | 75-A, 76-B |
| Waters, David | Q | ........ | 76-E |
| Waters, Henry | Q | ........ | 75-A |
| Waters, Israel | N | New York | 74-T |
| Waters, Jam's | Q | ........ | 75-A |
| Waters, Jno. | Q | ........ | 75-A |
| Waters, John | Q | ........ | 75-A associator |
| Waters, John | Q | ........ | 76-B, 76-E |
| Waters, John J. | Q | ........ | 76-E |
| Waters, Mary | N | New York | 75-R |
| Waters, Oliver | Q | ........ | 76-E |
| Waters, Oliver, J.P. | Q | Newtown | 75-B |
| Waters, Peter | Q | ........ | 76-E |
| Waters, Peter H. | Q | ........ | 76-E |
| Waters, Thomas | N | New York | 74-R |
| Waters, William | Q | ........ | 76-E |
| Watkins, Mary | N | New York | 76-I |

| | | | |
|---|---|---|---|
| Watson, Abraham | Q | ........ | 76-B |
| Watson, Jacob | N | New York | 74-A, 75-F |
| Watson, Jacob | N | New York | 76-G |
| Watson, Jacob [2] | N | New York | [on] 76-A |
| Watson, Jane | N | removed upstate | 76-P |
| Watson, Jno. | N | New York | 74-A |
| Watson, John | N | New York | 74-A |
| Watson, John | N | New York | 74-V |
| Watson, John, cabinetmaker | N | New York | 75-R |
| Watson, Josa. | N | New York | 74-A |
| Watts, George | Q | ........ | 75-A, 76-E |
| Watts, George Jr. | Q | ........ | 76-E |
| Watts, John | N | New York | 76-A, 76-I |
| Watts, John | Q | ........ | 75-A |
| Watts, John | Q | Jamaica | 75-D |
| Watts, John Jr., Judge | N | New York | 74-R to 76-R |
| Watts, John Jr., Major | N | New York | 76-Y |
| Watts, Robert | N | New York | 74-T2, 8/18 |
| Watts, Seaman | Q | ........ | 76-E |
| Watts, Simeon | Q | ........ | 75-A |
| Watts, William | Q | ........ | 76-E |
| Watts, William | Q | Jamaica | 75-D |
| Way, Elezar | S | Southold | 76:1.0.0.1.0 |
| Way, Elezer | S | ........ | 75-R |
| Way, James | Q | Newtown | 75-G |
| Way, John | Q | ........ | 75-A associator |
| Way, John | Q | ........ | 76-E |
| Way, John | Q | Newtown | 75-G |
| Way, John Jr. | Q | Newtown | 75-G |
| Way, Samuel | Q | ........ | 76-E |
| Wayman, Wm. | N | New York | 76-B |
| Wayman; see also Weyman | | | |
| Waynman, William | Q | Hempstead | 75-H |
| Weandell, James | N | New York | 74-A |
| Wear, James | N | New York | 76-A |
| Weaver, Micher | N | New York | 76-L |
| Weaver, see also Weever | | | |
| Weaver, Will'm | N | New York | 74-A |
| Weaver, William | N | New York | 74-R, 75-R juror |
| Weaver, William Jr. | N | New York | 76-A |

| | | | |
|---|---|---|---|
| Weaver, Wm, leather dresser | N | Chappel Street | 75-D1, D2 |
| Webb, _____ a cartman | N | New York | 76-B |
| Webb, Buckride | N | New York | 74-A |
| Webb, Ebenezer | S | Southold | 75-N |
| Webb, Ebenezer | S | Southold | 76:1.1.0.1.0 |
| Webb, James | N | New York | 76-A |
| Webb, James | S | Southold | 76:0.1.1.1.1 |
| Webb, James, millstones | N | Little Queen St. | 74-T2, 6/16 |
| Webb, John | N | New York | 74-A |
| Webb, Orange | S | ........ | 75-R |
| Webb, Orange | S | Southold | 76:0.2.2.2.0.1.0 |
| Webb, Thomas | S | Southold | 76:0.1.1.1.0 |
| Webb, William | N | New York | 76-A |
| Webb, William | S | ........ | 75-R |
| Webb, William | S | Southold | 76:0.1.3.1.1 |
| Webber, Isaac, joiner | N | Kings Street | 75-D1, D2 |
| Webbers, Arnold | N | New York | 76-A |
| Webbers, Isaac | N | New York | 75-D3 |
| Webbers, Jacob | N | New York | 76-A |
| Webbers, John | N | New York | 76-G |
| Webbers, Mary | N | New York | 74-R witness |
| Webbers, Philip | N | New York | 74-A, 76-A |
| Weber, Michael | N | New York | 76-A |
| Webster, Edward | N | New York | 76-A |
| Webster, Elihu | N | removed upstate | 76-P |
| Webster, George | N | New York | 74-A |
| Webster, George, grocer | N | Leary Street | 74-T2, 3/3 |
| Weecks, Berard | N | New York | 76-L |
| Weed, Jehiah | S | Brookhaven | 75-B6 |
| Weed, Jehiel | S | Brookhaven | 75-B3 |
| Weed, Jehiel | S | Brookhaven | 76:0.3.1.1.3 |
| Weed, Jehoel Jun' | S | Brookhaven | 75-B6 |
| Weekes, Abraham | Q | ........ | 76-E |
| Weekes, Ant. | Q | ........ | 76-E |
| Weekes, Daniel Jr. | Q | ........ | 76-E |
| Weekes, Daniel [2] | Q | ........ | [on] 76-E |
| Weekes, Edmond/Edmund | Q | ........ | 75-A, 76-E |
| Weekes, Edmund Jr. | Q | ........ | 76-B |
| Weekes, Geo. Sr. | Q | ........ | 76-E |
| Weekes, George | Q | ........ | 76-B |

| | | | |
|---|---|---|---|
| Weekes, George | Q | Oyster Bay | 75-A |
| Weekes, George, Capt. | Q | Oyster Bay | 75-H |
| Weekes, George Jr. | Q | ........ | 76-B |
| Weekes, George [2] | Q | ........ | [on] 75-A |
| Weekes, George [2] | Q | ........ | [on] 76-E |
| Weekes, Isaac | Q | ........ | 75-A, 76-E |
| Weekes, Jacob | Q | ........ | 76-E |
| Weekes, Jacob Jr. | Q | ........ | 76-E |
| Weekes, James | Q | Oyster Bay | 75-A |
| Weekes, Jesse | Q | ........ | 76-E |
| Weekes, John Jr. | Q | ........ | 76-E |
| Weekes, John Sr. | Q | ........ | 76-E |
| Weekes, John [2] | Q | ........ | [on] 75-A |
| Weekes, John [2] | Q | ........ | [on] 76-B |
| Weekes, John [3] | Q | ........ | [on] 76-E |
| Weekes, Joseph | Q | ........ | 76-B, 76-E |
| Weekes, Levi | Q | ........ | 76-E |
| Weekes, Micha | Q | ........ | 76-E |
| Weekes, Michael | Q | ........ | 75-A |
| Weekes, Michael | Q | ........ | 76-B, 76-E |
| Weekes, Nathaniel | Q | ........ | 76-E |
| Weekes, Nicholas | Q | ........ | 76-E |
| Weekes, Pen | Q | ........ | 75-A |
| Weekes, Pen/Penn | Q | ........ | 76-B, 76-E |
| Weekes, Refine | Q | ........ | 76-E |
| Weekes, Richard | Q | Oyster Bay | 75-F |
| Weekes, Richard [2] | Q | ........ | [on] 76-E |
| Weekes, Samuel | Q | ........ | 76-B |
| Weekes, Samuel [2] | Q | ........ | [on] 76-E |
| Weekes, Seaman | Q | ........ | 75-A, 76-E |
| Weekes, Townsend | Q | ........ | 75-A |
| Weekes, Townsend | Q | ........ | 76-B, 76-E |
| Weeks, Bisset | N | New York | 74-A |
| Weeks, Jesse | S | Huntington | 76-H3 |
| Weeks, John, Lieut. | N | New York | 75-A |
| Weeks, Stephen | N | New York | 75-R |
| Weever, Michael | N | New York | 74-A |
| Weiss, Johannis | N | New York | 76-A |
| Weissenvelt, John, Capt. | N | New York | 75-E |
| Welbank, George | N | New York | 75-R |

| | | | |
|---|---|---|---|
| Welch, Edward | N | New York | 74-R |
| Welch, Elizabeth | N | to Westchester Co | 76-P |
| Welch, Jane | N | to Westchester Co | 76-P |
| Welch, Mary | N | New York | 74-R |
| Welch, Nancy | N | to Westchester Co | 76-P |
| Welch, Redmond | N | New York | 74-R witness |
| Welch, Robert | N | New York | 74-T insolvent |
| Welch, Thomas | N | New York | 74-A |
| Welch, William | N | New York | 74-R witness |
| Welch, Wm. | N | New York | 74-A |
| Welden, Jonathan | S | ........ | 75-R |
| Welding, Jonathan | S | Southampton | 76:0.1.1.1.3 |
| Well, Giels | S | ........ | 75-R |
| Wellding, David | S | Southold | 76:0.1.1.2.4 |
| Welling, Charles | Q | Jamaica | 75-C |
| Welling, Samuel | Q | Jamaica | 75-C |
| Welling, W. | Q | ........ | 76-E |
| Welling, William | Q | ........ | 75-A |
| Welling, William | Q | Jamaica | 75-C, 75-D |
| Wells, Abner | S | Brookhaven | 75-B10 |
| Wells, Abner | S | Southold | 76:0.2.3.1.3 |
| Wells, Benj. | S | Southold | 76:1.0.0.2.0.1.4 |
| Wells, Benjamin | S | Southold | 75-N |
| Wells, ---- Capt. | S | Southold | 75-N |
| Wells, Cravat | S | Southold | 76:1.2.0.3.0 |
| Wells, Cravet | S | Brookhaven | 75-B10 |
| Wells, Daniel | S | Brookhaven | 75-B10 |
| Wells, Daniel | S | Southold | 76:1.2.0.2.4 |
| Wells, David | S | Brookhaven | 75-B10 |
| Wells, David | S | Southold | 76:0.1.2.1.1 |
| Wells, David | S | Southold | 76:0.1.2.3.1 |
| Wells, David Jr. | S | Brookhaven | 75-B10 |
| Wells, Fragift | S | Southold | 76:1.1.1.4.1 |
| Wells, Fregift | S | ........ | 75-R |
| Wells, Giels | S | ........ | 75-R |
| Wells, Hennery | S | Southold | 76:1.2.0.2.0 |
| Wells, Isaac | S | Brookhaven | 75-B10 |
| Wells, Isaac | S | Southold | 76:0.1.2.1.3 |
| Wells, James | N | Little Dock Street | 75-T |
| Wells, James | N | New York | 75-R, 76-R juror |

| Wells, James | N | New York | 76-A |
|---|---|---|---|
| Wells, James | S | Brookhaven | 75-B10 |
| Wells, James | S | Southold | 76:0.1.0.1.1 |
| Wells, Jeremiah | S | Brookhaven | 75-B10 |
| Wells, Jermiah | S | Southold | 76:0.2.5.1.2 |
| Wells, John | S | Brookhaven | 75-B10 |
| Wells, John | S | Southold | 76:0.2.1.2.2.0.1 |
| Wells, Jonathan | S | ........ | 75-R |
| Wells, Jonathan | S | Southold | 76:0.1.1.1.1 |
| Wells, Joseph | S | Southold | 76:0.2.2.2.1 |
| Wells, Joseph & Duis | S | Brookhaven | 76:1.2.1.3.1 |
| Wells, Joseph [2] | S | Brookhaven | [on] 75-B10 |
| Wells, Joshua | S | Southold | 76:0.1.1.1.2 |
| Wells, Joshua | S | Southold | 76:1.1.0.1.3 |
| Wells, Joshua Jr. | S | Brookhaven | 75-B10 |
| Wells, Joshua Jun[r] | S | Southold | 76:0.1.4.1.2 |
| Wells, Joshua [2] | S | Brookhaven | [on] 75-B10 |
| Wells, Manly | S | Brookhaven | 75-B10 |
| Wells, Manly | S | Southold | 76:0.1.2.1.2 |
| Wells, Matthew | S | Southold | 76:0.1.1.1.1.0.1 |
| Wells, Micah | S | Southold | 76:0.2.2.2.4 |
| Wells, Michael | N | New York | 76-R |
| Wells, Nathaniel | S | Brookhaven | 75-B10 |
| Wells, Nath[l] | S | Southold | 76:1.0.0.2.0 |
| Wells, Obadiah | N | New York | 74-R juror |
| Wells, Obadiah | S | Southold | 75-N |
| Wells, Oliver | N | New York | 76-A |
| Wells, Paul | S | Southold | 76:0.1.2.1.1 |
| Wells, Phinehas | S | Brookhaven | 75-B10 |
| Wells, Sam[l] | S | Southold | 76:0.1.0.1.0 |
| Wells, Samuell | S | Southold | 76:1.2.3.1.2 |
| Wells, Selah | S | Southold | 75-N |
| Wells, Selah | S | Southold | 76:0.1.1.1.0 |
| Wells, Thomas | S | Brookhaven | 75-B10 |
| Wells, Thomas | S | Southold | 76:0.1.6.2.0 |
| Wells, Timothy | S | Brookhaven | 75-B10 |
| Wells, Timothy | S | Southold | 76:0.1.1.1.0 |
| Wells, Timothy | S | Southold | 76:1.0.2.3.0 |
| Wells, William | S | Southold | 76:0.2.1.1.3 |
| Wells, William | S | Southold | 76:1.0.0.1.0 |

| | | | |
|---|---|---|---|
| Wells, William Juner | S | Brookhaven | 75-B10 |
| Welsh, Cath. | N | New York | 76-I |
| Welsh, Edward | N | New York | 76-I |
| Welsh, Edward, Sergt. | N | New York | 76-G |
| Welsh, George | N | New York | 76-A |
| Welsh, John | N | New York | 74-A |
| Welsh, Patrick, Lieut. | N | New York | 75-A |
| Welsh, Ralph | N | New York | 76-I |
| Welsh, Thomas | N | New York | 76-A |
| Welsh, Thomas | N | New York | 76-I |
| Wendell, see Weandell | | | |
| Wendle, Barberie | N | removed upstate | 76-P |
| Werden, Isaac Jun' | S | ........ | 75-R |
| Wernir, Christian | N | New York | 76-A |
| Werth, Anna Maria | N | New York | 76-K |
| Werts, George | N | New York | 74-R |
| Wessells, Evert | N | New York | 74-A, 76-A |
| Wessells, Gilbert | N | New York | 76-A |
| Wessells, Isaac | N | New York | 74-A |
| Wessells, James | N | New York | 74-A |
| Wessells, James | N | New York | 74-R, 75-R juror |
| Wessells, James, Lieut. | N | New York | 75-A |
| Wessells, John | N | New York | 74-A |
| Wessells, Peter | N | New York | 74-A |
| Wessells, Samuel | N | New York | 75-D2 |
| Wessels, Ann | N | removed upstate | 76-P |
| Wessels, Anne | N | New York | 74-V |
| Wessels, Evert | N | New York | 76-L |
| Wessels, Gilbert | N | Pearl Street | 75-T2, 1/5 |
| Wessels, John | N | New York | 75-D1 |
| Wessels, John, turner | N | Water Street | 75-D1, D2 |
| Wessels, Margrit | N | removed upstate | 76-P |
| West, John | N | New York | 75-C, 75-R |
| West, John | S | Huntington | 76-H3 |
| West, John, bricklayer | N | Batteau Street | 75-D2 |
| West, Zephaniah | N | New York | 74-A |
| Westerfield, Andrew | N | New York | 75-D2 |
| Wetherhead, Jno. | N | New York | 76-A |
| Wetzell, John | N | New York | 74-A |
| Weyman, William | Q | ........ | 75-A, 76-E |

| Weyman, William | Q | Newtown | 75-B |
|---|---|---|---|
| Weyman; see also Wayman | | | |
| Whaley, James | Q | ........ | 75-A, 76-B |
| Whaley, John | Q | ........ | 76-E |
| Whaley, Thomas | N | New York | 74-A, 76-A |
| Whaley; see also Wheyley | | | |
| Wheatcraft, Barzillai | N | New York | 74-A |
| Whedton, Jehiel | S | Brookhaven | 76:0.2.2.1.3 |
| Wheeler, Abraham | N | New York | 74-T insolvent |
| Wheeler, Amaziah | Q | ........ | 76-E |
| Wheeler, Charitee | N | New York | 76-I |
| Wheeler, Daniel | S | Islip | 75-I |
| Wheeler, Daniel | S | Islip | 76:0.1.2.1.3 |
| Wheeler, Daniel | S | Smithtown | 75-L |
| Wheeler, David | S | ........ | 75-R |
| Wheeler, Elias | Q | ........ | 76-E |
| Wheeler, George | S | Smithtown | 75-L |
| Wheeler, Gilbert | N | New York | 74-A |
| Wheeler, Gilbert, shoemkr | N | Water Street | 75-D1, D2 |
| Wheeler, Gilbert, shoemkr | N | Water Street | 75-D2 |
| Wheeler, Henry | Q | ........ | 76-E |
| Wheeler, Jacob | S | Smithtown | 75-L |
| Wheeler, Jeremiah | S | Smithtown | 75-L |
| Wheeler, Jeremiah | S | Smithtown | 76:1.1.2.3.3 |
| Wheeler, John Jr. | S | Huntington | 75-H |
| Wheeler, John Sr. | S | Huntington | 75-H |
| Wheeler, Jonas | S | Islip | 75-I |
| Wheeler, Jonas | S | Smithtown | 75-L |
| Wheeler, Josiah | N | New York | 74-A, 75-D1 |
| Wheeler, Josiah | S | Huntington | 75-H |
| Wheeler, Margaret | N | New York | 75-R |
| Wheeler, Mary | N | New York | 75-R |
| Wheeler, Micah | S | Islip | 75-I |
| Wheeler, Micah | S | Islip | 76:0.1.0.1.0 |
| Wheeler, Micah | S | Smithtown | 75-L |
| Wheeler, Nathan | S | Smithtown | 75-L |
| Wheeler, Nathan | S | Smithtown | 76:1.1.3.3.1 |
| Wheeler, Peter | Q | ........ | 76-A, 76-E |
| Wheeler, Platt | S | Smithtown | 75-L |
| Wheeler, Tho. | S | Huntington | 76-H3 |

| | | | |
|---|---|---|---|
| Wheeler, Thomas | S | Islip | 76:1.2.1.3.0 |
| Wheeler, Thomas [2] | S | Smithtown | [on] 75-L |
| Wheeler, Timothy | S | Islip | 76:1.4.3.3.2 |
| Wheeler, Timothy Jun' | S | Smithtown | 75-L |
| Wheeler, Timothy Sen' | S | Smithtown | 75-L |
| Wheeler, Zophar | S | Smithtown | 75-L |
| Wheeler, Zophar | S | Smithtown | 76:0.1.1.1.0 |
| Wheeting, Samuel | S | Southampton | 76:1.0.0.1.0 |
| Whelple, Joseph | N | New York | 74-A |
| Wheyley, Alex'r | Q | ........ | 75-A associator |
| Whilehand, Elisabeth | N | removed upstate | 76-P |
| Whippo, John | Q | ........ | 76-E |
| Whipps, Isaac | Q | ........ | 76-E |
| White, Charles | N | New York | 74-A, 76-A |
| White, Charles, coppersmith | N | New York | 75-T |
| White, Charls | S | Southampton | 76:1.0.0.1.0.1.0 |
| White, Ebenezer | S | Southampton | 76:1.1.1.2.0.1.0 |
| White, Elias | S | Southampton | 76:0.1.0.1.2 |
| White, Elnathan | S | ........ | 75-R |
| White, Ephraim | S | ........ | 75-R |
| White, Henry | N | New York | 75-F, 76-A |
| White, Henry | S | ........ | 75-R |
| White, Henry | S | Southold | 75-N non-signer |
| White, Henry, Doct' | S | Southampton | 76:0.1.1.1.0 |
| White, Henry, store | N | New York | 74-T2, 10/13 |
| White, John | N | New York | 74-R juror |
| White, John | N | New York | 74-T2, 11/24 |
| White, John | S | Southampton | 76:1.0.0.2.0.1.0 |
| White, John Ju' | S | Southampton | 76:0.2.4.2.2 |
| White, John, shopkeeper | N | Fly Market | 75-D1, D2 |
| White, John [2] | N | New York | [on] 74-A |
| White, Joseph | S | Huntington | 75-H1 |
| White, Mary, widow | S | Southampton | 76:0.2.0.2.0 |
| White, Patrick | N | New York | 74-T insolvent |
| White, Robert | N | New York | 76-A |
| White, Samuel | S | Southampton | 76:0.2.0.1.0 |
| White, Samu'' | S | ........ | 75-R |
| White, Silas | S | ........ | 75-R |
| White, Silas | S | Southampton | 76:1.1.2.2.1.2.0 |
| White, Silvanus | S | ........ | 75-R |

| White, Silvanus | S | Southampton | 76:1.0.1.2.1.1.0 |
|---|---|---|---|
| White, Stephen | S | ........ | 75-R |
| White, Stephen | S | Huntington | 75-H |
| White, Thomas | N | New York | 76-A, 76-I |
| White, Thomas, constable | N | New York | 74-R to 76-R |
| White, William | N | New York | 76-A |
| White, William | S | Southampton | 76:1.1.3.3.2 |
| White, W$^m$ Jun$^r$ | S | ........ | 75-R |
| White, Wright | N | New York | 74-A, 76-G |
| Whitehead, Benjamin | Q | ........ | 75-A |
| Whitehead, Benjamin | Q | Jamaica | 75-C, 75-D |
| Whitehead, Benjamin, Capt. | Q | Jamaica | 75-H |
| Whitehead, Benjamin Jr. | Q | Jamaica | 75-C |
| Whitehead, Daniel | Q | ........ | 75-A |
| Whitehead, Daniel | Q | ........ | 76-B, 76-E |
| Whitehead, Daniel | Q | Jamaica | 75-C |
| Whitehouse & Reeve | N | Wm st., jewellers | 74-T2, 9/29 |
| Whiteman, John | N | New York | 76-R |
| Whiting, George | N | New York | 74-R juror |
| Whitlock, Ephraim, crpntr | N | at John Waters | 75-D1, D2 |
| Whitman, Eliphalet | S | Brookhaven | 75-B8 |
| Whitman, Eliphat | S | Brookhaven | 76:0.1.2.1.1 |
| Whitman, Isaac | S | Huntington | 75-H |
| Whitman, Isaiah | S | Huntington | 75-H |
| Whitman, Jesse | S | Huntington | 75-H |
| Whitman, John | N | New York | 76-A |
| Whitman, Joseph | S | Huntington | 75-H, 75-H1 |
| Whitman, Nathaniel, 2d Lt. | S | Huntington | 76-H2 |
| Whitman, Stephen | S | Huntington | 75-H |
| Whitman; see also Wittmen | | | |
| Whitney, Justus | N | New York | 76-R apprentice |
| Whitney, Justus, shoemaker | N | at Goforths | 75-D1, D2 |
| Whittelsey, Elisha, clark | N | liv w/ Jno Holt | 75-D1, D2 |
| Whitten, Wm | N | New York | 76-N |
| Wick, Edward | S | Easthampton | 75-E |
| Wick, Edward | S | Easthampton | 76:0.1.1.1.3 |
| Wick, Silvanus | S | ........ | 75-R |
| Wick, Silvanus | S | Southampton | 76:0.1.0.1.2 |
| Wick, Zebulon | S | Southampton | 76:0.1.2.1.1 |
| Wickes, Abijah | S | ........ | 75-R |

| | | | |
|---|---|---|---|
| Wickes, Alexander | S | Brookhaven | 75-B6 |
| Wickes, Alexander | S | Brookhaven | 76:1.0.2.2.3 |
| Wickes, Ambrose | S | Huntington | 75-H |
| Wickes, Elijah | S | Huntington | 75-H |
| Wickes, Eliphilet | S | Huntington | 75-H1 |
| Wickes, Ezekiel | S | Huntington | 75-H, 75-H1 |
| Wickes, George | S | Huntington | 75-H |
| Wickes, John | S | Huntington | 75-H |
| Wickes, John, Capt. | S | Huntington | 75-H1, 76-H2 |
| Wickes, John Jr. | S | Huntington | 75-H |
| Wickes, Josah | S | Huntington | 76-H3 |
| Wickes, Joseph | S | Huntington | 75-H |
| Wickes, Josiah | S | Huntington | 75-H |
| Wickes, Josiah Jr. | S | Huntington | 75-H |
| Wickes, Marah | S | Brookhaven | 76:0.0.1.1.0 |
| Wickes, Moses | S | Huntington | 75-H |
| Wickes, Phillip | S | Huntington | 75-H non-signer |
| Wickes, Samuel | S | Huntington | 76-H2 |
| Wickes, Silas | S | Huntington | 75-H |
| Wickes, Thomas | S | Huntington | 75-H |
| Wickes, Thomas Esq. | S | Huntington | 75-H1, 76-H1 |
| Wickes, Zephaniah | S | Brookhaven | 75-B6 |
| Wickham and Sickles | N | New York | 75-F |
| Wickham, Daniel H. | N | New York | 74-A |
| Wickham, Daniel, Lieut. | N | New York | 75-A |
| Wickham, Jacob | S | Easthampton | 75-E |
| Wickham, John | S | Southold | 75-N |
| Wickham, John | S | Southold | 76:0.1.3.1.2.2.2 |
| Wickham, Joseph | S | Southold | 76:0.2.3.2.3 |
| Wickham, Noice | S | Southold | 76:0.1.3.1.4 |
| Wickham, Parker | S | Southold | 75-N non-signer |
| Wickham, Parker | S | Southold | 76:0.3.1.4.2.4.2 |
| Wickham, Thomas | S | Easthampton | 75-E |
| Wickham, Thomas Esq' | S | Easthampton | 76:1.1.3.1.2.1.2 |
| Wickham, William, attorney | N | New York | 75-T |
| Wickoff, Nicholas | Q | ........ | 76-E |
| Widdowson, James | N | New York | 76-I |
| Wier, Richard | S | Huntington | 75-H |
| Wiggains, David | S | Southold | 76:1.3.1.1.1.1.3 |
| Wiggains, John | S | Southold | 76:1.0.0.2.0 |

| | | | |
|---|---|---|---|
| Wiggins, Benejah | Q | ........ | 75-A |
| Wiggins, Benjamin | Q | ........ | 75-A |
| Wiggins, Benjamin | Q | ........ | 76-B, 76-E |
| Wiggins, Benjamin | Q | Jamaica | 75-C |
| Wiggins, Daniel | Q | ........ | 76-E |
| Wiggins, Daniel | S | Huntington | 75-H |
| Wiggins, David Jun. | S | ........ | 75-R |
| Wiggins, Henry | Q | Jamaica | 75-C |
| Wiggins, James | S | Southampton | 76:0.1.1.1.1 |
| Wiggins, John | Q | ........ | 75-A, 76-B |
| Wiggins, John | Q | Jamaica | 75-D |
| Wiggins, John [2] | Q | Jamaica | [on] 75-C |
| Wiggins, Richard | Q | ........ | 75-A |
| Wiggins, Richard | Q | ........ | 76-B, 76-E |
| Wiggins, Thomas | Q | ........ | 75-A |
| Wiggins, Thomas | Q | ........ | 75-A associator |
| Wiggins, Thomas | Q | Jamaica | 75-C, 75-E |
| Wiggins, Thomas | Q | Jamaica | 75-D associator |
| Wiggins, Thomas | S | ........ | 75-R |
| Wiggins, Thomas [2] | Q | ........ | [on] 76-E |
| Wighton, George | N | New York | 74-A, 76-A |
| Wilcocke, William, Lieut. | N | New York | 76-C |
| Wiley, Alexander, taylor | N | William Street | 75-D1, D2 |
| Wiley, Ann | N | removed upstate | 76-P |
| Wiley, John | N | New York | 75-B, 76-N |
| Wiley, John, distillery | N | New York | 74-T2, 7/28 |
| Wiley, John, Lieut. | N | New York | 76-C |
| Wiley, John, taylor | N | Nassau Street | 75-D1, D2 |
| Wiley, Joseph Sr. | N | New York | 74-A |
| Wilkes, James | N | Dock & Broad sts | 75-T |
| Wilkes, James | N | New York | 74-A |
| Wilkes, Thomas | N | New York | 76-A |
| Wilkins, Isaac | N | New York | 75-T |
| Wilkins, Jacob | N | New York | 74-A, 76-A |
| Wilkinson, Robert | N | New York | 76-A |
| Will, Henry | N | New York | 74-A, 74-V |
| Will, John Michael | N | New York | 74-A, 76-A |
| Willcocks, Wm. | N | New York | 75-D3 |
| Willcocks, Wm., Capt. | N | New York | 76-N |
| Willet, Abraham | N | New York | 76-A |

| | | | |
|---|---|---|---|
| Willet, Marinus, Capt. | N | New York | 75-D3 |
| Willets, David | S | Islip | 75-I Quaker |
| Willets, David | S | Islip | 76:1.1.1.2.0 |
| Willets, Jacob | S | Islip | 75-I Quaker |
| Willets, Jacob Jun[r] | S | Islip | 76:0.1.0.1.0.0.1 |
| Willets, Jacob, second | S | Islip | 76:0.2.3.1.1 |
| Willets, Jacob Sen[r] | S | Islip | 76:1.4.3.2.1.1.1 |
| Willets, Jacob the third | S | Islip | 75-I Quaker |
| Willets, Job | S | Islip | 75-I Quaker |
| Willets, John | S | Islip | 75-I Quaker |
| Willets, John Jun[r]. | S | Islip | 75-I Quaker |
| Willets, Richard | S | Islip | 76:1.1.1.3.0.4.1 |
| Willett, Charles | Q | ........ | 75-A |
| Willett, Charles | Q | ........ | 76-B, 76-E |
| Willett, Edward | Q | ........ | 76-B, 76-E |
| Willett, Elizabeth, Mrs. | N | New York | 76-V |
| Willett, Gilbert C. | Q | ........ | 76-E |
| Willett, John | Q | ........ | 75-A, 76-B |
| Willett, John | Q | Flushing | 75-H |
| Willett, Marinus | N | New York | 74-A, 76-N |
| Willett, Mar[s], Corp'l | N | New York | 75-D3 |
| Willett, Thomas | Q | ........ | 75-A, 76-B |
| Willetts, Ewd. | N | New York | 74-A |
| Willetts, Richard | S | Islip | 75-I Quaker |
| William, George | N | New York | 76-A |
| William, Jonas Jr. | S | Huntington | 75-H |
| Williams, Benjamin | N | New York | 76-A, 76-F |
| Williams, Benjamin, store | N | Wall Street | 74-T2, 9/29 |
| Williams, Eliz. wf of Wm | N | New York | 75-R late Irvin |
| Williams, Elizabeth | N | New York | 76-I |
| Williams, Eras. | N | New York | 74-A |
| Williams, Erasmus | N | Mount Pleasant | 74-T2, 4/21 |
| Williams, Jacob | Q | ........ | 75-A |
| Williams, Jacob [2] | Q | ........ | [on] 76-E |
| Williams, James | S | Huntington | 75-H1 |
| Williams, John | Q | Hempstead | 76-D |
| Williams, John, drummer | S | Huntington | 76-H2 |
| Williams, John [2] | Q | ........ | [on] 76-E |
| Williams, Jonas | S | Huntington | 75-H, 75-H1 |
| Williams, Micah | Q | ........ | 76-E |

| | | | |
|---|---|---|---|
| Williams, Nathaniel | N | Burling Slip | 75-D2 merchant |
| Williams, Nath[l] | S | Huntington | 75-H |
| Williams, Thomas | Q | ........ | 76-E |
| Williams, Thos. Sr. | Q | ........ | 75-A |
| Williams, William | N | Bowry Lane | 76-H, 76-I |
| Williams, William | N | head of Broadway | 76-I |
| Williams, William | N | New York | 74-A, 75-R |
| Williams, William | N | New York | 76-A |
| Williams, William | Q | ........ | 75-A |
| Williams, William | Q | ........ | 76-B, 76-E |
| Williams, Wilson | Q | ........ | 76-E |
| Williams, Zeb[n] | Q | Hempstead | 76-D |
| Williams, Zebulon | Q | ........ | 75-A associator |
| Williams, Zebulon Esq. | Q | ........ | 75-D1, 75-F |
| Williamson, David | S | Brookhaven | 75-B8 |
| Williamson, Jedediah | S | Brookhaven | 75-B8 |
| Williamson, Johannes | Q | ........ | 75-A |
| Williamson, Johannes | Q | Jamaica | 75-C, 75-D |
| Williamson, John | N | New York | 74-A |
| Williamson, John | N | South Ward | 75-R overseer |
| Williamson, John | Q | ........ | 75-A, 76-E |
| Williamson, John | Q | Jamaica | 75-C, 75-D |
| Williamson, John | S | Brookhaven | 75-B10 |
| Williamson, John | S | Southampton | 76:0.1.0.2.0 |
| Williamson, John | S | Southold | 76:1.1.0.3.1 |
| Williamson, John Juner | S | Brookhaven | 75-B10 |
| Williamson, Thomas | N | rem. to Bedford | 76-J |
| Williamson, Thomas | N | to Dutchess Co. | 76-P |
| Willing, W. | Q | ........ | 76-E |
| Willis, Daniel | Q | ........ | 76-E |
| Willis, David | N | New York | 74-A |
| Willis, George | N | Murray's Street | 76-I |
| Willis, George | N | New York | 74-A |
| Willis, George Jr. | N | New York | 74-A, 76-A |
| Willis, George Sen[r] | N | near ye Colledge | 76-H |
| Willis, Joseph | Q | ........ | 75-A |
| Willis, Mordecai | Q | ........ | 76-E |
| Willis, Oliver | Q | ........ | 76-E |
| Willis, Stephen | Q | ........ | 75-A, 76-B2 |
| Willis, W. | Q | ........ | 76-E |

| | | | |
|---|---|---|---|
| Willis, William | N | New York | 75-R apprentice |
| Willis, Wm | Q | ........ | 75-A associator |
| Willmot, Jesse | S | Huntington | 76-H2 |
| Willson, Abraham, furrier | N | Bridge Street | 74-T2, 9/15 |
| Willson, Jos., peace officer | N | New York | 75-T |
| Willson, Nicholas | Q | ........ | 76-E |
| Wilmot, George, age 20 | N | runaway | 74-T |
| Wilmot, Henry | N | New York | 76-N |
| Wilmot, Henry, store | N | Hanover Square | 75-F; 75-T2, 1/12 |
| Wilmot, James | N | New York | 74-A |
| Wilmot, James | N | Peck's Slip | 74-T2, 5/5 |
| Wilmoth, Jesse | S | Huntington | 75-H |
| Wilmoth, Nath[l] | S | Huntington | 75-H |
| Wilmoth, Selah | S | Huntington | 75-H |
| Wilse, Jacob | N | New York | 74-A |
| Wilse, Peter | N | New York | 76-L |
| Wilson, Albert | N | New York | 74-A |
| Wilson, Elizabeth | N | rem to Ulster Co. | 76-P |
| Wilson, Isabel | N | rem. to Bedford | 76-J |
| Wilson, Jesse | Q | Jamaica | 75-E |
| Wilson, Joseph | N | New York | 74-T |
| Wilson, Joseph, Constable | N | Elbow Street | 75-D1, D2 |
| Wilson, Joseph, pewterer | N | Dock Street | 75-D1, D2 |
| Wilson, Robert | Q | ........ | 76-E |
| Wilson, Sarah, Mrs. | N | rem to Ulster Co. | 76-P |
| Wilson, Wm [2] | Q | ........ | [on] 76-B |
| Wilt, George | N | New York | 74-A |
| Winchell, Pelitya | N | removed upstate | 76-P |
| Wincoop, ——— Capt. | N | New York | 76-B |
| Windisch, Fredrik | N | New York | 74-A |
| Windish, Fred[k] | N | New York | 76-A |
| Winds, Abijah | S | ........ | 75-R |
| Winds, Abijah | S | Southold | 76:1.0.2.2.2.1.0 |
| Winds, Barnabas | S | Southold | 76:1.0.0.1.1.2.0 |
| Winds, Barnabas Jun[r] | S | Southold | 76:0.1.2.2.5 |
| Winds, Thomas | S | Southold | 76:0.1.1.1.2 |
| Wines, Barnabas, Capt. | S | Southold | 75-N |
| Wines, Barnabas Jr. | S | Southold | 75-N |
| Wines, Thomas | S | Southold | 75-N |
| Winfield, George | N | New York | 76-A |

| | | | |
|---|---|---|---|
| Wingfield, John W. | N | New York | 74-A |
| Winslow, ____ widow | N | to Dutchess Co. | 76-P |
| Winter, Daniel | N | New York | 76-N |
| Winter, Joseph, 1st Lieut. | N | New York | 76-S |
| Winter, Joseph, Ensign | N | New York | 75-A |
| Winterbottom, James, ae 16 | N | New York | 75-V runaway |
| Winterton, William | N | New York | 74-A |
| Winterton, William | N | New York | 76-A, 76-F |
| Winthrop, Peter | N | New York | 75-D1 |
| Wintwort, Peter, gentleman | N | liv w/ S.Vanhorn | 75-D2 |
| Wiseham, William, Lieut. | N | New York | 75-A |
| Witnell, Wm. | N | New York | 74-A |
| Witter, Catharina wf Thos. | N | New York | 75-T, 75-V |
| Witter, Thomas, merchant | N | New York | 75-T, 75-V |
| Witterhorn, Jno. | N | New York | 76-A |
| Wittmen, Biony | N | New York | 74-A |
| Wittmer, George | N | New York | 76-A |
| Witzell, John | N | New York | 76-A |
| Woglom, Abraham | N | New York | 74-A |
| Woley, Garrad | S | Brookhaven | 76:0.1.1.1.1 |
| Wolf, Christopher | N | New York | 74-A, 75-D1 |
| Wolf, David, Lieut. | N | New York | 75-A |
| Wolf; see also Walf | | | |
| Wolfe, Christopher, 2d Lt. | N | New York | 76-S |
| Wolfe, David | N | New York | 74-A |
| Wolfe, David, Capt. | N | New York | 76-S |
| Wolfe, David, gentleman | N | Fair Street | 75-D1, D2 |
| Wolfes, Frederick | N | New York | 76-V |
| Wolhaupter, David | N | New York | 74-A |
| Wollffse, Friedrik | N | New York | 74-A |
| Wonderlick, David | N | New York | 74-A |
| Wood, Abel | S | Huntington | 75-H |
| Wood, Abel | S | Huntington | 75-H1, 76-H1 |
| Wood, Alexʳ | S | Huntington | 75-H |
| Wood, Caleb | S | Islip | 75-I non-signer |
| Wood, Caleb | S | Islip | 76:1.1.1.1.2 |
| Wood, David | S | Huntington | 75-H |
| Wood, Ebenezer | S | Huntington | 75-H |
| Wood, Ebenezer Prime | S | Huntington | 75-H1 Ensign |
| Wood, Elijah | Q | ........ | 75-A |

| | | | |
|---|---|---|---|
| Wood, Elijah | Q | ........ | 76-B, 76-E |
| Wood, Elnathan | S | ........ | 75-R |
| Wood, Elnathan | S | Southampton | 76:1.0.1.1.1 |
| Wood, Epenetus | S | Huntington | 75-H, 76-H3 |
| Wood, Epenetus | S | Smithtown | 75-L |
| Wood, Epenetus | S | Smithtown | 76:1.2.0.4.0 |
| Wood, Gilbert | S | Huntington | 75-H |
| Wood, Israel | S | Huntington | 75-H |
| Wood, Israel, President | S | Huntington | 75-H1, 76-H1 |
| Wood, Israel, South. | S | Huntington | 75-H |
| Wood, James | Q | ........ | 75-A, 76-E |
| Wood, James | S | ........ | 75-R |
| Wood, Jeremiah | S | Huntington | 75-H1 |
| Wood, Jeremiah Jr. | S | Huntington | 75-H |
| Wood, Jesse | S | Huntington | 75-H |
| Wood, John | S | Brookhaven | 76:0.1.2.1.1 |
| Wood, John | S | Huntington | 75-H |
| Wood, John Esq. | N | New York | 74-T |
| Wood, Jonah | S | Huntington | 75-H |
| Wood, Jonah, 2d Lieut. | S | Huntington | 75-H1 |
| Wood, Jonas | S | Huntington | 76-H3 |
| Wood, Joseph | Q | ........ | 76-E |
| Wood, Joseph | S | Huntington | 75-H, 76-H2 |
| Wood, Mary | N | removed upstate | 76-P |
| Wood, Patrick | N | rem to Ulster Co. | 76-P |
| Wood, Peleg | S | Huntington | 75-H non-signer |
| Wood, Richard | S | Southold | 75-N |
| Wood, Richard | S | Southold | 76:0.1.1.2.3 |
| Wood, Sam[l] | S | Huntington | 75-H |
| Wood, Samuel | Q | ........ | 75-A, 76-B |
| Wood, Stephen | Q | ........ | 76-E |
| Wood, Timothy | N | New York | 74-A, 76-L |
| Wood, Timothy | S | Brookhaven | 75-B1, 75-B7 |
| Wood, Timothy | S | Brookhaven | 76:0.1.0.2.0 |
| Wood, Timothy, Ensign | N | New York | 75-A |
| Wood, Timothy, shoemaker | N | Broad Street | 75-T |
| Wood, Unity | N | removed upstate | 76-P |
| Wood, Wm., J. | N | New York | 74-A |
| Wood, Zopher | S | Easthampton | 76:0.1.0.1.1 |
| Woodard, Lambert | Q | ........ | 75-A associator |

| | | | |
|---|---|---|---|
| Woodard, Philip | Q | ........ | 75-A associator |
| Woodard, Philip | Q | Newtown | 75-G |
| Woodard, Thomas | Q | ........ | 75-A associator |
| Wooden, Absalom | Q | ........ | 76-E |
| Wooden, James | Q | ........ | 76-E |
| Wooden, Solomon | Q | ........ | 76-E |
| Woodhool, Benjman | S | Brookhaven | 76:0.4.1.1.3.1.0 |
| Woodhul, Merrit S., Sgt. | S | Brookhaven | 75-B2 |
| Woodhul, Nathaniel | S | Meritches | 76:2.1.0.3.1.4.11 |
| Woodhull, Abel | S | Brookhaven | 75-B8 |
| Woodhull, Abraham | S | Brookhaven | 75-B8 |
| Woodhull, Abram Coopper | S | Brookhaven | 76:0.1.3.3.3 |
| Woodhull, Benjamin | S | Brookhaven | 75-B1, 75-B6 |
| Woodhull, Benjamin | S | Brookhaven | 75-B7 |
| Woodhull, Caleb, Lieut. | S | Brookhaven | 75-B2 |
| Woodhull, Gilbert | S | Brookhaven | 75-B2 |
| Woodhull, Hennery | S | Brookhaven | 75-B2 |
| Woodhull, James | S | Brookhaven | 75-B2, 75-B9 |
| Woodhull, Jeffery | S | Brookhaven | 75-B2 |
| Woodhull, John | S | Brookhaven | 75-B9 |
| Woodhull, John | S | Brookhaven | 76:0.4.1.1.1.2.1 |
| Woodhull, John | S | Brookhaven | 76:1.5.0.2.1 |
| Woodhull, John, Justice | S | Brookhaven | 75-B2 |
| Woodhull, Josiah | S | Brookhaven | 75-B2 |
| Woodhull, Josiah | S | Southold | 76:0.2.2.1.2 |
| Woodhull, Josiah, *Clark* | S | Southold | 75-N |
| Woodhull, Nathan | S | Brookhaven | 75-B4, 75-B8 |
| Woodhull, Nathan | S | Brookhaven | 76:1.2.2.2.0.2.3 |
| Woodhull, Nathan, Junior | S | Brookhaven | 75-B8 |
| Woodhull, Nath[ll] | S | Brookhaven | 75-B6 |
| Woodhull, Richard | S | Brookhaven | 75-B4 |
| Woodhull, Richard | S | Brookhaven | 75-B8 |
| Woodhull, Richard | S | Brookhaven | 76:1.2.0.3.0.1.0 |
| Woodhull, Sarah | S | Brookhaven | 76:0.0.1.1.2.1.0 |
| Woodhull, Stephen, Doctor | S | Brookhaven | 75-B11 n.s. |
| Woodhull, William | S | Southold | 75-N |
| Woodhull, Zebulon | S | Brookhaven | 75-B9 |
| Woodhull, Zebulon | S | Brookhaven | 76:0.1.6.1.1.1.0 |
| Woodroff, Nathaniel | S | Brookhaven | 76:1.1.0.1.0.1.1 |

| | | | |
|---|---|---|---|
| Woodroof, James | S | Brookhaven | 76:0.1.0.1.3 |
| Woodroof, Matthew | S | Brookhaven | 76:0.1.1.2.1 |
| Woodruf, John | S | Southampton | 75-M |
| Woodruff, Benjamin | S | ........ | 75-R |
| Woodruff, Benjamin | S | Southampton | 76:0.1.2.1.3 |
| Woodruff, Daniel | S | ........ | 75-R |
| Woodruff, Dan¹ | S | Southampton | 76:0.1.1.1.0.0.1 |
| Woodruff, David | S | ........ | 75-R |
| Woodruff, David | S | Southampton | 76:1.1.0.2.0.2.0 |
| Woodruff, David Jun. | S | ........ | 75-R |
| Woodruff, David Junʳ | S | Southampton | 76:0.1.1.1.0 |
| Woodruff, Isaac | S | Brookhaven | 75-B3, 75-B6 |
| Woodruff, Jabe | Q | Jamaica | 75-C |
| Woodruff, Jabesh | Q | Jamaica | 75-D |
| Woodruff, Jabez | Q | ........ | 75-A |
| Woodruff, Jabez | Q | ........ | 76-B, 76-E |
| Woodruff, James | S | Brookhaven | 75-B7 |
| Woodruff, John | S | Southampton | 76:0.1.0.1.1 |
| Woodruff, Matthew | S | Brookhaven | 75-B3, 75-B6 |
| Woodruff, Nath'l | Q | ........ | 75-A, 76-E |
| Woodruff, Nathaniel | Q | Jamaica | 75-C |
| Woodruff, Nathaniel | S | Brookhaven | 75-B6 |
| Woodruff, Silas | S | ........ | 75-R |
| Woodruff, Silas | S | Southampton | 76:0.1.2.1.2 |
| Woods, Jeremiah Sr. | S | Huntington | 75-H Quaker |
| Woods, John | N | New York | 74-A, 76-A |
| Woodside, James | N | New York | 74-R |
| Woodward, John | N | New York | 74-A |
| Woodward, John, merchant | N | New York | 74-T2, 4/28 |
| Woodward, Sam'l Jr. | Q | Newtown | 75-G |
| Woodward, Thos. | Q | ........ | 76-E |
| Woodward; see also Woodard | | | |
| Wool, David | N | New York | 75-R |
| Wool, Ellis | N | New York | 74-A |
| Wool, Isaiah | N | New York | 74-A |
| Wool, Isaiah, Corp'l | N | New York | 75-D3 |
| Wool, Jeremiah | N | New York | 74-A, 76-N |
| Wool, Jeremiah, Capt. | N | New York | 76-G |
| Wool, Josiah, stonecutter | N | Great George St. | 75-D1, D2 |
| Wool, Robert | N | New York | 76-N |

Woolegrove, see Walgrove

| | | | |
|---|---|---|---|
| Wooley, Benjamin | S | Southampton | 76:0.2.2.1.2 |
| Wooley, Jared | S | Brookhaven | 75-B9 |
| Woolley, Benjamin | Q | ........ | 76-E |
| Woolley, Benjamin | S | ........ | 75-R |
| Woolley, Charles | S | ........ | 75-R |
| Woolley, Charles | S | Southampton | 76:0.1.0.1.0 |
| Woolley, Henry | Q | ........ | 75-A |
| Woolley, Henry | Q | ........ | 76-B, 76-E |
| Woolley, Jno., Capt. | Q | ........ | 75-A |
| Woolley, John | Q | ........ | 76-E |
| Woolley, John Jr. | Q | ........ | 76-E |
| Woolley, Philip | Q | ........ | 75-A |
| Woolley, Philip | Q | ........ | 76-B, 76-E |
| Woolley, Samuel | Q | ........ | 76-E |
| Woolley, Silas | S | ........ | 75-R |
| Woolley, Thomas | Q | ........ | 75-A, 76-B |
| Woolley, William | S | Southampton | 76:1.1.2.1.0 |
| Wools, Christopher, shoemkr | N | Broadway | 75-D2 |
| Worth, Jonathan | S | Brookhaven | 76:0.1.2.1.0 |
| Worth, Seth | S | Brookhaven | 76:0.1.2.1.4 |
| Wortman, Garret | Q | ........ | 76-E |
| Wortman, Jo. | Q | ........ | 76-E |
| Wragg, William | N | New York | 76-A |
| Wright, Allison | S | Huntington | 75-H |
| Wright, Anthony | Q | ........ | 76-E |
| Wright, Anthony | Q | Hempstead | 76-D |
| Wright, George | Q | ........ | 76-E |
| Wright, George | Q | Hempstead | 76-D |
| Wright, Gideon | Q | ........ | 76-E |
| Wright, Gideon | Q | Oyster Bay | 75-F |
| Wright, Gilbert | Q | ........ | 76-E |
| Wright, Gilbert | Q | Oyster Bay | 75-F |
| Wright, Hallet | Q | ........ | 76-E |
| Wright, Jacob | Q | ........ | 75-A associator |
| Wright, Jacob | Q | Jamaica | 75-D associator |
| Wright, Jacob, 1st Lieut. | Q | Jamaica | 75-E |
| Wright, James | N | New York | 74-A |
| Wright, James, engraver | N | New York | 75-T runaway |
| Wright, John | Q | Oyster Bay | 75-F |

| | | | |
|---|---|---|---|
| Wright, Jonathan | Q | ........ | 75-A associator |
| Wright, Joseph | Q | ........ | 76-E |
| Wright, Jotham [2] | N | New York | [on] 74-A |
| Wright, Nathaniel | Q | ........ | 76-E |
| Wright, Nicholas | Q | ........ | 76-E |
| Wright, Samuel [2] | Q | ........ | [on] 76-E |
| Wright, Sarah | N | New York | 76-K |
| Wright, Theophilus | Q | ........ | 76-E |
| Wright, Thomas | N | New York | 76-A |
| Wright, Thomas | Q | ........ | 76-E |
| Wright, William | Q | ........ | 76-E |
| Wright, William | Q | Oyster Bay | 75-F |
| Wright, William, carpenter | N | St. James Street | 75-D1, D2 |
| Wright, William, oysters | N | New York | 74-T2, 12/22 |
| Wright, Zebulon | Q | ........ | 76-E |
| Wyley, George | N | New York | 76-A |
| Wyley, John | N | New York | 74-R |
| Wyley, ____ widow | N | New York | 74-T |
| Wylley, John | N | New York | 74-A |
| Wynkoop, Jacobus, Capt. | N | Dey Street | 75-D1, D2 |
| Yarington, Jonathan | S | Brookhaven | 76:0.0.3.2.3 |
| Yarranton, Wᵐ | S | Brookhaven | 76:0.1.3.1.2 |
| Yarrington, Jonathan | S | Brookhaven | 75-B7 |
| Yarrington, William | S | Brookhaven | 75-B7 |
| Yates, Jno. | Q | ........ | 75-A associator |
| Yates, Richard | N | New York | 75-T2, 5/4 |
| Yates, Richard | N | Wall Street | 74-T |
| Yeamans, George | N | New York | 75-B |
| Yeamans, George [2] | N | New York | [on] 74-A |
| Yeamans, ____ Lieut. | N | New York | 76-C |
| York, Henry, 1st Lieut. | N | New York | 76-S |
| York, Henry, Lieut. | N | New York | 75-A, 76-G |
| York, Henry, taylor | N | Frankfort Street | 75-D1, D2 |
| Yorks, John | N | New York | 74-A |
| Youel, Rebecca | N | New York | 76-I |
| Yough, John | N | New York | 74-R |
| Youle, James, cutler | N | Fly Market | 74-T2, 1/13 |
| Young, Ab'm | N | New York | 76-A |
| Young, Alexander | N | New York | 75-D1 |
| Young, Althe | N | removed upstate | 76-P |

| Young, Daniel | Q | ........ | 76-E |
|---|---|---|---|
| Young, Daniel | S | Southold | 76:0.1.0.3.1 |
| Young, Daniel | S | Southold | 76:0.4.4.3.1 |
| Young, Elsie | N | to Dutchess Co. | 76-P |
| Young, Elsie, Mrs. | N | rem to Ulster Co. | 76-P |
| Young, Hamilton | N | New York | 75-T2, 6/29 |
| Young, Hamilton | N | New York | 76-A |
| Young, Isaac | N | New York | 74-A |
| Young, Isaac | S | Huntington | 75-H non-signer |
| Young, John | N | New York | 74-A, 75-B |
| Young, John | N | New York | 76-A, 76-L |
| Young, John | S | Southold | 76:0.1.3.2.3 |
| Young, John, sadler | N | Queen Street | 75-D1, D2 |
| Young, John, servant ae 21 | N | New York | 74-V runaway |
| Young, Joseph | N | New York | 74-A |
| Young, Joseph Jr. | S | ........ | 75-R |
| Young, Nath¹ | S | ........ | 75-R |
| Young, Peter | N | rem to Ulster Co. | 76-P |
| Young, Peter | N | to Dutchess Co. | 76-P |
| Young, Philip | Q | ........ | 76-E |
| Young, Sarah | N | to Dutchess Co. | 76-P |
| Young, Saunders, wheelwrt | N | Fresh Water | 75-D2 |
| Young, Thomas Esqr. | S | Southold | 76:1.2.2.4.1.3 |
| Young, Wm | N | New York | 74-A |
| Younge, Thomas | Q | ........ | 76-B |
| Youngs, Abram | N | to Westchester Co | 76-P |
| Youngs, Catharine | N | to Westchester Co | 76-P |
| Youngs, Christopher Jun. | S | Southold | 75-N non-signer |
| Youngs, Christopher Jun' | S | Southold | 76:1.0.1.2.2 |
| Youngs, Dan'l Jr. | Q | ........ | 75-A, 76-E |
| Youngs, Daniel | Q | ........ | 75-A, 76-B |
| Youngs, Daniel | S | Brookhaven | 75-B10 |
| Youngs, Daniel [2] | S | ........ | [on] 75-R |
| Youngs, David Jr. | Q | ........ | 76-B |
| Youngs, Elizabeth | N | to Westchester Co | 76-P |
| Youngs, Gedion | S | Southold | 76:1.0.0.1.0 |
| Youngs, George | Q | ........ | 76-E |
| Youngs, George | S | Huntington | 75-H |
| Youngs, Hinckey | S | ........ | 75-R |
| Youngs, Isaac | N | New York | 76-M |

| | | | |
|---|---|---|---|
| Youngs, Israel | S | Brookhaven | 75-B10 |
| Youngs, Israel | S | Southold | 76:1.1.1.2.1 |
| Youngs, James | S | Brookhaven | 75-B10 |
| Youngs, James | S | Southold | 76:0.1.2.2.1 |
| Youngs, James | S | Southold | 76:2.2.0.3.1 |
| Youngs, James Jr. | S | Southold | 75-N non-signer |
| Youngs, John | N | to Westchester Co | 76-P |
| Youngs, John | Q | ........ | 76-E |
| Youngs, John | S | ........ | 75-R |
| Youngs, Jonathan | S | ........ | 75-R |
| Youngs, Jonathan | S | Southold | 76:1.2.0.4.0 |
| Youngs, Jonathan Junr. | S | Southold | 76:0.1.3.1.3 |
| Youngs, Joseph | S | Southold | 76:1.1.0.2.0 |
| Youngs, Joshua | S | ........ | 75-R |
| Youngs, Mary | N | to Westchester Co | 76-P |
| Youngs, Nath. | S | ........ | 75-R |
| Youngs, Nathanael | S | Southold | 76:1.0.1.3.2 |
| Youngs, Richard | S | ........ | 75-R |
| Youngs, Rufus | S | Brookhaven | 75-B10 |
| Youngs, Samuel | Q | ........ | 76-E |
| Youngs, Samuel | S | ........ | 75-R |
| Youngs, Thomas | Q | ........ | 75-A |
| Youngs, Thomas | Q | ........ | 76-B2, 76-E |
| Youngs, Thomas Jʳ | S | Southold | 76:0.1.1.2.1 |
| Youngs, Thomas Jr. | S | Brookhaven | 75-B10 |
| Youngs, Walter | S | Southold | 76:0.1.0.1.0 |
| Youngs, Waren | S | Southold | 76:0.1.1.1.1 |
| Youngs, Watham | S | Brookhaven | 75-B10 |
| Zedtwitz, H. | N | New York | 75-V |
| Zedwitch, Herman | N | New York | 74-A |
| Zeimermann, Antres | N | New York | 74-A |
| Zent, Charles | N | New York | 74-A |
| Zimmerman, Andrew | N | New York | 74-R |
| Zindall, George | N | New York | 76-A |
| Zise, Michael | N | New York | 76-F |
| Zoper, Daniel | S | Easthampton | 76:0.2.2.1.3 |
| Zuricher, Johannes | N | New York | 74-V |
| Zuricher, John | N | New York | 74-A |

www.ingramcontent.com/pod-product-compliance
Lightning Source LLC
Chambersburg PA
CBHW060139280326
41932CB00012B/1567